LIVE

FROM

NEW

YORK

LIVE
FROM
NEW
YORK

The Complete, Uncensored History of
SATURDAY NIGHT LIVE
as Told by Its Stars, Writers, and Guests

JAMES ANDREW MILLER *and*
TOM SHALES

LITTLE, BROWN AND COMPANY
New York Boston London

Little, Brown and Company
Hachette Book Group
237 Park Avenue, New York, NY 10017
littlebrown.com

Revised edition, September 2014
Originally published in hardcover by Little, Brown and Company, October 2002

Title page image: Color Day Productions/Getty Images

Little, Brown and Company is a division of Hachette Book Group, Inc.
The Little, Brown name and logo are trademarks of Hachette Book Group, Inc.

The publisher is not responsible for websites (or their content)
that are not owned by the publisher.

The Hachette Speakers Bureau provides a wide range of authors for speaking events.
To find out more, go to hachettespeakersbureau.com or call (866) 376-6591.

All images new to the 2014 edition (the second group of photographs) © 2014
NBCUniversal Media, LLC

The Library of Congress has cataloged the original 2002 hardcover edition as follows:
Shales, Tom.
    Live from New York: an uncensored history of Saturday Night Live /
Tom Shales and James Andrew Miller—1st ed.
        p.   cm.
    Includes index.
    ISBN 978-0-316-78146-6
    1. Saturday Night Live (Television program)   I. Miller, James Andrew.   II. Title
PN1992.77.S273 S52 2002
791.45'72—dc21   2002072958

ISBN for the 2014 edition: 978-0-316-29504-8
LCCN for the 2014 edition: 2014943177

10   9   8   7   6   5   4   3   2   1

RRD-C

Printed in the United States of America

For Zachary, Sophie, and Chloe Miller
with love

It's a turnaround jump shot
It's everybody jumpstart
It's every generation throws a hero up the pop charts

Paul Simon
"The Boy in the Bubble"

Contents

Acknowledgments   *xi*

Preface to the 40th Anniversary Edition   *3*

Prologue   *7*

1. Exordium: 1975–1976   15

2. Heyday: 1976–1980   100

3. The Stars Come Out: 1980–1985   191

4. Behemiel Rising: 1985–1990   288

5. Overpopulation: 1990–1995   354

6. Still Crazy After All These Years: 1995–2002   424

7. Politica: 2002–2008   526

8. One Man's Family: 2008–2014   608

9. Lorne   700

SNL *Cast Lists*   747

Index   757

Acknowledgments

Participation is the lifeblood of an oral history; speaking with so many funny, talented, and smart people was not a chore but a delight. To all the interviewees who shared their stories, thoughts, and professional lives, no amount of gratitude is sufficient.

As he did with previous editions of this book, Lorne Michaels neither requested nor received input on its content. Amid the many tales and myths about him, one fact is inarguable: he is a man who can make things happen and prevent things from happening. Fortunately, in this case, he elected to do the former, and that is much appreciated.

Thanks are also due, once again, to those who helped on the original and paperback editions of *Live from New York*. More than a decade has passed, but their efforts are still remembered and much appreciated. This time out, researcher Adam Khatib joined the team and proved invaluably skillful. He, Benjamin Korman, and Reed Dunlea formed an A-Team of ace transcribers. Rya Gershcovich marched into the forest of celebrityhood and helped track down important interview subjects. To that end, much appreciation extends to their agents, managers, and publicists. Dana Edelson, Colin Graham, Heather Karpas, and Lauren Rosenman simply made things better and easier.

Back at Little, Brown, special thanks goes to Reagan Arthur, Judy Clain, Heather Fain, and Evan Schnittman, all of whom brought indispensable experience to the project. Ben Allen, Peggy Anderson, Barbara Clark, Catherine Cullen, Nicole Dewey, Peggy Freudenthal, Pamela Marshall, and Allie Sommer each made a valuable contribution as well.

Although change is a major theme of *Live from New York,* one thing remained, comfortingly, *un*changed over the past dozen years: Sloan Harris continues to be an agent without peer and a beacon of light in stormy seas. The idea for this book was first mentioned to him at lunch one day, and by close of business a few hours later, the project had been pushed to prominence at Little, Brown.

Unfortunately, change *has* taken place there. The departure of Geoff Shandler, one of the finest editorial guardians imaginable, represents a serious, dispiriting loss. His professionalism will be greatly missed, but thankfully our personal ties (including those with his wonderful wife and children) survive, and with it, a friendship that will withstand any and all changes that might lie ahead.

LIVE

FROM

NEW

YORK

Preface to the 40th Anniversary Edition

In the twelve years since the paperback edition of *Live from New York* was published, *Saturday Night Live* has gone through many changes, as have we all. Twenty-eight cast members have been hired; twenty-six have left. Some departed for sitcoms or movies; others simply vanished from the public eye. There have been uproars, embarrassments, firings, budget cuts, a writers' strike that nearly derailed an entire season, and the construction of a new stage in Studio 8H. Women anchored "Weekend Update" and played a hugely prominent role in a presidential election.

This new expanded edition of *LFNY* is meant to chronicle those changes and others, help mark the show's fortieth anniversary, and document further its lasting imprint on American culture. After thirty-nine seasons, this much is still true: through triumphs and troubles, through incomparably memorable moments and fitful flirts with mediocrity, *Saturday Night Live* marches on as the most successful comedy show in the history of television.

As with previous editions of this book, here we endeavor to write history through commentary and reminiscences from the show's cast members, hosts, and writers—this time including those who have been part of the show since the original book was published. We originally conceived *LFNY* as a book of record, and we welcome the chance to make that a *living* record—an illumination, we hope, for those who have lived their entire lives within the time frame of the show and for those old enough to remember its first tumultuous years.

One consistency through the decades—despite all the changes and upheaval—is that *Saturday Night Live* still hews to tradition. It began as and remains the expression of primarily one man: Lorne Michaels, the creator and executive producer, who, except for a five-year hiatus during which others ran the show, hasn't missed a performance. He is the guiding spirit, and many of the standards he championed in the beginning are still evident in each subsequent iteration.

So even when its content may be sophomoric or semismutty, *Saturday Night Live* continues to reflect its old established values—no canned laughter, no fake breakups by cast members, stringent technical standards. Indeed, one of the most common refrains from hosts involves awe at how expertly and impressively the machinery of *SNL* operates; live television has no margin for error.

As a result, even in its own middle age, and with many cable channels now proclaiming themselves as major players in the comedy business, Michaels's creation stands out. It has, let's face it, a better pedigree than do pretenders to the throne, and beneath the ballyhoo and profits it evinces a palpable sense of purpose—something rare for commercial television.

You don't get to be forty without a little paranoia. *SNL* has always tried to stay ahead or at least abreast of industry developments, repackaging material for cast-member "Best of" home-video releases, DVD boxed sets, network specials, and exposure on Hulu and other Internet sites. In the past decade, though, *Saturday Night Live* has managed even to co-opt candidates for its own replacement. Former cast member Andy Samberg, along with writers Jorma Taccone and Akiva Schaffer, convinced Michaels to feature weekly digital shorts on the program just as YouTube was becoming part of America's daily routine. More people now see *SNL*'s digital shorts on computers than they do when watching the show itself on Saturday night.

Of course that digital ecosystem has put the show under a brighter and, arguably, harsher spotlight than ever, with each episode being analyzed and pounced upon by the Internet's cacophonous chorus of opinionators. The show has ridden a roller coaster of ups and downs, sometimes making news as well as commenting on it—or doing both at the same time. A "sketch that kills" can go viral now in a flash and be seen by millions who no longer watch the show. As a result, *SNL* has had to face, from Twitter and elsewhere, a huge new array of would-be satirists and commentators.

The same Internet that supplies perpetual criticism for *SNL* supplies perpetual competition for it, with a seemingly infinite array of satirical or pseudosatirical voices clamoring for attention. Competition has become even fiercer, especially against the bottomless pits of programming on cable and satellite television. Cable stars like Jon Stewart and Stephen Colbert try to do nightly what *SNL* does weekly on the "Update" desk, making it even harder for *SNL* writers and performers not only to be funny but also to say something distinctive and unique about the week's news and pop-culture parade.

To his credit, and even though there has sometimes seemed to be a lag between criticisms of the show and attempts to address them, Michaels has remained vigilant in maintaining the show's prominence in the zeitgeist and in the increasingly hasty march of time; he and the writers, producers, and performers under him try desperately each week to keep the show fresh and relevant. Obviously, currency is the show's most important single attribute.

NBC has exploited the success of *SNL* at every opportunity: its reruns often plug holes in the NBC schedule and are licensed to play on cable channels (some partly owned by NBC). Michaels's own domain and wealth have vastly expanded; with the ascendancies of Jimmy Fallon to *The Tonight Show* and Seth Meyers to *Late Night,* Michaels became executive producer and guardian angel of NBC's entire late-night schedule, Monday through Saturday.

The flagship broadcast, *Saturday Night Live,* has developed into a relatively dependable audience delivery device, so much so that it has become common for *SNL*—where the resident troupe used to be self-mockingly called the Not Ready for Prime Time Players—to score higher Nielsen ratings than any show in NBC's Saturday prime-time lineup. Of course that's attributable not just to *SNL* doing well but also, in the thousand-channel universe, to everybody else being in the dumps, or almost in the dumps. The size of the pie stays relatively the same, but the slices grow ever smaller; the audience now must be divided among new channels, new networks, and new media.

Can there be anything left, meanwhile, of *SNL*'s original rebellious, maverick swagger? Can *SNL* continue to satirize what it has, arguably, become?

Maybe these worries are spurious, perhaps as irrelevant as some claim the show has now become. But week after week and year after year, perpetually replenished with new young talent who claim Studio 8H for their own, *Saturday Night Live* continues to push on, and the man whose name remains first in the credits at the end of each show has vowed to stay there as long as he lives. Michaels still manages to identify with the audaciousness and irreverence that have always been vital to the show's DNA.

For us, this journey has proved a hilarious pleasure at times and a daunting challenge at other times. But always, more than anything else, it has been an honor.

No kidding.

—James Andrew Miller and Tom Shales

Prologue

Saturday Night Live is more than a television show. Since its premiere in 1975, it has served as a trendsetter in American humor and had a remarkable effect on American mores, manners, music, politics, and even fashion. It can't be said that there'd never been anything like it in TV history, because one of its bold strokes was reviving a format as old as television itself—in fact, older: the variety show, with music and comedy sketches intermixed. Though the basic form wasn't entirely new, the content was, and so were the show's attitude and approach and collective mind-set. Tea had been around for centuries, after all, but the notion of throwing mass quantities into Boston Harbor was new. It was revolutionary. So was *Saturday Night Live*.

The people who own and run commercial television networks don't put a show on the air because they imagine it will break bravely with tradition or set grand new aesthetic standards or stretch the boundaries of the medium—or for any reason whatsoever other than to make money. *Saturday Night Live* wasn't created because NBC executives yearned to introduce something new and bold into the television bloodstream or the American mainstream. It came to be because Johnny Carson wanted the network to stop airing reruns of his *Tonight Show* on weekends. For years, NBC's affiliated stations had been given the choice of slotting *The Best of Carson* late on Saturday or Sunday nights, or neither. One fine day in 1974, Carson told NBC to yank them altogether; he wanted to air reruns on weeknights to give himself more time off. NBC brass had the choice of returning the weekend time to local stations—and thereby kissing a chunk of ad revenue good-bye—or trying to fill the time slot with other programming. And so the word went forth from network president Herbert Schlosser: Develop a new late-night show for Saturday.

In 1974, when the decision to annex late Saturday nights was made, nobody knew what was coming. Ideas that circulated among NBC executives included a weekly variety show hosted by impressionist Rich Little, then under contract to the network. Somebody suggested Linda Ronstadt as costar. Even bland Bert Convy, actor and game-show host, was considered. But all those cockeyed notions were trashed when a brilliant and ambitious young writer from Canada born Lorne Lipowitz was named executive producer of the new show. He'd made a name for himself with his work on *Rowan and Martin's Laugh-In* and a few Lily Tomlin specials and, before leaving Canada, with a fanciful film about a failure in the annual hockey puck crop. His vision would turn TV on its head, turn TV on itself, and prevail for decades to come, even during a few years in which he himself was *in absentia.*

The man Herb Schlosser took a chance on, Lorne Michaels—then crossing the Great Divide into thirty—gave NBC much, much more than it had bargained for, probably more than it wanted: an adventurous "live" topical satire series that, had executives and advertisers known of its form and content in advance, might never have seen the light of night.

NBC's Saturday Night, as it was originally called, would be the television generation's own television show—its first. Except in superficial ways, it was unlike anything else then on the air, and it would be years before flummoxed rivals would even try to imitate it. From the ground up it was built to be new, unusual, arresting, surprising, and attractive to baby boomers, the largest generation in American history.

In the decades to come, the success of *Saturday Night Live* sparked a renaissance in topical, satirical, and political humor both on television and off it; launched the careers of innumerable new talents who might otherwise have had little hope of appearing on network TV, including some who'd had little interest in it; hugely expanded the parameters of what was "acceptable" material on the air, bringing it much closer to the realities of everyday American life; and helped bestow upon the comedy elite the hip-mythic status that rock stars had long enjoyed.

And it made a nation laugh — laugh, even when it hurt.

During its earliest weeks on the air, celebrity hosts and musical acts were the essence of the program. As weeks went by, the show's repertory company of young comedy players, recruited mostly from improvisational troupes in a few major cities, got more time on the air. Even before the original cast left, the show itself had become the star and a new American institution — a kind of keepsake to be handed down from generation to generation, both by the performers who served time in its stock company and by the audience that is perpetually replenished as new legions of viewers come of age.

All that and more because Johnny wanted additional time off. At first skeptical about the new show, he was later openly appalled by some of its more outrageous gags (foremost example: An aged comic known as Professor Backwards drowned in the ocean, Chevy Chase reported on *SNL*'s "Weekend Update," because onlookers ignored his desperate cries of "pleh, pleh"). But the King of Late Night, quite the icon himself, eventually came to terms with the show (and friendly terms with Chase). Michaels said he annually invited Carson to guest-host as a goodwill gesture but was just as annually turned down.

Lorne Michaels propelled TV forward partly by returning to its origins — his philosophy tidily embodied in the seven words that exuberantly, and somehow threateningly, open each edition: "Live from New York, it's *Saturday Night!*" Though it blazed new trails in the areas of what could be said and done on TV, and initially made censors batty and sponsors skittish, *Saturday Night Live* always had its roots showing: the early golden days of live TV from New York — the days of *Studio One* and, more relevantly, *Your Show of Shows* and *Caesar's Hour* with Sid Caesar and his troupe. The audience at home watched and laughed, thrillingly aware that "this is happening now" and that there was thus an element of daring and peril to what otherwise amounted to mere entertainment.

The story of *Saturday Night Live* is the story of the people who made it work—people there at the beginning; people who passed through as if attending some rarefied college of comedic arts; crafts-people and technicians as well as actors and comics and musicians. They and the show weathered many a storm along the way: the tragic premature deaths of cast members, drug abuse among the performers and writers, temper tantrums, office romances, and a near-fatal stumble when, five years into the run, someone underqualified took over as producer. There was also Michaels's own pratfall when he returned after a long absence with a casting concept that largely bombed and, in more recent times, an anthrax scare that had the entire cast evacuating 30 Rockefeller Center, the show's longtime home, on a frightening Friday in the terrorist year of 2001.

As executive producer for most of its nearly three decades, Michaels has had to contend with virtually every sin the flesh is heir to among his cast members as well as with his own fallibilities. He was a father figure even at the beginning, when he was only a wee bit older than the rest of them, and that continues now that he is twice the age of many of those who work for him and plays host to surviving members of the original cast who bring teenage sons and daughters to see the show in person. He watched as two of his brightest comedy stars died of drug abuse, saw others come perilously close, and has had to deal with the grimness of a disproportionately high mortality rate overall.

There have been cast members who drank too much, snorted coke too much, freebased too much, God-knows-what-else'd too much. A writer recalls walking into an office and finding three members of one of the world's most famous rock bands shooting heroin into their veins before a show. One brilliant but insecure member of a recent cast slashed himself with razor blades during bouts of severe depression. Talent may itself be a form of neurosis; it usually comes with troubles attached.

To those who work on the show, success and failure become close to matters of life and death. It's all there in the argot; a good joke "kills," while a bad sketch "dies." Having an audience "crushed" by material is devoutly to be wished. Many a sketch will "kill at dress"—meaning get big laughs at the dress rehearsal staged in front of a separate audience a few hours before the real show—only to "die on-air" when it's the show for real.

Among Michaels's nemeses over the years have been network censors, less conspicuous now but a constant source of friction at the outset; network executives who hated the program or wanted to produce it themselves; hosts who panicked at the last minute and wanted to bolt, or who canceled just before their week's exhilarating ordeal was about to begin; and an uncountable number of protests and condemnations from special interest groups offended by this sketch or that portrayal or a news item on "Weekend Update"—or the way a seemingly imperiled pig squealed during a sketch about a TV animal show.

Even in its maturity, if that state was ever actually reached, the show remained a troubled child. Brandon Tartikoff, for years NBC's much-loved uber-programmer, reluctantly canceled the series in the mid-1980s, only to give it an eleventh-hour reprieve. Essentially, the warden made the fateful last-minute phone call to himself.

The show made stars of unknowns and superstars of stars. There were also those who entered anonymous and left the same way. Some were made famous, some were made bitter, some were made rich. Some found nirvana and others a living hell. They never really knew, going through those portals, how or if they would be changed as a result. But they virtually all had one thing in common, even if they had joined the show simply because they needed work and liked to eat: It was much more than a job. They were the chosen because it was the chosen. They could look down on people working even on the most successful prime-time sitcoms or dramas because *Saturday Night Live* was something entirely unto itself, a towering edifice on the landscape, a place of wonder and magic, a sociopolitical phenomenon.

With the arrival of *SNL,* the TV generation, at least for ninety minutes a week, could see television not just as a window on the past or a display case for the fading fantasy figures of their fathers and mothers, but as a mirror—a warped fun-house mirror perhaps, but a mirror just the same, one reflecting their own sensibilities, values, and philosophies. Television, which had shown them the world, had heretofore neglected to show them themselves.

When *Saturday Night Live* began, its competition was mostly local programming—syndicated shows and old movies—since ABC and CBS, then the only other networks, went dark late Saturday nights. Today *SNL* faces an onslaught of competition in its time period from dozens of channels, including many cable networks and broadcasters fighting for the same demographically desirable, youngish audience that *SNL* helped define. And yet, though the competition has multiplied exponentially, *SNL* still dominates. Its viewership now includes parents who have children as old as the parents were when they first watched the show. Or older. They may say it isn't as good as it was then—but they still watch. They may go to bed much earlier than they did in the seventies—but they'll still try to stay up at least through "Weekend Update." Or they tape it or TiVo it and watch it the next morning, an option not available when *SNL* first appeared.

This book tells the *Saturday Night Live* story for the first time almost entirely in the words of the people who made it and lived it— the performers who found glory or agony there, the writers and producers who stayed for decades or only a year or two, and many stars who served as hosts. Elated or disgruntled, they talk with abandon and candor and represent a wide array of views about the show, what makes it tick, whether indeed it still does tick, how it has lasted, and whether Lorne Michaels is a comedy genius or a cunning con man.

Although *Saturday Night Live* spans five decades, some of the newness and even the nihilism of the early years survives and bursts forth every week. New talent is always coming in and shaking things up. To them, Studio 8H is not a hallowed hall because Arturo Toscanini once conducted the NBC Orchestra there (in fact, the studio was built for him) but because John Belushi, Gilda Radner, Dan Aykroyd, Chevy Chase, Laraine Newman, Bill Murray, and Garrett Morris reinvented television there; because the place echoes with the inspired hilarity of Belushi's mad Samurai, Aykroyd's fusty male prostitute, Radner's loopy Loopner, Chase's stumble-bumbling Gerald Ford, Murray's capricious Oscar-picker, Morris's shouted headlines for the hearing impaired, Newman's curiously sexy portrayal of young Connie Conehead, teenager from outer space.

People always point to those first years as the show's best, but in fact the years that followed have maintained a standard as high as that of any long-running television show, whether Ed Sullivan's or *The Simpsons*. MGM once boasted of "more stars than there are in the heavens," and *Saturday Night Live* could make the same claim for its current stock company and all those illustrious graduates. Too many of them, alas, really are in heaven now.

With this book, we aspire to come close to doing them justice and celebrating the gifts they lavishly shared with the world. Most of them would balk at being sentimentalized or romanticized, but we have no problem with that, no problem at all. They reinvented the wheel and made it funny, and as Art Carney once said, "Make people laugh and they will love you forever." Now, live, from New York—it's *Saturday Night*.

1

Exordium: 1975–1976

Like all show business successes, Saturday Night Live *had many fathers. Several mothers too. There is still, so many years after the birth, disagreement over who the real father is. The show had a gestation period of more than a year, during which the concept took various forms, none identical to that of the show we know today. Adjustments and refinements continued after the premiere. Whatever the evolutionary variations in structure and format, however,* Saturday Night Live *was from the beginning a lone pioneer staking out virgin territory and finding its way in the night, its creative team determined to make it television's antidote to television, to all the bad things—corrupt, artificial, plastic, facile—that TV entertainment had become.*

ROSIE SHUSTER, *Writer:*

Lorne Michaels arrived in my life before puberty, let's put it that way. I swear to God. There was not a pubic hair in sight when he arrived on my doorstep. We were living in Toronto in the same neighborhood. I was with my girlfriend. We were jumping on boards, just letting go—we were just wild prepubescent kids, and Lorne observed me from the sidelines. And I guess he was struck by my mojo, or whatever, and he basically started following me around. We were inseparable after that.

HOWARD SHORE, *Music Director:*

As kids, Lorne and I went to a coed summer camp in Canada. And that was really the beginning of our friendship. I was thirteen and

Lorne must have been about fifteen. Rosie Shuster was there, too. We did shows you do at summer camp, like *Guys and Dolls, The Fantasticks,* things like that. And on Saturday nights, we did "The Fast Show," a show Lorne and I put together quickly—hence the title. We did comedy, we did sketches, we had kind of a repertory company and some musicians. If you think about it, it was truly the beginning of *Saturday Night Live,* because it was a show we put on every Saturday night, and it was a live show, and it was somewhat improvisational, with comedy and music. We always had a bunch of people around us who were writers and actors even at that age. And that kind of progressed from summer camp to other things that Lorne and I wrote together.

ROSIE SHUSTER:

My dad really mentored Lorne in terms of comedy. Lorne had a partner and did radio shows just like my dad had done, and then did CBC specials just like my dad had done. I saw the whole thing unfold, and felt like *Saturday Night Live* was so much a part of something that grew from my home. Something about the show came from inside my family.

Lorne visited my dad inside his little showbiz pup tent where he shared his wild enthusiasms. Lorne was a very avid, eager sponge for all of it; he heard all of the names of everybody backstage at the *Ed Sullivan Show,* and all the ins and outs of the movies. My dad grew up watching the Marx Brothers and Chaplin. He was just spellbound by all of that, and he shared that love with me and with Lorne.

LORNE MICHAELS, *Executive Producer:*

I grew up in Canada, where we had all three American networks and later a Canadian network. So I was watching CBS and ABC when I was eight or nine, and grew up on the same television that everybody else grew up with. I saw the same kind of movies, but my grandparents owned a movie house and my mother worked in it and my uncle had been a projectionist—the Playhouse on College Street. My mother, who died in 2001, could still play music from the silent movies, from the sheet music the movie companies sent around. My maternal grandmother, who was an enormous influence on me, and my aunts and uncles and my mother of course, all talked about movies and show business in whatever form, and books. That was all a part of my growing up. I don't think I ever thought that's what I'd be doing with my life, although when I was at my peak seriousness, at twenty-two or twenty-three, I thought I'd be a movie director.

In 1972 I had presented this pilot to the CBC. They said they were thinking about it, but the head of the CBC—whose name I am clearly blocking—said to me one afternoon when I was talking passionately about why this show would be a breakthrough show, he said, "If you're that funny, why are you here?" And I thought, "Oh my God, it's that Canadian thing of 'If you're good, you go to America.' "

SANDY WERNICK, *Agent:*

When I met Lorne, he was in Canada, producing and starring in *The Hart and Lorne Hour* with his partner, Hart Pomerantz. I had never met anybody who had a gift of gab like Lorne. He would just mesmerize me with what he was talking about. If you talked about comedy, all of a sudden he would just light up and turn on. I remember introducing him to Bernie because I knew that would be a marriage.

BERNIE BRILLSTEIN, *Manager:*

I met him when he was working on *Laugh-In* with his partner, who wound up going back to Canada. We were doing the Burns and Schreiber summer show with Jack Burns and Avery Schreiber, and there was a spot for a writer. Sandy Wernick from ICM told me Lorne was available. I said to bring him in to fill the last slot. And I fell in love with him. He wanted to know about old show business, and he had done a short film, *The Hockey Puck Crisis,* which was great: Hockey pucks grew on trees, and there was a blizzard that destroyed the crop, so they couldn't play hockey in Canada that year. Being a hockey fan and a comedy fan, I thought it was hysterical.

LORNE MICHAELS:

Bernie's a larger-than-life character. He was also an antidote, because I was deadly serious about everything I was doing in those days. Bernie had the gambler's love of the sheer larceny of it, whether it was *Hee Haw* or whatever, it didn't seem to matter. He knew the good stuff from the bad stuff, but it didn't stop him from dealing with either—whereas I thought if I was involved with anything bad, it would destroy my life.

ROSIE SHUSTER:

I had done television shows with Lorne in Toronto and in Los Angeles. On one of Lily Tomlin's specials we did "Arresting Fat People in Beverly Hills" together. Bernie Brillstein played one of the fat people. Vertical stripes, you know, only vertical stripes. It got nominated for an Emmy.

LILY TOMLIN, *Host:*

Lorne was used to being a star back in Canada. We were quite close at that time. When Lorne worked with me on my specials, he would spend too much time editing and be too fanatical about everything. Jane Wagner would say, "You're going too far and you're spending too much money and the show needs to be rougher." Lorne and I would get into the editing room and get too perfectionistic, you know. I must say I think some illegal substances had something to do with it.

ROBERT KLEIN, *Host:*

I remember before there was any *Saturday Night Live,* an actually humble Lorne Michaels used to come to the office of my manager, Jack Rollins. Lorne was a kid from Canada married to Rosie Shuster, who was the daughter of Frank Shuster of Wayne and Shuster, the duo that used to be extremely unfunny on the Sullivan show years ago. Lorne was looking for some work, and Jack was very helpful to him.

TOM SCHILLER, *Writer:*

My father, Bob Schiller, was working on this show called *The Beautiful Phyllis Diller Show* in 1968, and he said there was a junior writer on the show that he'd love me to meet. And I said, "Why?" And he said, "Well, he knows all of the best restaurants in L.A."

So one day Lorne comes over wearing a Hawaiian shirt. He seemed like a nice enough guy—a little nebbish, you know. What struck me though was that after my dad introduced me, Lorne lit up a joint right there in the house. I was scared—but I was impressed too, that he had the boldness to do that. We sort of became friends and I started hanging out with him at the Chateau Marmont.

CBS still ruled the ratings in the mid-1970s, but executives at RCA, which owned NBC, had high hopes for the network's aggressive and competitive new president, Herbert Schlosser, a onetime Wall Street law-yer who took over in 1974. He was anxious to make his mark on tele-vision history. And he would.

DICK EBERSOL, *NBC Executive:*

In the spring of 1974, I was approached by NBC to come over there and essentially run their sports department. At that time, I was Roone Arledge's assistant at ABC. I said no. I think they were like in shock; how could somebody who was twenty-seven turn that down? But I felt they didn't take sports seriously, that they wouldn't put real resources into it, and besides, I didn't want to compete against the best person who'd ever done it before or since: Roone.

My saying no apparently impressed Herbert Schlosser, the presi-dent of NBC. So, lo and behold, in the summer of 1974, Schlosser invited me to his place on Fire Island—along with Marvin Antonowsky, one of his programming executives—and essentially laid out the whole thing: how Johnny Carson had given them fair warning that he did not want weekend repeats of *The Tonight Show* to exist after the summer of 1975. They had begun to order up some specials. One had Burt Reynolds sort of hosting. It was talky and had some comedy bits. Herb said he was very much interested in finding some regular stuff for that time period. I was intrigued, even though I had no back-ground whatsoever in late night. I'd been a sports kid since I dropped out of Yale to work for Roone in 1967.

I told Roone I was leaving the same morning Nixon resigned. I had a whole deal to come over to NBC as head of weekend late-night pro-gramming. I had one year to come up with a show to go into that time period, and if the show was creatively sound, I had Herb's word it would get at least six months on the air.

HERBERT SCHLOSSER, *NBC President:*

I had played a role in hiring Ebersol. I can remember when I interviewed him, it was out on Fire Island on a weekend, and he was wearing a pair of pants where one leg was one color and the other leg was another color. Which I guess is what you wore in Connecticut.

Johnny Carson was the biggest star NBC had, unchallengeable in his time period. It wasn't like Leno and Letterman fighting each other now. Johnny was very, very important to the network, and we were getting emanations that he was not pleased about the weekend repeats of his show. They'd been on for ten years, and we ourselves weren't that thrilled, but it had been an easy thing for us to do—just put 'em on.

So I thought we should try something new.

FRED SILVERMAN, *NBC President:*

When Herb looks back on his days at NBC, he's the only guy that had worse days than I did. He really doesn't have much of a positive nature to look back at. So I can see where he would remember the beginnings of the show so well. *Saturday Night Live* was a big deal for him. It was Herb's biggest endeavor.

GRANT A. TINKER, *Former NBC Chairman:*

I think Herb Schlosser gets credit for letting *Saturday Night Live* happen, or even causing it to happen for all I know, and I think that's particularly important because Herb is such a tight-ass guy. And the fact that it started on his watch says a lot.

I'm not sure if it would have started on mine.

I give Herb credit because he's the one who would take the heat when there was heat from the RCA directors or whatever. Those were very straight guys, in the old-fashioned sense of the word, on the fifty-third floor where RCA had its offices. There wasn't a laugh in a carload up there.

DICK EBERSOL:

I spent September and October of 1974 roaming the West Coast, Canada, Chicago, and New York, looking for comics and comedy producers. I came to the conclusion rather quickly that the only way this show would work would be if the young embraced it—if it was a show for a younger audience. Johnny was the most brilliant person in the world but his show wasn't for teenagers.

One piece of talent I thought would give us credibility was Richard Pryor. We had these meetings with Richard, and they went fairly well. He finally agreed to a deal. After that, Lily Tomlin agreed to fall in. So did George Carlin. Someone was trying to sell me Steve Martin and Linda Ronstadt as a twosome.

While all this was going on, Sandy Wernick at ICM, who had Lorne as a client, set up a meeting for us in L.A. I didn't know Lorne but discovered he had substantial credits in specials and that he'd been involved in *Laugh-In*. Lorne pitched an idea based on Kentucky Fried Theater. I decided right away that it wasn't for me. I just didn't really dig it. But Lorne and I hit it off. Meantime, I'm buying up a lot of talent.

Just after Christmas of 1974 I get a phone call from a manager-lawyer in Atlanta, now dead, who says that he represents Richard Pryor and has convinced Richard that television is a disaster and whatever career he has, he'll never be able to do what he does well on over-the-air television. He could not be himself. So the deal was off. I came back right after the first of January and told Schlosser that Pryor was out. Some day subsequent to that he wrote me a memo and said, "Why don't you bring the show back to New York and even think about doing it in old Studio 8H?" So that part was his idea: "Use 8H."

Then I got hold of Lorne, the closest contemporary to me I'd met in this whole process. He did not have an idea at this point. We goof now about the number of people who've talked about how "the idea" was "sold to NBC." No idea was sold to NBC. I adore Bernie Brillstein, but anything in his book about selling an idea, it never happened. Get the lie detectors out; ask Lorne. It's all bullshit. What did happen was that Lorne just took my breath away in the way he talked about things, how he wanted to have the first television show to speak the language of the time. He wanted the show to be the first show in the history of television to talk—absent expletives—the same language being talked on college campuses and streets and everywhere else. And I was very taken with that, among other things.

So I told NBC there were two people I wanted to do the show, which would be a live comedy show from New York: I wanted this guy Lorne Michaels to produce it, and I wanted a guy named Don Ohlmeyer to direct it.

BERNIE BRILLSTEIN:

You know that at one point NBC suggested Rich Little as the host? I swear to God. We had a meeting with a guy named Larry White. He was head of NBC programming. And we went to see him with the first real pitch of *Saturday Night Live* ever. Lorne told him what he wanted to do, and Larry White said, "That's the worst idea I've ever heard in my life."

DICK EBERSOL:

The night Lorne picked me up at the Beverly Hills Hotel to go see Kentucky Fried Theater—he never said a word about being married—there was this really, really gorgeous dish who got out of the front seat and into the backseat. So we all went to this play, and Lorne and I sat together and this girl sat next to me. And they had introduced her as "Sue Denim," because Rosie loved having these various names. And we finally got back to the Beverly Hills Hotel, and I'm thinking, "This girl is really a knock-out and smart as hell, maybe I ought to ask her out." Because I wasn't anywhere near married in those days. And at some point, when we walked into the hotel to have a drink, it came out that she and Lorne were married, though they weren't living together at that time. But I know they pulled the wool over my eyes for at least three hours.

ROSIE SHUSTER:

Dick thought that I was procured for his delight or something. There was a little fuzziness around my introduction.

MARILYN SUZANNE MILLER, *Writer*:

Other than Herb Sargent, I was the television veteran of *Saturday Night Live,* which is to say I had worked in TV for two and a half or three years, and I had started on *The Mary Tyler Moore Show,* having had the sort of Lana Turner-ish Schwab's discovery made of me by Jim Brooks, aided and abetted by Garry Marshall. So I was writing *Mary Tyler Moore* and *Rhoda* at twenty-two, and I was on the staff of *The Odd Couple.*

I met Michael O'Donoghue and Anne Beatts through a friend when I was doing *Rhoda* and living in New York. When Lorne was putting the show together and asked me to be a part of it, I had an overactive thyroid and was living with this guy I really wanted to be with. So I told Lorne, "I can't do the show because I want to get married, but you've got to hire this guy O'Donoghue, because he's brilliant." Lorne of course had his own access to the Second City people and already knew Chevy, which had nothing to do with Michael. So thanks to me, Michael O'Donoghue got hired.

ANNE BEATTS, *Writer:*

I was living a very sort of style-based existence with Michael O'Donoghue, which was severely crimped by the fact that he'd quit the *Lampoon* and we were completely broke. Michael was rather laid low by the whole experience. At one point I had achieved this thing where we had a gig doing restaurant reviews for the *Village Voice*— every reporter's dream, right? And free meals. And it was Christmastime and Michael and I cowrote a review of Luchow's, this restaurant where Diamond Jim Brady had gone to romance Lillian Russell. It was very Christmassy because it had a giant Christmas tree in the middle of it. Anyway, Michael insisted on putting some reference to Hiroshima and the Nazis into the review. The *Village Voice* did not go for this, especially in a restaurant review. Michael quit in a huff and we lost the gig. And I was like, "Oh, no." We were at the bail-out point when Lorne showed up and offered first Michael and then me jobs on *Saturday Night Live.* And I turned it down because I had sold a book: *Titters,* the first collection of humor by women. I said, "I can't do this stupid television show." And then a friend of mine was like, "Are you crazy? You have to do it." And thank goodness I did. So then Michael and I were working on it together.

DICK EBERSOL:

NBC set up a meeting for eight o'clock in the morning. And Lorne said, "Dick, eight o'clock?!? You know I can't function at that hour." I said, "Lorne, it's breakfast. We've got to do it."

BERNIE BRILLSTEIN:

Lorne said, "I can't get up." I said, "Lorne, this is the one time I'll call you and get you up."

DICK EBERSOL:

So he came to this breakfast, I don't know if he'd even been to bed, and he's sitting with these two guys who, despite whatever nice things they did for me, I have to give the title of "stiffs." They're basically asking if Connie Stevens is going to do the show. Lorne goes into his best BS. When it's over they say, "Well, he's awfully young. But okay—you can have him." The next morning I bring in Ohlmeyer, who's more akin to their world, and they liked him very much. But Roone would not let Don out of his contract at ABC, and it would be almost two years before NBC got Don away from them.

HERBERT SCHLOSSER:

I wanted to do the show live if possible, and I wanted to do it in New York City, because New York had lost all of its entertainment shows. Everything had moved to Burbank. Even Carson had moved to Burbank. Which left a void in 30 Rock. I originally thought it should be two hours and so forth. But the research department was very conservative. Nobody seemed to be enthusiastic at the meeting.

Now I'd had an experience with the *Tomorrow* show, which I didn't want to repeat. I had wanted to put it on, and we went through the procedure as you should of having a financial analysis and a research analysis and so forth, but I never could get an answer from my own network people.

So I was talking to Julian Goodman, who was the chairman of NBC, about my frustration with my ideas for Saturday night, and he said to me, "You should just call Les Brown"—the reporter from *Variety.* "Have lunch with him and just tell him you're putting the show on." So I did. And it was in *Variety* a couple days later. Sure enough, the wheels started moving more rapidly.

DICK EBERSOL:

I would go to the Chateau Marmont, where Lorne lived, and basically for nine or ten days, between going out to dinner and all this stuff, we worked out a loose thing of what this show is going to be. It's going to be a repertory company of seven, and a writing staff and fake commercials and all that.

BERNIE BRILLSTEIN:

About this time, Lorne invited me to his birthday party—his thirtieth, I think—the only party ever held in the lobby of the Chateau Marmont, where they all used to stay. So the party supposedly starts at nine. I was the old man of the group, so I arrive at nine-thirty. And there's not a soul there. Not one. And finally Lorne comes down in slacks and pajama tops, just waking up or something. He said people would be there in a while. This is so Lorne. And about eleven o'clock, here's who walks in: Richard Pryor, Lily Tomlin, George Carlin—the entire underground of Hollywood comedy. And that's when I knew Lorne was a real somebody.

NEIL LEVY, *Production Assistant:*

Lorne's a cousin of mine, and he had brought Paul Simon up to a cottage where I was staying. I didn't actually know who he really was. That's what an idiot I was. I asked him if he was from Simon and Garfunkel. He said, "Yeah, used to be." They had broken up four years earlier, I didn't even know. I did some magic tricks for Paul Simon. I think that impressed Lorne. After that he took me down on the dock and asked me if I wanted to be his assistant on this new show. Oh man, I think my bag was already packed. I thought I had died and gone to heaven. I was nineteen when I first came on the show—the youngest person on the staff. I just watched the whole thing come together with all these famous people slowly gravitating toward the show.

I slept on Lorne's couch for a couple of weeks, long before the show ever started, and one day I came in and Mick Jagger was sitting there—in Lorne's apartment, on the couch. I don't know how Lorne knew Mick Jagger, because at that point he wasn't even "Lorne Michaels." But people were drawn to him.

ROBERT KLEIN:

Some time had passed between when I met Lorne and the forma-tion of this show. Next thing I know, I was immediately sought out as the host. Lorne came down to see me with Chevy Chase, who'd been in *Lemmings,* and checked me out at the Bitter End on Bleecker Street in Greenwich Village. And I remember Lorne suggesting—he was no longer humble—that I should be more "vulnerable" in my act. He said this not directly to me, but through my manager, Jack Rollins. Anyway, it was definitely agreed that I had too big a reputation already to be, quote, "one of the kids," but that I should host the show.

ALBERT BROOKS, *Filmmaker:*

Here's how *Saturday Night Live* came about. I was doing clubs and performing a lot, and Lorne used to come a lot to the shows. I knew that he was a fan. And something was brewing. They decided, I think around September of 1974, that they were, in fact, going to open up eleven-thirty on Saturday. I was first approached in the late fall, early winter of 1974. I was sort of asked by Dick Ebersol if I wanted to have a show—be the permanent host every week. Lorne Michaels was around. I mean, you know, it was both of them. I think I met with Ebersol alone, and Lorne alone, and then both of them together. But that was the first time I heard, "Do you want to host your own show?" And I actually had just done a short film. I wrote this article in 1971 for *Esquire:* "The Famous School for Comedians." PBS had that *Great American Dream Machine,* which was a show of short films, so I made the "Famous School for Comedians" into like a fake infomercial, and it was hugely successful. The PBS stations ran it during pledge drives, and it just turned out to be a great experience for me. So this is what I wanted to do. But in any case, I knew I didn't want to do television, and I told that to Ebersol and Michaels.

And then, you know, a month later, they come back: "This is going to be a big thing. Why don't you do it?" Now, as I did with everything—every time I said no to someone in my life—I always felt compelled to come up with an alternative idea so I didn't sound like an asshole. So I swear to God on my own life, I said to them, "You don't want a permanent host anyway. Every show does that. Why don't you get a different host every week?" And so I really have to tell you, when I said that, they both went, "Oh, okay!" So that was *my* suggestion.

LORNE MICHAELS:

Wait a minute. I made the presentation to NBC on April first, and I didn't talk to Albert until June, so what do you think was in the proposal? But Albert felt, as did a ton of other people in that first year, that they had a big part in the creative effort of the show. It was a big part of their identity.

ALBERT BROOKS:

Then November, December, January, I get another call. They had not really done anything. They hadn't proceeded in any one direction. So what was said to me was, "We want you involved." And at that time there were no cast members. There was nothing. I think serious auditions started in the late spring. So I said, "I want to get into the film business. I want to make short films. What if I make a short film for you?" They all liked the idea and they all said yes, but they didn't have a show yet. So, you know, no one had thought far enough ahead to think, "Well, gee, okay, so then this show is going to have at least a short film."

Now, in turn for that, what I did for them is that in February or early March, there was a junket at the Sheraton Universal for the affiliates about the new season. You know, you'd walk in and the guy from New Orleans would put a palm tree and a bottle of booze there, and you'd stand in front of it and he'd say, "Welcome to New Orleans, Albert." I was there standing with Lorne, and the day was filled with people asking the same question: "So, what's this new show going to be about, Albert?" And I said, "I'm going to do some short films, but I don't really know anything other than that." Then Lorne said, "Well, we're not sure but, you know, we're going to do cutting-edge comedy."

So I am positive that I was the first person brought on. Because I never saw anybody else, and nobody else was ever mentioned.

DICK EBERSOL:

Long before anyone else, Albert had signed on to do those short films. They were inordinately important, because if you look at the early shows it's not really until show ten or eleven, with the exception maybe of Candy Bergen, show four, that you see anything roughly akin to what the show evolved into. So Albert's stuff from the beginning was wildly important. And it came from just running into him one day on Sunset Boulevard.

ALBERT BROOKS:

I always said one thing to these guys—and they didn't take my advice, and in this case I'm sure it's good they didn't—but I said, "This 'live' stuff, it's absolutely meaningless to me. I grew up on the West Coast. I didn't see anything live. It was always tape-delayed. If Ed Sullivan takes his pants down, I'm not going to see him."

To me Johnny Carson was as live as you want to get. If you were bad, you were bad; nobody did it over again. But you did it earlier. You didn't have to stay up until eleven-thirty. So what happens when you stay up until eleven-thirty? Guys like Belushi do nine gallons of coke to make it up that late. I know from being a stand-up, the late show, the midnight show, was the one I hated the most. So my suggestion was, tape a show without stopping tape, do one at four, do one at six-thirty, put the best of those two together, and show me that at eleven-thirty. I'm in California; nothing's live.

DICK EBERSOL:

So now we get to early April, and we're summoned back to New York to make a presentation to the then–NBC program board, a fine group that I don't think made it out of that year. And when it's time to make the presentation, a guy whose name is Bob Howard, then president of the network under Schlosser, tells me a few hours before the meeting, "You can't bring Michaels to the meeting because he's not an NBC employee, he's a freelance producer. We want to hear about the show from you." I said, "What?!?!" So here's this presentation, which is largely Lorne's, and they won't let him in the room. Schlosser does sit in on it. I outlined the whole thing and finished and got stunned silence. Nobody says a word. Nothing. Herb finally says to Bill, "What do you think of it?" Bill Rudin was head of research, and he never wanted to have an opinion in his life until he heard the lay of the land, but he then uttered the famous words, "I don't think it'll ever work because the audience for which it's designed will never come home on Saturday night to watch it."

I went back and told Lorne how it had gone, and tried to keep him from being completely in a snit. Two weeks later, Dave Tebet, the network's head of talent, tells me, "You've got to go to Burbank right away. Carson wants to see you." Neither of us—Lorne or me—had a relationship with Johnny. We're both thinking our lives with this whole thing may be over, because this man, not only is he a genius but our show is going to exist only because he doesn't want his repeats airing on the weekend.

So we get to Burbank and we're taken to Johnny's office. He's there with his producer, Fred DeCordova, who's dressed like Mr. Hollywood, and there's Johnny in a dirty undershirt, sweat stains under each arm, gray slacks. It's maybe one-thirty in the afternoon. Johnny said very little at the meeting, he just wanted to know a few things about the show. Then Fred DeCordova started into this thing about separation. They were talking about guests. We said we didn't have guests, but they said yes you do, you have these hosts. So we worked out this thing that nobody could be booked on the show for a month before a *Tonight Show* appearance and we couldn't have them for a week or two weeks after. We were scared to death the whole time. So when we got out of there, we just went, "Whew."

TOM SCHILLER:

The hip thing to do in those days was to go to the desert and eat hallucinogenic mushrooms. So we went to Joshua Tree and Lorne did the mushrooms. I don't think I really took them myself; it just seems like I did. He was talking a blue streak about this television show he was going to do; he would just never stop. I was really surprised that he could still take phone calls from New York at the pool after he had ingested those mushrooms. He never becomes noticeably different under any circumstances. You can't get through the glaze of brown eyes. You can't go behind them.

I didn't want to work in television; I wanted to be a great director, but I said yes to Lorne because I hated L.A. so much. When I first arrived in New York, I slept on the couch in Lorne's apartment. He would entertain people like Mick Jagger at the apartment, and Jagger would be sitting on the very couch that I was going to go to sleep on. I just couldn't wait for him to leave, because the second he got up, I would go to sleep.

LORNE MICHAELS:

So much of what *Saturday Night Live* wanted to be, or I wanted it to be when it began, was cool. Which was something television wasn't, except in a retro way. Not that there weren't cool TV shows, but this was taking the sensibilities that were in music, stage, and the movies and bringing them to television.

HERBERT SCHLOSSER:

No matter what anyone else tells you, the guy who created the show, and made it what it is, is Lorne Michaels.

DICK EBERSOL:

If you asked Lorne what I contributed to the show, what I think he would say is that during the development stage and the launch, I created an island on which he could exist and no one else could touch him.

Michaels continued his search for talent, listening to suggestions from network executives that he never for a moment considered, protected to some degree by Ebersol from direct interference. Some performers had to be pursued, others threw themselves at Michaels. He also relied on the many contacts he'd made as a performer and writer in Canada and on talent gleaned from improvisational groups like Chicago's and Toronto's Second City and the Groundlings in Los Angeles.

DAVE WILSON, *Director*:

I got involved because I was editing a show called *A Salute to Sir Lew Grade.* British television decided to salute him on his eightieth birthday or whatever it was, and they did an all-star show at the New York Hilton. Gary Smith and Dwight Hemion were actually the producers, but they couldn't stay so they left it all in my hands to get edited. And while I was editing, the production assistant on the show said she was going for an interview, there was a new show starting at NBC, some late-night thing that a Canadian kid was going to be producing. And I said, "Oh, what's it called?" And she said, "I don't know. I think it's called *Saturday Night*." I said, "Isn't that Howard Cosell and Roone Arledge at ABC?" And she said, "Oh no, that's the prime-time *Saturday Night*. This is the late-night *Saturday Night*."

I called my manager and said I was interested and could he get me an interview. The funny thing about it was, I had to fight with my manager. He kept saying, "Oh, you don't want to get involved with a late-night thing, you want to be involved with a prime-time show." I said, "No, I don't want to be involved with a prime-time show, this late-night show looks like it's got some very interesting people involved."

I got an interview in a weird way too, because Lorne wasn't seeing anybody. I guess he had just had it with people being forced down his throat. But luckily my manager was a very good friend of Bernie Brillstein, and I had worked with Bernie on a Muppet show, "Sex and Violence with the Muppets." And Bernie said, "I know Dave Wilson, he gets along great with Jim Henson. And if he can get along great with Jim Henson, he can get along great with anybody." So he put in the word to Lorne that maybe I was somebody he'd be interested in seeing.

HOWARD SHORE:

I actually had to find the band. I'm an avid collector of music and of jazz and R&B, and I just called people I'd listened to on records. I got in touch with as many people as I could that I was interested in. I knew they were in New York. I started to put the band together, started to write original music for the show, themes and original music for the band itself. The Carson show was big-band music. Although I sort of grew up in that a bit in the fifties—Glenn Miller and Ellington and Basie I listened to—the big-band thing was not really my generation. My generation was more R&B and rock and roll.

PAUL SHAFFER, *Musician:*

Howard Shore called me to be in his new band for *Saturday Night Live.* Howard had worked for me in a theatrical show in Toronto on saxophone. I was conducting *Godspell,* the Toronto company. We had a wonderfully talented cast. Gilda was in the cast. Also Andrea Martin, Eugene Levy, Marty Short, and Dave Thomas, among others. These were the funniest people I'd ever come in contact with.

I met Lorne up in his seventeenth-floor office. For some reason I have this recollection of him looking at two pots of coffee brewing and saying, "Which one of these coffees is fresher?" And I'll always remember that. I thought, "This is a guy who speaks in comedic pentameter." I remember that and the fact that his skin was all broken out, because he was nervous. He was putting this show together from scratch, and he hadn't hired anybody yet.

DAVE WILSON:

I first met with Lorne up on seventeen in his office, back in the days when he was wearing a T-shirt that said "Dracula Sucks" and jeans and a ponytail. I was there in my interview suit. I remember coming home from the interview and telling my wife, "Well, I guess I didn't get that job," because Lorne kept saying things like, "This is a young person's medium" and "I'm going to go off in a new direction." Luckily, by happenstance he also said, "For example, our first host is going to be George Carlin. Do you think you and he could understand each other?"

What he didn't know, and what I wasn't even sure that George would remember, is that George and I went to camp together as kids. So I said, "Of course, George Carlin and I are old friends—old, *old* friends, from when we were like little kids." And he said, "I'm going out to the coast to meet with him, I'll say hello for you." I kept praying, "I hope George Carlin remembers me after this whole thing." Turns out he did, and Lorne, I guess, was sort of impressed by that. Then I went for a second interview and got the job.

DICK EBERSOL:

We were walking through the rain one night after dinner, sort of going from awning to awning, and Chevy ran ahead. A couple hundred feet away, he goes into a pothole, does a complete ass over tea-kettle into this immense pothole, and comes out of this thing just soaked. And he walks back and he and Lorne look at me and say, "Now how could you say no to somebody who was crazy enough to do that?" So Chevy became a cast member. And he ended up with a magnificent loophole, since he already had a signed one-year contract as head writer. From the time the show launched, every time the performer contract was put in front of him, it never got signed.

BERNIE BRILLSTEIN:

I had to call Gilda Radner in Vancouver and urge her not to do the David Steinberg show, a syndicated show. It was an offer she'd been considering. I had never met Gilda. That's how I got to know her—over the phone. I made her laugh, you know. Lorne, of course, wouldn't make the call himself, so I had to do it. Even then, there was no direct route. Why it's that way with him I don't know. Fear of rejection, I guess. And clean hands—you know, it's like, "I have nothing to do with it."

DICK EBERSOL:

Late April, early May, Lorne started laying out the cast. One day he's got this really bizarre guy with smoked glasses, Michael O'Donoghue, and I'm thinking, "Oh God, what have we gotten into here?"

And then one day he told me, "This girl is the funniest thing and just a super human being, you're going to be crazy about her," because I had okay over these people. So this thin young woman shows up with a kid who says hello and excuses himself. But the woman is Gilda. And here I am talking to this young comedic actress, and I'm absolutely mesmerized by her. So she's the first person signed to do the show after Lorne.

DAN AYKROYD, *Cast Member:*

I went through so many auditions. Live auditions, tape auditions. After the first one, I thought, "I'm not going to get hired," and I ended up driving across country with John Candy to do Second City in Pasadena. We went from Toronto to L.A. in thirty-eight hours in a big old

Mercury Cougar with me and him switching off driving. And then we got to Pasadena and I started my first week of rehearsals and Lorne called and said, "Well, come back out." So at my own expense, I got on a fucking plane, flew back to New York, and had this other series of tape auditions. I think I did like newscaster guy, announcer guy type of thing, and if anything got me on the show it was that type of fast-rap announcer, the Ron Popeil sort of thing.

There was one audition in the summer, a live thing, a cattle call. I came down with a friend from Toronto. We had a song prepared, but then I saw all the people lined up, waiting outside in the hall there. There were a hundred people waiting to get in, and I was at the end of the line. And I thought, "Boy, it's three o'clock now, it's going to be seven o'clock at night when we get on. This song ain't going to go over too well."

So I just kind of cut through the line and busted into the room — because I knew Lorne from Canada — and walked up. "Hey, how are you boss, what're you doing, nice to see you." I said, "Well, I'm here," and I did a sort of quick five-minute kind of fast rap and then got out of there. And I think they were impressed. After that audition, it was clear I had the job. I went home to Canada, got my motorcycle, and drove down into the city for the first season in '75. I had just turned twenty-three.

PAUL SHAFFER:

Gilda and I had both worked on the *National Lampoon Radio Hour* here in New York, so we became friendly with John Belushi and Doug Kenney and this cast of characters associated with the *Lampoon.* I remember Gilda was trying to get Belushi hired for *Saturday Night Live.* A lot of people were telling Lorne he had to hire Belushi. And I remember seeing Gilda with Belushi one day, and she said, "We're sitting shiva because Lorne won't hire John."

CHEVY CHASE, *Cast Member:*

In fact, Belushi was an afterthought. I mean, he had told Lorne at some point that he was not enchanted with TV per se and he didn't want to do TV. And Lorne didn't particularly care if he saw him or didn't see him. Then John did an audition and Lorne said, "Well, he's funny, and we could use somebody who looks like him."

DAN AYKROYD:

Lorne was concerned that Belushi and I would be a duo that would give him a lot of trouble. He thought, "Oh, get these guys together and their strength will be my weakness, because they'll be rebels." And you know, in a way, he was right. Certainly there was an energy around us.

John was a kid out of Chicago, the Chicago Second City troupe, and I was out of the Second City in Toronto. I came from the capital city of Ottawa, the child of two government workers; his father ran a restaurant, was in private business. But we grew up loving the same things: *The Twilight Zone, The Outer Limits,* old black-and-white TV. When we first came up with the Blues Brothers, that was prior to *SNL.* John came up to Toronto to recruit for the *National Lampoon Radio Hour;* that's when I first met him. He managed to get Gilda to come down to New York to work with him. I had this gig on a kids' TV show at four in the afternoon, I had my job at Second City, I did radio and television commercials, and I had my speakeasy bar, which was all cash, no tax. So I was flush. I had rockets going everywhere. I was making more money than the prime minister of Canada. I had a car, a bike, an apartment in the city, my tent at the farm. I was living a beautiful life up there. There was no way I wanted to go to the States.

JUDITH BELUSHI, *Writer*:

In John's first interview with Lorne, one of the first things he said was, "My television has spit all over it." That's how he felt about television. He was asked to do a few television things. He was offered a guest shot on *Mary Tyler Moore,* which everyone thought could easily turn into a character role. And it was kind of a big deal to say no. He even liked Mary Tyler Moore. But he needed to be political and outrageous.

LORNE MICHAELS:

I had worked in television for eight years, so I was bored with people who go, "I don't do television." I had no patience for it, for people putting it down. They say, "I'm not doing television," and then I go,

"Well, then, there's no point to us talking." I told John, "I hear what you're doing is great, but I don't want you to have to do something that you don't want to do." My instinct was that he was going to be trouble.

JUDITH BELUSHI:

John went to talk to Lorne because, he said, "Well, if he's hiring O'Donoghue and Anne Beatts and Gilda"—they were people John liked working with, and so he figured the show was going to be something different.

ANNE BEATTS:

They had been paying us the same amount, which was a big $750 a week. You can imagine, if we were happy to accept free restaurant meals from the *Village Voice,* $750 a week represented a considerable sum to us in those days. I mean, our rent was $675 a month, which everyone thought was just horrendously high for what Belushi called "the Winter Palace" on Sixteenth Street.

And then NBC told me, "Oh, we're not supposed to be paying you as much as Michael. We've been paying you $750 a week, but that's a mistake. And we want the money back." They said it had been a bookkeeping error. And I basically said, "Go fuck yourself." You know, "The money's gone and you're not getting it back. Furthermore, you better start paying *me* $750 a week." Why shouldn't I make the same as him? I don't know. Because he had more credits or something. Or because he had a penis.

DICK EBERSOL:

Some of the auditions took place in a Steinway rehearsal hall on West Fifty-seventh Street. When we came back over to 30 Rock, even after John's incredible audition, Lorne was really troubled about how one could discipline him. John was always the best person available in New York, bar none. But he always made it perfectly clear that he thought television was shit. Everything about television was shit. And yet he kept showing up for all these meetings and auditions. And Lorne was very worried about it. Finally, on the day the decision was made, the three of us—Michael, Anne Beatts, and I—really argued for John in a big way. And I think Lorne said at the time, the thing that finally turned his mind was I said I would take responsibility for him. I made a vow to Lorne that if he's the nightmare some people think he'll be, I'll take care of him. I'll be the minder of Belushi—which led to some awfully fun stuff for me, including him almost burning my house down. He did the same thing to Lorne's place in New York.

JUDITH BELUSHI:

Just before John and I were married, I kicked him out of the house for this or that, and he went and stayed at Lorne's place. He fell asleep with a cigarette going, and the mattress caught on fire. He didn't burn the whole place down, but I'm sure it caused some damage. Lorne called me afterward and said, "Can I send him home now?"

BERNIE BRILLSTEIN:

I went down there after the fire, and there were odors I had never smelled before in my life. I mean, it was terrible. I was an old guy. I was used to comedians in tuxedos and ties.

CHEVY CHASE:

John was wonderful. He was trouble later on for me. Jesus, oh God, was he trouble.

GARRETT MORRIS, *Cast Member:*

I'd been a licensed schoolteacher, taught two years at PS 71 in New York plus five years at the projects with drug-addicted kids. And you know what, I hadn't worked in like a fucking year and a half. I'd done *Cooley High* and that was it. I left the school system to go back into a thing called *Hallelujah, Baby!* My license had even expired.

I didn't have a job. I was starving. So Lorne offered me a job. I won't tell you how much it was, but it was good money.

LARAINE NEWMAN, *Cast Member:*

I worked for Lorne the first time on a Lily Tomlin special. He had come to see me when we had just formed the Groundlings and we had our theater over on Oxford and Santa Monica. It was just the armpit of Hollywood, and he came to see the show. I was doing my characters and my monologues. They really were looking for men for the Lily Tomlin special, they didn't need any more women. But they ended up hiring me. And that was just thrilling. I was twenty-two.

The following year, Lorne told me he had been approached to do a weekend replacement show for *The Tonight Show* and said it would be a cross between *Monty Python* and *60 Minutes*. And I thought, "I'd watch that," you know. It was a big break and I thought, "This'll be great."

JANE CURTIN, *Cast Member:*

John and I were the last two people hired, and John was hired about a week after me, so I didn't have any idea of what was going on there. But I knew John, because John and I were also auditioning for the Howard Cosell show. So I was working with John in those auditions too. He was much sweeter back then, I think, because he couldn't afford the drugs. He was more in control. He was accessible. I actually liked him when we were working on the Cosell show auditions. I thought he was a lot of fun, and I thought he was very talented. And then when he got hired by *Saturday Night,* I thought it was a very good idea.

LORNE MICHAELS:

Gilda and John and Danny had known each other from before. Danny and I had known each other because when I came down, I brought him down from Canada. Gilda and I went back forever. And so you had Laraine, who I brought from L.A., Jane Curtin, who we kind of heard about, and the girl we were going to choose, this girl named Mimi Kennedy. But Gilda was worried that they were too similar.

GARRETT MORRIS:

The way I got on the show as an actor is that a couple people on the writing staff were trying to get rid of me as a writer. Mind you, I had two plays that had been produced in New York City. In fact, New York commissioned a play from your boy, okay, and then I wrote another play, which was produced in New York and in L.A. I'm a playwright, so I was having trouble getting my stuff down to a minute or a minute and a half, to fit into some sketch.

The first three months or so, a guy there stole an idea and then added a little something to it, and he didn't even give me credit for cowriting. This guy stole from me and then told Lorne I couldn't write. Lorne's response was even-tempered. He wasn't necessarily stroking me like I was a pet, but he was fair. When the challenge came to get rid of me as a writer, Lorne let me audition for the Not Ready for Prime Time Players. He did not fire me. And to this day, I am thankful for that. So I got with the Not Ready for Prime Time Players, and the look on that guy's face for the next four years was the only thing that saved me from jumping on him.

BERNIE BRILLSTEIN:

Lorne really stuck to his guns at the very beginning. He told the network, "I must have seventeen shows. Give the show time to grow." They thought we were insane. And maybe we were. But it wasn't until the tenth show that they really hit their stride. Lorne was this great young writer who had this vision of this type of show. He was also a good producer, but everybody forgets what a great writer he was, and certainly a great editor. He was like a conduit for all the comedy brains at the time. He was just "The Guy."

JOHN LANDIS, *Film Director:*

This is all hindsight, okay? I don't want to take anything away from Lorne, but he was in the right place at the right time. There were comedy movements going on everywhere. In England you had the Pythons, in San Francisco you had the Committee, in Chicago you had Second City, and then in New York — starting in Boston but then moving to New York — you had the National Lampoon Show. If you look at *Saturday Night Live*'s cast for the first three or four years, you'll see they were all either Lampoon or Second City. He cherry-picked people of great skill and talent that had been trained and gotten their chops.

BARBARA GALLAGHER, *Associate Producer:*

Lorne was very shy, very funny, kind of quiet. We were exactly the same age. He called me and said that Dick Ebersol and he were going to do a show. It sounded like a "Look, we've got a barn, we're going to put on a show" kind of thing. And because I'd had live TV experience by working on the *Ed Sullivan Show,* Lorne wanted me to come and write and be part of the team. I didn't want to go back to New York, and I didn't want to be a writer, so Lorne said, "How about 'creative associate producer'? I just like the fact you've been on a live show." So I said okay. I went back to New York in June of 1975.

I didn't have a clue what the show was going to be. It just sounded fun and kind of groundbreaking.

EUGENE LEE, *Set Designer:*

I can remember Lorne—he would *not* remember—saying to me, "God, this is going to be so great! We all get to just hang out in New York together." I was living on a sailboat in Rhode Island, working with what was then called the Trinity Square Repertory Company— where I still work—and someone called my boat about this Canadian producer doing a comedy-variety show. They wanted to know if we— my wife, Franne, a costume designer, and I—would be interested in talking. He was at the Plaza, we could call and make an appointment. Well, why not?

ALAN ZWEIBEL, *Writer:*

In 1975 I'm this Jewish guy slicing God-knows-what at a deli in Queens and selling jokes to these Catskill comics for seven dollars a joke. At night I would go on at Catch a Rising Star. I had taken all the jokes that the Borscht Belt comedians wouldn't buy from me because they said the stuff was too risqué for their crowd and made them into a stand-up act for myself, hoping that somebody would come in, like the material, and give me a job in television.

Everybody hung out at Catch a Rising Star and the Improv in those days. And I'd just met Billy Crystal, who was starting out the same way. He lived on Long Island, three towns over from where I was living with my parents; he was married and had a kid already. We would carpool into the city every night. One night about four months into this horror show, it's about one in the morning and I'm having trouble making these six drunks from Des Moines laugh, and I get off the stage sweating like a pig and I go over to the bar, and I'm waiting for Billy to tell his jokes so he can drive me home to Long Island. And this guy sits down next to me and just stares at me. Stares at me. And I look over — "What?" And he just looks at me and he goes, "You know, you're the worst comedian I've ever seen in my life." And I went, "Yeah, I know."

I said that I wanted to have a wife and kids someday but they'd starve if something else didn't happen soon. He said, "Your material's not bad. Did you write it?" I said, "Yeah." He said, "Can I see more?" And I said, "You bet." I didn't even ask who he was; I mean, I would have shown it to a gardener at this point.

But it was Lorne, and he was combing the clubs looking for writers and actors for this new show. So I went back to Long Island and I stayed up for two days straight and I typed up what I thought were eleven hundred of my best jokes, jokes that I wrote for the Borscht Belt comics, jokes that I practiced writing for other comics, jokes I heard in third grade — I mean, I just went nuts. And so I took my phone book full of jokes and went into the city for my interview with Lorne.

Oh, but first I called Billy Crystal, because he had been talking to Lorne about him being a part of the show from the beginning, either as a cast member or some sort of rotating player. So I said, "Look, I'm supposed to meet with this guy Lorne, can you tell me anything about him?" So Billy told me he used to submit jokes to Woody Allen, he's produced a *Monty Python* special, and the new show is going to have these little films by Albert Brooks. Oh, and he hates mimes. Lorne hates mimes. So I said fine, I went over to the Plaza Hotel and met with Lorne.

He takes the phone book of jokes, opens it, reads the first joke, and goes, "Uh-huh." And closes it. And he says, "How much money do you need to live?" I said, "Well, I'm making $2.75 an hour at the deli — match it." So he said to tell him more about myself. He figured before he'd commit to that kind of money, he wanted to know what he was buying. I said, well, Woody Allen's my idol, I love *Monty Python,* and maybe my career will go like Albert Brooks's — you know, short films and then bigger ones. "But," I said, "if there's one fucking mime on the show, I'm outta there." And he gives me the job.

The joke that I had as the number one joke in this compilation of jokes was, just to show you how long ago this was—because of the reference in it—was that the post office was about to issue a stamp commemorating prostitution in the United States. It's a ten-cent stamp, but if you want to lick it, it's a quarter.

We even did it on the show. I remember we were short on jokes. Chevy might have done it. Yeah, I think he did. I think that was my one contribution to the first show, the one that George Carlin hosted.

ROSIE SHUSTER:

I read Alan Zweibel's book of one-liners that came to the Marmont and discussed it with Lorne. I remember talking a lot about Chevy as a writer. Marilyn Miller we knew from Lily Tomlin. Anne Beatts and Michael O'Donoghue were celebrities, especially O'Donoghue, who was, you know, the darling of the *Lampoon,* so they came presold. O'Donoghue had a lot of charisma and he was very dark. He was an exciting character in his subversiveness. Al Franken and Tom Davis were a two-for-one kind of bargain basement. They were just starting and anxious to get into the business—you know, let's give them a tryout. I was definitely in the conversations about all that stuff.

ANNE BEATTS:

I truly think you can say that without Michael O'Donoghue, there wouldn't have been a *Saturday Night Live,* and I think it's important to remember that. I think Lorne would probably be generous enough to acknowledge that. Because I always said Michael was Cardinal Richelieu. He wasn't very good at being the king. He was much better at being either the person plotting revolution or the power behind the throne, telling the king what to do and think. I'm not saying he was manipulating Lorne. It doesn't always have to be about manipulation. It could be about actual helpful guidance.

AL FRANKEN, *Writer*:

Tom Davis and I had known each other since high school in Minnesota. In 1974 we were a comedy team out in L.A. We were the only writers hired by Lorne who he didn't meet. We always thought that if he had met us, we wouldn't have gotten the job. We weren't making money at the time, and the only variety shows around were Johnny Carson's—and we're not joke writers, so we couldn't do that—and Carol Burnett's, which was a good show but not our territory. Oh, and I think *Sonny and Cher* was on, which was a piece of shit.

Actually, we wrote a perfect submission for *Saturday Night Live,* a package of things we'd like to see on TV—a news parody, commercial parody, and a couple sketches. Basically from that, we were hired. We heard that Dick Ebersol wanted to hire a team from New York instead of us so he could save on the airfare, but Lorne insisted on us.

Michaels was aghast at the condition of NBC's historic Studio 8H, which despite its noble traditions was technically primitive and had been allowed to deteriorate. He didn't think it had hosted a weekly live TV show since Your Hit Parade *succumbed to rock and roll and left NBC in 1958.*

Meanwhile, NBC brass were consumed with nervousness about the content of the show—about giving ninety minutes of network time a week to Lorne Michaels and his left-wing loonies. On the first show, with sometimes-racy comic George Carlin hosting, the network planned to use a six-second delay so that anything unexpected and obscene could be edited out by an observer from the Department of Standards and Practices (the censor), who would theoretically flip a switch in the control room and bleep the offending material before it went out naked onto the American airwaves. Over the coming months and years, various hosts or musical acts would make NBC executives more nervous than usual, and the notion of making the show not quite precisely literally live kept coming up.

JANE CURTIN:

NBC sent me out on a limited publicity tour weeks before we went on the air. I didn't really know what the show was going to be like, but I was the only one in the cast that they weren't afraid of. They knew I wouldn't throw my food.

BERNIE BRILLSTEIN:

In the first six months, Lorne threatened not to come in to work a lot. He had no way of dealing with these network people. Because Lorne had a vision, and they didn't understand his vision. This was a new show at that time. He made them rebuild the goddamn studio, and they didn't understand that. And he made them get great sound in the studio because they were going to have rock acts, and they didn't understand that.

HOWARD SHORE:

I remember going for that first tour of the studio, and they had game show sets in there and they were doing very low-tech productions in there because it didn't have any of the technology that was really needed to do a live broadcast. It was stuck in the late fifties.

BERNIE BRILLSTEIN:

When Lorne told NBC they had to spend like three hundred grand to rebuild that studio, they nearly had a breakdown.

BARBARA GALLAGHER:

Dick Ebersol was really the buffer. He'd worked very hard to get the show on the air. And the NBC guys all thought we were from Mars. The bureaucracy at NBC was terrible. They thought we were a joke at the beginning. Trying to get through the red tape really took a lot of time. We couldn't even get stationery with the show's name printed on it. They had no faith in us at all.

The network really irked Lorne at the beginning, big-time.

CRAIG KELLEM, *Associate Producer:*

He was in a constant battle with the network as it pertained to the economics, particularly about the set. Lorne wanted the set to be like almost this architectural prototype. The argument was, "Hey, you can't even see that on camera," and Lorne's attitude was, "Yes, but I want it. I want it anyway."

EUGENE LEE:

They hired Dave Wilson to be the director. He'd done a lot of TV. Dave was a nice man, but he had very strong opinions about things and said them. And there was a lot of incredible feuding about the layout of the studio. Dave and I fought tooth and nail about how it would be laid out. I laid it out my way—longways. There was a lot of muttering about how there wouldn't be enough space. I said, "The cameras are on wheels, let the cameras roll to the scenery and not the other way."

One day just out of the blue, Lorne comes by and says, "Hey, we've got to go upstairs." And I went with him, and we took the model of the set up to whoever—I think it was Herb Schlosser. We laid it on the coffee table. And Lorne hadn't said much about any of this. But he explained it perfectly to Schlosser. He was like brilliant! I mean really, no kidding. I was knocked out. He said, "This thing goes here, and the camera moves here, and it all stretches around this great big environment." And after that, money didn't seem to be a problem.

DAVE WILSON:

The idea of having part of the audience sitting around home base was not that new. I'm sure that kind of thing had been done many times. But the idea of putting an audience in front of those side stages was a little different. It worked well because it gave performers more of an intimate feeling of audience, that they were performing not just for cameras but for a live audience.

HOWARD SHORE:

It's true—there is no theme song for *Saturday Night Live* in the traditional sense. This is inherent in the nature of the show. I wanted the theme music for the show to have an improvisational feel, like the show itself, and I wanted it to grow and change from year to year. And that's why when I listen to the show now after twenty-five, twenty-six years, it still sounds fresh to me and sort of classic, and it wouldn't have if you kept hearing the same hummable melody over and over. Because the nature of the music on the show was interplay between the ten musicians, which is completely different than what you have in a big band or the Carson sound, which is very formalized arrangements written very specifically, and everybody plays what is written on the page.

It's the same thing as the cast. You have to think of the musicians in the band the same as you think of the cast and how they would play off each other and kind of riff off each other. That was the same feeling that I wanted to create in the music. So it had to have an improvisational nature. The saxophone was just a thing that I loved, and I am a saxophone player, so it was inherent in my soul that it be the predominant voice. Instead of a band playing a piece with a melody, it was an improvisation by a great blues soloist.

On September 17, 1975, only a few weeks before the first live broadcast of what was then called NBC's Saturday Night, *Lorne Michaels and several of his cast members got together in a rented midtown studio for forty-five minutes of "screen tests" to see how the performers looked on-camera.*

Dan Aykroyd, Laraine Newman, Gilda Radner, Chevy Chase, Garrett Morris, Bill Murray, token older actor George Coe, John Belushi, guest Andy Kaufman, and musical director Howard Shore took turns before the camera, most of them improvising material or summoning up routines they'd done in stage shows like the National Lampoon's or at comedy clubs in the United States and Canada.

The tape is a hot underground item but has never been shown on network television, though Michaels considered using parts of it in the fifteenth- and twenty-fifth-anniversary specials. What is Bill Murray doing there? Michaels had hoped to sign him for that first crop of Not Ready for Prime Time Players, but at nearly the last minute he learned from NBC bean counters that the budget would not allow him to hire Murray, at least not now. He instead became a member of the repertory company known as the Prime Time Players on Howard Cosell's short-lived ABC Saturday-night variety show.

The tape shows the young performers at the tender and relatively innocent moment before they burst onto the American scene. Aykroyd, leading off, goes through a series of wacky riffs, starting with his recitation of mangled lyrics from the song "Till There Was You" from The Music Man: *" 'There were birds in the sky, but I never sore [sic] them winging, till there was you.' And 'you,' of course, is the Mashimilov UT-1 rocket that Russia has just developed."* In a Walter Cronkite voice he reports on *"troop movements across the demilitarized zone into North Korea today,"* then does a mock commercial for *"Lloyd Manganaro Deltoid Spray . . . made from the extracted liquid from the spleens of perfumed sheep."* Then he turns into a Louisiana swamp farmer who claims to have been briefly abducted by aliens in business suits: *"Now you can believe it if you want to or you can just say that I'm making up this story, but to me it was very, very important, because it killed all the crabs in the area, and my livelihood is threatened, and I'd like somebody to do something about it."* Then he assumes the voice of a man narrating a documentary and talks about *"shale and the influence of shale on the topography of the world and how shale was superimposed and brought down by the glacial formations."* This evolves into a discussion of glaciers, which ends with, *"We have a lot of things to thank the glacier for—but who do we write to?"*

To offscreen director Dave Wilson in the control booth, Aykroyd asks obligingly, *"More characters? More accents? Cleaner look?"* But he's dismissed to be replaced in front of the camera by Laraine Newman, who instantly becomes a chirpy and perky airline attendant: *"Hi, my name is Sherry and I was made to fly. . . . When I was first thinking about becoming a stewardess, all my friends were really bugging me. They were coming up to me and saying things like, 'Well, God, Sherry, why do you want to be a stewardess,' you know? And I had to just sit down with myself and get super-reflective and ask myself, 'Well, gosh, Sherry, why do you want to be a stewardess,' you know? And I really realized that it's because I love people. I really do. I love to serve 'em and try to help 'em fall asleep sitting up, you know?*

"Well, the real reason was, I had to get out of the Valley. I'm not kidding, man, it was really getting hairy. My boyfriend, Brad, and I were just falling apart. We had this really nice relationship, we were going to get married and everything, and like, he installed stereo systems and customized fans, you know, and all he ever talked about was woofers and tweeters and push-pull rods, man, and it was really boring. It really grossed me out royal. And my relationship with his parents wasn't too cool either, because I wasn't Jewish, you know, and I, like, made a peach

cobbler and I heard them say, 'Well, look. The shiksa made us a Presbyterian pie.'..."

Bill Murray follows, introducing himself as Washington Redskin Dwayne Thomas and saying, "You know, professional football has been good to me." He laments having been sentenced to "one-to-twenty in Texas for possession of herb," then turns into interviewer "Jerry Aldini" and soon is doing an early version of Nick, the awful lounge singer, a character that helped establish him, after some early audience resistance, as a true star on Saturday Night Live. First he does a freewheeling version of the show tune "Hey There" from The Pajama Game: "Hey there, you with the starrrrrs in your eyes. Nobody told you what day it was, Nobody was surprised." He pantomimes playing a cocktail piano, using the desk in front of him as a keyboard, threatening to sing and play "something by Bobby Vinton, something from his new 'Polish Is Cool' album...."

Gilda Radner, surprisingly, seems the least at ease in front of the camera. She giggles, looks off toward the wings where Lorne Michaels is standing. "I'm not going to talk about food," Gilda says, "I'm not going to talk about guys... so I don't have anything to say at all." She rambles for a few seconds, then asks, "Wait—can we get an audience in here?" Aykroyd, just out of camera range, tries to help by asking such questions as what Gilda would do "if your period came on right now," then pretends to be Peter Marshall, host of The Hollywood Squares, and poses a question to Gilda: "Is it true that women accelerate more than men on expressway ramps?" Gilda: "Only if they're with a man."

She offers to do her "only character, Colleen," a clueless girl with the same goofy and faraway look no matter what the circumstances. Thus she looks exactly the same, blank and baffled, as she goes through a brief series of impressions: "This is Colleen at a Nureyev ballet.... This is Colleen going to an Irish festival.... This is Colleen having her first sexual experience." All are the same.

Frustrated and restless, Gilda announces, "Lorne said if I just sat here and stared down the camera, it would take a lot of guts," then asks plaintively, "Can I go now—back to Toronto?" Lorne, off-camera, shouts, "Gilda, that was great."

Chevy Chase, in contrast to Gilda, looks supremely comfortable when he sits down in the chair and starts to talk: "You want me to do something here?" No member of the Not Ready for Prime Time Players, perhaps ever, has been more at home and less inhibited on-camera, ironic considering that Chase originally wanted to be only a writer on the show.

Immediately, Chevy becomes the fatuous anchorman he would immortalize in the "Weekend Update" segment of Saturday Night Live. He is holding a few sheets of paper and reads from them—or perhaps simply recites the material from memory:

"Our final note concerns the birth of a baby sandpiper at the Washington Municipal Zoo this morning at 9:13. It's the first such birth in captivity on record. The chick weighed in at just under fourteen grams, and it is said to resemble its mother quite closely.

"A final note of humor: the bird was stepped on and crushed to death by the baby hippo that was born on Wednesday.

"Said zookeeper John Pinkett: 'Well, I guess I'll have to pour kerosene on the mother and light it and hope for the best. Later, perhaps, we can take an electric cattle prod and drive it into the ears of the baby hippo. Or perhaps shove a couple of cherry bombs up its ass, light them, and hope for the best.'

"Well, that's the news this Wednesday. Good night, and have a pleasant tomorrow"—basically the same ending that would be used for "Weekend Update" once the show premiered. Chevy is asked to hold up a few of Edie Baskin's New York photographs so the camera can zoom in on them. Baskin's pictures will be used for a montage under the opening credits of Saturday Night Live. Originally those credits featured only images of the city at night and no pictures of cast members.

Jane Curtin, up next, performs what seems for her unusually "sick" material, once she gets a mock commercial for "Jamitol" (Geritol, an iron supplement) out of the way. "In show business, I've had a fairly limited career," she continues. "It's hard to perform onstage in a wheelchair. However, I entertain a lot of people at my parents' family parties. Having a catheter, a lot of people think, is funny, and they like to see me dance. Thank you."

A voice from the wings asks about what she does "in the privacy of your own home," and Curtin replies, "That's between me and my cat, isn't it?" Murray steps into the frame and begins massaging her shoulders.

Garrett Morris—who, like Chase, signed on only to be a writer—materializes next. "As I have nothing prepared, I decided I might do some imitations," he says. "The first imitation I will do is of James Mason: 'This is James Mason speaking.'" Morris makes only the most minimal effort to sound anything like James Mason. "That's James Mason. Okay, I'll do another imitation. There's a guy named Cross-eyed Jim that used to live on Federal Avenue in Marble City when I was a kid. Here is Cross-eyed Jim." And he, of course, crosses his eyes. As a "general West Indian," Morris talks about going to the second floor of Barney's and buying clothes from the Johnny Carson Collection.

Aykroyd comes in to feed Morris straight lines, asking him about having spent ten minutes with an unnamed congressman. "He asked me for a joint," Morris says, "and I didn't have any on me. He usually gets a little high.... The indictments against him haven't been proven yet, and I think we should give him the benefit of the doubt."

Aykroyd, changing subjects: "You're the man who saw the first mastodon come across the plains. Am I correct?"

Morris: "Yes, I did, I saw a mastodon. It wasn't across the plains, though. It was in my backyard. And it was sort of noisy.... It was three o'clock in the morning, man. I just got in at 2:45 and I needed some rest." Told the mastodon left footprints fifteen feet wide, Morris says, "Jeez, that was a big mother."

John Belushi's turn before the camera that day was brief and very visual. And the instant Belushi sits down, he takes effortless command of the camera. He already has a compellingly "dangerous" look about him. "Okay," he says, "we're going to do some loosening up exercises." He practices doing "takes" and "double takes" and then, as only Belushi could, some "work on the eyebrows." He alternates left and right eyebrows, moving them up and down independently of each other in a series of eyebrow calisthenics.

He shifts gears. "Good evening, ladies and gentlemen. Welcome to the Saturday Night *show. The show is live, the show is not on tape, so all the mistakes you—" He suddenly fakes a horrendous gagging sound, then regains his composure and continues: "So all the mistakes happening on this show are real. We don't plan anything, because everything is real." Now he breaks into a ghastly hacking cough, pretending to spit up into his hands.*

"With tape you have the advantage of editing things that don't work. With live television, anything goes." He attempts to attach strips of tissue to his eyelids, using spit to hold them on. Someone calls for an imitation of Marlon Brando and Belushi does part of the taxicab scene from On the Waterfront: "Don't you remember that night in the garden you came down and said, 'Kid, it ain't your night?' Not my night! Charlie, it was you, Charlie." He grabs more tissue, stuffs it in his cheeks, and does Brando in The Godfather, followed by a quick impression of Rod Steiger: "Teddy! Teddy! What're you talking about?! What're you talking ABOUT?! Don't talk to me that WAY!"

Finally, the definitively eccentric comic and performance artist Andy Kaufman, who'll appear on the Saturday Night Live premiere (lip-synching to the Mighty Mouse theme), sits in the chair looking incredibly young and bright-eyed, and simply recites the lyrics to "MacArthur Park" in a calm, conversational voice: "Someone left the cake out in the rain. I don't think that I can take it, 'cause it took so long to bake it, and I'll never have that recipe again. Oh, no." He covers his eyes with his hands mournfully.

When he finishes, the voice of director Dave Wilson comes over a loudspeaker: "Andy, could you do that again, please?" "The same way?" "Exactly the same if you can." And he does.

The tape ends with music director Howard Shore, very much the scruffy hippie, modeling a pimpish-looking outfit for Lorne, who directs his movements from the wings. The Saturday Night Live cast was on the brink of success, poised to revolutionize television, looking fresh, brash, and golden. The premiere was less than a month away—October 11, 1975. A date which will live in comedy.

BRAD GREY, *Manager:*

Bernie was there for the first dress rehearsal. He looked out and he saw the band rehearsing. And it was getting close to starting time. So he turned to Lorne and he said, "Hey, Lorne, you know the band doesn't have their tuxedos on yet. Better get them into wardrobe." That always made me laugh, because it was so honest of Bernie. Tuxedos! And that's sort of, I guess, the merging of two generations.

DICK EBERSOL:

Lorne's telling me every day that Chevy's got this great idea to open every show with a fall, and I am absolutely opposed. But Chevy was the only one who was funny and could write television for television.

We were reading scripts in those early days where people would have a three- or four-minute sketch take place on five sets, and it didn't take a real scholar to know you couldn't do that if we were going to do a live television show in a box the size of 8H.

DAVE WILSON:

Many of them had written for magazines or the *National Lampoon Radio Hour* or that kind of thing, so it wasn't as if they were brand-new to writing, it's just that they weren't familiar with the medium of television. So of course we'd always go through things where you'd read their script and it says, "We start with a flooded studio." And you'd say, "Well, you better rethink that."

JANE CURTIN:

Before the show went on the air, we would all have to hang out on the seventeenth floor with the writers and pitch ideas and do all of that kind of stuff, and Lorne would call us all into his office for whatever reason, and he would always end up by telling us what "stars" we were. And I'm thinking, "Hey, we haven't earned it yet," not understanding the machine—the PR and all this stuff that was going to happen and that they were going to make happen. I think Lorne was trying to pump up the arrogance and the adrenaline in the room—which wasn't hard—and I understand now that in order to do that kind of a show or any kind of a comedy show, you have to have arrogance and you have to have adrenaline. And by telling people they're stars, maybe that's one way of doing that.

But sadly, a couple of days later, I think some poor elevator operator was punched because he dared to ask somebody in the cast for an ID. I just kept fighting that kind of thing. I just kept thinking, "No no no no no, it's just a TV show. It'll be okay, and I'm fine."

BILLY CRYSTAL, *Cast Member:*

Three months before the show was supposed to debut, Lorne had found me in a club called Catch a Rising Star. I went, "This is a television producer?" He sounded like David Steinberg the comedian because he was from Canada. He was very appealing, he was very smart, and he was funny in a different way than I envisioned television producers to be. He asked me if I was interested in being a resident in the company. He felt I would do six appearances on the show, and then he saw me becoming a host of the show, among all the other hosts, in two years. They'd be grooming me to be one of the main guys. That's how it came down prior to the show.

BUDDY MORRA, *Manager:*

Billy turned down a Bill Cosby special, who was the hottest thing in the country at that time, to take *Saturday Night Live,* because they said, "If you do the Cosby show, we're not interested in having you do this." And so we opted to do *Saturday Night Live.* We had agreed in advance for Billy to do his special piece on the first show, and that the piece required a certain amount of time; it wouldn't work in less time. So Billy was coming in every day from Long Island, and he just sat around all day long. They never spoke to him, they never got to him, they never said anything to him. He'd leave at the end of the day, after spending eight or nine hours waiting around, and then come back the next morning again. This went on for pretty much the entire week.

BILLY CRYSTAL:

Then we get to the Friday night. We had a run-through for a live audience and some NBC executives. Now my routine was an audience participation piece and it utilized Don Pardo and it was this African safari thing with sound effects. I played Victor Mature—it's not going to sound funny—walking across the camp in Africa to knock the tarantula spider off Rita Hayworth's chest. So that was the setup. Don Pardo, who we never saw on camera, had his hands in a big bowl of potato chips, and every time I took a step, Don would crunch the potato chips so it was like this whole sound effects thing. It was really funny on Friday night. And it ran six, six and a half minutes, because

EXORDIUM: 1975-1976

53

it took a long time to explain it. But there were laughs in the explanation and then the piece just sort of went on its own. And Friday night, it was the comedy highlight of the night, and I thought, "I'm in great shape here." George Carlin's hosting this new show and I knew everybody in the show and this is going to be sensational.

Lorne sent in notes after the Friday night run-through and he said to me, "I need two minutes." And I said, "Cut two minutes?" And he said, "No, I need two minutes. All you get is two minutes." So it was a drastic cut in the piece, and frankly as a new performer then I didn't have a little hunk like Andy Kaufman's Mighty Mouse. I didn't have a two-minute thing that I could plug into the show, and I didn't have a stand-up piece that felt like what the show should be that I could have scored in two or three minutes. So we had a big dilemma. And after being involved with Lorne and the show for so long, we were all kind of confused as to what to do. And then when we saw the rundown, they had put me on at five to one. The last five minutes of the show, how can you score? This wasn't what we had talked about. So my representatives said they were going to come in on Saturday and talk to Lorne.

BARBARA GALLAGHER:

Lorne said to me, "We have to cut Billy," after dress rehearsal. "Why don't you go tell Buddy?" I said, "Me? Me tell Buddy? What're you, crazy?" He said, "Yeah, you've got to tell him." Lorne didn't like confrontation. He hated it. So I went and told Buddy. I said, "I think it's a mistake, I know Lorne feels terrible that he has to do this." I said, "Buddy, don't kill the messenger. I love Billy."

LORNE MICHAELS:

Buddy was a strong advocate for Billy, and I think what I objected to was him telling me what I should cut as opposed to just making the pro-Billy case. He made the who-was-funnier case, which was not a good thing to do. He said I should cut Andy Kaufman.

I probably didn't have the nerve to cut Carlin. One, he was our host, and two, he'd lent his name to the show, which was, at the time, a big deal. I think Andy, because he was surreal and there was nothing else like him on the show, had the edge. Albert had submitted his first film, which was thirteen minutes long. Fortunately he also sub-mitted his second one, which was a lot shorter, and that was the one we ran.

I thought Billy was really funny, or else I wouldn't have put him on the show. But I also thought that he was the one thing we could hold, the one thing we had the most of — stand-up comedy, because of Car-lin. Buddy turned everything into high drama. It became very heated.

BUDDY MORRA:

We took him off the show Saturday because they weren't living up to what we had agreed to. Jack Rollins and I decided if we couldn't get what we were promised early on, we would take Billy off the show. Earlier in the week, I had said just that to Barbara Gallagher, who was the associate producer. The piece was supposed to run about six min-utes or five and a half minutes, and it just wouldn't work in any less time. You could shave a few seconds off, but that would be about it.

LORNE MICHAELS:

Buddy had no idea what was going on. I don't think Bernie did either. They were from another time of show business. We were eat-ing vegetables; they were eating doughnuts. It was a different world. We were much more like a crusade. It was a very passionate group of people. Billy was sort of one of us — but now suddenly it went into this other kind of mode.

The talk with Buddy was of another time. And it made Billy *not* one of us. And I think that was unfortunate for all of us, because he had been.

BILLY CRYSTAL:

I was waiting in the lobby with Gilda for the dress rehearsal to take place at eight o'clock while my managers talked to Lorne. We had asked for five minutes in the first hour which, given what we had been through with Lorne in the preparations, didn't seem like an out-landish request. About seven o'clock, my manager, Buddy Morra, and Jack Rollins come out and suddenly said, "Okay, we're going, that's it." I said, "What happened?" They said, "Lorne went, 'I can't do it, I can't do it, I can't do it. I can't promise anything.'" So Buddy said, "We're going to go, there's no time, you're being bumped, and that's it." I had my makeup on! Gilda got all upset and angry. I was totally confused about the whole thing.

BUDDY MORRA:

It comes down to a matter of what they thought was most important. I know how bad Billy felt for a long time. I'm talking about several *years* after that. It still always bothered him. And it bothered me too. We walked out of NBC that night, and I can tell you my stomach was not in great shape, and it wasn't for several days after that. It wasn't an easy thing to do, but we felt it was the right thing to do.

BILLY CRYSTAL:

I was upset — mad, I guess — because I had wanted to be there. I was mad at my own managers, because I wanted to do the show. And I didn't want it to look like I was the guy who stormed off the show. That wasn't the truth. But my managers were protecting me, and Lorne was protecting his show, which I respect.

LORNE MICHAELS:

We were all under enormous pressure. None of us had done this before. It was a big night for an enormous number of people, Billy included. To be cut was I'm sure terribly hurtful for Billy, but there was no implication at all that it was about his not being good enough or of not wanting him on the show. This was straight confrontation. It was Buddy; it wasn't Billy.

BARBARA GALLAGHER:

It was a mistake when you look back on it. Billy was hysterical during dress. Very funny.

BILLY CRYSTAL:

I was friendly with John and especially with Gilda. They were always confused and blamed my managers. Especially John; he used to say, "They screwed you, man!"

And then after that, things weren't great for me for a while. I felt bad. I did come back the next year when Ron Nessen hosted the show and I did a routine and that was great. But after that, there was eight years when I didn't do the show.

BERNIE BRILLSTEIN:

Five minutes before the first show, I came through the back door where the food and coffee was and there was Belushi, sitting on a bench with Craig Kellem, who was the associate producer, and Craig was saying, "John, you've just got to sign your contract. NBC won't allow you on the air until you do." And I just happened to walk by at the time, and I didn't really know John well at all. I couldn't believe NBC in its stupidity was pressuring him at such a time. So John said to me, "Should I sign this contract?" and I said, "Of course you should sign this contract." He said, "Why?" I said, "Because I wrote it"—which, by the way, wasn't true. But I knew I had to get him to sign it. He said, "Okay, I'll sign the contract if you manage me." I swear to God, it was five minutes before showtime.

Belushi knew I managed Lorne. So why shouldn't he be managed by the same guy who is managing the boss, right? At that time, I didn't know how great Belushi was, so I just said yes to get him to sign the goddamned contract. It worked out great, and he turned out, obviously, to be one of my best friends.

TOM SCHILLER:

Before the offices on seventeen were filled up with furniture and stuff, I somehow got the key and went up there one night, and I was still enough of a hippie or a spiritual person that I lit a candle in each office as a sort of general mantra or prayer that the show would be successful and that it wouldn't hurt anybody. So at least that part came true.

And then on the first night of the show, still in my hippie phase, I went to every point underneath the bleachers and every point around the studio to try and send out good vibrations to the home viewing audience. Knowing we were sending out a signal across the ether that would be received all across the country, I wanted us to be sending it out with good wishes.

HERB SARGENT, *Writer:*

The very first night of the show, between dress and air, Chevy and I went down and had a cup of coffee at Hurley's bar downstairs. And Chevy said, "What's going to happen to me?" Because it was a big moment, you know, for all those people. He says, "Where am I going to go from here?" I said, "You'll probably end up hosting a talk show." I was kidding. But it's strange, you know. He wasn't frightened—but he was very curious. And it was like an empty vista out there. The interesting part of that for me is that even before the first live show, he was already thinking about what the next step was.

NEIL LEVY:

There was a feeling even before it started that something important was happening. It was almost like all the leftover spirit of the sixties found its way into this show—that spirit of rebellion, of breaking through whatever boundaries were left. There was something so special about being there that you knew from the moment you got there that this was going to work.

Of course, some writers weren't so sure. Even Dan Aykroyd—he had a bag all packed. He said, "Neil, this show could fold in a second, and I got a nice little spot picked out on the 401, and I'm going to open a truck stop." He had a whole plan!

CRAIG KELLEM:

We almost didn't get on the air, because dress rehearsal went so poorly. I remember Lorne seriously asking the network people—or having me ask them—to have a movie ready to go, just in case. And I don't think he was kidding.

George Carlin was the host when the show—still called NBC's Saturday Night—*premiered, on October 11, 1975. Only about two-thirds of NBC's affiliated stations carried the show, which had received very little advance publicity from the network. Over the course of its ninety minutes, Carlin—"stoned out of his mind," according to observers—delivered three separate comedy monologues, probably two too many. Iconoclastic comic*

Andy Kaufman lip-synched the Mighty Mouse *theme song, a seminal and now legendary moment. There were also several numbers by musical guests Janis Ian and Billy Preston, an appearance from a new group of "adult" Muppets invented for the show by Jim Henson, and a short film by Albert Brooks.*

The Not Ready for Prime Time Players—so named, by writer Herb Sargent, because Saturday Night Live with Howard Cosell *over on ABC at eight* P.M. *had a small comedy ensemble known as the Prime Time Players (one of whom was Bill Murray)—actually appeared very little on that first night. When they did, they were dressed as bees. The young performers were supplemented by an older Broadway actor named George Coe, who helped with narrations and commercial parodies and stayed around for one season only. The format was more like that of a traditional variety show, with nearly as much music as comedy and the repertory players there as laugh insurance, even filler.*

Among the consistent elements from the beginning was the "cold open" prior to veteran announcer Don Pardo's recitation of the bill of fare and the opening credits. Many a modern movie had started this way, with a "grabber" or "teaser" scene prior to the credits, but it was something new for a TV show. The very first cold open was new, too: an absurdist encounter between bad-boy writer Michael O'Donoghue, playing a teacher of English, and bad-boy actor John Belushi as a semiliterate immigrant who repeats everything O'Donoghue says—including, "I would like—to feed your fingertips—to the wolverines." When O'Donoghue suddenly keels over with a heart attack, Belushi's character dutifully does the same, falling to the floor. Thus did John Belushi feign death within the first three minutes of the very first show.

Then, Chevy Chase as the floor manager, wearing a headset and carrying a clipboard, sticks his head in, sees the seemingly dead bodies, smiles broadly in that phony-television way, and says—for the first of more than five hundred times that it would be said in years to come—"Live from New York, it's Saturday Night!"

LORNE MICHAELS:

I made the decision Thursday to open cold with "Wolverines." It seemed to me that, whatever else happened, there would never have been anything like this on television. No one would know what kind of show this is from seeing that.

EDIE BASKIN, *Photographer:*

For the title sequence, I just went around and photographed New York at night. Actually, the first titles had no pictures of the cast, only pictures of New York. Lorne had loved some pictures I'd done of Las Vegas and some of my other work, which was very different for that time.

LORNE MICHAELS:

The major focus of the night, weirdly enough, was over a directive we got that Carlin had to wear a suit on the show. He wanted to wear a T-shirt. The directive came from Dave Tebet; he was head of talent and very supportive of the show, but he was also trying to anticipate. The fear was that if George was in a T-shirt and it looked like the wrong kind of show, we would lose affiliates, and we weren't anywhere near 100 percent as it was. And the compromise was a suit with a T-shirt instead of a tie. That was a much greater distraction than can possibly be understood right now.

CRAIG KELLEM:

Tebet was the Don Corleone of network executives. And at that time I didn't look all that good—people dressed pretty sloppily there—and I went up and Tebet was reading the riot act about the prerequisites for Carlin's performance. And they included, "He's going to have to get his hair cut and have it look neat." And he went through this whole diatribe about what Carlin was not going to do, and it was uncomfortably close to the way I looked in the office. He went through the list—suit, tie, hair—and then he looks down at my bare ankles and says, "Socks!"

DICK EBERSOL:

If you go back and look at the first show on the air, the two people by far who had the most to do on the show were Chevy and Jane. There were only four or five sketches. The rest of it was four songs, six monologues—three by Carlin, one by Andy Kaufman, his Mighty Mouse bit, and one by what's-her-face, a comedienne who ended up in the show instead of Billy Crystal—Valri Bromfeld, from Canada.

ROSIE SHUSTER:

We were buzzed. I don't think we had any clue what kind of phenomenon was going to happen. Carlin later confessed that he was pretty loaded. Andy Kaufman was on that show. There were a lot of featured guests—there wasn't a lot of comedy on that show. But there was the live buzz you just got from that studio audience and it was pretty upbeat. I think everybody knew there had to be a lot more comedy sketches and that the cast had to be used more.

LORNE MICHAELS:

I taught at an art school in Toronto, I was teaching improvisations, the conceptual art movement which was being talked about and on the edge of things in the early seventies. Where that and entertainment met was what Andy Kaufman was doing. It wasn't just that he lip-synched to "Mighty Mouse"; it was that he only did that one part in it, that one line, and stood around for the rest. It was very conceptual, and it instantly signaled to the brighter part of the audience that that was the kind of show we were going to do. And they weren't getting that anywhere else on television. In the first couple years, Andy must have been on close to ten times. One night he even read from *The Great Gatsby*. In the beginning I had Penn and Teller on a few times, because that was the DNA, but I couldn't do that now. The pure variety show part of it is over. It's a straight comedy show now.

STEVE MARTIN, *Host:*

I do remember when I first saw the show. I was living in Aspen, and it came on and I thought, "They've done it!" They did the zeitgeist, they did what was out there, what we all had in our heads, this kind of new comedy. And I thought, "Well, someone's done it on television now." I didn't know Lorne at the time. I didn't know anyone.

HERBERT SCHLOSSER:

I can remember the first time I saw it. I was in Boston staying at the Ritz for the Cincinnati–Red Sox World Series and I had been with Bowie Kuhn. You always sit with the commissioner if you're president of the company. That was a truly great World Series. We had dinner, and I asked if he'd like to see a new show we were putting on. And that was the first show in October of 1975, with George Carlin. Neither of us knew what to expect. Now Bowie is a nice man but very straitlaced, very proper, and a religious man. I sat on a chair, and he and his wife sat on the couch. He didn't laugh. And I thought, "Well, that's Bowie."

And then after a while, he started to chuckle. And then he'd actually laugh. And I figured, "Well, if he likes it, it's going to have a wider audience than most people think."

AL FRANKEN:

I felt very confident that the show was going to work. It was youthful arrogance, I guess. I looked around and I thought, "This has never been on TV before, and this will work, this should work, and of course it's going to be a hit"—which is an attitude I've never actually had since.

LORNE MICHAELS:

The only note we got from the network on the first show was, "Cut the bees." And so I made sure to put them in the next show. I had them come out and talk to Paul Simon. He says, "It didn't work last week. It's cut." And they go, "Oh," and just walk off.

PAUL SIMON, *Host:*

I was up for doing the very first show. It didn't seem like there was much downside risk. Then Lorne said, "No, let me just work out the kinks on the first show." But I would've been happy to do the first show. It would've been more historical. But he went with George Carlin, and I did the second one.

EDIE BASKIN:

They had used publicity pictures of Carlin for the first show. I already had pictures of Paul Simon, so my pictures of Paul became the bumpers. And then Lorne said to me, "I think you should photograph next week's host instead of using publicity pictures." And that's how it all started.

PENNY MARSHALL, *Guest:*

I met Lorne when he came out and talked to Rob about hosting the third show. I wasn't anybody; I'd been on *The Odd Couple,* but *Laverne and Shirley* didn't go on until four months later. Rob was on *All in the Family.* I listened to Lorne talk to Rob at Lorne's apartment, and I kept my mouth shut. At the end, Lorne said to me, "Penny, what do you think?" And I said, "I think you're the most manipulative human being I've ever met, and you do it beautifully." And we've been friends ever since.

NEIL LEVY:

Rob Reiner refused to go on after dress rehearsal. I was in his dressing room. It was hilarious because it was like a monologue, him going, "I can't do this show, I can't do this show! It's bad, it's horrible, I'm going to make mistakes, I don't know the lines, I can't do it, I'm not doing it, I'm sorry, that's it!" And it was like he was not going to do it. And Lorne just talked him through it. And of course Rob did a good show.

ALBERT BROOKS:

We had agreed on how I would make these movies, and certainly I wasn't going to make a living off of it. If I remember correctly, we agreed on a budget of like a thousand dollars a minute, which I bring up because it's funny that I was actually able to do that. I think all six films probably cost, you know, fifty grand. Most of the films were four minutes, but one—the open-heart surgery movie—ran thirteen minutes, and Lorne refused to air it. But then Rob Reiner, who is my close friend, hosted the show and insisted on showing it. Otherwise, it would have never been seen.

LORNE MICHAELS:

My agreement with Albert had been for films of three to five minutes. I'd wanted three, he wanted five. Because the heart surgery one was thirteen minutes, it necessitated commercials in the middle and on either end—which meant we were away from the live show for close to twenty minutes.

BARBARA GALLAGHER:

Albert was always wanting more money. Lorne only needed like tiny pieces and we were getting ten- and twelve-minute pieces. And he'd be on the phone complaining and I'd say, "Albert, we have a whole show here, you can't do those things, we don't have the time." He was good about it, but it was constant, constant, "You can't do this, Albert."

JUDITH BELUSHI:

In the first three shows, John was the opening scene of the first show and I don't think he had a good scene again for three shows. Something that made a break of sorts was the third or fourth bee scene, when he went off on "I hate being a bee" and this whole "bee" thing, and he had his antennae swinging around his head in some special way. It was really the first time he got to show his personality and show that there was more to him, and he got a great response. But it took a while. It was slow to grow.

CHEVY CHASE:

On "Weekend Update," I was being a newscaster; I was being Roger Grimsby, actually. You know, it came out of that: "Good evening, I'm Roger Grimsby, and here now the news." One of the strangest pieces of syntax I've ever heard in my life: "And here now the news." But I knew I should say *something*. And on the fourth show, it just came out: "Good evening. I'm Chevy Chase, and you're not." And that was it.

CRAIG KELLEM:

There was a momentum from the beginning, but what was interesting was that, even though I don't remember the ratings being unbelievable after the first couple of shows, Lorne—ever the decider of what was what—decided the show was a hit right from the beginning and acted out of that belief, and it was infectious. I remember what he said. He said, quote, "I guess we're a hit." I thought, "Where's that coming from?" But it was vintage Lorne Michaels. He believed it was a hit. He felt good about it. It got on the air. He looked on the bright side of the numbers and the bright side of the reviews. He certainly got good feedback from friends and family. And that was it. It was a hit show. It's wonderful, the strength of his belief in how he sees things in this world.

CANDICE BERGEN, *Host:*

After the first couple shows, the dynamics of everything became so complicated and so loaded. People were learning things. They realized that you couldn't do the show stoned, because they were missing their costume changes. A live show was not compatible with grass. And then the burnout rate was so high, especially for the writers, because they were really just putting in all-nighters routinely.

DICK EBERSOL:

Lorne and I never had any real disagreements between us until the fourth show, the first time Candice Bergen did the show. There was a complete fuckup that night with NBC, where they made this enormous electronic mistake. They basically cued real commercials off of fake commercials. Somebody wasn't paying attention in broadcast control. And Lorne went nuts.

LORNE MICHAELS:

Candy's show, the fourth show, was the first show, I would say, that was a *Saturday Night Live* like the ones we have now. The week before, when Rob Reiner hosted, Andy Kaufman did a long piece, there was a long Albert Brooks film, and a long monologue by Rob. On the Candy show, we sort of hit our stride. We'd had our first week off, and we worked hard on the writing.

DICK EBERSOL:

Now comes week five. *New York* magazine comes out with Chevy Chase—on the cover. John is radically pissed off, because he sees Chevy running away with the show; now it's going to be all about Chevy. Onstage, John had been the star, not Chevy.

We do show six, which is a wonderful week, Lily Tomlin's come to do the show. Now we got Thanksgiving off. On Friday, we all get an advance copy of the Sunday *New York Times*. Major story: *Saturday Night Live* is called the most important and most exciting development in television comedy since *Your Show of Shows*. It's this drop-dead blow job. It was just unbelievable. And this is the same *New York Times* that did not even review show one with George Carlin.

They also printed a review that John J. O'Connor wrote on the second show, where Paul Simon and Art Garfunkel got together again for the first time, and his review essentially was that the show was not very good, but he couldn't be entirely fair in saying that because he missed connections on his way home from dinner on the subway, and so he missed forty minutes of the show. Can you believe that they fucking printed that thing?

LORNE MICHAELS:

It was humiliating that the critic thought it was a music show and reviewed it that way. He said, "Another Simon and Garfunkel reunion," of which there hadn't been one since 1968.

MARGARET OBERMAN, *Writer:*

I remember being really disappointed when Lily Tomlin hosted. Because we got so few women hosts, and growing up I always thought she was so funny and everything, so it was a little bit of an idolizing thing. And then when she came to the show, she was so condescending to us, especially to me and the other women writers. It was like, you know, "You should really write about something you know about, or something from real life." It was one of those kinds of things. It was like, "Oh my God!" And she seemed completely oblivious to the fact that she was being so insulting.

ROSIE SHUSTER:

One of the things we heard about the first four or five shows, while it was becoming the sensation that it would be, was that Chevy kind of jumped ahead of the pack, so to speak, and that started a kind of a resentment on the part of some people, particularly John, toward Chevy.

Chevy was writing his own segment using his own name—"I'm Chevy Chase, and you're not"—plus doing the physical shtick at the beginning. He was easily identifiable, whereas it took people so many years to catch on to what Danny's talent was, because he would disappear into characters. And Chevy just shot ahead. It wasn't that surprising. It was going to take John a little while longer. He was used to being beloved on the stage of the Lampoon Show and had a following of people, but to translate to television, especially if you have an attitude about television, takes a little while.

CHEVY CHASE:

I felt it was relatively easy. I'd come in and pick stuff up and learn stuff and simply walk through it, basically. I don't remember it being particularly difficult. You know, I have to say that, going in, one of the things that made the show successful to begin with that first year and made me successful was this feeling of "I don't give a crap." And that came partially out of the belief that we were the top of the minors in late-night television and that we wouldn't go anywhere anyway. So we had no set of aspirations in the sense that this would be a showcase to drive us to bigger and better things.

ALAN ZWEIBEL:

We worked on "Update" to the very last minute. Between dress and air on Saturday nights, I would go up to my office and I would watch the eleven o'clock news and if something hit me, I'd write it and it would be on television a half-hour later. You know, there were two shows where I was literally under the "Update" desk writing stuff and handing it up to Chevy while he was actually on the air.

ROBERT KLEIN:

Everyone was quite terrified about the live television aspect of the show. Most of the people in that building at NBC in New York hadn't done a live show since *Howdy Doody*. As a matter of fact, one of the first *SNL* shows had a blank gray screen for forty-five seconds. A network show and nothing but gray for forty-five seconds because of the improvising and screwups of doing it live.

NEIL LEVY:

Lorne quit on the Robert Klein show. They took away his lighting man and his sound man. Lorne had promised his guests the best sound and the best lighting. That was one of his promises to the people he'd gotten to do the first ten shows. He was furious that NBC had taken away his people. I think he realized at the time that if he didn't make a stand, they'd be stepping all over him. So he told NBC that he would walk unless they returned his lighting guy and his sound guy.

He left. He went back to his apartment and stayed there most of the week playing poker. Robert Klein showed up and said, "Where's the producer?" And we said, "Oh, he's around. He'll be here soon." And the whole week went by and he wasn't there. But Lorne won. It was a victory. I think he came back Friday or Saturday. A lot of people would have said, "We'll make do with this sound guy and this lighting guy," and he said, "No, I've got to have the best." And that philosophy has served him well.

HOWARD SHORE:

We were really kind of subversive in a number of ways. O'Donoghue and I were always trying to book acts on the show and then do things to them. They were so happy to be on the show, they didn't really notice. I remember when Robert Klein hosted, O'Donoghue put Abba on a *Titanic* set and tried to drown them. He thought Abba was kitsch.

LORNE MICHAELS:

Abba was the first and only act that lip-synched. And that was Dick. Dick was Abba. That was all he cared about; he left the rest of the music to me and Howard. But with Abba, he just wouldn't take no for an answer.

DAVE WILSON:

Lorne did not like lip-synching, and Lorne did not like—and I always thought it was a tribute to him—Lorne did not like close-ups of fingers on instruments. He always said, "We're not giving music lessons." Because you want to see the man's or woman's face; it was their inner feelings in creating this music that was worth seeing, not where their fingers were placed on the strings.

LILY TOMLIN:

I don't remember entirely the first time I saw the show. I think I just thought it was a good, young comedy show. What do you think I should have thought?

I think Belushi always thought he was so cutting-edge or so ahead in some ways, or he thought he was a rebel. Even though we liked him, we couldn't get him to come on our special. Jane had seen a lot of the Lampoon kids, and we tried to get some of them for our show.

Live TV was old, basically, but this was like new because they were doing it in a different time frame. Jane Wagner and I had always wanted to do a live TV show because we had to spend all our money editing anyway. A live show is great, but you're always going to have rough spots, and there's always the chance of something happening. Having been on *Laugh-In,* and I guess just doing comedy for a long time, I thought it was hip, probably—hip and current like that.

I don't think that I thought it was something I'd never seen before.

CHRIS ALBRECHT, *Agent, Comedy Club Manager:*

I ran the Improv in New York from 1975 to the very end of '79. Everybody came through there. Especially in the first year, several of the performers from *Saturday Night Live* would come in to the Improv on a semiregular basis to go up onstage and try out characters and work out stuff. Belushi would come in a lot, Laraine came in a few times, Gilda came in at least once. Belushi also came in to buy quaaludes from his dealer every other week.

On Saturday nights, we would always watch the show from the bar. At 11:30, we were just starting our second show at the Improv. So it was funny people watching funny people. I was impressed that *Saturday Night Live* was on the air at all. Because we worked in a New York nightclub, all of us had this kind of snobby opinion that the New York comedy sensibility was the best that there was. The fact that this was a show in New York was always particularly pleasing to us.

HOWARD SHORE:

By the time Lily Tomlin hosted, Lorne was sending the host over to the music department, which essentially was me in an office with a desk. NBC had a wonderful record library—phenomenal. When NBC started, I believe they actually filed every recording ever released. I couldn't believe I had access to this library. I found this old blues recording of "St. James Infirmary" there and thought of doing an arrangement for the band. And I played that song for Lily and she liked it.

And O'Donoghue said, "Have the band dress as nurses to do it." So we did. And I sang it with Lily. We did another show at Christmas where we all dressed as angels. It's just something that we got into— we've got these ten guys and one girl and what could we do with them that would be funny?

CRAIG KELLEM:

Lorne had us working hard to induce Richard Pryor to host the show. Richard had a lot of questions and was playing very hard to get. We went to a jai alai arena in Miami where he was performing; that was the beginning of the Richard Pryor saga in terms of trying to get him to do the show. He wanted his ex-wife on the show, he wanted a couple of writers, performers on the show, and he wanted a tremendous number of tickets—which was an issue, really, because it wound up being the majority of the seats in the studio. So it was tough going. With Richard, as wonderful and as adorable as he was, it was also very tense being around him. Lorne loved Richard. He thought he was quote-unquote the funniest man on the planet. But it took so much work and effort to go through this process of booking him that Lorne, in a moment of extreme stress, sort of candidly looked around and said, "He better be funny."

Once he was booked, Herb Sargent and I were assigned to go to his Park Avenue hotel and greet him and hold his hand. He was there in a suite with his guys, and the first thing he wanted to know was, where was the script. What we couldn't tell him was, there was no script. Everyone was just recovering from the last show, and there was the usual chaos. So we were in this uncomfortable situation. Now Herb is a very gentle and sensitive guy, and in the course of this meeting, the pressure became so intense that Herb suddenly said he was going back to the office to get the "script." He left the suite—and never came back. And guess who was stuck there with seven or eight very angry guys? Richard knew there was a certain amount of bullshit going down. He was saying, "Where is that guy? What happened to him?"

That was the beginning of the host game, which is, "There is no script. Try to make them feel comfortable and quote-unquote trust me."

BERNIE BRILLSTEIN:

When Richard Pryor hosted, NBC wanted a five-second delay because they thought Pryor might say something filthy. We ended up with a three-second delay, I think. But it was a new negotiation every week.

LORNE MICHAELS:

I resigned in preproduction over Richard Pryor in December. It was like an absolute "you can't have him" from the network. And I said, "I can't do a contemporary comedy show without Richard Pryor." And so I walked off. There was a lot of me walking off in those days.

Richard did wind up hosting, of course. But he wouldn't come into the office until we started rehearsing, so I brought John over to his hotel to see him. John had done his Toshiro Mifune for his audition, and he did it for Richard, who thought it was funny. Richard wanted to do it on the show, and so we wrote "Samurai Hotel."

CANDICE BERGEN:

I remember the terror. You know, the total exhilaration of it. I just didn't know you could have that much fun after thirty. It was like the inmates taking over the asylum. Totally.

On the Christmas show, we did a skating routine, a sort of Sonja Henie Bee-Capades skating routine. We went down to shoot the Bee-Capades after Rockefeller Center had closed, after the rink had closed, so we were in the elevators at midnight and I was dressed in a red velvet skating outfit with an ermine muff and then Belushi and Aykroyd and Chevy and everybody were dressed like bees. And the elevator operators, who still, after two months of the show, didn't know how to deal with it, just never looked at any of us, never said a word. I think it was like that for a long time. You just couldn't understand how they took control of a place like NBC.

LORNE MICHAELS:

The Candy Bergen Christmas show was not as good as the other Candy show, so I went into a tailspin. Chevy and I and Michael went into the office and worked over the holidays, and that's when we wrote the Elliott Gould show, which later won the Emmy for writing that first season. We wrote a sketch where the Godfather goes to the shrink, and we were in a "let's just blow it out" state of mind. By that point, I'd hit stride, we all had, and everyone was focused. The Gould show was our first big show which wasn't about the host. Gould was just a big goofy guy who'd been in *M*A*S*H.*

ELLIOTT GOULD, *Host:*

The first show I ever hosted was a very good show. One of the sketches was written by Michael O'Donoghue. It was a psycho group therapy session, with Belushi as the Godfather in it. I heard it replayed on the radio recently and it was so funny, it even worked on radio. Laraine Newman being in group therapy with Vito Corleone. I was the psychiatrist. My contribution was that I smoked a pipe. At this point I don't think I would, but then I needed a prop. Also I think it was the first show that I was the head of the Killer Bees, which was very, very funny.

Through the show there was a thread where Gilda Radner had a crush on me and at the end of this first show that I did, we married; Gilda Radner and I had a wedding ceremony, and Madeline Kahn's mother was cast as Gilda's mother and Michael O'Donoghue married us at the end of the show. And that was the representative show they submitted, and it won them their first Emmy. I was really pleased to be a part of it.

BUCK HENRY, *Host:*

On the first show I hosted, I made a suggestion for an ending for a sketch, because I came up in the school that says you end a sketch with an ending. And I heard one of the writers behind me say to the others, "Hmm, 1945." And I nodded inwardly. "I see. I get it." It was considered really corny to go for a joke. They thought somehow it was like Carol Burnett.

LORNE MICHAELS:

Buck Henry came in to host and taught me a whole other level of things. Buck so totally got it. When he got there he said, "Do you want to do the Samurai again?" And we had never thought of repeating things until that moment.

ALAN ZWEIBEL:

I wrote all the Samurais with the exception of one. Belushi auditioned for the show with the Samurai character. On the Richard Pryor show, Tom Schiller wrote a piece called "Samurai Hotel," about a two-minute piece or so, and that was that. That was like the seventh show we ever did. The eleventh show we ever did, Buck Henry was hosting. Lorne came by my desk and said, "You used to work in a deli, didn't you?" I said, "You name it, I sliced it." Lorne said, "You would be perfect to write 'Samurai Delicatessen.'" I said sure. I had no idea what he was talking about. But I wrote "Samurai Deli" and all the other Samurais after that. What started as that one two-minute sketch ended up being a franchise.

When I say I wrote all the Samurais, what does that mean? It means I wrote all the stuff for Buck Henry or whoever did it that week and then I go, "John throws up a tomato and slices it," and "John indicates in his gibberish whatever," you know. I wrote no dialogue for John. The only time I wrote anything that looked like dialogue for him was when I had to indicate what the gibberish was meant to convey.

BUCK HENRY:

On the Samurai sketches that I did with John, one never knew where it was going because John's dialogue could not be written. You never knew what was going to happen next. In "Samurai Stockbroker," he cut my head open with the sword, but it was really my fault; I leaned in at the wrong time. And I bled all over the set. It was a very amusing moment. You would not believe how much blood from a forehead was on that floor. A commercial came on right after the sketch and someone shouted, "Is there a doctor around?" And John Belushi's doctor was in the audience—which made me a little suspicious. So the guy came and put this clamp on my forehead. We went on with the show. It didn't require stitches, darn it, but it required a clamp for the rest of the show.

When "Weekend Update" came on, which was about ten minutes later, Chevy appeared with a bandage on his face. Then Jane had her arm in a sling. They featured the moment when I got hit by the sword on "Update" like it was a hot news item. Only *Saturday Night Live* could do that. By the end of the show, when the camera pulls back, you see some of the crew are on crutches, others have bandages or their arms in slings. As if the whole show caught a virus. It was pretty funny. And the genius of *Saturday Night Live,* it seems to me, is encapsulated in that event.

John didn't say anything to me right after it happened, but then we didn't see each other for another half hour at least. I was in one place and he was in another. But it wasn't John's forte to apologize anyway.

NEIL LEVY:

When Buck Henry got nicked by the Samurai sword and everybody started wearing Band-Aids, they all bonded. I think it was the same show where Lorne had done that Beatles offer and they got a phone call that John Lennon was over at Paul McCartney's house and they were both coming over. Lorne was thinking, "What are we going to do when they get here?" He had an idea, he said. "How about this, they get here and they want to play a song and I ask them where their guitars are and they say they didn't bring their guitars and I say, 'Oh. Well, then you can't play, because there's a union rule that you have to have your own guitar.'" His whole thing was to have the Beatles there and not let them play. I don't know if he would have gone through with it. But they never made it, because they realized it was too late. Just the fact that they were on their way was good enough.

TOM HANKS, *Host:*

I remember the first time I saw the show. I was working as a bellman in a hotel and got off late and came home. And one of the first things I saw was a parody of a razor blade commercial. Remember the one? It was in the first season, and it showed this cartoon of here's how it works, the triple-header. And they'd be yanking out this hair and doing this very painful thing. And I honestly couldn't figure out what I was looking at. Who would sell such a ridiculous product? And then I saw the first time they were in their bee costumes, and I could not figure what was going on.

I just thought, "Wow, okay, we're into the undiscovered country here, if they're doing this kind of stuff on TV."

LORNE MICHAELS:

We wanted to redefine comedy the way the Beatles redefined what being a pop star was. That required not pandering, and it also required removing neediness, the need to please. It was like, we're only going to please those people who are like us. The presumption was there were a lot of people like us. And that turned out to be so.

In its first weeks, the show looked little like it does today — different even from the episodes that aired mere months later. The repertory players got relatively little time at first, but that grew along with their popularity. Albert Brooks's films didn't turn out as Michaels had hoped, and there were frequent arguments over the fact that they weren't short enough.

Brooks was angry — and is still irked to this day — that in its first review of the show, Newsweek *gave credit for some of the clever parodies of network shows included in his short film not to him but to the show's writers and performers. In fact, Brooks was working in a virtual vacuum on the other side of the country. He went on to a brilliant career as comic and filmmaker. The Muppets didn't starve either; soon after being dumped, they were signed by England's Lew Grade to star in* The Muppet Show, *a hugely profitable, globally syndicated half hour that made Jim Henson a millionaire many times over.*

ALAN ZWEIBEL:

Whoever drew the short straw that week had to write the Muppet sketch. The first time I met O'Donoghue, I walked into Lorne's office, and Belushi's there, Aykroyd's there, people the likes of which had never crossed my path before, and I look in a corner of the room and there's a guy I learned was Michael O'Donoghue. What was he doing, you ask? He had taken Big Bird, a stuffed toy of Big Bird, and the cord from the venetian blinds, and he wrapped the cord around Big Bird's neck. He was lynching Big Bird. And that's how we all felt about the Muppets.

Franken and Davis and I were the rookie writers, and the others always rigged it so we were the ones who wrote the Muppet sketches. So I went over to Jim Henson's town house on like Sixty-eighth Street with a sketch I had written. There was one character named Skred, and I remember we're reading the sketch, Jim Henson's reading the pages, and he gets to a line and he says, "Oh, Skred wouldn't say this."

And I look, and on a table over there is this cloth thing that is folded over like laundry, and it's Skred. "Oh, but he wouldn't say this." Oh, sorry. It's like when I was doing Garry Shandling's first series, we wanted to have Shari Lewis and Lamb Chop on. I said, "Of course we'll fly you out," and she said, "Well, what about Lamb Chop?" What *about* Lamb Chop?!? She says that Lamb Chop gets a seat. I swear to God, I almost threw my back out giving her the benefit of the doubt that she wasn't insane. I laughed and she said, "Lamb Chop doesn't sit in the back." I said, "If I'm not mistaken, are we talking about the same Lamb Chop? Because, you know, *it's a sock! It's a sock with a button, okay?!?*"

And it ended up we didn't use her because it was too insane.

BERNIE BRILLSTEIN:

O'Donoghue had the best line about the Muppets. He used to say, "I won't write for felt."

CRAIG KELLEM:

There was this shit-or-get-off-the-pot moment when Lorne turned and looked at me and he said, "How do you fire the Muppets?"

GARRETT MORRIS:

A lot of people are very patronizing toward so-called handicapped people. They can take care of themselves. One thing about the kind of comedy we do is that it's a deeper realization of the fact that with all comedy, with all jokes, somebody's on the bottom.

ALBERT BROOKS:

I think Lorne resented the fact that I was in Los Angeles. But the very reason that I set it up that way was so I could function and do what I knew I could do, and I didn't want to participate in the New York thing. And once the cast made it, then these little helper things like my films became, in Lorne's mind, less important, and the reasons for getting me were pretty much over. Because what function did I provide for him? I made him something that got him great attention and great reviews. And, more importantly, I did the publicity for them.

After those six films, that was it. Because I don't think Lorne Michaels would ever, ever again, do anything outside of New York. I think that really was something that he never wanted. He didn't like not having control over all of the product.

DAN AYKROYD:

At first I stayed at Belushi's house—living with him and his wife, sleeping at the foot of their bed, having their cats attack me. I lived there for two months. Finally—*finally*—I said, "I gotta get out of here." John loved having me there, and Judy was very sweet. But I met a guy who worked in the graphics department at NBC, and we had a loft downtown for a while. Had some great parties there.

JUDITH BELUSHI:

John and Danny had met much earlier and they liked each other instantly. Danny had come in at one point and stayed at our house for a couple nights. I know he says he slept at the foot of the bed. It wasn't literally the foot of the bed. Actually, it was another room. He remembers it that way, though. It *seemed* like the foot of the bed to him.

HOWARD SHORE:

Dan had bunk beds because we had no money, we were paid so relatively little money, really, by NBC. I think they were paying me

$500 per show, not per week. I think the first year I made $10,000 when we actually created the show. So we had no real lives.

PAUL SHAFFER:

We were young, and nobody had much else to do. We used to be there all night writing. Lorne was a night owl and he encouraged this; those were the kind of hours he wanted to keep. So that was his schedule, that Monday night would be the first meeting pitching ideas, Tuesday he'd start after dinner and just stay up until you had some stuff written, and then you'd drag yourself out of bed Wednesday and come in for the first read-through of the material, which used to start, theoretically, at one. Not only was it weird hours, but it was long hours. People were really devoted to the show. There was not necessarily much social life. Our whole life was the show.

LORNE MICHAELS:

The thing I was worried about the most in those days was the dry cleaners, and getting my clothes back. I probably only owned two or three pairs of jeans and four or five shirts, so you could get in a jam where there were no clean clothes. I lived above a Chock Full o' Nuts at Fifty-seventh and Seventh, so I could always go down in the morning and have coffee and a whole wheat sugar doughnut.

When Buck Henry came to the show he carried *The New York Times* around with him the whole day, and he would read it A-1, A-2, A-3 — all in sequence. He didn't consider himself done until he'd read the whole paper. And I went, "Wow." I certainly didn't think of myself as unsophisticated, but you could make up a whole world out of what I didn't know back then. But there was no time for anything but the show.

Around the offices, I think early on I realized that if I looked like Henny-Penny, then pretty much that would be infectious. So when I was really frightened—when I was young, thirty, when I began—I would hold a glass of wine and people would go, "Well, he seems pretty cool and relaxed."

BUCK HENRY:

One problem was, Lorne couldn't fire anybody. He was constitutionally unable to do it, at least early on. Once hired, it was sinecure. I think Lorne felt it was an admission of failure if you have to fire somebody you've hired.

ALAN ZWEIBEL:

You know, Lorne did a thing which was really, really, really brilliant, and I don't know how long it lasted, it might have just been the first year. He wanted the public to know the cast as people beyond the roles that they played, so he would have a cast member just say, "Hi, I'm Dan Aykroyd, dah dah dah dah dah," just a little personality thing. With Gilda, she would sit on the edge of the stage, and she only did it twice maybe, and it was called "What Gilda Ate," and she would tell what she ate during the week. There weren't jokes in it, it was mostly personality things.

ROSIE SHUSTER:

Beatts and I were sort of thrown together to write, and we were the first two females there. Marilyn Suzanne Miller wasn't there at the very, very beginning. We sort of circled each other suspiciously for a short amount of time. I was always romantic about the idea of feminism, but the first time she saw me she exclaimed really loud, "Jesus, look at those tits!" So it got a laugh in the room and that was sort of unsettling, you know. But we were thrown together and then we definitely bonded, because there was a lot of testosterone around there. There was a lot of energy and it was combustible and it was exciting.

It was hard to be female; it always was, you know. Gilda had a good coping device for that somehow, because she could just be charming and darling. When you're actually pushing your own material, when you're in the trenches with the guys, it's a little harder. We were in the front lines, like Vietnam nurses. It was intense. It was very, very intense.

LORNE MICHAELS:

In the beginning, there were two things John didn't do: He wouldn't do drag, because it didn't fit his description of what he should be doing. And he didn't do pieces that Anne or Rosie wrote. So somebody would have to say that a guy had written it. Yet he was very attached to Gilda and to Laraine.

DAN AYKROYD:

There was a correspondents dinner that we went to in Washington. John and I played Secret Service agents to Chevy's Gerald Ford. Chevy invited us to come. It was at his behest. He was supposed to do Ford and he said, "I want to bring John and Dan down with me."

That John even went on that trip was interesting, because he had his problems with Chevy. Just—who's the bigger star, who's doing more important work, that type of thing. Of course, they had a history because they'd worked in the Lampoon Show together. So I think there was time for issues to foment there.

LORNE MICHAELS:

That was a magical day in Washington, but we couldn't get over the fact that Belushi went to the White House without an ID. We get to the White House, the car's pulling up, we give our names at the gate, and they ask for ID. And John says, "I didn't bring any." All of us: "John, how can you not?! How can you not bring ID?!?" But we vouched for him and they let us through.

JUDITH BELUSHI:

He had no ID with him when we got married. We eloped and went to get married in Aspen on New Year's Eve—and he has no ID. And when he's asked for any kind of identification, it's like he doesn't have any.

And John says, "Have you ever seen a show called *Saturday Night Live*?" The woman says, "No." Then he pulls out this review of the show that he carried around and says, "See, here, this is me, John Belushi." And she's looking at him like, "You must be crazy." And I said, "You're telling me no one has ever gotten married without an ID, no one, ever? There must be someone who lost all their stuff. What did they do?" She said, "Oh, well, if he had a letter from a judge." We said, "Okay," and went to the phone and called a judge. And John said into the phone, "Hello, Judge, I'm sorry to bother you at home, but have you ever heard of a show called *Saturday Night Live?*" And the judge says yes. And John says, "Oh good, I have this problem, I'm here with my girlfriend and we're trying to get married." And the judge came down, and he did an affidavit and okayed it. John showed up everywhere with no ID. He had trouble holding on to his wallet.

AL FRANKEN:

I went up to New Hampshire with my brother, who is a press photographer, to follow the campaign in '76. And I ran into Ron Nessen, who was the White House press secretary. I told him I was the writer of this show. And I was surprised that he had seen it — and that he liked it. I said, "Well, you should be on the show," and I went back to the office a few days later and I told Lorne. He kind of had to remind me that he was the producer of the show, and that I had only been in show business for about ten minutes. I was a writer. But anyway, Nessen ended up coming on.

LORNE MICHAELS:

I had to shoot Ford saying "Live from New York" and "I'm Gerald Ford and you're not" for the show. And I suddenly find myself in the Oval Office, and it's just me, the president, and this little crew. There's security too, I'm sure. And Ford does it, but the line reading is wrong, and I realized that it's just the same as working with anybody else and getting them to relax and do the line properly to camera. We'd done two or three takes, and to relax him, I said to him — my sense of humor at the time — "Mr. President, if this works out, who knows where it will lead?" Which was completely lost on him.

CANDICE BERGEN:

I had one sketch with Gilda and Chevy, I think it was "Land Shark," and I messed it up. I dropped a line. And Gilda, of course, handled it beautifully. I just started laughing and threw the sketch to the wind.

MAYA RUDOLPH, *Future Cast Member:*

Obviously in 1975 I was four years old, so who knows how much information I was retaining, but I know I was watching when Gilda was on, because I was doing Roseanne Roseannadanna impressions. I thought I looked like her, because we had the same hair when I was that age. I was probably five or six. I don't think I could have stayed up late enough to watch the show, but I remember seeing it when my mom was alive. My mom was Minnie Riperton. She died in '79. I remember crawling in bed with both my parents and seeing the "Land Shark." I know my mom was around when I was watching that show. Somehow I was obsessed with it and I loved Gilda. I always did. I think I related to her because she was a girl and I thought she was so pretty, and I also just felt sort of connected to her.

ALAN ZWEIBEL:

I was nuts about Gilda. I was crazy about her. I had first seen her in the Lampoon Show with Belushi. There was one sketch where she was dressed like Jackie Kennedy in Dallas, with the pillbox hat and everything, right? And every time there was what sounded like a gunshot in the sketch, she would start crawling backwards in the opposite direction. And just the way she did that, I swear to God, she didn't say anything, but I couldn't believe how much I was laughing. It made me nuts. And then the first day in Lorne's office, and it's God's honest truth, I was really intimidated by what was going on in this room. There was Danny, O'Donoghue, and Belushi and stuff like that, and in the corner of Lorne's office was this potted plant, and I hid behind it. I actually squatted down because Lorne was now going around asking people their ideas and I couldn't compete with this. So I'm there and I'm hiding when all of a sudden through the leaves I hear someone say, "Can you help me be a parakeet?"

So I parted the leaves and it was Gilda. I go, "What?!" She said, "I have this idea where I get dressed up like a parakeet, and I'm on a perch. But I need a writer to help me figure out what the parakeet should say. Can you help me?" I had no idea what she was talking about, but she was a human being calling me a writer so I go, "Oh yeah, I'm great at parakeet stuff." And she said, "Why are you behind there? You're scared, aren't you? Just look at this room, it's pretty intimidating, all this talent that's here. And so that's why you're here, because you're scared." I said, "Yeah." She said, "I am too. Can I come back?" And she came behind the plant with me. So now we're both behind this plant and we get to talking and all of a sudden she says, "Uh-oh, he's calling on you" — this is about five minutes later — and I get tongue-tied, you know, one of those things. Lorne's going, "Alan? Is Alan around here?" She says, "I'll take care of it." She gets up, goes around the plant to the front of the room, and she says, "Zweibel's got this great idea where I play this parakeet and I sit on a perch." So she attributed her idea to me. And I went, "Wow." I got up enough nerve to come out from behind the plant and Gilda said, "Wait a second. He's also got this funny, funny idea where I also play Howdy Doody's wife, Debbie Doody, and we're going to write this and all sorts of stuff," she said, "like a team." That's how I found out that I was going to be teamed up with Gilda. She just took pity on this puppy behind the plant.

CANDICE BERGEN:

Gilda was so great. She was such an angel. And so gifted, so sweet. Everybody bonded with Gilda, because she was irresistible.

DAN AYKROYD:

I was involved with Gilda, yeah. I was in love with her. But that was in the early days of Second City in Canada. Our romance was finished by the time *Saturday Night Live* happened. We were friends, lovers, then friends again. By the time we came to New York, we weren't involved by any means.

LARAINE NEWMAN:

I had a thing with Danny for a while. He was just adorable and irresistible and we had a lot of fun. And I always knew, you know, exactly what I could expect from Danny, so I never really got hurt.

PAULA DAVIS, *Assistant:*

I started hanging out at *SNL* when I was a kid. I was thirteen or fourteen when the show started, and I watched the show with my friend Toby. We just loved it, and we decided to sneak in, because I think at that point my mom was working in the building on game shows. So we were confident we could sneak our way around the *SNL* studios, which we did. And we got in and we hung around, kind of like stage-door Johnnies, for probably a year. Everybody was very, very friendly to us. Chevy was very friendly to us. Belushi and Aykroyd talked to us a lot. Even Michael O'Donoghue was nice. So we did a lot of hanging around.

I remember one day when I was in high school, Rosie Shuster asked me to help her out. It was one of those things like come over, pick up my dry cleaning, pick up my lamp from the lamp repair place— because they had no free time. When I got there, I remember Aykroyd getting out of her bed, and I was totally surprised. Because last I knew, Aykroyd was with Laraine at that point.

PAUL SHAFFER:

I was a little naive. I didn't get involved with anyone. I was friends with everybody, but I wasn't lucky enough to score with anybody.

DAN AYKROYD:

I don't know what goes on backstage there now, but I remember the dressing rooms were put to some good sexual purposes back when we were there. But those were just fleeting. They weren't really serious relationships. It was more clinging to someone, attaching to someone in the face of all we were going through.

CHEVY CHASE:

The "sex appeal" thing, I don't know where that came from. I know that I had sex appeal because I know how much sex I had.

You know what made me good was simply not giving a flying fuck. I had nothing invested there emotionally. I made sure that I had a contract that read that I had the option to leave after a year—the only one there. And I'd never had a job for more than a year before that with anybody.

ANNE BEATTS:

The only entrée to that boys club was basically by fucking some-body in the club. Which wasn't the reason you were fucking them necessarily. I mean, you didn't go, "Oh, I want to get into this, I think I'll have to have sex with this person." It was just that if you were drawn to funny people who were doing interesting things, then the only real way to get to do those things yourself was to make that connection. Either you had to be somebody's girlfriend or, sadly and frequently, then you'd be somebody's ex-girlfriend. And then someone else's girlfriend, as I ended up being, and Rosie did too.

MARILYN SUZANNE MILLER:

Did I date anybody on the show? I don't know that I'd use the word "date." I had intimate encounters. We were young, and the guys were single and the women were single and we were together twenty-four hours a day—you do the biology.

We slept around then. And it wasn't weird. Yes, you could have sex with someone at night and write a sketch for them, or with them, the next day. Totally. It happened a lot. Certainly to me it happened. That's the way life was then. You could sleep with a guy who worked on the show and just know it was de rigueur not to make a big thing out of it and just go to work with him.

ALAN ZWEIBEL:

I guess Gilda and my secret was that we *weren't* sleeping with each other. Our relationship was platonic. It had, with the exception of the sex part, everything else that a boy-girl relationship has. Emotions, the ups, the downs, the yelling, the screaming, the highs, I mean everything. She had said something very early on, when it was close to not being platonic, she had said something along the lines of, "Look, every relationship you've had and I've had with the opposite sex has pretty much ended in disaster or crashed and burned. And we have a good thing going here creatively; let's try not to be boy-girl." That made sense, you know. Years later, now, I think she just wasn't attracted to me.

The first generation of Saturday Night Live *is remembered for more than its comedy or its cleverness or its revolutionary contributions to television. Most of the cast members and writers had come of age in the sixties and hewed to that era's values — turn on and tune in, if not quite drop out. These were heady days, some of the headiest ever at NBC. Open an office door in the* SNL *suite on the seventeenth floor and you might well be enswirled in marijuana smoke. Harder drugs were used as well — at least one cast member freebased cocaine, others dropped acid — right there in the haute-deco halls of the RCA Building.*

CHEVY CHASE:

Fame is a huge thing that is in your life, and we know now that taking drugs is self-medicating. What are we medicating? Something that is hurting us. Usually it's a depression of some kind or some sort of sadness or something stressful, right? That's what we're self-medicating. Fame is extremely stressful. That's why so many people who become famous so fast self-medicate. And what is there to self-medicate with? A hundred-dollar bill and, if it's 1975, some cocaine, or some pot or something. The point is that it all follows, it's as natural as a guy going home and having a drink at the end of a stressful day. But this kind of stress, this fame thing I was talking about, is huge.

I was already thirty-two, I had already been through many, many years of writing and working and being around this business, so in my own mind, I should have been able to not lose any perspective. And, of course, in retrospect, I had lost *all* perspective. I think if there is one perception that the public feels about people who become famous, it's that it is a great, wonderful, marvelous, magical thing. And that's true up to a point. But in fact it's also a very, very frightening thing, because it's one of the most stressful things. There's a certain amount of post-traumatic stress involved in being a regular guy and then suddenly an extremely famous one.

By and large, people who are performers are looking for some sort of immediate gratification to begin with, some validation of what their identity is, who they are, some acceptability. They're not novelists who are waiting after ten years to see how they did. They want it right away. They're children, basically. And in all children there's this reservoir of self-doubt and guilt and sense of low self-esteem, I think. And so one lives with this kind of dualism, this disparity between the marvelous magic of becoming accepted by so many so fast and, at the same time, a lingering sense that one doesn't deserve it and sooner or later will be found out.

Lorne used to say that coke was God's way of telling you that you have too much money. He used to say, "Don't stay on one thing. If you're going to take anything, rotate them." This was a long time ago.

DICK EBERSOL:

There were drugs, but I was not nor have I ever been a drug user. I'd been around them in college. I just made different choices. I fell in love with business.

LORNE MICHAELS:

The widow Belushi was quoted in a book about a time when she found coke on John in the first season of the show and she said, "Where did you get it?" and he told her that Chevy and I gave it to him. But he had been doing coke for years.

CHEVY CHASE:

Everybody was supplying him, supposedly. No—I was supplying Lorne, who was supplying John, it was a middleman kind of thing.

CRAIG KELLEM:

John Belushi and I have the same birthday, January 24th. In 1976 they had a party for John but kind of included me. And the cake that they gave him was a facsimile of a quaalude. My cake was a facsimile of a Valium.

TOM SCHILLER:

Belushi was the first person to show me how to roll a joint. It was very exciting. You would come to the seventeenth floor, and as you walked down the hall, the stench of marijuana would greet you like about a hundred feet away from the offices. They kind of turned a blind eye to all that. It was like suddenly it was okay to do that. These "kids" were doing a show and it was all right. I remember Lorne at one of the earliest meetings, when we were sitting in his office, the first thing he did was light up a joint and pass it around. It was like saying, "It's okay to smoke up here."

Maybe Jane Curtin didn't smoke and maybe Marilyn Miller didn't, but that was about it. That was our drug of choice. Then it turned to coke. I didn't like coke. I tried it for one week and I just got diarrhea.

DICK EBERSOL:

My office was on the fourth floor. The writers basically never got there before one o'clock in the afternoon—ever. We had so little space. Herb Sargent was back in a corner. In the hallway to Herb's office were like Franken and Davis and Alan Zweibel, the three apprentice writers. Al and Tom had bought their first-ever cocaine, and they had it all out on the desk. First time they were ever able to buy any. As apprentice writers, their pay was, I think, $325 a week. So they have the cocaine on the desk, they're like literally staring at it. I'm off in the distance. I'm in a tough place because I'm supposedly the executive, but I decided it wasn't my job to play the policeman.

Suddenly this figure comes roaring through the room. Unbeknownst to us at the time, he had a straw in his hand. He gets to the table, and he has half of that stuff up his nose by the time they knew who it was: Belushi. They didn't know whether to be thrilled that Belushi had just done this to their coke or be absolutely decimated, because that represented about half the money they had in the world at that time.

The drugs didn't bother me, yet I knew they could be the end of the world for the show. And when I found out there was a partially available space on the seventeenth floor I said to Lorne that's where we're going. It's the best place because of the elevators. One elevator bank says fourteen and up, the other elevator bank one through sixteen in the old NBC. That's where everybody was, every executive was on that side, from the head of the network to the chief lawyers, between the first and the sixteenth floor. You could go up either elevator bank to the sixteenth floor, but if you got on the other elevator bank you only had three floors in common. Fourteen and fifteen were sports and press, sixteen was personnel and I figured, "Fuck them." But if they were on the other elevator, they'd be on the same elevator with Schlosser. And so we were somewhat insulated, but initially in an area that was too small.

EUGENE LEE:

That was a mistake, choosing the seventeenth floor, because we never thought that we'd have to wait for elevators. The elevator door used to be full of big dents where people had kicked it. They couldn't bear waiting.

EDIE BASKIN:

Drugs were definitely part of the times, but I just think if you wanted to do it, you did it, and if you didn't want to do it, you didn't do it. It didn't have anything to do with pressure. I didn't think anybody was cool because they did drugs, and I didn't think anybody was cool because they didn't. People just made their own choices.

NEIL LEVY:

Franken and Davis I think shared an apartment, and they threw a party so we could get together to watch Howard Cosell's *Saturday Night Live*. It came on before us, which is why we weren't allowed to call our show *Saturday Night Live* at first. We wanted to see this other *Saturday Night*. All the writers showed up, Michael O'Donoghue, Dan Aykroyd. They were passing around these joints. I had never smoked before, or not really gotten stoned, and I didn't want to seem like "the kid," so I started smoking. This pot was from Africa or something. You didn't even have to smoke it; you just looked at the joint and you were unconscious. It kept coming around and around to me, and then I just got so incredibly paranoid. Never in my life had I been that bad before. I locked myself in their only bathroom, and I was terrified, and I kept praying to God that it would stop. Every once in a while someone would come to use the bathroom and I'd flush the toilet and go, "I'll be out in a minute!" And I just got worse and worse, because people had to know I was in the bathroom and something was going wrong.

Finally Dan Aykroyd knocked on the door and he said, "Neil, this is Dan. You probably smoked some of that weed, you're probably paranoid, and you probably think you're the only one. Let me tell you, my friend, you're not the only one. We're all paranoid, we're all stoned." And he talked me out of the bathroom into the bedroom. And he started making me laugh. One of the things he did was he pulled his pants a little of the way down and pretended he was fixing the radiator as a radiator repairman. And later I remember he used that as a refrigerator repairman in a Nerds sketch. I think I saw it first.

MARILYN SUZANNE MILLER:

Alan and I were so young when we did that show, and we had so much extra fuel that after being up all night writing, we still had to think of other stuff to do. So one night we went into Franken and Davis's office and took out all the furniture—all the desks, ripped the phones out of the wall, took the chairs, took the file cases, took everything in the middle of the night and shoved it into Herb Sargent's office where it couldn't be seen. And then all we did was take a piece of paper and leave it on the floor that said, "See me. Lorne." This is like the first season, when they were apprentice writers! Alan and I thought this was hilarious. Needless to say, Franken wasn't too happy. But we did stuff like this all the time.

GARRETT MORRIS:

People suppose that if you are in a cast, that means you automatically go everywhere together twenty-four hours a day and you can tell what every other member is doing and that in fact you think that's good. I have always been an asshole with any cast I've been with. I was gone as soon as I could be. The fact that I didn't hang out with the gang at *Saturday Night Live* is no reflection upon anybody but me. At that time, I was in my Carlos Castaneda thing, and so I was doing a whole lot of mysticism and stuff. I was a loner. And that actually cost me. Because with *Saturday Night Live,* I learned that the social life is just as important as your own talent. Particularly with writers, they have to hear you talk and get to know you.

I'm not saying anybody was racist, but there are stereotypical things people draw from action that is devoid of me sitting down, talking, and getting into people's minds about what they think, et cetera, et cetera. For example, one time I said something about a particular duo of intellectual Jews at *Saturday Night Live* which was then spread all over the whole Jewish world and for like a year I had the reputation of being anti-Jewish because I told these particular Jews that they were for shit. The point is, no, I didn't hang out, but later I realized it was something I should have done.

ALAN ZWEIBEL:

We loved television, quite frankly, and we had our own sensibility and we were given the opportunity to do it. But I think it was because of the love for television that anyone who ordinarily didn't do television did this show. So Belushi could say, "I hate television." I think what that really meant was, "I hate what they've done to television," or "I hate what television is right now." I don't think that was anything against Newton Minow or the medium itself.

The one rule that we had, if there was a rule, was if we make each other laugh we'll put it on television and hopefully other people will find it funny and tell their friends. So there was a purity about the intent.

There was a nobility to me and Gilda taking a subway ride, saying something to make us laugh, and then we would go back to the office afterwards and write it up and it's on television a day later. There was an immediacy to it; it was just like, "This is the way the world works."

HERBERT SCHLOSSER:

The word of mouth was starting to get around. It was either in our November or December board of directors meeting at NBC. Boards of directors, then as now, had old guys with ties and gray hair. And we did get flak about the show—bad taste and this and that. But one of the directors pulled me over and asked me if he could get tickets for one of his kids who was coming home from college.

CRAIG KELLEM:

We were beginning to get some action out there in that first year, but people were not making a lot of money. Then some guy came along—I cannot remember his name—who was doing commercials for the United States military, and the *Saturday Night Live* gang were hired to appear in these commercials. And Lorne, being a kind of a born snob, wanted no part of dealing with these people, but it was a good way for everybody to earn money. So I became the guy who was the link to the commercial guy and did all the coordinating and producing, as it were.

And we actually made a series of commercials for the military. I never saw them. I've never even heard about them since. But it's a fact. This guy spent thousands of dollars on this thing. Belushi did them because he wanted that money, and fast. They all made money, including Lorne, but Lorne kept a very pronounced arm's length from the whole venture.

BERNIE BRILLSTEIN:

I knew Belushi was going to be a hit when Paul McCartney called and offered me $6,000 for Belushi to perform his Joe Cocker impression at his birthday party. John was making $800 or $1,000 a show. Six thousand dollars to sing like Joe Cocker? Oh my God, oh my God, he was so happy—not the money, just singing for McCartney. Oh my God.

LORNE MICHAELS:

I remember exactly how much money I made in 1975. I made $115,000, and it was more money than I'd ever imagined. I'd been offered the season before four Flip Wilson shows, four specials, for a little over a hundred thousand dollars and I said I would do one. The experience wasn't a special one for me. It wasn't a show I was terribly proud of, but it did a 46 share, and what I remember learning from that was if you did a show you really cared about, it didn't matter if anybody watched it. But if you did a show that wasn't any good, it was much better if everyone saw it. If it was highly rated, you knew you'd be able to work again.

JEAN DOUMANIAN, Associate Producer:

I didn't start working for Saturday Night Live until the eleventh show in 1975, because I had been working on the first show called Saturday Night Live, with Howard Cosell on ABC. We were canceled after the seventeenth show, and Lorne called and asked if he could use the title of the show.

CRAIG KELLEM:

That was a signature issue as far as Lorne was concerned: he wanted to call his show Saturday Night Live. It totally pissed him off that the title was taken by Howard Cosell. And when the other show went off the air and he got the title back, I kind of chuckled inside, thinking how Lorne had decided that he wanted that title and he was going to get that title. And you know what? He ended up with that title. That's Lorne Michaels to a T.

JEAN DOUMANIAN:

Lorne had one corner office. And I had the other corner office. I liked Lorne a lot, we got along very well. But I was never intimidated by him. And I was never part of the family. I didn't do drugs, and I had a life outside the show.

LORNE MICHAELS:

The Desi Arnaz show in February was a great show. He wouldn't stay at our normal hotel; he had to stay at the Waldorf. The great moment was when he was doing "Babalu" live on the air with Desi, Jr. I was in the control room watching and we were trying to figure out when to cut away. He throws himself into it so much, I'm like seeing his lips turn blue. He's going into it totally, like he's thirty. And I'm thinking, "Oh my God, he's going to have a coronary. What happens if he dies on live TV?" And so we finally cut away to commercial.

JANE CURTIN:

There were huge highs and huge lows. I think that because of the talent, and because of the people's temperaments, you could have these incredible moments of sheer exhilaration and excitement, and then moments where you just feel like you're a pill, you're a tiny little piece of lint. You feel as though you don't deserve air. So the highs and lows were huge, but there was a middle ground, because the show had to go on. At eleven-thirty, you had to put all of that stuff aside and hit the ground running and do what you were trained to do—and, hopefully, have a good time. More often than not, you did.

LILY TOMLIN:

Laraine was always good. And of course Gilda was a very adorable person. I don't know Chevy really well, but I've always liked Chevy. And Jane Curtin—I was never close to her and I don't know that anyone was, but while the other girls were just kind of spinning around her, Jane was always just kind of centered, and ironically she's the one that's had the biggest career. She was always very anchored. I was always impressed with Jane.

The original, still-most-famous cast in the history of Saturday Night Live *actually remained intact for only one season. Chevy Chase, the only performer who regularly identified himself by name on the show and who was the player most featured in magazine and newspaper stories— even as possible successor to Johnny Carson as host of* The Tonight Show *— left at the end of the first season, returning in later years only for cameos and guest-hostings. Because he had signed a contract with NBC as a writer and not a performer, and stipulated a one-year term instead of five, he was free to go. In August 1976, when the parting was announced, Chase radiated self-effacing graciousness, saying he had "a very strong love affair with the show" but that "my leaving won't affect it. It has its own momentum. There's more talent in Danny Aykroyd's right hand than in my entire body." Twenty-three years later, at the unveiling of a Lorne Michaels star on the Hollywood Walk of Fame in Los Angeles, Chase would tell a crowd assembled for the event that leaving the show when he did was a mistake — and that he still regretted it.*

BUCK HENRY:

I thought Chevy shouldn't have left. I thought it was really stupid to leave that early in the run, because he was so great on it. The show made him. He should have gone and done his movies later. Maybe Belushi wouldn't have blossomed so much, though, if Chevy had stayed. Because John was so happy to see him go.

JUDITH BELUSHI:

John and Chevy were always antagonistic *and* friends. It was a love-hate kind of thing. They worked together well when they were trying to. A funny thing they used to do on the side — underwear ad posing. They would just strike a pose together, like Chevy's arm on John's shoulder, one knee up on a chair, like the underwear poses in the Sears catalog.

I'd say John had mixed feelings about Chevy leaving. The whole thing around *Saturday Night Live* was, if you were in the circle with Lorne, you could get a lot more of what you wanted. Chevy was part of that circle, and Paul Simon and whoever, I forget. And Chevy was getting a lot of airtime and John felt *he* should get more, and that Chevy was sometimes cast for things that John thought he could do better.

ALAN ZWEIBEL:

There had come a point in the first season where Chevy wasn't writing for the show as much as he was writing for Chevy. And that didn't help things.

JOHN LANDIS:

The part of Otter in *Animal House* was originally written for Chevy Chase. Ned Tanen at Universal said to me, "Here's this script, *Animal House.* If you can get me Chevy Chase and John Belushi and a movie star, I'll make it." So Ivan Reitman was desperate to get Chevy.

But I was adamantly opposed to casting him. I had nothing against Chevy, I just believed that he wouldn't feel honored, and that he was too old. So I had this wonderful, famous lunch that Ivan Reitman will remember differently but where Ivan and Thom Mount desperately blow smoke up Chevy's ass, trying to convince him to take *Animal House* even though he's been offered *Foul Play* as well. Chevy was smoking a huge cigar; this was the first time I ever met him. A good-looking guy in good shape, and I was doing everything I could to sell it to him. And finally I had a masterstroke. I said, "Chevy, if you take *Foul Play,* you're then like Cary Grant; you're opposite Goldie Hawn, a major sex star, you're like Cary Grant. But if you take *Animal House,* you're a top banana in an ensemble, like *SNL.*" And under the table Ivan gave me I think the most vicious kick I've ever had. He was furious, but it worked: Chevy took the other movie.

CHEVY CHASE:

For me at the time, the question was, could I actually be in a movie with somebody who's talented—Goldie—and actually be in something

I'd never done before and actually try to act? You know, what would that be like? It wasn't a question of could I do something that was marginally subversive for movies, when I'd already done five years of underground television on Channel 1 and had written for *Mad* magazine, the *National Lampoon,* et cetera. *Animal House* is an ensemble piece any way you look at it.

DAN AYKROYD:

It's fair to say that John's mood, on a read-through day or whatever, was infectious to the point where he could dominate—like if he was in a jovial mood, it became a jovial table reading, or if he was down, it didn't. I think when you have great people that have charisma like that, that's probably a truism. Yeah, for sure, it was him and Chevy, him and Chevy were the ones primarily that could make the room, bring the room up or bring the room down. O'Donoghue to a certain extent too. You know, the giant talents like that.

CHEVY CHASE:

Look, I would have stayed. There was this girl I wanted to marry who ended up throwing a candelabra at me. Lorne knew she was wrong for me, but I thought I was in love. I also felt after one year that we should all leave, that we should all take off at least one year and think this over, because otherwise it was going to become solipsistic—jokes about ourselves, showcases for characters as opposed to what it should be, which is a vehicle to take apart television. Satirize it and rip it to pieces, show it for what it is—and we'd done that. We had a year to do it, we did it, there wasn't a hell of a lot more that you could do except start on something else. That was the way I felt then. But I'm still hurting, I still grieve for all those years that I could have had there.

And you know, if Lorne had put his arms around me and given me a hug and asked me to stay, then I probably would have. But he didn't.

BERNIE BRILLSTEIN:

Bullshit. Chevy was my client, and he said in my office, "The reason I'm leaving is I am a producer and a writer, and Lorne's a producer and a writer, and that's a conflict." The real reason was he got a fucking car and more money. William Morris was blowing smoke in Chevy's ears as well as his wife at the time, that he should leave the show. They weren't getting big commissions from the show, I think eighty bucks a week or something. I thought he should stay on the show for at least two or three years, for no other reason than that the exposure he was getting was great. But William Morris went to NBC, and NBC was so unsure about *SNL,* they just wanted to make sure they kept Chevy, because he was a good-looking guy and he was like a television star. They gave him two specials. William Morris got a package commission for the specials, and NBC gave Chevy a car. I think it was a Porsche. So NBC attacked its own show.

Chevy was very gentlemanly. He came to me and paid all the money he owed me and he said, "Look, I want to do it on my own. I'm competitive with Lorne, I want to produce too." He went and did the movies, you know, and for a while he was fine, but he destroyed himself.

DICK EBERSOL:

Lorne just felt totally betrayed when Chevy left, not because he was losing his biggest star, but because this was his biggest partner on the show.

LORNE MICHAELS:

I'm sure I was devastated by it, but I knew there would have been a struggle: was the show going to become the Chevy Chase show or was it going to stay an ensemble show? I think he'd become too big a star.

ANNE BEATTS:

I don't know exactly when Michael and Chevy's relationship went sour. I know that Chevy said—I'm sure you've heard this—that Michael told him once in a taxi, "One day you'll be a B-movie star." I know that Chevy has really taken that remark to heart. And so I think that perhaps the Michael-Chevy going sour thing was part of Michael calling it as he saw it, which he unstintingly did even when it was detrimental to his best interests.

CHEVY CHASE:

You have no idea what my life was like as a kid, you have no sense of that at all. You're probably looking into books and saying, "Hey, he went to a private school," as if that somehow is an explanation for my personality. You have no sense at all—nor would I share with you what my childhood was like.

ANNE BEATTS:

Chevy was the Waspy golden boy that neither Michael nor Lorne would ever be.

ALAN ZWEIBEL:

It was emotional. We were a colony. I don't mean this in a bad way, but we were Guyana on the seventeenth floor. We didn't go out. We stayed there. It was a stalag of some sort.

LORNE MICHAELS:

No one thought we'd have a summer holiday, because nobody at the network thought they could rerun these shows. I said, "No, we're going to put on reruns." And when we put on the Richard Pryor show, it rated higher than it had originally. And I won the case.

Some of us spent the summer together. We went to Joshua Tree in California. I'd been there many times before. It was a spiritual place for me, and so I was showing them this place that had a lot of meaning for me. We stayed at the Joshua Tree Inn, a motel with a pool in the center. John and Danny were in the room next to mine.

One night we had a barbecue. Chevy, who came with his girl-friend, cooked. I remember it was a very beautiful night, and we were all sort of grateful for each other and just beginning to soak up whatever that first season was. This was late June or early July, and we were just beginning to understand what being on a hit show was like, the full throttle of that.

We drank a lot and stayed up really late. Then at about five o'clock in the morning, the sun was way too bright and woke me up. There was some sort of noise outside, so I staggered to the door. When I opened it, I saw Danny standing in the archway just a few feet away, and he's in the same shape I'm in, and we look out and there's John, on the diving board, doing these cannonballs. He goes straight up, hits the board, comes down, and then flips over into the pool. This was just for our benefit, Danny's and mine, because there was nobody else awake or watching it. And we were like completely wrecked, the two of us, and just barely conscious, and Danny looked at me and he said, "Albanian oak."

And that's what we believed. We believed this guy was absolutely indestructible. He was like an animal. You couldn't have been through the night we'd just been through and be up at five o'clock doing cannonballs—neither of us could live that hard—but there was John.

The beauty of all that for me is that we were comrades-in-arms in the way that, growing up after World War II, you'd hear people talk about army buddies, or say the only people they could talk to were people who had been through it with them. A year earlier, we hadn't been in any way linked or close, and now we were suddenly on a holiday together. All this stuff was swirling around in the press and we were together at the center of it. We'd gone all the way to the finals and we'd won the Emmys and here we were on the road. We all liked each other. We had more in common with one another than with any other group of people.

To me, our first season was "that championship season." That said, I'm not sure it was the best season in terms of quality, but the freedom was intoxicating. And so was the success.

2

Heyday: 1976–1980

By the beginning of its second season, Saturday Night Live *was the talk of television, a national sensation both hot and cool, and the first hit any network ever had at eleven-thirty on Saturday night. Chevy Chase had become a star and flown the coop, though he would continue to make the occasional cameo appearance. Some cast members and writers saw his leap into greener pastures as tantamount to treason, but it kept* SNL *from turning into "The Chevy Chase Show" and cleared the way for John Belushi, Dan Aykroyd, Gilda Radner, Laraine Newman, Garrett Morris, and others to become the kind of household name that Chevy had managed virtually overnight.*

The Muppets were gone. Short films by Gary Weis and Tom Schiller would replace those of Albert Brooks. NBC censors were virtually forced by the program's surging popularity to become less strict—this was well before people could say "pissed off" or "that sucks" on television—and as other programs took advantage of the liberation, a new candor and a new realism came to American TV—for better and, sometimes, for worse. The way people talked on television was becoming closer to the way people talked in everyday life; a longtime boundary was being erased. Today one hears language in prime-time sitcoms and even commercials that was unthinkable on early editions of Saturday Night Live. *(In time, the show would break the "penis" and "vagina" barriers, among many others.)*

They couldn't fully know it at the time, but the cast, writers, and producers of Saturday Night Live *were living through the program's golden age, from 1975 to 1979, the era of the original cast (with Bill Murray replacing the departed Chevy Chase), the founding writers, and occasional visits from such off-the-wall novelties as quixotic comic Andy Kaufman and Mr. Bill, a little clay man who each week would be mauled and mangled. This was a time of exuberance, adventurousness, and unbridled excess. It would become legendary and infamous and set standards by which every subsequent manifestation of the show, including all future casts, would be judged.*

LARAINE NEWMAN, *Cast Member:*

There was one point in the second season where we were onstage rehearsing a Nerd sketch or something, and we were all talking about what we were naming our corporations. And I think it was Gilda who said, "Listen to us, for God's sake. We're talking about our corporations! What's happened? We've joined the establishment." And we were really kind of being hurled into all the trappings of a successful adult life at a young age.

TOM HANKS, *Host:*

It was the cultural phenomenon of the age. It was truly as big as the Beatles. It was this huge riotous thing and it was on every week and everybody gathered together on Saturday nights to watch it.

We would get together in college and then, later on when I was working in the theater, we would all get together after shows at a house and watch. Everybody from the theater that I was working at in Cleveland was in the living room of this rented house watching a ten-inch black-and-white television with a coat hanger for an antenna. And that's just what you did every week—got together and had something to eat and sat around waiting for *Saturday Night Live* to come on.

BRIAN DOYLE-MURRAY, *Cast Member:*

The show felt like it was the center of the universe. There was such a clamor about it. People at parties would stop and turn on the show and watch it. So it felt like the big high point of TV. Half your job seemed like arranging for tickets for people you knew.

JAMES SIGNORELLI, *Director of Commercial Parodies:*

By the autumn of the second year, I remember walking around with Gilda and not being able to go fifty feet down the street without people stopping us warmly and saying, "Hi," "I love you," and "I love your stuff," and so on. At first Gilda was pleased and delighted, and then later—much later—felt kind of put-upon.

TOM SCHILLER, *Writer:*

There were all kinds of people like Mike Nichols who thought the show was hip, and Norman Mailer, and you'd see them at restaurants and they'd nod to you and stuff, and you thought you were so great. And then, some nights you would come out of the show and you would see these really strange geeky people with eight-by-tens and marking pens to have you sign your autograph, and they were like troglodytes, these people. They were strange people who were your fans. So it was hard to reconcile who really liked you.

ROBIN SHLIEN, *Production Assistant:*

You would look around and Jerome Robbins would be in the back of the control room one night, or Michael Bennett. It was this place where the toasts of the town would show up.

ALAN ZWEIBEL, *Writer:*

To this day, I look back on those first five years with incredible fondness. I tend to romanticize the experience, because it was way more good than bad. But when it was bad, it was very painful. It was very, *very* painful.

JANE CURTIN, *Cast Member:*

I loved doing the ninety minutes of the show, just loved it, but I couldn't do the other stuff. I couldn't be in the writers' meetings; it was too frustrating. I just didn't function well in that situation. I didn't know how to push my ideas. So I would come in for the read-through on Wednesday and then go right home. On Thursday, when I came to work, I came to work on time. In the second season I had "Update," so I had something to do on the show and didn't have to fight to be on the air.

"Update" was my anchor. Everything else was gravy. The Nerds—I loved those sketches. I loved working with Buck and Billy and Gilda, and we always laughed, because they were just so dumb. And sometimes things like the Widettes, because they would just make you hysterical. I loved the epics and the costume dramas, and some of the talk shows that we did were just yummy. There were a lot of other things, but the fact that I had "Update" and didn't have to plead for material kept me sane. I had the luxury of being able to leave and come in when I needed to. I didn't hang around. And so I approached it from a totally different point of view than I think anybody else.

ROSIE SHUSTER, *Writer:*

Those first five years, only Jane amongst the cast really was able to have a total personal life. I think a few of the guys maybe could have someone back home. Of the girls, you lived and slept and breathed the show. You stayed there. I remember Danny and I, after sleeping over at the office, would walk each other like dogs around 30 Rock just to get a little fresh air. In those first years it was just pure gonzo, total commitment. There was this phenomenon that was exploding and we all threw ourselves into it 200 percent.

The whole thing sort of marked the beginning of comics being thought of the way rock stars had been. The rock stars had that real pulsing energy and immediacy, and this particular show, because of its live, New York danger vibe, gave you that same kind of raw immediacy. It was just raggedy-ass a lot of times.

PAUL SIMON, *Host:*

I don't think they necessarily changed for the worse with that metamorphosis into success. They became more confident. And they were still young so that they hadn't burned out and weren't cynical yet. Maybe they had more offers and distraction; that might have been a negative, I don't know. But they weren't jaded.

BILL MURRAY, *Cast Member:*

I remember my very first show. I had a sketch that was a little tricky to do, a telephone sketch. They were making me up for the first time and they were trying to make me look old and—well, you don't feel really comfortable the first time they make you look old. I was twenty-five or twenty-six, and they're trying to make you look like you're seventy-five, and it plays a little on your confidence. There was like a committee of people going, "Maybe if you put some gray in his temples," and you're thinking, "Oh my God, we're going to be in trouble out here." But that's one that I sort of pulled together on the air. I read it well the first time in the read-through, but you're not thinking about what it looks like, and even in rehearsals it's like you're still Bill, you know. My confidence sort of dropped, because I thought, "This isn't really helping me."

So I had to do it two times that day, the run-through and the dress rehearsal in that makeup, then for the air there was still that "put some gray in his temples" business, and at a certain point about forty seconds before I had to do it, I just said, "That's enough. Stop." And I just walked away and it was just on me to make it work. So I made that one work. That was pretty successful.

I did three shows and they were on a look-see basis. I think they hired me for three shows. And I remember just walking out onto the street after the first show and Lorne said, "I guess you're going to be moving to New York." And it felt great, you know. It felt really good. And so I thought, "This is great, I did it." But then I didn't get any sketches for weeks after that. That's when I became the second cop. Most of the rest of the year I played the "second cop" in sketches.

That speech I did to the audience—the one where I said, "I don't think I'm making it on the show"—that was during my "second cop" period. I'd really been there a pretty long time, and they were sort of stuck with me. I was there, they'd sort of hired me, I was getting paid, but I was playing that second cop every week. You sort of have to break through, be noticed by the audience. They have to understand you a little bit, see a little bit of who you are, but as the second cop you don't really get those opportunities.

I'd actually had the idea to do something exactly like what it was, and that day when I went to work, Lorne said, "You know, I think you should do a direct appeal." He had the same idea too. So I did this thing, I wrote the thing, and it was kind of funny, and I wasn't too full of myself or anything. There was a couple tablespoons of humility in it, I got laughs in it, and I think the combination of the two broke some sort of ice, not just for me but for people watching, and they thought, "Well, okay, he's going to be funny. He made us laugh with that sort of 'I'm dying here' thing"—which I've seen people do and die at. You know, I've seen people make that move before and fail, so the fact that I made that move and it was funny sort of took the pressure off. I felt pretty good about that. And it is sort of a funny watershed. It's a moment.

ROBERT KLEIN, *Host:*

I had hosted during the first season, but the next time I was on the show wasn't until the third season, in '77. And Lorne called me into the office that time and said, "You know, a lot has changed since you hosted. The kids have become celebrities—stars, you know—and the host is just one of the gang now." I said I understood that fully. But the real difference was Belushi. He was a changed person. There was a lot of difficulty rehearsing with him.

JANE CURTIN:

When John started making too much money, and started doing too many drugs, the sweet John was gone, and the ambitious John took over, and that's what was difficult to deal with. His ambition was just overwhelming, as was his need to self-medicate.

STEVE MARTIN, *Host:*

Once when it was very late after the show and everybody was in their limos and we were on like Seventy-second Street or something, Belushi got out of the car in the middle of the night and stood in the street screaming and directing traffic and being funny. And I thought, "Oh." There was something about it that was forced. I remember feeling like John felt he had to do this stuff. It was what he wanted to be. He also did things that were unforced, but at that moment he was trying to fulfill an image.

CARRIE FISHER, *Host:*

I was hanging around with Belushi, though Lord knows how I got to him. Everybody kind of knew each other. These were people who were abusers, people who liked to drink and use and stay up all night. Once one got into that little society, you were well in.

Danny used to call John "The Black Hole in Space," because if anything got near him, it disappeared into it. And he was also "America's Guest," because he literally could go to anybody's apartment or house—and did—and say, "Hi, can I use your kitchen or your bathroom or your bedroom?" Or your anything. John was always kind of a little bit of an emergency happening—but a fun emergency. At that time, I don't think anyone had said to me yet, "If John keeps this up, he will die." That was like two years away. It wasn't that dark.

HERB SARGENT, *Writer:*

I happened to be the one who broke the news to Belushi that Elvis had died. He had wandered into my office, there were just the two of us, and I told him I'd just heard it on the news. And he just froze for ten minutes. He didn't move. He couldn't talk. Nothing.

JOHN LANDIS, *Film Director:*

I've seen this attributed to John Lennon, but I know Michael O'Donoghue said it, because I was there when we heard Elvis died. My secretary came in and she said, "Elvis is dead," and Michael O'Donoghue said, "Good career move."

JUDITH BELUSHI, *Writer:*

John apologized a lot. He knew when he was wrong. And I think that he always came back and made sure to do that. He had a childlike way of seeing things, which is what I think artists and comedians need. He'd see things fresh. He'd see the thing that everyone is looking at a little differently.

DAN AYKROYD, *Cast Member:*

John would watch tape on whoever he was impersonating. He was meticulous in the preparation in terms of wardrobe, hair, makeup. He was always concerned with doing an accurate impression. He was very well read in English and history and theater. He counted among his friends Lauren Bacall and Judge Jim Garrison, and he was a student of American politics. John just astounded me with his references to English literature, American literature, history, politics—he was so well versed in things that you would never expect. He was a football star when he was a kid. An all-American guy—Albanian blood, and his father had an accent, his mother had an accent—but to me he was totally all-American.

He was extremely bright—really, really smart—a great administrator and executive. When we were doing our Blues Brothers thing, he was clearly in charge. He was the front man, he was the boss, he was the guy that was calling the shots, everything was brought to him for decisions, and ultimately his decisions were correct ones. He was very together as a businessman, understood the creative world and the business world and the marriage between the two. He was just one of the smartest people I have ever met.

MARILYN SUZANNE MILLER, *Writer:*

If you look at the Samurai, if you look at the Beethoven piece he did, there's no plethora of words. A lot of times he's doing a lot of acting, he's just acting all over the place, but he's not using words to do it. I wrote a piece where he crossed over into using words—and he was brilliant! The piece is really a great piece—about this young couple who are having trouble with their sex life and the guy can't get it up because he secretly believes she's thinking about somebody else. And John was so bound and determined to get every fucking word. That's what was so great about it, he was really acting and he was really using words. That was proof that John Belushi was meant to live to be a great actor.

I cried at the end of it, because it was so thrilling.

AL FRANKEN, *Writer:*

On one of the shows where Belushi played Fred Silverman, he was like totally out of it, almost unable to perform. I remember it very, very well because I was one of the writers of the sketch. Between dress and air, I went with another writer, Jim Downey, to John's dressing room. I had the script in my hand and I knocked on the door, and when I went in, I saw that John was kind of out of it, sitting in a chair. And I said, "John, I want to read the script to you so that when you say the lines on the air, it sounds familiar." And then he threatened to hit me. At which point Downey started to back out the door.

But I knew John would never hit me; he just wouldn't do it. So he held his fist up, and I just read him the sketch. And then I left. And it was marginally better on-air.

JUDITH BELUSHI:

I don't remember John ever hitting anybody. I tried to punch *him* once, though. It was very aggravating. Because he was like a fellow that you really cared about and you could see him hurting himself. You'd see him sinking. And it made you want to say, "Stop it now! Or I'll stop you!"

LORNE MICHAELS, *Executive Producer:*

One of the things you realize after a while is you can be having a talk about whatever you're thinking is important or matters with a comedian, and more likely than not he's just getting an impression of you down. You think it's about the content of what you're saying, but they're just sort of seeing your lips move and going, "Oh, he holds his head like that." It's like people caricaturing you but you don't see the drawing. So John Belushi used to have heart-to-heart talks with people, particularly when they were talking about drugs, and they'd say, "I had a really, really good talk with John." And—no. John was using his time in another way. He'd already heard the content of that message.

AL FRANKEN:

Yes, there were some people on the show doing coke. I don't like to get into this. John died of it. He had a problem, he got addicted. We didn't know about that, we didn't know at the time. When I say "we," I mean Americans didn't know what cocaine did, and about addiction, and that kind of thing.

DAN AYKROYD:

The powders and the pills were never attractive to me. It was just John. One of the nights when he played Silverman—that was pure blow. Pure blow, yeah. It made me angry. God knows I poured a lot of it down the toilet. But there were times when he was clean, and then of course there were times when he was at his peak—you know, the Joe Cocker stuff. And he really took the work seriously. It's just that he had an addiction.

He would also get screwed up on painkillers. We were doing a lecture in Rhode Island once and he jumped off the stage and shattered his shin. It was a Catherine the Great sketch, and he had a long, long wig. He was really fucked up that day.

RICHARD DREYFUSS, *Host:*

I remember that during the final dress rehearsal, John Belushi couldn't stand up. He'd been like falling around and mumbling and forgetting everything. I thought, "Whoa boy, this won't be great. He'll never make it through this show." Then the show came around and he was perfect, he was incredible, and I remember being astounded by that, because at the time I was very admiring of anyone who could take drugs better than I could.

BILL MURRAY:

John was great. John was very good to all of us. He was tough on the hosts, though. The better an actor the host was, the sicker Belushi would be. He would be at death's door. He would be hours late and at death's door, and he would come in in a robe, unable to speak. He'd have doctors in his dressing room. It would be just incredible. And the host would be thinking, "Belushi isn't even going to show up, he's too sick even to work"—and then John would come out on the show and just blast them away. He would sucker-punch guys that just didn't see it coming. And the more actorish they were, the worse they got it.

If it had been someone who'd won an Academy Award or something, they didn't have a chance and you knew it. Somebody would write a great sketch for them, and Belushi would be in it, and he'd rehearse it at sort of like 40 percent, too sick to really work, coughing into Kleenexes and pockets full of Kleenex. They'd be out there on the set waiting to rehearse and he'd come in assisted, and in a robe and looking like hell, barely speaking and coughing the whole time, and just completely distracted. Just like barely alive. And he'd be that way pretty much through dress. The doctors would be there. You'd be waiting for him during the run-through and the dress rehearsal. You'd smell vaporizers from his room. He had the smell of Vicks VapoRub and salves and creams and all sorts of medicines—and he would come out and just kill. Just *kill*.

I think he did it to Richard Dreyfuss. He did a Dreyfuss impression the week before Dreyfuss hosted. He did Dreyfuss in *The Good-bye Girl:* "I don't like the panties hanging on the rod." He just hated the performance in the movie, and he did it the week before the guy got there and murdered it, just murdered it.

There was no point in warning the host. They had too much anxiety anyway. They'd run to the next sketch going, "What happened? What happened to my sketch?" He would come out of nowhere, off his deathbed—and he was on his deathbed a couple times a year. And, you know, it was, "He's been doing the Blues Brothers all week and he just came back from rehearsal last night and he hasn't slept." He had the Dr. Feelgood guys there giving him shots and stuff. It was delightful.

LARAINE NEWMAN:

We did this one sketch about fishing in Alaska, and right before we went onstage I was in back of the set with John and he was green. Just *green*. I knew he would go on—I just didn't know how long he was going to live.

TOM SCHILLER:

When I started making films for the show, the third one I made was *Don't Look Back in Anger,* the Belushi-in-the-cemetery one. It was based on the idea that I can look at people and I can "see" how they are going to look when they get old. Of course, I didn't know John wasn't going to get old, but I was intrigued with the idea. When he shot it, he did every line perfectly and went to every spot perfectly without even blocking it beforehand. It was shot at some cemetery in Brooklyn. It was creepy.

ROBERT KLEIN:

In a sketch about giant lobsters attacking New York, I played the guy who said, "Oh, the humanity!" Like the radio reporter from the

Hindenburg fire. There was a very revealing line in there that was pretty awful when you think about it: "Oh, John Belushi is dead. We knew he'd die young, but not this young!"

Another time, in one sketch we were rehearsing, Belushi had the part of the father—miscasting, but it was just a sketch. And he just was sort of shaking and quick-tempered and impatient, and finally we were almost going to hit each other. And Aykroyd breaks it up and calms everything down quickly and says, "Oh, I'll do the part." It was like a terrible flare-up—a very bad memory—and Aykroyd, ever the mensch, stepped in and settled everything.

And it was nothing permanent with Belushi and me, but I do recall in subsequent weeks Belushi was off the show. I called it "getting docked," like at camp or something, where you're being punished. This is another of Lorne Michaels's talents that I'll have to give him, that he was able to juggle this stuff. Because there were drugs around. There were cocaine lines the length of a desk, you know. And most people could handle it, but a few people fell very badly through the cracks.

JANE CURTIN:

Lorne and I stopped speaking. It was during the second year. He wouldn't answer my questions. I would say, "Why aren't you doing something about John? I found him going through my purse. He set your loft on fire. His behavior is reprehensible. He's not coming to rehearsals or if he does come, he comes three hours late. Do something!" And he didn't. He would just sort of throw his hands in the air. Lorne doesn't deal with issues. Lorne cannot confront an issue. So I thought, "Well, this is pointless, I'm not going to talk to him anymore."

Gilda became our go-between. When Lorne wanted me to do something, he would call Gilda and say, "Would you ask Jane if she would do this?" And Gilda would come up to me and say, "Lorne was wondering if you would mind doing this?" And I'd say, "No, that would be fine." This made life so much easier. We would say hello, but beyond that, there was nothing I needed from Lorne. I had "Update," so I didn't need anything. I didn't need a father. I had a husband who loved me, and a great little dog. Life was good.

KATE JACKSON, *Host:*

I got a phone call from Bob Woodward when he was doing his book *Wired,* and he wanted to talk to me because he had heard that the show I had hosted was John's worst in terms of drug abuse. I didn't know that, because I never saw anybody do anything, so I didn't talk to Woodward. I heard later that paramedics had been called over to the studio and were standing by for John all through the show.

But John didn't miss the show. He was perspiring a little bit. But he never, never went way off on a wrong tangent, never went off the cards, or never messed anything up that made it hard for me to get back on track. He did what he was supposed to do.

John called me afterwards. For weeks he would call me on Thursday afternoons just to say hello and to thank me for saving his life. "Wow," he'd say. "Katie, man, you really saved my life, wow, and thank you." And I frankly didn't know what he was talking about. I didn't know why he was calling; he was just so sweet, you know. Danny had told me, "John is a bad boy, but a good man."

NORMAN LEAR, *Host:*

I loved in John and also in Aykroyd what I loved in Carroll O'Connor and Bea Arthur—a madness that would allow them to go anyplace. I have to say, whatever year I am destined to die, I have five years or ten years on top of that because those people who offered me that touch of madness gave me time, added to my life.

NEIL LEVY, *Production Assistant:*

I was at Catch a Rising Star trying to pick up a girl one night. When I first started on that show I looked like I was about twelve, and this girl didn't believe I worked on *Saturday Night Live.* And then suddenly everyone turned toward the door because Belushi had entered. Whenever he entered a room, there was an energy about him that made people turn their heads. And this girl saw him, and John saw me, and he went, "Neil!" and starts coming right toward me. And I'm thinking, "This girl is going to be putty in my hands now." And he comes right up to me and gives me a big bear hug and says, "You got any money?" I'm thinking, "Not only do I know John Belushi, but he's going to borrow money from me." So I take out my wallet and he takes the wallet out of my hands, rummages through it, hands it back, goes "Thanks," and disappears into the crowd. Well, he'd left me with a dollar. And there were no ATM's back then. When I went to find him, he had disappeared.

If he did something like that, though, I remember more than one time him coming around later and saying, "Was I with you last night?" And you'd go, "Yeah," and he'd go, "I'm so sorry," and be really contrite. Then you'd hear him knocking on other people's doors and going in to apologize about things.

AL FRANKEN:

There was not as much cocaine as you would think on the premises. Yeah, a number of people got in trouble. But cocaine was used mainly just to stay up. There was a very undisciplined way of writing the show, which was staying up all night on Tuesday. We didn't have the kind of hours that normal people have. And so there was a lot of waiting 'til Tuesday night, and then going all night, and at two or three or four in the morning, doing some coke to stay up, as opposed to doing a whole bunch, and doing nitrous oxide, and laughing at stuff.

People used to ask me about this and I'd always say, "No, there was no coke. It's impossible to do the kind of show we were doing and do drugs." And so that was just a funny lie that I liked to tell. Kind of the opposite was true, unfortunately—for some people, it was impossible to do the show *without* the drugs. Comedians and comedy writers and people in show business in general aren't the most disciplined people, so the idea of putting the writing off until you had to, and then staying up all night, was an attractive one. And then having this drug that kept you awake in an enjoyable way was kind of tempting too. But I only did cocaine to stay awake to make sure nobody else did too much cocaine. That was the only reason I ever did it. Heh-heh.

ROBIN SHLIEN:

The band scored an ounce of coke on the air one night. According to the band member who told me, they got it during a commercial and divvied it up. I couldn't attest to whether it was gone by the end of the show.

The dealer used to be to the left of the stage, and the commercials were a couple minutes long. I thought that was kind of an amazing story.

TOM DAVIS, *Writer:*

Dick Ebersol was the only real network suit who would pop into the offices on seventeen. And it didn't bother him so much. I remember getting in an elevator with Tom Brokaw once, though, and I was just reeking of pot. Just stinking up the elevator, because I had really skunky pot. He couldn't help but notice. He just got very quiet. Everybody on the elevator stopped talking. Brokaw kind of looked at me out of the corner of his eye. I just smiled. What else are you going to do?

RODNEY DANGERFIELD, *Host:*

I never saw anybody do hard drugs there. Pot, sure. Put it this way: I've been smoking pot all my life. I've found it tremendously relaxing. I do it a lot. The doctor told me, "Don't smoke cigarettes. Just smoke pot."

CARRIE FISHER:

Lorne was the token grown-up in a sea of children and coeds. He was very professorial. He was only rated R while the rest of us were unruly, not well behaved, but fun-loving. I think he was trying to keep everything together without it looking like that's what he was doing. But certainly he wasn't fully participating in all the drug nonsense. He would look at it and shake his head laughing—that kind of thing.

LARAINE NEWMAN:

I came there with a drug habit. I'd had a drug habit since I was fourteen. It just got worse. I never worked intoxicated or high or anything. It was so much a part of me that it just permeated my outlook on things. It was also a very lonely time for me. I was pretty young, I didn't know that many people in New York, I was terribly homesick, and I was frustrated about the amount of airtime I was getting. So those things made me want to escape what I was thinking and feeling a lot. Drugs were very available. That's how I coped. I know they did their damage.

JANE CURTIN:

Laraine was in a horrible position. She was a baby. She was like twenty or twenty-one, and she was uprooted from this very comfortable lifestyle in L.A., with all her friends, and into New York, where she was in a hostile environment and she was alone. She didn't have anyplace to put that creative energy, so she had it tough. She was not happy. And I don't blame her, because it's hard enough to do that show in a comfortable environment, but when you're totally at sea—when your surroundings are different and you're just not comfortable—it's extremely hard.

DICK EBERSOL, *NBC Executive:*

The second year of the original show, I would take John to California with me every Sunday. By then I was married to my first wife, and I would take him home with me on Sunday and bring him back on Wednesday for read-through. And what I didn't know at the time was, my first wife and he, after I fell asleep, nothing romantic about it, but they would go out again. They'd go out all night and just manage to get back before six o'clock in the morning when I would wake up. And I woke up one morning at six o'clock, still not having doped all of this out, and walk by our guest bedroom, which was smoldering, and John had fallen asleep smoking a joint.

BRIAN DOYLE-MURRAY:

After I left Second City, John and his wife came to visit, and I had one of those floor heaters, you know, where the heat comes out from a grate on the floor. And they were fooling around on the couch and knocked a pillow on top of it. All of a sudden I woke up and there was smoke in the house. They didn't even realize that the pillow was on fire.

PENNY MARSHALL, *Guest:*

I'd get calls about John in the middle of the night. "John just burned down my apartment, John just started a fire," that type of thing. Sometimes he would just knock on my door at three in the morning. We'd know when John got up in the middle of the night to eat, because there'd be spaghetti sauce imprints all over the kitchen. "Oh look, John was up. I guess he got hungry."

JUDITH BELUSHI:

The second or third year of the show we were walking downtown, and there was an empty bar for rent. We got the idea of renting it ourselves. At that time we actually had a pretty good-sized place, on Morton Street, but we didn't want to invite fifty people over. So we thought we'd use this bar as a place to hang out. After the show or other nights, we'd invite people over. We had instruments there, and we kept the bar stocked. For a while it was pretty crazy. After the show, there was always a *Saturday Night Live* party. We'd usually go by that for a little while. The hosts would be there and all that. Then afterwards we'd go to the bar. It was just a big party. The hosts sometimes came down to the bar, but more often musicians, writers, actors, friends, and sometimes even people we didn't know.

DAN AYKROYD:

We opened the first Blues Bar in '77, I think. So for a few years we had a great place to party after the show. It was pretty easy to get in — you just had to show up and knock on the door. We used to go to the after party for the show, and then we'd take all the writers and our friends and the musical guests and the host of the show and invite them down for a party where you didn't have the public hanging around. Because usually at the after parties, they let the public come in at some point. And we just wanted the inner circle there, so we needed a bar where we could entertain.

ROBIN WILLIAMS, *Host:*

Years and years and years ago, before I even did the show, I'd come to the studio those nights when they were shooting, and then after they'd go down to the Blues Bar. Way back when. Dan brought me down there the first time. I said, "What is this?" He said, "Just step inside, don't be afraid, Robin, just step inside. You'll see — there's amazing people, wonderful music, just step inside." It was like, you'd walk in and it was funky. "Funky" is a good word. The old sense of, "Was that a rat?" "Maybe." The rat's going, "Hey, shut up." The crowd was a really mixed bag, you know — a lot of the performers, musicians, Michael O'Donoghue — always good for an unusual laugh—and Dan bartending and kind of being maitre d'. A really wild, mixed group of people.

BRIAN DOYLE-MURRAY:

There would always be a party, usually at some chichi restaurant. There was a velvet rope and it was supposedly, you know, the event. Actually, it was usually pretty grim. But Lorne would hold court at a table, usually with whoever the guest host was, and people would hang out in their own little cliques. Then there would be some talk, you know, about who the good-looking girls were, and things like that. But then people would bail out of there and go down to the Blues Bar. And there'd usually be a band, and Danny and John would be performing, and it was a lot looser atmosphere.

BILL MURRAY:

I was one of those Blues Bar people. Stayed until the sun came up. You had to blow off a lot of steam. You had an amazing performance high that lasted because it had built to this explosive point at an odd hour of a normal person's day, between eleven-thirty and one A.M. You couldn't really just say good night and go home and go to sleep. You were up for hours. You had all this energy and this uplift and you had to sort of work it off, so you could go to the Blues Bar, where you could dance and you could drink and you could be funny and could meet a lot of people and really carry on. It was necessary to have a place to go. You couldn't just go to an ordinary place, because there were a lot of people who would crash into it.

You had a very weird energy; it was just a completely different energy after you did that thing. You weren't fit for normal people. You had to go someplace where you could let yourself down gradually. So that was great that they provided this place where you could go and you'd be safe.

At any point, if there was someone that was bothering you, every person that was already in was a bouncer. And you'd just say, "You've got to go." And it was kind of funny, because they would think they'd just walk away from you, like, "No, that's all right, man, I won't bother you anymore." "No, no, you're not going to bother anybody else either." And it was a shocking moment when someone would get in and start working it and then get evicted by anybody. The women would just go, "He's out. Danny? Billy? This guy—out." And out he'd go. I know famous people got tossed out too. Famous people in their own area came, and when they obviously were just sucking blood, they were just evicted. We had no time for that. We were really just trying to get down to a safe level so you could sleep. Because you couldn't really sleep until six in the morning no matter what you did.

LARAINE NEWMAN:

When I saw *Trainspotting* they had a sign, "the filthiest toilet in Scotland." Well, the toilet at the Blues Bar was the filthiest toilet *anywhere.* It was so vile. Nothing short of Turkish torture with a hole in the ground. And the walls had water damage and were peeling and stank unbelievably. The floor was always wet, completely wet. Wadded-up tissue on the floor. And yet it was a fun hang—a windowless hole with lots of cool music people and the Stink Band, named such because they stank too. It would be John and Danny, plus people like David Bowie and Keith Richards and James Taylor. And then they had the backup group, the Natural Queens, one of which was my best friend, Lynn Scott, who is married to Tom Scott, who was in the Blues Brothers band. You'd go in, it was dark, you'd come out, it was dawn. Nothing more depressing than that. If there was sex on the premises, I never saw it. And I shudder to think if it took place in the bathroom. That person couldn't be alive today.

It really looked like it had been maybe a bar from the *Titanic* that had been exhumed after several hundred years of submersion and just hastily dropped onto a sidewalk. It was practically rotting, which is probably how they got it, because the rent was reasonable and at the time none of us had that much money. We were still getting probably maximum $2,000 a show. I think our fourth season we all got $4,000 a show. We started the first year at $750.

ROSIE SHUSTER:

I was hanging with Aykroyd at that point in time, so it was kind of amazing watching the whole scene—the Blues Bar and everything—

take off. It was kind of like boys' fantasies of the blues, and then heavy saturation of the blues, and then, having played out all these different fantasies in TV sketches, suddenly there was this manifestation and they really inhabited these characters. And you could see that whole thing start to unfold in the Blues Bar. Some of those parties were pretty intense and wonderful, and just great music and dancing. I remember that really fondly. Just watching those characters explode.

And it was the end of the week and, well, you were psyched. It was like you were buzzing, you'd get turbocharged from the intense effort of it, and then there's like adrenal burnout later. I remember sleeping at the Blues Bar, you know, as the light broke. Also probably there were other substances involved besides alcohol, and the party just spilled over. People really had a lot of energy they needed to shake off.

DAN AYKROYD:

By the time you're done at one o'clock Saturday night, that pump's still going at full race. And you can't just go home and go to bed. So we needed a place to party. And frequently I remember rolling down the armor at the Blues Bar and closing the building at eleven o'clock Sunday morning—you know, when it was at its height—and saying good morning to the cops and firemen.

PENNY MARSHALL:

The Blues Bar was a zoo, but it was fun. It was people getting famous at the same time, which is always very scary. We held on to each other desperately because we trusted each other. In hanging out with each other, we knew we weren't going to tell on each other.

STEVE MARTIN:

The first time I did the show, there was a fire in the studio. We had to go out to some other studio to do it. The cast was a little upset because they were not in their home world. We had to go to Brooklyn. I remember being very nervous and thinking, "Oh my God, it's live." It was very tense but a lot of fun.

I ran into Dan early one afternoon, and he was sort of black and blue, and I said, "What happened?" and he said, "Oh, I got pushed out of a moving taxi." They were wild, Dan and John. I never went to their bar, the Blues Bar; I wasn't that kind of guy.

JANE CURTIN:

I didn't even know where the Blues Bar was. I sort of stopped going to the after-show parties after the first year, just because they weren't fun. They were strange. I'd just go home.

JOHN LANDIS:

I went up to the *SNL* offices, John was giving me a tour, when a very sexy girl walks by. Tight jeans and a T-shirt, no bra, curly hair. "Oh my God, who is that?" And John says, "That's Rosie Shuster. That's Lorne's wife and Danny's girlfriend." Which is true. It was wild. Rosie's the one who coined the best line about Aykroyd. Danny had studied in a seminary to be a Jesuit priest the same time he was doing second story jobs in and around Ontario. Rosie's the one who said, "Danny's epiphany would be to commit a crime and arrest himself."

HOWARD SHORE, *Music Director:*

When the band did warm-ups for the show, some members of the cast wanted to get involved. I knew Danny from Toronto, so I let him do a few things. Then Danny wanted to bring John into it and I said okay, and I did a couple of things with Danny and John. I used to introduce them as "those brothers in blues, the Blues Brothers." I think John looked to us as more serious musicians, something he wanted to be.

DAN AYKROYD:

When Carrie Fisher did the show, we used the Blues Brothers to warm up the audience, but we had played a couple of times prior to that. We played with Willie Nelson as our backup band, and Mickey Raphael on harp, and Willie Hall, and then the Uniforms at the Lone Star, and then we had Duke Robillard and Roomful of Blues playing behind us as well. We wanted Duke to be our backup man, but he was with Roomful of Blues, and I think he felt that Belushi would dominate, so he kind of backed off that gig. And we ended up recruiting through Tom Malone, the horn player in the *SNL* band; we ended up getting Steve Cropper and Donald Dunn, and Lou Marini and Alan Rubin and Matt Murphy. Matt Murphy we found in a bar on Columbus Avenue, and we heard him play. He was playing with James Cotton, and we said, "We want this guy in the band." And then Cropper and Dunn, they had to be convinced, because they weren't sure that we could acquit ourselves to the music. But they saw the respect, the reverence we had, and that we wanted to do a Memphis-Chicago fusion band—which ultimately the Blues Brothers turned out to be, doing Chicago electrified blues, and Memphis Stax R&B, and that was our set. They came on, and we did the first appearances with Carrie Fisher and then with Steve Martin.

JOHN LANDIS:

Lorne was hysterical that Chevy was making a movie, and he refused to give me Danny for the part of D-Day in *Animal House*. He refused. He wouldn't release Danny and he told him, "You have to be here and write or I'm going to fire you." He threatened Danny, and it was ugly. And by the way, that's what happened on *The Blues Brothers* later, which is he wouldn't release Paul Shaffer, who was a member of the band, who was the star, who put the band together.

As the stakes got higher, the atmosphere at SNL *grew more fractious. Actors fought for airtime and for the attention of writers. After Chevy Chase's ascent, and then Belushi's, appearances on the show came to be looked upon by many performers as auditions for movie careers, as if the show itself were no longer the object all sublime.*

Many of those who were there for those first five gold-standard years look back not in regret but in rueful resignation, or a kind of pained joy. Some had required chemical stimulation merely to maintain the show's mind-bending schedule, working through the night, especially Wednesday and Thursday nights, and virtually living in the building. Taking a cue from Dan Aykroyd and his office bunk-beds, Anne Beatts famously demanded that the network install a hospital bed in her office during a contract negotiation and got her wish. They and their cohorts were not just the staff of a TV show. They were still a commune, a subculture, and most of all, a family; sadly, the family was splitting asunder. That became evident when the prodigal prankster Chevy Chase returned to host a show. His stint as host set a new ratings record for SNL, *but behind the scenes he was not warmly embraced.*

JANE CURTIN:

My husband and I had tickets to the ballet, and I had on my best clothes, and Lorne called about ten minutes before we were leaving to go uptown and said, "I need to talk to you. Can you come up to 30 Rock?" I said, "We have tickets to the ballet," and he said, "It will only take a minute." So I went up there, and Chevy proceeded to say that he thought that he should be doing "Update" that week, and I said okay, and then he went through this whole thing about how his fans wanted to see him—I said okay—and Lorne was backing him up, and backing him up, and I'm going, "Okay, okay." They were expecting a fight, and I honestly didn't care, because it was just one week and I wanted to leave! I wanted to go to the ballet. But they had to make their point. So we were late. The two of them were on this feeding frenzy in the sense that Chevy was expecting something that he wasn't getting from me, and he became more intent on selling his point of view and then Lorne would jump in. You sit there and you have pieces of your arm bitten off and then you leave. But it heals. It grows back.

CHEVY CHASE, *Cast Member*:

It was difficult the first year I went back to host. Because I went back feeling that I was still part of the family there and at the same time feeling probably, in retrospect, full of myself because I had become pretty famous. And I think that I had never really realized how envious John had become of me or had been while I was on the show. In fact, it was Lorne who verified that for me later on—that John had been pretty upset that I had become the star and not him, even though I told John many times that it was because I said my name every week, because others couldn't pronounce his or spell it, and it would happen for him—that these things were more luck than talent or ability and that, of course, *he* should have been the star.

And that he could become one, you know, albeit dead later on. But what the hell, who knew? I wish he were around today.

So that first time I came back, two things were at work. One was my feeling that if I were to come back the audiences would really want to see me do a fall, and they'd want to see me do "Weekend Update." That was somewhat egocentric of me, because Jane had been doing it all year. It was not thoughtful in that sense, I think—in retrospect again. But in any case, John had also, as I later found out, been spreading some pretty apocryphal stories about me out of his jealousy and anger or whatever to Billy Murray, who was protective of Jane and also, generally speaking, a feisty fellow. And I'm sure Billy wanted to take me down, you know. So Billy and I got into a kind of a preliminary fistfight that never really came to fruition but came close. And it happened just before I went on the air. It was not very good timing. That was painful for me.

In a sense, John caused that fight with Billy, but we both ended up hitting John by mistake. Billy was out of line. I'd been out of line to some degree—certainly in Billy's mind, initiated by the things that Lorne later told me about. So Billy came after me and tried to throw me off a little bit just before I was going on the air. Ultimately, Billy's still Billy and I'm still me, but it didn't faze me for the show. I was sure upset, but I noticed John when I was going into Billy's dressing room, and John was like the Cheshire Cat—sitting there like "mission accomplished."

I felt at the time I was a lot tougher kid than maybe Billy or anybody might have thought. I had grown up on the edge of East Harlem. I had been in a lot of fistfights. And I didn't feel like anybody could take me—Billy Murray or anybody else, for that matter. And so, as intimidating as he can be, at the time I just let it pass. I was angry and I just let it go, thinking, "Big deal. This happened but I've got a show to do." Others might have withered. I had a certain tensile strength about me from childhood with an older brother who had already kicked the crap out of me through much of my younger life. And there'd been a number of times where I was in violent situations. So it wasn't as if I was simply some guy who had never seen the other side of the tracks. I had. And so I guess I simply weathered it. In other words, rather than be filled with the adrenaline that gives you the shakes and doesn't allow you to concentrate on what you're doing, that simply passed, and it may be because I was in shape and I played a lot of soccer and had been in situations where I could calm down readily after something like that happened.

I think Billy was trying to take me down a rung, and I probably was up a rung. I was probably a little too full of myself, you know.

I realized when I left that maybe I hadn't been such a great guy. Maybe we weren't so close. Maybe I'd been somewhat of an asshole. I left with self-doubts. And as time went on, it was a little easier to do it over the years because, you know, it was water under the bridge. But it did change my perception, because my perception had been all along that that first year was really a tight, close-knit family and that I just happened to emerge because of something someone had written and because people were responding to me as the first breakaway star.

BILL MURRAY:

I got in a fight with Chevy the night he came back to host. That was because I was the new guy, and it was sort of like it was my job to do that. It would have been too petty for someone else to do it. It's almost like I was goaded into that. You know, I think everybody was hoping for it. I did sense that. I think they resented Chevy for leaving, for one thing. They resented him for taking a big piece of the success and leaving and making his own career go. Everybody else was from the improvisational world, where you didn't make it about you. You were an ensemble, you were a company. So when he left, there was resentment about that. It was a shock.

At the same time, Chevy was the big potato in the stew. He got the most sketches, he had the most influence, he got the most publicity— all of those things. So they didn't miss that part of it. But there was still a hangover feeling that he shouldn't have left until everybody had that. You make sure everybody else is there and then you do it.

It did leave a big vacuum, because he was really heavy in those shows. And so you had a whole year when the writers ended up writing, like writers do—they write for the guys who can get it done, who can get it on the air—and Chevy's sketches got on the air because he was "the man," you know. The other actors had to start over from scratch and teach the writers how to write for them. They were "new" people who had to be written for, but they weren't new people, they'd been there all year; they just hadn't gotten on. So the show had to sort of start up again from the beginning without him. I remember just sort of a general animosity that they felt, and he did come back as a star.

When you become famous, you've got like a year or two where you act like a real asshole. You can't help yourself. It happens to every-body. You've got like two years to pull it together — or it's permanent.

JOHN LANDIS:

I've only been to *SNL* three times, and one time I was there, Chevy and Billy were having a huge screaming fight in the hallway, and Michael O'Donoghue and Tom Davis were holding them back, and John and Danny jumped in because Chevy and Billy were really going to come to blows. I mean, it was a huge argument. And the thing I remember about Bill Murray — I don't know Bill Murray, but he's screaming, you know, foaming at the mouth, "Fucking Chevy," and in anger he says, "Medium talent!" And I thought, "Ooh boy, that's funny. In anger he says 'medium talent.'" That really impressed me. I went, "So, Bill Murray — wow, who is that guy?"

LARAINE NEWMAN:

It seems like there was a tension between Chevy and Billy all along during the week. I don't know why. I don't know if Chevy provoked it or not. But it culminated with Billy saying to Chevy, "Why don't you fuck your wife once in a while?" And I don't even remember who threw the first punch, Billy or Chevy. But it was ugly. I'd never seen guys fighting like that, let alone people I knew. And you know, I don't know how he did it, but Chevy went out and did the monologue a few minutes later. Watching him from the floor, he seemed shattered.

LORNE MICHAELS:

Billy Joel, the musical guest, was out there singing his heart out while all this was going on backstage.

ALAN ZWEIBEL:

There had come a point in the first season where Chevy wasn't writing for the show as much as he was writing for Chevy. And that didn't help things. I can't put it in the degree of who was despised more or whatever. I know that when he left the show and he did the specials, there were some interviews with him where he was talking about the future of *Saturday Night Live,* the show that he had just left. And I seem to remember him being quoted as saying things like, "I've used that show for everything I can, that show has no future other than to get weirder as opposed to smarter." As if the first year we'd just shot our wad. Those were the kinds of things that were coming back to us, and so those of us who were still in the coal mines shoveling seven days a week had to ask, "Why are you doing this? We worked really hard with you and for you. That made no sense."

I remember Chevy coming back after one of his specials and talking about it or raving about it, you know, proud of something he just did, and I remember Al Franken saying something like, "That's good, Chevy, but we do one of those every week." So there were some ill feelings, I think.

In those first five years, Saturday Night Live *not only had its best cast ever, but also the best and ballsiest collection of writers. The sketch form was older than television itself, but the way they approached it, bent it and shaped it, was their own, and it resulted in sketches that are remembered vividly to this day by the first generation of* SNL *viewers—such recurring classics as the Coneheads, the swinging immigrant Czech brothers, romantic nerds Lisa and Todd, the Greek diner where all one could order was "cheeseburger cheeseburger"—and such beloved or notorious sketches as Danny Aykroyd's hemorrhaging Julia Child, his virtuoso performance as the immortal "Bass-O-Matic" pitchman, the violent and controversial "Stunt Baby," Buck Henry as pedophilic babysitter Uncle Roy, and the hilariously businesslike comportment of Aykroyd as Fred Garvin, Male Prostitute.*

STEVE MARTIN:

When you're young, you have way fewer taboo topics, and then as you go through life and you have experiences with people getting cancer and dying and all the things you would have made fun of, then you don't make fun of them anymore. So rebelliousness really is the province of young people—that kind of iconoclasm.

DAN AYKROYD:

Michael O'Donoghue was one of the really great writers on the show, and he really taught me how to write for television. He taught me to have the confidence, he taught me to go with the concept, to embrace the absurdity. He taught me structure, he was meticulous in the way he laid out structure bits, he taught me the discipline of writing for television.

LILY TOMLIN, *Host:*

I enjoyed hosting. At least I think I did. I do remember that after the show got to be such a big hit, I hosted it again. By that time, I just remember everybody—not everybody, but people like Michael O'Donoghue—was a little bit manic. The dress rehearsal did not go well. And Michael was so eccentric and he must have been so angry with me, he was like putting the evil eye on me or something. And it was so kind of ludicrous that I burst out laughing.

It was so important to them at that point, because they were creating that show and getting it off the ground and everything, so that was their identity, and I can understand their intensity—their wanting it to be this or that or great or whatever, and being put out with someone. I think I was forgiven.

CARRIE FISHER:

I was around Michael O'Donoghue until he was deeply offended that I married Paul Simon and his ex-girlfriend was maid of honor and he wasn't in the wedding, and he never spoke to me again. I went up to him again at some point and said, "Can't we put this aside?" He just screamed at me. It was horrible. But I loved Michael. Michael and I had gone to Ireland together, and I think we were actually the first people to do 'ludes and mead. I was shooting the *Star Wars* movies, and John and Danny wanted to be in them as space creatures or something. I think it was mostly John.

DAN AYKROYD:

I was never proprietary about pieces. Look, if a piece didn't work, you know, please get it out and let's do what works for the show, let's put someone else's piece in there. But I had a lot of strength behind me, because I had Franken and Davis and Downey and O'Donoghue as my cowriters, and oftentimes we'd come in, and there'd be three or four of us real strong writers, and so we knew we were going to get on. The goods had been created.

LARAINE NEWMAN:

Lorne urged me to repeat characters. I refused to do it because I wanted to, you know, dazzle everybody with my versatility. And that kept me anonymous. That was the same pitfall for Danny. He was much more comfortable doing characters, and I think that it made him less recognizable than John, who was always John even when he was the Samurai. And Billy was always Billy. He did Todd in the Nerds but basically he was Billy. So even though I loved the kind of work that I did, and still do—I love the character work—I think it keeps you more anonymous than people who play themselves.

BUCK HENRY, *Host:*

I never had a problem with repeating characters, saying, "Oh, we've done enough Coneheads," or that we had done enough of, you know, anything that worked. I thought, why not keep going and doing it? You would only stop it if you had a concept that didn't live up to the characters. Then you would say, "Oh, this is not strong enough for the characters, and we can't do this."

DON NOVELLO, *Writer:*

I wrote the Greek restaurant sketch the second week I was there. It is like a hit song, I guess, in a way. The restaurant is called Billygoat's. I used to go down there all the time to this Billygoat Tavern—I worked in advertising then—just to hear these guys going, "Cheeseburger cheeseburger cheeseburger." It's still there. They've really played it up. They have a sign outside, "Cheeseburger Cheeseburger." It's on some Chicago tour, they drop by. And they opened a few other places. They sell them at the stadium, but it's always "cheeseburger cheeseburger," they play it up big. The people at the diner recognized it right away on the show.

It was a big thing to do at the time. We had a live grill there, a working grill, they were really making cheeseburgers. I'd say we did six, seven, eight of those sketches.

BRIAN DOYLE-MURRAY:

Don Novello and I came in at the same time, and we got put in a former storeroom that abutted the elevator shaft. You could barely hear because of the noise from the elevator shaft. There were no windows. That's where we started out. And they were trying to make us work together. And then when he wrote that "cheeseburger cheeseburger" thing, he got a decent office. The next year I got a decent office after I did a series of like Knights of Columbus meetings, which introduced the character of Garrett Morris's Chico Escuela.

GARRETT MORRIS, *Cast Member:*

Chico was my favorite, but I also really liked "I'm going to get me a shotgun and kill all the whiteys I see." Now that was when we were improvising. Lorne actually said, "Look, I want to do a thing called the 'Death Row Follies.' You be a prisoner, you be so-and-so, you be so-and-so, go away and come back with something." That's what we did. See I liked it when they did it like that, even though I was desperately learning the technique that these guys were masters at—John and Gilda particularly. I'm the kind of guy, "Throw me out there, I don't give a shit." I knew I could always react to your ass.

A lot of stuff on *Saturday Night Live* was really my kind of stuff, because I like to do stuff that's really new and exploratory. If stuff was on the line either racially or sexually, I didn't give a damn. If you want to try it, let's try it.

JAMES SIGNORELLI:

If we gave every sketch that anybody ever complained about not having an ending an ending, the show would fail. I don't think people say that as a criticism. I think they just say it.

BILL MURRAY:

Danny was the best at saving sketches, when things were really deadly, when things were really dying. When you're dying, you just play for yourself: "Let's make ourselves laugh. If we're not making *them* laugh, let's start over again and just make ourselves laugh." And that fearlessness would then turn the audience.

When people talk about the old cast versus the later casts, I think that was the one thing that our group had; we had that training, so there were more tricks. We'd learned working together as a group in a service way. Nowadays there's probably more stand-ups that end up on the show, sort of more individual guys, than there used to be, and they're individually good but they maybe don't have that particular skill or training or as much experience in that area.

I think the old cast made bad sketches work, or made sketches that were incomplete work. You were always in process, you were always in play. You weren't trying to get the laugh on that line. You were always seeing like a bigger movement of the whole sketch and the other characters in it, and you were watching them and trying to make them look good.

That was another thing we learned, that you make the other person look good and then you don't have to worry about how you come off. Make the other people look good and you'll be fine. Sometimes there'd be sketches that would be incomplete and the writers may have never found how to make it work. And maybe we didn't even figure out the literary resolution of the sketch precisely. But in the performance of it you managed to shape a roundness, a completeness, the wholeness of it. And if you were alert in the middle of the scene, you'd see: "Okay, now these people are really fully developed as much as we're going to do, and now this character will drive the resolution of it and these characters will satisfy it enough." That was what we did.

DAN AYKROYD:

If you look at Carol Burnett or *Your Show of Shows* with Sid Caesar, they rely on something to take you out of it, so that whenever you have a great ending, you've got a great piece. We struggled with the endings, yeah, and they were probably the hardest part of the sketch.

I think the ending to a movie is hard, the ending to a television show, the ending to anything is tough. You kind of want to wrap everything up with a bow and button it all up and hark back to what you have done before and end on a high note or great joke. And that's not always possible.

JAMES SIGNORELLI:

Nobody really understood what Lorne's contribution was, which was integral to the whole thing, not only in selecting the people but in creating an atmosphere where people could endure the pressure and where the pressure was, in fact, a good thing—a cumulative pressure with a release. And that rhythm, you know, that kind of—I don't know what to compare it to—but that rhythm is what kept the show going, because everybody could start, start, rush, rush, rush, rush, peak, and crash—and then start again.

DAN AYKROYD:

Fred Garvin, Male Prostitute was developed in the lab. That started with me doing guys I'd seen up in Canada—the local tire salesman, whatever. And then when I was living with Rosie, I used to do that at home with her, you know. As part of our love life, that character would emerge. And she said we have to do this, so we wrote it up. It started in the bedroom—you know, "Come here, little lady." I do that with my wife today and still get a laugh. No sex, but a laugh.

PAUL SHAFFER, *Musician*:

I wrote a piece with Marilyn Miller about Shirley Temple being named an ambassador. And the idea of the sketch was Shirley Temple bringing the leaders of two warring nations together by going into an old-fashioned Shirley Temple song. And that worked, and Marilyn went to Lorne and said, "Paul should have a position on the show as a guy who writes this kind of material." Lorne agreed and put me on. But the credit was a problem, because the traditional credit is "special musical material." This worried us because it sounded, as we said then, "too Carol Burnett." We loved Carol Burnett, we respected her, but we were trying to be different than that.

DAN AYKROYD:

On the "Little Chocolate Doughnuts" parody — that was a Franken and Davis thing that John didn't want to do. His vanity sort of got in the way there, but ultimately, as with all of us, once the writers presented their concept, you could see the merit in it right away and sometimes you'd go, "Well, it may not make me look great, or it is not my humor, but this is going to work and this is going to be funny."

JAMES SIGNORELLI:

Belushi had been a high school athlete and he didn't really want to do the sketch. The thing was not whether John thought he could do it; the thing was that John was in his recalcitrant stage. Anne Beatts was along on that ride too. At one point, John is supposed to jump over a bar like a track star. John insisted that he would do the "stunt" himself. All we did was put some cardboard cartons with blankets over them on the other side of the bar and the bar was only a couple feet high. I got down as low as I could get with the camera, you know, the widest lens I could get, and so John jumped over this table and landed on the couch. Okay?

We did it once for practice and again to refine some element. The second time he did it, he screamed out in pain and he tensed up in his most melodramatic way, he clenched his knee to his chest, and everybody ran over and John goes, "Get me an ambulance! Get me a medic!" John wanted to be taken to the hospital. He was absolutely not going to do this thing. He was, you know, "crippled for life." He was mad at all of us. And Anne went in and smoothed that over with him and got him to go back and finish. John at that point was just, you know, feeling his oats.

At the end of the spot he's at the breakfast table. John comes on the set wearing a green crewneck lamb's wool sweater and he's supposed to look like Bruce Jenner, right? And a shirt with a button-down collar. He insisted that was how he should look. And there's a huge moth hole in the front of the sweater and a white shirt underneath. So I made him wear it backwards. If you look at it again, you'll see he's wearing the sweater backwards. And, of course, he wanted to smoke a cigarette, but he couldn't for the life of him figure out how to smoke and take a bite of the doughnut at the same time. So finally we came up with this awkward solution where John holds the cigarette in his hand, takes a puff, then—"I like a good breakfast"—and picks up the doughnut and the cigarette in the same hand.

AL FRANKEN:

"Julia Child" came from Tom Davis having seen her cut herself on the *Today* show. I had written the sketch for Walter Matthau, but it didn't get picked the week he hosted. So I had to convince Aykroyd to do it. We tried it once, but we didn't have the hose working properly the first week, so we held it until we got control of the blood spurting. And it's really a consummate Danny performance. I mean, it's live TV, and just the timing of the spurts, it's beautiful. I was so admiring of that performance. It was in the right hands. Walter Matthau wouldn't have been able to handle the technical aspect nearly as well.

Danny and I had a good relationship, and I always felt that if I cared about something enough, he would do it. You can only call those in so many times. You've got to be sure about something in order to say, "Do it." Or you've got to be thinking at least it's worth trying, worth the risk. That's when you feel good. When you make somebody do Julia Child and it turns out the way it did, then you've got some credibility for the next time you want to make him do something.

It's always a tug-and-pull of how much direction you can give somebody, how much they trust you, how much they don't, how much they trust their own instincts, the mood they're in. It depends on the cast member. You have to know each cast member to get the best work that you can out of them.

STEVE MARTIN:

I think Lorne was reluctant to have me on. I was never reluctant. I wanted to be on the show from the first moment I saw it. But—it was one of those timing curves where, when the first show hit the air, I was not, you know, popular enough to really host it. Then there was a synchronicity in my rise to stand-up and records, and we sort of hit at the same moment.

In a strange way, I was new and old-fashioned at the same time.

And maybe the irony of my performance hadn't reached Lorne yet. I really don't know. Lorne's been one of my oldest friends and oldest supporters, so whatever you feel about somebody at first really doesn't matter. I found that, in performers and sometimes movies, and especially art, that it takes a while to come to something that's new. And a lot of times when the resistance finally turns to acceptance, it makes you a greater supporter of it or them.

JEAN DOUMANIAN, *Associate Producer*:

Nobody wanted to put Steve Martin on the show. I'd seen him on *The Tonight Show* several times. And I kept trying to get them to let Steve do the show, because I thought he was so funny. But, you know, the writers also wanted to be on the show. They said, "He's our same age. If he could do the show, we could do the show." I remember somebody falling out. And I remember running into Lorne and saying, "Lorne, give this guy a chance, he's really, really good." Lorne was reluctant to have him on, but when he finally did, Steve's manager sent me a dozen roses. I was just so thrilled.

DAN AYKROYD:

The Czech brothers were, I guess, a combination—a grafting of characters. Steve had this character, the continental guy, and I had the Czech expatriate, the "swinging" Czech who was trying to talk like an American, trying to be an American, trying to have the inflection in the accent, the clothes. And so we took his continental guy and my Czech guy and we fused them into the Czech brothers. That's essentially what happened there.

MARILYN SUZANNE MILLER:

I did something kind of different from other people. I started writing these things which they called in those days "Marilyn pieces," which were pieces about either men and women or dramatic pieces, the most notable one of which I did with Belushi and Sissy Spacek, for which I won the Emmy. The pieces were like dramatic and they came from the tradition of those Richard Pryor, Lily Tomlin sketches that weren't about the jokes but were about the character builds and were often kind of bittersweet.

One day Danny came to me and said, "Okay, you know those guys that come over and paw you and they used to be an engineer in Poland and now they drive a Camaro?" And I said, "Yes!" So he and Steve Martin kind of talked like them and left, and then I wrote the sketch, including that patois they use—"I will put my hands on your big American breasts."

STEVE MARTIN:

At that point I was doing "I'm a wild and crazy guy," and I said, "That's the only act I have, wild and crazy guy," so I did my thing that I was doing onstage. Danny's was actually the more authentic character. And it was funny, because when we rehearsed it during the week it seemed so funny to us, *so* funny, and we went on with it and it seemed to go fine. It wasn't anything special. But we decided to do it again, and for some reason when we did it the second time, the audience was prepped. It stuck in their heads or something, and they were right there cheering and laughing and going overboard. Between the first time we did it and the second time we did it, something jelled or happened. The crazy walk was something that was supposed to indicate coolness.

BILL MURRAY:

The original Nick the Lounge Singer sketch was one that I walked into the read-through. They'd read all the sketches for the week and I said, "Oh, I have one more." I had never written really anything, and I was just dying on the vine, because like I said, as the new guy I was pretty much the second cop through the door every week, the second FBI guy, whatever. Danny was always kind enough to write me in as the second something; no one else even bothered. That was my life-style. Then, I don't know, something happened and somebody gave me this shower soap thing in the shape of a microphone and I took off with it and wrote this sketch. But basically it wasn't even written; it was half-written. I started doing it at the read-through, and you're supposed to have a copy of the script for everyone—you're supposed to duplicate them for the entire crew—but I was the only one with a copy. I just started doing it, and I was getting huge laughs, and then I said, "I haven't finished the ending yet."

Well, there was this silence. This bone-crushing silence. And Tom Davis said, "I would love to help Bill finish writing that sketch, Lorne." And it was the grandest gesture of like, "This son of a bitch needs this badly, and you know I can make sure he gets it done." At that point it had gotten a lot of laughs, so it was like okay. So Davis helped me finish that sketch, that was the shower-mike sketch, and then we started writing all the Nicks.

PAUL SHAFFER:

Billy decided to do a version of the kind of character that he had been doing in Chicago: Nick the Lounge Singer. And of course I would be the pianist, but I also got to participate in the writing of it with Billy, Tom Davis, and Danny. Danny would always make an appearance in it as an Indian guy. At ski resorts in Canada, there were always guys like that who operated the chair lift, and they always found a dead animal in the sewage system or something, and that was his appearance. Marilyn Miller was also instrumental in writing this.

Billy's performance was so over-the-top, it almost superseded the writing. We did five or six of them—I'm just guessing. They always had to come from Billy, and I never knew what his criteria were, but whatever he wanted to do was just right. "Star Wars" of course was his idea, but then we would collaborate on the lyrics once he got the idea. Most of it came from him, though.

ROSIE SHUSTER:

I wrote a lot of Gilda's first sketches. Like I did the first Emily Litella. I did the first Roseanne Roseannadanna before she had a name. I did a lot of the Baba Wawas. And I did all the Todd and Lisas. I watched every one of those on the live show because I loved it so much, and it just didn't seem like it had been done the same way at dress or even, you know, a couple times before. It just seemed so amazingly live and raw.

PENNY MARSHALL:

Gilda went with Paul Simon. She also went out with Billy. One night I was about to see Billy and he said, "I'm no good, ask Gilda."

He was drinking, you know. Everyone went through their periods of bad behavior.

ANDREW SMITH, *Writer:*

I remember there was this wonderful Puerto Rican maid that Gilda had based the character of Emily Litella on. She was a lovely, lovely gal, and very small. She actually became a great friend, and we used to play tricks on her and chase her down the hall. But she was afraid to come into my office and clean because my office used to be Garrett Morris's, and that's where he used to freebase. She was afraid to come in, since that was where fire was. So for a long time my office never got cleaned, until I assured her it was totally safe to come in.

LARAINE NEWMAN:

Billy and Gilda's relationship didn't really affect me, except that I can remember them coming to read-through and fighting. And she was furious with him and she'd just told him not to talk to her and he'd be begging her—and this would be acted out in front of all of us.

JANE CURTIN:

Billy and Gilda? When you're changing clothes backstage right next to two people who are involved, oh yeah, you know what's going on between those two people.

BILL MURRAY:

Lisa Loopner was a great character for Gilda because she could actually laugh inside of it. That sketch was all about making her laugh. There was a lot of extra in that. Those sketches were always tragically overwritten. They couldn't edit worth a damn, and they wouldn't edit. It was a turn for both of us, because she had this thing that was so extreme that you could throw anything at it and it would hit the mark, partly because she was such a bright target and partly because of the way she reacted to it.

You never saw nerds enjoying themselves before. No one ever saw nerds enjoy themselves, really get funny. You never saw what really tickled them. This was before the *Revenge of the Nerds* movies. I played a nerd and Gilda played a nerd and I was going after her, personally, whatever it was, and it made her laugh and it made all the stuff so incredibly stupid—the fact that even nerds had stupid humor—it was a blast. It was really a blast to do.

But they would never edit the stuff, never cut the stuff. And I'd say, "Look, the sketch is running eight minutes, it's never going to go, can't we just cut some stuff?" And they'd never cut it. And finally between dress and air, Lorne would say, "You've got to take two minutes and fifteen seconds out of that sketch." And we'd already figured out what was wrong with it so we'd never even committed to the stuff we didn't like, so they'd be there doing all these cue card things and saying, "Here, I've got the new changes," and we're like, "Yeah, sure. Whatever." We already knew what the hell was going to go. Both Gil and I knew what was working and what wasn't, so we never got attached to the garbage part of the sketch, the thing that was going to be gone, but we still had to rehearse the damn thing for hours and hours and hours.

Pulling my pants up as Todd—that was my skill. I remember guys that I knew that were like that. You stick your belly out through your pants, your belt's over your belly, it's sort of like you have your emotional armor in your belly and you're banging at people with your armor. You go at people with that emotional armor. You lead with it. Rather than being attacked first, you sort of lead with that belly. And it was great to have it with Gilda, because her body was this other thing with these crazy goofy shoulders and stuff, and she was like almost getting hit from behind all the time in the back of the neck. You'd get the feeling like somebody was thudding her with a mallet or something.

ROSIE SHUSTER:

Todd and Lisa also became a medium for Gilda and Billy to work something through on television. There was definitely some of that going on. They went through different permutations where they were together, they weren't together, you know. You could probably track what was going on by seeing how they related to each other on the air. Beatts and I would really write for them with a mind to letting them take off. We thought we had a sense of how the chemistry was operating. And sometimes, when our foreknowledge of that came together at a particularly juicy point in their relationship, you could see the results on-screen. On the "Prom Night" sketch, they were really present. They were both really playing and they were both really good. And they just took off. The best of that was fab, just to see them together like that.

CARRIE FISHER:

There was a time when Gilda had gotten a very big crush on Paul and then I went out with Paul and then there was sort of a drama and I didn't want to be in a drama and somehow I remember being on the phone with Gilda and there was crying. I was just twenty-one. I didn't know how I got into this thing. But it was sort of a fun drama, I suppose.

I couldn't figure Gilda out. The thing that happened, whatever that was with Paul, kind of estranged us. The horrible thing was, years and years later I went to this stomach doctor, and he had treated Gilda when she was very, very ill, and she had talked about this thing that had happened with Paul and myself and her.

NEIL LEVY:

There was a profound sadness inside Gilda. At the same time there was this boundless joy and energy. She fluctuated. It wasn't like bipolar. She didn't go on periods of horrible depression and then elation. They existed side by side. And sometimes she'd just disappear. She would just go away, and maybe that's when she was sad.

I remember somebody was coming to town, somebody very important to her, she said, because she had tried to kill herself and this guy had saved her. I remember her telling me that.

I loved Gilda, that's the thing. If I ever had a problem, I could talk to her. She was totally accessible and one of the wisest women I ever met. She had an understanding of human nature that most people don't have. That cute Gilda on TV is not the Gilda I saw—although she was incredibly cute in real life. She had that quality, but she was also incredibly bright.

MARILYN SUZANNE MILLER:

You know the legendary story of Gilda going over to Jane's house to look at Jane and Patrick being married? And just watch them? That's what it was like. Gilda would just watch them and say, "Oh, now you're going to turn the TV on together, how will you decide what to watch?"

Gilda projected the most extreme vulnerability, and it translated into whatever she did. And when she did physical comedy, you could feel her fall.

JANE CURTIN:

I'd invite her over for dinner. She'd come and sort of sit there while I was cooking. My husband would be there. And she wouldn't participate, wouldn't carry on a conversation; she just wanted to watch us live. It was off-putting in the beginning, but after a while it got to be very funny. You know—it was Gilda, so it was okay.

RICHARD DREYFUSS:

I thought Gilda was fantastic. She was like a combination of Judy Garland and Martha Raye. She was an extraordinary creature. Of course no one could see the future, and I certainly didn't. She wasn't walking around with a cloud of doom over her head. She was just a hysterically funny and sweet person.

DAN AYKROYD:

The Coneheads started out as the Pinhead Lawyers of France. I had been looking at TV—I guess I'd smoked a "J" or something—and I thought, "Everybody's heads don't really reach the top of the screen. Wouldn't it be great if you added four inches to everybody?" So I drew up this design. And we would be the Pinhead Lawyers of France. But then people were afraid that we'd be disparaging encephalitic people or retarded people with that, so we changed it to the Coneheads. And Lorne said, "Why don't you put it in an alien setting, aliens coming to work?" So we tried it out in a comedy workshop downtown, and that's where that came out of. It evolved in the writing.

ROBIN SHLIEN:

The production assistants used to play a game. We'd get the sketches and then it would be like, "Hmm, what drug were they on when they wrote this one?" The pot sketches were all a certain way. That was one of the funny things about getting all those handwritten pages that we had to type up.

A lot of the pot smoking went on when people were writing. Like the Coneheads, that was a total pothead sketch—the quintessential pot sketch. Here they are, these really weird people with things on their heads, and they say they're from France—you know.

BUCK HENRY:

Uncle Roy was an idea written by Rosie Shuster and Anne Beatts that I like to think was inspired by my own tawdry life. The thing I wanted to do, which we did the second time, was to have the setup be something about the uniqueness of Uncle Roy—Jane and Danny as Mom and Dad, after coming home and almost catching us doing something really disgusting, would say, "Oh Roy, you're so wonderful. You are unique. There's only one like you." And I look into the camera and say, "Oh, no, no. There are hundreds of thousands of Uncle Roys." Or something like that. My assumption being, of course, that in a huge number of families across North America, children would be casting a sidelong glance at their uncles or their mother's boyfriends or their stepfathers or whatever. In other words, I talked myself into the fact that we were performing— or that *I* was performing—a public service.

ROSIE SHUSTER:

Uncle Roy came from—I had a babysitter that I just adored, though he was *not* touchy-feely. However, I did used to ask him all the time, "And what else did you do that was bad?" And he would just fill me full of lurid tales, and then I sort of put that together with Buck's natural salaciousness. I think Dan was sort of pissed that I didn't do Uncle Roy for him. Because I used to call him Uncle Roy sometimes, and then that kind of got grafted onto Buck because Buck had that special thing.

The way we excused doing it was that Gilda and Laraine as the little girls had so much fun and loved Uncle Roy so much that, even though he got his jollies, they were sort of unscathed and had the best time of their lives. I don't think you could ever do it now; it would just be considered like disastrously politically incorrect. But like I said, the saving grace to me was they just had so much fun. If they were on a glass-topped coffee table, they pretended they were in a dinghy and they were having a wonderful time deep-sea fishing.

BUCK HENRY:

I did a lot of material that no one else would do. They would save the stuff that other hosts wouldn't do for me, because they knew I would do it. Except for one. Once I didn't do it. It was a takeoff on *First, You Cry,* the TV movie about breast cancer. I didn't do it—one, because the girl who wrote *First, You Cry* was a friend of mine, but also because I had a very close friend who was dying of it. And I just couldn't quite see my way clear to do a sketch about it.

I don't think anyone but me would do "Stunt Baby." That was very notorious—a sketch about doing a movie on child abuse, and whenever it was time for a violent scene, they called in the stunt baby and it got batted around. Both "babies" were dolls, of course; Laraine did the babies' voices. I liked the sketch so much, I asked them to do "Stunt Puppy," which was equally rude. I heard they got more mail protesting "Stunt Baby" than anything else they'd done up to that time. "Stunt Baby" really offended people—and it was one of my favorites.

ROSIE SHUSTER:

I loved Bill Clotworthy, one of the censors. I used to always talk to him like Eddie Haskell and go, "That's a really attractive tie you've got on, Mr. Clotworthy." To me, comedy writing was all about flirting with taboos and seeing how far you could push it. Not just gratuitously, though; it had to be funny. It had to make you laugh. Beatts and I wrote a "nerd nativity" sketch and it all came down to that screaming thing. There was a meeting, I'm trying to remember—this happened twice, because it also happened with a sketch about "What if Jesus had gotten five to ten instead of a death sentence?"—where the censors were pulled out of bed and came running down to 8H right between dress and air. The question was, were they going to put it on or not. And the censors sort of defanged it, declawed it, took the balls out, and removed the spine and then sent it out there, kind of mushy.

ROBIN SHLIEN:

Audrey Dickman was the associate producer. She was English to the core and she loved to laugh. Audrey really was like a mother hen. I think she was very protective, certainly of the production department, and she really loved the cast and the writers—and Lorne. She didn't ever want to say no to people. Someone would ask her a request sometimes and she would turn around and roll her eyeballs, but she would never say no.

So one time Danny sent me to the censor to try to get the word "muff diver" approved. We had a substitute censor that week, so he thought he'd try his luck. They were always merciless to the substitute censors. I considered not doing it, but Audrey taught us it wasn't our job to say no, especially to the writers. So I waited until the censor was eating lunch in the control room. I opened my script in front of her and said, "These are the new lines," trying to be nonchalant. She scanned the pages and pointed to "muff diver": "What's that?" Since the scene took place on a window ledge, I said the first thing that popped into my head: "I think it's someone jumping out a window." She nodded okay. But when the scene played in dress, as soon as Danny yelled it to Laraine—"So long, muff diver"—like four phone lines in the control room all lit up at once. Somebody knew what it meant. It was like instantaneous, as soon as he said the word. During dress the advertisers and other executives were watching from other rooms.

So "muff diver" never made it onto the air. Audrey never asked what had happened; there were some things she knew even she couldn't control.

ALAN ZWEIBEL:

There used to be a Japanese restaurant downstairs in the Woodward Hotel on Fifty-fourth Street that was open 'til like four in the morning; so we used to go there all the time. I remember a Friday night I was there with Gilda. It must've been about one-thirty in the morning. There was a newsstand in the hotel lobby. When I went to the men's room, I saw the latest edition of the *Daily News;* it said that Mr. Ed had died. I went back into the restaurant and I said to Gilda, "Mr. Ed just died." She said, "Wouldn't it be great if tomorrow night on 'Update'"—and I completed what I knew she was going to say—"we interview the grieving widow, Mrs. Ed."

So I'm mulling this over and I can't stop thinking about it; somehow we have to do this. I go to a phone and call Lorne at home and tell him, "Listen, Mr. Ed just died, can I interview Mrs. Ed?" He said, "You get a horse, you can do whatever the fuck you want." So it's two o'clock in the morning; how do I find a white horse? I wouldn't know how to find a white horse at noon. So I call a prop guy at home, and tell him Mr. Ed just died and I want a white horse for this "Update" thing.

Now in those days I used to come in at seven on Saturday morning to get a start on "Update." There was a restaurant downstairs; I'd get all the newspapers and sit there and write jokes. So I start writing this Mrs. Ed interview. Bill Murray was going to interview her and Gilda was going to do the voice. Now Audrey in the production department finds me at the restaurant and she says, "Who's getting the white horse?" I said, "I called a prop guy, he'll take care of it." She threw her hands in the air. She says, "You don't ask them about white horses." I said, "Who do I ask?" She says, "I'll take care of it."

I swear to God, an hour and a half later there's a white horse in the studio. I went up to Audrey and said, "Where did you get the horse?" She wouldn't tell me. But she was the person who could make anything happen.

TOM DAVIS:

We were going to do a Franken and Davis sketch—I think it was in the fourth year—and we're dressed as sumo wrestlers. And I suddenly stop and just announce that we're gay.

AL FRANKEN:

Tom says he can't stand it anymore, we're gay lovers, and I go, "My wife and kid are here." "They don't know?" "No, they don't know!"

And the kid is in the audience going, "I hate you, Daddy! I hate you, hate you, hate you, Daddy!" Then I go back behind the curtain, you hear a gunshot go off, and my legs sort of flop out from under the curtain. Then our music plays and I come out and we go, "Good night, everybody!" And that was it; that was a "Franken and Davis Show." And for a while we would say, "Brought to you by the International Communist Party—working for you, in Africa!"

TOM DAVIS:

And where the censor got involved is, we're dressed in these sumo outfits, basically naked. Our genitals are covered in the front, but our asses are hanging out. Just being naked. And the Standards and Practices people hadn't seen the costumes. So Al and I put on the sumo outfits and went down to the fourth floor, and we're just walking around NBC naked, and we walked into the office of the head censor, Herminio Traviesas, and he just started laughing, and he said, "All right, I give up!"

DAN AYKROYD:

Naturally the censors didn't like the refrigerator repairman sketch, where I kneeled down and the audience could see the crack of my ass. And the censor said, "Don't put that pencil in there." I was checking this fridge and I had to put the pencil *somewhere*. "Don't put the pencil there!" And of course I said I wouldn't, but then on the air, I did. And you know—*massive* laugh.

ALAN ZWEIBEL:

Gilda was doing Emily Litella, who would get some topic rolling because she was so hard of hearing, and so she would try to defend violins on television and Chevy would correct her and tell her, "No, it's not violins, it's violence." "Oh, that's very different. Never mind." So that worked and it was cute for about a year, and now Jane Curtin is on "Update" and we wanted to give more life to Gilda's character— we already had done endangered feces and presidential erections and so on, and now the laugh at "never mind" was obligatory and we wanted to get rid of it. So I wrote this Jane thing where she says to

Gilda, "You know, every week you come on and you get it wrong, and you're disgusting, you're an insult to the integrity of journalism and to human beings worldwide. Am I making myself clear? I don't want to see you anymore." And I had Gilda say back to her, crystal clear, she took a beat and she went, "Bitch."

Now this is 1977, okay? We do it in the dress rehearsal and the place goes nuts because "bitch" on television was groundbreaking. But Jane Crowley, who was this five-hundred-pound censor and an ex-nun or would-be nun or something, she comes around and says, "You can't do that." "Can't do what?" "You can't say 'bitch' on television." And I said, "Jane, listen to me. What Gilda is calling Jane Curtin, when she's saying 'bitch,' she is effectively using the adverb form of the word. In effect she is saying, 'You are acting bitchy toward me,' which I have heard on television before. She's not saying, 'Jane, you are a bitch,' which is a noun, which I agree should never be in television nor even in streets. She's using the adverb form." And would you believe it, she bought this crock of shit. She goes, "All right, all right, the adverb then," and went on.

BUCK HENRY:

I remember there was a really odd argument between me and Lorne and the Standards and Practices woman in a bit where I played a censor. There's a moment when, in trying to describe something, I poke my forefinger through a hole made by my other forefinger and thumb, if you see what I mean. And the argument was, how many times I could do that and whether, having once poked the finger into the hole, could I move it around, or must I withdraw it immediately? It got pretty silly. It's easy to be dirty, but hard to be incisive.

NEIL LEVY:

There was a time in the third season when the writers all thought they were being cheated out of their paychecks and there was an insurrection. Everybody got paranoid at one point that they weren't getting paid enough. They discovered there was a certain amount of money in the writers' budget, but when they divided what all the writers were making, where was all this extra money? It was going into sets and other things, and it wasn't their business what was happening to it. But there was an insurrection, really. Somebody kicked a hole in a wall and then Lorne came in and said, "What's going on here?" And he was confronted by this mob. And he didn't say a word—he just turned and walked away and went back into his office and closed the door. And then there was dead silence, and then en masse, all the writers stood in front of Lorne's door begging his forgiveness, banging on the door and pleading, and he wouldn't talk to them—'til later.

TOM DAVIS:

When we did the "Franken and Davis Show" sketches, our theme was usually that we were breaking up. Once we had Al's real parents in town, coming to the show, so we dressed up in SS uniforms and we dressed his parents in these death-camp stripes. It was going to be something. In the sketch, Al's father would say, "You know, Al, your mother and I are very uncomfortable with this piece. We think it's tasteless." And Al would say, "Oh come on, Dad, you wanted to be on TV. This is funny." Elliott Gould was the host and Elliott was going to go along with it. But Standards and Practices was really sweating. And Lorne and Bernie Brillstein were like, "Oh God!" And then Lorne finally decided, "No, no, you can't do it." And Joe and Phoebe, Al's parents, were really dejected. They were excited about being in the piece and being on TV.

So there we are up in Lorne's office in our SS uniforms, black skulls on the hat and everything, and Joe and Phoebe, this old feeble Jewish couple, are dressed in the prison outfits. And we got cut. And Al's parents walked out of the room. And Lorne said, "Don't ever do that to me again. I don't want to ever cut your parents like that."

One charge that plagued Saturday Night Live *was that the show was a boys club, which meant women had to struggle first for admission and then for recognition. Women writers were easily among the most prominent and creative of the first group yet still remained in the minority—a state that would worsen rather than improve in years to come. Among cast members, men who stood out or became stars have outnumbered women, partly because better roles are written for men on the show—by male writers. During the 1976–77 season, the writing staff consisted of thirteen men and three women—Rosie Shuster, Anne Beatts, and Marilyn Suzanne Miller.*

MARILYN SUZANNE MILLER:

There was a sort of sisterhood that extended—you know, there weren't that many people, so we were like each other's best friend, because we didn't even know anybody outside the building. By "we" I mean all six girls, the writers plus the performers.

GARRETT MORRIS:

Either it's that they were all niggers with me or I was a woman with them—because I got the same raw deal.

LILY TOMLIN:

There was a lot of misogynist stuff that I considered to be demeaning to women—or to any group—on *Saturday Night Live*. It was not my style, you know. You can do anything about anything if there's some artistry involved, but I never was very big on imitating celebrities and putting them down either. It was too limited to me. It was too easy in some sense.

JANE CURTIN:

John absolutely didn't like being in sketches with women. He told me women were not funny. Actually, Chevy said it to me as well. And I found it stunning.

Lorne didn't help, because that isn't what Lorne did. Oh, it was ridiculous. It was just insane. There's no way you can respond to that, so you just have to learn to live with it, plod on, and hope that Marilyn will get a piece on that week.

LARAINE NEWMAN:

I think Lorne was really a champion of the women writers and gave them an even break. His background was working with women. He started writing for Phyllis Diller, he produced most of the Lily

Tomlin specials. He hires women and he's supportive of women. He is not one of those people that thinks women are not funny.

But the boys got away with a lot. They were bad and we were good. We were punctual and they were late. We were clean and they were dirty. We were prepared and they weren't—it was that stuff. I don't think we really got into personalities, because we didn't really have that many. Jane certainly didn't have relationships with the guys on any level. She had a life and was married. I was very fond of everybody. It was a family. I always think of that scene in *The Right Stuff* when they've gone to that event that Lyndon Johnson planned for them, and they're backstage before they're introduced at this big party on their behalf, and they're all just sitting around realizing what they've all done, and they're just kind of looking at each other like, you know, "Here we are." And that is how we all felt. It's like we'd been through this incredible lifeboat of a situation and we're all tied together because of it.

DAN AYKROYD:

I think if you look back on the first four years, it was pretty evenly balanced. The women were pretty strong. Jane, Laraine, and Gilda were strong and played strong characters. So I would question whether it was a boys club, just because what would it have been without those women there? It would have been very empty.

MARILYN SUZANNE MILLER:

I'm not sure how to say this, but everybody sort of thought I was good, and when I wrote something, people wanted to do it. It was a little niche I created for myself.

ROSIE SHUSTER:

Was Lorne prejudiced against female writers? I think we sometimes had to try harder. I remember being instructed by Lorne to write at least nine separate drafts of this stupid sketch called "Backstage Banter" that I just wanted to throw in the garbage can. I wanted to chuck it and say to him, "You're not the boss of me." There were times we were dismissed, or there were times that I would quietly pitch something in the room in a little voice, 'cause I would not, you know, jump on Lorne's desk and tap dance it out. I was quiet. Someone else would pick up the idea in the room and then sock it home. Stuff like that happened all the time. But I don't have any bitterness. I just think we did have to pave the way. We were on new ground. And it was challenging, let's say. Lorne had a real way of juggling a lot of hot egos. I'm sure he saw backbiting and infighting that we didn't see; he was probably privy to more of that than any other person. I know he was, because he used to confide certain stuff to me.

AL FRANKEN:

My daughter was the first *Saturday Night Live* baby, the first new child born to anybody who worked on the show.

TOM DAVIS:

Gilda and G. E. Smith, the musician, were living together in the Dakota, and Gilda wanted to give Al's wife, Franny, and the new baby a shower. G. E. and I are in the back room of the apartment where all his guitars are, because the shower's for women—all the secretaries, all the wives, Jane is there, Laraine is there. Everyone is waiting for the baby to arrive and there's a knock at the door and G. E. and I peek in from the other room.

AL FRANKEN:

My wife came with her sister first and I was to bring the baby. My other sister-in-law came with me. So I got a doll the exact size of the baby and swaddled it—I told Franny I was going to do this—and there's like thirty women, and I walk in and they're all going like, "Ohhh...ahhhh," and I walk in and I hit the baby's head on this piece of furniture and I go up in the air and I come down with everything, *everything,* going onto this doll, so that there is no way I didn't kill the baby. And the screams, the screams!

TOM DAVIS:

The scream that came out of these women, it just made everyone's hair stand on end. They just witnessed this man kill his newborn baby. To this day, I've never heard a more terrifying sound than all those women witnessing this baby being killed by its father.

AL FRANKEN:

And then my sister-in-law Carla walks in with the real baby.

TOM DAVIS:

I'm telling you, Al did shit like that. I love him for it.

STEVE MARTIN:

And then there was Gilda, who was the sweetest, kindest, funniest person. She was so happy on-camera, she had such a happy face on-camera, you really did grow to love her. You understand what it means when people say they "love" a performer, because they're bringing such happiness into their world.

BILL MURRAY:

Gilda was really an extraordinary and spectacular person. And she was tough. She was really, really tough. Gilda would just give herself up to a moment, she really gave herself up, she sacrificed herself. She knew how to serve a scene or another person in the scene just so devotedly. She really had the most of that of anyone. As a result, because she made other people look good, she herself looked fantastic.

And she had a charm about her and people could write things for her and sketches would be written and somehow she always took it back to that level of her childhood play. They wrote a lot of sketches to that—you know, of her Judy Miller dancing and bouncing on her bed and stuff—but her own sense of childhood play was really her touchstone.

She was a fantastic laugher. I never enjoyed making anyone laugh more than her. Never. I remember one day, I made her laugh so hard—you know there are girls who say, "Oh my God, I wet my pants," all the time—and I made her laugh so hard, she thought she was going to die. And I just couldn't stop. I used to be really funny, and in those days I used to have almost like a vengeful thing; I could just go for a long period of time and try to be funny. I don't do it like I used to. And I miss that. I'm still funny, but back then I would take something and not let go of it, just take something and not let go of it.

PENNY MARSHALL:

Cindy Williams wasn't even sure she wanted to go into television, having done movies. So I was like reading with the world for who would play Shirley on *Laverne and Shirley*. And I called Gilda, because I needed someone strong. I said, "What's your contract? Can you get out?" But she had a loyalty to Lorne, which I understood. Gilda was funny. Gilda was great.

ROBERT KLEIN:

Once Gilda made me laugh so hard, it was one of the hardest and longest laughing jags I ever had in my life. Do you remember years ago there was a yogurt commercial where they show these old Russians in a village and they live to be a hundred and six because they eat yogurt? Well, she played the old woman with the babushka, and yogurt was going all down her face. She was as good as it gets.

KATE JACKSON:

I was so shy and nervous when I hosted, because these were the Not Ready for Prime Time Players. They were better than anybody else on television and everybody knew it. After the cold opening I rushed to change clothes and was doing my wardrobe change and waiting for the lights to come up, and Gilda just very quietly said to me, "You're really good at this." And that just sent me flying. She just absolutely released me and allowed me to have the kind of confidence that lets you do the best you can do. That was the most generous thing. It was just wonderful of her to do that.

MARILYN SUZANNE MILLER:

We were aware of Gilda's eating problems, but we didn't know it was called bulimia. We thought it was this incredibly brilliant idea that Gilda thought up, and I underscore that and I suggest you put it in your book. Yeah, we thought it was a great idea. There were a few girls in my sorority house that went into the bathroom and threw up right after dinner. Which we also thought—by "we," I mean the entire female population thought—was the most wonderful idea and many of us tried to do. It didn't have any name like bulimia, and nobody had said it was a disease. We just thought it was a great idea. And then when it went on for a while we thought it was a great *weird* idea.

LARAINE NEWMAN:

I was concerned about Gilda's bulimia because I'd had a very close friend who was bulimic all through her teenage years. I knew the things that could happen, so I was really worried about Gilda in that context. She was very open about it—not covert, which I always thought was typical of people with that illness. They're usually very hidden. But she was so funny about it, because she would really announce it to us.

Jane and I and Gilda shared a dressing room until the third year. The boys always had their own dressing room; we had to share one. And Gilda used to make this joke about how when we were tired we would have to split a couch three ways. We would all be on the couch together. Then at one point, Gilda would get up and say, "Well, I've got to go into the bathroom." And there were times when she and I would hang out at her house and I would be snorting heroin and she would be eating a gallon of ice cream. And I remember her staggering to the bathroom to make herself throw up, and saying, "I'm so full, I can't hear." And I laughed so hard. There we were, practicing our illnesses together. She was still funny throughout all of it.

ELLIOTT GOULD, *Host:*

Gilda became a very close friend of mine. She was the greatest. Just the most lovely and sensitive human being you could imagine. Gilda told me that when she couldn't sleep, she would order food at about two or three in the morning, and she was so bulimic she would order enough for six or seven people, even though it was just her alone. And then when the delivery guy came and rang the bell, she would say, "The food's here! The food's here!"

TOM SCHILLER:

"La Dolce Gilda" was an attempt to capture the sadness of Gilda when she was at parties and all these sycophants would come around her, done in the style of Federico Fellini, my favorite director. We shot it in black and white after the show, at a place where we had our parties sometimes. For the end of the film, where she says, "Go away, leave me alone," we stayed up all night in order to get the real feeling of dawn coming up. Then I realized you could shoot that at dusk and it looks the same. So I was learning filmmaking at the same time.

I eventually got to show the film to Fellini himself. I went to Cinecittà Studios in Rome and said I was a friend of Henry Miller's and Paul Mazursky's, which was true, and they let me in to watch Fellini direct one of his pictures there. I met him and said, "Look, I made this homage to you, I'd love to show you." He said, "We must arrange a screening." So they showed him the movie, and he said it was "very sweet" and "it had the feeling of some of my work." Oh, I was in heaven when I saw him there.

ROSIE SHUSTER:

I really enjoyed doing the "Perfume for One-Night Stands" commercial parody. That one I really had a great fondness for, because it brought together a lot of what was going on at the time in terms of casual sex and waking up next to somebody whose name you didn't remember and hobbling out in the morning in last night's dress. It was a great character for Gilda. I mean, I can't imagine Jane Curtin doing that one.

LARAINE NEWMAN:

I had a situation involving Gilda when Christopher Lee was host. I was the one who wanted him to host. I'm a big horror movie fan and I just knew his work from that. And he turned out to be an excellent host, even though he dropped a bomb on us the first day. He walked in and said he refused to do Dracula on the show.

I know there is a story about me threatening to quit over that show, but I would like to set the record straight on that. They had written the sketch "Dr. Death" for a couple of shows before that, and I knew it was Gilda's sketch but I'm thinking, "Fuck!" This is the conversation I had with Lorne: "Why does she get to do that sketch? She gets so much airtime. This is a character that I could do. Why can't I do that sketch?" So it got turned into this big thing that I had threatened to quit unless I got that sketch, which I never did. Lorne said, "If you really feel that way, you should quit," and I said, "I'm not going to do that. I'm just saying that this is really difficult for me. This is very hurtful and unfair." So I don't know who told who what, but that is really what happened.

The day of read-through, when we went in there, Danny was furious with me, because he had heard I'd threatened to quit. I only found out years later that Gilda had partially written that sketch. Now if I had known that, I would *never* have asked to do it, because my sense of fair play would never have allowed me to want to do something that someone else wrote. She wrote it with Alan Zweibel, but no one told me at the time. I just thought it was something that Alan wrote that I could have easily done—and what hardship would it have been on Gilda, when she had so much to do in the show? Especially with Christopher Lee, who was the host that I wanted?

And as it happened, I was cast as the little girl. And the sketch turned out okay.

NEIL LEVY:

I had to go fish stars out of bars all the time, especially the first and second seasons. Oh God—Broderick Crawford was completely drunk all the time. He actually disappeared. He'd always try to get to the elevator. I'd say, "Where are you going?" He'd say, "I gotta go find my script, I left my script downstairs." I'd say, "I'll go with you." "No, you don't need to come with me." But Lorne had given me very explicit instructions: "You have to stay with him all the time." And Crawford tried to trick me, and then he'd get angry when I caught him at it. He did get away from me once, and I found him in a bar.

Kris Kristofferson was completely wasted during dress rehearsal. He couldn't say his lines, sloshing around, slurring the words. Lorne said, "Just get the biggest pot of coffee you can." I remember Louise Lasser on her hands and knees crawling into my office looking for pot. Why she was on her hands and knees, I don't know. And then the day of the show, she decided she wasn't going to do the show unless a certain sketch was cut. And we were all preparing to do the show without her. In fact I remember Aykroyd getting excited about it: "We can do it, Lorne. We can get out there and we'll improv it. We'll do a helluva show." And they were ready. And Lorne told her agent that he would make sure everyone knew if she walked out.

DON NOVELLO:

The Frank Zappa show was like one of the worst ever. And I looked at that recently and I really liked seeing how awkward he was in that. Zappa's a genius, but he doesn't trust people, he does everything by himself. A lot of performers after dress are shaken; it doesn't go well and all of a sudden, "Oh God, in two hours I'm going on live." With Zappa what happened was we had a terrible dress and what was he going to do? What he did, not telling anybody, was he turned into Dean Martin. The approach he took was, he read the cards like he was reading the cards — he made a point of it. He was obviously reading the cards. That was his approach to the humor. No one else in the sketches knew it. It was real bad, because I always liked Zappa, I think everybody did, but it was just a terrible show. Lorne was really upset.

HOWARD SHORE:

Hugh Hefner wanted to sing "Thank Heaven for Little Girls" when he hosted, and we rehearsed it endlessly all week and did the dress, which was great. Then we did the show, and during the show he stopped listening, which a lot of amateur singers do. He saw the audience and just stopped listening to the band and went off into his own world. And I looked at Shaffer, who was playing piano, and it was just like, oh my God, he was bars ahead of us and we're on the air and we're trying to catch up.

RICK LUDWIN, *NBC Vice President for Late Night:*

Belushi was thrilled to hear that Milton Berle was coming on, because Belushi admired Milton Berle, and it was one of those things where they were all hanging around Milton's dressing room for the first day or two of the week, you know — Milton, tell us about this, tell us about that. And then Milton assumed he was not hosting *Saturday Night Live,* Milton assumed they were doing *Texaco Star Theater,* and as Milton sometimes did, he took over the production and tried to make it his own, as opposed to being the host. And Lorne disliked the show to such an extent that it's never been seen on Comedy Central, it's never been seen anywhere, since. Lorne was so upset with the way Milton had just steamrolled his way over everyone that he never wanted that show to see the light of day again.

ROSIE SHUSTER:

Anne Beatts and I had written this sketch for Gilda and Milton Berle when he hosted. He was to play an old man in an old folks home, and she was going to feed him dinner. And during dress rehearsal Uncle Miltie did these painfully broad spit takes, enough to make Danny Thomas cringe. So I was sent to Uncle Miltie's dressing room between dress and air to deliver this one simple note, which was, do not go overboard on the spit takes. But he was totally focused on his opening monologue, which was looming in an hour, and he was trying out jokes on me. He was pacing around in his boxer shorts, very proud to parade in his shorts in front of me. Thank God they weren't briefs, because it was already too much information.

He left me no verbal airspace. I could not get a word in. He was like a totally crazed tennis ball machine spitting shtick at me, a comedy filibuster on my little one note. He just drowned me out. And finally wardrobe fetched him, and I found myself running after him screaming, "Don't be broad!" Of course he went even broader, if that was possible. It was sort of like watching a comedy train accident in slow motion on a loop.

ALAN ZWEIBEL:

Milton Berle took a liking to me and gravitated to me, I think because in the early seventies, I had written all these jokes for Catskill comics. And I wrote jokes for a lot of the Friars Club roasts, where Uncle Miltie was usually the roastmaster. You played to people's stereotypes with those jokes — Jack Benny was the cheap one, and so on — and with Berle, all I had known was he wore a dress on TV and supposedly stole everybody's jokes. And also I learned early on that he was the guy with the big dick, one of the biggest in show business. So I started writing big dick jokes about him for these Friars roasts.

Now fast-forward a few years and I'm in Milton Berle's dressing room at *Saturday Night Live.* He's sitting on a couch behind a coffee table and he's wearing a very short kind of bathrobe, the kind that comes down to about midthigh. And somehow I just say to him, "You know, it's so weird that I'm here talking to you, because for years I was writing jokes about your dick." I said, "I wrote all these jokes about your cock and now I'm talking to you—I feel like there's some violation or something here."

He says to me: "You mean you never saw it?" I said, "Uh, no, I don't believe I did." Then he said, "Well, would you like to?" And before I had a chance to say, "Not really" or "Can I think about it?" or whatever, he parts his bathrobe and he just takes out this—this anaconda. He lays it on the table and I'm looking into this thing, right? I'm looking into the head of Milton Berle's dick. It was enormous. It was like a pepperoni. And he goes, "What do you think of the boy?" And I'm looking right at it and I go, "Oh, it's really, really nice."

At which point Gilda opens the door to the dressing room. It's like an *I Love Lucy* sketch, but this honestly happened! She opens the door to his dressing room just in time to see me looking into his dick saying, "Yeah, it's really, really nice."

I tell Milton, "I'll talk to you later," closed the door, and left.

LORNE MICHAELS:

I had resisted having Berle on, but Jean Doumanian talked me into it on the basis of "How could we not?" I knew we were heading for disaster from minute one. The sketch in the old folks home was supposed to be sentimental, but during rehearsal, when Gilda would feed Milton, he was letting the food dribble out and all over his face. So I go, "Milton, she's giving a speech here and you're completely upstaging her with the mashed potatoes coming down your chin." And he'd say, "Now you're getting two laughs instead of one." And I'd say, "Well, no," and then he'd pat me on the shoulder and go, "I know, I know—'satire.'" He'd say that whenever I'd say anything.

Just before the close of the live show—and it's not a very good show—he said to me, "Don't worry about a thing, the standing ovation is all arranged." He was singing "September Song," and I swear to God there were ten people, which was the number of seats he had, who stood up in the balcony. The only time it's ever happened. I was quite clear in the booth about not cutting to it. We don't do that.

I have great affection for old-time show business. But it had become corrupt. It wasn't what it had been. The show was trying to get away from that.

Saturday Night Live invigorated viewers because it represented so many departures from the safe, the sane, and the expected. One of Michaels's rules was, no groveling to the audience either in the studio or at home. In those first five years especially, SNL writers were not pleased when a studio audience applauded some social sentiment or political opinion in a sketch or "Weekend Update" item. The writers wanted laughs, not consensus.

In its earliest days, the SNL company exuded a contempt not for the medium but for the bad habits it had developed over the years—and the innocuousness that infected virtually every genre, including sketch-comedy shows. Pandering to "the folks at home," a near-sacred TV tradition, was anathema to the original SNL writers and performers, who felt it was better to aim high and miss than aim low and get a cheap laugh. The collective approach of the show's creators could be seen as a kind of arrogance, a stance of defiance that said in effect, "We think this is funny, and if you don't, you're wrong." The show reflected and projected writers and performers who strove first to please themselves—to put on television the kinds of things they'd always yearned to see but that others lacked the guts to present.

To viewers raised on TV that was forever cajoling, importuning, and talking down to them, the blunt and gutsy approach was refreshing, a virtual reinvention of the medium. The stars of Saturday Night Live *were saying, "We're not coming to you, you have to come to us—or at least meet us halfway." They produced television that commanded attention because it demanded attention. Everything wasn't made easy and lazy and served up predigested.*

It could be argued that in time, Saturday Night Live *became as eager to please as any other TV show—even the kind that its writers and actors despised and derided—and that, probably inevitably, it became what it belittled. But in that first burst of glory, there was still a captivating, rebellious purity to it. It was on a wavelength of its own, proudly above the fray, brash and brave and youthful and honest. Television without guilt that was still entertaining as all get-out.*

BILL MURRAY:

It was Davey Wilson who didn't want us ad-libbing more than Lorne didn't want it. But the thing about the ad-libbing is that the camera cues, the camera cuts, are all on the script. They're supposed to go from this person to that person on this line. So that was a technical thing that was sort of a limit that you had. You'd screw things up if you ad-libbed at the end of something.

Davey caught a lot of stuff because he was fast. If he could see in your eyes that something was coming, he'd hold on it. You'd hear him in the booth: "Oh Christ, where's he going?" You learned that if you were going to fix something, the easiest way for everybody was to figure out how to fix it and still say the last line so they had the cuts right. You could actually watch them go, "Awgh!" You could hear six or seven people in the booth go "Awgh!" like he got it, and there'd be this glee as the technical director would push the camera button switch; there'd be this delight that you did it right, that you respected their technology and what they had to do. That was when you got good at it. It takes a while to learn how to do that. Not everybody did.

I shot off a flash camera into the lens one time during "Update." Yeah, I burned out the TV camera. Oh and they were furious. God, they were angry. They thought, "Oh you fucking rookie, you idiot." Well of course it turned out to be just a temporary thing. It burns a hole for a moment and then they have to redo the white balance or something, but they were so mad, because there was this bubble in the screen for the rest of the "Update." The whole floor was like, "Did you hear what he did?" And people were walking out of the booth going, "Do you know what he did?!" Of course—it's on the screen and everyone sees it on the monitor anyway, the whole crew sees it, and people know.

JAMES SIGNORELLI:

With the exception of Don Novello, who had worked at Leo Burnett in Chicago, no one here had any background in advertising. My background was in documentary filmmaking and feature film cinematography, so I had passed through the world of low-budget commercials that everybody does at one point, and I knew the silliness of it and what some of the excesses were, and I knew how to do them from the production and visual points of view. One of the things about commercials is that they're very good storytelling devices.

By the beginning of the third year, the typical short movie for *Saturday Night Live* cost between $10,000 and $13,000. It was kind of a watershed period because of what was going on in commercials in general. For one thing, money was no longer an object. Phenomenal sums were being spent on advertising. And new techniques were being born there. The other thing was that it was becoming acceptable — even with the most staid client — to use humor.

We at the show, of course, were on the cutting edge. So nobody could do what we did. And whatever we did in commercials, the attitudes that we took, the archness or the surrealist approach, was making a big impact on the creative people at the ad agencies. So they started pushing the wave further and further to the left. Editorially, we were doing things that were very sophisticated back then.

DAN AYKROYD:

I did "Update" for one season, I think, and I wasn't comfortable in it. I didn't like it. They only gave it to me because Chevy had gone. "Jane, you ignorant slut" really caught on — that was great — but delivering the jokes and being the newsreader was not something that I was comfortable with. I was very happy to be relieved of that.

LORNE MICHAELS:

In the seventies, I was much more proud of who I wouldn't allow on the show — people who had just been all over Las Vegas and prime-time television. There were even people I always thought were really great but they were of that other generation. And now we were coming along, and we were shaped by a different set of things. And any association with the Rich Littles and the John Byners and the original *Tonight Show* guys like Dayton Allen would have been antithetical to what I was trying to do.

PAUL SHAFFER:

The idea that some of the things would not be necessarily accessible to everybody didn't matter. As long as there were a few people out there who thought it was hilarious, that's what mattered. I kind of learned that from this show, that concept. It was a show for our generation, which was, let's face it, a sixties-style generation.

AL FRANKEN:

I heard Spiro Agnew was going to be on Tom Snyder's show, so I just wanted to meet him and harass him a little bit. I brought a tape recorder and went down to their studios on six. Agnew was in the makeup room, so I sat down in the next makeup chair as he was getting made up and I said something like, "You called student protesters bums, and aren't you the bum"—I think that's what I said—"because you took money?" And he just said, "I never called them bums. That was Nixon." It was like beneath his dignity to address this kid with long hair and to spend too much time on it.

I thought I'd pressed the button to start the tape recorder, but I didn't. I'd had it on and turned it off or something. So I didn't get it on tape. And then I also felt stupid because I checked it out and I was wrong: Nixon had called students bums. At least I did get to say to Agnew that he was a bum.

And then the producer of the Snyder show called me up and said, "Don't do that. If there's somebody on our show that you hate, don't come down and harass them. That's not good for our show."

LORNE MICHAELS:

When Al went down to the fucking sixth floor to berate Spiro Agnew, Chevy and O'Donoghue and I were like, "Al, what the fuck are you doing?" Al took that "nattering nabob" speech personally. He was probably twenty-three when the show started, I was thirty. It has always seemed to me that the people who made the most noise about artistic integrity were the first people to buy a Mercedes, and the more people railed about things, when you examine their lives twenty-five years later—well, you know.

TOM DAVIS:

One day Henry Kissinger calls up, and the call is picked up at an NBC page's desk. And the page goes, "Henry Kissinger's on the phone. He wants tickets for his son." And Al grabs the phone and yells into it, "You know, if it hadn't been for the Christmas bombing in Cambodia, you could've had your fucking tickets!"

PAULA DAVIS, *Assistant*:

My first official job was working for Michael O'Donoghue. I was dying to get into *SNL*. It was all I wanted to do. And I found that there was an assistant position open in the talent department, which I really wanted. So I had Michael write a reference letter to Lorne. He wrote me this long recommendation and then, at the end, he wrote, "P.S., I'd rather stick my dick in a blender than write another one of these letters."

ROBERT KLEIN:

Rockefeller Center was one of the better-run office complexes, and it was beautiful. They don't like you putting things on the wall or anything like that. Aykroyd and Belushi had a little corner office with barren walls, and they had nailed against the wall panties sent in by girls, some of them soiled, and many other odd things as well. And it was sort of like rebellion, you know, in these stodgy halls.

DAN AYKROYD:

I had one episode of rage. And that was when this guy—an accountant, a unit manager—billed me for a hundred and fifty bucks for some meals we were having when we were writing. "Wait a minute. These are expenses that should be picked up by the show." But he kept sending me these bills. So finally I wrote a satanic message on the wall in lipstick—I think Michael O'Donoghue came in and saw it and approved of it—and it was something like, "Your relatives will all burn in hell forever." It was very effective.

CARRIE FISHER:

Danny was always into weapons and cars and doing his little imitations. He was always hanging around with the person who does the autopsies — the coroner. That's who he would hang around with. And of course he really took care of John. He loved him.

I was set up with Danny by John. John invited me over and then passed out. That was the setup. That was a blind date, John-style. Danny was adorable. He was lovely. He's just your classic codependent and caretaker. Once I almost choked on a brussels sprout and he did the Heimlich maneuver on me. He wound up saving my life. When he asked me to marry him, I thought, "Wow, I probably better."

PENNY MARSHALL:

Yeah, Danny proposed to Carrie. Then she ran away and bought him some clothes. That's how she handled that.

STEVE MARTIN:

Dan Aykroyd rode a motorcycle and wore leather clothes and everything. I was trying to be friendly and I said, "Hey, you want to go shopping for clothes over at Saks?" And he said, "Well, I'm really not into that."

NEIL LEVY:

Aykroyd is great. He's an atomic mutant — a web-toed atomic mutant. He actually had web toes, you know. I've seen them with my own eyes, at least one foot. I asked him about it and he said, "I'm an atomic mutant." He's also got a photographic memory and instant recall. He can take a book and once he's read it, you could ask him any page and he could recall it. Unfortunately, I think the only book he's actually memorized is like a 1974 meat packagers guide.

JAMES DOWNEY, *Writer*:

My brother was an air force career guy, and when Aykroyd and I did a thing a long time ago that involved Napoleon having a B-52, Aykroyd supplied all the references for the armaments and the weaponry and stuff. In fact the term "daisy cutters" was probably first used on television in that piece. And my brother had been watching it in Thailand or something on the Armed Forces Channel and he called up and said, "My God! Who there knows what a C-130 is?" I said that was Aykroyd. He goes, "Wow, we were amazed, because you guys actually had the stuff right, and we've never seen that kind of thing."

JAMES SIGNORELLI:

During the first five years, the show changed a lot of stuff that you don't think about. It changed this business of dinner at eight into dinner at ten or dinner at midnight. The way Franne Lee, our costume designer, dressed Lorne for the show suddenly became the way everybody in New York was dressing. Lorne used to come out onstage wearing a shirt, jacket, and blue jeans. Nobody had ever seen it. But before you knew it, everybody was sitting around in Levi's and a jacket.

Riding a tsunami of success and acclaim, Lorne Michaels proposed sending the entire show on location to New Orleans for the 1977 Mardi Gras. Since NBC figured the production cost of that to be at least $700,000, executives decided to put the show in prime time on a Sunday night, stretching it to two hours and making it an entry in a weekly anthology called The Big Event. *Penny Marshall and Cindy Williams were among the guest stars. But this was one big event that went busto, and in a spectacular way — a live show in a city full of drunks and near-naked revelers turned out to be much harder to control than one mounted in a TV studio. It was such a fiasco that it almost became self-parody, a sort of instant legend, and thus didn't really do a thing to impede the surging popularity of* Saturday Night Live.

ALAN ZWEIBEL:

We had Buck Henry and Jane Curtin at the "Update" desk waiting for this Bacchus Parade to come, and all our jokes were about the floats and the specific things that would pass by the reviewing stand where they sat. But then somebody got killed — there was this horrible accident at the beginning of the parade route, two miles away. So for the entire hour and a half or so that we were on TV, there was no parade. Every time the bright lights came on Jane and Buck, millions of kids were vomiting and drinking and throwing balloons at them. And I'm under the desk while they're on live TV being pelted, and I'm writing jokes about there not being a parade—what you would have seen had somebody not been killed, okay?

And I remember the last joke I wrote, the concluding joke, was something along the lines of, I'm paraphrasing, "Mardi Gras is French for 'no parade.'"

PENNY MARSHALL:

Oh, was that a disaster! That was ridiculous. The parade was rerouted because there was an accident. People were throwing things at Buck and Jane. Meanwhile, Cindy and I had to do this Apollo Ball thing, but Cindy got lost and didn't make the first part of it. There were men dressed as women, but we weren't allowed to say that on television. We couldn't say they were men because it was prime time. In those days, we couldn't even say "do it" on *Laverne and Shirley*.

BUCK HENRY:

It was a very, very bad week for Garrett Morris, because that was his hometown and his sketch was canceled and he didn't have much to do. He was severely pissed off. He wandered off. Everyone felt very badly about it. And yet the show wasn't bad, considering there were, I think, fifteen live locations. O'Donoghue even got to do his reindeer dance, or whatever the hell that was, and there was Belushi doing, of course, Brando doing *A Streetcar Named Desire*.

GARRETT MORRIS:

I was unhappy about it, because I had a song I wanted to do, a song called "Walking Down Bourbon Street." I'm a composer, and here I'm also a native son and I would have been doing a song about New Orleans. But Lorne didn't see it, and I think he was influenced by a lot of people. So now I'm not in one thing on the show, and nobody is saying anything about that. The only thing I could do is walk off, but I don't want that reputation. By the way, the cast went to my aunt's house and ate 'til they could hardly leave the house. They had to like put their stomachs on wheelbarrows to get to their cars.

PAUL SHAFFER:

Naturally I wanted to do more performing. The fifth season, Lorne made me a featured player, which was a supporting actor, and I was in certain sketches that year playing various characters and things. And then there was the famous time when I said "fuck" on live television. The sketch was about a medieval band rehearsing. Did you ever hear of the Troggs tape? The Troggs were a band in the sixties; "Wild Thing" was their song. There's a tape that circulates in the music business of them in the studio trying to make a follow-up to "Wild Thing" and not being able really to communicate. They didn't know musical terminology so they just kept saying "fuck" over and over: "*You* had the fucking beat," they kept saying. They couldn't seem to re-create what they had done before. It's a famous music biz tape.

Anyway, Franken and Davis had the idea to transcribe this Troggs tape and make a sketch out of it but make it into a medieval band rehearsing and saying those lines. I remember James Taylor was in it too, because he was the musical guest that week, and Laraine Newman. We made up our own word, "flogging," instead of "fucking," and we would say, "Well, you had the floggin' beat before" and we were all doing British accents, some more successfully than others. So it went very well in the dress rehearsal. And Al Franken said to me, "You're getting big laughs. If you want to add any more of those 'floggings' go ahead." But I got carried away, and just without thinking I said, "You had the fucking beat before." And then I, oh my God, I watch the tape of it and I go white. And I look off, you know—what am I going to do?

But nobody noticed I said "fuck," because we were doing these bad English accents. You couldn't hear it, it wasn't really clear, and there were no phone calls or anything. Everybody in the sketch heard it, though, and I remember Laraine coming over to me right after and saying, "Thank you for making broadcasting history." And then Lorne came over and said, "You just broke the last barrier." But I didn't get in trouble, because it was clearly an accident. I didn't get fired or anything.

ROSIE SHUSTER:

I wasn't actually in a couple with Lorne when the show started; that's the real folly of all of it. But I never really actually got divorced from him, I don't think, until like 1980 or something. I just didn't want to deal with that. And so I didn't.

DAN AYKROYD:

By the time Rosie and I became involved, it was over between Rosie and Lorne. They might have been married in name, and all that, but he was seeing other people. There was definitely separation there.

TOM DAVIS:

When Rosie and Danny first started dating, Danny was sure that Lorne was going to kill him because Rosie was his ex-wife. I was very close to Danny, and he was like, "Don't tell anybody, Davis, don't tell anybody." And of course everybody knew anyway. Finally Lorne said to me, "Danny and Rosie sure are hitting it off," and it was like, why are we going through all this hiding and charade kind of thing? I mean, Danny and Rosie and I went on vacations together. But somehow, Danny was sure that Lorne was going to kill him.

DAN AYKROYD:

My thing with Rosie never really got in the way of work until near the end. I was pretty upset, because Rosie was breaking up with me and going with a guy who is one of my best friends now.

LARAINE NEWMAN:

I always had these long-distance romances, which were about as much as I could handle. I really didn't get involved with people I was working with. I liked keeping it light. I was involved with lots of people who were just numb lotharios, but because I knew that about them I could just enjoy them and not get involved. I was in no shape to be involved with anybody.

ROSIE SHUSTER:

On Wednesday mornings, people were scrambling for the showers. We did bunk there and it was pretty fun—and pretty funky. Sometimes people would crawl out of their offices in the glow of those fluorescents, and it was not pretty. It was dormlike. Gilda came in once in her pajamas to write in the middle of the night.

BUCK HENRY:

John and Danny left the show at the same time, and I thought they shouldn't have. I thought they owed Lorne another season. The kind of spontaneity and cleverness and responsiveness that went into that night when I was injured and they all ended up in bandages, I don't know why, but I just have that feeling that wouldn't happen today. It's too homogenized now. It's too mechanized. It's corporate. And to a certain extent I think it's because Lorne's still the only one who can come and say, "No, don't do that."

But you also get the feeling that people are there because, first and foremost, it's their launching pad or stepping-stone or way station or whatever, not as a destination in itself. They all know that it's a franchise which leads to making bad movies.

HERBERT SCHLOSSER, *NBC President:*

Once I invited the whole cast to come up and have lunch in this big dining room that the chairman and I shared. And the cooking was not nouvelle cuisine. We were used to having heavy stuff, so we had roast beef with all the trimmings. And I said, "Bake an extra batch of chocolate chip cookies." Well, you've never seen people eat like this—second portions of roast beef and so on. And then the cook gave each of them a little bunch of these cookies, tied up in paper napkins so they could take them with them. And I remember Bill Murray told me, "I've heard you're a good guy and I'm going to give you a noogie." And he came over and rubbed his knuckles into my head. My God, they really were wild.

HARRY SHEARER, *Cast Member:*

Three years into the show, I got an offer to join the writing staff, and I sent back a fairly brusque letter to the effect that, if I wanted to write for television, I could do that very well in Los Angeles, I didn't have to move to New York—the implicit message being that I'm a writer-performer and I don't take writing jobs. So two years further on, I'm in Washington, D.C., being interviewed to be the host for what ended up being *Morning Edition* on NPR, and I got a message to come up to New York; Lorne wanted to meet with me. And I came up and the meeting was in the darkened auditorium of the Winter Garden Theatre, where Gilda was doing *Gilda Live,* and there Lorne offered me a job as a member of the cast and as a writer.

LORNE MICHAELS:

In 1979 I was doing Gilda Radner's show on Broadway, which I was directing. Belushi was definitely leaving *Saturday Night Live,* and Aykroyd was coming back as a performer only and not going to write. We all thought we'd do just one more season. So we made some additions to the writing staff. We hadn't added any cast. That was the plan.

Just before Gilda's show opened, I got a call first from Bernie Brillstein and then from Dan Aykroyd saying they had a chance to make the Blues Brothers movie in November and that Danny wouldn't be coming back after all. That happened in July. Now I didn't have a plan. Al Franken was a big fan of Harry's from the Credibility Gap, which we all were, and it seemed like yeah, that would work.

HARRY SHEARER:

I thought fairly early on that the show betrayed a certain desperation to try to repeat anything that got a laugh—which I thought was, given the show's advertised adventurousness, a little puzzling. The times they ran "News for the Hard of Hearing" in the first season probably numbered in the double digits, and it seemed to me a tip-off that the show's agenda was to develop running bits and running characters as quickly and as determinedly as possible, whether or not they really had legs.

But by the fifth season, the show had serious career implications for anybody who was involved in it, obviously. I overestimated my ability to put my mark on it.

AL FRANKEN:

I had sort of recommended Harry, so Lorne held that against me. And Harry did too. That's the wonderful part about Harry. Harry actually held it against me that I had recommended him for the show.

LORNE MICHAELS:

Harry's working style was just so completely different. I think he was also less innocent than we were—much more experienced. He'd been a child actor. He'd been around. And whereas Chevy with Gerald Ford would make no effort whatsoever to look like him, if Harry was doing Reagan it took twenty minutes of prosthetics. *Now* we do that. *Then* we didn't. So I think Harry is obviously very talented, but his comedy was mostly industry.

HARRY SHEARER:

I would say that when the first words that a guy says to you when he's offering you a job are, quote, "I've never really hired a male Jew for the company before. I've always gone for the Chicago Catholic thing," unquote, that puts you on a certain notice that the relationship is going to be interesting. It was said fairly seriously as, like, "I'm changing my strategy." I was filling basically two slots, because John and Danny had left and he was bringing in only me. So I don't know if Lorne remembers that or would choose to remember it. I sure remember it, because it was remarkable that he said that.

I had also worked with Albert Brooks on most of his films in the first season, and had seen the relationship between Lorne and Albert, and while I'm perfectly familiar with the difficulties of working with Albert, because I've done so myself, I empathized with what Albert experienced at his end. I knew what I was getting into—or I thought I did, let's put it that way. I was fully prepared for a difficult situation. I wasn't prepared for how difficult.

I was pretty fucking miserable for virtually the entire season. I was explicitly hired as a member of the cast as well as a writer. That was pretty much the sine qua non of my taking the job. So I began to be a little curious when I was not included in the opening montage of the cast. There was some talk about, oh, you know, deadlines, and blah, blah, blah. I don't believe I was in there in the montage in the early part of the season. I couldn't be sure. But I don't think so. I'd have to go look at the tapes. I have the tapes.

What I do know was that, about five or six weeks into the season, Billy Murray invited me to go to a Knicks game. Billy was telling me about the difficulties he'd had in his early days of the show and how basically the rest of the cast treated him like shit. And I said, "Yeah, but there's something else going on. I can't figure out exactly what it is. I'm getting this weird vibe from the other members of the cast when I read my pieces at read-through." And Billy says, "Well, a lot of people think it's not really appropriate for a new writer to come in and write himself into a lot of the pieces." And I said, "But I'm a cast member as well." And he says, "Oh? That's a little piece of information Lorne hasn't shared with the other members of the cast." Now I know that I'm in for a really interesting ride.

The first big piece I wrote that got on the air was a piece I quite dearly liked. I wrote it with Paul Shaffer, and it was a backers' audition for a rock musical about Charles Manson. At the party after that show, Lorne called me over and said, "That moment at the end of that sketch when you were mouthing the words to the final song silently, that was the moment that you became a star on this show." And, of course, the very next week I was not on the show at all. So much for stardom. The whole place was just full of the most insidious mind games.

LORNE MICHAELS:

The amount of things that have to come together for something to be good is just staggering. And the fact that there's anything good at all is just amazing. When you're young, you assume that just knowing the difference between good and bad is enough: "I'll just do good work, because I prefer it to bad work." I think what distinguishes great work for me is — I remember when I saw *The Graduate* in 1968. I thought, "I won't be doing anything like that." It so got you and moved you, and it was smart. And I think when you see the real stuff it's always an elevating thing. It may make you question where you are and the kind of work you're doing. And if we weren't fans of it we wouldn't be doing what we're doing.

HARRY SHEARER:

Late in the season, February or March, there was this sketch in which Garrett Morris played Anwar Sadat. And the year before, on ABC, Billy Crystal and I were in a show in which Billy played Begin and I played Sadat. And I thought to myself, "I was a great Sadat. Garrett is a truly mediocre Sadat. I'm here. I'm going to go over to Lorne and say why shouldn't I do this?" So I went over to Lorne's apartment on a Friday night, and he was the soul of friendliness to the extent of inviting me to have a sauna with him. So there we are in the sauna and I said, "Lorne, I do a great Anwar Sadat, and Garrett really does a pretty shitty one, and I really think I should be doing Sadat in this sketch. It's sort of infuriating to me to watch." And Lorne goes, "All right, you know what, I'm going to call Al." And he gets out of the sauna in front of me, calls Al Franken, and says, "Al, I've been thinking and blah, blah, blah, and Harry should be Anwar Sadat." I go home.

The next day I show up for the show, open the script to see what changes have been made. And Garrett is still playing Sadat. I mean, it just was insoluble. I could not figure it out. I have no idea. All I know is, we're on the set twenty seconds before going live, and Garrett turns to me and says, "Hey, man, you do Sadat—how did he sound again?"

ANNE BEATTS, *Writer:*

I remember asking Lorne once about somebody that I felt had really done me dirt and saying, you know, what should I do about it? And Lorne said, "Be perfectly friendly and civil to them, but just never work with them again." So I would guess that that would be more his style.

FRED SILVERMAN, *NBC President:*

At that point in time, *Saturday Night Live* was doing very well in the ratings. Which is why although occasionally it would annoy me, I never let it annoy me too much, because it was like an oasis in the schedule. It was extremely profitable—it and *The Tonight Show* brought in hundreds of millions of dollars every year.

But then we began very serious conversations about giving Gilda Radner her own variety hour in prime time. That was very, very much a part of my planning for midseason. I think it was 1978, the first midseason I was there for. And, you know, she was doing it, she was doing it, she was doing it, and then we had a lunch—just Gilda and Lorne and myself—and I found out at that lunch that she decided with Lorne that they weren't going to do it after all. And that was an enormous disappointment on several levels. On a personal level, but also because I thought she would have been an absolute smash doing the kind of show that Carol Burnett used to do. It would have been great. When you're running a network, you search for a signature program. And in the days of *BJ and the Bear* and *Sheriff Lobo,* to put on a smart variety show with Gilda Radner, coming out of the studios in New York, would have been a home run. So that was an enormous disappointment. It certainly didn't help my relationship with Lorne at that point in time.

LORNE MICHAELS:

Somewhere around the time she did the Broadway show, Gilda decided she did not want to do the variety hour. And somewhere in that time, Bernie Brillstein claims, he conveyed to NBC that Gilda did not want to do this prime-time hour. So imagine my surprise when I was summoned to Fred's office and shown the board and there on Wednesday nights is Gilda's show. So I say, "Fred, that's not happening, she said no." Well, it got very heated between the two of us. He said some unpleasant things about her. I defended her. We stood toe to toe and had a very deep exchange. I think he thought I wasn't delivering Gilda as promised.

ALAN ZWEIBEL:

By the fifth year there was a mass burnout. There was the thought, for me personally, "Gee, I'd like to try to do something else."

MAX PROSS, *Writer:*

When Tom Gammill and I worked for Lorne, I thought, "Oh my God, this is the best job I'll ever have in my life." Coming out of college, it just seemed like, oh, this is great, you know. It was 1979 and we were, what, twenty-two, and probably the two funniest people in the world for me were Bill Murray and Steve Martin. And I got to meet them both my first day of work. How cool was that? Not only met them, I got to, like, work with them.

TOM GAMMILL, *Writer:*

And you had all these amazing bands. I mean, the Grateful Dead hung out there for like a week. We went out to restaurants all the time. Plus you only worked twenty-two weeks out of the year, because the weeks that the show wasn't in production, people didn't come in to the office. Although Max and I used to come in just because we wanted someplace to go.

MAX PROSS:

We got such a skewed idea of what the working world was like. We get this job where people act like college kids, staying up all night and smoking pot and drinking beer all the time. Boy, were we in for a let-down when we saw the way the rest of the world operated.

TOM GAMMILL:

Our next big job was at Letterman, where it's like, "Wait, where are the parties?" "You'll get a party if we last a year." There wasn't any beer.

HARRY SHEARER:

Chevy was back as the host of the show, and it was the first of many occasions when Lorne assured the cast that, I don't know, "Chevy's cleaned up." I learned that wasn't exactly true when I saw the sweat on his brow when we were actually doing the show on the air. But anyway, we were doing this talk show bit and Garrett's not there, we're doing camera blocking and Garrett Morris is nowhere on the floor. And then I heard the euphemism — "Garrett's on seventeen."

That meant that Garrett was up on the seventeenth floor where the offices were and that he would be indulging in some substance, rather than being down at the stage on eight where he was expected.

GARRETT MORRIS:

I've been described as being the worst person in the world in terms of drugs. Now we know that that turned out not to be so. My attitude toward drugs has been indifferent. I'm not saying that excuses it. I don't know why marijuana is still illegal. It has never killed one single individual in all the time we've known about it, yet tobacco kills 300,000 each year, alcohol kills 250,000 each year, and they are legal. The laws, the whole thing has been the right wing trying to get back at the civil rights movement: "What can we do to reverse it? If we can put them in the fucking buses we would, but we can't do that." As far as I'm concerned, that's all I see.

JANE CURTIN:

Garrett was treated horribly, horribly—by the writers, by some of the performers, and Lorne. They just dismissed him. I used to have conversations on the set with Garrett about, "Why do you put up with this?" And he said, "I can't pass up the money. I'm going to make the money and get out and go on and do something else." I found it amazing that he let it go on for as long as it did, but it took its toll, it clearly took its toll on Garrett.

GARRETT MORRIS:

I got so many years of Uncle Tom letters, especially when I did the monkey in *The Wiz.* I like to do stuff that's out of line. Nobody tells me how to think, not even black people, so that's why I did the monkey. The rest of them can kiss my ass. Now the same people who criticized me for doing the monkey in *The Wiz* are doing donkeys in *Shrek* and making millions of dollars. I guess that's what I get for being ahead of my time.

I had five years of building what everybody knows is a chair there, the only nonwhite chair in that whole thing, and I shed the blood for that. So at least if people don't want to say something good, they should not say anything at all, because I've done nothing to deserve anybody to come after me saying a lot of bullshit.

HARRY SHEARER:

I knew that everybody in the original cast had a five-year contract. And this was the fifth year. So I knew that, despite Billy and Gilda—you know, poor Gilda, but I called her up and went over to her place because I was trying to find some advice from everybody there as to what the fuck I should do. And Gilda just said, "Do whatever Lorne says"— which I understood, coming from her, but which was of no use to me.

FRED SILVERMAN:

Saturday Night Live was an enormous hit and a major profit center. It was the only show on the network that was reaching that particular demographic. I looked at *Saturday Night Live* and said, "Thank God it's here." And I really tried my best just to stay out of their way. And if they wanted to take some shots at me—fine, let them do it. I didn't care.

DICK EBERSOL:

Fred fired me in 1979, although he did not have the guts to do it himself. He had a triumvirate of folks do it. I was running comedy, variety, and specials at the time.

ALAN ZWEIBEL:

John was on the cover of *Newsweek* by himself when *Animal House* came out, and there wasn't anyone from the rest of the cast there with him. I think if there was a demarcation point, as far as I was concerned, that may have been it. Things changed. All of a sudden there was a world that was dangling temptations. John's a star now by himself, John's getting a million dollars or whatever it was, by himself. Gilda was given a one-woman show on Broadway. Billy did *Meatballs.* John did *Goin' South,* and he and Danny did the Blues Brothers movie. And I think those last few years that I was there, one of Lorne's greatest tasks was to keep everybody together. So it wasn't just, "Let's put on a fun show," it was, "Let's keep this together." And what happened was, there was a competition. There were studio executives starting to hang out in 8H during blocking asking, "Who wrote that sketch?" They were looking for sitcom writers or movie writers.

MARILYN SUZANNE MILLER:

Lorne died with the show. If things didn't go well, he torpedoed. They'd go up there in those first years immediately after the air show and watch the tape within seconds. In the earliest years, they were together night and day, day and night. At night it's the party; the next morning you'd go to the Russian Tea Room and have brunch. And it was always about, "We will try harder." Everybody was this animatronic personality who was going to do better, and it was all for the show, and giving up things for the show. The emotional component was so great for everyone involved.

DAN AYKROYD:

It's too stressful, because you worry about quality, you want things to be so right, and that really weighs heavily—plus the adrenaline pump, it's like being in combat or a cop or something. You can't take that week after week. It's a young man's game, there's no doubt about it. It is satisfying when you pull something off, and it is tremendously debilitating and anxiety-producing when you don't.

BILL MURRAY:

I only became sort of important to the show after Danny and John went to do *The Blues Brothers* and quit. When they were doing *The Blues Brothers,* all of a sudden I started getting a lot to do, and when they were gone, then I really got a lot to do. Then I was in lots and lots and lots and lots of sketches.

When you have this celebrity thing, different things change, your vision is different, and I was sort of like in the wake of all these people. I didn't have as many famous friends and I didn't necessarily work certain parts of town. So I was just doing what I was doing and happy enough to do that. I was still trying to be not-famous on some level— and I still was not-famous on some level—so I was able to enjoy that part of it and see that the famous part of it had its downside. I was busy mining the parts of my life where I was not famous, because I saw that those were not going to last forever.

Professionally, I just kept doing my job because I was pretty good at it, and I became valuable those last couple years, and I was proud of the work I did. I thought I worked hard. I was a little late sometimes, but I thought I worked pretty well and I never had like brawls or feuds with the girls or anything.

Even network executives became embroiled in backstage melodrama— especially toward the end of SNL's raucous infancy, when NBC was getting a double drubbing: terrible ratings in prime time and even worse press. Fred Silverman, having a spectacularly stormy reign as network president and already feeling under siege, saw Saturday Night Live *graduate from being a source of occasional irritation to being a major, gaping trouble spot. Al Franken picked this painful moment to compose a savage piece of satire called "Limo for a Lame-O," one of the meanest acts of character assassination in the history of—well, in the history of mean acts of character assassination. Franken, addressing the camera, told viewers Silverman had done a lousy job running the network and didn't deserve the limousine that was one of his lavish perks, whereas Franken, star of a hit show, did. He invited viewers to write to Silverman demanding that Franken be given the use of a limo. More than five thousand letters—nastily addressed to "The Lame-O"—deluged an infuriated Silverman's office.*

Already incensed about losing the Gilda Radner variety hour that he thought would rescue his regime, and assuming the Franken sketch to have been part of a staff conspiracy at Saturday Night Live, *Silverman broke off communication with Michaels and never consulted him about who his replacement as executive producer should be. Michaels wanted Franken. The "Limo" sketch certainly put the kibosh on that.*

LORNE MICHAELS:

I was going back and forth about whether to come back or not. All I really wanted was time. Since the election was coming up in the fall and they always threw us out of 8H for election coverage in those days, I was looking for some downtime after the season ended. I'd worked the summer before on Gilda's Broadway show, and I wanted this summer off, plus just a month or two of recovery time. So basically, I wanted to start up again after the 1980 election. That was what I wanted creatively. The business questions of what I wanted, or of what I have to this day, had been solved at the end of the third season, when my contract was first up. So it wasn't a money issue at all.

And that fifth season, Fred Silverman was running a *Best of Saturday Night Live* in prime time for thirteen weeks, so in every way we were at the peak of being exploited—or to put it another way, the peak of overexposure. We were limping to the finish line.

Gilda had said she would stay with me. There were a couple people I knew would still be there. But the big piece of information was that I was going to have to really recast and reinvent the show. I was going to have to fire some people, many of whom had lived up to the top of their talent, but the mistake was made five years earlier in the hiring. Quite often the least talented are the ones who most want you to know how loyal they are. And if I did return, I'd have to give up all thoughts of directing movies or whatever else I thought I might want to do with my life.

Brandon Tartikoff had been given the task of either trying to get me to come back or getting a replacement. I think he had more than enough problems with Silverman as it was. And Freddie was a screamer. I was supposed to have met with Fred, but he had stayed out late the night before and canceled the meeting. Bernie took this as a sign of lack of respect. I did know they were making Tom Snyder's new deal and Johnny Carson's new deal, so the emphasis seemed to be on on-air talent as opposed to dealing with a producer, which they weren't used to. It just wasn't a priority. I don't think they understood the part a producer played in that kind of a show.

Anyway, Fred apologized profusely and our meeting was resched-uled for the following Monday. That weekend, Al Franken does "Limo for a Lame-O," which is a direct fucking assault on Fred Sil-verman. I see it for the first time, as I do with "Update," at dress rehearsal. Brandon Tartikoff comes over to me, and he's laughing at it because it's very funny and it killed with the audience. I say to Bran-don and Barbara Gallagher, who worked directly for Fred, "You should let Fred know. Don't blindside him on this. You don't want to be sitting in your house and suddenly Al Franken is attacking Fred." But neither Brandon nor Barbara made the call—I think because, at the time, they were both frightened of him.

So what happens is, Fred Silverman *is* blindsided by this thing at home and goes into a complete rage. He thinks that I'm responding to his canceling the meeting with me by calling him a lame-o on national television. And what are you going to say—that it wasn't me? Then he'd think I'm such a wuss that I allow Al Franken to just steamroll me against my own better career instincts. Anyway, it all blows up and that's that. And then his hurt feelings lead to my hurt feelings. It all seemed to be end-of-season emotions, which are just end-of-season emotions—that time when you never want to see anybody again ever.

The upshot of it all was that Fred took it personally, and that put a further strain between him and me, and we never did meet.

FRED SILVERMAN:

I never liked Al Franken to begin with. You don't mind it if somebody like John Belushi gets up there and makes jokes about you, because I respected his talent and he was funny. But I thought this piece that Franken did was just very mean-spirited and not very funny. I don't think I called Lorne about it. I think I sent a letter, a note or something, to Franken and said in no uncertain terms that I thought he was way off base and that I wasn't going to forget it. And I believe he left the show shortly thereafter. I don't believe he stayed on the show very long. I don't think Lorne put the sketch in there to be mean. He never did a sketch to be mean. That was not his style. I never blamed Lorne personally.

WARREN LITTLEFIELD, *NBC Executive:*

Brandon was sitting in the audience and they had just done the "Limo" sketch and a page comes over and says, "Mr. Tartikoff, you have a phone call." And he says, "Who is it?" And the page goes, "A screaming Mr. Silverman." Brandon stopped for a second and then asked, "Did you tell him that you knew where I was?" The page said, "No, we were just told to find you." Brandon said, "Okay then, tell him you can't find me."

Brandon just couldn't take it. Here it was, midnight on Saturday night, and he just couldn't take Fred screaming at him at that hour. We always thought that was a wonderful lesson that Brandon was imparting to us about survival in the executive ranks.

BARBARA GALLAGHER, *NBC Vice President:*

I went to Lorne when I saw the "Limo for a Lame-O" sketch in rehearsal. He said, "Too much, huh?" I said, "Yes." He said, "Go talk to Franken." So I go over to Al, and Al goes, "Wasn't that the greatest?! Didn't you love it?!" I said, "Al, I'm not going to censor you, it's not my job. I'm just telling you it's pretty dicey right now. Fred's in a bad way, and this is really going to hurt him." And Al said, "Good, because he hurt Lorne." So I went back to Lorne, and Lorne said, "I'll take care of it."

Well, the bit was worse when it came on the air. I was home watching the show. The phone rang; it was Fred. When he couldn't get Brandon, he called me. He said, "Did you know about this?" I said, "I did." He said, "And you didn't do anything about it?" I said that I'd told Al we weren't going to censor him but that it was too much. Fred said, "You call Lorne and tell him how hurt I am and how could he do that, how could he let that go on at this time?" Fred had offered Lorne the world to stay on at *Saturday Night Live.* He wanted him to stay. He'd said, "Whatever you need, whatever you want—just stay."

So I call over to Lorne and Al gets on the phone and says, "So, Fred's pissed at me?" I said, "No, Al, he's not mad at *you.*" Al said, "Well, it's not Lorne's fault." I said, "Yeah, it is. He's the producer." Al said, "Lorne lets us do what we want to do." I said, "Fred is really hurt. If you heard his voice, he is really hurting." So Lorne gets on the phone. He says, "Is he mad?" I said, "No, he's hurt, and he's blaming you."

I was right in the middle of all this. And if you know me, I hate confrontation. I'm worse than Lorne. I will run 3,000 miles the other direction or get a root canal before I have a confrontation. I hate it. And I really like Lorne. We'd gotten along great.

But he has been cool to me now for a long time. I think he feels I betrayed him, and I didn't. I truly didn't. I was walking a fine line, and I was ready for a loony bin. It was horrible. I saw what was happening to Fred too. And if Lorne didn't take time off, Lorne would have been in a loony bin as well. He was hanging by a string, he was so tired. I frankly worried about him too. Both of them.

AL FRANKEN:

"Limo for a Lame-O" maybe had implications for what happened that next year, because I think it ruptured the relationship between Silverman and Lorne. Fred knew Lorne was leaving, but instead of going to Lorne and asking him who would be a good successor, Fred relied, I think, on Barbara Gallagher, who was a friend of Jean Doumanian's. So it sort of led to Jean's selection.

LORNE MICHAELS:

I'd given so much energy to holding things together all those years; I had been truly drained, just spent. I was just burnt out and emotionally very vulnerable. So I told Brandon I couldn't do another year. He didn't try and change my mind, and I said to myself, "All right, I guess that's it. I've done my five years." It was very hard for me. In retrospect, to be relieved of the show was an emotional withdrawal that took me, truly, years to get a perspective on.

I began looking at studio deals and went back and forth between Paramount and Warner Brothers. And I met with Jean Doumanian about it and I said, "If I go to Paramount, I'd love you to come with me." And she implied yes—that's what I came away with. Several weeks later, I was on my way to the opening of *Urban Cowboy* when I got a phone call from Brandon saying, "I'm going to name Jean Doumanian as the next producer of the show." I go, "Really. That's an interesting choice." I was startled because I always think of the show as a writer-based show, and you have to be a writer to say what is funny or not funny. To control that many people in comedy without having any credits yourself in comedy is impossible.

Jean called me five minutes after Brandon did. I asked her, "When did they talk to you?" and she said, "Six weeks ago." That was the part where I went, *"Wha—?"* And then she said, "They made me promise not to talk to you." That was the very first moment of my growing up: "They asked me not to talk to you."

And this was when I'd been talking to her about coming to Paramount with me. Now Brandon was not an innocent in all of this. I don't mean that meanly. I mean it in the sense that I had thought, because he and I were friendly, that he would at least listen to me about my replacement. I had told him I would use some combination of Jim Downey and Al Franken and Tom Davis, because it had to be someone with writing credentials who understood how the show really worked. Jean wasn't even there for meetings between dress and air.

BARBARA GALLAGHER:

It wasn't a conspiracy to do Lorne in. Lorne was leaving. He wanted Al, Fred wasn't buying it, so there we were. They also didn't want to leak it to the press, they didn't want anyone to know yet, and if Lorne knew, it would have been all over the town. So that was the reason for not telling him. It wasn't a conspiracy to do anything to Lorne.

FRED SILVERMAN:

The decision to hire Jean Doumanian was made by Brandon Tartikoff based on a recommendation from Barbara Gallagher. I didn't know Jean. I knew she had worked with Woody Allen. I said, "If you recommend her, fine."

BARBARA GALLAGHER:

Lorne didn't want Jean Doumanian in there for some reason, probably because she's not a writer. But Fred Silverman did not want an outsider coming in. He wanted someone from the show, who'd been with the show. And Jean had been there forever, worked with the talent, and Jean wanted the job. I said, "Jean, I'll talk to Fred about it." Lorne wanted Al Franken and Tom Davis to produce the show, and Fred said no, he didn't want Al, because of what they'd gone through.

Brandon was there at the time, and I said the only other person down there who knows how to run the show because she's been sitting there all the time, although she's not a writer, is Jean. And he said, "Oh, all right, let's run it by Fred." I said, "I know Lorne doesn't want her, so if you tell Lorne, you're going to have a big craziness going on." Fred said, "Well, if that's the only person down there and you think she'll be all right." And I said, "Everyone likes her, they all know her, what problem could it be?"

ROBIN SHLIEN:

Woody Allen was best friends with Jean Doumanian, who was the associate producer when I was there, and he would call the control room constantly and talk to her. Woody Allen would always call as "Mo Golden." And the second day I was there, I got this call for Jean Doumanian and had to say, "Jean, it's Mo Golden calling." We always had to answer the control room phone. I didn't think anything of it, and then somebody said, "It's Woody Allen."

We never knew if she knew that we knew. We had to pretend that we all thought this guy calling her was Mo Golden and not Woody Allen. He called all the time. Sometimes it was like every five minutes. And we were just like, "What the fuck?"

JAMES DOWNEY:

Jean was like a fashion person. It was all about restaurants and clothes and stuff. She didn't seem to me to have much of a sense of humor. The only time I've gone to a party where I was kind of awe-struck was when she called me and said, "Woody Allen's going to have a party," and Woody apparently never had parties. And when she called me she said, "Don't tell anybody else." It was like 1980, '81, and I went with my college girlfriend. It was in Woody's house, I thought it was his house, because it was a town house. You went upstairs. You actually met him at the door and he like stayed there the whole evening with Jean, who would assure him that whoever came through the door was not a dangerous or menacing person.

Walt Frazier was the first person I saw, then John Lindsay. It was a very New York thing, and the best collection of camera-shy, publicity-shy, retiring type people I'd ever seen. Paul Newman was there, Truman Capote, even Jackie Kennedy.

In one of the last sketches of Saturday Night Live's *fifth season, Laraine Newman played a noblewoman, Garrett Morris played a butler, writers Jim Downey and Tom Davis played Lords Worcestershire and Wilkinson—of sauce and razor-blade fame, respectively—Jane Curtin was Lady Wilkinson, Bill Murray played the Earl of Sandwich ("I'm afraid nothing has been named after a member of my family," he lamented), his brother Brian Doyle-Murray was a servant, and host Buck Henry joined Gilda Radner to play the principal characters of the sketch, Lord and Lady Douchebag. The setting was the manor of Lord Salisbury, whose steaks were served to the guests, and the year 1730. "My dear Sandwich," said Henry, in character, "Parliament has always had its share of Douchebags, and it always will."*

And on this mildly satirical and intentionally ridiculous note, what was left of the original cast and creators of Saturday Night Live *would soon part, never to perform together again. The stakes were being pulled up and the circus was leaving town. It was May 24, 1980, the end of the fifth season but also of an era. Lorne ended the last show on a shot of the* ON AIR *sign going off.*

JEAN DOUMANIAN:

I think Lorne would've stayed on, but NBC wouldn't give him the deal he wanted. So he went away. Lorne wasn't very happy about me getting the job. Because after all, it was Lorne's baby, and he wanted Franken and Davis to get it. But Silverman didn't want them, and Brandon didn't want them either. They thought that I could do it.

I had been in every writers' meeting when Lorne was producing. I had seen how the writing was done. Besides, Lorne really wasn't writing, he was editing and selecting. I took the job because I thought it would be a challenge. There was no other woman doing a live ninety-minute television show, and I wanted to see if I could do it. I did want to keep several writers, but I think everybody was advised not to stay on. I don't know who advised them, but four writers said they would stay, and then they had a change of heart and came back and said they couldn't. In fact, everybody who said they would stay reneged once word got out.

LORNE MICHAELS:

I had no problem with people staying with their jobs. That was not a problem for me. I think in the case of Franken, Davis, Downey, and a couple others who were the people I had nominated to succeed me, because they embodied the writing perspective, Jean didn't want them. What happened was, everyone got a memo from Jean to clear out their offices by July. Now this had been a group that had lived there for five years. That was what killed everything, when she made that one big mistake. It was a signal of, you know, "a new broom." I didn't get the memo, because I'd left. For guys like Franken and that, it was the first sign that they weren't even being considered to stay.

LARAINE NEWMAN:

I was dying to go home. On the other hand, I knew, having grown up in Los Angeles, what it was like to have been on a series and to no longer be on one. I knew what it was that I was facing, to have been on a hit show and then be an unemployed actor. So I was a little worried about that. Mostly I was glad to be back in L.A., because I love New York for about five days, but after that it's just utter toil. I came from a car culture. Not to be able to drive myself around is like imprisonment to me.

JANE CURTIN:

I was happy to move on, I was tired. You get very burned out after doing something like that. And you get very jaded. It was very hard to deal with going from relative obscurity to everybody knowing who you are. I had to deal with what I had become. It was hard to deal with on the show, because you were busy doing the show—so I had to come to terms with what I had become and try to adjust to that. I needed time off.

ALAN ZWEIBEL:

I left when Lorne left, in May of 1980, and I was there from day one, which was July '75. What had happened was the show changed. It stopped being fun the way it was originally. At the risk of sounding naive, this is what was going through our minds at the time, and it was only after all of us left that there was some perspective on it. We were all these neophytes that got together. You know, it was Marilyn Miller saying, "Hey kids, let's put on a show." Nothing was sacred, and we had fun.

ROBIN SHLIEN:

I dream about those days, actually. I dream about those people a lot. When I was transitioning into my new career I had a lot of dreams from that old time. As a psychotherapist, I realize what an amazing and important life experience it was for me and I think for everybody else who worked during that time there. I now give talks on therapeutic humor, and I'm always thinking about the time that I was in a work situation where I had so much laughter in a day. Working on that show gave me great confidence in my own sense of humor, because I was able to make people like John Belushi laugh.

JAMES DOWNEY:

We all left in 1980. The cast and the writers all sort of agreed we would leave and take the show with us.

In fairness you'd have to say that the only reason we're even talking about this, the only reason the show's still on the air, is because of what went on in the first five years. First, it gave it this tremendous momentum that it could survive anything, like the Jean Doumanian period or some other bad period. Then it reached the point where it was beyond good or bad. Gilbert Gottfried said a great thing one time; he said at this point "it's just a restaurant in a good location." But even so, it's a good location because of those first five years. It had been a blighted neighborhood. It was Saturday night, when no one was watching TV and they were showing reruns of Johnny Carson. And so it was gentrified. People went in there and did the equivalent of cleaning up vacant lots and forming neighborhood watch committees and just spiffed it up and took a chance and turned it around.

ROSIE SHUSTER:

I left at the end of year five—after the first five years that Lorne did. After that, the Ayatollah Doumanian came in.

ANNE BEATTS:

Lorne sheltered us from the realities of show business. It's interesting, because while some people might have thought *SNL* was a dangerous world, I think in many ways it was a very safe world. We were protected. We were in this little cocoon in the RCA Building. We were pampered, and we got our way most of the time. When I got to Hollywood and found out the harsh truths, I wasn't really prepared.

BILL MURRAY:

I was definitely going to go when everyone else left. I'd been at Second City when that sort of thing happened. I knew there was no point in being the one guy who knows how to do it. You've got to get the hell out of there. It's a little like *Lifeboat,* you know. It was just time to go. I would never have wanted to start up with a whole new group.

It was really a great thing to be a part of it. The fact that it was live made it performance-driven. You were always pushing yourself physically to keep your spirit going and get out there and do it. The writing had to be good too. It was great fun—and really hard work. That's the part nobody seems to know: how hard it was, what it was like to be young and exhausted all the time. Lorne did build in this great thing where we had every fourth week off. We all got a chance to blow off some steam and to rest. After three weeks, we'd be pretty beaten down. We'd come walking in there on our knuckles or our knees.

When the show ended, it was difficult for some of us in the outside world—difficult for each person relative to how much they'd already been working on the outside. None of us wanted any TV jobs, because we'd had the best TV jobs there were. Once you saw what the other jobs were like, you knew they were not half as much fun as *Saturday Night Live* had been. On sitcoms, you're working on these little bitty scripts for hours and hours and hours. They just keep shooting and shooting and shooting. Ours was the best situation because you had the pressure of having to do it when the time came. Then at one o'clock in the morning, you were done. It was over. So nobody wanted regular TV or prime time. We'd all made more money than we needed in the short term, so we just went out there and got into the movie business.

KATE JACKSON:

After I had hosted the show, we went to the bar that John and Dan owned. And Joni Mitchell was there, and there were musicians and other writers, and it was a terrific group of people to be around in such a small room. But it got to be time for me to leave, because I had an early flight in the morning, and Billy Murray walked me out to the car. I got in and closed the door and as we were beginning to pull out, I turned around and looked behind me and there was Billy, standing in the street, waving. Snow was falling all around him—just the sweetest thing. I had been terrified of hosting. I was so afraid. But I knew that I had to do it, it was one of those things where you're really afraid to do something and you know you have to take the chance. You just have to push yourself and do it. And I remember saying to a friend of mine who went with me, "Well, I'll never do that again, because it will never get that good again. That was as good as it gets."

LORNE MICHAELS:

I took my name off the show and I left.

3

The Stars Come Out: 1980–1985

PAM NORRIS, *Writer:*

I have my personal conspiracy theory, which is that whoever came in after Lorne and the original cast was going to be killed—because, you know, you can't replace the Beatles. Somebody thought, "Well, we'll just let things get extremely bad, and then when we pull it back up a little bit afterward, it'll be considered a triumph."

BARBARA GALLAGHER, *NBC Vice President:*

I said to Jean Doumanian, "Look, I think you can have it, but if I were you, I wouldn't take it. First of all, the network is going to jump on you like a bad suit. They'll want to cut the budget, I can tell you right now, and they're going to cut it to the bone. They have been waiting all this time to get even with Lorne."

I knew that because after they had squeezed Lorne at the beginning, he told me he was going to let them have it when it became a hit, and he did. He started demanding things. And when you're a hit, you get them, especially when you have advertisers scrambling to be part of the show.

I remember telling Jean, "Any producer who comes in here now is doomed to fail. It's not going to work."

JEAN DOUMANIAN, *Executive Producer:*

I had to get an all-new cast and all-new writers in two and a half months. When I took over the show, the first thing they did was cut my budget. The budget under Lorne had gotten up to a million dollars a show. They cut my budget to $350,000, as I recall. And I was supposed to do the same show for that amount of money.

I don't know this for a fact, but it would seem to me that if a woman could actually mount a show and get it done in such a short time, it minimized the importance of those who preceded her. And nobody liked that. So I was attacked viciously. How dare I take this job? How dare I think I can do the show? Most of that was said by men. You have to remember, the show had been biased against women for a long time.

ALAN ZWEIBEL, *Writer:*

When we left, I remember Gilda would call me up on Tuesday nights at two in the morning and we'd still be up because our bodies for five years had been up all night on Tuesday, staying up and writing.

LORNE MICHAELS, *Executive Producer:*

I never watched Jean's show. I didn't watch it when Dick was running it either. I never watched it that whole time. Not once. It would have been too painful. I didn't have anything to do with the show, so I didn't feel compromised. To walk away clean is at least to have your honor intact, and I felt I'd taken the honorable way out.

The Jean Doumanian era—all ten months of it—marked the first but not last time Saturday Night Live's *very survival was at stake. After five years of enormous and trendsetting popularity—replete with breakout stars, iconic characters, and now-classic sketches—the show zapped back to square one in 1980 following the departures of Lorne Michaels, the cast he had assembled, and all the original writers.*

Viewers may not have been immersed in the backstage politics, but they couldn't help noticing that the quality of the show plummeted. Many in the business thought Doumanian lacked the experience and expertise necessary for the job. She was further beset by skullduggery among staff members who wanted the usurper ousted from the throne almost the instant she assumed it.

NBC was doing badly in prime time, and within weeks of Doumanian's accession, Saturday Night Live *was added to the network's list of gaping wounds requiring medical attention. An audience that expected to see fresh new Gildas, Belushis, Chevys, and Aykroyds refused to settle for the paltry replacements that initially dominated Doumanian's cast—Charles Rocket, Denny Dillon, Gail Matthius, Ann Risley.*

Saturday Night Live fell apart in less time than it took to come together five years earlier. The show still had no real competition in its time period—"Our competition is sleep," as one cast member put it—but its predicament was perhaps worse than if it had. Saturday Night Live was competing against the memory of itself. And losing.

JOE PISCOPO, *Cast Member:*

When we came in—after Lorne and all the original guys had left—the offices were completely empty. They even cleaned all the desks out. The pencils were gone. And when I tell you pencils, I'm not exaggerating. The offices were all reconfigured. It was like somebody came up there and just kind of bombed out everything, man. It was pretty wild.

ANDREW KURTZMAN, *Writer:*

I think we had the feeling of being a bit beside the point. Coming in the aftermath of this big cultural juggernaut—the first five years of the show—we were a little like the guy with the handcart behind the locomotive. *Saturday Night Live* had its own mythology in place. The big show had left town. We had a certain cheese-ball feel. It was hard work to book guest hosts for a while. "Pamela Sue Martin's on the bubble, but she might say yes"—that kind of thing. You never really had the feeling that you could open your suit on the observation deck of the Empire State Building and yell, "I own this town," because people were always saying, "Yeah, but you weren't nearly as good as the original show."

BILL MURRAY, *Cast Member:*

I knew Jean and liked her. I'd known her a long time. I'm not sure that she did the worst job in the world. They gave her no credit for trying. She had great connections in the music world and she got some great acts for the show. They didn't really give her a full shot.

She did find Eddie Murphy and a couple other people who were really talented; they just needed some confidence. She was struggling, and they were having a hard time getting quality hosts. So I called up and I said, "I can't get arrested. Is there any way I could work on your show?" So I went in there. It was a tough week. We worked really hard writing and rewriting, and the show turned out good, and I thought, "This could work."

The cast saw how hard you have to work to do that show. I don't think most of them ever worked that hard before. They were going through their first brush with fame, even at the level they were at. The world just wasn't ready for a brand-new group, so it was incredibly tough for them.

ANDREW SMITH, *Writer:*

If you want to get philosophical about the problems of the subsequent years after the first five years, the actors were so cognizant of the success of the group that had gone before them — that Chevy and John and Gilda had broken out into these huge stars — that they began to have one eye on the audience and on the fact that Steven Spielberg might be watching, and only one eye on being funny. The first group that came through before me didn't know how big they were going to be, so they were much freer and much more open and thus, I thought, a lot funnier than the subsequent people.

As soon as *SNL* or the Not Ready for Prime Time Players became a launching pad, then it wasn't about just the comedy that was happening there. It was about future earnings or future career moves. And that's kind of the cancer that is always threatening to eat away at the comedy on the show, even to this day. God knows, if I was an actor, I would feel the same way. It's like a loss of innocence. You can't not think about the fact that if you make the right moves on *Saturday Night Live,* you could become a huge, huge star. And so therefore when somebody wants you to play a turtle or something like that, you say, "Well, I don't know. I don't think that would look good." I bet if those original guys knew how big they were going to be, they probably wouldn't have done Killer Bees.

GILBERT GOTTFRIED, *Cast Member:*

Back then it was a big deal that the cast was changing and the producer was changing. Before we even hit the air, there were already articles being written in every paper and every magazine saying disaster was coming and how dare they continue *Saturday Night Live* with a different cast? And that this producer is not equipped to do the job and this cast is terrible.

DAVID SHEFFIELD, *Writer:*

A friend of mine named Patrick was auditioning as an actor on the show. Patrick got his big break as a men's-room attendant at Studio 54. He worked the stalls there a bit. He knew everybody. I think he actually had an agent at that point. He got an audition and called me and said if I would write some material for him, he would see the producers got it. I wrote a couple of sketches, thinking nothing would come of it. He called back and said, "They love your stuff, man, they want to hire you." I said, "*Who* wants to hire me?" He said, "I don't know, some guy with glasses." That guy turned out to be Jean Doumanian's producer.

CHRIS ALBRECHT, *Agent, Comedy Club Manager:*

I became an agent at ICM in 1980. My client list as an agent included people like Jim Carrey, Whoopi Goldberg, Billy Crystal, Dana Carvey, Paul Rodriguez, Sandra Bernhard, Keenan Ivory Wayans, Joe Piscopo, and other people. I actually ended up putting a lot of people on that very ill-fated Jean Doumanian one-year tenure. The fact that there were new opportunities for *Saturday Night Live,* that they were going to recast this quickly legendary show, made for very exciting times.

BARRY BLAUSTEIN, *Writer:*

When I got there the first day and I was taking off my jacket, a writer from the office next door came in and said, "I want you to sign a petition to get rid of Jean Doumanian." It was total turmoil already.

I think one of the reasons David Sheffield and I survived that year is we stayed away from the turmoil as much as possible. We just concentrated on the writing and not the politics. Everyone was bitching and no one was writing.

Dave had worked in local television in Mississippi; I had worked on *The Mike Douglas Show* in L.A. We were hired separately. We met on the show. We were the last writers hired that year, as a matter of fact, and I think we both realized what a tremendous break and opportunity this was for us. We were surrounded by people going, "I don't need this job! I don't need this job! To hell with this!" And I was thinking, "I *do* need this job. This is the big break. This is the big opportunity."

JEAN DOUMANIAN:

I made Barry and David write together. Barry's Jewish humor was wonderful, and David's southern humor was great as well, but very different. And they were both very smart guys. I thought between the two of them, they'd come up with something that was really original. I think they're still together on things. I was also very lucky to have Pam Norris as one of my writers. She was a terrific writer, and quite an individual.

PAM NORRIS:

I had been at the *Harvard Lampoon,* and this was before the *Harvard Lampoon* was a rocket—when the people working there were goofing off, basically, when you were supposed to be doing something else and instead you were goofing off with the *Harvard Lampoon.* But there was a writer on the original show, Jim Downey, who had seen some of my stuff in the *Harvard Lampoon.* And he encouraged me to think about going to the show, and he put in a good word for me with Jean Doumanian.

I was working on Wall Street that summer and had not finished Harvard. So I wrote a few sketches and sent them over there, got interviewed, and got the job. I finally finished college during the writers' strike of 1981, when I went back to Harvard. Actually, my diploma was mailed to me. I didn't get my Harvard diploma handed to me in Harvard Yard; it was handed to me by a production assistant at *Saturday Night Live,* with very little ceremony.

DAVID SHEFFIELD:

I have mixed feelings about Jean. She gave me my first big break at the networks, and for that I'm eternally grateful, and she had an eye for talent—like finding Joe Piscopo. Her background was in talent, because she was the talent booker for the show, so you could see the network's logic. They were losing Lorne and they wanted to maintain continuity.

But Jean knew zilch about comedy. She didn't have a clue. It was almost a lesson in how not to run a comedy show. She had a knack for pitting people against each other that was just antithetical to comedy. I don't know why she thought that was a good way to work. She actually started rivalries where none existed before among the writers and cast, thinking somehow the strongest would prevail. That was *not* a formula for comedy.

JOE PISCOPO:

I didn't want the job as a cast member on the show. And I told my agent at the time, Chris Albrecht, "I can't do the show, man." I'd be taking a pay cut, because I was making more money doing commercials — just being the working stiff — and I said, "I don't want to do this." But he said, "You've got to do it, it's *Saturday Night Live*."

HARRY SHEARER, *Cast Member:*

I went to Jean and said, "I know you're not a fan of Lorne's, and you know that I'm not a fan of Lorne's, so you're not going to have a loyalist sitting around saying, 'Lorne wouldn't have done it this way.'" I told her, "I'm willing to come work on your show. I think you really need to get some people around us, if you want me to come, who've got some experience, because you're not going to have the slack that Lorne had at the beginning. You're going to have to hit the ground running." I suggested Christopher Guest and a couple others as people who should come in, and she said, "I'm not really sure I want people who know what they're doing." At that point, I knew I wasn't coming back.

GILBERT GOTTFRIED:

If they just did reviews of the show and said it sucked, they would have been right. But the articles were like a whole other thing. It became like, even though the writers going in were considered terrible writers because she hired them, the minute she'd fire them, all of a sudden they became great writers. There was even an article in *People* magazine about three writers as if, because they were fired, that made them great, and they talk about how terrible she was. It was a weird period.

JEAN DOUMANIAN:

Even the censors became very, very tough on me. I couldn't say something like "rolling off a log." They thought there was an innuendo there. Then you think about what we got away with from '75 to '80. I mean, we were saying things like "golden shower" and they didn't do anything about it. But the censors really became so tough on us, it was incredible.

PAM NORRIS:

I think a lot of people were there saying, "Why couldn't I have been on the *good* show?" And it's like, why don't you make a good show yourself? One person has a tremendous amount of power at that show. At least they did when I was there. One person can write a great sketch. One person can write two great sketches. One person can write three great sketches. I mean, if you can sit down and write, you know, seventy minutes of pretty good material, you could have the whole show. So I just felt that when writers complained about things, they could have been writing something.

GILBERT GOTTFRIED:

Basically on that show they hire you as a performer and expect you to be an unpaid writer. They didn't use me that much. I think the low point of what the writers thought of me was in one sketch. It was a funeral scene, and they used me as the corpse.

BARRY BLAUSTEIN:

Some people say Woody Allen was kind of a hidden producer of the show that year, because he was a friend of Jean's and he supposedly had an adviser role. But we never saw him.

JEAN DOUMANIAN:

Woody Allen was not involved in the show in any way. I say that unequivocally. You can put that to rest. He was not involved at all, aside from the fact that he was a friend.

PAM NORRIS:

I lived in those offices for a long time. They had a great shower. And they had a color TV and food and soda, and I found myself staying later and later every night, and finally I just said, "Oh, what the hell," and I moved in. I don't think anybody knew that I was living there. What made it really great is that they had this bank of metal file cabinets—down next to where the secretaries typed the scripts—that had every sketch that had ever been written for the show filed away in them. And this is every sketch ever *written,* not just every sketch ever aired. So I had the access to what seemed like the Rosetta stone to me—every sketch written and rejected for the first show, every sketch written and rejected for the second show. It was all this very seminal material by the people who became, you know, gods and goddesses. And that was an amazing experience.

JEAN DOUMANIAN:

My numbers weren't bad at all, considering it was a new show with a whole new cast. Some of them, I think, were higher than the last of Lorne's, because the last year of Lorne's regime was not as good as one would expect. They were all thinking about what the future was going to be.

BARRY BLAUSTEIN:

One executive from the network called me and Dave into his office and said, "I want to show you something." And he shows us this footage of a boa constrictor eating a mouse. And he says, "This is exactly what we should be doing on the show." It was such a bizarre meeting.

JEAN DOUMANIAN:

I was so busy doing my job that I never saw any writing on the wall. I thought the shows were getting better. We were all working so hard. I was really not aware of anything going on behind the scenes. That's how unaware I was. I was putting in eighteen hours a day, easy. I knew I could do it.

JOE PISCOPO:

I could never describe to you in words how painful those first ten months really were. You just knew that this was America's favorite television show, and yet here we were, taking it right into the toilet.

Saturday night, after the show, it was pretty much like a funeral, like you were mourning. Oh my God, oh my God, did we really do this, oh my God—and then we had to turn it around on Monday all over again.

Hopeless as the situation seemed, Doumanian actually had a tremendous secret weapon in her arsenal—so secret that, sadly for her, even she didn't realize it. This was a young, brash cast member who spent most of the season in small bit parts, except in the seventeenth-floor offices, where he kept coworkers continuously entertained. He was not a "great white hope." Au contraire. *Definitely great, however. His day would come, but not in time to save the very doomed Doumanian.*

NEIL LEVY, *Talent Coordinator:*

Jean had cast an actor named Robert Townsend to be "the black guy" on the show. And then this guy Eddie Murphy started calling me—it sounded like from a pay phone—and I told him, "I'm sorry, we're not auditioning anymore." But he called again the next day, and he would go into this whole thing about how he had eighteen brothers and sisters and they were counting on him to get this job. And he would call every day for about a week. And I finally decided I would use him as an extra.

So I brought him in for an audition, and he did a four-minute piece of him acting out three characters up in Harlem—one guy was instigating the others to fight—and it was absolutely brilliant. The timing, the characterizations—talent was just shooting out of him. And I went, "Wow," and I took him in to Jean and I said, "Jean, you've got to see this." He did his audition for Jean, and she sent him out of the room and she said to me, "Well, he's good, but I like Robert Townsend better." And I went nuts, you know. I threatened to quit. At that point there were so many mistakes, I was actually heartbroken, because I'd been on the original show, and it went beyond mistakes for me. It was like there was a spirit that I knew that existed in that show and she had no idea what that was, and she was missing it. She would choose Robert Townsend over Eddie Murphy—not that Robert Townsend isn't great, a good actor, but the difference in terms of what was right for that show was so obvious, and compounded with all the other crap that was going on, I couldn't take it.

So she hired Eddie as a featured player just to spite me. He was the only featured player that year. He should've been a regular. She hired him only because I pressured her, and then to spite me she wouldn't make him a regular. She only wanted to hire one black actor and Townsend hadn't signed his contract yet, so she signed Eddie.

The point of it is that she didn't want him, and she's been claiming that she discovered him for years. Now Ebersol I heard is claiming he discovered him, and Ebersol wasn't even on the show when Eddie came. But Ebersol used to take credit for all the Not Ready for Prime Time Players, so that doesn't surprise me.

JAMES DOWNEY, *Writer:*

When I first met Eddie Murphy, I was up there visiting Jean—I'd recommended a couple of writers to her—and Eddie was hanging around. He'd been hired as a featured player, but he would just go around to everyone's office and make everybody laugh. He made me laugh the first day I met him. And he was just so clearly the funniest person on the floor. I remember saying to Jean Doumanian, "You've got to use this kid Eddie Murphy, you've *got* to put him on." And I remember her going, "He's not ready."

JEAN DOUMANIAN:

I didn't have enough of a budget to put Eddie on as a member of the cast, because I had already selected the cast when I auditioned him. So I let him be a featured player. They said okay. After the first two shows, I said to the administration, "Listen, you have to make this guy a member of the cast, you just have to, he's so great." He was eighteen when I found him. They finally said okay. And then I found out from Eddie that a network vice president was trying to tell him to leave the show and that he'd get him a sitcom on NBC. But Eddie wouldn't do it.

NEIL LEVY:

One night Jean was five minutes short in the show. She had nothing, whereas Lorne always had something in the bag, a short film, something so you go over instead of under. If you're under you're left with nothing, and she had nothing. This is fifteen minutes before the end of the show when Audrey Dickman, who was timing it, realized it was going to run short. Dave Wilson was sitting there saying, "What are we going to do, Jean?" And she was pacing and she didn't know what to do. And I remembered Eddie's monologue from his audition like three months earlier. So I said, "Why don't you see if Eddie can do the monologue that he did for his audition?" And she said, "Oh no, that won't work." And then about a minute later, she said, "Why don't we get Eddie and he'll do the audition piece?" And they laughed in the booth, and I said, "Yeah, okay, great."

And I ran up and I found Eddie and I asked him. And his face lit up like he'd been waiting for this moment his whole life, and he said, "Yeah!" So we rushed him downstairs and he did that piece. And in another week or two, I think, he was made a regular.

Doumanian's fate was sealed on a night in late February 1981. Charlie Rocket was playing the victim of a shooting in a show-length spoof of the then-popular prime-time soap opera Dallas *and its famous "Who shot J.R.?" cliffhanger. Mere minutes before the one A.M. closing time, Rocket, in a wheelchair ostensibly because of injuries suffered in the assassination attempt, complained about having been shot and said—for all those watching at home and in the studio to hear—"I'd like to know who the fuck did it."*

FRED SILVERMAN, *NBC President:*

Doumanian got out of control. I think the thing that really did it was that there was a kid on the show by the name of Charlie Rocket, and one night he did the unpardonable: He said the fuck-word on live television, and it went out to the whole network. And that was it. I said, "Who needs this aggravation?" I think we'd made the decision even before then that we had to get rid of her. This woman was a train wreck, and the shows were just not watchable.

GILBERT GOTTFRIED:

I was sitting in the offices talking to Eddie one day, when all of a sudden some woman comes in and says, "Eddie, somebody from NBC wants to speak to you." And he gets on the phone and he goes, "Yes, yeah, okay, no. No, I won't tell anybody." And he hangs up. Before the phone even hits the cradle, he tells me, "Jean Doumanian's been fired."

The next day or so, Jean Doumanian was going to make this announcement to the cast and crew that she'd been fired, but by then everyone knew it. And it was weird, because they had this improv teacher named Del Close hired there for some reason, and so she calls everyone into her office, and everyone's sitting there, and she's tearfully telling everyone that she's been fired and everything but that she wishes everyone the best and whatnot. And, in the midst of all this, all of a sudden they walk in with a cake, singing "Happy Birthday," and it's put in front of this Del Close guy. It was a very surreal situation.

JEAN DOUMANIAN:

I was down in Irwin Segelstein's office for maybe four hours, trying to convince him to please give us more money for the show, but I also found out that some of the people on my show, that I'd hired and helped, were going downstairs and talking to the brass behind my back. I don't know this for a fact, but I was told. They were really sabotaging the show and me.

He had sent me some wine when I got the job, as a congratulatory thing. But before I told anybody anything, I broke open about five bottles of wine and I said, "Everybody, come on in. I have something to tell you, and don't be upset about it, because I'm not upset about it. I just want to tell you you've done a wonderful job. I think you're all terrific. I want you all to go on and try to make the best of it, but they told me that I've served my purpose and that's it for me." And that was it. In retrospect, I think really they put me in there on purpose, because after a very successful show, the second guy usually fails and then the third guy comes in, takes over, and succeeds.

PAM NORRIS:

I've sort of learned, in the subsequent twenty years I've been in show business, that people just aren't that clever, and sometimes things that look like clever schemes are just people stumbling over their own feet.

CHRIS ALBRECHT:

In retrospect, what Jean did was just take the hit that was going to come to anybody who was going to try to recast that show with new stars. I liked Jean. I really did. She was very direct. She had bad press and not a lot of support from the network. I'm not so sure it's not tough being a woman in that job.

JEAN DOUMANIAN:

I must say, my friends were very happy that that part of my life had ended. Because they thought I was working so hard and I was so determined that they were concerned about my health. But I was really disappointed. I thought Brandon and the network were going to stick behind me, and they didn't at all. If you read the newspapers, they didn't support me at all. So that's when I kind of discovered that I had been used. I don't consider that show a failure for myself. I consider it truly an accomplishment.

GILBERT GOTTFRIED:

After I was fired from the show, I kind of was like walking around with this feeling that everybody was looking at me going, "Oh, that's the guy who was on a bad season on *Saturday Night*." I hated it for the longest time when someone would recognize me from *Saturday Night*.

Network chief Brandon Tartikoff felt an emotional attachment to the show and desperately wanted to keep it on the air, even when other network executives advocated cutting the umbilical and letting it float off into space. In his desperation, Tartikoff turned to old pal and fellow Yalie Dick Ebersol, a man who had never produced a comedy show or professionally written a sketch in his life and who, in fact, had not so long ago been fired from an NBC executive post by Tartikoff's bellicose boss, Fred Silverman. But Brandon's friend had also been present at, and instrumental in, the creation of Saturday Night Live. *The embalming process was halted and shock therapy began.*

Michaels and Ebersol had little in common when it came to style and personality, but they did have this: Each thought the other wanted too much credit for the creation of Saturday Night Live. *It took both of them working together at the very outset to bring* Saturday Night Live *to life, but once it premiered, Michaels would have preferred Ebersol to have disappeared.*

When Ebersol was asked to rescue the show after the Doumanian cliff-hanger, he wisely sought Michaels's approval and blessing before taking over. That meant that creative people loyal to Michaels wouldn't feel they were committing heresy or poking him in the eye if they went to work on the Ebersol version—a problem that had reputedly helped sink Doumanian.

Though Michaels and Ebersol weren't close, they were both close to Tartikoff, who felt the show represented more to the network than a profit center; it was a badge of honor too, and Tartikoff was one network executive who cared about prestige in addition to profits. For Ebersol, the situation was rife with irony. After helping create the show in 1974 and then being sentenced to a certain anonymity for his efforts, he would be called back to keep the show going by his old nemesis Fred Silverman, the guy who fired him. And Tartikoff, the longtime friend who did the actual recruitment of Ebersol, had become head of programming when Ebersol was passed over for the job.

What Ebersol lacked in imagination, he made up for in iron-willed determination. Swinging a baseball bat or just lugging it around like some swollen scepter, Ebersol pitched a ferocious battle to make Satur-day Night Live *a hit again. He would save the show, whatever it took.*

DICK EBERSOL, *NBC Executive:*

I remember Jean's last show. It was just beset with problems. It was the night that Charlie Rocket said "fuck" on the air. And I stayed up with Brandon quite late, and he asked me again, "Would you consider fixing it?" I said I would come as long as I could hide inside 30 Rock, watching on the internal system how the show works, the camera blocking, watch to see if the talent is mature enough to save a piece, because I could think of a million pieces from the earliest days of the show which absolutely sucked on Wednesday and had at least an

80 percent life by the time they went on the air. The talent was that good, and some of the writers were good enough to fix it.

And I said, "Number one, only if it goes off the air. This is not something you can fix in a week. And number two, I get to pick what airs all the weeks it's off the air." I wanted to put on four or five of the greatest shows from the first five years, just to get people back in the sense of "this show was *about* something." Actually, I think I said to take it off for two months.

So this meeting was set up in Fred Silverman's apartment on a Sunday afternoon. And Fred is so uncomfortable to have me there, because there is no love lost between the two of us and I just did not respect him. So they go through this whole thing about will I do it, and I said, "Yeah, under certain circumstances." And we argued and debated, and finally it became five weeks that the show would be off the air. I didn't want a lot of money; I just wanted a guarantee that I would get series commitments for every year that we managed to keep the show alive, and this would be stuff I would develop myself. That's how *Friday Night Videos* and the Bob Costas talk show *Later* came to be. And finally, I said, there was one last condition: "We don't have a deal until I have a conversation with Lorne. I'm not doing this show unless Lorne wants it to survive." And Fred felt like he had really been set up. He wasn't happy, but he grudgingly said, "All right. But I want to know where this is tomorrow."

I called Lorne and we went to dinner and wound up over at his apartment, and we sat there basically all night talking. And I honestly believe it's one of the five or six most important nights in the history of the show, because I'd hired Lorne when we were first sitting in L.A. putting it all together back in the spring of '75. I said, "Lorne, I'm willing to do this only if you'll bless it." He just had to put the word out. Anyway, around five or six in the morning he finally said, "I do want to see it go on. I won't go back, but I will completely support it."

And that word was out by the time Lorne woke up the next afternoon.

LORNE MICHAELS:

Michael O'Donoghue's manager, a guy named Barry Secunda, explained to me the simple fact that Michael had no money. And

Michael was very proud, but he really needed a job. Barry wanted to know if I would speak to Ebersol on his behalf, which I did. Of course, the very first thing Michael did was to meet with everyone and say, "We have to obliterate Lorne Michaels, we have to pour gasoline on him and set him afire." And then he burned some picture of me. Pretty soon after, he was fired.

I love Michael. And I would have expected no less. It wasn't as if I helped him thinking I'd get the thanks of a grateful nation. After all, it was Michael. Of the three of us — the senior three males in the first months of the show — Chevy went on to fame and stardom, I got what I got, and Michael wanted more performance time. The rewards for him weren't as great as he felt he deserved.

DICK EBERSOL:

Lorne told me I should hire Michael. He persuaded me it would be a good idea. O'Donoghue thought the show was shit and he thought the people involved were shit. He wanted to give it a "Viking funeral." He was going to be, quote, "in charge of the writing staff."

Since Ebersol was determined that the show regain its lost luster as well as its lost ratings, it may seem odd for him to have installed O'Donoghue as head writer, especially since O'Donoghue was so fond of proclaiming Saturday Night Live *dead. But what made him attractive to Ebersol is that he represented a link to Lorne Michaels and his era, and Ebersol was anxious to establish such links. Few were available, but O'Donoghue had been a very conspicuous and productive presence during those first five years. Ebersol wanted to be a member of that club, and O'Donoghue seemed one way — however risky — to gain acceptance. It would be a recurring theme of Ebersol's stewardship.*

NEIL LEVY:

Dick wanted to be Lorne, basically. The first words out of Dick's mouth to the writers was, he broke them into two teams at the first meeting and said, "Here's what we're going to do. I have two ideas and we're going to make short films. And half of you are going to do this one idea and the other half are going to do this idea about a bag lady." I forget what the first idea was. And the writers kind of scratched their heads—a bag lady? What's funny about that? But Dick said to go and do it.

So the team of writers for the bag lady did whatever their short film was and it was shot and Denny Dillon was in it and it came back and it was a disaster, totally unusable. And O'Donoghue was sitting there smoking one of those long brown cigarettes with his hat and sunglasses on and he said, "Well, it's all there on the screen." Something like that. It was a huge embarrassment to Dick, because it was the first thing he had asked for and it was his idea and it was horrible. So he says to Michael, "Is there anything we can do to make it work?" O'Donoghue says, "If you took out all the sound and used outtakes of Denny as the bag lady sitting there on a bench, maybe we could put some funny voice-overs or something—but I don't think so." And Ebersol jumped on it and he said, "Great, that's great," and he looked at me and he said, "Neil, get the writers together and tell them we want lines for passersby to say about a bag lady." I didn't realize I'd just been handed the bag. I went and told all the writers and came back and reported to Dick they were all working on it.

So now they've finished their lines and Dick sends me to collect them. I show them to him, he crosses a few off, he says, "Great. Now get the actors and get it done." All right. So I told the actors what we had to do. Basically I didn't want to do this, I was just following instructions on what Dick wanted. I didn't realize I was suddenly producing this piece.

The night of Dick's first show, Lorne comes. And it was like God visiting. You know, "Make way! Make way! He's in the building!" Dick even let Lorne sit at his own desk on the ninth floor. And I come in and Dick looks at me and says, "Oh Lorne, your cousin made this great bag lady film." And I was about to say something and he told me to leave the room. He said, "I need this list for tomorrow and I need this and that," and I said, "But Lorne—" and Dick said, "Just go." And of course the bag lady was just a total embarrassment. I don't know why he even bothered showing it. It made it as far as dress rehearsal. That nearly killed me. I didn't get a chance to talk to Lorne about it, actually. I don't think I ever mentioned it to him—that I was set up and had nothing to do with it.

BOB TISCHLER, *Writer:*

I was actually a record producer, had worked with the Blues Brothers and had worked with a lot of the people from *Saturday Night Live* on the *National Lampoon Radio Hour,* which I had produced. That's how Michael O'Donoghue knew me. He said, "Come on to *Saturday Night Live.*" I said, "Well, you know, I kind of have this other career going." And he said, "It'll be fun, and by the way, the show is just going to go down anyway, so don't worry about having to be stuck on the show." And he actually described it as a "death ship."

TIM KAZURINSKY, *Cast Member:*

John Belushi pretty much got me hired and recommended me for *Saturday Night Live.* The evening that Dick Ebersol came to Chicago and hired me, I assumed I was being hired as a writer. I'd never thought of myself as an actor. And then, as he was wrapping up, he said, "You have your AFTRA card, right?" And I said, "Why do I need an AFTRA card if I'm going to write?" He said, "No, no, you're going to be in the cast." I said, "You want me to *act?!?*" He said, "Yeah, I didn't even know you wrote." I was completely stunned. I was driving home in my Volkswagen going, "That's weird," because I'd never really thought of myself as an actor.

JOE PISCOPO:

They kept Eddie and me, and fired everybody else. O'Donoghue said to me, "Piscopo, I'm not crazy about you, but that Sinatra thing is not bad." And in essence he told me, "You're going to have to prove yourself to me."

Then he put us all in a room. O'Donoghue came in, spray-painted DANGER on the wall, and said, "This is what the show lacks."

PAM NORRIS:

I remember the day Michael was writing DANGER on that wall. The spray can stopped working halfway through. And I was like on my back laughing, because he'd just written DAN on the wall and the spray can temporarily stopped working. I thought, "Oh my God, this guy's going to go down in history writing DAN on the wall." But he shook it a few times and it started up again.

NEIL LEVY:

Dick told me that if I could get Catherine O'Hara to come to New York, he would let me stay on. It was sleazy. But I thought, "Well, I can do it." So I went and asked Catherine O'Hara. She wasn't really interested. But I talked to her and she came down. Then she saw the flaming Viking ship going under and she went, "Uh-oh, gotta run."

DICK EBERSOL:

Meantime, I'd hired Catherine O'Hara. It had taken a lot to lure her, because live was not her style. So in that very first meeting with Michael, when he was telling everybody the show is shit, and spraying all over the writers' wall the word DANGER, it really scared Catherine O'Hara—scared her right off the show. She packed up her stuff and went home to Canada that night.

TIM KAZURINSKY:

O'Donoghue had this vision of taking the show down. He wanted to destroy the show. His motto was "Viking Death Ship. Let's all go down in the Viking Death Ship." I grew up in the slums, you know, starving, and I'm thinking, "Can't we like keep it afloat just until I can buy a condo?" Yeah, he wrote DANGER on the wall. It was like carefully orchestrated. He was a drama queen. But I loved Michael. He was great.

He did bring on Terry Southern. Terry had been one of America's great writers. But he was not a sketch-comedy writer. It's absurd. I don't know if he ever wrote anything that actually got on the air. But he ran a fine wet bar out of his office. It was a really odd time, because it seemed like that first year, half of them really worked at trying to have it go up in smoke. In retrospect, maybe O'Donoghue had the right idea.

ROSIE SHUSTER, _Writer:_

I was having this big fight with Clotworthy about a sketch called "The Taboosters," which is just a normal, regular family, and they have lots of rules and stuff, but no taboos. And I couldn't win this argument. And then afterwards, when I showed the censor out of my office, I saw that Terry Southern, who was writing on the show at that time, had left a *Hustler* magazine sitting there with this big female pink genitalia flashing right in the censor's face. I had no idea. That was Terry's idea of being hilarious. It *was* pretty funny afterwards. I thought, "Oh my God, no wonder the censor was mad."

BOB TISCHLER:

The day that Michael was going to do his DANGER thing, he actually asked me not to come into the room, because he knew he was putting on a show and was going to be very theatrical. He knew I wouldn't have bought into it. It would have been very hard for me to sit through something like that. Michael lost a lot of people with that one. He was trying to shake everybody up, but there's always a second agenda with Michael. I have to categorize it as his own combination of sadistic and masochistic tendencies. Michael loved to play those roles, and he loved to be the focus of everything.

There were certain periods where he would just break down and throw temper tantrums—breaking things, throwing things, screaming. And you just had to stay away from him. Michael really had something wrong with him, a chemical imbalance. He complained of migraine headaches all the time and would flip out occasionally.

He was most interested in shocking the audience. I don't mind shocking the audience, but you have to make them laugh too, and entertain them. He was really just into the shock value, or doing something that was weird and boring.

I never called myself a writer before *Saturday Night Live.* I produced a lot of comedy and I did writing, but I wasn't a member of the union or anything and didn't go sit down and write. And when I came to *Saturday Night Live,* I was all of a sudden brought in as head writer, and what happened was we did one show and the writers' strike happened. So at that point it was an opportunity to basically clean house of the Jean Doumanian people that we didn't want and come back the next year with our own staff. There was an opportunity to upright the death ship and let it sail again. I've never been one to work on anything with the intent of it failing. But Michael would not give up on this death ship thing. So Michael and I kind of disagreed on that, and that's where we started to lose our friendship.

At one point Michael had been an incredible genius, an incredible writer. At a certain point, the panache and the desire to be recognized and to get the accoutrements of *Saturday Night Live* became more important than his craft. It was very sad for me to see this happen.

JAMES DOWNEY:

Lorne at that time was anxious to get into movies in a big way, and he had a deal with Paramount. And different writers and teams of writers—like Tom Schiller wrote a movie—each had movie ideas. Lorne was pushing Franken and Davis and myself the most to do a movie. But we didn't really have an idea. We had the deal before we had the idea, which is not a good way to do anything. So from like the summer of 1980 on and off for the next two years, we just in a desultory way wrote the screenplay, which once we finished it Paramount was then able to officially reject. Then, like the summer of '82— Letterman had just started up in March, and he had asked me to come in when he was first putting his NBC late-night show together. I knew that I probably wouldn't be able to do it, at least in the very beginning, because of the movie thing, but I went in to meet him because I was a big fan of his morning show. And then in August we had finished up the movie, so I went to the Letterman show. Later I became head writer for about a year and a quarter.

The biggest difference between writing for *Letterman* and writing for *Saturday Night Live*—well, obviously it would be the sketches, per se. I hope this doesn't sound pretentious, but I think that the principle in operation at *Saturday Night Live* seemed to be that—I didn't feel this way myself—but the principle was that we wanted to be hip. And at *Letterman,* we wanted to be smart. And I liked that much better.

It's not like I can identify even a single person at *SNL* who would say that being hip was what was most important to them. It was just that what made *Saturday Night Live* distinctive was not that it was so smart or brainy in that sense; it was more that, when it appeared, television had been kind of middle-aged and square for a long time. And *Saturday Night Live* set a tone of being cool. And certainly it was pretty clear that that was never a concern of the Letterman show.

BRAD HALL, *Cast Member:*

I came in the second year of Ebersol, and we were there until the end of Ebersol. When Ebersol first started, he hired a bunch of people from Chicago—Mary Gross, Tim Kazurinsky, those guys—who we knew peripherally because we were from Chicago. And when we had the show in Chicago that we were doing next door to Second City, we shared the bar with Second City. And when Ebersol and Tischler came out to do their usual pilfering from Second City to get actors, they went to Second City, they saw the show, and the owner of Second City, who was sick of losing people to *Saturday Night Live,* said, "Hey, go next door, because we have a big hit show going on next door." And they came over and saw our show. And that night, right after the show, they said "You're all hired. You're all coming to *Saturday Night Live.*" It was very exciting. It was crazy.

Julia and I were really lucky that we'd been going out for a while before that. We had a really solid relationship, and we came to the show together.

JULIA LOUIS-DREYFUS, *Cast Member:*

Audition? No, we didn't do an audition, that's the thing. We were just hired off the show we did in Chicago. And then when we came to New York, Dick wanted us to do some of the material we'd done onstage. It's a real quirky show that we did. It was funny, but it was not straight-down-the-middle improvisation comedy, and they made us perform a rather substantial section from the show. Dick set it up so that everybody sat on folding chairs, and the four of us performed sketches from our show for these jaded writers. It was just grotesque. It couldn't have been a more hostile crowd. It was so painful, I can't even believe I'm talking about it. There was no team spirit.

BRAD HALL:

It's a funny place to work, that seventeenth floor. People act as if it's so important, that it's the only thing in the world. And the hours are ridiculous. But at the end of the day, how about just being funny? Those of us who didn't get so much material had a lot of time to hang out with the band. I spent a lot of time with the *SNL* band and with the guest bands. And when I look back, I think less about comedy and more about music, to tell you the truth. We got the Clash, we got Squeeze, we had Joe Jackson.

GRANT A. TINKER, *Former NBC Chairman:*

I never visited their offices on the seventeenth floor, never went up there once. I didn't want to go up there and fight my way through all that marijuana smoke, which I'd been led to believe was quite thick. So I felt, why cause trouble?

JACK HANDEY, *Writer:*

I went over to this house one time for a Halloween party, and Cheryl Hardwick was playing the piano and they had a Poe reading, and then Michael O'Donoghue announced that he was going to unveil this painting by a new young artist that he had discovered. And so we were all sucked into it. Like here's the artist, supposedly, and he's standing there and looking kind of embarrassed. And the name of the painting is *Desi Arnaz as a Young Man.* There were, I don't know, thirty or forty people there. So the painting is up on the wall and Michael pulls off the cover and he goes, "Ladies and gentlemen, I give you *Desi Arnaz as a Young Man.*" And there's the painting, big oil painting, and sure enough, it is Desi Arnaz as a young man, seated on a chair facing you, but with female genitalia instead of male. And there was just an audible gasp from the room. That was the kind of thing Michael liked to do.

JUDITH BELUSHI, *Writer:*

I did a little writing, but only on one show, when Dick Ebersol came in. The first year there was a writers' strike and we only did one show. John said to me, "Why would you ever want to write for *Saturday Night Live*?" And I said that I had been around it so much and sometimes had even participated—giving somebody a line or something. And I'd worked on the *National Lampoon Radio Hour* and other things. So I thought, "I can do that." And I thought it would be interesting. But I really didn't like it. I call it "My Week in Television." It was actually three weeks of working.

TIM KAZURINSKY:

It was too crazy. Everyone was out of control. Finally, I decided to quit the show. I called John Belushi and said, "I'm going home. I'm flying back to Chicago tonight. I quit." Pam Norris, Blaustein, a few others, and I were pretty much coming up with the show almost every week. O'Donoghue's writers were hopeless. They did nothing. When they did do something, it was horrible. But I didn't get to quit—because John said, "Okay, Judy and I will drive you to the airport." They came by my house, got my bags, and, instead of taking me to the airport, they took me to a psychiatrist. John said, "If you want to quit that show, you've got to be crazy." He told me, "Here's the thing you can't lose sight of: It gets bad, it gets ugly, but you're an improviser, you're a writer, you have access to network airwaves. You have a chance to reach some hearts and minds out there. You have a chance to say something. You cannot walk away from this." And he sent me in to this psychiatrist, who I saw every week for the next year and who kept me healthy enough to stay on the show.

BOB TISCHLER:

There was a lot of lying going on, a lot of deception. And it became furious between O'Donoghue and Ebersol. I kept on trying to defend him; Ebersol really wanted to get rid of him a long time before he did. I had known Michael for years before the show. He and I were great friends and actually ended up not remaining friends as a result of our experience on *Saturday Night Live* together. Michael had this history with everybody. Anybody who really got close to him ended up being on his enemies list at a certain point.

ELLIOT WALD, *Writer:*

I hit it off badly with Michael. He passed judgment on things. He and my first partner, Nate Herman—he didn't like Nate too much, and since Nate was a performer, he was always hilarious in meetings. So it was hard for him to fire on Nate, but Nate's quiet partner was easier to pick on. I was afraid to speak up at meetings in the first half of the season. He had made life difficult for me. He almost got me fired—"Just get him out of here"—because he was trying to get somebody else hired. But before that could be executed, he got himself fired over the "Silverman in the Bunker" piece. This was a piece he wrote, with Silverman as Hitler in the last days. The sketch didn't make it to air, and that's why Michael quit—or put himself in the position to be fired. He talked to somebody in the press about what a bunch of morons everybody up there was, how they couldn't see the brilliance of this piece. And the network said, "Well, you do have a clause in your contract about doing things like that," so they fired him. He was asking for it. He was, in essence, quitting.

But Michael and I made our peace after the show. We did a couple of panels together at the Museum of Television and Radio and actually were on pretty pleasant terms. Then the shock came, when he died.

ROBIN SHLIEN, *Production Assistant:*

When Michael O'Donoghue got fired, he left this amazing note: "I was fired by Dick Ebersol. I did not leave the show, and if he should claim otherwise, he is, to steal a phrase from Louisa May Alcott, a lying cunt." It's very Michael. He posted it on the wall. Dick wasn't in yet, so those of us who were there immediately took it off and Xeroxed it and made copies, knowing that Dick would rip it down, which he did. But it survived.

BOB TISCHLER:

There were two wakes for Michael. The one on the East Coast was the original, official wake, and they actually had the graph of his aneurysm from the MRI. And then they had a second wake at the Café Formosa in Los Angeles. You have to realize that a lot of people who were once friends or who once worked together—who had lots of issues between them—were suddenly in a room together. When anybody dies, everybody gets pulled together whether they like to or not. At Michael's wake, there were a lot of egos flying. A lot of people needed to be the center of attention.

JACK HANDEY:

I went to Michael's wake. There was food and drink, and his wife, Cheryl, was there, and toward the end of the evening, people got up and sort of talked—telling stories about Michael. They had put the X-rays of his head up as decorations so people could see where he had his massive stroke or something like that.

There was some controversy after Lorne and Chevy Chase spoke. Buck Henry got up and said something to the effect that it was interesting that they got up to speak "when I think we all know what Michael thought of them."

LORNE MICHAELS:

That's the blackest period for me. Buck later wrote me one of the most beautiful notes I ever received in my life in which he said, a year or two later, that at the time there were attack dogs running at me and he had joined the pack, and he apologized.

What happened was, Michael died on a Tuesday. He'd gone into St. Vincent's Hospital on Monday. My son, Eddie, was born on Wednesday before read-through in the same hospital. Friday night was a wake that I helped organize at Cheryl's. After visiting at the hospital and going to the studio around eleven o'clock, I went to the wake—with Chevy Chase. He and John were not on the best of terms but on another level really loved each other. Meanwhile, John was considered the real deal in Hollywood and Chevy was—well, you know. I remembered a time before all these people had joined the Belushi camp, they had been professionally in the John Belushi business. Then they switched over to the Michael O'Donoghue business. And somebody in their remarks took a shot at Chevy, as if you had to make a choice between loving Michael and loving Chevy.

JANE CURTIN, _Cast Member_:

The fact that here we all were, our lives forever intertwined, and you had these love-hate relationships with people, and things got said that were just so incredibly perfect and mean and funny and honest. Some people laughed, some people gasped. It was pretty cool.

ANDREW KURTZMAN:

I came into the show through Tim Kazurinsky. He brought in several of us. My father had been a creative director at Leo Burnett in Chicago, and Tim had been in his creative group along with Jeff Price, who went on to be a screenwriter. A couple of playwrights and a lot of odd people came out of that agency. I was an accidental hire. I wrote Tim a funny letter asking for tickets to the show. Tim said, "This is quite funny. You should write a couple of sample sketches." And I won't say I dashed them off, but I wrote a bunch of sketches and then went back to a $90-a-week job at Barnes and Noble. I forgot the whole thing for about two months, and then I began to get these strange phone calls at odd hours in the middle of the night from Kaz, saying things like "Blaustein loved the stuff." Shortly thereafter I was brought in.

BRAD HALL:

Dick didn't really have a lot to say about the comedy. He would sort of go into the room and pick the sketches. It was much more like he was a judge than he was involved in the process at all. I noticed very quickly that on Wednesdays when we had these gigantic read-throughs that the very funniest sketch at the table would almost always get in the show. But so would the worst sketch.

DICK EBERSOL:

The sets were made in Brooklyn in those days. And then they had to be broken down so they could fit on an elevator, whereas, you know, everything in the West Coast is horizontal. I mean, the big studios. They make the sets in one end of the building; they can be as big as you want. You push them down the hallway. The studio doors open up; they're thirty or forty feet high, and the thing wheels in. With *Saturday Night Live,* everything has to fit into one of those small Rockefeller Center elevators. And so not only does it take a while to build the set, you have to then build it in such a way it can be broken down and then reassembled. So, from the end of read-through, you go back in a room and pick the elements of the show you want to take to dress.

I think one difference between Lorne and me was that I never wanted to go to dress more than three sketches too long. He has stronger feelings about the ability to repair things late. So he oftentimes will go to dress much longer than that. I mean he'll go a half hour or forty minutes longer going to dress, and obviously it's worked for him for a quarter of a century. I was more comfortable being about three long. But that's the big thing that you're facing, that Wednesday night deadline because of the sets.

DON NOVELLO, *Writer:*

This was an amazing thing. I'm not sure of the year, but I would say early eighties. Bill Murray was hosting, I was a guest as a performer, and I really was like a writer for him. And at the end of the show, everyone's going up onstage to say good night, and there's a commercial break — two minutes, four minutes, whatever — and during the break, Ebersol suddenly comes running up and says, "It's on the news, Russia's invading Poland, and you should announce it." Bill said, "What should I do?" And I told him, wisely as it turns out, "That's a news thing. This is a comedy show. Why would you want to do it?" Ebersol says, "Come on, we've got thirty seconds, you're going to do it." Well, I was not going to stand there when he announced it, so I went and stood way in the back, even though I was one of the main guests. So Bill announced it to America that Russia had invaded Poland and "the poor people of Poland, our hearts go out to them." It was really almost teary-eyed. And it didn't happen. The "invasion" didn't happen, at least not that night. But I guess Ebersol wanted this to be the comedy show that broke it to America that Russia invaded Poland.

ANDREW SMITH:

Dick was tremendously successful with the network. He could get anything out of the network, whether it was money or one thing or another. He understands network politics and that side of it, you know, better than anybody else. And, of course, his best friend was Brandon Tartikoff, which didn't hurt. He was brilliant at that side of being an executive producer. But he obviously wasn't a comedy writer and was somewhat foreign to comedy, although I guess there are some issues as to whether he invented the show with Lorne or not.

FRED SILVERMAN:

There are very few people who can produce that show. I never got along particularly well with Ebersol, but I think he did a pretty good job, actually. He walked into a real mess and kept it going, to his credit. The show had had its ups and downs, but he managed to hang in there.

DICK EBERSOL:

It was like a war, and most of it was about the fact that Fred just didn't like having a show that had that level of freedom that was attacking Fred. *Saturday Night Live* does not work if it censors itself about its own company. You have to attack. I made a point the very first show I did by myself, in April of '81, of letting Franken do a piece on "Update." We were friends, but deep inside he thought he should produce the show, and I let him do a piece on "Update" the sum of which was that "Dick doesn't know dick."

DAVID SHEFFIELD:

Ebersol is a guy who walks the halls slapping a baseball bat into his palm. He is not easily intimidated. We were at a meeting one time, twenty minutes until air, and this pipsqueak guy from the network says "I just think we really ought to—" and Dick turned around and said to him, "Just shut the fuck up and sit in the corner."

He ran defense between us and the network. He kept the wolves away while we did the show. This is a good executive strategy. His great strength as producer of the show is he didn't try to do comedy. He left that up to us.

BRAD HALL:

My big run-in with Dick came when there was this very funny sketch that got cut for time and he said, "Don't worry, we'll do it next week." And then, of course, it wasn't on the board the next week, and so I said, "You said we'd do it 'next week.'" And he denied having said it, of course. I'm a very even-tempered guy, but once in a while I'll get mad. I was absolutely in offense, because it just wasn't true. And good old Mary Gross, to her credit, goes, "We were all there, we all heard it." It was typical. I think everybody had things like that.

GRANT A. TINKER:

I had so many larger problems that had to be dealt with that I just didn't get around to *Saturday Night Live,* and no one was the worse for wear as the result. The show went on, and I did what I did, and just because the twain never met, it wasn't advertent on my part. I guess you could say it was inadvertent.

PAM NORRIS:

I did not find Dick difficult to work for. I did not agree with a lot of his decisions, but he had what to me is a magical quality in a boss in that I felt like I could say anything to him. And I really quite often said very harsh things. He was okay with that. I never felt like he was going to be angry with me if I told him something he didn't like. I really am glad in a lot of ways to have dealt with Dick, because I never felt like he was some kind of royalty and that I needed to curry his favor somehow.

TIM KAZURINSKY:

Somebody pointed out to me at read-throughs that Ebersol didn't really know what was funny. He would look over to Davey Wilson, the director, for some sort of indication. And, of course, Davey had done the show for so long that he was very tired. He only cared if it was easy to shoot. If it was difficult, he would just move his head from side to side and Ebersol would kill it. So he took a lot of lead from Davey.

ANDREW SMITH:

His real name is Duncan Dicky Ebersol. He used to have a Dutch boy haircut. He would come to the office dressed like he was going to a country club — golf sweaters, plaid madras pants, that kind of stuff. He certainly had no embarrassment about being a Wasp. It was really fascinating. It's as if he hadn't been down in the city very long.

When I first started working with him, he had this thing about contractions. I think his mother put the fear of God into him and told him that nice people don't use contractions. I cannot even do an imitation, but if you can think of talking without ever using a contraction, you will be able to assume what it is that I am talking about. It made him sound like a foreigner. And then he had this thing that you don't talk a certain way in front of women. You know, "You had better get that woman out of here before we talk about that." He wouldn't swear in front of them. He wouldn't say "fuck" or "shit" or anything like that. Or he'd spell it out or use a euphemism. He was much more comfortable in the company of men, which is not to make any kind of sexual aspersions. Women were sacrosanct to him.

JIM BELUSHI, *Cast Member:*

I supposedly threw a fire extinguisher at Ebersol. I don't remember throwing it at him. I remember going down the hall and getting really pissed and grabbing the fire extinguisher off the wall and heaving it toward his office. I was a hungry, aggressive young man. I was a pain in the ass to Ebersol, but not to the other actors.

Ebersol didn't even really hire me. Brandon Tartikoff was always a fan of mine, and he saw me do a big Second City benefit show that started the John Belushi Scholarship Fund. We invited everybody in the industry, and every studio gave like $7,500. Brandon saw that show, and I did quite a few Second City routines there, and he said to Dick, "Why don't you hire Belushi?" And Ebersol goes, "You think so?" Brandon said, "Yeah, he was really funny." So Ebersol did.

TIM KAZURINSKY:

The thing with Ebersol was that he was always looking for the lowest common denominator. The moral majority was really big then, and he didn't want to do anything to piss anybody off or do anything controversial. I had just come out of Second City, and he tells me, "I don't want to do political things. I don't want to do controversial things. Who do you do impersonations of? Can you do Mickey Rooney?" I was like, "Fuck off!" I remember John Candy's saying that was like the bottom of the comedy barrel. Mickey Rooney!

BARRY BLAUSTEIN:

Reagan's election set the tone. There was a kind of impending doom hanging over the country, and there was palpably a move toward conservatism at the network. We tried ideas for sketches that the network would shoot down. The censors would say, "You can't do that." We'd point out they did something similar with Aykroyd three years earlier, and the censor would say, "Yeah, but that was then, this is now. Things are different." There was to be no mention of the Iran hostage crisis. Ironically, when the crisis was over, we did a whole show with every hostage sketch we could think of.

DAVID SHEFFIELD:

Barry had an idea for a great hostage sketch, which was, a guy knows this woman's husband is being held hostage, and he goes over to console her and winds up hitting on her. The network said no. It was a strange time.

JAMES DOWNEY:

I liked Dick Ebersol a lot. He gets a bad rap. He developed a playbook to run the show which I would argue they are definitely using these days. The way the show works now is Ebersol's formula: the popular characters in heavy rotation, the kind of pieces they pick. It's not a writer's show. Ebersol made no bones: "I'm pushing Eddie Murphy, there's going to be a 'Mister Robinson's Neighborhood' or a Buckwheat every other show in alternation. I'm going to pretend 'The Whiners' are popular characters whether the audience thinks so or not, and we're going to keep doing it. It's going to be about the performers. The sets are going to be very simple."

I think Ebersol kept the show on the air at a point where it might have been canceled. It's like Sam Houston holding the Texas army together long enough to hang on.

ANDREW KURTZMAN:

Tim Kazurinsky, who came from a business environment, sort of clued me in by saying, "Watch Ebersol. Watch how he leaves the door opened or closed during a meeting. Watch who he has in his office." What was it they said about Lyndon Johnson? He never had a telephone conversation without needing to win a point. Even when Dick was yelling, he was subtly turning things so that the argument would go his way.

ELLIOT WALD:

I don't remember who said the line—I've said it so much that someone said they thought I said it originally, but I didn't—but one of the writers said, "Every time somebody in the world lies, Dick Ebersol gets a royalty."

BOB TISCHLER:

I had one big run-in with Dick before our last year. I said, "I know you're a publicity hog and you can't control yourself, but at least give me some kind of credit for this. I'm doing all the work. I think you should be much more in the background." He was dealing with the network and dealing with a lot of the nuts and bolts, and I was really running the show much more from the creative point of view, because he really did not have a good rapport with the writers. So I would do all the rewriting, and that would be a hell of a lot of work. But he would just take all the credit, and I was very troubled by it and told him so. At one point I was going to leave the show—he was thinking of firing me, I was thinking of walking out. But we came together and settled it, so I stayed.

I ended up liking working with him a lot, because he is an excellent producer. He really knows how to deal with the network more than anybody I've ever met. It's just that he had a lot of shortcomings in knowing how to deal with creative people. Dick is a very strange animal.

ANDREW KURTZMAN:

The toughest it ever got between me and Dick was at one point he said, "You're talking pretty big for a guy who was making $90 last week." That's sort of a Dickensian moment in my life. I had to get between Dick and a couple of people several times. With Dick there was always an element of fear. Like his argument with Andy Kaufman. I was standing there backstage where they screamed at each other. There was a certain amount of "fuck you" and screaming down the little entranceway leading into the studio there. It was a big confrontation. It was the show where Andy was voted off the air. I will say Dick was always in control. Even when Dick was out of control, Dick was perfectly in control.

ELLIOT WALD:

There was one piece I remember very well that Jim Downey wrote that we were falling off our chairs about. It was hilarious. It was an alien spaceship landing on Earth. The aliens come out and say, "We are superior, you shouldn't even bother to oppose us," and it becomes obvious as they talk that they stole the spaceship and haven't really read the manual or anything and really don't know how to run it very well. And in four minutes, it just had half a dozen wonderfully funny things. I remember that piece—and there were a million like it— where Dick just didn't get it. The writers all got it. Dick didn't.

TIM KAZURINSKY:

I had done this running thing called "I Married a Monkey," where my wife was played by a live chimpanzee. And I did it because I knew that something would screw up and people would see that it was live. People would always ask me, "When do you tape the show?" No, it's called *Saturday Night Live*. It's *live*. It became so slick, people forgot that it was live. So I thought, "I'll do this soap opera thing with a live chimp, and inadvertently I'll get to improvise." And it got to be very popular. And anything that took off, Ebersol wanted: "Let's do that again," you know. "Let's do another monkey thing." Even when you think it's played out, you still have to do them. "We need a monkey for this week." And I'd go, "Christ!"

And we used to hire these midget chimps Butch and Peppy, because they supposedly worked with Ronald Reagan in *Bedtime for Bonzo*. And the trainer told me one time, "Watch out for the chimps. When the hairs go up on their arms, they're ready to attack." So I was on the show one night, it was dress, and Madge, my "wife," is in a hospital bed with amnesia. So I'm sitting there next to her and suddenly I see the hairs on her arm go up. And I make this dash trying to get out of there, and she grabs me and gets my head in a headlock that was like steel. Fortunately she was tethered by a chain at the back of the hospital bed and I was able to pull my head free before she crushed my skull. Then she went berserk and ripped off her leopard skin negligee and diaper and revealed to the audience that Madge was really a male chimp. So, standing there on the bed now, he grabs his monkey member and starts masturbating—as if to say, "I'm a guy." Out in the audience, mothers are shielding their kids' eyes, and I thought, "Oh God, if this ever happened on-air, I'd probably have stayed and wrestled with the chimp. But for a dress rehearsal, get the hell out of there."

So they sedated the chimp for the air show. I look over and he's just totally glassy-eyed. And the next time I worked with a chimp, its teeth had been removed. Then I found out from a production assistant that Ebersol was secretly taking out like massive amounts of insurance on me when I worked with the chimp! And that's when I said, "No more. I'm not doing it anymore." I thought, "He's taking a million bucks of insurance in case I get killed. And fuck that. It's too bizarre. I mean, I'm *not* going to die for *him*."

JIM BELUSHI:

Ebersol's an executive network manager. He's one of the tops in that field. I think he knew what worked, and what didn't work, and I think he really knew how to program the first thirty minutes to be the most successful. He knew the first thirty minutes of the show was the most-watched, so he really kind of messed around with the commercials to try to hold them back. As far as being a writer or a comic and telling you, "Why don't you try this gag," he was a little dry that way. Ebersol is like a lot of people in our industry; they're heat-seeking missiles. What they're looking for is the heat. He put that heat up there in the first thirty minutes. Sometimes, though, people like that don't know how to nurture something.

JOE PISCOPO:

The Sinatra stuff was early on, and they had to talk me into that, because I didn't want to disrespect my hero. When I first started doing him, I wrote him a letter and I sent him an album through his attorney—we put out this "I Love Rock and Roll, Sinatra Sings the Rock Tunes" kind of thing. I was a North Jersey Italian American just like the Old Man, as we affectionately referred to Mr. S., and he couldn't have been nicer. Matter of fact, he sent out cease-and-desist letters to anybody who'd even think of doing him and he never sent me a letter. And he used to call me Jusep, which was Italian for Joseph.

He would invite me to everything. He just liked it. And when I look at it now, it had a real edge to it, you know?

But he couldn't have been nicer, and I have the fondest memories, rest his soul, of the Old Man. He was just the greatest. When I first did him on *SNL,* he was at Caesar's Palace in Atlantic City and he was about to step onstage—the opening act was an old comic named Charlie Callas—and everybody was waiting for the Old Man, and at eleven-thirty for the first time it was me doing him, and everybody stopped in the room, and I heard this from everybody, and they just said, "How is this guy crazy enough to do Sinatra?" And Callas breaks his silence and says to the Old Man, "What do you think, Captain?" And Sinatra looks at me doing him and he says, "He's pretty good—the little prick."

And when I met him, he said, "Hey Joe, baby, come here." I felt so comfortable, I said, "Can I call you Frank?" He said, "No." It was great, you know? He was just a wonderful, wonderful guy.

BOB TISCHLER:

We had a piece on one show where people were jumping off a building, and in the sketch Frank Sinatra was supposed to jump, as was Mayor Koch, who played himself, and Joe says, "Frank wouldn't jump off a building." And Eddie turns to him and says, "Oh yeah—and Mayor Koch would?" That was one of many "Frank wouldn't do that" stories. There was another time where Billy Crystal was going to play Sammy Davis, Jr.—Billy and I wrote this piece—and Joe was supposed to play Frank, and it was supposed to start in the Carnegie Deli and end up where Sammy would break-dance in front of the NBC studios, which we did. But when we told Joe that we wanted to start in the Carnegie Deli, he said that Frank would never eat in the Carnegie Deli, and he refused to do it until we put Frank in a limo.

Then there's the Stevie Wonder story. It was a sketch called "Ebony and Ivory," and it was supposed to be Frank Sinatra and Stevie Wonder—Joe and Eddie. In the sketch, which Barry and David wrote, Frank was supposed to be waiting for Stevie Wonder to show up at the recording studio, and Joe said, "Frank wouldn't wait for Stevie. Stevie would have to wait for Frank." And refused to do it that way.

It was sick.

ANDREW SMITH:

Joe needed to think he *was* Frank Sinatra. All that stuff about Frank. And we wanted to write a sketch called "Frank Wouldn't Do That," because we'd pitch a sketch or something, and Joe would say, "No, no, Frank wouldn't do that." I once wrote a sketch — "The Gay Frank Sinatra Club." And, "No, not that, Frank wouldn't do that." So he really got a little squirrelly about this whole Frank thing. Joe saw his Frank thing not in comedy terms but as a tribute.

TIM KAZURINSKY:

I always said I would love to have done *SCTV.* There were smarter producers and smarter people involved. Watching the talent wither on *Saturday Night Live,* that was painful. You had really good writers trying to dumb down — and getting depressed about it and turning to drugs.

Good performers — Mary Gross, Julia Louis-Dreyfus, Robin Duke — were given so little to do on the show that their confidence eroded. Robin Duke was hysterical in shows at Second City. And they gave her nothing. And the less they give somebody — well, you know what they say: If you have one line it's harder than if you have a big part. The confidence erodes week by week, and it can just destroy people. And that was a hard thing to watch. The Second City environment was much more nurturing back then, and to come from that into the *Saturday Night Live* snake pit was not pleasant.

ANDREW SMITH:

If Joe thought he'd done a bad show — well, I remember one time sitting in Ebersol's office, and Joe went around the corner into Ebersol's bathroom and started banging his head against the wall in the shower, and there was this *thud* as, you know, he's thumping his head against the wall. And his wife, his first wife — this long-suffering, very sweet, mild girl — turned to us and said, "Joe is such a perfectionist. Poor Joe, he's such a perfectionist." What? *Thud, thud, thud....*

JIM BELUSHI:

Let me put it this way. Those two years of *Saturday Night Live* — '83–'84 and '84–'85 — were the toughest years I've ever spent in show business. Everything has been easy since. If you were a young physician and they threw you into Cook County Hospital or Bellevue for two years, that's what I equate it to. I'm really glad I did it. I'm very proud to be part of the legacy of *Saturday Night Live*. The only thing I regret is I didn't have two more years to really kind of hit that full fruition of it.

Even my brother John left after four years. I said, "John, what are you doing leaving? It's like the hottest thing going." He goes, "Well, you know, Jimmy, it's like high school — freshman, sophomore, junior, senior year, and then you've got to move on."

Dick Ebersol's initial version of Saturday Night Live *was efficient and commercial but fundamentally uninspired. It had little soul or spark, except for that provided by one magnificently conspicuous member of the cast — the man whom Doumanian had failed to feature. Now, allied with two of the show's best writers — Blaustein and Sheffield — Eddie Murphy blossomed forth during the Ebersol regime. He was fresh, funny, electrifying. He lit up the screen. Audiences who had wearied of the show's sameness and dropped away were lured back to see this spectacular new kid in town. Murphy had another loyal ally, or perhaps fervent disciple, in cast member Joe Piscopo. Offscreen, Murphy and Piscopo played the role of campus cutups — though to some observers, Piscopo seemed sycophantic in his adulation of Murphy and basked to the baking point in Murphy's refracted glow. And more than one insider reportedly remarked, "Eddie Murphy's success went to Joe Piscopo's head."*

BRIAN DOYLE-MURRAY, *Cast Member:*

Eddie Murphy wasn't too happy. He wasn't being used when he first started. And then he proved himself and he moved up. He was trying to get a spot on there at first, and they weren't really giving him a shake. I always liked Eddie, yeah. Yeah, in fact when Del Close came to teach improv, Eddie wasn't too up for that. He went, "Hey, I'm funny. I don't have to learn that shit."

NEIL LEVY:

I had this tape of Elvis Presley's 1968 comeback concert, where he wore that black leather jumpsuit thing, and Eddie used to come in and watch that over and over—and a few years later he was wearing black leather.

I also remember sitting in the bathroom and you could see in pencil on the wall, "Eddie Murphy No. 1." And as he got famous, it got bigger. He put it in bigger writing and switched from pencil to pen. He told me when he was nineteen that he was going to be a millionaire before he was twenty-one. He said that to me. I never met anybody so sure that once he got his foot in the door he was going all the way.

MARILYN SUZANNE MILLER, *Writer:*

Eddie Murphy had been some kind of a part-time guy under Doumanian, and Michael and I screened something, or saw some of his work, and Dick went, "This guy is unreal! He's got to be on the air." And we met with Eddie, and Eddie was very quiet. You know if you're great, and he just seemed to be saying, "Yeah, I'm great, what do you want to do?"

ELLIOT WALD:

To his credit—and I think Dick deserves credit for certain things—they made some good hires. Doumanian hired Eddie, but it was Ebersol who immediately realized that he was going to be a star. Dick saw Eddie's potential right away. He sort of picked Piscopo out of the mix; I am not a huge fan of Joe's, but he stuck in people's minds, which gave them kind of a peg.

MARGARET OBERMAN, *Writer:*

All you had to do with Eddie at that time was be a real good stenographer. Because you'd get him in the office and he'd have the character down, and he'd have the voice down and then if you had a good ear, you could kind of figure it out and give him the stuff right back, and he would just kick ass.

I likened him a lot to Bill Murray. I think Billy and Eddie are probably the most talented people to ever come out of the show. There's a drive that they both have. I think they're both really unique talents.

NEIL LEVY:

One time Eddie asked me if I'd be his manager, and I said no, I wasn't interested in doing that. Like a fucking idiot!

DICK EBERSOL:

When I came back and did that first show in the second Saturday in April of '82, the writers' strike happened at midnight that night, and so I never produced another show that season. We got picked up based on the positive reaction to that one show that I did that night. And Eddie had been wonderful in that show, but not enough to show the outside world what he could do. I would say that in that next year, '82–'83, he was at least a third or more of the draw of the show, so you could say he was worth a rating point and a half or two rating points.

During those two years, Eddie, Sheffield, and Blaustein had as much to do with keeping the show alive as anything or anyone. They were a wonderful marriage, the three of them. Eddie was clearly a genius then, at eighteen or nineteen years old. They were able to take his rough stuff, and they became his transmitters.

BARRY BLAUSTEIN:

What happened with our first Eddie Murphy piece was, my dad was always calling me up with ideas for sketches, and they were always terrible, but this was the one time he came up with an idea that was decent. He'd read this article about a high school basketball team in Cleveland, where the court ruled that there had to be at least one white player on the team. We wrote something for Eddie based on that, showed it to him, and worked with him on it. It was his first piece. And you could tell the first minute he was on the air that whatever "it" is, he had it. He completely connected with the audience. He just jumped off the screen.

PAM NORRIS:

The idea that Eddie got too much attention is hard for me to swallow, just because he earned it so much and he was ignored for the longest time. But he didn't get bitter, and he didn't quit. He kept writing, and he kept working with writers that would write for him. He kept coming up with new characters over and over again. I'm sure it's frustrating to work with him, because he could do everything. I mean, he could write for himself, he could create characters for himself. How do you compete with that? That could be extremely frustrating. I just saw how dismissed he was for the longest time, so if he got a little special later, he certainly deserved that—and way more.

ELLIOT WALD:

My era never was lionized the way the people in the first years were. In that first show, those people were the toast of New York, and I don't think anybody from my era was that way. Even when Eddie turned twenty-one, he held his own birthday party at Studio 54. It was well attended, but he still had to hold it for himself. No one really knew of us. They just knew of us as "the successors."

BRAD HALL:

Eddie was the one guy that really stood up for us. And if we were light in the show he was always, "Come on, let's give these guys something." He was really a team player from that point of view and an easy guy to talk to and always funny and fun to have around. That's definitely where the show was focused—on him. He'd had a big movie come out when we got there. And he was a big star. And that's where they were going to hang their hat. And who can blame them? The guy was great. But it did make it frustrating for us.

DANA CARVEY, *Cast Member:*

I was in New York stuck on a sitcom with Mickey Rooney, Nathan Lane, Meg Ryan, and Scatman Crothers called *One of the Boys.* Mickey Rooney was always talking—"I was the number one star in the *worrrld,* you hear me? The *worrrld.* Bang! The *worrrld!* Judy Garland never owned a car. They pumped her so full of drugs they killed her! How long has Robert Redford been in the business, ten years? I've been in the business sixty-one years!" He was sixty-two at the time. He would act out entire movies that he thought of, with lines like, "How are you, Mr. Fuck? I'm Mrs. Shit."

We were taping in Letterman's, now Conan's, studio on the sixth floor at 30 Rock, and to clear my head, I would go up to the eighth floor and watch Eddie Murphy rehearse. He was great.

BARRY BLAUSTEIN:

Eddie would go full-out on all our stuff. I don't think we ever wrote a sketch that didn't make the air that we wanted, or had to say, "They should've used that." The show's at its very best when the writers and the actors are in a room together writing stuff, the way Eddie was with us. Eddie would come in and say, "Hey, what about this?" and then we'd just start writing together. You can't write in a total vacuum. Pretty good rule of thumb: If you're laughing when you're writing it, it will be funny.

Eddie was up for everything. That was just one of the reasons for his success. In his stand-up, Eddie used to mention Buckwheat, from the old Our Gang comedies, and every time he did, he'd get a laugh. So we decided to do a tribute to Buckwheat—have Eddie impersonate him.

ROBIN SHLIEN:

I have a very specific memory of typing the first Buckwheat sketch and almost falling off my chair because it was so funny. Having been at the show and knowing what it took to have a great character and get a big response, I remember thinking, "They nailed it. This is going to be huge." It was "Buckwheat Sings," and they had bothered to put the mispronunciations in the script. So it was "Untz, tice, fee times a nady." I was typing this and I couldn't stop laughing. That was always a good sign.

DICK EBERSOL:

Eddie did Buckwheat for the first time in October of '81, so I would guess it would've been just after the first of the year, January of '83, that he came in to see me late one night in the office that's now Lorne's again and said, "I want to kill Buckwheat." It was one of the hottest characters in late-night television at that time. But he said, "I can't stand it anymore. Everywhere I go people say, 'Do Buckwheat, do this, do that.' I want to kill him."

His instincts were so good. I said, "Go sit down with Barry and David." They came back into my office about two, three o'clock in the morning, and it was a two-part thing: "The Assassination of Buckwheat." It probably was the best piece of satire in the four or five years that I was there. The first part was the actual shooting, out in front of the building as he got out of the car. The assassin's name was John David Studs, because they always have three names. Piscopo was funny in it too—he was too on-point for what a lot of *SNL* should be, but he was a brilliant Rich Little of his time.

They really wanted to do a satire on how far the media had gone. And that was to be the end of Buckwheat.

BARRY BLAUSTEIN:

Part one aired and went real well. And then we thought, "What if we do this: We take the next step, they catch the killer, and that will be like Lee Harvey Oswald getting killed." The censors were kind of unhappy, there were problems upstairs. What? Well, "Grant Tinker is very sensitive on this. He doesn't want to make fun of the Kennedy assassination." And we were like, "Oh, come on." The censor, Bill Clotworthy, was an old friend of Reagan's. They had been in *GE Theater* together. He's actually a really decent guy, Clotworthy, because he had a sense of humor about it. And I remember saying, "Goddammit, we always make fun of Reagan, why can't we make fun of Kennedy?"

DAVID SHEFFIELD:

We staged it downstairs at Rockefeller Center. We shot it two ways on tape. We actually brought in a guy from special effects to place squibs on Eddie's body so that we had blood gushing from each shot. But just as an afterthought we said, "Let's shoot one without the blood, for safety's sake." And that's the one we used. And it was lucky we had it, because the blood just looked too real to be funny.

DICK EBERSOL:

That sketch gave me my best battle ever with the censors. Part one airs on a Saturday night. The following Thursday, I'm summoned to the office of Corydon Dunham, who was then the corporation counsel to whom broadcast standards reported. I went to his office in jeans and a sweatshirt and he's Savile Row to the nth degree—but a nice man. And he said, "Dick, I just have to tell you that we will not be able to air 'The Assassination of Buckwheat, Part Two' this weekend." I said, "What are you talking about? It was read at read-through yesterday, it was a killer piece, there are no language problems, everybody loved it." He said, "But there's real violence implications here. Somebody gets shot in this piece." I said, "Cory, that aired *last* week. Buckwheat was assassinated *last* week. Everybody laughed." He said, "Yes, but do you realize that on Sunday night, the night after your show airs, we're presenting your friend Don Ohlmeyer's docudrama *Special Bulletin,* and we're having real problems with that because people will think it's real." It won the Emmy that year as the best single program shown on television. It was about nuclear terrorists at Charleston Harbor. Cory was convinced it was going to be Orson Welles's *War of the Worlds* all over again. He said, "People are just going to think we are out of our minds with all this violence." I said, "Oh, come on—we're on the night before, we're finishing off a comedic premise, and you're telling me I can't air it?" And I had sworn I was never going to do something like this, but I told him, "In forty-five minutes I'm going to hold a press conference announcing that I'm not doing the show anymore." I'd never done that; that was always Lorne's trip, threatening to quit. But I said, "I'm leaving, and I'm going to make abundantly clear the height of insanity that went behind this bullshit decision." And I said, "See you," with a smile on my face and I left. Cory called Grant Tinker and Grant laughed in his face when he heard the story. And before the forty-five minutes were up, Cory called me and said, "Never mind."

ANDY BRECKMAN, *Writer:*

There was this rumor circulating that over the summer Ebersol was on a private NBC plane talking to the network brass about how badly they needed Eddie Murphy to come back in the fall—and I think at the time Joe Piscopo was also a linchpin—but they needed Eddie Murphy or they didn't have a show. There would be no show without him. And they said, "We have to pay them whatever it takes." You know—bend over backwards as far as scheduling and pay. And the rumor that we heard was that this phone call was picked up by a ham radio operator somewhere in the Midwest, and he recorded it, and that tape somehow got back to Eddie Murphy. And so he went into negotiations knowing that he had them over a barrel. It's a great rumor, and I remember it circulating. Unfortunately, I don't know if it's true.

JOHN LANDIS, *Film Director:*

After the accident, the tragedy of *The Twilight Zone,* I was so freaked out I just said to my agent, "I'll take any job offered. I just want to work." So Jeff Katzenberg sent me this script of *Black or White*—later changed to *Trading Places*—and I said that Pryor would be brilliant in it. But Katzenberg said, "What do you think of Eddie Murphy?" and I had to say, "Who?" And he said, "We've made this picture called *48 Hrs.* and it just previewed." They tried to fire Eddie off of *48 Hrs.,* but Walter Hill saved his job. When it previewed, Eddie tested through the roof. So they gave me a tape of all his things he'd done on *Saturday Night Live,* and I said, "Kind of young, but he's funny. I especially love the James Brown Hot Tub. I'll meet him." So I fly to New York to meet with Eddie, who's a baby, like nineteen, whatever, and we come down onto Fifth Avenue and he said, "You have to get the cab, because they won't stop for me."

MARGARET OBERMAN:

We always had to go down and get cabs for him at two in the morning, because no cab drivers would stop for a young black man. Not even him.

DICK EBERSOL:

By the end of the '82–'83 season, Eddie already had had *48 Hrs.* It had come out at Christmas of '82, and then all through that winter, late '82–'83, early '83, he was making *Trading Places.* It became really apparent that, just on the launch of *48 Hrs.,* which had those glorious reviews for him, he was a movie star. I remember the *Times* in particular saying that his scene in that country-western bar was maybe the greatest scene an actor ever had in his debut movie. That, coupled with the fact that Paramount had already signed him, upon seeing the dailies before the film came out successfully, to a long-term deal that guaranteed him millions of dollars and had signed him and had him shooting *Trading Places* in Philadelphia and New York through that winter. It was going to be pretty hard to hold on to him. We had him for one more year, but they were making all the noises of, you know, being very resistant about it, and it could have been kind of a legal thing.

So I came up with this idea that, for the '83–'84 season, which would be his last, he had to appear in ten shows, and I think that year we were committed to doing twenty. He had to appear in ten of the twenty and we would be done with him by March. And we also had the right to tape up to, oh, I think it was fifteen sketches to put in the other shows. We weren't going to hide that he wasn't physically there. That wasn't the intent. But this was just to keep him available. They jumped at it and signed the deal. We kept ourselves from losing him, which would have hit us pretty hard.

ROBIN WILLIAMS, *Host:*

The first time I did the show was when Eddie Murphy and Joe Piscopo were on. Eddie had done a lot of great characters. I think he had just started to kick in the movies, but he was still on the show, which was great. It was an interesting time, because it was the new regime, not Lorne.

PAM NORRIS:

Before the beginning of the season, we knew that Eddie was going to be away a lot of the time doing movies. So what we wanted was a backlog of Eddie taped sketches. I wrote a lot of those. We basically just did a private show that was one Eddie sketch after another that we taped with a studio audience. And then those were later put into the shows.

ANDY BRECKMAN:

For the live shows, they didn't make any announcement that Eddie wasn't really there, but he certainly didn't show up to wave good night at the end.

DICK EBERSOL:

It would have been very difficult, I think, to have kept the show on the air without Eddie. The show would absolutely have launched for the '83–'84 season, but he was still the main draw. And it would have been pretty hard, I think, to keep up the show long enough to get to the next year—which Brandon labeled my Steinbrenner era in the spring of '84.

MARGARET OBERMAN:

I remember when Eddie was really starting to make the big money. One night Jeffrey Katzenberg came up to the offices—*48 Hrs.* had just opened—and he was sitting in the writers' room on the ninth floor, waiting for Eddie. And when Eddie came in, Katzenberg gave him a check for a million dollars. And none of us had ever seen a check for a million dollars before.

When Eddie wasn't at read-through, we'd have to go find him; he'd be downstairs buying jewelry in the jewelry store.

HERB SARGENT, *Writer:*

Eddie came to me one day and said, "I don't know who my friends are anymore." And he was frightened, you know. He said that people would patronize him or compliment him, and he wasn't sure that they were serious. Maybe it was only because he was on television. And he was scared. It wasn't showing up in his work, but it was a real personal fear that he had. And so I got Harry Belafonte to come and talk to him. Because the same thing had happened to him when he was young.

Harry came up, and I put him in a room with Eddie and let them talk. I think it worked out okay.

ANDY BRECKMAN:

I remember he got a million dollars for appearing in just a few scenes of a Dudley Moore movie. Eddie framed that million-dollar check and put it on his wall. It was one million dollars for a few weeks' work. Oh yeah, he cashed the check; the one on the wall was a copy.

JOE PISCOPO:

Eddie got death threats and—I don't think he'll mind me telling you—he was upset with that. That was as insane as it got. And I remember saying, "Eddie, these are just jealous creeps that don't know what they're doing, don't even worry about it." He was upset about it and in retrospect rightly so. Just think about it, a brilliant talent like that. I hate to even bring it up now, because there's always a nut out there. Even after he left *Saturday Night Live,* I remember him being pulled over a lot by cops in Los Angeles. He was thrown against the car once. That is really sad.

BARRY BLAUSTEIN:

I think it was hard for Eddie. It was hard for both of them. I think when Joe saw Eddie eclipsing him tremendously, it was hard. The relationship changes. They're no longer equals. Joe was a really good impressionist. He worked really hard on mannerisms, to get an impression down. And Eddie would then just be able to do that same impression—boom—like that.

ANDREW KURTZMAN:

People thought that there was a big blowup between Eddie and Joey. They drifted apart. We all heard later that there were some Sinatra-like moments between them. It was that period where Joe was going on talk shows and talking about being friends with Eddie a lot—all that talk-show stuff about things he did with Eddie. And I remember someone saying that Eddie got really ticked about that.

CHRIS ALBRECHT:

Joe looked after this kid from the moment he showed up. And more than a couple people noticed that when there was an opportunity to return the support, none came. Eddie never helped Joe later on. Never gave Joe a part in a movie, never did anything. Never, ever helped Joe. Why not? I couldn't answer that.

ELLIOT WALD:

It was really hard to get hosts the first year I was there. We lost Nick Nolte the first night. He supposedly went into rehab, but he was seen preparing for rehab at Studio 54. But Eddie came in and took over as host and of course did great. That was the year Eddie was half there and half not.

TIM KAZURINSKY:

Ebersol was not a writer and he's got cheap tastes. So—this is the frustrating thing—all the good scripts went into the wastebasket on Wednesday. And you'd stay up, and people were fueling themselves with cocaine from Monday through Wednesday, because Wednesday morning we had the read-through at eleven. And you literally had that fifty hours to get a show written. So you would kill yourself to get good scripts done. Ebersol was looking for scripts that would make Eddie and Joe bigger stars. He was looking for impersonations of showbiz people. Anything that had an idea or a political notion or that he thought was a little too smart—bang, dead, into the wastebasket. And so the writers would get more depressed, they'd do more drugs, and pretty soon most of the scripts were written for Eddie and Joe. It was like publish or perish—you had to get a piece on the air, so everybody wrote thinking, "If I don't do a piece for Eddie, it won't get on, and I'll get fired"—which people often did. It was really fucking crazy.

DICK EBERSOL:

John Belushi had become convinced that Fear, which was this punk kind of rock group, were on the verge of breaking out and convinced me that I ought to book them and personally vouched that they were terrific and so on. Anyway, their musical number—in the last fifteen or twenty minutes of the show—was so dark. They had films in it showing pumpkins that, as you carved the pumpkin, blood came out of each carving. It was just like O'Donoghue at his darkest. And I, quite frankly, had given him too much freedom. But now here I am with Fear itself. We're on the air. And all of a sudden they're out of control and there are dancers around them—including John, who you can't see on television—and they're slam-dancing, that's what it was called, banging off each other, banging into the audience, banging into cameramen. None of this was really foreseen. And things got really, completely, and totally out of hand. And so you're sitting at home and you're watching this, and you don't really have the total sense of what we could see, because Davey Wilson in the booth was not shooting what was breaking out in the lower areas of the audience, where people sit on those movable chairs.

And I think probably, for the only time in the history of the show, I had been worried about it enough to have told Davey to at least have a film standing by. It was a sensational film that had aired in the first show, four weeks before, on October third, with Eddie playing a black inmate who wrote poetry in iambic pentameter or something like that. It was a takeoff on whoever Norman Mailer loved at the time, who was a wronged guy in prison, and a wonderful piece of character. And so I told them to roll it. And so we just rolled the film.

We let Fear finish in the studio, and I don't think they knew until they were back in their dressing room that the last half of their song had gone away. Anyway, the total damage that was done in the studio was about $2,500. But the *New York Post* headline on Monday was, "Saturday Night Live Riot Destroys $250,000."

DAVE WILSON, *Director:*

It was like mosh pit kind of stuff, with people diving off the stage into the audience. And all I remember is Dick Ebersol actually running around, ducking underneath the cameras, trying to quiet it all down.

The death of John Belushi on March 5, 1982, at the age of thirty-three, brought the festivities to a sorrowful, traumatized halt. No matter how many people might have predicted a premature demise for this ebullient man of vast and varied appetites and legendary overindulgence, the death came as a dark, cold shock. It told his friends at Saturday Night Live *not only that John was mortal, but that they were too. It had the sobering impact of a biblical warning: Your parents were right after all, dammit— drugs can destroy a life, excess can be fatal, self-abuse can have severe consequences, there's no free lunch, and all that other antihedonistic claptrap.*

Belushi's death seemed tragic on many different levels. That his death was linked to drug abuse only reinforced the mistaken public perception that Belushi was some childish party animal, undisciplined and wild— much like the slobbish Bluto whom he played in his triumphant movie hit Animal House. *But those who knew Belushi even superficially knew him as tender, sensitive, painfully vulnerable, and lovable. The only time Belushi and Bluto really resembled each other was during a scene in which Bluto tries to cheer up a despondent fellow frat boy. He romps, he mugs, he cracks a bottle over his head, and then he pantomimes a big happy grin, propping up the corners of his mouth with his fingers. The gesture recalls the sweet innocence of Harpo Marx.*

Saturday Night Live's *resident ensemble had been called the Beatles of comedy, and now they had their own dead Lennon. They could never go back, never regroup, never be together again. It would never be just like it was.*

In Don't Look Back in Anger, *a famous short film made by Tom Schiller for the show in 1977 and set sometime in the distant future, an elderly but dapper Belushi visits the wintry graves of fellow alumni and explains that though some predicted he'd be the first to go, it was in fact he alone who survived the intervening decades. And the reason? "I'm— a dancer!" he exclaims, just before launching into some sort of Greek-Albanian folk stomp. John's death came well after the original Not Ready for Prime Time Players had disbanded, and yet it seemed to shut down this exclusive club once and for all.*

ANNE BEATTS, *Writer:*

I had a friend who was in Vietnam. We were talking about our experiences—his in the war, mine on the show. And it seemed somewhat equivalent. Then I said, "Well, but nobody died in mine." And he said, "Yes, they did." I thought about it for a second. "Oh. You're right. They did."

BARBARA GALLAGHER:

I ran into John at a restaurant in Los Angeles, where I'd moved. I didn't want to go over to his table because I didn't know what to expect. I hadn't seen him in years. But he was really sweet. He came over to me and said, "You know what? I'm clean." I said, "John, I'm so happy for you." He said, "I am too. I'm on the right road again. Danny's been my savior." And then two months later, he was dead.

LORNE MICHAELS:

I'd lived at the Chateau Marmont for three years, so the irony of John dying there was, well, whatever. About two weeks before he died, I was out in L.A. for a movie meeting, and Buck Henry invited me to go with him to the Playboy Mansion. I had only been there once, and that was to ask Hefner to host the show. Buck said, "He shows his *Saturday Night Live* show every Saturday night in the screening room." So I went there with Buck, and John was there. He was a little fucked-up but not crazy-man fucked-up, just a little fucked-up. And we were sitting in the screening room watching an Armand Assante movie. Hefner sat in the front row on the aisle and there was a little table with a bowl of popcorn on it next to his seat. I was sitting in the back with Buck. And John, to make us laugh, crept down the aisle and started taking popcorn out of Hefner's bowl. So when Hefner would reach over, there would be less and less each time, because he wasn't looking at it. It was a nice visual.

Later, in the game room, John and I talked. He was enormously effusive about *Noble Rot,* the script that Don Novello was writing for him, and how hilarious it was. It was very warm between us. Lots of hugs. It was good. It was the last time I saw him.

NEIL LEVY:

Exactly one week before John died, I was trying to get into the Ritz to see Mink DeVille, and I had forgotten my *Saturday Night Live* ID and the guy at the door would not let me in. And Belushi came by and says to the guy, "Do you know who this is?!" And the guy backed up in horror, because Belushi was really on a rant about his not letting me in. Then John grabbed me and took me in and took me right to the dressing room. I thanked him and then afterwards I wanted to thank him again, and Judy was sitting there and I asked her how he was and she said, "Not good." I think this was just before he flew to L.A.

DICK EBERSOL:

John got back into drugs the weekend Lorne married Susan. John's movie *Continental Divide* had come out around Labor Day of 1981 with Blair Brown, and there were two diametrically opposed reviews. I can't remember who was which. But either *Time* or *Newsweek* wrote that he was the new Spencer Tracy, and the other one wrote that the movie was a massive disappointment to all of John's fans. And the box office showed the latter. And it was only a day later that John fell back into everything else; he had been clean for two or three years at that point. And it was pretty much downhill from there.

Lorne got married the weekend after Labor Day, and I remember John was out of control at Lorne's wedding, which was held out at Lorne's house in the Hamptons. And nobody knew what to do. Nobody would handle it. And I remember pleading with Bernie Brill-stein to help me with John and he wouldn't. And then finally I grabbed John and literally dragged him out of the reception, across Lorne's lawn, into the downstairs bedroom, where I laid him down and he fell asleep. That was mid-September.

ROBIN WILLIAMS:

A friend came over and said, "Your friend John died." I said, "Excuse me?" The night before, I had been told by a guy at a bar called On the Rocks that "John wants to see you over at the Marmont." I went, "Okay, that's weird."

The next morning, they say he's dead. And I had to go testify in front of a grand jury about what I'd seen — which was nothing. It was wild. I could never find that guy to ask why I was sent there. He had said that De Niro and John wanted to see us. When I got there I called Bob and he was like, "Not right now. I'm busy, okay?" Okay, great. It was weird — maybe a setup, maybe not. Maybe someone was trying to set up a big bust. Who the fuck knows?

The sadness is that John could have done anything. He loved music, but the fact is he could have acted and done some really great drama. Kind of like almost Elvis on that level. He was like a comic Brando. He had "the thing." They just started to pull him out, because he started out doing those great comedies. He kicked ass in *Animal House.* Even in *1941,* you remember him as being this life force.

BERNIE BRILLSTEIN, *Manager:*

I was one of the last people to see him alive. I gave him $1,800, but it wasn't for drugs, it was for Bill Haley's guitar. I owed him a birthday

Lorne Michaels, executive producer of *Saturday Night Live,* in the year of its birth, 1975. NBC president Herb Schlosser said, "No matter what anyone else tells you, the guy who created the show, and made it what it is, is Lorne Michaels."

© EDIE BASKIN

Magnificent Seven. The original Not Ready for Prime Time Players (from left, clockwise): Chevy Chase, John Belushi, Gilda Radner, Garrett Morris, Dan Aykroyd, Jane Curtin, Laraine Newman.

© EDIE BASKIN

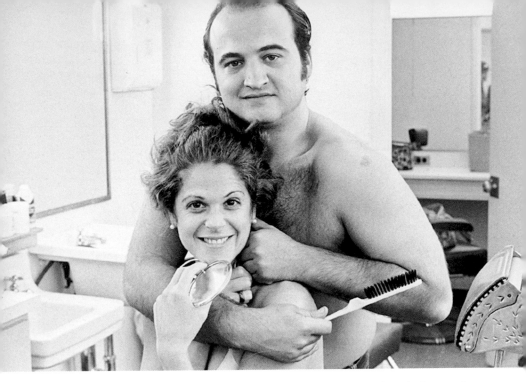

Gilda Radner and John Belushi in the makeup room. Gilda "sat shiva" for John because Lorne Michaels didn't want to hire him for the show. Michaels changed his mind. © EDIE BASKIN

The *Star Trek* sketch, a pivotal ensemble production from the first season (May 29, 1976), began a long *SNL* tradition of biting the network that fed it. Dan Aykroyd played Dr. McCoy, John Belushi was Captain James T. Kirk, and Chevy Chase played Mr. Spock, who vainly tried to prevent a network executive (host Elliott Gould) from canceling the series. © EDIE BASKIN

We, the women: Jane Curtin, Laraine Newman, and Gilda Radner. Laraine shot up heroin, Gilda binged and vomited, and Jane went home each night to her husband and dog. © EDIE BASKIN

Lorne, Chevy, Dan, and John clown around at the Lincoln Memorial during a trip to Washington in 1976. John forgot his ID, but guards let him into the White House anyway.

© 1976 THE WASHINGTON POST. PHOTOGRAPH BY GERALD MARTINEAU. Reprinted with permission.

Jane Curtin emcees "Mr. U.S.A.," a male beauty pageant that flip-flopped gender roles.
© EDIE BASKIN

"Samurai Hotel," with Belushi taunting host Richard Pryor. The network was so nervous over Pryor's appearance that executives ordered a five-second delay to catch obscene ad-libs before they aired. But director Dave Wilson says nobody was ever able to make a "delay" work anyway.
© EDIE BASKIN

LEFT: Two insatiably wild and crazy guys: Steve Martin and Dan Aykroyd as those swinging would-be babe magnets, the Festrunk brothers, not-so-fresh off the boat from Czechoslovakia and perpetually in search of "foxes" with "big American breasts." © EDIE BASKIN

RIGHT: Jane, Dan, and Laraine as the Coneheads, beer-guzzling visitors from another planet. Aykroyd originally conceived the characters as Pinhead Lawyers from France while smoking a joint—but there were worries that encephalitics in the viewing audience might be offended.
© EDIE BASKIN

That (Second) Championship Season: Stars and writers from the show's second year. Standing (from left): Al Franken, Dan Aykroyd, Alan Zweibel, Herb Sargent, Michael O'Donoghue, Chevy Chase, Bill Murray, Tom Davis, Lorne Michaels. Seated: Rosie Shuster, Marilyn Suzanne Miller, Tom Schiller, John Belushi, James Downey. Foreground: Anne Beatts. Chevy and Bill got into a fistfight backstage; Chevy thinks John made it happen. © EDIE BASKIN

Some of the real musicians in the *SNL* band may have scoffed, and musical director Howard Shore had his misgivings, but Aykroyd and Belushi as Elwood and Jake Blues, the Blues Brothers, went from *SNL* warm-up act to a blockbuster movie directed by John Landis. © EDIE BASKIN

Bill Murray and Gilda Radner, as nerds Todd and Lisa, are convulsed in laughter at Dan Aykroyd's overexposed refrigerator repairman. Network censors told Aykroyd to keep his pants pulled up. He didn't care; he let them slide down anyway, and the audience roared. © EDIE BASKIN

Gilda Radner and NBC president Fred Silverman at an *SNL* party. Silverman's dream of turning Gilda into NBC's "Lucy" or Carol Burnett, and giving her a prime-time variety show, went up in smoke when Gilda simply said no. Silverman blamed Michaels and excluded him from conversations about his successor. NBC PHOTO

Bill Murray, self-described "adopted" child of the *SNL* players. Given the daunting task of replacing Chevy Chase when he went off to Hollywood, Murray won over the audience with such inspired characters as Nick the (lousy) Lounge Singer and a speech in which he confessed, "I don't think I'm making it on the show."
© EDIE BASKIN

Eddie Murphy, the biggest star, at least in terms of box office receipts, ever to emerge from *Saturday Night Live*. Producer Jean Doumanian claims to have discovered Murphy, but he languished in the background until Dick Ebersol took over the show. If not for Murphy's talent and popularity, *SNL* would probably have died in the early eighties. © EDIE BASKIN

Joe Piscopo plays straight man to Eddie Murphy's hilarious impression of Gumby, the children's cartoon character, as a hardened old show business veteran. Fellow cast members were heard to observe, "Eddie Murphy's success went to Joe Piscopo's head." © EDIE BASKIN

Guests Barbara Bach and Ringo Starr flank Billy Crystal as Fernando, one of the durable characters Crystal created in the last year of Dick Ebersol's reign as *SNL* executive producer. Crystal was supposed to appear on the premiere of *Saturday Night Live* in 1975, but an argument over the timing of his sketch led to his walking out the night of the show. He returned in triumph nine years later. NBC PHOTO

One of the greatest of all *SNL* political sketches: A 1988 debate among contenders for the Republican presidential nomination, brilliantly written by James Downey, Al Franken, and Tom Davis and starring, from left, Kevin Nealon as Pierre "Pete" DuPont, Al Franken as Pat Robertson, Dan Aykroyd (making a special cameo appearance) as Bob Dole, Nora Dunn as Pat Schroeder, Dana Carvey as George Bush, and Phil Hartman as Jack Kemp. The sketch helped reestablish *SNL*'s credentials as America's leading political satirist. NBC PHOTO

LEFT: Martin Short and Billy Crystal as "Kate and Ali" — Katharine Hepburn, whom Short imitated flawlessly, and Muhammad Ali, another of Crystal's virtuoso impressions. With Christopher Guest and Harry Shearer, they formed an "all-star" team that once again saved *SNL* from going under. NBC PHOTO

RIGHT: Norm Macdonald. Chevy Chase thought he was the best "Weekend Update" anchor since — well, Chevy Chase — but his stint in the anchor chair provoked the wrath of NBC West Coast president Don Ohlmeyer, who mounted a relentless, obsessive campaign to get Macdonald removed from the post in 1994. © EDIE BASKIN

Sometimes the envelope got pushed too far. Sinead O'Connor (center), host Tim Robbins, and Lorne Michaels during rehearsals for a 1992 show in which O'Connor shocked the audience — and everybody involved with the show — by tearing up a photo of the Pope at the end of a song. Director Dave Wilson ordered that the "applause" sign not be lit, and the sequence ended in deathly silence. © EDIE BASKIN

LEFT: Mike Myers and Dana Carvey as Wayne and Garth in "Wayne's World," a sketch that began life modestly in the "ten to one" spot (the last sketch on the show) and eventually became the basis of the highest-grossing movie ever spun off *SNL* characters. Carvey and Myers got along fine in the TV version; the movie set was another matter. © EDIE BASKIN

RIGHT: "Two guys named Chris, hired on the same day, sharing an office....One's a black guy from Bed-Stuy, one's a white guy from Madison, Wisconsin. Now—which one is going to OD?"—Chris Rock on himself and fellow cast member, officemate, and friend, Chris Farley. © EDIE BASKIN

Letting it all hang out. Chris Farley romps through an "audition" for male strippers, with host Patrick Swayze. Farley idolized and emulated John Belushi even to the point of wearing Belushi's pants when he found them in the wardrobe department. But inner demons similar to Belushi's led to Farley's death at the same tragically early age, thirty-three. © EDIE BASKIN

"Good-nights" from one of the great shows of the nineties, with host Tom Hanks, musical guest Bruce Springsteen, and regular Chris Farley in the foreground. Hanks was one of the most frequent and hardworking guest hosts, pulling all-nighters with the writers and never behaving like a prima donna. © EDIE BASKIN

More stars than there are in the heavens—but too many of them really are in heaven. A rare reunion of cast members, writers, hosts, and producers from several eras of *Saturday Night Live* at the Aspen Comedy Festival. At left, *60 Minutes* correspondent Steve Kroft moderates the discussion. Michaels sits front row, far left, and former executive producer Dick Ebersol is fourth from the right. © NEAL PRESTON/2002

Comic Andrew Dice Clay with Michaels and a studio technician during rehearsals for what would be one of the most contentious *SNL* shows of the nineties. Cast member Nora Dunn refused to appear on the show because she found Clay's humor misogynistic. Clay insisted he was only playing a character in the same way members of the *SNL* cast did every week.
© EDIE BASKIN

The Gap Girls in a sketch from the early nineties: David Spade, Adam Sandler, Chris Farley. Network executives were at the gates demanding changes and threatening Michaels. Among other things, they wanted Sandler fired because they didn't "get" his comedy; he went on to become a major movie star of hugely successful comedy films.
© Norman Ng for EDIE BASKIN

Like Buttah. Barbra Streisand makes a surprise appearance during a special edition of "Coffee Talk," the Mike Myers sketch in which Myers (left) played talk-show host Linda Richman, a gabby yenta who sometimes told viewers to "talk amongst yourselves." Madonna and Roseanne look on.
© Norman Ng for EDIE BASKIN

Dana Carvey as George Bush, Phil Hartman as Bill Clinton, and David Spade as Ross Perot greet the audience from "home base" in Studio 8H. For many younger viewers, *SNL* became a primary source of political information. © EDIE BASKIN

Molly Shannon as the beleaguered Catholic schoolgirl Mary Katherine Gallagher, with Ana Gasteyer, Cheri Oteri, and host Gwyneth Paltrow. Though *Saturday Night Live* was often criticized as a "boys club," women writers were prominent from the beginning, and the casts of the nineties included some of the most talented women in the show's history. © Mary Ellen Matthews for EDIE BASKIN

Monica Lewinsky as herself and Darrell Hammond as Bill Clinton. Beginning in the nineties, celebrities spoofed on the show were more and more likely to make appearances—from Robert DeNiro to Janet Reno. Veteran writer James Downey thought it was a bad idea and that inviting infamous presidential fellationist Lewinsky onto the show was a "tacky" thing to do. © Mary Ellen Matthews for EDIE BASKIN

Saturday Night Live reborn—again. In the second half of the nineties, the show went through yet another resurgence, thanks largely to a talented and relatively drug-free cast that included (from left) Will Ferrell, Chris Kattan, and Cheri Oteri. Frequent host John Goodman joins them. Ferrell, the most versatile "utility player" since Phil Hartman, left at the end of the 2001–02 season. © Mary Ellen Matthews for EDIE BASKIN

Friends of the producer. Michaels (right) greets host Alec Baldwin and musical guest Paul McCartney in 1993. Baldwin, one of the most popular recurring hosts, once asked Michaels if Rosemary Clooney could be his musical guest. Request denied.
© EDIE BASKIN

Opening the twenty-fifth-anniversary special. Bill Murray reunites with Paul Shaffer for their first Nick the Lounge Singer sketch in years, doing the Bruce Springsteen song "Badlands." Murray later called it one of the highlights of his career. The sketch "killed" and got the show off to a rousing start. © Mary Ellen Matthews for EDIE BASKIN

Onstage at the twenty-fifth-anniversary prime-time special. Writers Robert Smigel, James Downey, and Tim Herlihy—arguably three of the show's best—with star Adam Sandler. The special earned spectacular ratings and reunited all the living cast members from a quarter-century of comedy—with the exception of Eddie Murphy, who refused to appear. © Mary Ellen Matthews for EDIE BASKIN

Jeopardy!, *SNL*-style: Will Ferrell as Alex Trebek hosts one of the show's most popular and hilarious recurring sketches, with Michael J. Fox as Tom Cruise, Jimmy Fallon as former cast member Adam Sandler, and Darrell Hammond doing his wickedly ridiculous impression of Sean Connery. © EDIE BASKIN

Last-minute rehearsal. Jimmy Fallon and Tina Fey, in background, go over jokes for a "Weekend Update" segment—always the last thing to be written. Fallon and Fey brought "Update" back to its former prominence as the show's satirical centerpiece. © Mary Ellen Matthews for EDIE BASKIN

Cleaning up on Emmy night in 2000 (from left): supervising producer Ken Aymong, coproducer Mike Shoemaker, Michaels, and coproducer Marci Klein. During the 2000s Michaels relied on these three colleagues, along with producer Steve Higgins, to handle the crises and complications of each week's show. © AP/WIDE WORLD PHOTOS

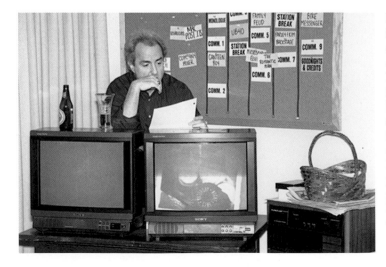

Michaels in his ninth-floor office, which opens onto the balcony of Studio 8H. Behind him: the all-important lineup board on which each show's list of sketches is arranged on index cards. At right, Michaels's ever-present basket of fresh popcorn, religiously kept filled by his staff. © EDIE BASKIN

present and he said, "I just found out what you could get me," because I didn't know what to get him, his birthday had already passed, and he said, "I saw Bill Haley's guitar at the Guitar Factory," whatever it was, and I said, "How much is it? I'll give you a check." And he said, "Eighteen hundred dollars, but they only take cash." And me being a moron, I gave it to him. He bought drugs with it that night. I always felt responsible, but he would have gotten it someplace else.

He used to come and say, "Give me a hundred dollars," and I'd say, "I'm not going to give you a hundred dollars." And he said, "It's my money, I'll call my business manager." Okay. Because I used to get all his checks. So you see, there was no way to stop it.

JIM BELUSHI:

I trust Bernie Brillstein. I don't think he's the bad guy. I'm going to tell you a little something about my brother. I don't care how strong-willed you are, after twenty minutes, you'd be doing whatever he wanted you to do. And you'd love it. He'd have you dancing on a cigarette machine in two hours. And loving it. He was just that powerful.

Did Bernie "enable" him? You know, we all enabled him, because we never knew what it was. Everybody was getting high. It was not a big deal. And then you turn around and say, "Did they enable Chris Farley?" No. They sent him into rehab seventeen times. That disease comes into your life, comes into your family's life, and it slowly strangles until someone dies. If Bernie was an enabler, so were we all, because we were all under the spell of John's charm, and none of us knew any better. We just didn't know better. Remember, the Betty Ford Center started in 1982. It wasn't popular to get cleaned out until after John died. He led us in comedy, he led us in film, and he led us into rehab. He was before all of us.

John ate up all his adrenaline. He ate it all up. He lived three lives. He lived to ninety-nine.

LORNE MICHAELS:

Bernie had to stop one of John's cousins from taking a picture of John's body naked. It was a fifteen-grand thing, to sell the picture. The guy's argument was that John wouldn't have cared.

BILL MURRAY:

John never gets enough credit from the world. John made that show possible in a way, because he brought all the people out from Chicago to do the National Lampoon Show and then the *Radio Hour*. I got the job from him on the *Radio Hour*. He brought all these people out. He was responsible for bringing a lot of those people to the party.

He was the best stage actor I've ever seen. He walked on the stage and you couldn't look at anyone else. People that only knew him from television really missed something. Onstage he was a monster. He was an absolute bear. And he was brilliant. He had the ability to see what an improvisational sketch needed. He would enter scenes and "solve" them in ninety seconds. He was really gifted, really gifted. And obviously he lived life hard, but he lived well. You could have more fun with him — and as time went on, you had less of those moments with him because he was sort of spun out there in the world — but he could have more fun in the simplest situations than any person I've ever met of my ilk, you know — any entertainer type.

He ended his life like a rock-and-roller and an enormous celebrity, a big star, but in the simplest situations, he really shone. He really could find the essential in a moment and in an experience. He was something.

BOB TISCHLER:

It was horrible. John had been a really close friend of mine for years. He picked me to produce *The Blues Brothers*. He was horrible to a lot of people, but he had many sides to him, and he was always a great friend to me. When he died, it devastated me. I wasn't surprised by it, because I had been with him through a lot. I used cocaine like everybody else used it. It was not a problem for me, but it was a real problem for him, and during the Blues Brothers years he would take just a little hit of cocaine and become an animal. And that was horrible.

When John died, it changed me. I gave up doing drugs. And I haven't done any since.

TOM DAVIS, *Writer:*

I was very open about smoking pot. I got away with it until Belushi died. That was the end of that. I couldn't smoke in the office openly anymore. No more of that shit. As long as we were a hot show, I felt I could get away with it. But when Belushi died, and then everyone started having babies, that was the end.

JOE PISCOPO:

When Belushi died, rest his soul, everybody stopped. All the drugs stopped. I always got such a kick out of that.

TIM KAZURINSKY:

Bob Tischler called to tell me John was dead. I ran into the office to help make calls and try to contact everybody in his family that I knew, and also get the Second City tribute going. I think Judy Belushi kept John alive maybe longer than he would've been. She had bodyguards. She had him watched, and her life became keeping drugs away from John, until she began to shrivel. How much can you do? Can you really watch somebody twenty-four hours a day? I think Judy fought the good fight. I don't know that his agents, managers, and producers and bosses did as much as they could. At some point, you have to represent reality to the person in trouble.

JANE CURTIN:

It was very sad. But it wasn't shocking.

CARRIE FISHER, *Host:*

When we heard he had died, we were all waiting to find out what he had done. We didn't know. And everyone was hoping it wasn't their drug of choice. It was horrible. What I recall happening was, we were all in the room and we heard that it was heroin and it had been injected, and that was just farther than this group went. So everyone kind of breathed a sigh of relief—not because you weren't distraught over his death, but because he had gone farther than anybody else went. One always hopes that things like that are cautionary tales, and they are not. I think I overdosed two years later.

BILL MURRAY:

When John died, it was like, "Oh God, what a drag this is going to be. What a drag this is." And when they said he died of an overdose, my brother Brian said, "He died from four beers." The guy was a real short hitter behind the bar. Really, four beers would put him into like an absolute delirium. He didn't have a high threshold in some ways. Because he was a finely tuned instrument, it didn't take much to set him a-kilter. The fact that he died was like, "Oh Christ, why'd you go and do that?"

When you're with somebody who does stuff which is either incredibly pleasing, incredibly amusing, or incredibly disappointing in some way, you're sort of glad it's not you that did it, because it could have been any one of us goofing off somehow. We've all been through stuff, and we've pushed limits and crossed lines in order to establish where the line was, sort of, or to reestablish the line. So when he died, I think it was, "Okay, now someone has crossed this line here; where does that put us? Where does that leave us? What does that say?" Because he really was the icebreaker in so many ways. He was the first one to come to New York from Chicago of our group. He was the first one to do a lot of things. He really was a leader in so many ways that the idea that he was the first to die was probably not surprising. That he was the first to do anything was not a surprise. That's really the truth.

John's funeral was great theater. It was our first funeral together, and there were TV cameras, and it's like, "Whoa. There's nothing funny going to happen and these cameras are here." And Danny did the motorcycle thing, and the night before I think we'd gone out on John's property and fired shotguns at the moon and stuff and tried to do something sort of epic that involved howling and sort of displaced rage.

God, the song James Taylor sang—chills. "Walk Down That Lonesome Road," you know that one? It's chilling. He sang it with his brothers and a sister, I think. All the press and everything were at a fencepost like a hundred yards away. When he sang that song, it was just, "Ooooh okay. That is the lesson, I guess."

Whenever I hear it, I'm right back there at John's grave.

EDIE BASKIN, *Photographer*:

Right after John died, *People* magazine called me and asked, "Do you have some pictures of John when he was doing the sketch with the powdered sugar doughnuts?" They wanted me to give them pictures of John with powdered sugar all over his nose so it looked like he was doing coke. I said, "You're sick. Good-bye."

GARRETT MORRIS, *Cast Member*:

One time I saw his picture in *People* magazine, and he was like a balloon. I thought, "Oh my God." I couldn't believe it. I was worried about his heart or his circulatory system. During the previous two years or so, I was thinking he personally didn't like me, because he was saying a lot of things that just were uncharacteristic. And then when I saw the picture in *People,* I began to realize what had happened.

The way I found out he died was an *L.A. Times* lady got my number and had the nerve to call me and tell me he was dead and then try to elicit a response. She didn't take into account at all that it broke me up. I said to her, "Look, I don't want anything about drugs or anything." And she said, "Well, I don't let people put restrictions on my interviews." And of course I hung up, because I didn't want to have AT&T sue me for using words like—well, "motherfucker" is not a four-letter word, it's a twelve-letter word, but I was going to call her a motherfucker at least twelve times.

TIM KAZURINSKY:

The day Belushi died, I went in to help out with making calls, because I was very good friends with the Belushi family. John and I were supposed to have had dinner on March third, to celebrate my birthday, and he was in L.A., and he killed himself March fifth. So there were a bunch of us up there, and guys were crying, and I was going to call Second City to get hold of Jim so they could get a medical unit over to John's mother, because she had a bad heart. They wanted somebody that knew CPR to be there with defibrillator panels when she was told the news.

So I'm off making calls trying to find Jim Belushi. I run back into one of the executive's offices on the floor and the executive's on the phone making arrangements for funeral stuff and he has tears in his eyes—and he is leaning over his desk snorting coke! And I went, "What the fuck are you doing?! Jesus! You're making funeral arrangements for a dead man and—" You know, it was almost laughable. I get sick when I think about it.

PENNY MARSHALL, *Guest:*

None of us knew about the other life he had, if he had that life—or if he was just starting or experimenting. All of us were smoking grass and doing coke once in a while. We did what we did, but it wasn't like he was more abusive than anyone else. We knew there were drugs, but he had a whole different set of friends, I think, that none of his good friends knew about. He didn't do any more than anybody else unless a fan came up and he wanted to be bold. Fans would just come up and hand him a gram. He represented that to them, a wild person. My fans wrote with crayon on lined paper; I had different fans. But we never saw needles, we never saw heroin, we never saw any of that shit.

LARAINE NEWMAN, *Cast Member:*

I was at my house in Los Angeles when I heard that John had died. A friend of mine called me on the phone and said, "Hey, did you know that guy John Bell-utchee?" And I said, "Yeah." "Well, he's dead." And I remember being annoyed that the guy didn't even know how to pronounce John's name and then hanging up and turning on the TV and seeing all the coverage and it being so unreal. This was the first time that someone I was close to had died. And unfortunately it wasn't going to be the last. So it was unreal to me. I just couldn't believe it—the sight of a covered body being carried out of the Chateau Marmont, and me knowing that that shape had to be him. And the sordid image that the details elicited in my mind, you know, of probably all the shades being drawn and here was this woman giving him a fix and letting him die. Whether she knew he'd OD'd before she left or not, it's just so hideous.

CARRIE FISHER:

John had offered me some drugs once, and I said, "John, should you be doing this?" and he said, *"Do you want some or not?!"* And I just thought, "You know what? I can't do this. I am not a cop, and he is three times bigger than I am." Danny was always trying to get him to stop. We all were. But you couldn't stop him, you couldn't stop him. You couldn't have stopped me. I always think about people who say, "We should have blah, blah, blah." You can't. As much as you'd like to think so, you can't.

The thing I regretted about John was that he hadn't had a scare, he hadn't had some sort of overdose, or hospitalization or something, some warning. He just went straight to death.

TIM KAŻURINSKY:

Having grown up in the sixties, I was kind of done with my drugs by the seventies. And so here it was the eighties, and I particularly hated cocaine. And whenever a new shipment arrived on the floor, I would come in and see everybody grinding their teeth. I came in one day and pretty much the whole floor was just craving it heavily, and I went, "Oh, this is not good. I'm going to write at home." Because everybody was running into my office with gigantic pupils and grinding teeth saying, "I've got an idea." And you know, I've always found that cocaine causes constipation of the brain and diarrhea of the mouth. In the time it would take to sit and listen to people's idiot ideas while they were coked up to the tits, I could get more work done at home. It seemed like the secretaries, the PA's, everybody, was tooted that particular day, so I just took off. A couple of friends of mine who were Chicago writers, I called their wives and said, "I got your husbands hired on the show and I really don't want to send them home in body bags. You have to come to New York and stop them, because they are doing way too much coke." And they did. They came and took care of their guys.

JIM BELUSHI:

John would have been happy that I made it onto *Saturday Night Live*, but he actually wanted me to be a dramatic actor. When I started at Second City, I called him and said, "I got in at Second City." There was a long pause on the phone. He goes, "Uh, shouldn't you be at Goodman Theater or something, be more like a dramatic actor?" I said, "I'm really enjoying this here." He said, "You're a better actor than me, don't you think you should be, like, doing drama?" I said, "I can probably do both, John." He goes, "Okay." That was it.

BRIAN DOYLE-MURRAY:

John and I were quite close. He had replaced me at Second City when I left initially. I lived on his couch in New York City for six months. He was bigger than life. No matter what he did, he didn't think he would die. When he died, Lorne asked me to say something at the end of the show, because we had been together a long time. I recounted this one incident: He and I were walking down Bleecker Street and it was snowing and he had one of those hood things up. And a truck hit him and it flipped him into the air and he rolled up against the curb. And he just jumped right back up. An ambulance came and took him to the hospital. And he was fine. I mean, he got hit *hard* by a truck. And no problem. So I thought he was pretty indestructible.

DAVID SHEFFIELD:

I did go to a party one time at the Blues Bar. It was 1980. Belushi had done a guest spot on the show. We walked in. Robin Williams was behind the bar passing out beers. And Belushi stood at the door as we walked in and looked me up and down and said, "Who the fuck are you? I don't recognize you." He said, "Did you bring any beer?" I said, "No, but I got a J." "Oh, all right, come on in."

LORNE MICHAELS:

When I got the call from Bernie, I was at Broadway Video. I had lost my father suddenly when I was fourteen—he was only fifty. It was a big surprise. So I feel like since then I've always been prepared for the worst. It was easier for me to go into a withholding mode. I dealt with John's family, and Judy and I arranged for airplanes to get everybody there. It was the first time in my life I had ever chartered airplanes. When I walked out of my office, there were cameras and lights everywhere.

Bernie flew in with John in a body bag on the Warner corporate plane. Danny and some other guys were waiting at the airport on motorcycles to salute him. The plane landed. And then they took off. Bernie had to take the body to the mortuary.

I didn't deal with anything until I saw John in the coffin. I had seen him look worse, but it was awful. Standing at the grave, we all just sobbed.

TIM KAZURINSKY:

When we made the movie *Neighbors,* that was probably the most fun I had. We would work on Staten Island on the movie in the daytime and then every night go back to John's house and order in food and hang out and watch old movies. And John would do impersonations of Brando as the Godfather and make us howl until our sides hurt. He was the greatest guy to hang with. Half of him was this poor peasant Albanian kid from this small town where he'd been much looked down upon. And he said to me once, "Fuck them, I'm going to go out and become the most famous guy in the world just to spite them." And he did that, and he could be that person, but the other half of John was that he was just this really lovable guy who did go out and become the most famous guy in the world and that wasn't the answer. And he would go out on what I call that three A.M. to six A.M. club crawl in New York, where I don't imagine he was the same person around Mick Jagger and Robert De Niro and Francis Ford Coppola as he was around Tim Kazurinsky. He had this old homebody self, but then he felt he also had to play the role of King of New York. It was really a schizophrenic way to live.

LORNE MICHAELS:

John, as I've said many times, lived his life in three eight-hour shifts. And if you spent eight hours with him and then you went to bed, you thought he did too. But he just went on to the second shift. And there, waiting, was a whole other group of people who knew John.

TIM KAZURINSKY:

My theory on Bob Woodward and John Belushi goes like this: They're both from the same town. Woodward, he's like Salieri. No matter what the fuck he did—*All the President's Men,* winning the Pulitzer, whatever—unfortunately he grew up in the same town where John Belushi grew up. And so he's always going to be number two. And that's why he wrote *Wired.*

DAN AYKROYD, *Cast Member:*

I wasn't happy, because I think Woodward just gave up on it and handed it over to his researcher. Plus there were certain things that he just got patently wrong. He painted a portrait of John that was really inaccurate—certain stories in there that just weren't true and never happened. So no, I wasn't happy. This was my friend that was being besmirched. That's the posture I took, and I live by it today. The book didn't fill John out to the measure that he could've been appreciated. He just overlooked a lot. It was all about the drugs and the excess, not about the quality of work and the background in theater and the preparation and the respect that John's friends had for him.

JIM BELUSHI:

Woodward—that cocksucker! That motherfucker. Hey, Bob, what's with the girl who won the Pulitzer Prize, what's with the eight-year-old junkie? "Oh, that just got right by us." Bob! You're the fucking editor, Bob! How did that fucking get by you? You check your fucking sources? My ass! Yeah, Woodward did a really nice job of making John look like a Bluto junkie. I don't think Woodward's capable of understanding what love is, or compassion, or relationships. He is one cold fish.

DAN AYKROYD:

I had eight years with John, and we had a ball every second, we had a ball. I mean, we had our disagreements, naturally, but we sure made each other laugh.

In any group you're going to have people who precede the others. I just hope he's waiting for me on the other side. I'm sure he will be.

Many stars were created by Saturday Night Live, *but many talented people also passed through the show little noticed and little utilized. Billy Crystal might have hit it big ten years sooner if he hadn't been bumped from the premiere back in 1975. Eddie Murphy was all but ignored during his first year in the cast. Jim Carrey failed an audition and wasn't hired. Lisa Kudrow and Jennifer Aniston, both later stars of* Friends, *were passed over.*

With Eddie Murphy having ascended to movie superstardom, Joe Pis-copo's services were no longer in great demand in Studio 8H, and he was not invited back after 1983–84. Other cast members who'd failed to make much of an impression also departed, and SNL was looking severely talent deprived. The show had the blahs and needed a new direction. The remedy decided upon was simple and yet, considering the show's traditions, theoretically heretical: Instead of spending time and effort looking for new talent to introduce and nurture, the producers would turn the show over to established comedy stars—fairly well-known performers who could generate their own material. The remedy didn't come cheap: Crystal, acclaimed for his portrayal of a gay son on the ABC sitcom Soap, *finally signed on as an SNL regular, at $25,000 per show. Revenge was sweet.*

Martin Short, a stunningly imaginative comic actor who'd played a wide, wild range of characters on the SCTV *satire series, got $5,000 less per show, but only because he waited until the last minute to say yes. They were joined by writer-comedians Christopher Guest and a return-ing Harry Shearer and given the daunting assignment of bringing* Satur-day Night Live *back to life. It wouldn't be the show Lorne Michaels had daringly envisioned half a decade earlier, populated by virtual unknowns, but at least it would exist.*

DICK EBERSOL:

I went to Brandon and said, "I have an idea for next year." By then I'd had Billy Crystal come back to host the show, and subsequent to that, he did a couple other cameos. And I said, "Just grant me the notion that, if we stop this whole process of believing everybody we hire has to be unknown, we can really build a hell of a cast." And he said, "Who do you have in mind?" And I said, "Well, I think I can get Billy, Marty Short, probably could talk Chris Guest into it." Others ultimately fell into the mix. But those were the names. And also Andrea Martin, who subsequently we chose not to get, because the guys I was hiring fell in love with Pamela Stephenson. And so we didn't make Andrea the offer. But Brandon said yes, and that repre-sented the first time in the history of the show, and I don't know if it's true anymore, that we broke favored nations among the cast.

Everybody received the same thing except for Billy, and Billy got a deal at a higher level.

BOB TISCHLER:

I said to Dick, "You know, this is really going to be our last year here, let's bring in people we know who are funny on-camera and off-camera and who can work together." And I basically suggested bringing in some big names, including Chris Guest, the person who actually was responsible for me getting into show business. Dick did suggest bringing Billy in.

DICK EBERSOL:

There's a very interesting story there that I've never told publicly, which is, having gotten Brandon's okay to do all this, I went out to California in May of '84 and sat down with Billy's management. And Buddy Morra was one of the managers at the time; I can't remember who the other ones were. But we had a lunch and they explained to me that Billy moving back to New York to be a cast member of *Saturday Night Live* was a nonstarter. They didn't think it would be good for his career at that stage. He'd had a few movies, and *Soap* had been on the air and had a lot of notoriety and was, by that point, off the air. And they were adamant and told me no at lunch. And I went upstairs to my room at the Beverly Hills Hotel and, without hesitation, called his house to talk to his wife, Janice, who I heard say in New York when Billy had hosted, "I'd love to bring my daughter back to New York for one year at some point in her life." She wasn't talking about *Saturday Night Live,* but I just overheard her say that. And I said, "Janice, look, here's what's happened. This is a great opportunity, at least I think, for Billy to come back. He'll certainly be well paid, and I'm not going to get you into that. But he could come back to New York, be a cast member on *Saturday Night Live,* do what he really loves—which is all of his characters, where he'll be free to write them and do all of that—and you'd have a wonderful year before you lose a daughter to college, and so on, and have everybody living under the same roof." Well, how she did it or what she did, I don't know, but by that night, Billy called me back on the phone and said, "Forget whatever you've been told by my managers.

Provided we can make the right business deal, I want to come to New York." And that deal was made in about the next twenty-four hours.

I knew Janice at that point maybe about a decade, from the time I'd first seen Billy in the clubs in New York in the midseventies, when I was roaming around that year before — or those months before I knew Lorne. In any case, Billy helped me get Chris and Marty and subsequently Harry Shearer, who, sadly, didn't work out for me any better than he did for Lorne. There were just too many problems behind the scenes. He's a gifted performer but a pain in the butt, unfortunately. He's just so demanding on the preciseness of things and he's very, very hard on the working people, you know, whether it's the makeup people or the prop people, or the engineering people. He's intolerant of other people's issues. He's just a nightmare-to-deal-with person.

BILLY CRYSTAL, *Cast Member:*

I wasn't having the career I always envisioned myself having. I wasn't doing the work I should actually say I really always wanted to do and felt I could do after doing *Soap* for four years. And my own variety series was short-lived, and I was headlining clubs and concerts all across the country. That two hours onstage was always satisfying. But as a whole I wasn't where I wanted to be, I wasn't doing movies, I wasn't doing other things, but more importantly I don't think I was showing the country what I felt I had in myself, what I could do.

I think when I came to the show, I was sort of a piñata of ideas and thoughts and characters, and all kinds of things happened. Every day I was excited at the discovery of what we could do. I never put a time limit on how long I would be there or what it would give me or get me. I didn't approach it like that. I just felt personally as a performer and as a creative person I had to give it my shot. I was thirty-seven years old, I was looking at the chance to finally say to everybody, "This is what I can do." That's why I said yes to come in and do the show after hosting it twice the season before. It was everything I wanted it to be.

LILLY TARTIKOFF:

Billy didn't have an apartment when he was first on *Saturday Night Live*. We just gave him our apartment for like a month, until they got settled, and he and his wife and his girls used it. It seemed to work out okay. And it helped save the show.

HARRY SHEARER:

Spinal Tap appeared on the show as a musical guest in the spring of '84. We got treated so well. I didn't realize that guests are treated better than the regulars. So it was my own stupidity; smart people do dumb things. So I really thought, because we'd been treated pretty well as the guests, hmmm, this might be a better situation. Dick basically extended the offer to all three of us; Michael McKean passed, Chris and I accepted. I knew Marty Short by reputation; he was a friend of Paul Shaffer's and Paul just raved about him, and I'd seen a little bit of his work on *SCTV.* We had not been told, I don't think, that Jimmy Belushi was coming back. That came as a surprise.

Dick put on a pretty elaborate show. He got Chris, Marty, Billy, and I together and said, "Now guys, you know Mary Gross and Julia are coming back, and I want a third girl for that slot and I want you guys to help choose her." Well, we went through this elaborate process of meeting people. Geena Davis met with us in the lobby of the Century Plaza Hotel. And Geena had just been on a couple of sitcoms and it was all quite awkward and uncomfortable for everybody involved. But it boiled down to Andrea Martin and Pamela Stephenson. And Marty, of course, had a number of ties with Andrea and really wanted Andrea there, and I thought, after we saw her tapes, that Pamela was an incredibly versatile actress and just brought something really different, so we tossed it back and forth and finally Pamela got it. To her everlasting dismay.

MARTIN SHORT, *Cast Member:*

I had a one-year contract. I certainly approached that show not as someone who was going to be around, obviously, for more than one year. So I felt that I had to do a lot and be in as many interesting things as possible, because it was only a limited time.

I never wanted to leave *SCTV,* and I had to find out for sure *SCTV* was officially gone, which it was. I'd been asked for my last two years there to join *Saturday Night Live,* but I didn't want a change.

It was important to me. I had already done *SCTV* for three years and I had a new child. But I never figured out how to do *SNL* particularly. After the third show, I still hadn't cashed any checks, because I was not happy there at all. And I went in to talk to Dick and said, "I want to leave the show." And he thought I was kind of insane, of course. But he figured out how to keep me there, which was to say, "Look, if by Christmas you're still unhappy, kid, you can go free of that contract." I think he figured out that, by that time, I'd figure out how to do the show.

ANDREW SMITH:

I always say the "kings of comedy" came in to deign to do the show. It was my third year, and I became part-time because they took me down in order to pay for them. Or maybe it wasn't the money. Anyway, they said, "You can come and write on the show, you can be on the staff, but you can't be head writer anymore with these guys." And of course I got on my high horse—which was a bad, bad mistake—and said, "I don't think so," and left. But then I did come in and do freelance on, I don't know, ten shows.

Because these guys were coming in as stars to do their year in New York—stopping by to do *Saturday Night Live*—and even though some great comedy came out of it, I don't think it was the best thing for the show. Because it was not home-grown talent—finding new people and making them stars. These were sort-of-stars coming in for a year. I think it affected the style of comedy, to tell you the truth. The comedy after them became much more about characters and star turns, so that a sketch, instead of being an ensemble piece, became one of these character pieces—a Brimley or a Grimley or whatever his name was.

The show before that was much more of an ensemble piece and a lot more democratic. In their year, because they were stars, the sketches were about a central character doing his sort of turn, regardless of anybody else in the sketch. I think there was a little shift. And since then, the thing seems to be driven much more by these sorts of characters that the actors come up with. Then they sort of build a situation around this person to do this character, rather than a situation sketch.

ANDREW KURTZMAN:

The resentment directed at Dick's big stars was never about money. The resentment was simply that they were a little clannish, and that they leaned toward a certain style of their own. We'd had Joe Piscopo doing Reagan, but suddenly here comes Harry Shearer, and he felt very proprietary about his Reagan. "Well, sorry, but I don't think we have to check out every joke with you, Harry. He's president of the United States. We've got to do stuff on this guy." I have not had much contact with Harry recently. I understand he's much more relaxed now. He was a bit depressed then. He had the office next to mine, and sometimes he would be in there alone playing bass late at night. It was a real dorm-room kind of thing. You'd hear these depressed bass lines thudding through the walls next door.

ELLIOT WALD:

Harry's impossible—impossible to get along with. And if he wasn't as bright and talented as he is, nobody would put up with him for one minute. But the fact is that he is one of the smartest guys doing this stuff, and I'm always impressed by him.

BILLY CRYSTAL:

Dick Ebersol was a great producer for all of us in that way. It was an awkward situation where Harry, Marty, and Chris and I came in and yet there were still some remaining cast members from the year before—Jim Belushi, Julia Louis-Dreyfus, Mary Gross, Gary Kroeger. So it wasn't Us versus Them, but there was definitely the sense that they were veterans with perhaps different sensibilities. This had been their turf, and here we come in. And there had to be a melding of the two. We had very specific ideas about what was to be the tone of that year after coming off some bad times for the show.

Setting the tone began that summer when we filmed some of the pieces that would become the strongest things for us during the year—the *60 Minutes* piece we did that introduced the Minkman character and Nathan Thurm, and Harry as a great Mike Wallace; the two black ballplayers that Chris and I did—that was one of the finer pieces that we did that year; "Relatives of the Rich and Famous" had a really different tone to it. So matching all the tones was Dick's job that year—and keeping everybody happy.

MARTIN SHORT:

They certainly paid us a lot of money, much more than what other people had ever been paid on the show. And gave us one-year contracts, so all of it was rare. I guess they didn't assume there was a tremendous future to the show. They had lost Eddie Murphy and then Joe Piscopo within, I guess, half a season of each other. And there was a tremendous concern that the show had become a star vehicle, and that without stars, the show would falter.

JIM BELUSHI:

You bring an all-star in, you've got to pay him, and these guys were all-stars. I didn't consider myself equal to Billy. I was not prolific. He'd write all night and he'd come up with these great things. He understood the medium. But anyway, I think I was making like fifteen grand myself, writing and acting—it wasn't *that* far off. That show was not about money; that show was about launch.

ELLIOT WALD:

It was tough for the writers, especially since at the end of the season before, Brandon Tartikoff came down and said, just to the writers, "You guys have really carried the show. No, we have not had the stars that we used to have"—at that point Eddie had been off the show for a year—"but the show has gone on, the ratings have gone up, and it's because of you guys. And you guys should be very proud of yourselves." And then we come back in July or August and here are the new guys, and they all write for themselves, they all fit as a group, they've already been working together, and it's like, "Well, if we need a piece, we'll give you guys a ring." It wasn't, "We've got this brilliant new cast, and you guys should really learn to work with them."

Now when Billy Crystal comes into your office and pitches a funny idea, I will guarantee you it's funnier than when Elliot Wald walks into your office and pitches a funny idea. And I think the producers fell a little in love with being performed for. Marty and Billy and Chris *are* incredibly funny. But we found ourselves at the back of the bus virtually overnight.

Chris Guest is impossible to talk to. As Eugene Levy said in a piece about him, "Chris brings new meaning to the word 'dry.'" The man is an emotional desert. He will not break his deadpan for any force on earth, so it's very hard to interact with him in a friendly way. On the other hand, Marty is very nice, Billy is very nice — they were all great, but they knew what they wanted to do.

Billy Crystal is the only star-actor I ever saw at the show who wrote stuff for other people, for sketches he wasn't even in. Billy is really a sweet guy in a lot of ways. I don't hang around with him, so I don't see the negative side at all. I'm sure there is one. In fact, they were all a pleasure to work with, but we were very much out of the limelight, and I think after the little speech, and after being on the show for three years, it was a bit of an emotional trauma.

ANDREW SMITH:

Billy Crystal was probably the most insatiable performer I have ever worked with. Once I saw him sitting on the stairs looking very, very depressed. It was the day before a show and I asked him what the matter was. He said that he felt he "just had to do more" on that week's show. I told him he was in six out of eight sketches and that seemed a heavy load, but he was not to be soothed. He kept repeating that he had to do more.

I remember hearing him say on more than one occasion, "I think the kids need another Sammy," meaning he thought it was time again for him to do his Sammy Davis, Jr. turn — which would indicate he maybe suffered slightly from the Piscopo-Sinatra syndrome. I think it was Billy who turned to Martin Short in the middle of a large ensemble sketch and said, "It's been three minutes since either of us has had anything to say. Maybe we should leave."

MARTIN SHORT:

I was so conditioned from *SCTV* to be doing the same kind of work but just having endless fun. And this was different pressure. I think for me it was mainly tied to the writing. At *SCTV,* you would write for six weeks, then you would shoot for six weeks, then you would edit as you were writing again. So it meant that if for two weeks you didn't have an idea, it was okay. Maybe the third week you'd make up for the first two weeks.

Now you're a star on Saturday night, but if forty-eight hours later you haven't come up with an idea, you're a failure. Billy Crystal and I were always the ones who would leave at six fifty-nine A.M. after handing in last scripts. Oh, it was terrible. And then the read-through was at eleven, which I think Lorne made it later for that reason. So you went home, slept for a couple hours, and came back. I remember on my wife's birthday—it was a Tuesday night, and that was always the worst night—stopping off at an all-night market and picking up a cake. It was just so pathetic. You know, you have no life. But I didn't know how else to do the show. You would think they would make some adjustments when they had big stars doing it.

I always thought it was like final exams. I was always exhausted and never home. But then the more I did it, the more I was able to figure out how to do it and not work so insanely.

BILLY CRYSTAL:

One thing you learn on the stage is, you've got to cover your ass, because nobody else is going to. I remember one week there were eleven comedy sketches in the show and our "group," I'll call it, did nine of them. The pressure was always on that way. Some were good, some were bad, that was the nature of the beast. The time you have to do the show is so short. We just filled up the time as much as we could and tried to integrate the other cast members as much as we could, but certain teams just grew. Chris and I did tons of stuff together that year, and Marty had Ed Grimley. We all had our things. And so when it got light Dick would come to us and go, "I need a Grimley." And he'd look at me and go, "I need a Fernando."

BOB TISCHLER:

Billy started becoming very popular and doing characters like Fernando and other characters. Dick, who is a whore, would try to get him to do the same characters over and over. And Billy, who loves attention, would feel no compunction about doing Fernando every week, even though a lot of us were tired of it. Harry Shearer looked at Billy as selling out and made no bones about it. Where other people might see the audience laughing at what Billy was doing—they may not have liked it themselves, but they weren't abrasive or abusive about it—Harry was just vocal and insulting. He could be insulting to anybody at any time, but he especially picked Billy to mistreat. He was just horrible to him.

MARTIN SHORT:

As a performer, you only found the repetition of a character boring if you had nothing else to say comedically about it. But in the case of Ed Grimley, it was totally interesting to do because Ed Grimley on *SCTV* is an actor who works for the network and is in different movies, and that's the way we use Ed. Now suddenly we saw him in his apartment. We saw where he lived. We saw him musing about life. So this is all different.

BILLY CRYSTAL:

We could always say, "No, we don't have it." And if it got really desperate, you'd try and do one. I don't remember ever being forced to do anything, but Dick would come to us with a plea: "Please."

What was great about the "Fernando's Hideaway"s was they were all improvised, so nobody had to write anything. That's what I loved most about him. The danger of it was doing it in the dress rehearsal and getting screams and then trying to re-create it three hours later. But the danger was intoxicating too. Once the set was rolled out, the hideaway, the audience started to get excited, because it was the first sketch they would see where there were no cue cards. And they knew it. They knew it was dangerous. It was a talk show within the show. A whole different energy hit the studio when it happened. I loved seeing the host squirm a little bit, because it was, "What's he going to say to me now?" Because I had to switch off from the dress show to the air show, otherwise it would be flat.

I had people in the hideaway crack up on the air. Mr. T and Hulk Hogan. When I show clips of highlights, that's one of the big ones. The two of them just go. I said to Hulk Hogan, one of his pecs was heaving with laughter and he was wearing a tank top, and I said, "Look at your chest, it looks like Dorothy Lamour from behind walking to the commissary." They just went, and when that happened the audience went wild, because it was live and it was right in front of them.

MARTIN SHORT:

When I did Ed Grimley on *SNL,* it moved into a kind of live energy. What I did love about Ed on *SNL,* particularly, was the pure joy when the phone would ring and before he'd answer it he'd say, "Gee, I love the phone. There's always such a sense of mystery." I remember one time years ago, my sister-in-law was flying to California, and she had never flown before, or at least not that much. And she said to me, "I got dressed four different times. I couldn't decide what to wear for the plane." And I thought, "How seductive is that? To be that unjaded that you're still that enthusiastic?"

HARRY SHEARER:

I watched the synchronized swimming on television in August. In late August we were already assembling in New York, and as we were talking, I was just fulminating about the outrage of these people, you know, getting the same medals as real athletes. And Chris and Marty and I were, I guess, in my office, and I don't know whose idea it was to do the sketch, but we just started writing it. Dick said, "You know, by the time we go on the air in mid-September, nobody will remember the Olympics," and I said, "We'll make 'em remember." Marty and I got to go to the pool every day to rehearse for a week, you know, devising a routine. I had brought tapes of all the synchronized swimming routines with me from L.A., so we just sat and watched the tapes. "Oh, we can do those. Oh, we can do that, we can do that." And sort of put together our own routine. We didn't have a choreographer, so we just did it ourselves. And then I think I selected the music, and we just sort of devised these routines and then went out and shot it.

ANDY BRECKMAN:

I was there when Larry David wrote for *Saturday Night Live.* He was there for one season and he did not get one sketch on the air. Not one.

And then he went on to do *Seinfeld* and be Mr. NBC. It was a Dick Ebersol year, and I'm sure Larry has nothing good to say about Dick Ebersol, but of the sketches that Larry David didn't get on, some of them made it to dress rehearsal and some became the seeds of *Seinfeld* episodes. The other writers would love Larry David pieces, because you just admire the work, but they were very subtle pieces and the audiences were never into them. There were never audible laughs. One sketch was about a guy who left a message on his girlfriend's answering machine that he regretted leaving, and he broke into her house to retrieve the tape. And I believe, if I recall the sketch correctly, that it ended with the girlfriend coming home and the boyfriend killing her.

LARRY DAVID, *Writer*:

No no no. No murder. I haven't dealt with murder yet. I can't believe that I would write that. I think it was a courtroom sketch. Because my guess is he'd been arrested. But yes, I finally wound up using that on *Seinfeld*—the guy who wants to get back a message he left on a girl's answering machine.

I did get one sketch on the show that season. Just one. It was a sketch about—let's see, the host was Ed Begley, Jr. The sketch got on at five to one in the morning. And this is for the entire season. Ed Begley played an architect, and Harry Shearer was the developer, and he was looking at the plans for a new building. And Harry Shearer noticed something in the blueprint. He says, "What's this?" And Ed Begley, Jr. says, "That's an elevator." Harry goes, "No, what's this little thing?" And Ed Begley, Jr. says, "That's a stool for the elevator man." And then Harry Shearer kind of pauses and goes, "Well, I don't want the elevator men sitting on stools." And then Ed Begley tries to explain: "Well, they won't be sitting on stools all the time, only when there's nobody in the elevator." And then it just deteriorated into this fight about whether they should be sitting or standing. This too showed up on a *Seinfeld* episode but was changed to a security guard in a clothing store.

BILLY CRYSTAL:

There was another thing Larry got on which he's forgetting. We wrote a thing that became a running character which was a big hit named Lou Goldman, a weatherman. He was an old crazy Jewish weatherman who would give the forecast only for where his family lived. It was very funny. And the forecasts were, "Monday is *feh,* Tuesday continued *feh,* Thursday and Friday—don't be a big shot, take a jacket." Then he'd do "Miami, where my sister Rose is—" And then he just went off on rants. And we did that two or three times. Larry and I did those.

BOB TISCHLER:

We let the new cast members read the new writers that were coming in, and I remember Chris Guest, in particular, not getting Larry's stuff at all. I liked his stuff; I don't remember what Dick's position was. But he came on. It wasn't a total unanimous decision to put him on. He came on, and because of who Larry is—and one thing Larry is is always true to himself—he did not compromise. Even though you could tell immediately that he was a really good writer, it was more stuff about him than it was about stuff that the cast members could do as characters. Some people are just not meant to write for *Saturday Night Live.* Larry was one of them.

He was certainly not meant to work for Dick Ebersol. They locked horns immediately, and their relationship was just horrible. I think some of Larry's sketches were prejudged. Some of the sketches I wanted to put on, but Dick didn't want to put on, and Dick won out. It got to be almost a personal thing between the two of them. If it just had the name Larry David on it, Dick shied away from it. These are two people who were very far apart. I felt sorry for Larry. Everybody—but Dick—did.

ELLIOT WALD:

Part of my job that year was going to Larry David and trying to explain to him why his pieces didn't get in. Larry's and Dick's senses of humor were just completely different. Larry would write pieces that, you know, we'd just be falling on the floor over. Some of those became great *Seinfeld* episodes. The one about trying to get someone's apartment at a wake? Elaine did that in *Seinfeld,* but Larry wrote it first as a sketch. And we were falling down laughing. And Dick would say, "That's not going on the air; that's not funny." And it's like, Whoa!

So we were what—*faking* our laughter? And so my job became com-miserating with Larry. And he's so smart and so funny.

LARRY DAVID:

I think Dick Ebersol did the best he could for what he wanted to get out of the show. What's he going to do? He doesn't have a comedy background. He was a good guy, a decent guy, and I don't have any problem with him. I do remember this, though: It was the day before read-through, which was, let's see, Tuesday, around seven o'clock, and I'd been there maybe three weeks to write material. And so for that first read-through I had already written maybe two or three sketches and maybe two news pieces for the "Update" thing. So I was all set.

So I'm waiting for the elevator to go home, and I remember Dick came out of the elevator, and I said, "Good night," and he said, *"What are you doing?!?"* I said, "Oh, I'm going home." And he looked at me like I was out of my mind. He said, "What do you mean, going home?" I said, "Well, I've written three sketches and two news pieces and that's it, you know." And he goes, "But we stay up all night." I go, "What for?" He says, "To write the show. That's when we write the show." I said, "But I've already written three pieces." And he goes, "Well, we stay here all night." I just couldn't believe what I was hearing. And I said, "I'm not staying up all night. For what? What am I going to do—just walk around? I'm all done." So we kind of looked at each other and I said, you know, "Good luck," and I got into the elevator and left. I think that was the beginning of the end for me.

It was frustrating, yes, not getting pieces on the air. One Saturday night, five minutes before air, after getting probably six or seven sketches cut from the show, I went up to Dick right before we were going to go on and I said, "That's it. I'm done. I've had it. I quit. It's over." And I walked out and started walking home, and it was freezing out and I was in the middle of walking home going, "Oh my God, what did I just do? I just cost myself like sixty thousand dollars!" I'm adding up the money from the reruns and all this. At that time I needed every penny I could get my hands on. So yes, I went back the next week and pretended I hadn't quit — which I also used later in a *Seinfeld* episode. I went in on Monday morning and just pretended the whole thing never happened. And Dick never mentioned it. I think maybe he said, "Is that Larry David down at the end of the table?" But that was it. The writers were looking at me, that's for sure. I was getting some very strange looks from the writers — like, "What the hell are *you* doing here?"

ANDREW KURTZMAN:

Whether or not you were getting stuff on the air affected your life, but I don't think anyone ever thought Larry David was anything but sensational — and comically, a bad fit with Ebersol. Neither us nor Julia Louis-Dreyfus ever figured out really what to do with her on TV, but Larry did. We were all there. She was the same person. But what Larry saw was that peculiar force of hers.

ANDY BRECKMAN:

Larry didn't even want the typists in the typing pool — it used to be all typewriters — to type his scripts up. He would type them himself. He was always finicky — George Costanza finicky, you know.

JULIA LOUIS-DREYFUS:

Larry was just miserable there. And he almost came to blows with Dick Ebersol. I forget what, I'm sure it had to do with a sketch. I think Dick told him that something he'd written wasn't funny, and Larry went berserk. There was a lot of tension on that floor, and people were always sort of threatening each other. Brad got mad once too. He went crazy. That's one of the reasons I liked Larry so much — because he lost his temper. Somebody threw a chair through a wall too. I think that was Jim Belushi.

LARRY DAVID:

I did meet Julia there. Yes I did. And obviously that had some impact. I didn't really write for her then. I didn't really write for anyone in particular. I would cast after I wrote. But I remember thinking that she was terrific — and underused.

JULIA LOUIS-DREYFUS:

I did a couple of things that for some reason are still played in gay bars around the country—like "Spit-Take Talk Show." A bunch of my friends who've been in gay bars say they've seen that played a lot. Mary and I once did a parody of *The Rink,* a Broadway show with Liza Minnelli. Our parody was called "The Womb," and it's also playing in gay bars. I have no idea why. I guess it has a certain campiness to it.

BRAD HALL:

It was particularly frustrating as a writer. We'd have these massive read-throughs of thirty sketches or something. That everybody had just sort of vomited up all these sketches, with no real focus as to what the show was going to be about that week. And there was a lot of news going on, Reagan era. There was stuff we could've been parodying. I don't think Ebersol wanted that. And I don't think NBC did. Someone's taste did not run toward satire. And so the very thing that originally made the show popular was really resisted. We had people that could do good impressions of all the right people. You look back, it's kind of bizarre, the election in 1984, there's almost no political humor during an entire political election. Nothing. And for me, doing the news, it was really frustrating. My brilliant idea was that I should've been a real news guy. I should've gone out and covered real news stories from the *SNL* perspective. That's what I wanted to do. But they were much more keen on doing "President Reagan had his hand stuck to his head today" and show a picture.

JULIA LOUIS-DREYFUS:

It wasn't a particularly happy experience for me. To begin with, I will take responsibility for some of it, because I was extremely young. I hadn't graduated college and I was very naive about how things work in real show business. So I went into it very green. I had been in their audience. I was a teenager when the show was sort of at its height. So then to be plucked out of Chicago between my junior and senior year of college to go on the show was head-spinning, to say the very least.

I thought it was going to be a congenial experience; my head was in the clouds. I wasn't aware of the politicking one had to do, and I think there were a lot of drugs going on at the time, but I was unaware of that as well, to tell you the truth. I was always surprised at read-through, though, when certain writers' sketches were eighteen pages long and they were laughing and laughing, and I was so confused as to how they could possibly have found it so funny—and made it so long! Everybody was doing a lot of coke and smoking dope. Everybody would stay up late. All the work was done between eleven o'clock at night and six o'clock in the morning; that's when everybody was functioning. And that wasn't, in my view, conducive to comedy.

Doing *Seinfeld* was, of course, just the opposite experience. It was pure joy from beginning to end. I thought, "No one will ever get this, because we're having too much fun."

MARGARET OBERMAN:

There are certain people who really go after *Saturday Night Live* because of that "boys club" business. I think that element certainly existed, but I think it was like anything else: You had to be a survivor to make that show work for you, and that was true of men and women. There was a certain political kind of thing that went on there, and you had to know that and function within those rules. And if you didn't know that, then maybe you weren't as happy as some other people were.

ELLIOT WALD:

Herb Sargent said at the end of one season, "Our biggest fuckup this year is we did not find stuff for Julia to do. She is really talented." A lot of people didn't see that, but the fact is, Herb was right and we were wrong. Not that I thought she wasn't talented, but I thought she was limited and hard to write for. It was my own inability to write for her, and obviously not any lack of talent on her part, that was the problem.

MARGARET OBERMAN:

Julia is one of the people who doesn't like to talk about the show. It's my opinion that she shouldn't be so negative about it. I love Julia, but I just feel like that show really helped her. It got her out there, and she met Larry David. So how bad could it have been? It complicated things for her that Brad Hall, her boyfriend—who joined the show when she did—didn't stay the full time with the show, and there was a lot of acrimony. He was very, very unhappy, so that complicated things for her. But I just feel like she'd be better off not saying how horrible she thought it was. I don't know what she's going to gain from that. She's had so many great things happen to her.

JULIA LOUIS-DREYFUS:

Dick Ebersol was always wielding a baseball bat. He would always hold this bat when he would have these meetings. The writers and the actors would be there, and he would have the bat in hand. It was really very Al Capone-y. And he always wanted me to straighten my hair. He was always trying to get me to straighten my hair. Well—he's in sports now.

ANDREW KURTZMAN:

To this day, I miss working live. There is nothing quite like that. There was a sketch we did in which Chris Guest dropped his script. He was doing a voiceover from the announcer's booth, but he dropped the script and couldn't retrieve it right away. And so we just went dark for a while. We stayed on a title card or something and Chris was pawing around the bottom of the booth, looking for this lost piece of script and unaware that he was being cued. He'd just dropped it, and to reach it he had to take off his headphones and thus missed his cue. So we just stopped TV for a while. It's like stopping time.

ANDY BRECKMAN:

I mostly wrote for the "B" cast—like Julia Louis-Dreyfus and Gary Kroeger—and my sketches were usually on at twelve-fifty. That used to be the time for high-concept stuff—the "writers' sketches."

MARTIN SHORT:

If you're just a performer, you were at the mercy of what they would hand you. You had more control of your fate as a writer-performer. If you were just an actor on the show, it was not as gratifying as if you were an actor-writer. I love that control, you know, making it actually funny. Other people did write for me. Jim Downey was there that year, and Andy Breckman—two strong writers. But there was a tendency to write for yourself, particularly if you were perceived as someone who did strange material. People would sometimes feel like they wouldn't know how to write for that.

I must admit, when the live stuff would work, there was a great excitement that you could never capture anywhere else.

DICK EBERSOL:

Billy and Chris and Marty, and Harry for that matter, were writers. And they were a pleasure. Billy's contribution on the writing side was so enormous. He was writing two, three, some weeks four pieces a show. In the history of the show up to that point, only Chevy in the first two or three months was ever that prolific.

BILLY CRYSTAL:

I think maybe in a way we represented the age group that stayed with the show from beginning to end. We were, let's see, nine years later. The audience that started with the show was now thirty-seven, thirty-eight also—so we hit a big chord with those people. And that was good. Some of our pieces were really funny and inventive. And you had people who could play characters and do voices. Marty and I did "Kate and Ali," where I played Muhammad Ali and he played Katharine Hepburn.

And bringing Grimley, and bringing Fernando, and finding "I hate when that happens," which is something Chris Guest and I used to do as friends, and that being a big hit, was another part of the success of the show.

JIM BELUSHI:

Ebersol fired me the first week of December in my second season. I wasn't on the Christmas show. I begged for my job back, and I came back in January.

Why did he fire me? Because I was uncontrollable—throwing things down halls and angry and disruptive. I might have been an asshole, really, because of my own frustration and being in the middle-child syndrome. Then he let me back and I stopped drinking, because every time I'd gotten upset, I went down to Hurley's bar and shot some whiskey. So then you have behavior you're not proud of. I don't regret any of it, though. I've taken all those experiences and learned from them. I got more serious about my work and my craft after that. So in a way I thank him. It was the best firing that ever happened to me.

Hosting had become a hip, chic thing to do in the first years of Saturday Night Live, *and the list of hosts was audacious and eclectic. During the Doumanian and early Ebersol years, that gig lost luster, but with the rise of Eddie Murphy, and then the year that starred Billy Crystal and Martin Short, hosting status rose again.*

Brandon Tartikoff, the seemingly ever-youthful NBC programmer who survived the Fred Silverman regime and went on to success and acclaim under Grant Tinker, felt protective and brotherly toward Saturday Night Live, *even though at least once during his reign he actually canceled it—then about twenty-four hours later gave it a reprieve. He believed* SNL *was one of the network's signature shows and that to kill it would be almost sacrilegious. When in New York and not at his office in Burbank, Tartikoff liked to drop by the eighth-floor studios and seventeenth-floor offices of the show—and a dream of his came true when his old friend Ebersol invited him to host.*

Tartikoff was involved in his own far more dramatic and consequential life-and-death struggle, having been diagnosed years earlier with Hodgkin's disease. Through it all he showed an unflappable resiliency. He hosted right after an exhausting round of chemotherapy, wearing a toupee to hide the attendant hair loss.

DICK EBERSOL:

It was late 1982 and Brandon was clearly back into serious problems with cancer. And at that point Grant knew, Lilly knew, and I knew, and maybe one or two other personal friends and his parents knew. And that was it. And so he starts heavily into chemo and, actually, when his daughter Calla was born in November of '82, Lilly delivered Calla and then went, not that many hours after, to another part of the same hospital to hold Brandon's hand while he had a chemo treatment.

Lilly said to me, "He's really pulling this off, or he thinks he is, but I know deep down inside that he's kind of down." And I got the idea at the time to put something in front of him. I called her two weeks later and said, "I have an idea. Brandon's the ultimate ham. How about if I give him the ultimate moment? I'll offer him hosting the season premiere of *Saturday Night Live,* and he'll have five or six months to look forward to that if he successfully completes his chemo at the end of the spring." And that's how he ended up hosting that show. It was really initially done to give him something to look forward to as he went through the chemo. And you know, for those next six months, all I got from him were ideas about "I'll do this, I'll do that."

LILLY TARTIKOFF:

When they asked him to host, he literally had just finished chemo. If you look at the footage of Brandon, he is totally moon-faced. The steroids were still very much in his system. And at the time they asked him to host, he didn't have a hair on his head, and yet you have no idea how thrilling it was for him. I don't think he ever anticipated that anybody would ever ask him to host *Saturday Night Live.* But that was one of the great moments of his career that literally has nothing to do with his career. I had to remind him that that was not what he was supposed to be doing. In fact, when he said he would do it, I was furious, because I thought, "How much pressure can you put on yourself, and on me?" I took everything personally. I tried to talk sense into him, you know. I just said, "You're not Steve Martin. You're Brandon Tartikoff. You're supposed to, like, wear a suit and run the network. Who do you think you are? What makes you think that they're going to roll out that carpet and you're going to know what to do?" But really, there was no way that I was going to get in the way of that. I think Brandon would have given up his day job to work on *Saturday Night Live* if they had ever asked. I think it symbolized every reason for him for ever being at a network and being able to put on a show, a *Saturday Night Live.* He was completely attached to it and loyal, and he wouldn't, and couldn't, give it up. It was a place all unto its own for him. He would leave the network before he would sever those ties or end that show.

Brandon said that when he did the dress rehearsal, he was really relaxed. But when they said, "Live from New York, it's *Saturday Night,*" he said he had never been that frightened in his life. And

normally nothing scared Brandon. This is a man who just had survived nine rounds of chemotherapy.

MARGARET OBERMAN:

Jerry Lewis hosted the show when I was there. That was a total
trip. It was so out there, so insane. We had one writer who was just out
of Harvard, he was twenty-one, and Jerry Lewis literally said to him,
"I've got ties older than you." He just was such an odd guy. It was his
second marriage to a woman he's still married to. I remember so vividly him taking the gum out of his mouth and her holding her hand
out and him putting the gum in her hand. He told me some outra-
geously foul story about how he'd just done *Hellzapoppin'* with Lynn
Redgrave and somebody asked him what he thought of Lynn Redgrave and he'd said, "I'd like to take my cock out and piss all over
her." It was just insane.

TIM KAZURINSKY:

One little test I used to do was on a Monday morning when we'd
meet the host, I would ask the host if he would be interested in doing
a sketch called "The William Holden Drinking Helmet." I would
always gauge by their reaction, because poor Bill Holden had fallen
and cracked his head open and bled to death. So I always thought, if
they laughed at that at least, I knew it would be a good week. And if
they went, "What?! Aw, no, that's sick," then I thought, "Aw-oh, we're
dicked." That was my little running gag to see if they had a sense of
humor or if they were going to be a dickhead like Robert Blake.

DAVID SHEFFIELD:

My vote for worst host is Robert Blake. He was sitting in a room
and a sketch was handed to him by Gary Kroeger, who was a writer-
actor—a sketch called "Breezy Philosopher," a one-premise sketch
about a lofty teacher who's kind of a biker tough guy, talking about
Kierkegaard. Students kept asking questions while he combed his
hair and he'd say, "Hey, I don't know." Blake sat there and read that,
with his glasses down his nose, then wadded it up, turned to Kroeger,
and said, "I hope you got a tough asshole, pal, 'cause you're going to

have to wipe your ass with that one." And he threw it and bounced it off Gary's face.

MARTIN SHORT:

Jack Palance was on once and no one laughed at the sketch, and it was so strange. Jim Downey wrote it, it was just the strangest scene, and it got cut at dress. I remember that some of those scenes that didn't make it to air are just kind of classically funny to me in their way. This scene was something like, "What would you do if I told you Jack Palance was standing behind that door?" That was it, and then he would come out. And it died at dress. I remember I said, "Isn't there an applause sign someone could have turned on or something?" And Billy Crystal said, "They *were* flashing the applause sign. The audience still wouldn't clap."

To me, Ed Grimley's most memorable encounter was with Jesse Jackson—two people you just don't expect to see in the same sketch—when Jesse hosted the show. We were supposed to be sitting next to each other on an airplane. They kept saying, "Now when you climb over Jesse, you mustn't actually fall on him," although it was in the script. I never did fall on him at rehearsal; I just did it for the live show. They didn't want me to do anything that made him look silly or foolish. But he was terrific about it. He was great. He loved it.

DICK EBERSOL:

About eight shows into that season, just before Christmas of '84, we did a show which Ringo Starr came to host. And everybody was exhausted. I think it was the second of three in a row or something. But everybody was just worn-out. And the Wednesday night read-through was a travesty. And I took Ringo and Barbara Bach, his wife, and walked, as you can from NBC, almost underground all the way back to the Berkshire Hotel over on East Fifty-second Street and kept saying, "Don't worry," to them, which you often tell a host. Lorne used to say—maybe he still does—you're basically bluffing the host from Monday 'til Friday.

In this case, I leveled with Ringo. I said, "What you saw today won't be the show," and I went back with Billy and Chris and about ten people on the writing staff. I think this may be the only time it happened in the history of the show. I said, "We have nothing. I know everybody is exhausted. But let's take all of our best characters and let's write a show around them. And let's break the rule that you go three or four shows between great characters," whether it be Fernando at that point with Billy, or whether it was Marty doing Grimley. I said everything's fair game. We just have to show this guy a great show. We've got nothing now.

And that night, with no sleep for two days, each one of them wrote a piece, and it turned out to be a pretty good show. I offer all that as evidence of the fact that here you have mature adult stars, as they were in the world of comedy—all of them—and they easily accepted, with no complaint, starting completely from scratch that late in the week, which up to that point never happened in the history of the show. They were pros.

MARTIN SHORT:

When Ringo hosted, that was exciting. I remember my wife coming in on a Friday, and when she saw Ringo, she got so flustered she was shaking. I said, "I can't believe you're shaking," and she said, "That is a Beatle!" She was totally overwhelmed. That part of *Saturday Night Live* was always the most fun—meeting the celebrities and going to the parties.

ANDREW KURTZMAN:

Sid Caesar came in and was absolutely stunned at the way we did things. And I was given the task of working with Sid. He had a rather elaborate parody of, I think it was *Tootsie* and *Rocky* combined. I wasn't quite hip enough to know I was writing the vanity piece that wouldn't get on the air, because I knew *Your Show of Shows* and I guess Sid kind of locked onto me; they made me Sid's boy for the week. He took me to a dinner at some hotel, not the Algonquin, but one of these faded-glory places where they knew him when he was the TV god of the fifties. The carpet was getting a little tatty but they still had the overpriced Italian dining room.

And he ate the strangest meal I've ever seen. Sid claimed to eat one meal a day. He starts with a veal chop as big as a baby's head. The thing is oozing cheese, and he eats his and then eats half of mine, because I couldn't get near it. He eats both our portions of spaghetti. As we're gasping after all this food, he says, "Wait—they do me a special dessert. You won't like it. It's just for me. It's this health thing." They bring to the table a salad bowl, a large-sized box of Shredded Wheat—the ones where the biscuits are the size of Brillo pads—and it's a full box, not your little individual serving packs. Then comes a thirty-two-ounce container of yogurt, an enormous bowl of berries, and an equally large bowl of raisins and nuts. I would say there were probably four pounds of food there. And he proceeds to combine this into a mash in the big salad bowl and then drops it on top of this Italian pasta we'd just been eating. It was the strangest thing I'd ever seen. And all the time he's talking about the sketch we were going to do—a sketch that never got on the air.

What astonished Sid, what he could not believe, is that we wrote thirty sketches to get nine. He was absolutely baffled by that. Because that's not the way they did it in his day. He said all of these things should be one line in a meeting. You kill it right there or you decide it's perfect, it's the right thing, and then you go work on it until it's great. He just didn't agree with the system. I don't know if it was Lorne's invention or what.

DICK EBERSOL:

I met Susan St. James when she came to host the show that was the second show of the next full season. At midnight the writers went on strike and we couldn't go back on the air. She was pushing the movie *Carbon Copy*. She does the show on Saturday, and five weeks after that show we were married.

ROBIN SHLIEN:

This is a very Dick story: When Susan St. James hosted the show, that's how they met—I guess it was immediate attraction—and he ended up with her at Xenon, a big disco back then. And they were like making out at Xenon and someone from some paper caught them and it was in the paper the next day. Now most people would be embarrassed about this, right? Dick put the clipping up on the wall of his office.

DAVID SHEFFIELD:

Favorite hosts included Stevie Wonder, who was a terrific host. It was an interesting week because cue cards were right out. He had a little earpiece, and someone was feeding the lines to him off-camera, his brother. He was just a great host.

There was one host who came on, he was drunk and senile. He kept going, "Where's Gilda? When's Gilda showing up?" He was so arrogant; he basically just did a monologue. Donald Pleasence.

DICK EBERSOL:

The first three shows of the '82–'83 season—the first show was hosted by nobody. That was the one where Jimmy Caan's sister had bone marrow cancer and he pulled out, so we did the show with no host. And Rod Stewart was the musical guest. And Tina Turner was in New York, and I suggested to whoever was managing Rod at the time, why don't they get together, and they had a memorable duet.

With John Madden, it was really about the closest I ever came to having a heart attack before I had a real one in February of '96. In the last half hour of dress, John had, in effect, a second monologue, and basically it was bringing him out to tell some stories that he told normally about various crazy football players who had played for him on the Raiders. But it was so funny, we had helped him shape it into like a two- or three-minute monologue about an hour and ten minutes into the show.

So we were in a break and John was up on home base to do the second monologue when he said, in a booming voice, "Ebersol, Ebersol." And I'm under the bleachers in approximately the same area that Lorne works at today. I stuck my head around the corner so he could see me. He said, "Come here a minute." I came to about halfway to the stage area with a full house, whatever it is, three hundred–plus for dress. And he said, "I just want to tell you now I'm going to finish this dress rehearsal and then I'm going to leave. I'm not happy with how things have been going, and I'm enough of a trouper to finish it for this audience, but then I'm outta here. This is just the pits."

I'm standing there and I'm dying. And he lets about two or three seconds go and then he gets the biggest smile on his face in the world and he said, "You know I'm a practical joker, don't you?" The place went nuts. But in the meantime, I had just about had a heart attack.

ANDY BRECKMAN:

When Sam Kinison hosted, I don't think I've ever laughed harder. He did a little bit of his act for the staff about necrophilia. There was an article in the paper about a guy who was caught having sex with a dead guy in a funeral home. The question was whether Sam could do the joke on the show. It was in the air all week whether or not it was something he would be allowed to do, and I guess they eventually decided he couldn't.

DANNY DEVITO, *Host:*

The first time I did it was when *Taxi* had just gotten a bunch of Emmys and they then promptly canceled the show. And we did a whole thing on *Saturday Night Live* where we blew up the ABC Building in the cold opening, and the taxi drove off the bridge.

The weird thing is that the show goes by so quick when you do it. They pull you from one spot to the next. You're putting a wig on or a mustache and going, "Oh, this is the skit we're doing, oh, I remember this is what we're doing." They're in tune to it. They lead you around by the nose, basically. And it's over before it seems like you started it. You have to go with the flow. And you can't sit there and think about it too much, you have to just accept a lot of things in trust and go for it.

MARGARET OBERMAN:

There were scenes. There were definitely scenes. One was particularly nasty. It involved Michael Keaton, who was a friend of mine who had come to do the show and who was very hot off *Night Shift*. And between the Monday when Michael came in and the read-through, Dick decided he didn't like him and brought in Michael Palin, who was a real friend of the show and would come in occasionally to do things and who everybody loved. And Dick sort of inched Keaton out and moved Palin in. And it was pretty nasty.

Keaton was really hurt and angry and never really understood it. It was aberrant behavior on Dick's part. Keaton was one of those guys who as an actor in read-through was very laid-back and wouldn't really give you too much, and Dick was convinced he was just bad and just lost all confidence in him. Palin didn't know what was going on. He was oblivious. It was really awkward, one of those yucky, strange things that leaves a really bad taste in your mouth.

HARRY SHEARER:

I had been writing this series of Reagan sketches called "Hellcats in the White House," none of which got on the air. And the last one, they had me in Reagan makeup from dress straight through air. So I spent eight straight hours in Reagan makeup, and I think Bob Tischler finally told me at twelve fifty-three the sketch was cut, and I said to him, "I kind of figured that out." So for three straight weeks, I wasn't on the air, and I just at that point decided I had better things to do with my time. I'm not the tantrum type, although I think I'm better at hiding my feelings than I am. I'm told that when I'm unhappy in a situation, people know it just by the cloud that gathers over me. So on January 13 at one forty-three A.M., Dick said, "You know, we should stop this." And I said, "Well, I do too, but I think you have to pay me for the rest of the year." He said okay and then I left. I had said to Bob Tischler early on, "Why is Billy Crystal getting all this exposure on the show?" And he said, "Billy's stuff is more commercial than yours." And I said, "But this is a late-night show. Why is that the calculation?"

When I left, Dick issued a press release saying "creative differences." And the first person who called me for a comment on it read that to me and I blurted out, "Yeah, I was creative and they were different."

DICK EBERSOL:

There weren't many ego problems to deal with there—none at all, other than with Harry Shearer, who just got out of control. So by the end of January, I let him go. I had talked to each cast member before I did, and for the most part they were okay with it. A couple of them, who should go nameless, were sad, but they had to admit that the problem had gotten out of hand.

MARTIN SHORT:

Harry wanted to be creative and Dick wanted something else. Harry's very smart and very prolific, and I think that he felt his voice should be represented on the show. When he wouldn't get a chance, it made him very upset. If someone had said, "Harry, here's eight minutes of show, do whatever you want, and the rest of the show will be what it is," I think he felt there was an audience out there that would be interested to hear what he had to say. So that was a source of huge frustration between the two of them.

JAMES DOWNEY:

I used to walk down the street with Bill Murray and have to stand there patiently for twenty minutes of like drooling and ass-kissing by people who would come up to him. And Murray would point to me and say, "Well, he's the guy who writes the stuff," but they would continue to ooh and ahh over him. Murray can be a real asshole, but the thing that keeps bringing me back to defend him is I've seen him be an asshole to people who could affect his career way more often than to people who couldn't. Harry Shearer will shit on you to the precise degree that it's cost-free; he's a total ass-kisser with important people.

Back when neither of us was making much money, Murray and I would take these cheap flights to Hawaii. We had to stop in Chicago, and at the airport there'd be these baggage handlers just screaming at the sight of him, and he would take enormous amounts of time with them, and even get into like riffs with them. I enjoyed it, because it was really entertaining. We went down to see Audrey Peart Dickman once, and the toll guy on the Jersey turnpike looked in and recognized Murray and went crazy. We stopped and people were honking and Bill was doing autographs for the guy and his family.

I've yet to meet the celebrity who was universally nice to everyone. But the best at it is Murray—even to people who had nothing to do with his career or the business.

TIM KAZURINSKY:

It got really, really depressing, and there was also the notion, I think from Ebersol—from Yale Business School, or wherever the freak he came from—of divide and conquer. I was like tops of the group. I was the old guy that people would come to for life advice and medical questions; I was Mom and Pop. And I noticed that Ebersol would keep the cast off balance. He would try and keep it divisive and pit people against each other, because if we were united, if we were unionized, he was fucked. And he always did everything he could to keep the cast from being cohesive. I remember my last year there, they offered me "Weekend Update" about three-quarters of the way through the season. And I said, that's really fucked. Brad Hall would feel horrible. I mean, that's just like yanking him in the middle of the season. Everybody's ego was fucked-up enough. If you're going to do something like that, do it at the end of the season. And I just said no. I didn't have the stomach for it.

BRIAN DOYLE-MURRAY:

I got along with Ebersol. He was kind of goofy, but he's basically a likable guy.

MARGARET OBERMAN:

I think Dick was made fun of by Lorne. They used to call him "Patches." He was the NBC guy, kind of a suit. But I think that in a funny way he knew what he was doing. Look what he did. It was trial-and-error. He didn't pretend to be a creative genius, and he did some really low-rent things. It was not at that time a very hip show to be on in a certain way. The first year I was there, the hosts were like—we used to call them "the Bobs"—Robert Culp, Robert Conrad. It was such a weird array of people.

But you know, Dick kept it afloat, and all these people came out of it, and there were some great moments. It wasn't consistently wonderful—but then I don't know if it was ever consistently wonderful since the original show, and even *that* wasn't consistent, but the level of talent was so high you just didn't care.

ELLIOT WALD:

I was always one of those people who stayed up late and loved to watch the sun coming up. By the time I left *Saturday Night Live,* I was phobic about watching the sun rise. I couldn't stand to watch it getting light, because it meant time was running out and the pressure was on. So that changed in my life.

From a distance, they were wonderful years, and it was a good experience. But the closer in I focus, the more I remember exhaustion, disappointment, and pressure. The individual days of those years were so hard.

Those four years took about ten years off my life. Just the number of hours, the amount of pressure. The fact is that it's enormous pressure to be funny, and beyond that it's enormous pressure to be funny at a particular time. You're funny on Monday and Tuesday. Being funny on Thursday just isn't the same thing. So you've got from noon Monday 'til read-through on Wednesday.

JAMES DOWNEY:

That last season Dick had, when Eddie Murphy had left, he had Billy Crystal, Martin Short, Chris Guest—that was one of the best years of the show ever. They did some really wonderful, original stuff. A lot of it sort of broke up the form of the show—a lot of it was on film and really had nothing to do with "live." But it was really good stuff.

MARTIN SHORT:

SCTV was different. I did it for longer and it was in my hometown and it was the first show of that kind that I did, so there's obviously a special place in my heart. But I have a great fondness for *Saturday Night Live* and that year. I think of it as more like an event than a working job. It was like putting out a paper or something.

MARGARET OBERMAN:

At one point I was asked to write for *SCTV* and I was pissed off at Dick about something, so I thought I'd go to Toronto and do that. I knew a lot of those people at *SCTV,* but once I went and thought hard and long about taking that job I decided not to and went back to *Saturday Night*. Because *Saturday Night* was really a writer's show and *SCTV* was really a performer's show. And there was a big difference. As a writer, it was a better place to be.

For five years Saturday Night Live *had gone through highs and lows, sometimes seeming like the distressed damsel in a silent-movie serial, tied to railroad tracks and then being plucked up just before the train roared through. But what had Ebersol and his stars saved—the show or merely the title? Glorious tradition or mere commercial franchise? To some of the purists present at the creation of the precedent-shattering show, it seemed to have strayed far from its original mission and looked like it couldn't shatter a precedent with a pickax. And yet anything that lasts has to change—and Ebersol's final year, the one that starred Billy Crystal and Martin Short, is widely considered one of the funniest in the history of the show. The laughs were there, if not the heart.*

BILLY CRYSTAL:

Here's a story I never really told before: I got a movie out of my year on *Saturday Night Live,* with Gregory Hines, called *Running Scared*. But right before that was to start, Brandon Tartikoff called me and asked me would I consider becoming the permanent host of the show. At this point I was in California, the night before the screen test for the movie—which was a formality, because I knew I'd gotten the part, but the studio wanted to see me on film. It was actually a test to see if I could be convincing throwing a punch, which is most of what I ended up doing in the test. I was staying at Rob Reiner's house because I had rented my house out; people were still living in it. I felt weird. I came home and couldn't go home.

Brandon calls me at Rob's and says, "Listen, this is what I'm thinking about. Would you be interested?" This is May or June, right after the season had ended. I said, "Of course I'd be interested, but let me know, because then I won't test for the movie. I'll turn the movie down, because I'll have to come right back to New York and start planning." Clearly I could not possibly do both the movie and the show. And he said, "Let me call you back."

And I was ecstatic, because I felt I was ready for it. I can't describe enough how *comfortable* I was on that show. And then we didn't get a call. And what had happened was—this is all within twenty-four hours—Dick Ebersol decided not to come back, Lorne decided to come back, and not only was I not going to get what Brandon was envisioning, I was also not going to be a part of the show. Lorne wanted to start fresh and start with a whole new group of people. So the decision was sort of made for me. I would have come back, I would have liked that to happen. I've loved my career since then, but that would have been an interesting time if that had worked out. It may not have been the right thing. It may be that the show is great because it has guest hosts. Even thirty years later, it's still fun to watch people do things you wouldn't expect them to do.

I look at my year on *Saturday Night Live* fondly, as my favorite year in my career. It was an exhausting, euphoric, creative, explosive kind of feeling working with Marty, Chris, and Harry. And all of this on a show I started out to be on back in 1975 and then got bumped from the first show as a guest comedian because of time. To come back and have this show set my career in motion, even though I always wanted it to be nine years earlier, was a great personal satisfaction.

ANDREW SMITH:

Lorne rules the reruns now. Any clips or anything like that, it's as if the Ebersol years didn't exist. Once in a while he'll throw in an Eddie Murphy, but whenever there's a clip show, it's like those years of Ebersol's just disappear. It's as if Lorne still has some kind of hard-on about Dick.

4

Behemiel Rising: 1985–1990

Lorne Michaels had wanted to take six months off at the end of the 1979–80 season of Saturday Night Live *so he could rethink and recast the show. Instead, as things turned out, Lorne's half-year hiatus turned into a five-year exile. Unfortunately, the creator's return was not an immediate raise-the-roof triumph. He had an act to follow for a change—the Billy Crystal–Martin Short* Saturday Night Live, *which had been a populist hit. Instead of scouring comedy clubs and improv groups for fresh young talent as he and his cohorts had done the first time, Michaels, as if borrowing a page from the Ebersol playbook, stocked the show with the known and near-known: veteran actor Randy Quaid, teenage star Anthony Michael Hall (who had played Chevy Chase's son in* National Lampoon's Vacation), *young actors Robert Downey, Jr. and Joan Cusack, newcomers Terry Sweeney and Danitra Vance.*

It was a more peculiar than colorful group, one that writers found it difficult to write sketches for. Among the saving graces, though, were eccentric newcomer Jon Lovitz, a male diva who popularized original characters like his Pathological Liar and Master Thespian; performer Nora Dunn, whose SNL *stint would end in public acrimony; and snide Dennis Miller, who turned "Weekend Update" into his own fitfully amusing soapbox, replete with cranky ranting, girlish giggling, and a hailstorm of obscure references—one of his favorite and more accessible being the character Boo played silently by Robert Duvall in* To Kill a Mockingbird.

Michaels was not completely bedecked in glory. His much-ballyhooed foray into prime-time TV, a tastefully inert variety hour called The New Show, was apparently not new enough; it lasted fewer than thirteen weeks in the 1984–85 TV season. Not only were the ratings puny, but Michaels experienced his first true trouncing from the critics. He also lost, by his estimate, more than $1 million of his own money. In addition, what had been envisioned as a prestigious and productive movie career—first, abortively, at Warner Brothers and then at Paramount— fell short of expectations and momentarily threatened his reputation as king of the comedy impresarios.

Now Michaels had to build a new mountain and didn't have much raw material to do it with. He was in somewhat the predicament that Jean Doumanian had been, except he had all those connections and a keen eye for talent. All that was on the line were his personal and professional reputation, his livelihood, and the fate of his life's most important creation.

TOM HANKS, *Host:*

I did the show for the first time in 1985, the year Lorne came back after being away for five years, and I asked him, "So, why did you come back?" And he just said, "I missed it."

BERNIE BRILLSTEIN, *Manager:*

Lorne Michaels loves a lot of things. He's not *in love* with anything but *Saturday Night Live.* That's it. It's that simple. That's why he came back.

HERB SARGENT, *Writer:*

The season before Lorne's return, Brandon called me. And he said he was on the fence between Dick and Lorne—between Dick staying and Lorne coming back. I said, "If you have Ebersol, you have a solid professional show. If you have Lorne, you have something unexpected—which is much more fun than anything."

LORNE MICHAELS, *Executive Producer:*

The reality hit me that I needed a job. I wasn't really focused on much other than *Three Amigos.* I'd spent the better part of 1984 writing it with Randy Newman and Steve Martin, and it was about to go into production, with John Landis directing.

Meanwhile there was the failure of *The New Show*. Not only did it sort of fail, noble failure though it was, but it was enormously costly, which I had to bear personally. This was the first time I was producing a show for a license fee. We were deficiting it, and I was losing $100,000 a week. We did eleven of them. When it was all over, what I was focused on was behaving well.

I felt I'd had such enormous success with *Saturday Night* that it was character building to have that kind of failure. I had won big—and now I was losing. The last thing I wanted to do was go back and do a television show, but there was a very strong financial reality. I won't say I was completely broke, but I was pretty close to it. I wasn't in any danger of going under, and I'd had lots of periods in my life when I didn't have much money. It was more the dealing with the failure. And then I was getting divorced later on in that year.

By the spring of '85, when *Three Amigos* started shooting, Brandon called me and asked me about coming back. Dick had just decided not to. I said I didn't think so. I think he'd had discussions with Buddy Morra, Billy Crystal's manager, about Billy being the sole host, at least for ten of them, or something like that. As with a lot of things with Brandon, I only know the part that I heard. Jobs like his are always about making sure you have options.

When I left in '80, I just thought it would go away. I never really thought of it as having a life of its own, because I'd been there at the beginning of it. Someone very powerful told me, "You don't want to do *Saturday Night Live*. Somebody who wants to be you wants to do *Saturday Night Live*." I thought about that a lot. I promised Brandon that he and I would talk again. And then I think we got to a point in the conversation that he was going to pull the plug on the show. And for me, that was the swing vote.

ANNE BEATTS, *Writer:*

Lorne called and asked me if I wanted my old job back. It was a compliment, I guess. I said no. I've sometimes regretted that, but I was working on other stuff, and being in L.A. more. His first year back didn't seem to go that well. I certainly wouldn't pass judgment on what it represented that he returned.

TOM SCHILLER, *Writer:*

In the early days I was pretty much left alone. I could go into a meeting and say, "I want to do a thing with John Belushi as an old guy; he does this and that." And then they'd say, "Great. Do it." I'd write a script and go around and show it to people. Herb Sargent usually added a line or two to make it better. Then I just shot it, and in two weeks it would be on the air. It was a dream come true.

But later it became difficult. After the five-year gap, I went back and worked there a little bit, and it was murder. They assigned some young writer to work with me, and it was bad. They had more checks and balances, and that was bad. Somebody said Lorne had become the corporate person that he used to make fun of. It became more of a business. Suddenly there was a guy with a clipboard walking around while you were writing your sketches and stuff, making sure you were working.

When the show first started, no one knew what was going on, and there was a wonderful flux period, which was incredibly creative. We were more individuals in the early days. Then in '85, the show had coalesced, and you found you were just an interchangeable part. Not that the drugs were good, but there were no more drugs. It was clean. It wasn't as rambunctious—that's the word.

ANDY BRECKMAN, *Writer:*

It had meant nothing for me to please Dick Ebersol or to have Dick Ebersol say, "That's funny," to get his seal of approval. He was a suit, more of an administrator. He never once made me laugh. So creatively, I didn't respect the man. On the other hand, I was born in 1955. So in my early twenties, *SNL* was so influential, so big, and Lorne Michaels was this mythical, legendary figure, that when I started working for him, making him laugh and having a pat on the back from him meant a great deal to me.

I was surrounded by writers who had come back to the show and were very cynical about him. They would always be telling "Lorne stories"—about his miscalculations, his posing for the press, his lying to the press, and Lorne supposedly taking credit for stuff that he might not have been entitled to. Clearly they didn't feel the same way about working for Lorne that I did.

BERNIE BRILLSTEIN:

Lorne didn't want to go back with the same type of show Ebersol had. There were no long discussions. Lorne just said, "Here's what I'm going to do, here are the people I'm going after." Robert Downey, Jr. was one of the people he really wanted, and it wasn't a terrible idea, but it wasn't a good idea either, in retrospect. It just didn't work. And there were a few problems among the cast; I mean alcohol and drugs and whatever. It wasn't good. But Lorne was still young then, thirty-nine or forty, and he was trying something different.

JON LOVITZ, *Cast Member:*

I'd only had one job in seven years—doing *The Paper Chase* in its second year on cable, when I was twenty-five. So now I was twenty-eight. I mean, I just couldn't believe I got the show, you know? Like you go, "You want me to do the Master Thespian?" I'd done it at the Groundlings, but originally when I was eighteen. I was like just goofing around, you know, saying, "I'm the Master Thespian." And now they've built a whole set for it, you know. It just blew my mind.

Or doing the Pathological Liar. And next thing you know, everybody's imitating it. It was just unreal, because I'd been working as a messenger. And then I finally started working and I got a movie and a series, then I got *Saturday Night Live.* I mean, I was broke, and then by the end of the year I got a deal to do a movie for half a million dollars. So that was just an amazing time for me, you know, amazing.

Well, everybody else went nuts. Everyone else started getting weird, and I was like, "What's going on?" I got the job, you know, and then a friend of mine sent me a book of quotes, and he underlined a quote from Kirk Douglas, and it said, "When you become famous, you don't change, everybody else does." That's what was happening in my life. Everybody had said no for seven years, and all of a sudden everybody was saying yes. And I couldn't believe it.

ANTHONY MICHAEL HALL, *Cast Member:*

I grew up watching Eddie and Piscopo and that cast from that era. I was just a kid at the time, and I was just enjoying what was happening to me, working on the John Hughes films. And then all of a sudden I got a call from Lorne and, you know, I was in shock. I was such a huge fan of the show and so many of the actors and actresses that emerged from it. So it was really an honor.

Even after I had decided to do the show, I remember walking around the city, just baffled that I had taken this on. I couldn't believe I was actually going to be a part of it. It really is one of the most creatively demanding mediums to work in, because it's a blend of a lot of things — theater and rock and roll and everything else.

DICK EBERSOL, *NBC Executive:*

I think Lorne's first year back in '85 was very dark. It was a very dark year. It was the roughest season Lorne ever had doing the show, and everybody came out of the woodwork to attack. It was the first time he'd ever been subject to that "Saturday Night Dead" stuff. And that just reminded me that I had left of my own volition, because when I did the show, I'd never gone through a diatribe year like he went through then.

ANTHONY MICHAEL HALL:

It was one of the most forgettable seasons of the show's history. I certainly didn't make a major impact on the show like a lot of people did. But just to be a part of it from my standpoint was amazing. It's far and away the most competitive environment I've ever worked in. Some guy who was based in the west, a fan of the show, would send me tapes of selected sketches where it was so blatantly obvious that I was reading cue cards. He had time to do an edited version of, like, my worst cue card readings, the ones that were most blatant. It didn't bother me; I thought it was hilarious.

TOM HANKS:

It was a sort of cobbled-together cast. Lorne put it together in like six weeks. Franken and Davis were back as writer-producers. I think they'd been gone. So it was definitely a sense that the whole staff was either finding their bearings for the first time or trying to refind their bearings after an extreme absence. But in some ways it was one of those years that *Saturday Night Live* showed itself to be this enduring show business tradition—this entity, this classic thing. Because you could easily say it should have been off the air; that's what everybody wanted it to be. You know—"Saturday Night Dead." How often did you read that by the time I was on the show for the first time?

AL FRANKEN, *Writer:*

The '85–'86 season was difficult for a number of reasons, one of which was that Tom Davis and I were nominally the producers but didn't have that much authority. The second was we had a cast that didn't gel, and it was very hard to write in the same way as for a cast that had worked. I don't know what was happening in Lorne's head when he put that cast together, but I think he was consciously going after youth. We didn't have enough people to play middle-aged males. It was impossible to write a Senate hearing.

I liked Danitra Vance very much, but it turned out she was dyslexic and couldn't read cue cards on the air. I remember her agent or manager coming to us and saying, "You wrote for Eddie Murphy, why aren't you writing for her?" And I said, "Eddie Murphy's Eddie Murphy and Danitra's Danitra. Just because they're black doesn't mean they're the same thing." It was a little out of control.

But we had Lovitz, who was great, and Dennis Miller started coming in and doing "Update," so the building blocks were definitely there, but it was a tough year. Youthful problems, attitude, absence of skills, not to mention what may be a case of talent lack—that confluence made it very, very hard for a talented group of writers to find stuff to do. When the show is doing well, it's usually overpraised, and when it's not doing so well, it's overcriticized.

LORNE MICHAELS:

Jim Carrey never auditioned for me personally. There is an audition tape which we almost played on the twenty-fifth-anniversary show—if he had come that night, we would have. We have all the audition tapes. Carrey, I think, auditioned for Al Franken the year I was executive producer and Tom Davis and Al were the producers along with Jim Downey. In '85, when Brandon got me to come back, his whole argument was I had to learn how to delegate. Dick had run it successfully that way, and so Tom, Al, and Jim did their stuff and I sort of approved things. But later that season, when Brandon was again thinking about canceling the show, he told me, "You have to completely take charge of everything again."

CAROL LEIFER, *Writer:*

Jim Downey and Al Franken were really the people who hired me. Jim had seen me doing *Letterman* pretty regularly around that time, and he came in and saw me at the Comic Strip and then just asked me if I wanted to join the staff. Of course I had to meet Lorne, to officially be hired. The meeting was like thirty seconds. I walked in — it wasn't even a sit-down meeting — and he said, "Jim and Al said some really good things about you. Are you familiar with what kind of goes on with the writers? It gets pretty intense. Are you prepared for that kind of thing?" I said, "Yeah, I'm down with it." And that was about it. What I realized later was, having been Jim and Al's person coming in, I was never going to be in the inner circle, because Lorne wasn't the one who found me.

TERRY SWEENEY, *Cast Member:*

I think Lorne hired me because I was funny. I don't think he hired me as a gay guy. I don't find Lorne homophobic at all. I think he deserves credit. He was the first. When he told me he was going to hire me, I said, "You know I'm going to be openly gay, I'm not going to hide it or pretend I'm not." And he was totally fine with that. I never got the vibe from him that he was homophobic in the least.

JAMES DOWNEY, *Writer:*

We opened the season with Madonna hosting the show, and there was tremendous hype. It was an offensive, dreadful show. I don't know how many shows there've been — more than five hundred. I would say the Madonna show has got to be considered one of the top five—I mean in an entirely negative way. It really crippled the season from the get-go, particularly since there were a lot of people anxious to see that new group of actors fail. That first show was like an albatross for us. Years later people would still say, "I haven't watched the show since that Madonna thing." It did so much long-lasting damage.

When we left in May of 1980, we averaged something like a 12 rating and a 36 share—something pretty high like that. And then after Jean Doumanian's third show, it was consistently halved. So it was like a 7 rating or something. When Ebersol did the show, he stabilized it and solidified it and kept it on the air, which I think he deserves a lot of credit for, but the numbers were never really huge. That Madonna show got like a 10 rating. That was big.

It was almost like, "The bad news is, a lot of people were watching."

ROBERT SMIGEL, *Writer:*

I wrote a song for Madonna to do in a Spanish talk-show sketch and it was surreal, because she was the biggest star in the world and I was just stepping into this show for the first time. I'd half-written this sort of medley for her to sing, and I was one of the backup singers in the sketch. It was a very, very strange way to start.

Then I didn't get anything on for four weeks and I was worried about getting fired, because the show was such a disaster. George Meyer was a great writer who took me under his wing, and he told me, "Don't worry, no matter what, Lorne doesn't fire people, he gives them a chance." But after about five shows, people started telling me, "Things are tough and the network's clamping down."

DAMON WAYANS, *Cast Member:*

The thing about Madonna was, she was terrified. She had never done this before. They were doing the "five...four...three" countdown for the show to come on live. And I looked over at Madonna and she had the biggest facial tic, like her skin was jumping off. One of her eyes was like jumping off her face. She was a wreck. Madonna's not the friendliest person in town but she was very, very professional, and throughout the week she kept saying, "Let's do it again, let's rehearse it again, let's rehearse it again." She worked her ass off.

JACK HANDEY, *Writer:*

The Madonna show was considered in bad taste. It was viciously attacked and the ratings started going down. We were actually worried. That was one year, I think, that people wondered whether the show was going to get canceled. But we had a good writing staff then, with people like George Meyer and Jim Downey and Franken and Davis.

TERRY SWEENEY:

Chevy hosted the second show, and we were all so excited because, to us, Chevy was like a god. This was someone returning who'd been one of the original people and was this legendary figure. And we were just excited to work with him. And when he got there, he was a *monster.* I mean, he insulted *everybody.* He said to Robert Downey, Jr., "Didn't your father used to be a successful director? Whatever happened to him? Boy, he sure died, you know, he sure went to hell." Downey turned ashen. And then Chevy turned to me and he said, "Oh, you're the gay guy, right?" And he goes, "I've got an idea for a sketch for you. How about we say you have AIDS and we weigh you every week?" It was out of place. So then he ended up having to apologize and actually coming to my office. He was really furious that he had to apologize to me. He was just beside himself. And it was just awful. He acted horribly to me. He acted horribly to everyone. When he got on the elevator at the end of the night—you know, we all go to the party afterwards—and everybody saw him coming, we hid. We wouldn't be on the elevator with him. We were all hiding. We were plastered against the wall going, "Oh, he's getting on the elevator, he's almost gone. Oh, he's gone." No one wanted to be near him. I don't know what he was on or what was happening to him mentally, but he was just crazy.

JON LOVITZ:

When Chevy Chase was hosting, there was a meeting of the writers and staff. So Chevy looks at Terry Sweeney and goes, "You're gay, right?" Terry goes, "Yes, what would you like me to do for you?" Chevy goes, "Well, you can start by licking my balls."

ANTHONY MICHAEL HALL:

I never knew that side of Chevy. Then again, to Chevy I was probably always the kid who played his fourteen-year-old son in *National Lampoon's Vacation*. He was always nice to me. I really had a good experience.

RON REAGAN, *Host:*

I went and saw Lorne at the Chateau Marmont, where he was staying. He was getting ready to go to some award show. We sat and talked for about a half an hour or so about me hosting the show. Initially, I was really just doing him a courtesy of telling him no to his face. They'd called before to ask if I wanted to host the show and I'd said no. And then he was going to be in L.A., and he said, "Why don't you come over and talk?" I said, "Well okay, fine." I just expressed my concern about I didn't want to be taken advantage of in some way and didn't want to see my family hurt because of my stupidity—going onto a show where it was really an opportunity to make fun of them— and in a cruel way, not a fun way. And Lorne just said, "We don't want to do that. That's not what we're about," and he promised I'd have final say over things. Nothing too awful was going to get by me. And that pretty much addressed my concern. Once I'd realized I'd have control, that was it. I said okay. It just seemed like a fun thing to do. Who at that age wouldn't want to host *Saturday Night Live*?

ANTHONY MICHAEL HALL:

People were pretty impressed by the job Ron Reagan did hosting the show. He was very willing to throw it up there to see what stuck, you know. He was quite fearless as an actor, I thought. And he really had a good sense of humor about his upbringing and his family and everything. I thought it was really cool.

RON REAGAN:

I think that once they got to know me a little bit, everybody was being fairly careful about not being cruel. To have family members sitting there, it takes a little bit of the edge off. You can't be too mean. I'm probably as far or farther left than anybody on that cast. So in terms of personal politics, nobody was going to out-left me. There's always a little bit of weirdness. I've discovered in my life, having been my father's son for years and years, that people have preconceptions about you. And you try to disabuse them of those pretty soon.

We actually rehearsed one sketch that had been my idea. When we were sitting around the table earlier in the week, I said to everybody that I thought it would be funny if Terry Sweeney and I did a kind of screaming-queen sketch. And we wrote one up and kind of put it together and did it in the dress rehearsal. And you could kind of see the audience was really just sort of confused by it, didn't really see the point.

TERRY SWEENEY:

In one sketch, Ron and I played these gay guys who were house-sitting for Nora Dunn in her apartment—and we just change everything around and redecorate, and do all this stuff. And he played the really flamingest queen in the world. But they cut the sketch. His manager made him cut it. But he was still a great host.

RON REAGAN:

The *Risky Business* sketch seemed like an obvious one. I got a little note from Tom Cruise afterwards—just saying that he enjoyed the sketch and thought it was really funny, and ha ha. A little polite note. And yet there were some people who were upset by it. I don't really understand why. I guess it was just the Jockey shorts. I was actually wearing three pairs of Jockey shorts. Every time we rehearsed, and right after the dress rehearsal, Standards and Practices would come back and say, "Could we put another pair on him?"

My parents probably were not thrilled that I was going to be doing something that would inevitably poke some fun at them. I don't think my dad really cared. But Nancy tends to get a little nervous about that sort of thing.

TERRY SWEENEY:

Ron said his mother did not care for my impression of her. But *he* thought I was eerily accurate. Ron thought I was more like his mother than his mother was. So I thought that's the highest compliment one can ever have. He was great. He used to call to me, "Hi, Mom," in the halls. Imagine how freaky it must have been for him. There's a man coming down the hall dressed as your mother, in the same red Adolfo suit, going, "Hello, dear. Hello, son."

RON REAGAN:

Later on I was in New York for something completely unrelated. And I dropped by the *Saturday Night Live* offices to just say hi, and they were in the midst of doing a show where Oprah was guest host. And they were having their first cast meeting with her in Lorne's office when I happened to knock on the door. I didn't know what was going on. I just came in to say hi. "Oh, come on in, come on in. Sit in on the meeting." So I did. I turned around and said hi to Oprah, who I really didn't know at the time. She wasn't as humongous as she is now. And I could tell she was really displeased I was there. It was like I'd really stepped into her thing. So I stayed just a few minutes and politely left.

AL FRANKEN:

We had some good things that season, like when Ronald Reagan, Jr. did the show. And Pee-wee Herman did a funny show. Lovitz started doing the Pathological Liar. And Joan Cusack was tremendously talented. They were bright spots. It's just that nothing else went right.

CAROL LEIFER:

I wrote a sketch about a husband and wife having an anniversary dinner. It's just basically, "We love each other so much, it's so great, our anniversary." And you know, "Isn't it wonderful we can just tell each other anything, that's how close we are." And at that point the husband goes, "That's so true. Here's something: Sometimes I have this fantasy that you die." Tom Hanks eventually did it. But it literally went through every read-through of every male host and got cut. When Tom Hanks did it, it was so great.

Otherwise, it was a terrible year. That was, I think, maybe the only year where at the end of the season, the show certainly was not guaranteed to come back. It seemed genuinely in danger of being canceled.

TERRY SWEENEY:

It was an unhappy time during that period for a lot of the actors and actresses involved, but I've heard from future casts that they were not so happy either. There was a lot of Al and Tom, definitely. Al Franken and Tom Davis were very much involved in the show and very hands-on and very opinionated. So I think that they had their own version of things. I think they had felt like, "We're back," and rolled up their sleeves. And I think Al very much wanted to be on the show, and now he's found his little niche, which is wonderful for him, but I think he was still looking then for what his niche was — what was his claim to fame and how could he move from being a writer to being on-camera, being up front.

TOM HANKS:

Hosting the first time is a very, very milli-close second to the first time you appear on the Johnny Carson show. You're that combination of absolutely petrified but also kind of dizzy. The whirlwind preparation that goes into that first week, if you've never done it before, is kind of mesmerizing. It honestly looks as though nothing is happening at first. You know, you're the host and you're just kind of escorted around and around and around, and you're getting your picture taken, you're getting fitted for something, and people come up to you and pitch ideas that you might or might not understand. And then, on Wednesday, you have that big long read-through that, for some reason, starts a full hour and a half late and then goes for about three hours and then, from that, they cull all these things. You read twenty-five, thirty, forty, fifty, six hundred pieces. I can't even remember. Then you go into this room and they have them all up there on cards posted to a bulletin board, and the next thing you know, you decide what's going to be on the show. So that by the time you get through that — that moment which, by the way, is after the full dress rehearsal — you've sort of done it already, but now you know that it's live. I mean, it's horrifying. And yet it's the most exhilarating thing, like being strapped inside of a huge explosive rocket ship and you're waiting for the countdown to go and it just might blow you to kingdom come or it might take you to the moon.

The thing that happens the first time you do the show is you're just completely swept away with the history of the place. I think there's still stuff tacked up onto bulletin boards that hasn't moved in seventeen years or so. So you're reading these things that have been up forever in hallways lined with all those photographs. But when you go down and you're actually on in Studio 8H, you're thinking you sort of recognize this place, but you can't believe it's as small or as crowded or as dark as it is, and that the band is actually playing as loud as it is.

The first time I did it, it was just the beginning of the Christmas season, so it was December and they were lighting the Christmas tree there in Rockefeller Center. And the offices of *Saturday Night Live* were like one extremely big and confusing family. Everybody who had kids brought them in, and everybody was staring out the windows of the seventeenth floor looking down at the big tree and watching it all on TV at the same time.

The show was, of course, a history of entrances and exits. Sometimes the entrance was momentous and the exit ignoble, sometimes the exits were en masse. Many of the show's stars left only to return sporadically in cameo roles; they were like alumni revisiting the campus of their youth. No one ever actually quit on the air, while the show was actually in progress—or, not quite. Damon Wayans came close, with one of the most memorable exits in the annals of exiting.

ANDY BRECKMAN:

I wrote a sketch for Jon Lovitz called "Mr. Monopoly." The idea was he was a lawyer. And you know the character from the Monopoly board, the character that they draw on the Monopoly game, the little man with the hat? The idea for the sketch was Jon Lovitz was that man, Mr. Monopoly, and he was a very successful lawyer because he had all these "get out of jail free" cards. His clients would go to jail and he would come in with these cards and the cops would hate him: "Damn you, Mr. Monopoly!" And that was the idea for the sketch. And Lovitz was very funny. And Damon Wayans I wrote as a cop who had one line. He would say, "Hey Larry, your lawyer is here to see you." That was it.

Dress rehearsal went fine. I didn't know any of the political bullshit that was going on, but I did know Damon had been angry about various things, including something apparently that was cut at dress rehearsal, and he was furious and he decided between dress and air he was going to quit *Saturday Night Live* right then and there, he was fed up. And this is how he quit. During the live show, he made his entrance in the sketch not as a cop but as his flamboyant queen gay character that he later did on *In Living Color*. He came in prancing and delivered "Your lawyer's here to see you" very swishy. He totally derailed the sketch, derailed the sketch completely. The audience was completely thrown: What's a gay cop doing in there? Is it about the cop or is it about Lovitz? It was just stunning. I was with Lorne watching, and Lorne turned to me and said, "That's it. I've got to fire him." Lorne had no choice. Damon had sabotaged a sketch live on-air and Lorne fired him that night, which is what I think Damon wanted anyway.

I was just sitting in the corner, thinking, "I'm sorry. I supplied the bullets." And then I was going to disappear at one o'clock forever. I remember Tom Davis, who I guess was also a guest writer or was just hanging out there, saying, "I'll bet anyone in this room that within three years, we will all be standing in line to see a Damon Wayans movie. This is not the end of his career." And he was right. That was the start of his career.

DAMON WAYANS:

What was I supposed to do? I was supposed to just be a cop. But I was frustrated, because I think Lorne Michaels thought he was protecting me by not putting me out there, letting me do my thing. So I started walking around wearing dark shades. When they asked me what was wrong, I said, "It's too white in here, it hurts my eyes." I was really on the verge of a nervous breakdown, or just taking a gun and killing everybody. The night in question, the "Mr. Monopoly" sketch, I didn't think the sketch was that funny. I thought it was a one-joke premise. I was supposed to play a cop and we were doing a takeoff on like *Miami Vice*—this was the hot show at the time—and I was supposed to be Tubbs and Randy Quaid was playing the other guy. So between dress and air, they pushed that button. I wore a suit, so I thought, "At least I'll look good in the sketch." And then between dress and air Lorne Michaels comes to me and goes, "The sketch is not working. You look like a pimp." It was because of me the sketch wasn't working! He wanted me to wear a uniform.

So I just got angry. Because I didn't think the sketch was funny. I had a bunch of straight-man lines. It was the fact that Lorne blamed me for the sketch not being funny when I had told him before that it was a one-joke premise. The guy's waiting to get out of jail and Mr. Monopoly comes in and gives him a "get out of jail free" card — that was the big joke. It's like twelve minutes until Mr. Monopoly finally walks in. And then they say the reason it wasn't working was that I looked like a pimp at dress rehearsal. And I just said, "Fuck it."

I was like, okay, I'll be a cop in uniform but I'm going to find a character. And it would've been funny if I had not done it with such anger. I was so angry, I basically wanted them to fire me. I wanted to quit, but I thought they would sue me. It was the Brillstein-Grey management company trying to manage everything at one time as opposed to getting on with my needs. They were representing Lorne. Lorne was the big dog.

LORNE MICHAELS:

Damon broke the big rule. I went berserk. The whole business of trust when you're in an ensemble — the whole deal with the network, in my mind, is that we operate on the level of trust. We have live air, we're not just going to go up there and say, "Fuck fuck fuck fuck fuck." And I think Damon, in his defense, he didn't get a big enough laugh with what he was doing. And he went back to a character that he'd done in *Beverly Hills Cop*.

DAMON WAYANS:

I'd never seen Lorne lose his cool. He had always been very logical and reasonable and we could talk about anything. But he came backstage and he was like, "Get the fuck out of here, who the fuck, what the fuck" — it was like talking to friends up in Harlem. He was cussing. He was like, "John Belushi never did anything like that." "You'll never work in show business"—he said that one to me. Or never work again in New York, whatever.

I didn't even say good-bye. I went home, gladly. It was the same management, so they were basically telling me, "You fucked up, this is it, word is going to spread," and all that. In hindsight I understand that, but I was a young kid. I didn't understand politics or how tough it was for Lorne Michaels coming back for his first year and how he wanted to be right and be the guru of comedy. I didn't understand any of that. All I understood was I wasn't funny and they wanted me to hold a spear.

TERRY SWEENEY:

I think the writers came to think of me as just "the gay guy." They'd go like, "Oh well, he's a hilarious gay guy, so if we want a gay guy, we'll just put him in this sketch where the guy can be really effeminate—the guy's *really* gay. But if it's a regular role, let's give it to Jon Lovitz or Randy Quaid"—who were very talented, but it's just a question where I would feel like, "Hey, I can do this too." So I think I felt the brunt of some prejudice.

Later on, I came to realize—as one matures, one realizes it's not always the homophobia; it's a lot of times just that's not your world. If you're straight, you're thinking about a straight guy and a husband, and it's not—it's just not something you're thinking about. You think that you find a gay guy over there, and a straight guy's over here, and it doesn't occur to people that they're ever in the same place.

CAROL LEIFER:

I really don't think during the season Lorne said much of anything to me. I never requested to speak with him by myself. I'm different now; if I'm getting the cold shoulder from somebody—at that time I'd stay out of your way—but now I'd want to investigate more to see how I could help the situation.

I do remember a very valuable Lorne lesson that I still use today. I remember him really clearly in one meeting saying he always hated the funny-name joke, you know, when a character had a funny name, like a punny name. That kind of thing. It's such an indicator of an amateur.

DAMON WAYANS:

I was so glad to be off the show. I was so relieved. I finally felt like I lived on the edge. My problem with that show is, and I used to say it all the time, we're so rehearsed, where's the thrill of being on live? I had an improv background, hung out with Robert Townsend and my brother and Eddie Murphy. We'd go onstage and play around, and I didn't feel we were doing that on *SNL*. And the group of actors that they had—great actors, but they weren't improvisational actors. You say a different line during rehearsals and they go, "Cut!" What about playing around? So when I got fired, I was thrilled, I was relieved, I had knots in my stomach, I was angry, and I would cry when I got home.

But you know, to Lorne's credit, he's never spoken bad of me. I think in his mind he respected me or something. He's actually given recommendations for me in films and stuff like that. And that was right after this happened.

TERRY SWEENEY:

I'm really happy. I'm still with my lover that I was with back then, who was a writer on the show. I went back to television writing and movie writing, and so I've made money and done well, so I'm really actually happy I had the experience. The training is invaluable and I've used it, you know. I've just used it in everything I've ever done since then.

DAMON WAYANS:

I was brought back for the last show of the season. There's a sick side of Lorne Michaels; he loves the rebel. Once he got over his own ego—what I did on the show that time was basically a "fuck you" move—he sat back and said, "Well, the guy's talented. I just don't think he's ready to be a Prime Time Player."

It was great except Dudley Moore was the host and I was doing this joke about—I was born with a clubfoot, and so I used to do this whole routine about when I was young, how I used to wear orthopedic shoes and I had a shoe with like a five-inch heel and I used to walk with a limp. And I did me walking with the limp and said people that knew me thought I was cool. Thank God I was in the ghetto. I did this thing about how I wasn't a fighter at the time, I was just a very passive kid, and I said you don't find many handicapped bullies, and I did, you know, "Imagine some crippled dude coming up to you, 'Gimme your lunch money!'"

But Dudley Moore walked with a limp too. When I started doing the guy walking with the limp, he walked over to Lorne and like, "You're not going to let him do it?" So Lorne also killed that bit. But then at the end, he let me do it. Dudley saw it at dress rehearsal. I was looking at Lorne like, "You know this is a live show and I'm going to do shit anyway." Dudley was just like, "I can't go on. My foot."

I didn't do it to mess with Dudley. It was in my stand-up, a really funny bit I used to do. But it was his own insecurity. The reason I came out with the bit was the same reason, the feeling that people were watching. It was like, even if I don't do the joke, don't people look at that boot on your foot and go, "Damn, that's big"?

BERNIE BRILLSTEIN:

Brandon calls me up in April and says, "I'm going to cancel *Saturday Night Live.*" And by then, I have to admit, I was happy to hear it—you know, rather than see it suffer. I wasn't in love with the persona of *Saturday Night Live* the way Lorne was.

So I go home that night and I said to my wife at the time, "Deb, they're going to cancel the show." She said, "You can't let them bring Lorne back and then cancel it." She got offended. And I said, "You know, sometimes you've got to hear it from someone else." I call Brandon back and said no way, you've got to give him one more year. Brandon said to have Lorne come out, which he did. We all met, and that's how it stayed on the air. It was that close, it was canceled. My wife knew nothing about show business, but she liked Lorne. She said you can't let them do that, bring him back and then cancel him, that's terrible. And she was right. Common sense.

WARREN LITTLEFIELD, *NBC Executive:*

Brandon was very involved in getting feedback to Lorne on the show and felt that it was struggling, and I do remember him saying, "It's over." I think many of us would, in our years as executives at broadcast networks, be in a meeting, focus on problems, sometimes lose sight of what had been accomplished and what we had. And that kind of piling on happens, and you push away from the table and you go, "That's it, goddammit. We're shutting it down. I'll be the decision maker." And God bless Brandon—in the light of day I think he woke up and went, "Oh God, am I really going to face Lorne today and tell this human being who I love and care about and believe in that I'm pulling the plug on him and the show?"

And that's when that cold executive maneuver that you said the day before—"I'm going to take control and take action"—that's when you finally realize, you know what, maybe I'll just wait a little bit. And part of that is not wanting to be confrontative, and also in the light of day, forgetting the posturing for a moment, saying, "You know what? It may not be perfect. What is? But does that mean we throw it out—and what do we have to replace it with?" One of the questions you have to ask yourself is, "All right, kill it, but what's your plan?" And sometimes faced with "what's your plan," you look at it in a different light.

ROBERT SMIGEL:

By the end of the season, the show was still a disaster. I had this idea to do a cliff-hanger like *Dallas*—one of those obnoxious cliff-hangers that really were new at the time—and I wrote one where Billy Martin sets the studio on fire and Lorne's in there and he runs out and he just saves Lovitz, which infuriated a few people in the cast. And he leaves all these other people and it's like, "Who will survive?" And then the whole credit crawl, everybody's name had a question mark after it.

Once more Saturday Night Live *had teetered on the brink and once more the program was spared the unseemly ignominy of cancellation. Now it was up to Lorne Michaels to reinvent the show one more time, and though he still disliked firing people, one of his first moves had to be to throw the "new" cast out and recruit a newer new cast, one that could help SNL win back America's heart. Michaels had learned the lesson of casting people for their talent rather than for their names, and he set about rebuilding the show in much the way he had first constructed it—*

he and his staff searching comedy clubs and improv groups for bright young performers, especially those who could write sketches and create characters.

Even though the search would prove to be successful, Saturday Night Live *still faced a future that was anything but certain. For the first time in its history, the show was renewed for only thirteen weeks, not a full twenty-week season.*

BRAD GREY, *Manager:*

I thought Dana Carvey was really special, and I wanted Lorne to see him. We all went to the Comedy Store—Bernie, myself, Cher, and Lorne. It turned out to be one of those silly circumstances where the moment Dana went onstage, Lorne had to go to the men's room. So I was sitting there and I knew that Dana would just kill, which he did. And just as he was finishing, Lorne returned from the men's room. So Dana didn't get the show then; we waited until the next go-round.

DANA CARVEY, *Cast Member:*

I'd auditioned twice before. This time, I went on at midnight at the Comedy Store, after Sam Kinison. I always had my own equivalency of the dumb blonde in my career, especially back then. I really looked like an innocent midwestern guy with blonde bangs, I just didn't look like a comedian, and it kind of threw people sometimes. But this guy had a little club on the West Side and Lorne saw me there. Rosie O'Donnell was headlining, and she let me come in and do forty minutes before her. And Lorne showed up with Brandon Tartikoff and Cher—just so we would be a little more nervous. And that's where I got the show.

My wife didn't even move out to New York. I said, "This will probably fail." I went out there early because Lorne said, "You could come out and, you know, just hang." So I came out in August and Lorne turns to me and says, "Paul and Linda are coming over tonight." I said, "Excuse me?" "Oh—Paul. McCartney. Over here." And literally the blood drained from my face. And I went into a room that Lorne called "Jack's Room" because it's where Nicholson would stay, and I called my friends back in the Bay Area and said, "I'm going to meet Paul McCartney tonight." And Paul and Linda came over for four nights in a row and we listened to demo tracks, we heard all about them. Being a Beatle fanatic, that experience was just absolutely mind-blowing.

TERRY TURNER, *Writer:*

When I got onto the show, there was a sense that this show is over. I remember sitting in a restaurant with my father-in-law in New York, and he said, "My son-in-law here works on *Saturday Night.*" And the waiter said, "God, I thought that thing was off the air. It's been bad for so long."

VICTORIA JACKSON, *Cast Member:*

I lived in L.A., had my own house, and I had already been on a canceled series. I remember I was pregnant in '85 with my first baby. I was twenty-six years old. I was doing a commercial in the desert for a truck company, and I was nauseous and everything and I didn't want them to know I was pregnant, because they might fire me, but I wanted the money 'cause I was the breadwinner since my husband never worked. And so I came back to L.A. from that commercial, and I heard someone say my name was on a list at the Improv to audition for *Saturday Night Live* and why wasn't I there? And I was like, "Huh?!" Nobody told me about that. William Morris was my agent, but nobody told me that there was even an audition.

Here's the cut to the chase: I had the baby. I did *The Pick-Up Artist.* And all of a sudden the phone rings in the summer of '86. And my baby's three months old and it was someone from *Saturday Night Live,* and they said, "Do you want to audition for *Saturday Night Live* tomorrow?" And it didn't even go through my agent. It didn't go through anyone I knew. It was like they called my home directly. I have no idea how they got my phone number. It's really mysterious. And I said, "Oh. Sure." And then they said, "There'll be a plane ticket waiting for you at LAX tomorrow morning at eight A.M. to come to New York and audition." And they said to be sure and bring all your characters. And I said okay. So I hung up. And I was like, "I don't have any characters!" I never was in the Groundlings and I never took improv and, you know, basically the way I got on Johnny Carson was I had a six-minute stand-up comedy act that was mostly doing a handstand while reciting poetry.

So I hung up the phone. I told my husband, "I'm going to New York tomorrow to audition for *SNL* and they said bring your characters." And I looked at him like bewildered, you know. I knew about *SNL* and Belushi just 'cause you know it as part of culture, but when I grew up we didn't have a TV, and then I was in college and I didn't have one, and then I was trying to get on TV so I was always busy. So then I flew to New York. I brought my ukulele and my handstand; the handstand traveled with me. And I got on the plane and I thought, "Now if they lose my ukulele, I have no audition," because, you know, I don't have characters. And they lost my ukulele.

So then I got picked up and they took me to a hotel where the other girls who were against me were staying. There were about ten other girls from Canada and Chicago. The next day they marched us all down the street in a row, like ducks, past that big guy Atlas holding the world. I wore my French maid costume from when I was a cigarette girl, because that's when I started doing the stand-up thing. I was really nervous.

We were all in the hallway waiting and then everyone was whispering that one of the girls had done a strip routine for her audition. And that's a really dumb idea, I think, because you can't really be naked on NBC, you know? Even if you look good naked, it's not going to help a comedy program. So then I did my little stand-up comedy act. I guess I had about ten minutes. I sang my songs and did my handstand poetry, and Lorne was watching with about three Lornettes. You know, they're called the Lornettes, the girls who work for Lorne and make sure he has plenty of popcorn. The bravest cast members would eat some of Lorne's popcorn but I was scared to. But one time I did and like one kernel fell on the floor and one of the Lornettes gave me a dirty look. They're not supposed to let any of them fall on the floor, you see.

So I did my audition and then they said, "Oh, spend the night. Lorne wants to see you tomorrow, but he doesn't come in until four P.M. because he wakes up late and starts the workday at three P.M."

Then he met with me and he said, "Well, you—um—I loved your audition. It was really funny, but I don't know if you're really strong in character." And I said, "Oh—well, I could talk like this and be British." And he goes, "Uh-huh, yeah." I go, "I could talk like *this* and that's a character." And he goes, "Uh, yeah." And he goes, "Well, like if I wanted you to be Annie Hall, you know?" And I said, "Well, then I would just wear men's clothing and kind of look at the ground a lot." And he goes, "Well, what if I wanted you to be—a housewife in the Midwest?" And I said, "Well, I *am* a housewife." So then I went home and I thought, "Oh man, I was so close, but he's not going to pick me."

So I was supposed to be on Carson again in two weeks, and I thought, "Hey, what if I continue my audition on national TV? That would really impress Lorne." So I asked *The Tonight Show* and they said, "Sure, but just don't say the name of the show." So I got all these tapes of people and tried to imitate them—like Tina Turner and Teri Garr and stuff. But it wasn't my strong point, you know. So I thought, well, if I just try to do the impression and people know who I'm doing and they laugh—well, all your goal is, is to make laughter, so it doesn't matter how you get there. So I sat next to Johnny Carson and I told him I was auditioning for a show and I had to do characters and I said, "Let me do them for you, and if you can guess who I'm doing, then I'm doing it good, right?" He goes, okay. So I went, "Oh, oh, Archie! I'm sor-ree!" And he goes, "Edith Bunker." And I go, yeah. And the audience claps. And I go, "I don't know why I'm here. Just go to a commercial. I don't have anything to say. I don't know why I'm here." And Johnny says, "Teri Garr!" And I go, yeah. And then I went, "What's love got to do, got to do with it." And I danced, you know. And he goes, "Tina Turner." And I go, yeah. And so then I was smoking a cigarette. And he goes, "I don't know, Bette Davis?" And I go, no. And he goes, "Who is it?" And I go, "I made her up." And then Johnny laughed so hard. The audience laughed too. And then he goes, "If you made it up, how am I supposed to guess who it is?" And I go, "Oh, I don't know. I'm supposed to make up characters in this show, you know."

So then my manager at the time took the video of that show to Lorne's L.A. hotel in case he wasn't watching that night. And then, about a week later, they called me at home again. It was ten o'clock on a Sunday night. And she goes, "Congratulations. You're in the cast of *Saturday Night Live.*" And I was like, "Oh, thank you." And she goes, "There will be a ticket waiting for you at LAX in the morning, and we're putting you in a hotel until we find you an apartment." I was like, "Oh, thank you." So I hung up the phone and then I screamed really loud. Because I had been trying to act real cool in front of her. And then my baby woke up and started crying, and then my ex-husband—he doesn't handle pressure very well—he threw up. On the bed.

TERRY TURNER:

When we got there, Bonnie and I had been married for a bit. One thing good about us is we've always worked together, and she could shore me up and I could shore her up, and we could yell at each other too. We both went in for therapy during the show. So that might have helped. Wait—I can't believe I just said that, that *Saturday Night* drove us both to therapy. I'd never thought about it until now.

BOB ODENKIRK, *Writer:*

They hired Robert Smigel as writer, and then while Robert wrote I would sort of work with him on the phone every week and pitch him ideas and help him with his ideas. And meanwhile I was continuing to write sketches in Chicago, and I would mail those in to Robert and he'd pass them around the office, and sometimes they would do a joke of mine on "Weekend Update." I think there was maybe even one sketch that I might have written that was done. And so people were kind of familiar with my work and I came in and did an interview the following year, which was Robert's second year, and then I was hired a few months later. I interviewed with Lorne, which was extremely weird. I basically had a huge chip on my shoulder, and mix that in with Lorne's traditional intimidation and it's not good. I didn't respond to the way he likes to approach young performers and set himself up as some kind of very distant, strange Comedy God.

KEVIN NEALON, *Cast Member:*

When Aykroyd and those guys were on—the original years—I moved out to California to do stand-up, so I was always out there in the clubs when the show was on and didn't get to see it that much. I never really thought that was my gig. I didn't do characters or impressions. My stand-up was basically off-the-wall, absurd. I was influenced by Andy Kaufman and Albert Brooks and Steve Martin, you know.

The clubs in 1975 were really tough. Audiences were really brash and heckling, and they're all crammed in these little rooms, and the comics were just tough New York guys, and there was a lot of profanity and heckling going on. And I remember seeing Larry David onstage one night follow some heckler right out into the street and slug it out with him. So I thought California would be a good place.

VICTORIA JACKSON:

Oh, another thing—in my audition, when Lorne said, "I think you're weak in characters," I said, oh, well, you know who's the greatest female character actress in America? Jan Hooks. And I didn't even know if he knew her, but I had already worked with her on *The Half-Hour Comedy Hour,* which was trying to be like *SNL,* and I was like a baby at the time. It was like my first TV show. Arsenio Hall was the star of it. And I had seen Jan be brilliant—like backstage when the cameras weren't even on, she would do a lesbian gas station attendant in Atlanta. And she would just go into these people and I thought she was like great. I mean, personally she pretty much hates my guts, but professionally I thought she was like a genius, so I told Lorne. And I told her later, "I told Lorne to hire you."

KEVIN NEALON:

I was renting a house in the Hollywood Hills and Dana was living in an apartment over the garage, temporarily, and there was another comedian I was living with and a writer, and I was dating Jan Hooks at the time.

JAN HOOKS, *Cast Member:*

Kevin was great. We were really, really good friends. And my mom got sick. My mom had cancer. And I just grabbed on to Kevin and he went down to Atlanta where my mom was. And we just started this relationship—it was a relationship out of a kind of trauma. And the only problem was that we both got *Saturday Night Live* in the middle of it.

He was hired as a featured player and Lorne wasn't quite sure what I was. He thought the year before I was too old, and then I heard through the grapevine that he thought I had a weird mouth and he didn't want to hire me because of my mouth.

TERRY TURNER:

Dana and Bonnie and I wrote a lot of the Church Ladys together, but it was Dana's creation. We sort of played support. We were the only people—because we were from the South and there was a cable industry in the South that hadn't quite reached into New York—we were the first people who really knew, next to Jan, who Jim and Tammy Faye Bakker were, and all of the nuances of who they were, which is sort of how we got into the Church Lady, because it became a target of that character. And we were sort of the people who could access it quickly.

JAN HOOKS:

I knew Tammy Faye Bakker from the seventies. She had a show in Atlanta—when I worked in Atlanta. I would just religiously, pardon the pun, watch. It was just unbelievable. And I turned my friends on to Tammy Faye. And I actually went in to Lorne and said that there's a woman that's on cable, Tammy Faye Bakker, and I would really love to do her. He said, "I've never heard of her." I said, "Yeah, but she's such a great character." And then, lo and behold, the scandal happened.

ROSIE SHUSTER, *Writer*:

Dana's audition tape was the most amazing audition tape I've ever seen, because he nailed impressions and pushed them to this surreal place but he also did these amazingly absurd, highly original characters like the chopping broccoli guy. I especially responded to this rudimentary version of the Church Lady. The smug superior attitude was there. And the consummately couchy "Isn't that special?" I think that character reminded me of a Waspy, repressed side of Toronto that was very big on shaming. So I mentioned that to Lorne and he teamed me up with Dana, who at the time was this sketch-comedy virgin, and together we anchored this character in a "Church Chat" talk-show format. And we added all this titillating talk of engorged naughty bits and all that kind of stuff.

"Church Chat" stole the rehearsal and it got moved up to open the show, the first show of the new season. So it was pretty prominent, pretty scary. But it struck a main vein pretty instantly, instant franchise time, and they were very fun to write. The Church Lady would project her filthy erotomaniac imagination all over the poor hapless guest, whoever they were. She would basically verbally slime them with her own repressed garbage and then she'd go to town shaming them. She had a black belt in shaming. And then she'd coyly suggest their behavior was the work of Satan.

Thinking back, I think the Church Lady was the forerunner of what Kenneth Starr did to Bill Clinton.

DANA CARVEY:

The very first night was a crisis. The Church Lady—which no one knew if it would work—was going to be the last sketch on in the dress rehearsal, right before the good-nights—in other words, the dumping ground. But then it *killed* in dress and they moved it up to be the very first sketch. And then I had this chopping broccoli thing, and then the show was sort of on my shoulders for some reason, and I felt just intense pressure. I would essentially cry in my dressing room. I'm emotional. And then I was swearing at myself in the mirror. There was so much pressure, because there I was, thirty-one, I never thought I would get on *Saturday Night Live,* and here was this first show, I was unknown, I had never done sketch comedy, the red light was going to come on, twenty million people, the pressure was so extreme, at least the way I felt—and then it came off great. So that was a huge moment.

JAN HOOKS:

The show changed my life, obviously. But I have horrible stage fright. And with all these, you know, stand-up comics who I love— you know, Dana and Dennis and Kevin and all these people—you know they wanted their shot, they wanted to get in there and do it, but I was one of the ones that between dress and air was sitting in the corner going, "Please cut everything I'm in!"

VICTORIA JACKSON:

The first live show of my life, my ex-husband had a hemorrhoidectomy performed in the hospital on the day of my show and he's like, "Why aren't you here visiting me?" I'm like, "I'm on *Saturday Night Live!* For my first time! Are you kidding?"

JAN HOOKS:

Victoria Jackson? I thought she had a pretty good gig. I just have a particular repulsion to grown women who talk like little girls. It's like, "You're a grown woman! Use your lower register!" And she's a born-again Christian. I don't know, she was like from Mars to me. I never really got her.

VICTORIA JACKSON:

When we would sit in his office, we'd be on the floor and he'd be on the desk, like we were little preschool kids. From that sense, it's kind of fatherly. He would never say, "You did a great show last week." He would say, "Well, the show was okay. Do we have one this week?" So he didn't play favorites and he didn't compliment us too much. But I was used to that 'cause my dad doesn't compliment me either. My dad was my gymnastics coach and he only said criticisms.

I never gained weight because I was on my toes all the time. Sometimes I walked down the hall and he would say, "Hi, Victoria." And then the next time he would walk down the hall, I would say, "Hi, Lorne," and he'd completely ignore me. I was one inch away from him, and he'd keep walking. It was a kind of scary, weird thing.

DANA CARVEY:

I'm too passive-aggressive to have ever had a fight with Lorne. But we had little snippets. You're working under conditions where you're exhausted. If I'd been assigned an impression that I didn't get and I just tanked at dress, he'd say, "Dana, are you ever going to get John

Travolta?" or whoever. "No, I'm never going to get it, Lorne, you should just cut it." "Really???" My thing was like, "Church Lady's not happening tonight." And I would just say, "Well, maybe we should just cut it."

"Rrrrrright. So you're saying we're going to cut the thing that's going to make the show."

"Well, that's my suggestion."

"Dana, no no no no no no, don't misunderstand me." Lorne is so brilliant at getting in your head. "No no no no no no, don't misunderstand me, I think it's fabulous, if you want to go that route, that burlesque route, um, it's fine, but I think you'll find if you keep it smart, it's where all the good stuff is."

See, I had to learn all that, because I thought a laugh is a laugh. And then Lorne and those guys were kind of like, well no, there's different levels, there's smart laughs and there's dumb laughs. Being a stand-up comedian to me, it was just, "Get the fucking laugh at all costs."

VICTORIA JACKSON:

I brought the writers food. They were all very intensely writing. Their goal wasn't to make me a star; most of them wrote themselves into the show to become stars. If you want to get in the show more, you could always bring the writers some food. Well, I tried that.

I asked Robert Smigel, "Robert, how come I never get to do any impressions? I never get to do any characters." And he says, "Because you're nasal." And I said, "There must be someone nasal I can do an impression of." He goes, "Roseanne Barr is kind of nasal." And I said, "Let me do her. She's hot now. She's nasal, can I do her?" And he's like, "Hmm." And so he wrote a sketch, and I was thrilled.

Jon Lovitz always tried to help me get in the show too. Dana and Kevin and Lovitz—they helped a little. Kevin and Dana wrote me into "Hans and Franz" as Roseanne getting liposuction.

KEVIN NEALON:

I think Hans and Franz made Dana and me laugh more than any other characters when we were writing them. It's funny how something like that will permeate the culture and become pop culture. It seems audiences are like parrots, they like to repeat phrases that either have some kind of cadence to them or are silly. Whether it's "Isn't that con-veeen-ient?" or "We want to pump—you up," or whatever it is—"Cheeseburger, cheeseburger." It's something that everybody can relate to, when they get around at the office on Monday morning and just kind of laugh, because everybody kind of recognizes it. They can all be in on the laugh. And they can use it as their own little personal joke. I mean I do that too, with other people's stuff. If I hear a lot of Mike Myers stuff, like "Yeah, baby," I find myself doing that. People need that occasional catchphrase in their life. The coolest thing for Dana and me is that on the space shuttle they were doing Hans and Franz, which was fun.

JON LOVITZ:

You're always competing. I mean, it's not like you want the other people to do bad, but it's just the way it's set up because, you know, you write all Tuesday night and then they pick like three of the forty sketches at read-through, and then they whittle that down to fourteen of them, then six would get cut. Only about eight or nine make it to air. It was competitive. I mean, it just was the way it worked. And when I was there anyway, it was almost like the writers against the cast, and if you got a lot of stuff on one week, the next week there'd hardly be anything written for you. I also think that the writers would just write for themselves really a lot of times. And just whatever they happened to think of, that's what they thought of. So certain writers you ended up hooking up with because, you know, your humor was more like theirs. I worked a lot with A. Whitney Brown doing the Liar character the first year. And then Al Franken would write for me a lot.

When I was on the show, like just say from '86 to '90, that group stayed the same for four years. You know, the eight of us. And it was very competitive but everybody was working really, really hard and really wanted the sketches to be great. And also I think our group was into saying let's do this sketch but also try to do great acting, like the best as actors. And play it really, you know, funny, but also trying to make it really real and believable.

My first year, I was doing well, so they pushed me a lot. And I got everything on. And then my second year, I got less. Lorne said, "You're going to have a lot of competition this year." And then, I don't know, I was supposed to do a Liar movie and it didn't work out. And so that caused problems between Lorne and me. So I would say stuff about him and it would get back to him, because I was angry about it. So it would get tougher for me to get pieces on. And then, you know, he was mad at me. I mean he just was. He was mad at me for the next four years. And then he was mad at me for leaving the show for six or seven years. Because I left. What happened was, he was mad. I mean, everybody would talk about him, but for some reason, everything I said got back to him. I wasn't saying anything different than anybody else. I would never say it in public and I still won't, because—because the guy hired me, you know, and he gave me the opportunity of a lifetime. So my beef with him was more about, I thought we were friends and I heard he said stuff about me. So I was hurt by that.

I was supposed to do two movies that summer and then come back to the show. So I was just thrilled, you know. And then one of the movies didn't happen. And the other movie, I would've had to miss two shows to do it, and Lorne said you can't miss shows. So I had to choose. Personally, I didn't think it was fair, because my contract was up and I thought, you know, I did a really good job for five years and I just asked him to miss the first two shows. But his opinion was, well, you know, this show is really important. If I let you miss shows, I have to let everybody else miss shows. And, you know, Belushi and Aykroyd do movies and fly back and forth. And so I asked the producer could I do that, and he said we can't—you can't do that. It wouldn't work out. Lorne was getting a lot of pressure too, from NBC executives who didn't like—especially Ohlmeyer—didn't like the idea of people running off to make movies, which to me was stupid. I'd say, "Look, I'll miss the first two shows and then you don't have to pay me, of course, or I'll make 'em up." If he'd said, "You can do the show, but if you get movies, you can do those too," I would've said, "Fine. Sign me up for the next five years." Because then what you would've had, from my point of view, is a cast full of movie stars. Wouldn't that have been something?

Of course Lorne later admitted it was a mistake and he should've done it that way. And then the following year, he let people miss shows. So, you know, for me personally, it's kind of upsetting, because I really wanted to stay. And then, of course, the movie I did came out for a week. It was a colossal bomb. It was called *Mom and Dad Save the World*. What happened was, they reedited the movie for kids, so if it had any edgy humor, they took it out, you know.

After the fifth year, when my manager said, "Why don't you just clear the air with him?" he was very angry. I went in there to do that with him, and he was very angry with me. He was shaking. He was furious. Not yelling but just shaking, you know. But after that, we cleared it and I said okay.

I think a lot of the problem that people have with Lorne is that they just know him as the genius from *Saturday Night Live,* right? Oh, he's picked you to be in his show. So it's the opportunity of a lifetime. So you're so grateful to the guy, you know, like here's this guy giving you the chance of a lifetime. So you're automatically like, "Thank you," and he's the boss and you have strong feelings for him and you want to please your boss. And, you know, he's not really demonstrative that way. But actors are.

Many writers got their starts, or their first major professional gigs, on Saturday Night Live *and then went on to write sitcoms or movies, hits and flops. The show truly was a talent processing plant and the most influential comedy academy in TV history. Among those who went through the process was a young, tall Irish American with skin as fair as Snow White's.*

CONAN O'BRIEN, *Writer:*

I was always a nervous *Saturday Night Live* writer. I found being a writer on *Saturday Night Live* more nerve-wracking than being the host of *Late Night* and replacing Letterman.

GREG DANIELS, *Writer:*

Conan O'Brien and I were a writing team at one point on this HBO show called *Not Necessarily the News*. And we did a packet of material for *Saturday Night Live* and then we didn't really hear anything for about a year. And in the intervening time we had gone on to a different show and then that show had failed.

We had an interview with Lorne. I remember when we went into the interview, he offered us wine and we said no and then he asked us some question, like, "How do I know you'll succeed here at the show?" And we said, "You don't, we might not." So we left the interview and Jim Downey, who was the guy that had brought us in, came up to us and said, "How can you answer questions like that? It was terrible." Eventually, I don't know why, we ended up getting the job. I think that they had said about ten minutes later that it was okay.

This was more like big-time showbiz stuff, and we didn't really know the rules of that kind of behavior. So we were still kind of rubes. I think we should've accepted the wine at least.

CONAN O'BRIEN:

Lorne kind of throws you into the pool. I remember, very early on, him bringing me into a room and—not that my view of him has changed at all—but when I was twenty-six years old, which I was then, and you put a gun to my head and said, "Who's the funniest person ever in the world?" I would probably say Woody Allen, Steve Martin, Peter Sellers, one of those three. But definitely Steve Martin was like a towering figure in my comic worldview. And I remember Lorne pulling me into a room early on. Like, "Conan, what do you think? Steve and I are trying to figure out this thing. What do you think?" He's not afraid to just throw you in there with those people. And he's not afraid like, "I don't know, this kid might embarrass me," or "This kid might be an idiot." He's not afraid to go, "Let's get Conan in here and maybe he'll have an idea."

GREG DANIELS:

Carl Weathers was the host the first week we got there. And he'd just been doing this movie, *Action Jackson*. And so our introduction to everybody was they had a screening of *Action Jackson* and we went and all the cast sat in the back and made cracks. I remember Kevin Nealon being very funny, sitting in the back.

It was intimidating, because we were the new guys and we were younger than most of the writers. And we did this thing where we'd close the door and go, "Okay, on three, we're going to laugh like crazy." Then—one, two, three, *HA-HA-HA-HA-HA!!!* And people would hear out in the hall and they'd come by and say, "You got something good?" We'd go, "Oh yeah, oh yeah." So that kept our spirits up.

CONAN O'BRIEN:

I think my favorite host, other than like a Steve Martin, is Tom Hanks. I remember he'd stay up all night and he'd write with you. I mean, literally there was the walk-through that some hosts did where they clearly were just being paraded around and pretending to listen to your ideas but they just couldn't wait to get back to the hotel room and let these idiots hash it out. But Tom Hanks would actually roll up his sleeves. Sometimes you'd pass him and it's like four in the morning, and he's in the corner scribbling away on something, just constantly trying to make it better. That's what always impressed me, people who looked upon it as, "I can make this better right up until the moment we go on the air."

A really difficult guy was George Steinbrenner. There was some idea that Lorne wanted him to do and he sent Odenkirk and me in there to talk to him. So Odenkirk and I go into this room and it's George Steinbrenner. He's got like the giant World Series rings and he's in a bad mood. He had just been banned from ever setting foot in Yankee Stadium, so he was really gruff. So these two nerds come in the room. I remember, like, "Mr. Steinbrenner, we just think, you know, this sketch is funny," and, "Yeah, yeah, I don't know, I don't know, I don't think I'm going to do that sketch." And we were like not taking no for an answer. And he just wheeled on us. He was like, "Hey, not happening! Out!" And he just threw us out of the room.

GREG DANIELS:

I met my wife, because she was one of Lorne's assistants, at the first party there. She was very briefly a Lornette and then she moved over and became a development exec at Broadway Video. So Lorne was very happy in kind of a weird way that we had this office romance. And I don't remember exactly when he realized it was going on, but he was saying that there hadn't been a real good office romance since Gilda Radner and G. E. Smith.

CONAN O'BRIEN:

I think one of the reasons *Saturday Night Live* has been so successful is that it's almost brutally unsentimental about its past. It just keeps trying to find who's the next person. Let's get him in here. What's the new thing? Let's do it. You always get the sense that the show is almost like a shark that's constantly on a mission to find what's new, what's hot, what are people into now? And chomp its teeth into it.

GREG DANIELS:

I remember one time Conan and I had a sketch that was supposed to be the cold opening and it was cut between the dress and the air. And we were kind of moping around, and then about twelve-fifteen they realized that the show was running long and they didn't have time for this other big sketch. So they came to us and said, all right, your sketch is back in. And we were so excited and then we realized that it ended with "Live from New York, it's *Saturday Night!*" from being the cold opening. And so we ran down there and the music was on, the musical guest was playing, and then right after the musical guest the sketch was going to start. And we ran down to the cue cards and we wrote a new ending directly onto the cue cards. And basically it was like from *Broadcast News,* we just kind of gave the cue card to the cue card guy and he ran out and the music ended and they started the sketch. But it was really one of the most exciting showbiz experiences I ever had.

CONAN O'BRIEN:

It definitely for me has a "my favorite year" quality to it. I'll never be that young and naive again. There's something about it; it's like going off to war. *Saturday Night Live* tends to get you when you're real young, you haven't seen a lot, and it throws you into this world of lots of pressure, big-name stars, crazy situations — and you can't get that combination again.

No matter what happens to me now — I've just been through so much and I am still thrilled by many things that happened in my career — when I think back to that big Art Deco lobby and the first time being in 30 Rockefeller Center and the first time you hear that "Live from New York, it's *Saturday Night*," and you're standing there and your sketch is about to come up and your heart's going, I can see why it affects people so much.

The magic to me is, it's show business. It's ostrich costumes, people dressed as Civil War soldiers smoking cigarettes out in the hall, dance numbers. I want to be in show business. I want there to be a crowd. I want there to be high highs and low lows. That's supposed to be what it's all about, and *Saturday Night Live* — it's not going to get more intense than that.

KEVIN NEALON:

I didn't know Dennis Miller was leaving, and then Dennis left, and Lorne offered the "Update" spot to me. I said, "Let me think about it over the weekend." I was kidding. Because, you know, it had always been something I felt that I could do pretty well.

I'd been on the show for I think five years at that point, and so it was a welcome change, a different kind of job description. But it wasn't going to work well, and it took me more out of the sketches and into writing for myself. It was just more of a workload. Tuesday night was rewrite and then Wednesday is the table read and then Thursday I started reading like five or six different newspapers every day.

My approach to it was more like Chevy Chase — you know, keep it dry and more of a straight newscaster, and as far as the audience laughing, I think everybody wants the audience to laugh, but if *you* think it's funny yourself — even if it doesn't get a laugh at dress — you leave it in there because to people at home it's funny. I'm not from the school of like broad comedy, throw-it-in-your-face stuff. I think the broadest thing I ever did was "Hans and Franz." You know, mine is just put it on the plate; if they want it, they'll take it.

Many SNL *cast members were discovered while working with a satirical improv group called the Groundlings. In the late eighties, one of the greatest Groundlings of all joined the cast: Phil Hartman, the man of a thousand characters — or so. In his eight seasons on the show, he played virtually every type, impersonated innumerable celebrities, and endeared himself to Michaels with his unflappable versatility.*

JON LOVITZ:

I'll tell you a story about Phil. You know, we do that sketch Jim Downey wrote, "Tarzan, Tonto, and Frankenstein." So they did it once where it was like a talk show and Nora Dunn was doing the "Pat Stevens Show" with Tarzan, Tonto, and Frankenstein. And Phil is Frankenstein and all of a sudden he starts laughing, right, like he just completely broke up — ha, ha, you know, he laughed out loud. And then he stopped.

And then about fifteen seconds later, he just completely lost it. So then of course we all started laughing, because he's just losing it. And I'm thinking, "What is he doing? We're on live television. It's not the Groundlings." And he's just laughing. And so I had like my face in my arms, trying to hide it, trying not to laugh, but I was laughing, of course. I was just laughing hysterically. I mean, he just completely lost it. And it was just hysterically laughing. So afterward I asked him, I said, "What happened? What was so funny?" So he said, well, he was thinking of himself sitting there as Frankenstein and something happened, and thinking about how silly the sketch was, you know, just the idea of it made him laugh all of a sudden. So he started laughing. And then he stopped, right? And then, he said, he was sitting there thinking how funny it must have looked to see Frankenstein laugh like that. And then that just made him like lose it.

VICTORIA JACKSON:

I was married. Phil was married. Lovitz was single. Dana was married. Nora was married. Dennis Miller was married the second half, and no, I never got the impression they were having a wild time. I think our job took up like everything — like 200 percent of our being. And I don't know, maybe they were having fun. I think the Belushi era was way different than ours, because in ours, nobody was doing — well, okay, I know one person who was doing drugs. But I mean, in our era, it was the "Just Say No" thing, and our cast was not full of drugs or drinking or anything.

JACK HANDEY:

Phil was a guy that I really loved to write for. I wrote so many pieces for him—like "Unfrozen Caveman Lawyer." I think that the show tended to become more performance-oriented than idea-oriented. And maybe that annoyed Phil.

JOE PISCOPO, *Cast Member:*

The Sinatra family was not happy with the impression Phil was doing at all, again rest his soul. To this day I'll go out and do these Sinatra tributes with a seventeen-piece band—which is a riot, by the way. It's all tongue-in-cheek, because they know me from the *SNL* thing. But I always check with Tina and the family to make sure it's okay. When we did the Brisk Lipton Iced Tea campaign, they had me do the voice.

There was a meanness there to the Hartman thing. That was Lorne too, man. And I think there's some kind of law: Don't even attempt to do Sinatra unless you're Italian.

BOB ODENKIRK:

Phil Hartman was amazing. He just delivered every time. He had amazing timing and great power and just—I don't know what to say about Phil, because he was a very genial guy and he seemed to have a great work ethic. He was an older guy when he got the show, which might have helped him, you know, be more of a steady personality while he did it. But when I got there, he'd been on the show I think for like two years or maybe three, and he just came in every day and it was like an office job for him, and he was very good at it. I don't think he ever again got caught up in the whole stay-up-all-night routine or worrying about status all the time. He was more sure of himself and he just came in, did his work, and churned out the sketches, and if they didn't get on, he didn't get too upset—he just delivered. And he seemed to have a good time doing it.

JAN HOOKS:

We were doing "Beauty and the Beast" with Demi Moore and Jon Lovitz, a sketch about the two beasts, you know, going out on a blind date. Phil and I were in the backseat of a car making out; he was the

Beast, I was the Beauty. I just have to tell you this about Phil. At the end of it, they cut to the commercial, and Phil had to rush off and be, you know, whoever. But first Phil said to me, "You gave me a huge boner. Oh God. I've got to run!" So there's like this mountain of manhood, and he had to go on and, you know, make a quick change with a big old boner.

KEVIN NEALON:

I got a death-threat letter once from some crazy person, just saying he didn't like what I did on "Update." He said, "How you became so unfunny, I'll never know, but your days are numbered. I'm going to put a bullet in your big fat head." Well, for about a week after that, I went around asking people if they thought I had a big fat head.

VICTORIA JACKSON:

I was always trying to figure out a way to make fun of the news, but I just never fit into the news. Then Christine Zander came by and laid this *People* magazine on my desk, and it said, "I am not a bimbo," with Jessica Hahn's picture. And Christine goes, "Hey, this would be perfect for you." And then she walked away, and I thought, "Write me the thing — you're the writer." But I went to my typewriter, because we all had our own offices, you know, but mine was mostly just empty all the time — I had pink and blue tulle stapled to the ceiling to look like clouds and I used the phone a lot to call long distance because it was free — but I thought, "I am not a bimbo," and in like ten minutes, I typed up the whole song.

But Lorne didn't put it in the show. And I met with him and said, "Lorne, everybody loved it." And he goes, "I don't know. It shouldn't be the blues." I asked him, "Could it be in if I changed the melody?" And he said, "Uhhh, go talk to Cheryl." So I went to see Cheryl, who was the piano player in the band. I told her Lorne wanted more of a pop sound, and she changed the melody.

Then I did it and everyone loved it. It was the Sting–Steve Martin show. I couldn't believe that a song I wrote was actually not only on national TV but that Sting and Steve were watching me, and it was perfect. At the party afterwards I could tell everyone was like loving it. And then it was in the paper the next day. The *Wall Street Journal* had an article called "1987 — The Year of the Bimbo," and they talked about all the bimbos in the news that year, like Donna Rice and Jessica Hahn, and they mentioned my song. So I framed it and it's on the wall.

CAROL LEIFER:

There were two women on staff, me and Suzy Schneider, and she got fired in January. I'm used to boys-club situations. From starting in stand-up to any staff I worked on, women are always the minority, and I'm used to it and I'm very comfortable in that situation because I've never felt alienated. I've always felt welcomed by the men in those situations. It's only when I'm in a situation where I don't know the guys that I see the boys-club mentality.

LORNE MICHAELS:

The Turners' big thing was "boys club," and that was a very hard thing to overcome. There was an incident, I think, when from what I've heard described—I wasn't there for it—I think Adam Sandler peed in a plant to make Downey laugh or something, and Bonnie Turner was disgusted by it—with, I'm sure, absolute justification. She was also, you know, a mother, and this all seemed to be wasting time. It was a natural complaint. And it was the end of a cycle: that it was a boys club and that women were not treated well.

VICTORIA JACKSON:

I was the first woman in the cast to get a lead in a movie—*Casual Sex?* And my poster was all over town. And we never talked about it, but I'm sure that was everyone's goal. So that probably really bugged the rest of them, you know. No one ever said a word about it. It was invisible.

My theory is that men compete better than women. The men were competing against each other too, for lines, but when they compete and then the show is over, they pat each other on the back and have a beer. Women are much more vicious and scary. They don't do that. And sometimes I actually thought the other women were going to try to poison my coffee and kill me. If I had a really good joke in a sketch that got a huge laugh and was like a really great moment that would be repeated for all eternity—as in the "Big Pill" sketch, where I got this huge golden nugget of a great moment—it got mysteriously taken away from me. And I was like, "Why don't I have a line all of a sudden? It got a huge laugh at dress rehearsal."

They weren't nice to me. Maybe they were jealous or something.

JAN HOOKS:

I had a huge ego. I just loved anybody that wanted me to show my stuff. I will do it. Oh man, let me go out there and show my stuff. And in my midtwenties, it kind of hit that it wasn't a hobby anymore, that it was my vocation, that I had to do this in order to live. And that shaded it in a whole different way. It made me afraid, you know.

Frankly I kind of miss those silly years of youth, where you're all ego and you just want to get out there and show your stuff. But now, I don't know. I'm in therapy.

NORA DUNN, *Cast Member:*

I hadn't been to church in years, but when I got the part on *Saturday Night Live,* I went right to St. Patrick's Cathedral and just wept, because it was monumental. It really came out of the blue. I'd never even considered in my head that I was ever going to be on television.

No one takes you under their wing at *Saturday Night Live.* There are no wings. I was also shocked that it was so hard for the writers to write for women.

JON LOVITZ:

I think that Nora Dunn got a lot of her stuff on because of her relationship with Lorne. She would get everything on. I thought that was the reason, and a lot of other people thought that was the reason. Then she would complain: "The show's against women." She got all of her stuff on—almost all of it. She had her own writer hired for her, Christine Zander. And then she would say how tough it was for women and stuff. I just was like, what are you talking about?

She fought with a lot of people. She fought with me the first year.

And then the second year she started again, and I said, "I'm not going through this with you for another year." She would pick a fight. She fought with everybody. And then one time, one of the funniest things was seeing Dana with her. It was Dana's first year, and I go, "You'll see." He asked me, "What are you talking about?" And then they did this *Star Trek* thing, or maybe it was a Church Lady. And he and Nora were just screaming at each other.

One of the funniest things was seeing her and Terry Sweeney both dressed as Diana Ross or Nancy Reagan—and the two of them screaming at each other over who gets to play which women.

VICTORIA JACKSON:

Nora told us the first day I was there that she had a close relationship with Lorne. I'm not spreading gossip, since she actually told everyone herself—probably to intimidate us. I don't respect people who do that. I just went, "Oooh."

We had this meeting and one of the producers asked us what was wrong with the show. And everyone was supposed to say something, but no one was saying anything. And it was all of us sitting on the floor like high school or kindergarten or whatever. And the door was shut and she said, "Okay, come on, *something's* wrong with the show." Because there was a lot of tension and fighting and anger and stuff. And finally I go, "Okay, I'll say it in one sentence. You really want to know?" And then I felt like I was Robert De Niro—"You really want to know?" Like, "You talkin' to me?" I repeated it three times to build up the courage to tell the truth.

So then I was shaking, and I stood up and told everyone that what was wrong with the show was those two women—I pointed to Nora and Jan—and all the things they did bad: They didn't cooperate in sketches and they slammed doors in people's faces and backbite and backstab and all that, you know. And then there was like silence and no one said anything. And so they both got up, really slowly, and walked out of the room. And then I said to the others, "Thanks a lot for standing up for me." Because everyone agreed, but no one said anything. And Dana goes, "You didn't hear anyone disagreeing, did you?" And everyone burst out laughing. And so then, after that, they were afraid of me and they didn't mess with me anymore. I mean, it was weird. It was kind of like you got rewarded for being mean.

TERRY TURNER:

Victoria ended up standing on a chair and said Nora was a bitch. And she turned to Jan and said, "And you, you're the devil." So this explosive meeting where everyone got together to discuss how we could make our work situation better just got immediately crazy.

There was more backstage melodrama to come. When vulgar macho comic Andrew Dice Clay was booked to host Saturday Night Live, *cast member Nora Dunn found his act so politically incorrect, so antifeminist, that she refused to appear on the same television program with him. SNL was making headlines again—and not loving it.*

RICK LUDWIN, *NBC Vice President for Late Night:*

I will admit to a professional mistake when Lorne first said to me, "What do you think, Andrew Dice Clay is being offered to us." Andrew Dice Clay was then the hottest thing in comedy, and my reaction was yeah, we should do it. I knew he was controversial, but *Saturday Night Live* had been no stranger to controversy over the years, and frankly, controversy can help ratings. Lorne obviously has the final say and agreed to do it, and it was only after that that I caught Clay's concert film on HBO or someplace. And after I saw it, I thought, "Oh my God, we're going to catch far more heat than I anticipated." Because I didn't realize just how misogynistic his act was and is.

On the night of the show, the network broadcast standards people insisted that *Saturday Night Live* be put on a delay so that if Andrew Dice Clay said something or did something that needed to be cut, it could be cut via seven-second delay or whatever it needed to be. Nowadays, you can do that electronically and it is a much, much easier method of delaying the video and the audio, but in those days it was still a matter of having one reel of tape on one machine recording the program and then literally the tape sort of going down to the floor of the tape room and back up to a second machine that would play it back. And Lorne was very wary of that system, because you just never knew; it was too untested and unreliable.

As it turned out, there was no point in the show where the censors wanted to cut anything, but because of the technical nature of this thing, this sort of jury-rigged system, the video got screwed up, and Lorne vowed never again. Whatever the circumstances, he would never allow that sort of tape delay on *Saturday Night Live*.

Saturday Night Live is *live* live. If someone were to say "fuck," it would go out over the air. At least the East Coast of America would hear it. They would make a repair for the West Coast.

BOB ODENKIRK:

Lorne waits until the last second and then he picks whoever's hot. He and Jim Downey picked Andrew Dice Clay, and I don't think they knew who he was or what he did. I don't think they'd ever heard his act. And so they were shocked.

NORA DUNN:

I didn't hear about Andrew Dice Clay hosting until Monday. I was very familiar with his work. He had a routine about sticking a woman's head into the toilet, fucking her up the ass, and then telling her to make him some eggs. Where's the joke?

VICTORIA JACKSON:

I think the Andrew Dice Clay thing was totally a publicity stunt on Nora's part. We'd had other comics that degraded women. Like Sam Kinison. Sam made fun of Jesus Christ and although I'm a Christian, I still went to work, because my contract wasn't based on, "I come to work if I approve of the host." If Nora's passionate platform of life is women's rights, she was meaner to me than anyone in my life, and I'm a woman, so obviously she doesn't really love women.

LORNE MICHAELS:

I came back on a Sunday. Nora Dunn announces to the press that she's not doing the show. It would have been nice if she'd called me.

Already it was like a circus. It all seemed so out of whack. The reason I got so furious and stubborn about it was, "Wait a minute. You haven't seen what he's done yet. You're just assuming that we're going to put him on in a full embrace." I was on *Nightline* the night before the show and some woman said something about Hitler and the Holocaust, and I went, "Whoa. Just a minute. How did we jump to the Holocaust? Because the Holocaust is really a giant thing, and we're here talking about a comedian with a bad act. And we haven't even done anything with him yet."

My sympathies were with him. One of the things you'll find is consistent from the beginning to now is that we've always obeyed the rules of hospitality. You don't invite somebody to your house to piss on him. My point is that this person has put themselves in your hands, they're completely vulnerable, the show only works if they look good, so why would you have anybody over that you don't like? What— because you need the ratings? It doesn't make any sense. He was completely vulnerable.

Nora painted herself into a corner, I think. We're not one big happy family, you've probably figured that out. That said, everybody plays by a set of rules.

NORA DUNN:

To me, Andrew Dice Clay hosting was the pinnacle of everything that upset me about the show. I still feel that it's a black mark that they endorsed him and let him walk through that door.

Anyway, I talked to a couple people at the show, told them I wasn't going to do the show, and then I made a statement. My brother had given me the name of a friend of his who was with the Associated Press, and he said, "You'd better just cover yourself here." So I made my statement to the guy, and he told me he wouldn't release it unless I wanted him to. I thought by Wednesday it would all be resolved and they would just tell him, "We'd rather you don't do the show." Then the reporter called me back to say that another statement had come out of *Saturday Night Live* saying that I wasn't asked back for next year, and that I was disgruntled, that I was doing this because I thought I was being fired—which was a complete falsity. So we released my statement because of the other statement. I think Lorne did the *SNL* statement and I was very hurt by it. I felt betrayed.

I know that Lorne felt I didn't talk to him, but he was not accessible. He was never accessible. The whole experience had a huge impact on my life, and ultimately it was a really, really good thing.

TERRY TURNER:

I remember there were metal detectors at the show for the first time, which was a little disorienting. People were calling up our house to talk to Bonnie, saying, "How can you write this week? How can you possibly continue working there when this man is hosting?" Some people called our house and harassed my wife about why go to work, and I wanted to say, "Well, there's tuition, there's a car payment," you know. There were a lot of reasons to work that week.

I felt that we were blindsided by Nora. Why not tell the people she had worked with for all these years that she was going to do this. So at least we'd know what to expect. And it really irritated me that suddenly Bonnie and other women who were writing the show were considered traitors and got a lot of harassment.

JAN HOOKS:

A writer for the *New York Post* called and it was like, "Do you have a comment?" And I said, "What are you talking about?" And she said, "Nora Dunn has walked off the show." And I was dumbfounded. I had no idea. Because Lord knows, through all of the trials and tribulations of *Saturday Night Live,* you go on with the show.

I called the office and there was kind of mayhem going on. What bugged me was that Nora had called the press. She didn't call Lorne. She didn't call the other women in the cast. She called the press. And I thought, "God, that's not fair." I mean, normally when you work with somebody, you call and go, "Look, I really feel uncomfortable with this and I would like to not do the show." Instead, she had no contact with us. That week was horrible. I got a lot of hate mail. It was like, "Why can't you be more like Nora Dunn and stand up for your rights?" — and all that shit.

I knew that her contract was up and I don't know if they had made an offer to her. But I was really disappointed. And it put us in danger, actually. I mean, all of these radical feminists were sending hate mail and we had to call in security. And I didn't even know who Andrew Dice Clay was. I didn't care. It's like just another host. Steven Seagal, we got through him. I just thought the whole thing was careless and unfortunate.

ANDREW DICE CLAY, *Host:*

I didn't watch *Saturday Night Live* every week. I was out. When that show started, I had to be—I don't know—fifteen, sixteen years old. And I really wasn't that into comedy at fifteen. So in those days, I was out on the weekends. I wasn't a *Saturday Night Live* freak at all.

My management got the call about hosting. I actually got the call from my dad, who was advising me back then. He worked with my manager. And I was back in New York. I was getting ready for my picture *Ford Fairlane* to open, and the funny thing was, I just wanted a nice relaxing week before it opened, because I was really going through it as far as controversy goes. I just wanted to take it easy. But my dad said it would be a good thing to do. It's *Saturday Night Live.* It's right before the movie comes out. You'll have a lot of fun. And I said, "All right, we'll do it."

So I'll never forget it. I show up and I'm waiting like in some reception area with my father, my sister, my right-hand guy at the time, Johnny West, and another guy who worked for me. And I'm waiting like a long time, like an hour. All of a sudden this girl walks in—I think it was actually Calvin Klein's daughter Marci, who was working for the show—and she says, "Lorne will see you now, and this is really crazy with what's going on." And I go, *"What's* going on?" She goes, "Nora Dunn walked off the show." And I go, right, you know, what do you want from me? So now I go into Lorne's office, and he sits down and he starts telling me about Nora Dunn walking off the show. And I'm sitting there looking at him like, "Who cares? What do you want from me?" And he goes, "She walked off because of you."

Now I look at him and I go, "Who is she?" Because I don't watch the show. I'm not interested. I mean, of course I know about Belushi and Chevy Chase, and I've seen their movies. But I was never an avid follower of *Saturday Night Live*. And Lorne goes, "Don't you know the cast here?" I go, "No, I'll be honest. I really never watch. I know Dennis Miller, because he shows up when I'm performing.

Then from there it just turned into mania, you know. Next thing you know, I'm getting calls from *Entertainment Tonight*. I'm getting calls from all these different tabloid shows. And what was supposed to be a fun, light week wound up the most stressful week I had in my entire career. To this day, if I turn on the tape for somebody, you can see the blood in my face, how high my blood pressure was.

I was out of my mind, you know, doing that show. It wasn't fun, I'll tell you that much. What really bothered me about the whole thing is, these performers that are supposed to know what character comedy is didn't know I was playing a character. When I heard this was the end of Nora Dunn's contract, I'm going, "This is a play to get publicity — to make herself into something." In my opinion, she was just looking to make something out of her career after *Saturday Night Live*.

The one good thing is, the ratings were incredible. It was the only time, you know, in the few times that I have seen *Saturday Night Live*, that they threw people out of the audience. I mean, I got heckled during my opening monologue and they had to throw people out. There was all kinds of security. There was a bunch of people in the balcony they threw out. Because the dichotomy between who I am as a performer and who I am as a father and a husband is very different.

I've never met Nora Dunn to this day. And obviously it didn't work out for her the way she thought it would. And, you know what, that's what she deserved. I guess she thought she was going to become like a major star from that. That's not how you become a major star. I thought it was a foolish move to start with.

And *Nightline* is this great show and look what they're putting on. It's not a world affair. I'm a comic. I'm a bozo from Brooklyn.

JAN HOOKS:

I know there was a meeting before Nora was due in the following week, so I think we had one more show. And we took a vote: Get her out of here! Get her out of here!

VICTORIA JACKSON:

I ran into Nora's manager a couple of years ago in L.A. He mentioned he represented Nora. I'm like, "Oh. Great." I couldn't hide that I wasn't thrilled. And he goes, "I'll tell her you said hi." And I'm like, "Yeah, okay." So the next week I saw him again, and he goes, "I told Nora that you said hi, and she said she kind of gave you a hard time when you were working together." And I went, "Oh, so she actually admits it. Cool. I thought maybe it was all in my head, you know?"

DON NOVELLO, *Writer:*

The first time I did Father Sarducci was at a place called the Intersection, a coffee house in San Francisco. But then I started driving down to L.A. to do comedy clubs in '73, and I started doing it at the Comedy Store. I was on the *Smothers Brothers Show*—I was a regular on their NBC show—and I did it there. When I got on *Saturday Night Live,* I think it was the fall of '77, I knew Franken and Davis from the Comedy Store and I had met John Belushi, and John pushed to get me on as well. I think Brian Doyle-Murray and I were the first new writers after the original group of writers.

People were just afraid of Father Sarducci, you know. Everybody always said, "We're not offended, but we think other people will be offended." When I began smoking, someone said, "Priests don't smoke." I never made fun of the religion. I never did the sign of the cross or talked about Jesus or anything like that. I just made fun of the hierarchy. One thing I did though was a thing about the bill for the Last Brunch. Actually I had wanted to do the bill for the Last Supper, and at that time the guy in Standards and Practices said we can't do the bill for the Last Supper, and so I worked it out that I could do the bill for the Last Brunch instead. Because of that it got much funnier. One guy only had eggs. Everyone else had all these big breakfasts. The moral of it was, if you're part of a big group, order the most expensive thing, because someone will always just say, "Let's divide it."

St. Pat's were our neighbors in Rockefeller Square, but I never had any problems from Catholics or from the Church or anything. I was arrested once in Rome when I was taking pictures of the Vatican, but that was for taking pictures without permission, they said. But I never had people complain.

ROBERT WRIGHT, *NBC Chairman and CEO:*

When I came to NBC, *SNL* was not on my radar of things that were broken, needed fixing, were under hospitalization, or were enemies of the people. I kind of stayed away from it. I knew by reputation that Lorne had a principality that had signed nonaggression pacts with other principalities. I didn't need to be there. I had so many other things I was involved in, and I didn't have any agenda with *SNL*. To me, if it was funny, that was good enough.

But I was only here a very short time when I got involved in an incident with Father Guido Sarducci. I'm a Catholic and I got a call from Cardinal O'Connor's office. His assistant, a very well thought of young priest who was made a monsignor, and was like an executive assistant, called me to say that the cardinal wanted me to come over and he had some things he wanted to talk about. The cardinal talked about labor unions, but in the process he also wanted to talk about Guido. And I was very defensive about it. They were politely saying to me how many Catholic organizations had been really offended by his portrayal. I didn't pretend to have any journalistic credentials, but I was really offended, because I thought it was very funny. And I felt that if I think it's very funny and I'm an upstanding Catholic, then "why can't you take a joke?" So I got very defensive about this whole discussion, it was something I kind of just stepped into, but I found myself defending it against, I think, the Catholic League at the time and some other groups. There are hundreds of them. I realized I had to stop defending the show in person because there were more groups than I had hours in the day. So that was my initial period. Nobody asked me to do this. I just got into this stuff and then I realized I had to get out of it.

When the show began, hosts—like musical artists—were chosen as much for their novelty as for their proven popular appeal. Hence the appearances of Ralph Nader, Julian Bond, Ron Nessen, and other non-performers in the host's spotlight. The practice continued over the

*years—sports figures were added to the mix—but generally, the host
pool became smaller and limited to stars of showbiz, oftentimes those
with a movie opening very near the date of their appearance.*

*There were good hosts and bad, those who came with their own entou-
rages and their own writers—thus alienating the SNL staff from the
get-go—and those who just came to have fun, to spend a week at a kind
of amusement park for the very, very privileged. Some tried to bail out as
Saturday night approached. Some canceled at the virtual last minute.
Some threw up. But most came and conquered and seemed to have a wonderful time. Some would say that, even having done it and enjoyed themselves, they still couldn't picture themselves doing it again, while others
took so naturally to the unnatural experience that they were invited back
repeatedly; they were old reliables who, because they pitched in with
gusto, inspired the writers and regular cast members to be at their best.*

BUCK HENRY, *Host:*

There were people outside the cast that I look at and say, "They
could have been cast members"—Tom Hanks, Alec Baldwin, John
Goodman, and Steve Martin. Those four people were essentially cast
members, because they really fit into the format and they understood
their work, and they were really great guest hosts.

DANNY DEVITO, *Host:*

They pitch lots of stories to you. You do the read-through, which is
really cool. You read everything and everybody sits around the table. I
was used to that kind of work on *Taxi,* because we were trying to get
the show ready on Friday every week and we did a lot of table readings. So it's less shocking, I think, for an actor who comes to it after
having had the experience of a table reading and trying to get a show
in shape for seven o'clock on a Friday night, which is what we would
do on *Taxi.*

When Jon Lovitz was on the show, he was hysterically funny. There
was one incident where I think I shoot him like in the foot and he
says, *"Ya shot me."* The way he said it was just so off the charts that
nobody could keep a straight face. It was just one of those things
where every time he said, *"Ya shot me,"* I went crazy. *"Ya shotttt me."*

And of course once you go, he just did it more and more and more and more to throw it out into the stratosphere. Even to this day, when we see each other we say, *"Ya shot me."*

JON LOVITZ:

The sketch was kind of dying so I said it a lot. Like about ten extra times more than I was supposed to, just to get a laugh.

JOHN GOODMAN, *Host:*

I was scared to death. I mean, I was petrified. It was something I always wanted to do. I remember stalking NBC when I first moved up here in 1975, you know, I would walk around after auditions and everything. I would always come through here just to see if I could see any of the cast members and stuff. And then I auditioned for the show in 1980 when they replaced everybody. It's something I've always loved, because I was a big fan of the *National Lampoon* and the *Radio Hour* and Michael O'Donoghue. So when I finally did do it, I was so damn scared I just wanted to disappear, fall through a manhole cover — anything.

I like the day on Friday. Saturday it's just too nuts. I'm getting to be an older man now, and all the running around and changing you've got to do, ugh. I've got to be rested and fit for that, so physically it's a little draining. But on Fridays I just like being there, I feel like I'm at home.

JAN HOOKS:

I loved Dolly Parton. She came in and said, "Look, okay, here's the deal. I won't use any cuss words and I won't make fun of Jesus." Those were her two demands. And anything else was carte blanche.

GREG DANIELS:

Mel Gibson did the show, and he has a pretty strong sense of humor. But I'm not sure if it's really the same sense of humor of the show. I remember him trying to pitch us doing a parody of *Brideshead Revisited* that he called "Bird's Head Regurgitated." He's like pitching that really strongly, and we were kind of politely nodding and thinking how do we not do "Bird's Head Regurgitated."

DANA CARVEY:

Robert Mitchum hosted once and I did a sketch with him, and he was like out-of-body. I think he had like half a gallon of whiskey in his room. He was of the old school.

TOM HANKS:

The second time you're back, you think you know how things are going. The second time I was on the show, Randy Travis was the musical guest. It was around the Winter Olympics in 1988. So by that time I had done it already once and the gee-whiz-bang aspect of being in the room was a little bit different. You fancy yourself a seasoned professional now. And you're just kind of in the middle of the show, middle of a season. Everybody's exhausted. Always a couple people around with the flu and just kind of like bang through it. I felt honored to be invited back, like I was in some sort of quasi-select club, but I don't think the show was all that great.

BOB ODENKIRK:

They have a pool of names of potential hosts. They have a few that are anchored down for one reason or another—they have a movie coming out or whatever—and famous enough. But then, outside of that, for a normal show, two weeks ahead of time they've got a pool of names, two or three people, and they ask these people to host the show. And these people say yes or no, or maybe these people all want to host the show, and they're tentatively scheduled for that week. And then, as the week gets closer, Lorne picks one of them. And what happens then is the other two people get burned. Supposedly John Candy was like the most-burned potential host, in that he would never host the show, because he'd been asked to do it so many times and then told "no thanks" at the last minute by the staff—which is all Lorne.

AL FRANKEN:

When there's a Beatle up in the office, nothing gets done. Because everybody is just following the Beatle around, you know? So here's my George Harrison story. I think it was the second season Lorne was back, so '86 or something like that. George went out to dinner with

Lorne, and it was on a Tuesday night — Tuesday night as you know by now is writing night, right? So it's about eleven at night or something and George comes back to the show, comes up to seventeen, and he's really drunk.

And he hung around until like two o'clock in the morning, and nothing had gotten done. He was just really drunk. He's at the piano in the read-through room playing and playing, and my office was the office closest to the piano. And he plays the piano for like a real long time, and again he's really drunk, so I take Phil Hartman aside and I go, "Phil, watch this." Phil stands outside my office, I go into my office, and I *SLAM* the door as hard as I can. And Harrison jumped about three feet off the bench — and finally left.

So that's my George Harrison story.

GREG DANIELS:

Judge Reinhold wasn't one of my favorites. The thing is, you get a lot of these guys right when they're at their maximumly famous, most fame-going-to-their-head moments. And they come in. They're in New York City. And they're hosting the show and they kind of give you like a couple of minutes and they want to run out and just have fun. That was definitely how Judge was that week. But I'm sure he's a nice guy now.

Even if all other attempts at livening up the show failed, it was almost guaranteed a new burst of energy every four years when election time came around. During the Ebersol years, SNL *dabbled only lightly and mildly in political humor, but once Michaels returned, the show began to build a stronger and flintier political profile. In time it became an integral if impudent part of the process. The line between observing and participating was sometimes blurred. Politicians who were roasted over a spit on* Saturday Night Live *would nevertheless appear on the program themselves if given the opportunity — everyone, over the years, from Gerald Ford to Janet Reno (Bill Clinton was a notorious bad-sport holdout). George H. W. Bush was so enamored of Dana Carvey's presidential portrayal that he invited Carvey to the White House and eventually taped a cold open for the show.*

Jim Downey was the best political satirist among the writers, though Al Franken wrote some great political sketches too. Among the all-time best was a 1988 primary "debate" by Downey and Franken and Davis which starred Franken as Pat Robertson, who then fancied himself a candidate, Dana Carvey as George Bush (Carvey then in the fetal stage of what would later become a classic Bush impression), and Dan Aykroyd making a gala return to the show as a hilariously petty Bob Dole.

DANA CARVEY:

I was just assigned George Bush, and I couldn't do him at all. It was just a weird voice and weird rhythm. It's one of those things where you go, "There's nothing to do." Reagan was so easy because you just go, "*Well,* everybody." But then over time, after Bush won the election, one night I just sort of hooked it, and it was that phrase "that thing out there, that guy out there doin' that thing," and that sort of hooked it for me, and from there on I kind of refined it.

He enjoyed it. I give him credit. He was just incredibly friendly. Lorne and I had done a benefit for Pamela Harriman and the Democratic Party in Washington, D.C., where I played George Bush, and he heard about that and invited us to the White House, Lorne and I, so he was just Charm Central. In '92 after he lost the election, he invited me back—which was really surreal, because I was actually talking to Jon Lovitz on the phone and I got the call waiting thing and the quote is, "This is White House operator number one, hold for the president." And I go, "Jon, I gotta go," and he goes, "Why? Is there a bigger name on the other line?" And I go, "Well, it's the president."

So he invited me out there to cheer up the troops, as he saw it. His sense of it was that it wasn't mean, that it was mostly silly. But I don't think he ever saw the one where we had him on his knees saying, "Please, God, don't make me a one-termer." I don't think they knew or wondered about my politics, whether I was incredibly left or whatever, but I was sort of in the White House and Barbara would bring up politics and George would say, "Let's not do it." And for my wife and me, it's still one of the peak experiences and most mind-blowing experiences of our life, to be in the White House with the president, who had just lost the election, during Christmas. It was just so gorgeous and surreal. And we're in the Lincoln Bedroom and suddenly he comes in, and he's six-foot-four and he goes, "How ya doin', meet ya downstairs," and he just sort of charmed the pants off us.

I only met him that one time for ten minutes in 1988, and then we just mercilessly made fun of him for four years. Al Franken's a pretty famous Democrat, Jim Downey's a real Republican, I refer to myself as a radical moderate. So in the beginning of George Bush's tenure, he was so damn popular, I think he saw some of those sketches where the angle was how happy he was. It wasn't until the last eighteen months, where we had the recession and the no-new-taxes thing, where some of the stuff was heavier hitting. I think between Lorne and Al Franken, they wouldn't have allowed me to make it soft. We make fun of liberals too, you know.

It's scary to go out there and know you don't have it. You just say, "I'm George Bush" and cop an attitude. When I was in college I would tape Dan Aykroyd off the television, tape his Jimmy Carter, shamelessly practice it, and then go to the clubs and just steal it, do his Jimmy Carter. Then eight, nine years later Danny's in the office going, "I really like your George Bush." It was kind of surreal.

I would actually give Lorne credit in terms of the way he worked with me. He sort of saw my potential before I did and kind of pushed me out there.

MIKE MYERS, *Cast Member:*

I wanted to be on the show since I was eleven years old, so I wear having done it as a badge of honor.

I didn't really audition. Producer Pam Thomas, who is the wife of Dave Thomas of *SCTV,* had seen me at the tenth anniversary of Second City Toronto—as had Martin Short. Pam called up Lorne and said, "Have a look at this kid"—and so did Martin Short. I got called in for an interview and I got hired from the interview, which was very lucky for me. But I wasn't quite sure I had gotten hired when I came out of the room. Dave Foley from the Kids in the Hall, who's a really great friend of mine—a great guy from Toronto as well—was there when I came out of Lorne's office, and he and I started walking downtown. We tried to dissect what Lorne had said. He said, "Would you want a job here?" And I didn't know if that was an offer, but I said, "Yes." So I just kept asking Dave, "So, does this mean I'm hired?" Foley and I walked all the way from Midtown down to the Village trying to decipher if I was hired.

CONAN O'BRIEN:

I remember very clearly when Mike Myers showed up. He was wearing a leather jacket with the American flag on the back. It was his first time there and he was very polite and proud to be at *SNL*. He was asking us all about what he should submit in our read-through and we were giving him advice, Robert Smigel and Bob Odenkirk, Greg Daniels, and I. And then he came to us and he described to us this idea, this character he had named Wayne who had a cable show in his basement, and the show was called "Wayne's World." We politely told him that we didn't think it was his best idea. But I remember very clearly sitting at read-through in my little folding chair, and I turned the page of the script and there's the "Wayne's World" we had dissuaded him from submitting. And I felt sorry for him. I thought, "This poor kid is going to have to learn the hard way."

MIKE MYERS:

If Conan's recounting that, he's recounting it modestly. My memories of Conan O'Brien are just that he was absolutely supportive, decent, fair, hilarious—the funniest guy in the room. So if he's saying he was a naysayer at any point, that's him being extremely modest. He'd always give you great positive encouragement, but he also had a great eye on how to make something better. You always came away with three great jokes that he would give you. He's a great collaborator and a generous, generous colleague.

As it happens, the first thing I did that went over big with the studio audience was on my fourth show, when I did do "Wayne's World." It was what they call the ten-to-one spot, the last sketch of the night. And it went really great. On that next Monday, as I was coming into work, I heard somebody working in the building singing the theme song from "Wayne's World." I was like completely blown away, because it had been on at ten to one. But somebody was going, "Wayne's world, Wayne's world." I was like, "Were you in the audience?" The guy goes, "No, no, we saw it on TV." I go, "Of course." And that was a really magical moment. The only thing I can describe it as is magic. Just unbelievable.

JACK HANDEY:

There are very few shows on television where writers are not forcibly rewritten. When we would sit around the rewrite table, it was up to the writer whether he wanted to take any changes that were suggested, even if Lorne didn't like it. I remember I wrote this sketch for Jerry Hall when she hosted. It was called "Sore Toe." And it was just that Randy Quaid had a sore toe, and the gag was basically all these things that were a danger to the sore toe. Anyway, there was a non sequitur ending where Jerry Hall said something like, "Your father has gone and hung himself." It was just out of the blue. And it made me laugh and Jim Downey laughed really a lot.

But Mick Jagger was there and just hated the ending, or so I heard. And he was trying to get Lorne to make me change it, and I said, "No, I like it the way it is." And to his credit, he left it on. *Saturday Night Live* is one of the few shows where writers really can control what they get on. Of course, you can fight really hard and produce the piece and then it's cut after dress. But at least if it does get on, you usually control it.

TERRY TURNER:

I remember at one point we were standing at the elevators on seventeen and we had been there for like thirty minutes pressing the button, going, "What the hell's going on?" Five or six people walk by, and finally somebody walks by—I think it was Al Franken—and he says, "Those don't run at night." So it was like you were on your own to discover anything. There was no handbook to figure out how this worked.

GREG DANIELS:

One of the reasons I felt like I didn't want to go in and talk to Lorne was, when I was there you could see Tom Davis there and Al Franken still being there, and it just seemed like it was possible to spend fifteen, twenty years working at *Saturday Night Live*. And it's a really great show and everything, but I was scared that I would end up putting in my whole career there. It's hard to really have your own voice there. I was more cowardly. I said, I'm leaving and I'm going to California and make my way.

TOM DAVIS, *Writer:*

My breakup with Al was hardly just a matter of shaking hands and going separate ways. It was a really ugly divorce. It was just hideous. It was precipitated by someone he knew having to enter a twelve-step program. And they really had to. They had a serious problem. And then Al wanted me to go into a twelve-step program. And I didn't want to go. And then I got married in '89 and we were already drifting apart significantly. Because Al was into Al-Anon at that time. And the show kind of became twelve-step comedy. I just wasn't going to join the program. That was one of the issues.

He thought I was an alcoholic and a drug addict. He called me a garden-variety alcoholic and drug addict. He did his share of my drugs. He did plenty of experiments. I don't want to embarrass him now, because I don't think he needs that for his current career or whatever, but it was common knowledge. I was rather brazen and open about it in a way that was very politically incorrect when I was still doing that. And I'm sure that was a major issue.

And there were money problems. We were so close that we had just pooled our money together and assumed that our business manager was keeping track. And he wasn't keeping track. And I discovered all of this when I got married. That's when the lawyers got involved. And it became a bitterly contested thing. It was just about the worst breakup you could have. And the irony of all those years of doing comedy about ourselves breaking up I'm sure did not escape Franken either.

We don't speak, except at funerals. Or at *Saturday Night Live* reunion shows. I saw him at the twenty-fifth reunion.

RICK LUDWIN:

I officially began working on *Saturday Night Live* in 1989. In the fall of that year, we had the celebration of the fifteenth anniversary of the show, so there was a big special that aired in prime time with every star there could be. That was my big first assignment after joining the show on the executive side of it. The show was doing pretty well at that time. It of course goes through hills and valleys, and that was one of the hills. The special did extraordinarily well for us. So I entered at a good time—only the usual crises, not any unusual ones.

But Eddie Murphy did not show up for the anniversary celebration. The story that's told is that Eddie saw the David Spade "Hollywood Minute" where David did a joke about "catch a falling star" and referred to Eddie Murphy, and the following Monday, Eddie Murphy got David Spade on the phone and was very upset. David took the call and took the heat, and there was plenty of heat. And I'm told that from that day forward, Eddie Murphy never set foot on that stage again.

Lorne Michaels would get a lot of wear out of his black suits over the years. Indeed, too much. He saw many former cast members meet heartbreakingly premature ends. No one broke more hearts, however, than the former SNL *star and member of the founding family of 1975 who died on May 20, 1989, at the age of forty-two. Anyone given half a chance, it seemed, had fallen in love with her, whether literally or vicariously. In the history of the show, there were no brighter lights.*

Gilda Radner.

Gilda—who got that name because her mother saw the movie Gilda, *with Rita Hayworth, the year Gilda was born—was someone who often expressed disappointment in herself, plagued by anxieties that she had somehow let herself or others down. She was chronically unhappy with her appearance, no matter how many people told her they loved her just as she was. Gilda was not disappointed in life, however; she did not complain about bad breaks or misfortune, no matter how misfortunate.*

Steve Martin touchingly eulogized Gilda on the first show to air after her death. A segment from the first five years was shown, a sketch without dialogue in which Martin and Radner, both dressed in white, danced romantically around the studio to "Dancing in the Dark" from the movie The Band Wagon. *Introducing the segment, Martin had a lump in his throat and tears in his eyes, and had trouble getting through his short speech — the first time viewers, or perhaps his own colleagues, had seen him so openly emotional.*

STEVE MARTIN, *Host:*

It's one of those things that come over you. You're introducing something and suddenly you just feel kind of emotional. I remember what it's like to have an honest lump in your throat on television. Because most lumps on television are phony.

I wasn't expecting it but, you know, I was just of that period. When we first did the dance, that was another period in our careers, where we were so young, so confident. It just felt like what we were doing was really funny to us and therefore it was going to be funny to "them."

Gilda was so lovable in person as a person. And so it was easy to get sentimental about her, because in looking back over her life, I know she had trials and tribulations, but knowing her, it was never expressed. It was just joy and happiness and funniness and comedy.

MIKE MYERS:

Gilda Radner had played my mother in a television commercial for British Columbia Hydro when I was ten years old. It was a four-day shoot, and before it was over I had fallen in love with Gilda. I thought she was awesome, funny and cool and beautiful. I cried on the last day of the commercial, because I had so fallen in love with her. My brothers used to taunt me mercilessly about it.

And then one day my brother Peter said, "Hey, Mikey, your girl-friend's going to be on this TV show called *Saturday Night Live.*" And I saw her, and I thought she was brilliant, and at that point I did turn to someone in my house and say, "Someday, I'll be on this show." Everyone laughed at me. I just really wanted to be on that show, and eventually I was. I got hired in February of 1989. I think it was May of 1989 when Gilda passed away, because it was on a Saturday, the last show of my first half-season. Somebody said to me as I was walking to work, "What's your feeling about Gilda?" And I didn't know she had passed away, so I said, "Well, you know, I think she's amazing." And they said, "Did you know she died?" And my blood ran cold.

MARILYN SUZANNE MILLER, *Writer:*

I would occasionally go up to visit Gilda in Connecticut. One time she was very sick. We had lunch with Gene, but Gilda said she couldn't really eat. What I didn't know is that her intestines were closed off. She'd chew the food and spit it out just to get the taste of it. She couldn't ingest it. Then she took me around the house to see some stuff that had been redone. She showed me this couch she had covered outside the bathroom. Then some friends of hers came over. She was like pumping me for everybody's love life — who's going with whom, who's dating that one, all the gossip, always. And her friends were really nice. So we just sat with them and chatted, and then finally I said, "Okay, I have to go. It's getting dark," and I don't like to drive in the dark. We go outside and Gilda gets in the driver's seat of my car so I can't leave.

I said, "Gilda, I've got to go, I've got to go." And she said, "Oh, everyone's working and having so much fun and I'm not working." And I said, "Not everyone's having so much fun, they don't like what they're doing," and so on. A lot of people were doing those bad boy-comedy movies at the time. Finally I said, "You *must* get out of the driver's seat so I can drive home." And finally she did. That was the last time I saw her.

And when she died, I read in her book that those people at the house were not friends. Those were nurses she had hired to give her chemo at home. She had set up a whole hospital in her house that she didn't tell me about. Because by that time they had told her there was no hope. So she was on this chemo that was some other option that some other doctor came up with, administered by nurses at home. All those people were nurses — acting and calling each other by their first names because she had made it clear that no one was to know how sick she was, and no one was to know that she wasn't going to live. So if you want to know how brave she was, that's how brave she was.

BILL MURRAY, *Cast Member:*

Gilda got married and went away. None of us saw her anymore. There was one good thing: Laraine had a party one night, a great party at her house. And I ended up being the disk jockey. She just had forty-fives, and not that many, so you really had to work the music end of it. There was a collection of like the funniest people in the world at this party. Somehow Sam Kinison sticks in my brain. The whole *Monty Python* group was there, most of us from the show, a lot of other funny people, and Gilda. Gilda showed up and she'd already had cancer and gone into remission and then had it again, I guess. Anyway she was slim. We hadn't seen her in a long time. And she started doing, "I've got to go," and she was just going to leave, and I was like, "Going to leave?" It felt like she was going to really leave forever.

So we started carrying her around, in a way that we could only do with her. We carried her up and down the stairs, around the house, repeatedly, for a long time, until I was exhausted. Then Danny did it for a while. Then I did it again. We just kept carrying her; we did it in teams. We kept carrying her around, but like upside down, every which way—over your shoulder and under your arm, carrying her like luggage. And that went on for more than an hour—maybe an hour and a half—just carrying her around and saying, "She's leaving! This could be it! Now come on, this could be the last time we see her. Gilda's leaving, and remember that she was very sick—hello?"

We worked all aspects of it, but it started with just, "She's leaving, I don't know if you've said good-bye to her." And we said good-bye to the same people ten, twenty times, you know.

And because these people were really funny, every person we'd drag her up to would just do like five minutes on her, with Gilda upside down in this sort of tortured position, which she absolutely loved. She was laughing so hard we could have lost her right then and there.

It was just one of the best parties I've ever been to in my life. I'll always remember it. It was the last time I saw her.

In 1980, with Saturday Night Live *just behind her and new careers in the theater and movies ahead, Gilda said, "I think I'd be a neat old woman—if I ever make it that far. I once said that to a guy I was going out with, and he said, 'You already are.'*

"But I feel with my life, somebody's been so generous with experiences for me—whosever controlling it. I mean, I've enjoyed a real generosity there. So sometimes I feel maybe I'm getting this all now and quickly because there's not going to be a whole lot later. I mean, maybe I'm going to die or something. I know that's an awful way to think, but I have been real fortunate. Real lucky."

5

Overpopulation: 1990–1995

BOB ODENKIRK, *Writer:*

Chris Farley was like a child. He was like an eight-year-old. One time when he was fucking, rip-roaring drunk in Chicago, he was tossing furniture around his apartment, actually picking it up and throwing it like ten feet. It was scary, man. Then all of a sudden, he turned to me and said, with complete innocence, "Do you think Belushi's in heaven?" I didn't know what to say.

Saturday Night Live *was growing older and younger at the same time, entering the third decade of its existence with a few cast members who were even wetter behind the ears than the founders had been. While some of the new comedy struck longtime* SNL *loyalists as juvenile (the negative adjective most often applied to the show in the nineties), new generations drawn to* SNL *loved the humor and identified with the younger cast members.*

The SNL *audience has always felt protective toward the show and concerned about its possibly becoming tamer, less impudent, less willing to take risks. And from the earliest episodes, Michaels made the show a regular topic of the show; criticisms were addressed, and lampooned, on the air. In a lavish and complex production number that opened a December 1991 show hosted by Steve Martin, the cast ridiculed both itself and the idea that the show was growing soft. Martin sang that instead of just "going through the motions" or "phoning it in," tonight was the night "I'm actually gonna try" and "do the best I can"—for a change. As he led* the singing cast through the studio (the number was a parody of the title song from the old movie musical Babes in Arms), Martin came upon Michaels, who—spoofing his own image—was having his portrait painted and getting a manicure, barely involved in the program, looking aloof and effete. Saturday Night Live defused criticisms of itself by turning them into comedy. But as the decade wore on, jokes wouldn't be enough to placate all the critics, especially those high up in the ranks of network management.

To one of its noblest traditions, the show remained conspicuously true: discovering and showcasing comic talent that might otherwise never have come to the nation's attention. Some of those who joined the cast in the nineties and had first watched the show in high school looked to Eddie Murphy as their ultimate SNL role model, rather than to members of the original cast, that comedy Mount Rushmore of Chase, Belushi, Radner, Aykroyd. Chris Farley was the exception. Belushi was his hero, his obsession, and he tried to pattern his personal and professional life after the wild Albanian's—the best and, alas, worst of it. Like Belushi, Farley demonstrated amazing physical agility for someone of considerable heft and girth. It isn't easy to be elfin when you weigh three hundred pounds, but Farley brought it off. Sadly, things he turned out to have in common with his idol included not only prodigious talent but an array of beckoning demons. And as with Belushi, the demons proved deadly.

ADAM SANDLER, *Cast Member:*

Farley was a whole other level. It was not even a question of who we all loved and thought was the funniest. When he walked into the room, that was it.

LORNE MICHAELS, *Executive Producer:*

As a kid, Chris had taped his eyebrow up to try and look like Belushi. We often said Chris was the child John and Danny never had but would have had if they'd had a child. Chevy came to see Chris once, and Chris was doing his falls, and Chevy said, "Don't you use anything to break your fall?" Chris said, "What do you mean? Did you?" Chris had welts all over his chest. He just assumed that that was the price you paid for doing it.

FRED WOLF, *Writer:*

I was in such awe of Chevy, and I know Farley was too. Chevy was very nice to Farley, and Farley would sort of sit at his feet and listen to him talk—because Farley was physical, Chevy was physical, and Chevy was telling Farley that he was worried about him throwing out his back or getting into the same problems that Chevy got into because of his physicality. Chevy would talk to Farley and be very nice to him. And Farley just loved it.

Farley looked at Lorne as the ruling patriarch. He goofed off to get his attention and then, when he got his attention and was chastised for it, he would be quiet for days, then furious at him. Chris got away with a lot because he was a really likable guy.

DAVID SPADE, *Cast Member:*

Chris was my best friend in the cast. I was close to Adam Sandler and Chris Rock too, but Chris and I always had a real good time together. *Tommy Boy* was Lorne's idea to make something based on how we are in real life, how we fight, how we laugh, and how we act. So we tried to make a movie to reflect a little of that; it was great.

We used to make fun of Chris at table reads. We were like, "Are you ripping off Belushi in this one, or just Aykroyd?" Because he liked those guys so much that he would incorporate them. He wore Belushi's pants from wardrobe if he could find any, and sometimes he wore two pairs of pants, which I don't even know how to explain. I used to get stuff that had old cast members' names in them, but when his said "Belushi," he loved that. He would keep those; he'd wear them.

Chris looked up to Belushi as the king. My argument was that I actually thought he was funnier than Belushi. And he wouldn't accept that. Then, when I would get pissed at him, I would say, "Was Belushi trying to be like anybody? No. He just did whatever the funniest thing that he could think of was. You're hysterical on your own, you don't need any of that, don't try to be like him, don't even look up to him. We all think Belushi is great, but you are fine on your own." And I thought that angle might get to him—that Belushi didn't try to copy anybody or be like anybody, or look up to anybody, so why should he? It didn't work.

JACK HANDEY, *Writer:*

Farley was such a sweetheart. He would come offstage after being in one of my sketches and put his hands together in a sort of prayerful motion toward me and go, "Was that okay, was that okay?"

I remember one time we went to Tom Davis's wedding at some resort in upstate New York. The resort had a bowling alley. In front of everyone, Farley would just throw his body out parallel to the lane and land from about a three-foot straight parallel drop to the bowling lane as a joke. That's the kind of stuff he would do all the time.

FRED WOLF:

Farley and this girl on the show were going out. She was really smart and pretty, and Farley really liked her a lot. But she couldn't put up with any more of Farley's stuff, so they broke up. And then she started dating Steve Martin. So one day Farley comes to me and he says, "Fred, I hear that she's going out with some guy. What can you tell me about it?" And, you know, nobody wanted to tell Chris Farley that she was dating anyone else, particularly Steve Martin. So I just said, "Well, I haven't heard. I don't know." And he goes, "I know she's seeing somebody. You've got to tell me who it is." And I said, "Well, I don't want to get in the middle of any of that kind of stuff." And Farley said, "Well, she may find somebody better looking than me, or she might find somebody richer than me, but she's not going to find anybody funnier than me." And what I couldn't tell him was, he was wrong on all three counts. He had hit the hat trick of failure. Steve Martin was richer, better looking, and even funnier.

CHRIS ROCK, *Cast Member:*

He was my man. I loved Chris. He was one of the funniest guys. Not competitive at all. We all knew he was funnier than us and it was totally acceptable. He would try to break me up on the air. He broke Spade up a lot. You have to watch the sketches.

Farley had no qualms running around naked. That wasn't a big thing to him. I probably saw his dick more than his girlfriend did.

MOLLY SHANNON, *Cast Member:*

I had some rituals before shows. Mostly I would pray. I'd say a little prayer. And Chris Farley did that too. I saw him once. It was so sweet. He'd kneel down and bless himself in his dressing room before every show. I peeked in one night and saw him, and I thought, "That's sweet." He was a very religious Catholic man. He was very Catholic. I was raised Catholic too. Lorne loves Irish Catholics. I don't know why, but he really does seem to like Irish Catholics a lot.

FRED WOLF:

Farley once stuck his ass out the window of the seventeenth floor at 30 Rock and took a shit. Another time, in front of twenty or twenty-five people in a very crowded writers' room—mixed company, women, men—Farley came in naked. He has his dick tucked between his legs and he was doing Jame Gumb from *Silence of the Lambs.* He took a golf club and shoved it about three inches up his ass, then pulled the golf club out and started licking it.

DAVID SPADE:

That Chippendales sketch where Patrick Swayze and Chris danced with their shirts off became pretty well known. It was early on, when we all thought you had to do whatever was asked of you. Chris took off his shirt then because he's a fat guy and it is funny, and that was really part of the sketch. But I think later on he didn't want to do that as much. Like most actresses—they'll do the Cinemax movie, but then after that, they keep the shirt on.

KEVIN NEALON, *Cast Member:*

Most of those guys who came in—Farley, Spade, Rock, and Sandler—were much younger than the rest of us. It was almost like they were our teenage sons. All their offices were clustered together way down the hall, and when you would go back there, the offices were messy, with *Playboy* magazines strung everywhere, and they'd be talking about what kind of action they got the night before with some model. But it was fun having them around.

Those guys probably knew Farley better than I did. He was always loud and acting up, and one time I caught his eye and said, "Take it down a notch." So after that, if I'd look down at him, he'd go, "Take it down a notch." I got to know his family; we had Mother's Day specials two years in a row, and he brought on his mother and his family—all great people. I think Chris just wanted to make people laugh. He wanted to make sure that he was funny. He always felt he *had* to be funny—that was his torture.

AL FRANKEN, *Writer:*

It got to be when cast members and new people came in, they sort of had this template to go by, which is do the show, become a star on the show, get movies, and become Eddie Murphy. And the problem was, many of the cast members that came in thought that would be their arc. And many of the people who came into the show thought it was sort of chapter two or chapter one in the incredible career of "Them." Like, "This is Manifest Destiny. This is meant to happen. I am Eddie Murphy."

And the worst of that was the attitude, "Get out of the way, old man," to any of us who'd been there awhile, instead of, "I want to learn something." Now Farley was not that way. Farley revered the show. And with anyone who had any contact with the old show, he just wanted to sit and listen.

JON LOVITZ, *Cast Member:*

I was in California and Brad Grey calls me and said, "Lorne called and said they're doing something on the show and it's just a joke and they love you." I said, "Oh. All right." So I watched the show that night, and it's a cold opening, and Lorne says, "You're really leaving, huh?" And Dennis goes, "Yes." And then Lorne says, "You're not going to keep coming back like Lovitz are you? It's pathetic." I was like really hurt. I was like, "You asshole."

And the audience didn't laugh. It bombed. But I was really pissed. And I was like, "Fuck them, I'm not going back." I thought it was really shitty. Because they kept asking me to come back. And then after that, they still asked me to come back! Lorne goes, "Oh, it's just a joke." I go, "Oh, what's funny? It didn't seem funny to me, and the audience didn't laugh." It was really mean-spirited.

*   *   *

Worried about losing cast members to the movies or prime-time television, Michaels overstocked the show and in the process proved that there can be too much of a good thing. A cast so large was bound to be fractious, with the competition for airtime fever-pitched. The SNL troupe of the early nineties tended to split along generational lines, with Sandler, Farley, and Rock—the new boys—pitted against veterans like Carvey, Hartman, Nealon, and Franken. Mike Myers sort of straddled the field, prepping for his own film career.

The show was turning another corner. Baby boomers who'd grown up with it were becoming less demographically desirable to advertisers. As the decade progressed, Michaels relied more and more on young, "hot" stars to host the show and lure younger audiences, knowing that viewers who'd been with SNL from the beginning might never have heard of them but that their kids—yes, now they had kids—probably had. It was a time of less than subtle humor but, often, huge laughs.

CHRIS ROCK:

I've been friends with Adam sixteen, seventeen years—since I started stand-up. I was a young comedian and he was a young comedian but also in college; he was going to NYU.

I was doing some movie, *Hangin' with the Homeboys,* and they wanted to meet with me. And little-known fact: Lorne Michaels makes you wait two, three hours to see him. There's many a funny comedian that couldn't wait. None of them are very successful now that I know of. So I waited.

We auditioned the same night. There were all these great character guys ahead of us and we really felt inferior. We didn't know why we were there. I didn't even wait around to meet Lorne after the audition, because I knew I wasn't going to get it. I guess Farley auditioned the same night too, but he auditioned at Second City. I got to audition, and then I stuck around and saw Adam's audition. We passed, we got hired. And I remember years later I asked Lorne why he'd hired us— because I didn't do any voices, anything particular that would help me on *SNL*—and Lorne said, "The reason I hired you guys was original thought." He said, "Anybody can do impressions. Like, my uncle does impressions." And I said, "Okay, good compliment." And when I did casting for my show, I kept that in mind, the "original thought" thing.

ADAM SANDLER:

I was in, I think, sixth grade when *Saturday Night Live* was the biggest thing. I'm sure the other guys who are my age probably said this too, but my big thing was trying to stay up to watch it. In the schoolyard the cooler kids were talking about the Bees and they talked about Belushi a lot, and I wanted to be part of that conversation. So I tried to stay up, and I'd make it to eleven o'clock and I was very excited; all I had to get through was the news. And I'd usually get to about eleven-twenty—and fall asleep. And then my brother would be carrying me to my room and while he was carrying me I'd be like, "Is it on? Is the show on?" He'd say, "Yeah yeah, don't worry, go to sleep, I'll tell you about it tomorrow." And so he would tell me what happened on Sunday mornings and then I would bullshit in the playground and pretend I saw the show also.

I loved Aykroyd. I loved Belushi. I loved Bill Murray. I loved Chevy. I think the reason I loved *Caddyshack* so much growing up is that all my favorite guys were in the movie together. No matter who they cut to, I was, "I love that guy. I love him too." The hosts back then were cool. Like when Reggie Jackson hosted—I was a huge Yankee fan—that was as cool as it got.

The show was a major part of the life of every one of the kids I grew up with. It was not only topical, because it dealt with current events; it was just like instilled in our heads. "These are the funniest guys of our generation, so whatever they say is funny is funny."

TIM HERLIHY, *Writer:*

Adam Sandler was my college roommate at NYU. He decided he wanted to do stand-up his sophomore year, so I just helped him out. We all kind of helped him out with some material. I started doing it more—more and more as his school progressed. I always figured that he would be successful. We both graduated, and then he went out to L.A. after graduation and I stayed in New York and actually went to

NYU Law School. When he got the job at *SNL,* I kind of helped him out. And then he got me a tryout in the spring of '94.

DAVID SPADE:

I remember there was a period when the cast members were bigger stars than the hosts. That was scary. I was thinking Mike Myers is a bigger star than the host, and Dana Carvey is a bigger star than the host. It was weird. After they left, it got back to normal, where the cast was all evened out and the hosts were bigger names.

When I got there, they were saying that Dennis Miller and Dana and Phil were horrible, that was a horrible cast, and then in a couple of years, when I moved up into the cast, they said *we* were horrible, why can't we be like Dana and Phil and those guys, back when it was good? And then when we left, they were telling Will Ferrell that when Spade, Farley, and Sandler were there, *that's* when it was funny.

JULIA SWEENEY, *Cast Member:*

I came from the Groundlings. I was performing there for a few years, and I think it seemed like every week an increasingly more important person from *SNL* would come and watch. And then, in the end, it came down between me and Lisa Kudrow. And so Lorne came and we did like a showcase for me and Lisa—we each got to do three sketches, and I ended up getting chosen. And I remember thinking afterward, "I hope Lisa does okay."

LISA KUDROW, *Host:*

Thank God I didn't get *Saturday Night Live!* I had met Laraine Newman at the Groundlings, and she let me know that she thought I was really funny and really good. So she called Lorne Michaels and said he should really look at me. Then I found out they were also going to look at Julia Sweeney. Julia and I got to be friends over this. I remember us being on the phone and talking about what a crazy, hideous situation this was for us. There was going to be one show that we were going to do, and based on that one show, a big chunk of our career was going to be decided.

So Lorne came out with Marci Klein, the talent coordinator, and there was one night set aside at the Groundlings for them to look at Julia Sweeney and myself. Julia had a lot of people in the audience. I had some friends in the audience. I even had some good friends who were writers on the show. Conan O'Brien was writing on the show, and I asked him if he could be in the audience. He actually thought that wouldn't look so good. So I just thought, yeah, the classier route is not to stack the audience. I don't think I did my best, and, rightly so, they picked Julia.

There've been a couple things that I didn't get or got fired from where friends of mine who had a little more experience said, "It's always a blessing when a door closes, because another door is going to open." And there's no such thing as your whole career being decided in one night. I just kept believing that I was being saved by not doing *Saturday Night Live* to do something else.

JULIA SWEENEY:

I felt really accepted and encouraged and appreciated right away. In some ways my trajectory was the opposite of other people's who probably were more successful there in the end. My first show was Jimmy Smits, and I did a sketch with Jimmy right after the "Update" spot, which is like an important sketch spot. And so I felt like I came in with a bang. I didn't come in and hang out and only do teeny parts in sketches waiting until I could get a bigger part. So that was really encouraging for me.

Lorne had wisely paired me up in an office with Christine Zander, and we hit it off immediately. She had been there a few years and knew how to navigate herself around politically there. So the beginning was really great.

ADAM SANDLER:

It helped my whole career when I went from a stand-up comedian who would write maybe a couple of jokes a week that I would be excited about to—I think I was twenty-three when I got on the show—all of a sudden writing a few skits a week and helping other guys out with their ideas and trying to do jokes for their skits. All of a sudden, I thought about writing more. I thought about what really makes me laugh.

FRED WOLF:

My little group that came up on that *Saturday Night Live* were Dana Carvey, Kevin Nealon, Adam Sandler, Rob Schneider, David Spade, and Dennis Miller. It was a giant cast. The first time I was there, I was writing for the guys who were featured players who weren't really getting on the air as much as maybe they'd want to. And so I concentrated on writing for Schneider, Spade, Adam Sandler, and, you know, whenever I could, I'd throw some stuff everyone else's way too. But I mainly wrote with those guys. And then, when Norm Macdonald was at it, he was another friend of mine and so I wrote with him and for him also.

DAVID MANDEL, *Writer:*

I was in the *Lampoon* and, between my junior and senior year, we did a project down at Comedy Central which was called "MTV, Give Me Back My Life." It was a fake ten-year-anniversary documentary for MTV. And Al Franken was an adviser to it. And the following summer, Al and a guy named Billy Kimble and a couple of the executives from Comedy Central who had been on the show that I worked on for the *Lampoon* went on to do the comedy coverage of the Democratic and Republican conventions.

And they all remembered me and hired me back. So I went and worked on that. I spent all summer doing the Democratic and Republican stuff with Al and, at the end of the summer, he basically said, "You're funny. I'm going to talk to Jim and Lorne and get you on *Saturday Night Live.*" Which was perhaps one of the great moments of my life.

TIM MEADOWS, *Cast Member:*

A well-written sketch is basically anything by Jack Handey or Robert Smigel. Those guys write sketches that are refreshing to watch and different takes on the subjects or comic premise. It's original.

BOB ODENKIRK:

I would like to state for the record that Robert Smigel saved sketch comedy in America. I think he was the best sketch writer in America for like that ten-year period, his first ten years there. And as great as Jim Downey is, and as pure as he is, I think Robert was really hitting his stride and, you know, doing amazing things—everything from a *McLaughlin Group* to the James Kirk sketch to a lot of Perot stuff to so much great stuff, like that opening where Steve Martin sings "I'm not going to phone it in tonight": Smigel. I mean just genius work. Solid, amazing, brilliant, and smart.

Partly because it really is a live show and not live-on-tape like The Tonight Show *or* Late Show with David Letterman, SNL *has a history filled with surprises, shocks, major and minor calamities, and, most of all, controversies. But all of the show's dustups were trifling compared to the brouhaha that erupted in September 1992. In a gesture that had not been rehearsed nor revealed to anyone on the show's staff in advance, singer Sinead O'Connor ended a haunting a cappella rendition of a modern protest ballad by tearing up a photograph of the Pope on the air, thus indicating the song had really been an attack on him and the Catholic Church. That turned out to be haunting too, but in the worst way.*

JOHN ZONARS, *Music Coordinator:*

I was in the control booth. I was the one who basically put the whole thing together, unfortunately. Essentially what happened was she was performing on the show with an orchestra on the first song she was doing, and the second song was a selection from a record that she had done a cappella. We rehearsed it that way on Thursday. Everything was all fine and well, and we got through it. She refused to tape a promo, which we all thought was really rude. And that was a difficult thing to handle, actually, at the time. On Thursday afternoons we always taped the promos, and Lorne was actually coming in and producing. These days the writers do it. But she refused to do it and left in a huff, and there was sort of blame cast around for that, which I was involved in.

Anyhow, I didn't think much of it until Saturday afternoon when they came in to do their audio balance at five-thirty— "they" meaning the band and Sinead and her manager at the time, who I think has passed away. They came in, and the manager cornered me and asked me a very poignant question, which was, "When something goes wrong on the air, do you use the dress rehearsal performance?" I said to him, "It's been known to happen for the West Coast, but for the live show, obviously it's live. It goes out live, I think as far as like the central time zone."

So then he said, "I want to change the second song to 'War' by Bob Marley. And she'll do it a cappella. And there's a very special thing she wants to do since 'War' is essentially about child abuse. At the end of the song she wants to hold up a photo of a child and make a statement about child abuse, okay?" So I went as far as to get her the photo of a child, talked to Lorne about it, talked to the director, basically tell him he's got to zoom in on her and get a close-up of her with this photo. And when we did the dress rehearsal she sang "War" and held up the photo of the child and I think she said, "This is what we have to protect," or something. The house was captivated. She's giving this exhilarating performance by herself.

And then during the actual show, I remember I was in the studio watching her and I started feeling nervous and I thought that my nerves were due to the fact that since she was doing it a cappella, she was taking longer than she had at dress, and I was afraid that she was taking too much time. So I walked into the control room and just as I did, it happened—and I looked up at everybody, and they were all in shock. And they refused to turn on the applause sign after she ripped up the picture of the Pope. And I think that was the classiest move in the whole history of television—not cueing applause.

And then everybody was basically just in shock except for Lorne. Lorne was the only one that didn't seem like completely out of his mind. One thing I've always respected about Lorne is that he has this real hard-on for any kind of censorship. He does not want anything to be censored. He wants things to happen as they happen.

The big issue at that point was, does she go on for the good-nights? Does she get up there and say good-bye with everybody like a legitimate cast member? And Lorne decided that she should, which is a decision that he got fucked for afterwards but I'm sure he would stand by today. Because there she was, she went out and she did something extraordinary—and blasphemous in some people's eyes—but he was able to maintain some kind of respect for her, some kind of respect for the whole process of the show by letting her do that.

LORNE MICHAELS:

I didn't know it was coming. Here's what I think was happening that week, which was the other story: Tim Robbins, whose film *Bob Roberts* we first ran as a short, like a three-minute film, in the '85 season, was the host and had written a piece about GE dumping PCB's into a river, which we had all heard at read-through. The sentiments behind it were heartfelt, but it didn't work as comedy. It didn't get picked because it didn't play. And I think Tim was fearful that I might be under some sort of GE thing that I was not going to allow that to happen. So after one of the musical intros, he wanted to wear a T-shirt that had a GE logo with a bar across it, and I said, "Be my guest," you know. "I don't think that General Electric" — which by then owned NBC, of course — "will suddenly grind to a halt because of this. *Saturday Night Live* is its own thing. It has its own sort of beliefs and standards" — or whatever.

What everybody forgets is that music wasn't the closing thing, there's an act after it. So now after Sinead tears up the picture, we have to go do a comedy act. Well, there's complete silence in the studio when it happens. The switchboard's lighting up, but we're not anywhere near the switchboard; we're just getting ready for the next sketch, which we know is not going to play. I was stunned, but not as much as the guy from the audience who was trying to charge her and destroy the show while she was singing. He had to be taken away by security.

Now there's silence and we've got to do a sketch. The sketch unravels. But now Tim Robbins has got to come out and stand beside her for good-nights. It wasn't like somebody holding up her LP — of course, saying "LP" dates me now. What I'm saying is, it wasn't promotional. I think Tim Robbins was wearing the anti-GE T-shirt. For him that would have been an enormously big statement, to be defying a corporation while you're on it. And that was sort of the revolution that was going on that week. That was what people were focused on. People at the network were very focused on what Tim Robbins was going to do about GE, and I was less so because I have more

confidence in GE. But there's a lot of people whose job it is to anticipate trouble, and they were all on the Tim Robbins issue. And suddenly this girl tears up a picture of the Pope. When she did the Dylan
concert the next week at the Garden, they booed her. I don't think she
understood the scale of what she was doing. It was martyrdom. We
didn't quite get what it was.

WARREN LITTLEFIELD, *NBC Executive:*

All in all, even when it was, "Oh my God, Sinead O'Connor tore
up a picture of the Pope," as I said to Lorne, "Lorne, when we go too
long without controversy, something's wrong. This show is supposed
to rock, it's supposed to be the adolescent that's not obedient to
authority. And if we lose that, then we don't have that show."

LORNE MICHAELS:

I think it was the bravest possible thing she could do. She'd been a
nun. To her the church symbolized everything that was bad about
growing up in Ireland the way she grew up in Ireland, and so she was
making a strong political statement.

RICK LUDWIN, *NBC Vice President for Late Night:*

That was truly a Danny Thomas spit-take moment on my part. I
jumped out of my chair. I was in Burbank watching the live feed in my
office. I just knew we were in trouble.

DAVE WILSON, *Director:*

It was a little unnerving. I was more upset that she had hidden it
from us than I was by the act itself. In rehearsal, her manager had
asked if we could use only one camera because of the type of song it
was; they would like it not interrupted with intercutting. And then he
asked if she could hold up a picture of starving children, and that's
what she did at rehearsal. It was a very tender moment, actually. And
then to change it all into this whole Pope thing—I think everybody
felt they had really been railroaded. I was angry.

I made sure that nobody pushed the applause button so we went
out on a quiet studio. I gave the order.

LENNY PICKETT, *Bandleader:*

Things like the Sinead O'Connor incident have happened from time to time, somebody's done something outrageous, and I hate to say this, but it's kind of more delightful than anything else—to see something that amazing on live television. It's what everybody secretly is waiting for. That's why it's still an interesting show after all these years, because people know anything might go down. And when it does, it's exhilarating as much as anything else. I mean, it's not like you want to see those sorts of things, but at the same time, when they do happen, you're aware that you were just participating in an event. And to know that there's always a potential for that to occur is sort of wonderful.

Once that uproar subsided, Saturday Night Live *returned to its version of normal, concentrating on comedy. Michaels was coming under increasing pressure from the network to churn out recurring characters that would bring the audience back week after week and maybe, potentially, be spun off into NBC sitcoms of their own. That turned out to be only a bean counter's pipe dream—though some* SNL *cast members have wandered off into prime-time sitcoms after leaving the show.*

JULIA SWEENEY:

I did the character Pat at the Groundlings, and it was part of my audition for *Saturday Night Live.* I'd been an accountant for like five years, and there was one person I worked with in particular who had a lot of mannerisms like Pat. This person sort of drooled and had the kind of body language of Pat. I started trying to do him. I was testing it out on my friends and they were just like, "Yeah, it's good, but it doesn't seem like a guy that much." Like I couldn't quite pull off being in drag convincingly enough. So then I thought, maybe *that's* the joke. I'll just have one joke in here about we don't know if that's a man or a woman just to sort of cover up for my lack of ability to really play a guy convincingly.

I think it was like the Christmas show or something—a John Goodman show. I put it up with Kevin Nealon in it. Just showing how humble I was about that sketch, I didn't even cast the host opposite me. I just thought, "Well, maybe the host needs a break." And they put it on as the very last sketch of the show. And I didn't think it got that great a response. I felt it was just okay. I felt happy with it, but it wasn't like, "Oh, new recurring character," even. And the audience responded, but I think they were also really confused by it, or creeped out by it.

A couple weeks later, though, Roseanne hosted, and she had seen that show and she said, "Oh my God, we've got to do that character." And I said, "Oh, okay." So Christine and I wrote a Pat sketch for Roseanne and I to do, and when I came on during the sketch, I got like this fabulous entrance applause, as if the audience knew the character. That was actually one of the most beautiful moments in my life. And it was completely unexpected. I knew there was never going to be a moment like that again.

People would always ask about Pat's sex, and I didn't have an answer. To me, Pat by that point had sort of taken on its own personality. It's almost like I was — this sounds really actor-y, but I felt like I was just playing Pat — Pat was this other person. And I didn't know Pat's gender either. It was more like I had channeled this person than created it.

DANA CARVEY, *Cast Member:*

Most of the writers want to be performers. But I was naive, I didn't know that. So there was this creative tension between writers and performers. But you made alliances. It had all the resident political machinations of any large bureaucracy. You found writers who were sort of symbiotic with what your sensibilities were and you worked with them. It was good to write with people who had Lorne's ear and could go into the special meeting where the sketches were picked.

Toward the last couple years I hooked up with Robert Smigel and I'd go around the office doing Johnny Carson. Not the Rich Little version, which I thought was great, but, "That's funny stuff. You're a funny young man. Will you come back and see us again sometime?" I think Johnny said that to me every single time I was on his show. Robert picked up on that and we wrote a sketch. He's a brilliant writer.

Johnny liked some of the sketches we did. The one that was called "Carsenio" he liked because he saw we were poking fun at Arsenio

Hall as much as at him. There was one that I thought was kind of mean. It portrayed Johnny as senile and out of touch, and that one I just regret, because it wasn't my intent. When you play Carson, when I was in the moment with Phil, what really comes through you is sort of just charm, just incredible likability and charm. He never really patronized a guest, and that's why he could sit out there with a five-year-old or a hundred-year-old and really make it work.

JAN HOOKS, *Cast Member:*

I remember during the Gulf War, when we were all so terrified. They had security guys with earphones in the studio who were pack-ing lead and all this stuff. There were even bomb threats. Phil and I had a sketch and I just looked at him and said, "I'm not doing it, I'm not going out there, I can't go out there." And Bonnie Turner came up and said, "Now come on, you're with Phil." Phil just offered his arm and I went out with him.

DANA CARVEY:

One night that was a breakthrough for me is, I'd done enough of the show that the audience knew me, and I'd done enough George Bush cold openings that I was comfortable, and I remember right before I went to air, I just said to myself, "The cue cards are sugges-tions." Because Lorne doesn't like ad-libbing. I thought I'd be in trou-ble when I went off the script, but that didn't happen. Lorne always likes it when the room is full of laughter.

DAVID SPADE:

One of the bummers was, we did a prime-time presidential spe-cial, an election special, and it was a debate among Bush, Perot, and Clinton. So they said, "You're going to play Perot." I wasn't on the show a lot. It was kind of exciting. Phil was going to play Clinton, and Dana was going to do Bush. I thought, "It'll be perfect. I'll do a funny accent; it'll be a lot of fun. So we did the special and we filmed the debate ahead of time. I got in the Perot makeup, Dana got into his Bush, Phil got into Clinton. We did the wide shot, and we all walked in. Clinton did his speaking first, then Bush did his. When it got time for Perot, they have me step out, they have Dana redo his makeup as Perot, and then he comes back in and does the close-up.

It was humiliating. It was me just walking out, and it was Dana doing the fun stuff. So I was basically an extra — after forty-five minutes of makeup. It was just that Dana is really good, and they want a cast member doing that, and I thought they were over a barrel because he couldn't do both. It was a special with all three of them, and they would all be in the same shot sometimes, so I was going to win. And I didn't. And I was like, are they finding new ways to humiliate me?

Michaels always looked for SNL *characters to be spun off into movies that he would produce and that would be box-office blockbusters. He'd seen how the Blues Brothers movie struck it rich and longed to make a movie that hit as big. The right character never seemed to come along — but that would finally change with* Wayne's World, *costarring Mike Myers as Wayne and Dana Carvey as his friend Garth, two cute goofs who ran a no-budget cable-access show in Aurora, Illinois. A gigantically successful movie (followed by a gigantically anticlimactic sequel), it would be the only film derived from an* SNL *sketch to gross over $100 million. It was Michaels's biggest coup as a movie producer. Myers would go on to make many other films — most successfully the* Austin Powers *sixties spy spoofs, which contain a wicked but apparently friendly homage: the character of Dr. Evil, one of several played by Myers, has the unmistakable speech patterns and mannerisms of Lorne Michaels (although, for the record, Carvey does a better Michaels impression).*

Myers did not suffer from an inferiority complex. Brandon Tartikoff loved to tell the story of the time when, having moved on from NBC to the presidency of Paramount Pictures, he was trying to convince Myers, in the wake of the Wayne's World *success, to agree to make a sequel. To sweeten the pot, Tartikoff asked Myers who he'd always wanted to work with. "I have a big Rolodex," Brandon said. "Give me the name and whoever it is, they're only a phone call away." Myers thought for a moment and then said, "Fellini." Tartikoff didn't believe his ears. Who? "Federico Fellini," Myers replied. "I have always considered him a great artist." He looked at a flabbergasted Tartikoff, waiting for his response, or maybe expecting him to pick up the phone and dial Italy. "That's when I real-*

ized," Tartikoff said, "that he was completely serious. He really thought he was in that league now."

DANA CARVEY:

Lorne said Mike needed a sidekick for the "Wayne's World" sketches. Basically I just showed up at read-through and there was this sketch and I was just in there. I don't think Mike resented it. It's so infamous that it's hard to talk around this—but obviously the show was fine, and then once we got into feature-film territory, defining the roles was a little harder. That's as delicately as I can put it. When it was just a sketch, I would just be reactive and laugh really hard and support him.

I remember I always thought, "Aren't we just doing *Bill and Ted*?" I thought we'd be nailed as doing a *Bill and Ted* ripoff. But I think Mike's a clever writer, and he put his own stamp on "excellent" and "way, no way." *Bill and Ted* did precede us, but I guess it didn't matter.

TERRY TURNER, *Writer:*

Mike was interested in us writing *Wayne's World* with him because we'd done some of the sketches with him and the collaboration seemed to work. And then Lorne came to us one day and asked us if we would like to write the movie with Mike. And we said, "Sure, absolutely. We definitely would love it." Because it was an opportunity. So we took it.

Oddly enough, Lorne's advice on the movie was don't make anyone angry at each other, because it will remind the audience too much of home, and we want them to have a good time in the theater. In a way, his light touch worked, because he only said about two or three things about the movie. And sometimes he made us a little crazy, because he didn't keep up with the dailies as much as he should have and we had to go back and then reshoot things which could have been done sooner. But I can't complain about it, because it certainly was a great opportunity for us.

I'm sure I'm not speaking out of school here when everyone knows that there was a problem with Mike and Dana on the set. I'm pretty sure everybody knows that. So there was some hostility and then some friendly hostility, and then people would band together and it spilled over into the show. I remember once, Lovitz said to Dana, he was just absolutely killing in a sketch, but when Dana came off the stage, Lovitz said to him, "Dana, Dana! You're coming off gay"—just to undermine every bit of confidence he had. Just like, you know, a jerk. They'd pick at each other, but everybody knew it was kind of a joke, and yet sometimes it wasn't so jokey.

DAVID SPADE:

I think the breakthrough for me was probably when I did that sketch as the receptionist saying, "...and you are?" and that kind of thing, which kind of worked. It was a little dry attitude, and it caught on fast, which was nice. That didn't really solidify me there, but the following year I did my first "Hollywood Minute," and that's the one Lorne liked.

I was just basically sitting at the table in the writers' room, bored, reading *People* magazine, commenting out loud about what was going on in the world, and just making fun of everyone. Someone was like, "Why don't you just do that on the show? That's what you're good at." And that was Lorne's opinion too. He said, "You've finally found a unique voice, just do that." And then about two weeks later, he said, "Why don't you write up another 'Hollywood Minute'?" And he had never asked me to do something like that, which basically meant it would probably be on the show. And I thought, "Great!" So I was such a whore doing that. I probably wouldn't have done it as much as I did, but it was actually getting in the back of my head that I might get fired at that point—because it was three years in, and I hadn't made much of a dent.

And I did it every couple of weeks. It was crazy, I didn't care who I took out, I was just an unknown guy making fun of million-dollar celebrities for no reason, just to take their legs out. A year or two later, it was less interesting, because I had turned into one of them.

FRED WOLF:

I would actually beg Spade to not hit the people that probably couldn't take a hit. It just drove me crazy to make fun of some of the celebrities that were already having their own troubles. I used to tell him, "Who knows where you'll be one day when you're turning on the TV and you'll see somebody say something as nasty about you as what you're saying about them, and it's going to just send you into a free fall?" And, you know, he listened to me somewhat. If you hit Madonna, she'll take it. If you hit Michael Jackson, he'll take it. But you can't hit the real easy targets.

AL FRANKEN:

I originally wrote Stuart Smalley for Mike Myers. But when he did it in read-through, it didn't work, because it was so specifically in my head and in my ear, and I think Smigel said I should do it, and I did it, and it worked. I felt while I was doing it that I had such good reactions that I did another one. And then, in the room between dress and air, I would of course demand that they cut other people's sketches so Stuart could be in the show.

One day, when I was picking up tickets for *The Producers,* the guy I got the tickets from asked me, "When are you going to do a Stuart sequel?" And I said, "Well, the movie lost about $15 million, and I've discovered that when you lose money for a studio, they don't want to make a sequel. Now if that doesn't tell you what this business is about, I don't know what does." This is my standard answer.

DAVID SPADE:

I thought "buh-bye" was good, and the good thing about it was that we only did it twice, and yet I still hear it. I used to think that you had to do something twenty-five times and beat it into their heads to get some catchphrase going, but "buh-bye" and the receptionist's "…and you are?" were just kind of stumbled into. We probably should have just left it at one—although it's never been the case, in any sketch that's worked in history, to leave it at one. It's usually "leave it at thirty."

ADAM SANDLER:

Before I was on the show, I didn't really know what I was doing quite yet. But once I was in a room with like Jim Downey—who if you wrote a skit and Jim liked it, you were high for a week—and Robert Smigel, the same thing, it was always about impressing those guys. If you had just one line in the skit that they would comment on, you felt like you were doing something special. It was just sitting in a room with the guys you idolized, and I guess after a little while you developed what you think was the kind of comedy you wanted to do—and the kind that those guys would disapprove of.

BOB ODENKIRK:

I think Sandler really seemed to take everybody by surprise. I mean, the things that Adam was doing were so sort of inconsequential—silly songs and just like basically dicking around, you know. I'd been there for a couple years, and I really believe in good sketch comedy and great sketches, really solid sketches, and yet I thought that Sandler brought a really great breath of fresh air to the show and relaxed the show when it was getting kind of uptight and formulaic. So I liked what Adam did. But I think his fame or his success did surprise maybe everybody.

ADAM SANDLER:

I remember in the beginning when I would be on-camera, Lorne would hear, "What are you using that guy for?" I remember one time they did a Q rating, and I happened to be on the show that they evaluated. They got all this stuff on who's likable on the show and who's not. It was like the second or third thing I ever did, and I guess whoever did the Q thing, they said I sucked and I was not fun to watch. And so I remember Lorne caught some flak from NBC saying, "Don't use that guy. People don't like him." But Lorne and Downey and Smigel, they kind of looked past that. Lorne always said, "When you first get on the show, it's going to take time for the audience to like you, because they're used to seeing Dana and Nealon and Hartman and guys that they're comfortable laughing with." Sure enough, they cut to one of us young buffoons and they go, "Who's that guy? How did this idiot get a chance?" But after a few times of being on the show, the audience grew a little more comfortable with you and they said, "Okay, this guy I guess is on *Saturday Night Live*," and then you get more confidence as a performer.

JACK HANDEY:

I was in a fraternity in college, and I thought I had heard some pretty graphic sex stories, but Sandler would just go into detail about some of his sexual adventures to the point where you would just be crying and laughing, it was so embarrassing—just the details he would go into. But very funny. Sandler was always a sweet guy to me and I think to most people on the staff.

ADAM SANDLER:

I remember actually my first skit. I was in a thing that Smigel wrote and that I helped write a little bit. And it was Tom Hanks and Dana Carvey, and I just came on, I just had two lines, and I remember that countdown. I remember telling Hanks right before, "Hoo, I'm nervous," and he goes, "Hey, it's going to be all right." I said, "Man, I feel like I'm going to faint or something." He goes, "Well, don't."

I wasn't always funny on the show. I remember sometimes I would be funny at dress rehearsal, because I felt loose and like, "Well, no one's really going to see this, just this couple hundred people," and I was used to doing stand-up in clubs and I felt pretty confident in front of a crowd of two hundred or so. But then the live show would come on—and this happened to me the first couple of years—I'd hear the countdown, and I'd be like, "Oh no, oh no, everyone's going to see this. I'd better do as well as I did in dress." And then I would choke and my mind would be spinning out. And right after I would get off I would say, "Is there any way you could run dress for the West Coast?"

MARILYN SUZANNE MILLER, *Writer:*

It was a boutique aspect. Each one was their own boutique. There was the Adam Sandler boutique, which presented writing and acting and music and lyrics by Adam. Which was not the way it was when I was at the original show; we were the writers, they were the actors. And indeed they were a different generation than me. Adam I loved. It was a whole other sensibility than mine, but I loved it.

JANEANE GAROFALO, *Cast Member:*

The only thing you could count on in my day, when I was there, was if it was a Sandler or Farley sketch, it was on. That was the only thing you could ever bank on.

ADAM SANDLER:

Herlihy and I wrote a movie, *Billy Madison,* and we said, "This could be pretty funny, maybe we could do this." And I showed it to Lorne, and he read it and told me, "There's some funny stuff" but that maybe this shouldn't be my first vehicle. And I remember saying, "Oh, okay, all right, I guess I'll just write something else." I didn't have my feelings hurt at all. I just thought that's okay, that's how he feels, and he picks what skits I do also. If I write a skit and it doesn't get on the show, I don't sit and cry about it, I just say I'll write another one next week. So that's how I felt about *Billy Madison.* I said, "Okay, Herlihy, he doesn't like this one. Let's write another one."

CHRIS ROCK:

I got hired because *In Living Color* was on. *SNL* hadn't had a black guy in eight years or something. *In Living Color* was hot, so they had to hire a black guy. Trust me, there was no black guys for eight years, man. Let's put it this way: It didn't hurt. I'm trying to help you with the backdrop of the time.

No black guy for eight years, and Eddie Murphy was under Dick Ebersol. So there was never really a black guy — a star anyway. Damon Wayans was on like six months or whatever and then he got fired.

I was a featured guy. Adam actually had to write for like a year. He might've got on here and there, but he basically was a writer for a year. We'd give each other jokes sometimes on each other's pieces. Adam actually gave me the best joke I ever had on the show. It was a Nat X sketch. My militant character, Nat X, used to do these Top Five lists, 'cause the Man wouldn't give him ten. So — "Top Five Reasons Why Black Guys Don't Play Hockey." Adam gave me the joke: "Don't feel the need to dominate another sport." Adam Sandler! Adam Sandler, man. Good guy.

FRED WOLF:

Rock is so smart. God, he's so smart, and he has such a unique sense of humor. We would talk sometimes, you know, we shared an office when he was there. We had these connecting offices in the back toward what's now "Update." But anyway, we would talk forever. He was so smart about things. And he appreciated Jim Downey as much as anyone else did.

CHRIS ROCK:

I watched it as a kid, sure. Loved it. Dreamed of being on it. It was my dream. I was twenty-one when I joined the cast. I got a duplex apartment in Fort Green. I bought a car, a Corvette. That stuff. My mom started making money doing stand-up too. That was cool. Prices go up. I had a big year. First *SNL,* then the movie *New Jack City* came out, so I was hot shit—at least I thought I was.

The live show was incredible. It was incredible to meet these famous people every week and see these great musical acts and see this whole show form around you and how they built it. The best thing about the show was that when you did write a piece, you were responsible for it. You were in charge of the casting. You were in charge of the costumes. You produced the piece. I wouldn't know what the fuck I was doing if I hadn't been on *Saturday Night Live.* It's the absolute best training you can have in show business.

Dana Carvey *was* the show. He carried the show on his back. Add to him Mike Myers, Jan Hooks, and the others, and I think it was a great cast. Our cast actually went on to the most success afterwards, probably. Even Rob Schneider is in big movies. History will say we were the best cast ever.

ADAM SANDLER:

That's why I love Rock, because he's got the balls to say anything he wants to. I think we had quite a cast, no doubt about it. You can list off our guys, and both on the show and hanging out with them, they are the guys that make me laugh the hardest.

When I got there, a lot of guys who were my age, the younger guys on the show, we respected the older guys. We knew that when Dana and Phil and Nealon and Dennis and Jan Hooks went out there, they crushed. They knew what they were doing. And we watched them when we were at home so that when we got there, we were just psyched about getting to say we worked with these guys. And the fact that a lot of younger guys were writers also, it made sense that we had to pay our dues and write stuff, and try to impress those guys and say, "Hey, we wrote you a good sketch—do you mind if I play the busboy?" It 100 percent made sense.

CHRIS ROCK:

Eddie was the biggest star. Anybody who says different is making a racist argument. Eddie Murphy has the biggest numbers in the history of movies. Grosses are people; it's not dollars marching in, those are people. Belushi didn't have a movie as big as *Trading Places,* and that's not even Eddie's biggest movie.

Blues Brothers is not as big as *48 Hrs.* It's not. *Animal House* had a cultural impact, but Belushi's not the star of *Animal House,* he's the breakout guy. It was still an ensemble; he was the best of the ensemble. Eddie Murphy's a *star,* man. He's probably the only guy of the *SNL* posse to embrace stardom—its Elvis.

He won't talk to anybody about the show. He's done with it. He's not bitter about it, he loves it. He totally credits the show. I don't want to speak for him, but I think he does get pissed when they make fun of him, only because the show would have gotten canceled if he hadn't been there. There would be no show. So he deserves a pass on that aspect. The show would have absolutely gotten canceled. There were really no stars. Have you watched the reruns on Comedy Central, when they do the intros and Don Pardo is saying the names? The yell on Eddie Murphy is so much greater than for anybody else in the cast.

LORNE MICHAELS:

As the fifteenth anniversary approached, I met with Eddie Murphy. He couldn't have been nicer, was very gracious, but there was a thing that Billy Crystal had said about him in a *Playboy* interview that Eddie didn't like. So what I was told was that Eddie would come on the anniversary show, but he wouldn't want Billy Crystal to be on. And I had already invited Billy Crystal. I think Eddie felt Billy was wrong for telling tales out of school.

TIM MEADOWS:

I think Chris Rock and I had a good time just being friends and experiencing and stuff, but I don't think creatively he had a good time. I think it was hard for him to express his comic thoughts and stuff and the kinds of things he wanted to do. A lot of his stuff didn't get on, and it's the same as it is now. Chris and I would have maybe one sketch a week or every other week or whatever. I mean, we never had shows like Dana or Mike. I've never been in more than four sketches in a show, in the nine years I was there. I've never had a show like Will Ferrell, or Jimmy Fallon for that matter. Even when Jimmy was a featured player he had more sketches than I would.

CHRIS ROCK:

I was on the bench. Three years, sixty shows, I probably was on fifty-five, fifty-two of them. I had a talk with whoever the new black guys are now, Tracy Morgan and the other guy, I forget his name. They don't really have stars now, so I told these guys they've got to assert themselves. When I got there, there were stars, real stars. Dana Carvey was a star of the show. Dennis Miller was a star. Mike Myers and "Wayne's World" was really popular. Phil Hartman was big on the show. There were a lot of big people on the show. So for me to not get on wasn't that big a deal.

Black people I guess stopped looking for me after the second year. You know what happened? It was like, when Eddie was on, there was nothing else for black people to watch. So his first year he didn't get on until the end of the show, I was one of those black people who'd wait until the end of the show to see my favorite guy. By the time I got on, there were all these other things on TV with black people in them, so you don't wait until the end of *SNL* to see a black guy. You watch another show. Eddie Murphy was for everybody, but we got him first. We knew.

My frustration was half that, and the other half like the black comedy boom was happening and I wasn't part of it. *In Living Color* was a big show, and *Def Comedy Jam* was on HBO, and Martin Lawrence was on. So there was all this stuff happening, and I was over here in this weird world, this weird, Waspy world. But the things I learned there—there'd be no *Chris Rock Show,* I never would have had the success that I had with that, if I hadn't been on *SNL* learning how to run a show. I didn't go to college. So it was all school to me. Everyone was a professor—Professor Al Franken, Professor Phil Hartman.

NORM MACDONALD, *Cast Member:*

I always hear about how Chris Rock was underutilized and stuff. That's not really true. I mean, they let you do whatever you want on that show. So you can't blame anybody. It's just that Chris is a great stand-up comedian, a great voice. Unfortunately, that doesn't mean he's a great sketch-comedy comedian.

CHRIS ROCK:

"Can't compete with white people, man. You'll lose your mind." My mother told me that a long time ago. "Just find your spot. Find your spot, work within that spot." Okay, everybody's writing sketches for the host. They've got to do something without the host, let me write something without the host. I was a separate thing.

With Tim Meadows being on the show, you know somewhere in your mind that if there's two nonwhite, pretty good sketches, they probably won't both get on. And they'll never go back-to-back, even if they have nothing to do with each other. One could be about medieval times and one could be a drag-racing thing, but you're never going to see this sketch with a bunch of black people, and this other sketch with a bunch of black people, back-to-back. One might go near the top of the show and the other would be at the end of the show.

That's how it was in comedy clubs too. One black comic goes on at nine o'clock, they will not be putting me on at nine-fifteen. Same goes with women. It was just men in power overreacting, overthinking things.

FRED WOLF:

The one thing I will say is that while Chris was on the show, I would walk somewhere with him and everyone was recognizing him. Everyone out there knew who he was, and typically he'd have more of a black slant to some of the stuff he was doing. And I think he felt like his audience wasn't really watching *Saturday Night Live,* and that may be the case. But I also think he's been able to cross over quite a bit, and I think some of the stuff he learned at *Saturday Night Live* or was able to sort of do at *Saturday Night Live* probably helped him prepare for that.

If he had started at *In Living Color,* maybe he would have jump-started much faster than he did at *Saturday Night Live.* My observation was, yeah, he was having a rough time. But I don't think *Saturday Night Live* hurt him in any way.

CHRIS ROCK:

Maybe I could have worked harder. As I think back on it, I worked just as hard as anybody else, but as my father raised me, "You've got to work harder than the white man. You can't work as hard; you're not going to get anywhere." I don't want to say anything bad about the place. They're good people.

It's not the place for a black guy, it's not the hippest place, man. We used to always get the black acts the year they were finished. Like the music acts. So we got Hammer when he did "Too Legit to Quit," when he did *The Addams Family* theme song, on his way out. We get Whitney Houston on the way out. I'm just telling the truth, man.

Who wrote for me? Me, man. Just me. No black writers and no one really got into that side of the culture. Half the culture's into some form of hip-hop sensibility, half of the white culture, it's not just a black thing, but the show's never really dealt with that part of the culture. Even now.

DAVID MANDEL:

I was a fan of Rock's from before I got there, and I had his original stand-up album. He's a genius, obviously. And his stand-up acts are as close as it gets to perfection. At the time, I just don't think what he was doing was just exactly right. I mean, even now, when you see the success he's having in the movies and stuff, he's basically still playing variations on Chris Rock. At the time, on the show, people were trying to write characters for him and things like that. And I just don't think that's what he does, and so it was sort of a bad match at the time. I don't think anybody was saying that was genius and it wasn't getting on. I just think it wasn't a good match.

Chris seemed incredibly frustrated. So were a lot of people.

CHRIS ROCK:

It was the best time of my life. The show, that's one thing. But then there's the hang. The hang was the best time of my life. I honestly tell you, I made friendships that will last for the rest of my life. Most people had to share, they had a partner in their office. I had a four-person office: me, Sandler, Farley, and Spade, we shared an office. And those are my boys for life. For life. I love those guys.

ADAM SANDLER:

Backstage with Chris Rock, Farley, Spade, was the best. Nothing was better than having a read-through. You stayed up all Tuesday night—all of us did that—and then we'd do the read-through and you wouldn't know what was getting on the show but you'd have an hour or so while those guys were figuring it out. So we'd all go to China Regency up on Fifty-fifth, and we'd eat and watch Farley eat more than us. Farley was so happy; I think we went there the most because they had a lazy Susan. It's easier that way. That's all we did, we just talked about comedy—what we just heard in the read-through, what was funny, what we didn't like, what we thought was going to get on, what was going to get past dress, that kind of stuff. We lived for comedy. We still do. Every one of us—sadly, I think. The women and the other people in our lives have to deal with the fact that we think of our comedy first. I'm not saying that when something important comes up we can't drop it, but it's on our minds more than you would think. We wake up thinking about jokes, we go to lunch together and that's all we talk about. I think we've become pretty obsessive with it. "Obsessed" or "obsessive"? I don't fucking know.

JANEANE GAROFALO:

I was on from September '94 to March of '95. Less than a year. I'd been a longtime fan of *SNL*. I mean, it certainly has had its highs and lows—lows being the Jean Doumanian era and then another low being the brief time that I was on it. Those are the two lowest of the lows. The season that I was on it, the system was geared toward failure. The prevailing comedy tastes were certainly none that I could support or get behind. I did not think we were doing a quality show, and if you mentioned that, you found you were an extremely unwelcome guest. You're a very unwelcome family member if you do not wholeheartedly accept whatever the level of comedy is at the time.

CHRIS ELLIOTT, *Cast Member:*

All the performers there are required to write. That was another thing that bugged me when I got there, was that there was this pressure that, if you wanted to get on the air, you had to write some material for yourself. And I had stopped doing that. I was at a point now where people were writing for me, and when I did write, I was getting paid for that. But at *SNL* performers are sort of just expected to write. For nothing. It's not a separate sort of deal. I remember mentioning that to Herb Sargent once while he was urinating. And he sort of, you know, blew me off. How does this show get away with having these guys write stuff and not pay them through the writers' guild? And I guess there's just some loophole about performers writing their own material that gets away from the guild.

The only thing I can remember actually enjoying doing on that show was something that was very Lettermanesque, where I just started a skit that was really lame and then, you know, broke in and just told everybody, "That's it for me. I'm leaving *SNL*. Good-bye." And walked out of the studio. And as soon as I went through the studio doors, it turned black and white and it was kind of obvious—it looked a lot like, you know, Lee Harvey Oswald being brought down the hallway at the Dallas precinct, and then I get shot at the end. Anything else that I did on that show, I didn't do very well.

JANEANE GAROFALO:

I had desperately wanted to live in New York City and do a live comedy show from that building—30 Rock. I just thought it would be the greatest job in the world, and I had friends who had done it and friends who were on it—even though, oddly enough, I had been warned by everyone who had been on it not to do it. I had friends who were writers who had left and a couple of cast members who had left who I was friendly with who said, "You're not going to like it." They just felt it would not be a place where I would thrive, especially coming off of *Larry Sanders* and Ben Stiller's show, which were very progressive, intelligent, and collaborative television programs.

CHRIS ELLIOTT:

I think people just thought I would go there and do my own thing and, you know, be great on the show. And I was thinking the total opposite—that I would go there and everybody else would write for me and I'd have an easy walk through the show. And neither happened.

JANEANE GAROFALO:

I can still remember one sketch in particular, where aliens had taken some of the male cast members on the ship and had anally probed them and written "bitch" in lipstick on their chests. Is that funny? It was a Maalox moment every five minutes. I had irritable bowel syndrome every day. My drinking just got out of hand. I would credit *SNL* with being very instrumental to some bad habits that certainly increased.

I wanted to quit after the first week. I phoned my agent and said, "This is not a good fit. There's something wrong here." There is a tangible, almost palpable—perhaps the word is "visceral"—feeling of bad karma when you walk into the writers' room. There is something rotten in Denmark.

CHRIS ELLIOTT:

There were so many people in the cast. There was no reason for there to be so many people. There were times when I'd get in my Munchkin makeup and sit until, you know, five to one and come out and do one sketch. There was no reason. When the show first started and there was a smaller cast, it was funny to see, like, Belushi doing Marlon Brando and then having to run and change and be in some other sketch back-to-back. And that never happened with us.

JANEANE GAROFALO:

Every Wednesday there was always a great show in there. There were always funny sketches on Wednesday. Just somehow, I don't know why, writers were doing some really great, funny stuff that was not getting on the air. I don't know. For whatever reason, that season seemed to be the year of fag-bashing and using the words "bitch" and "whore" in a sketch. Just my luck. I was always surprised that a chapter of ACT UP never showed up to protest—honestly.

If you stepped out of line presswise, you would hear about it, and if they didn't appreciate what you said in the press, there would be Xerox copies of it for other people to read. It was the tactics of intimidation. There was so much pressure not to complain. If anybody got anti-fan mail or a disparaging note, it would be posted. I didn't understand that. It was another tactic of breaking you. Lorne enjoys the house divided syndrome. I think he *prefers* the house divided.

I learned that I made the experience even worse than it should have been. I was defeated. I was weak. I drank too much. I will go with the Eleanor Roosevelt quote, "No one can make you feel inferior without your consent." I gave my consent freely. And every time I waited for Lorne for five hours—luckily, I didn't do it more than once or twice—but once I did it the first time, I gave my consent to feel inferior. I gave my consent to Marci Klein to feel inferior because I was intimidated by her. I gave my consent to the other writers and my coworkers that I was just weak, you know? I was a loser. And so I definitely learned from that experience. Other than that, I don't know what I took away from it. But I guess that's pretty significant.

FRED WOLF:

Janeane Garofalo was awful on the show. She had it completely and totally wrong. She's a very, very insecure person. She was my friend. I helped get her on the show. And she's a very insecure person and she's unwilling to sort of stand on her own body of work and ride on that talent. Instead, what she does is sort of tears everything down around her, (a) to make her feel better about what she's doing, and (b) so she doesn't have to really actually attempt anything upon which she could fail.

And so she was an infection in that show in that she was going to the press—at that point she was a darling of the press because she was sort of an articulate female—and going on about how it's a men's club at "Saturday Night Lifeless." And that's just bullshit. It's an absolute total bullshit label. It just so happens that men are wildly more successful than women at *Saturday Night Live,* but not by design. It's just genetic makeup, in my opinion.

Janeane Garofalo never spent an all-nighter. The writers and performers that went on to do very well never missed an all-nighter session. Janeane Garofalo never got with the writers and wrote sketches that she was dying to perform and would do anything that she could to get on the air. What she did instead was glom onto the host and just tear the show apart for the whole week, about how it's a boys club there, and how they don't let creativity flourish, and if they see certain initials on sketches they won't laugh at them at read-through. All these negative things that were just patently ridiculous. And then she was a spectacular failure on the show.

CHRIS ELLIOTT:

Janeane and I hung out a lot that year, because in a way she was in the same boat as I. But she was a lot more capable in that arena than I was. And I guess she had the whole female issue to deal with there, which was a big issue, especially with guys like Sandler and stuff who were at their peak. So a lot of the humor was not up her alley.

PAUL SIMON, *Host*:

Janeane Garofalo has no case. She wanted to be on the show. She came on. It was during one of the show's low points. She signed on for, you know, whatever—for the year. And she had a miserable time. And she asked to be released and Lorne released her.

You know, she messed him up. In the middle of his season, he had to go replace her. She could've had some aesthetic disagreement with the show, which she did. I mean, no doubt about it. I mean, she vocalized it. She actually said it in public. He didn't say in public anything about her. What harm did *SNL* do to Janeane Garofalo? Any harm that she was on *Saturday Night Live* for, you know, five months? Did anybody ever say, "Except for stuff you did on *Saturday Night Live,* what a great career you've had"? And nobody there bad-mouthed her either.

FRED WOLF:

It was all just such a crock of shit.

I had this one sketch. It was about five idiot guys who were working on oil rigs in North Dakota. And they're drilling a hole deep into the earth and out of the hole pops sort of a subterranean human—some crazy alien person. And it's Janeane Garofalo. And these five idiots see her come out of the hole and she tells them that she lives in an underground kingdom, that they've been watching earth's progress over millions of years and they have all the answers to any question that we might have about life on earth. And that she has five minutes until exposure to the air will kill her. "Ask any question you'd like."

Well, when she first pops out of the hole, Chris Farley screams a really high-pitched scream, so after she gives her speech about how they could ask any question they want, the next thing out of Adam Sandler's mouth is, he turns to Farley and says, "What the hell kind of scream was that? When you saw the fish lady pop out of the hole, you screamed like a girl." And then they proceed to spend one minute of her last remaining time on earth arguing over how he didn't scream like a woman, he screamed like a man. And back and forth. The point of the sketch was that these guys were idiots and that they were blowing their chance at, you know, at great knowledge.

Janeane Garofalo raised hell with three or four people before I got wind of it that I was being "disrespectful to women" in that it is a fault of a guy to scream like a girl, that because Farley screaming like a girl would bring chastisement, she said that meant that women therefore are deserving to be chastised for the way they scream. It was one of the most convoluted, strangest, most ridiculous reasons I've ever heard to dislike a sketch.

JANEANE GAROFALO:

There were nights where I had a really nice time. Actually, I had a great night the night Alec Baldwin hosted. My family was in the audience. It was super fun. It was the Christmas show. The party afterwards was incredibly enjoyable. The Beastie Boys were the musical guests. It was just like I had fantasized it would be. I actually had things to do in the sketches. It was very exciting. My family was really pleased.

But I was usually embarrassed. My family did not like the show that season. My father felt that his intelligence was being insulted, and I was always embarrassed by that too at that time.

JAMES DOWNEY, *Writer:*

The fact is that for all the people who talk about what a nightmare this place is, there've been remarkably few true assholes. People can be difficult, and artists are always difficult one way or another. But it's a trade-off and worth it for what you get. There are a few people where everyone agrees that nothing they give us is worth the pain they give.

I wouldn't consider Janeane one of those. In her case, I think she's a very good actress. She's smart and does great nuance. But to me, the most frustrating thing about her is her whole thing about how straight-ahead and honest she is, and "it's all about the work." I've never encountered anyone who's more into the whole working-the-press thing. Someone said she had her first press agent when she was like twenty, and I can believe it. The year she was here, she spent the entire year on the phone with the press, giving them searching, candid interviews about the show. That's fine, but then don't play like "I don't know the system."

CHRIS ELLIOTT:

My kids watch reruns on Comedy Central, and they'll come to me and say, "I just saw you half-naked doing this thing where you're walking into an alien spaceship and you're supposed to be naked." And I'm thinking, "Fuck, did I ever do that?" I seriously have no memory of it. And I think it was just such a miserable experience that I have sort of blacked out a lot of these things. That whole year I was just embarrassed.

I think I tried to quit once and, you know, Lorne said no, I'm the type of thing that the show needs. That kind of stuff, you know, blah, blah, blah. I was amazed Janeane actually got out. She had a movie offer and she was just incredibly miserable. And I guess somehow she got out of it. I think I was with Brillstein-Grey, who of course represented Lorne at the time, so there was more pressure on me to stay.

JANEANE GAROFALO:

Although I wanted out after the first week, it took—for whatever reason—until March to make it happen. I talked to my agent and I would talk to other people and then, finally, I couldn't take it anymore. I just couldn't take it. And I walked into Lorne's office and I basically told him I was leaving. It wasn't like a debate or a discussion. Plus, I did not sign a five-year contract, because I had a feeling it would come in handy, and I fought and I fought against signing for five years.

I think when I quit, it was the first time Lorne ever respected me, to be quite honest. It was the nicest he ever was to me, even though he was generally nice to me. The nicest he was was after I quit, and I think he had a bizarre respect and then also, in some way, he hated me, you know? He despised me and was pleased that I quit — pleased that I was leaving and pleased that I had shown some kind of backbone.

LORNE MICHAELS:

Some people, their whole lives, are just injustice collectors. They're going to find new injustices every day. That's what they do, and that's what they are.

There were disgruntled writers too. Tensions that had existed virtually from the beginning between writers and performers — and between performers who were also writers and those who weren't — flared up anew, perhaps because in the early nineties, SNL *had seemed so much more a performers' program than a writers' showcase. Writers may also have been dismayed at the fortunes amassed by some performers once they left the show and went to Hollywood (in one or two cases taking favored* SNL *writers with them), while the less fortunate stayed behind in New York.* Saturday Night Live *was apparently being looked upon even by some of its cast and creative team the way the network regarded it — as an ATM rather than as a learning experience or a creative challenge.*

TERRY TURNER:

Bonnie and I had done comedy writing before. We had written sketches before. *Saturday Night* did a great thing for us. It knocked all the rough edges off of us very fast — that, you know, you didn't go for certain jokes. You tried to stay smart. You tried to stay current. And if it didn't work, it was really an abrasive situation.

I remember one time at the end of one particular piece, Lorne got to the end of it, and he said, "And what did we learn from this?" Then everybody snickered and put our piece to one side. I thought, "I'm glad I'm not near the window; I would jump out right now." It's a tough environment. It's a good environment. I'm glad that Bonnie and I had each other to lean on.

JACK HANDEY:

Jim Downey likes to laugh. It seems to amuse him to think that I was fired from the show. He thinks I'm a really good writer, and so it amuses him to think that the show was so stupid that they would fire me. But I sort of decided I'd had enough of the show and they weren't going to put my "Deep Thoughts" on, and so I went to Santa Fe, New Mexico, and just did some writing there. And then, finally, toward the end of that next season they said, "Hey, come back and do some guest writing." I did, and everybody really liked what I did, and so they said, well, come back — come back and work on the show some more.

I'd written some "Deep Thoughts" for the *National Lampoon,* and there was a college magazine called *Ampersand,* and I just knew that getting them on television was sort of a key to promoting them. And I felt like it was really important. I did a book of them and that was the main point. I knew that to get a popular book of them, television promotion was important. But I think my worth as a sketch writer finally overcame the resistance to putting my name on it. And they proved to be pretty popular. And also they have a utilitarian purpose on the show which I didn't foresee, which was that a lot of times they need, you know, thirty seconds to move the cameras from one set to another, so they can just drop in something like that, and so it was helpful in that regard. I probably did more than two hundred of them.

JAMES DOWNEY:

To me it was always, number one, to do comedy about things that are going on in politics or the culture, and do it without confusing or offending the smarter people. I always thought that if comedy is going to confuse anybody, by rights it should be the stupider people. You shouldn't be punished for knowing more. Sometimes there are things on the show that really annoy me. The more you know about the target of the satire, the more you go, "But wait a minute. That's not right. He's precisely the opposite of that." But for people who only have a passing acquaintance with it, it just feels, "Yeah, that's right."

One time there was a Willard Scott thing on the show, and the basic idea was that he was a big, dumb buffoon, and it just made me crazy—and I was the producer at the time and I could have killed it, but of course it got big laughs from the audience. But my point was, "Wait a minute—he knows he's a big buffoon. That's his act. So for us to skewer him by having someone do an impression the point of which is that he's a buffoon makes us look like idiots." And if I were Willard Scott I would call up on Monday and go, "Hey, morons. I was joking, and you took me seriously."

ROBERT WRIGHT, *NBC Chairman and CEO:*

When Don Ohlmeyer first came in '93, we had the issue of replacing Letterman, who'd jumped to CBS, and Lorne had cleverly got himself the commission to do that. And so Lorne was going to be the executive producer of the show starring someone. "Someone" didn't exist, and Don was very anxious about this and wanted to participate in it. This was the first time they were really together. So we had this sort of open audition, and people were submitting tapes and whatever, and they'd gone through a number of people, and I saw the tape on Conan. Lorne already knew Conan was the one he wanted, and I thought it was the best of all the tapes we had seen, and there were lots. It was the beginning of our relationship with Conan. Don didn't particularly like this, but he did agree that he was the best. The fact that he was totally unknown presented some huge problems for us. But Lorne got support from Don and got support from me and was willing to take on the issue that he wasn't well known. Some of the other people were known, so that was a big deal. But it's worked out well for all of us.

ROBERT SMIGEL, *Writer:*

I left to do the Conan O'Brien show in '93. That's what got me to leave *Saturday Night Live.* I was always afraid to leave unless I had a really good job to go to.

MARILYN SUZANNE MILLER:

I got very, very little on the air. The performers who were good wrote. I did do a great piece with John Goodman and Mike on a cruise ship, where Mike was doing Linda Richman and they were playing old Jewish people who could only discuss food on trips. So they just discussed the menus of all their previous cruises. And that was great.

It felt like it was a very hard match. It was like a closet full of clothes. The tops were size fourteen, the bottoms were size twelve.

ANDY BRECKMAN, *Writer:*

For a while in the late eighties and into the nineties, Lorne would bring back the golden oldies, writers from the first five years, for a week or two when their schedule permitted. And it was actually great to be a guest writer. Suzanne Miller I met that way. Anne Beatts I'd met, I don't recall if she was officially on as a writer, but these people would come back for a season or for a show or two.

In those years when there were guest writers, I didn't sense any tension, and it was actually a great system, because everyone came in knowing the show and knowing what Tuesday nights were like and what was expected after read-through and how Thursday nights worked and how rewriting worked. Lorne had a pool of these writers that were experienced, and for me it was great, because I was starting work on features, but if you give me fifty weeks and a year off I can come up with three great sketch ideas. Doing it every week is tough, but I kicked butt doing it for two weeks. If I had three weeks in a row, I'd run out of ideas—but I could always do it for one or two.

I never noticed any resentment from the younger writers until recently. I came back with my friend Norm Macdonald, and there was tension. He brought me and Sam Simon in and the situation had changed, it was like going back to your hometown and, hey, where's the drugstore? I didn't recognize any faces, and we were not welcomed back. I mean, if I was a young kid writing on *Saturday Night Live,* I would love to be in a room with Sam Simon and just hear how he thinks about putting a comedy sketch together.

TIM HERLIHY:

I definitely wanted to stay, you know, in New York, and had no interest in going to Los Angeles. And I hadn't had my fill of it like maybe Adam and some of the other guys who left at that time did. They were sick of it. Oh, maybe not sick of it—but they just had done everything they wanted to do. And I still felt like I was learning the ropes.

For writers and performers alike, whether during one of SNL's *upswings or downturns, the experience of working on the show was singular in their lives and, for better or worse, unforgettable. Some of them look back on it the way marines look back on the torturous training they got on Parris Island: It was hell, it was horrible, it was mentally and physically excruciating—and they are extremely happy that they went through it and would do it again in a minute.*

CHRIS ROCK:

I left first. I left to go to *Living Color.* It was actually more of a machine than *SNL. SNL,* they had little rules, like no one was going to write a "Wayne's World" but Mike Myers; your character was your character. Lorne might say, "I need you to write a 'Wayne's World,'" or, "It would be very nice if we had a Church Lady this week," or whatever it was, Opera Man, but it still was up to you. At *In Living Color,* if you had a hit character, they didn't care who wrote it. Once it was a hit character, it was the show's. It was weird that way. It's not a better way, to tell you the truth.

The good thing about me being on *Living Color,* I got things on that had nothing to do with race. On *SNL,* I either had to play a militant or a hip-hop guy. If you watch my stand-up, race is ten minutes of an hour-long show. I talk about relationships, whatever. And *Living Color* allowed me to talk about other shit. I could do sketches about, you know, funny stores I was in.

DAVID SPADE:

It was weird when I left there, because when you are around Lorne and Jim Downey and some cast members and writers that you think are really funny, you are with some truly sharp, fast people. And I didn't realize it, but when you leave, and you do movies or TV, or whatever I've done since, it's not always the case. And that kind of bummed me out. I did a few movies after, and I did a few smaller parts in them, and I thought, "Wow. I didn't mind taking orders from guys I looked up to, but there is no one in this room that I think is that hysterical, and now they are telling me what to do." And that started to drive me crazy.

FRED WOLF:

There's no reason for me to kiss anybody's ass at *Saturday Night Live,* including Lorne Michaels, who I'm talking about. But he set it up so brilliantly in that it's like this enormous pool of talent, and they all have egos, and they have to have egos to survive the situation at *Saturday Night Live,* and it's almost set up like sports teams—a university and a varsity. I always thought that that was a great way to do it. And that you had your varsity, your first-string guy, out there doing these sketches in the first half hour or the first half of the show. And you'd have second-stringers that were so hungry to get on the air that they would do anything they could to make that happen. So they'd write sketches for themselves and they'd write sketches for the star that they could be included in.

And it just kept everybody sort of working as hard as they could to take advantage of the place. Because one of the things I loved about *SNL* is that it's one of the only showcases left on TV where you can actually vault into star status. Back in the days when Johnny Carson was hosting *The Tonight Show,* when he had a comic on, that meant a lot, and that comic generally would get a lot of attention in the industry. Those days of that being one of the best showcases for any comedian are gone.

Saturday Night Live is still the main place where you could actually say, "If I did three or four years of *Saturday Night Live,* I would become a star if I'm ever going to become a star." I think it's the case to this day. So anyway, these guys come in and they're so hungry to get on the air and there's like twenty-five, you know, very talented people and egos walking around there—I mean the writing staff and the performing staff. It's such a big mix, and I don't think there's ever been a show like that, really, where you just have a bunch of people out there vying to get on the air and trying to do their best once they do. It's a remarkable place, because if you survive that process, you're probably going to be able to survive the next ten years of your career.

DAVID MANDEL:

We were sort of trapped there. There was a bunker mentality. You know, there was the siege of putting the show up each week. And that ultimately meant you were sort of eating and drinking and, in some cases, sleeping with these people, the same group of people, and going to the bathroom with them and, you know, seeing them at their best and their worst. And so ultimately, it was very collegiate. I guess that's the best word. It was a lot like freshman year rooming experiences, where you don't necessarily get to pick your roommates but you ultimately have to try and get along. And then you think back and go, "Well, there were some bad times, but there were some really good parties too."

FRED WOLF:

There are definitely internecine rivalries and fighting and all that sort of stuff. But ultimately I don't feel that that's a bad thing. I mean, I think it's bad if you go in there in a fragile sort of psychological state. I don't think you're going to get cured by spending five years on *Saturday Night Live*. That's what I say about Hollywood: No one goes to Hollywood for the right reasons. No one goes to Hollywood to meet their future husband or wife and buy a house and have kids. They all go to Hollywood because they're kind of damaged and there's something they're searching for.

I think it's the same with *SNL*. You have a collection of twenty-five sort of damaged people—thirteen writers, you know, twelve performers—and they're all trying to get on the air. And the best way to do it is to be competitive and to work really hard and stay up all night and just make sure that you're in the right sketches and trying to get writers to write for you or write for yourself and figure out how to suck up to the host and do whatever it takes to get on the air.

And the people who lost that sort of battle are sort of bitter about it, because it really is one of the greatest showcases on TV. When I was going out to *Saturday Night Live* the first time, when I got hired, I had like a couple months to prepare for it. And I ran into an old cast member who was there from the original season and, I shouldn't tell you who it was, but she says to me, "I heard you're going out to *Saturday Night Live*." And I said, yeah. And she said, "I just want to tell you: That place is evil." And you know, her experience wasn't that great. But she was one of the few cast members that never went on to do anything beyond that show.

LORNE MICHAELS:

There's an enormous amount of pettiness in this place, on this floor. You have a lot of writers fighting for time on the show. There's an old Hebrew proverb that if you have six Jews in a town, you have seven synagogues. And I think it's about the same with writers. While they can acknowledge someone else's talent or work, there's always a qualifier.

DAVID MANDEL:

If a guy comes out to Los Angeles and becomes a writer, let's say he becomes a staff writer, and has never worked at a show before or anything, he can rise up, you know, from staff writer probably to like practically coexecutive producer or maybe an executive producer of a show and conceivably not ever talk much to the director, wardrobe people, lighting people, and never have been in an editing room. By the end of my three years at *Saturday Night Live,* don't tell the union, but they used to let me call my own edit session. I could film things. I could do small film shoots. I had had three years of experience talking to Dave Wilson about how to turn my comedy notes into notes that would work for him as the director. You learn how to talk to stars. You learn how to calm egos. You learn how to play to egos. You learn that the key to everything is the wardrobe people — get on their good side and everything gets smoother. And you learn how to make sure that you can talk to the design people.

I cannot tell you how important that was — getting to a show and having just some of these skills that (a) no one expects you to have and (b) no one teaches you to have. I can remember being in my first edit session on my first episode of *Seinfeld,* and you were sort of invited into the editing room to come in and take a look. And I was able to say things and solve some problems that helped cut some time out of the episode, because we were always long on *Seinfeld*.

DAVID SPADE:

It's kind of like surgery—*Saturday Night Live*—where you're glad afterwards, but it's hard during. And you say you would never do it again. But it was the reason I got everything else, it's what started me, and it was really the best thing that I could have done.

DANA CARVEY:

It's terrifying, and I can still be scared thinking about it. It's just when you're sitting there at eleven-fifteen and you're getting your makeup and, man, you're so tired you can't even possibly imagine having the strength to do the show. Just very, very, very stimulating. And nothing will ever be quite the same. So you do create sort of a bond, almost like war buddies, with people who were on the show with you. Kind of an instant bond.

CHRIS ROCK:

Saturday Night Live brands you as professional. No matter what is written about me to this day, *SNL* comes up. It's the Harvard of Comedy, you know. Everybody passed through it. You bump into people. I saw Randy Quaid the other day; he's like a frat brother. I never met him before, but we're frat brothers. I did a movie one time, it was an extra part, damn near. It was *Sgt. Bilko*. I had a little part, man, nothing big at all, but Dan Aykroyd let me use his trailer when he left for the day. Because I'm a frat brother. It was incredible—big-ass TV and a stereo system, a place I could relax. You know, frat brother. It will be with me—the fact that I was on the show and had any success—will be with me forever. And that's an important thing.

FRED WOLF:

Saturday Night Live is the rock and roll of comedy. All comedians envy rock and rollers, and the show has that mystique about it. I've written on a lot of TV shows and never really came close to seeing anything like it. There's something about that show that's phenomenal.

I don't know of anyone who was on *Saturday Night Live* as a performer who clicked—I'm talking about the Lorne Michaels years—and then years later didn't click in another capacity as a performer. If you've been there five years and you're not able to do a movie or star in your own TV show, then I think you probably failed ultimately in your career.

LORNE MICHAELS:

Very often the least talented people are the very first to declare undying loyalty. Because the other people have more choices. To me it isn't that people shouldn't leave or that it's a betrayal to leave, because I think people have an obligation to their own talent and to express it. The more artistic they are, generally the more restless they are anyway.

When people come up to me at the party at the end of their first year and say, "I can't tell you how much I appreciate this, and I'm so grateful for this opportunity," I always go, "Well, let's talk about this in year six, because that's when it will actually matter. Because now all the power is on my side and you have no power." The test of character is how people behave when they're successful and they have more power. Some people handle it really well.

On Saturday Night Live, *guest and host are one and the same. Hundreds of celebrities, not all of them from show business, some more notorious than famous, have filled that double role. Some ingratiated themselves with the* SNL *regulars, and vice versa, while others proved uncomfortable, antagonistic, and even, in one or two cases, sexually predatory.*

TIM MEADOWS:

The biggest problem with Steven Seagal was that he would complain about jokes that he didn't get, so it was like—you can't explain something to somebody in German if they don't speak German. He just wasn't funny and he was very critical of the cast and the writing staff. He didn't realize that you can't tell somebody they're stupid on Wednesday and expect them to continue writing for you on Saturday.

DAVID SPADE:

He didn't want to go along with what the plan was that week, and as a result, I think that was the first week that I heard talk about replacing the host and just doing a cast show.

JULIA SWEENEY:

When we pitched our ideas for Seagal at our Monday meeting, he gave us some of his own sketch ideas. And some of his sketch ideas were so heinous, but so hilariously awful, it was like we were on *Candid Camera*.

He had this idea that he's a therapist and he wanted Victoria Jackson to be his patient who's just been raped. And the therapist says, "You're going to have to come to me twice a week for like three years," because, he said, "that's how therapists fucking are. They're just trying to get your money." And then he says that the psychiatrist tries to have sex with her.

TIM MEADOWS:

I love Chevy Chase. I do. He rubbed some people the wrong way, but when he was here, it was like just watching a car accident over and over again just watching him deal with people. Because he didn't care about what he said. He has no qualm about telling you you're an idiot, but not just saying it but showing you, you know, treating people really bad and being a real smart-ass. But I actually like him, though. He didn't call me an idiot, he was nice to me.

CHRIS ELLIOTT:

I remember having dinner with John Travolta and Lorne. He talked to Lorne about *Saturday Night Live* and how it had influenced him and how he had always felt that *Welcome Back, Kotter* was kind of the prime-time sister show to *Saturday Night Live*. And I remember Lorne just politely sort of nodding and going, "Right, right," and then afterwards walking back to Rockefeller Center with Lorne and how that really bugged him, that Travolta brought that up: "I was surprised to hear that we were the sister show to *Welcome Back, Kotter.*"

DANA CARVEY:

Keith Richards I remember. There was a horse backstage that week, and I was in my dressing area and I saw Keith Richards go up, hold the horse's face in his hands, and go, "You're a fine horse, aren't you?" I'll never forget that. Working with the athletes was great, like playing catch with Joe Montana, because I had a "Church Chat" where he threw a football to me—playing catch and running patterns with Joe Montana. With Wayne Gretzky we did a "Wayne's World" thing. I had never been on skates or played hockey, so Wayne Gretzky kneeled down and put on my shin guards. Wayne Gretzky showed me how to hold a hockey stick. I mean, that's like unbelievable. He was the most humble superstar I guess I had ever met.

TOM HANKS, *Host:*

The second, third, fourth, fifth, sixth times I did the show were just a blast. It's a one-week performance camp where everybody's operating from a sense of just incredible amounts of glee and manic energy as well as vast amounts of fear and flop sweat. That's *Saturday Night Live,* and there is absolutely nothing else like it.

KEVIN NEALON:

Musicwise, it was just a dream come true, because I grew up with the Beatles and James Taylor and Paul Simon, and those are people who came through a lot. You know, sitting next to Paul McCartney as he's playing "Hey Jude" during rehearsal. And Mick Jagger came on the show. And Eddie Vedder from Pearl Jam, he's doing three songs and he's not sure which three to do, so he's asking during rehearsal, "So, what do you think I should do?" So that's why I loved the show and the only reason I stayed so long, is because I loved doing it, I loved living in New York City, and I loved being able to work with all of these talented people who came through every week. A lot of people just wanted to use that show as a stepping-stone to get out and move on. But I just loved being there.

AL FRANKEN:

Paul McCartney was the musical guest. The musical guest usually rehearses on Thursday afternoon, and if we had someone like Clapton or Paul McCartney, 8H would just fill up with people from 30 Rock to see the rehearsal. The place was just jammed.

Paul does two songs, and Lorne comes up to him and says to him, "Paul, could you do 'Hey Jude'?" And Paul goes like, "Huh. I'm not sure if I remember it really." And I go like, "Hey Jude, don't be afraid—" and he goes, "No, stop! Stop! You'll get it wrong." And then he thinks about it for a second and he goes, "Okay, okay, okay," and he goes to this guy and talks to him and then sits down and they do "Hey Jude." And "Hey Jude" was like the song that when you were sixteen and you were driving and got to your destination and "Hey Jude" was on the radio, you just sat there and listened to it.

He's playing "Hey Jude" and I'm beginning to tear up and think about what's happened to my life since I've been sixteen, where'd my life go, and everybody else in the place is beginning to cry. So Saturday, the music rehearses after dinner or during dinner and we stop blocking and they do the music rehearsal. So again it's McCartney and again the place is jam-packed with people. He plays "Hey Jude" and the same thing happens. People start crying and I get kind of misty. And then I see a set. We're doing the Gap Girls that week, and every time we do the Gap Girls we have the set that has thousands and thousands of dollars' worth of Gap clothes in it, including a shelving of jeans, and they always put a guard in front of it so nobody would take any of the clothes. And I'm looking at the guard and the guard is crying. And, you know, I haven't had any time to shop. So we get to dress and "Hey Jude," and the audience is going like, "Unbelievable! He's playing 'Hey Jude,' I can't believe it." I'm looking at the guard, who's still very moved. I'm thinking I'm not going to have time on Sunday to go shopping and I need some jeans. So on-air, the Gap set was dark and the guard was totally focused on McCartney singing "Hey Jude," so I just started looking for some 34–30 jeans and took them.

I went to Dan the prop guy and told him I took two pair of jeans. I was willing to pay for them, I just didn't want to spend the time shopping.

CHRIS ELLIOTT:

Joey Buttafuoco, that was the lowest point for me at *SNL,* walking back to my dressing room and seeing this guy just walk by me and go, "Hi, Chris," and I just said, "Hi, Joe." And then I had to be in a sketch with him.

It literally was the worst year of my life. I went there too late after I had a career. I had already done my own TV show and had eight years with Dave, and then I got there and it was a huge cast. I kept thinking every show, "Okay, I'll do something next week that's better," you know. And I never did. And the year got away from me. And it was devastating, because I think for everybody who's like my age and in comedy, *SNL* was probably the reason that we tried to get into it. For the first few years at *Letterman,* I thought, you know, it was a stepping-stone—to *Saturday Night Live.* And to fail that miserably there for me was a big deal.

DAVID SPADE:

They say that if you go with the flow it's always better, and that would be my recommendation to anyone going on the show: If you're going to go on, then just make fun of yourself and have a great time. It is always endearing to watch someone make fun of themselves. You can't hate someone that actually says, "I'm an idiot. I'm admitting I know you think so, and I'm okay with it," and it kind of goes away, and it's funny. But to fight every possible sketch and everything that makes you look not cool and all that is exhausting.

TOM HANKS:

"The Five-Timers Club" is still one of my favorite sketches. By that time I had figured that the secret of being the host of the show is to concern yourself only with the monologue. Because if you have a good monologue, everybody thinks the entire show was great. If you have a poor monologue, it means you have to go and win back the favor of the people who are watching at home. So by the fifth time, I was like pushing for something slam dunk. We must have a magnificent monologue. And I think Lorne said, "Well, why don't we do something like, you get to join a select club?" And that was that.

I think that was the first time I met Paul Simon. He did a cameo. So there was definitely truth to the idea that I felt I was entering a pantheon of *Saturday Night* legends. The other great thing about that "Five-Timers Club" was, they had Ralph Nader outside the door trying to get in, because he had hosted the show once. So it's a heady atmosphere, man. Suddenly you're like goofing with Ralph Nader and Paul Simon.

ALEC BALDWIN, *Host:*

I did a sketch once in the early days when we did this really silly send-up of Brando in *The Wild One.* We did "The Environmentally Sensitive One." I do my Brando impersonation and I roll into town, and Victoria Jackson is the girl I pick up in town, and she's got the tight sweater and the huge boobs sticking in your face. Phil Hartman plays her father, who's the head of a chemical manufacturing company that's dumping waste into the local lake and killing everybody. It was this incredibly silly, silly sketch.

In the end, when the chemical factory is exploding and killing everybody in town, I'm offering Victoria a chance to ride off on my motorcycle with me. Phil Hartman beseeches me, he says the line, "Take me with you," and it was just the way he said the line, I always remember that as one of the times I almost cracked up on-camera. He just grabbed me and with this incredible yearning, this incredible panic, said, "Take me with you." I thought I was going to piss in my pants in the middle of the show.

I can be sitting there in one of those NPR sketches saying "wiener" and "balls" and "lick my balls" and "sweaty balls," and I don't think that that's funny; I appreciate that other people do. But Phil Hartman could walk up to me and say, "Take me with you," and he had that little sob inside the line, you know, and I thought I was going to pass out. It was all I could do to keep from laughing.

TOM HANKS:

I think you figure out after a while that there are some sketches out there that are floating around and they have yet to land on a show and they keep bringing them back again. You realize there's a reason these sketches are still just floating around and haven't landed on the show. There've been times we've been at the read-through and you can tell by everybody's groans that you're reading for the fourth time some sketch that somebody just thinks is great, hilarious, and they're submitting again, hoping that the host will click with it or something will happen like that.

I know there was one sketch that we'd actually put on its feet—I can't remember what show it was, but it was called "The Penis Song." It was all about us singing this song called "Penis, Penis, Penis, Penis, Penis, All Day Long. Penis, Penis, Penis, Penis, Penis Song." It just went on and on and on—and it got cut. And so I thought, "Well, that'll never be seen again." But then it showed up about three shows later. Somebody else was hosting. And so somebody else got to sing "The Penis Song" on TV, God bless him. Can't remember who it was.

On one of the earliest times I did the show, when NBC still had Standards and Practices, we read a hilarious sketch called "Jew, Not a Jew," which was a game show in which you try to figure out who's Jewish and who's not. Standards and Practices wouldn't let it on the first time but, like when I did the show, I don't know, either the fourth, fifth, sixth time, by that time there was no Standards and Practices, and so we were trying to figure out something to do. Then Al Franken said, "Well, how about 'Jew, Not a Jew'?" I said, "You guys haven't done that yet?" And so we pulled out "Jew, Not a Jew" and it killed. It was hilarious.

But when you're there for a while, you begin to get—you recognize the patina of a sketch that has yet to be on the air because no one has quite fully committed to it.

VICTORIA JACKSON, *Cast Member:*

Lorne said I could stay as long as I want, but I was burned out. I was just tired of trying to think of ideas. The only thing I figured out how to write was "Update Handstands." How many different ways can you do a handstand? They had one with a flag on my butt.

DANA CARVEY:

By '93 I'd done seven years, George Bush had run its course, "Wayne's World," Church Lady had all been done—basically I thought I'd done as much as I could do. My younger friends who were right behind me—David Spade, Chris Farley, and Adam Sandler—were bursting with energy. They'd been on the junior varsity two or three years and it just seemed like a natural time for them to take over the show. Dennis Miller had left, Jon Lovitz had left, and Nora Dunn had left. Bonnie and Terry Turner were leaving right around that time. It was a close call, because Phil Hartman was still there, but it felt like the right time to go. I just didn't want to stay too long.

Very quickly you feel incredibly old after you leave the show. What happens is that people come in, you're thirty-one, and then all of a sudden you're forty in the blink of an eye, and then there's a cast member who's twenty-four, looking at you like you're Chevy Chase or Dan Aykroyd and shaking when they talk to you. And you go, "But I was just the new guy a second ago."

I know that Lorne didn't want me to leave, so it was bittersweet that way. He definitely wanted to keep me through the election, which I did until Clinton was sworn in and stuff, and that added a year and a half. I stayed. I definitely felt some sense of loyalty in that sense. I didn't want to leave him in the lurch.

I had such a lucky run on that show that it felt like the right time. I still feel that way. I have no regrets. If I'd left after five years, I'd have missed out on a lot, but if I'd stayed two more years, into nine years, I don't think it would have been the right move for me. A lot of people stayed a lot less. Martin Short only did twenty shows. I feel bad for those guys. They didn't get to really explore it.

TOM SCHILLER, *Writer:*

I left for good in 1993. It happened abruptly and without any human contact between me and Lorne, and it kind of threw me. Suddenly I went to the office and guys were putting my things in boxes. They said "management" had asked Lorne to clean house. But Lorne was nowhere to be found when I wanted to ask him why this was happening to me.

And yet it turned out to be the best thing that ever happened, in a way, because I should have left three years earlier.

JULIA SWEENEY:

I would say my first two years, and even up to my third year, were fabulous. And then my last year was just like one of the worst years of my life. I don't know exactly why. I think that Lorne was feeling a pressure to concentrate more on the younger talent, which wasn't even—particularly in age—years younger than me, but it was like going from like the Dana, Phil, me sort of emphasis, to the Chris Farley, Adam Sandler sort of emphasis. I think I got one sketch out of my whole fourth year.

I complained. I think Lorne really liked me a lot, but I could see in his eyes that I wasn't part of the new order. I don't think anyone cared whether I left or I stayed. And then finally I went to him in March. I had such a difficult time. It's like every week I was writing and writing and nothing was getting on and I hadn't really been the driving comedic force of a sketch like for—like until March, when I went just insane and forced Lorne to put on a sketch that I had written for Patrick Stewart. And the sketch went on last, and it did okay. But I could tell that it was sort of a favor to me to shut me up. Overall, I was over.

In April I went and told Lorne that I wanted to quit. My contract was five years, and it had only been four years. And he would never ever tell you, "Please don't go." I wasn't looking for him to say that. I knew that even if he felt that way a thousand percent, he would never say it. But I knew that he also didn't want me to go, not so much because he wanted me there but because he didn't want to have the drama of me leaving. Not like it would be that big of a drama. But it's almost like I felt like he just wished I would disappear and we didn't even have to have the conversations about me leaving.

But by then I had so made up my mind. My agents would say, "Don't leave a job 'til you get another job." And I had saved up like $70,000, which was like to me a zillion dollars. And I felt like I would have scrubbed toilets with a toothbrush rather than come back to that show. There was no job I could imagine having to do that would have been more difficult than returning to that show the next year.

LORNE MICHAELS:

Michael Eisner called and said he wanted to make a movie based on her character Pat, and I said I didn't think so. Then Julia came to talk to me. I had the right to stop her, because NBC owned the thing. But I said, "Good luck," and I let her make the movie. And ever since, it's been on *my* record. They say *"Saturday Night Live* movies like *It's Pat." And* she's unpleasant about the show! And I go, "What?" Well, why—because her life didn't turn out quite the way she wanted? Now it has, she's done a one-woman show, and she has a baby, and she's defeated cancer.

CHRISTINE ZANDER, *Writer:*

I got to know Phil even better. And this was after I had moved to L.A. and they had moved to L.A., after we worked together. Phil was a wonderful guy, incredibly generous and good-hearted, but I think he was difficult to get to know. I think maybe with his male friends it was easier, but I don't really feel like I knew him completely. I think he became unhappy, because the last two years the new talent started to come in, it got a little bit more cutthroat, because, you know, the old guard wasn't getting written for as much.

DAVID MANDEL:

The final season for me was really, really exhausting. I started poking around Los Angeles for sitcom writing and got an offer from *Seinfeld.* If I was 90 percent sure I was leaving before, knowing I had *Seinfeld* pushed me to about 140 percent.

TIM MEADOWS:

The worst year from my perspective was the year before the big changeover. The last year with Sandler and Farley and Spade and all those guys was, I think, the most fun backstage, but the least fun on-camera. We had good times and we enjoyed each other's friendships, but there were too many people. The writers and the cast people didn't gel, you know. I think after doing a certain number of years, it seemed like there were thirty people trying to race to the finish line, instead of people sort of like being a relay team and the writers handing out funny pieces for the performers to do.

There were a lot of talented people, and it was weird, because when you looked at the people that left during that big changeover, a lot of those people went over to write and produce for *The Simpsons* and *Seinfeld*. Sandler and Farley and Spade and Jay Mohr, and all these talented people that were in the cast, went on to do other things.

AL FRANKEN:

The last season of the show that I was on, Kevin Nealon had been the "Update" anchor and was going to leave as anchor next season. So the spot was open, and it was something I'd always wanted to do, so we had sort of a test. And I did it and Norm Macdonald did it. And it got sent out to Ohlmeyer. And this is something I'd always wanted. So Lorne and Jim take me out to dinner to give me the bad news, right? I know that's what the dinner is about, but neither of them can kind of get up the courage to tell me. So we're eating dinner. We're talking about everything else. We go through the appetizer, the entrée, it's a nice dinner at a nice Italian restaurant, some place downtown. Finally we get to dessert and coffee, and we're having our coffee, and I go like, "Guys—what's going on with the 'Update' thing?" "It's Ohlmeyer, it's Ohlmeyer." And I go, "Well, okay." But I'm heartbroken, and now I know I'm leaving the show. It's this big blow to me. And then the check comes. And neither Lorne nor Jim has brought their credit cards. So I have to pay for the dinner. But I got reimbursed. It has a happy ending.

LORNE MICHAELS:

The writing was on the wall with Al when he didn't get "Update" and Norm Macdonald did. Which was a very tough decision. I think there was a feeling at that moment, from Ohlmeyer in particular, that Al was too associated with the show—the "old" show.

NORM MACDONALD:

Adam Sandler liked me and he told Jim Downey about me, and then Jim Downey said I could come on the show. I wanted to be a writer and performer. I wasn't a very good writer and I wasn't a very good performer, but I could be a writer-performer. And the one place I could do that was *SNL,* because Lorne was always good with letting writers perform if they were funny.

I always thought Chevy was the best guy at doing "Update." Most people were not good at it, you know. So I didn't think if I was bad I'd be singled out. Just basically Chevy and Dennis Miller were the only good ones, ever. So I wasn't worried about it.

JAMES DOWNEY:

Most of my friends liked the Norm "Update." They thought it was better than previous incarnations of "Update." They liked the way we did it — deadpan, just very straight, no frills, and the jokes were smart — and they would say it was the reason they watched the show or the best thing in the show. The prevailing attitude at the show and at the network was that "Update" was the problem of the show, and I know Lorne felt it was really hurting the show. He would never say it to me directly.

When we brought Norm in, Herb was still in charge of it, but because Norm was my protégé, I had for the first time a lot of influence, and then I brought other people in. So "Update" was suddenly being group-written again. A lot of writers would kick in things. We liked writing stuff for Norm, because he was great at handling words. He worked with us at editing things down so they could be as tight as possible.

JANEANE GAROFALO:

I certainly am a big fan of Jim Downey as a person. I really like Jim. But he was not in control when I was there, when he should have been. He should have been looking out for some of the cast's best interests too, and he wasn't. And he was not available for meetings. He is a great guy and an extremely funny guy and, as a person, I would hang out with Jim Downey anytime. But at that time, he was not there for the cast.

NORM MACDONALD:

Jim Downey is the best. He was producer the first year I did "Update," and then after that he got fired as producer and I got him just to do "Update," which was good for me because I got to work with him full-time and he was great. He was a brilliant guy. He was the funniest guy there and the smartest. He would work as sort of like a great editor. You know, he would take the jokes and figure out ways to sharpen them and improve them and, you know, narrow them and stuff like that. And he knew about politics, which I had no interest in at all. So he could think politically and stuff.

JAMES DOWNEY:

There'd be some giant hack joke that you knew would destroy but it would be an embarrassing thing to do, and I could always say to Norm, "This thing will kill, but you know it's tacky." And he would not do it. Or I would say, "This is brilliant, but there's not a chance it'll get a laugh from the audience" — and we would do those.

ADAM SANDLER:

Downey taught us our taste. I'm not sure if Jim would like that, all the bad reviews I get, but I think I'm doing stuff that Downey would like. But if Herlihy and I wrote a skit and we showed it to Downey and he smiled and then said, "What if the Canteen Boy says this," me and Herlihy would bump chests and go, "Yes! Downey gave us greatness!"

FRED WOLF:

After Chris Rock left the show, he came back like six or seven months later to visit. And my office, at that time, it was me, Norm Macdonald, Adam Sandler, and David Spade. And we were back there and Chris Rock came to visit all of us. And he said he's been out there in the world, doing some other shows, doing some other comedies, and doing some movies, and working with *In Living Color,* and all this sort of stuff. And he said that it's really great but the one thing that he has recognized is that there is no one like Jim Downey out there. And that was a sad thing.

DAVID MANDEL:

Some of the greatest jokes that were ever added to other writers' sketches at the table came from Jim Downey. So even in something he didn't necessarily write, I just — I can't explain it except to say he impacted everything that went through, and this is not to take anything away from the current people at *Saturday Night Live,* who I think are great. But I've sat through the way they rewrite, and they rewrite relatively quickly, and you just know they don't stay until five in the morning. And that's not a bad thing. I'm not sure it was great that we stayed until five in the morning. But Jim Downey added things to sketches that no other human being could, and I've seen Jim like dictate a sketch from his head as if—it must be like the way genius chess players see chess. It's almost as if he's reading from a script in his head that the rest of us can't see, and he's trying to read and dictate it.

I sat in a room with him once when John Malkovich hosted. We did a Menendez brothers sketch, if you can remember, where Rob Schneider and John Malkovich played the brothers, and their testimony was that there were two other Menendez brothers—their twin brothers—who were responsible for the killing and were waiting in the bathroom, and then they would get up and go get the other Menendez brothers and come in. They would switch sides and sit down and pretend to be two other Menendez brothers. They would then be asked where the first two Menendez brothers were and be told that they were in the bathroom.

And this kept going on until then one left and never came back. I sat in the room at like six in the morning with Jim lying on a couch and basically, a couple of us got a few jokes in, but this came fully formed out of Jim's head. And to this day I've never seen anything like that.

JAMES DOWNEY:

That summer I never heard from Lorne or anybody from the date of the last show in May of 1995. The phone never rang, which I thought was kind of insulting. Finally Dana called me and said, "I can't believe those fucking assholes haven't even talked to you." And he said, "Do you want to come to work for my show?" I said, "That's very nice of you." And then like five minutes later Mike Shoemaker called and then Lorne got on the phone and said, "Hey, you want to write for the show?" And that's when I said I would only do it if I could just do "Update."

In the same years that he was getting the most grief from network executives that he'd ever received in his career, Lorne Michaels also got an exquisitely flattering offer. Howard Stringer, the CBS president who had lured David Letterman to the network partly by buying Letterman the Ed Sullivan Theater, and the office building above it, offered to do the same for Michaels. A great admirer, Stringer thought Michaels could put CBS in the Saturday late-night business the way Letterman had put CBS in the late-weeknight business for the first time in its history. He had a mock-up photo made of the Lorne Michaels Theater to tempt him.

But Michaels, even though under siege—really a constant barrage—turned Stringer down. He still felt a loyalty, if not to NBC, then to the show he had created.

CHRIS ROCK:

Was being on the show the greatest creative experience for me? No. But it's still the biggest thing that ever happened to me in show business. The jump from broke to famous is the biggest jump. There's no bigger jump than that. I could win five Oscars tomorrow, it wouldn't be a bigger jump than *nothing* to *something*.

Is Lorne arrogant? Yeah—but hey, man, I know arrogant cab drivers. I know arrogant hot dog guys. This guy produces *Saturday Night Live*. He made *The Rutles,* one of my favorites. So, you know, there's arrogance with no reason to be, and there's arrogance with plenty of reason to be.

TIM MEADOWS:

Lorne wrote me a couple of cold openings. Lorne can still write, you know. I guess he prefers not to, but he can. I forgot that he can write. I didn't know that he was such a great writer. But then people mention names like Lily Tomlin and the Smothers Brothers, it's obvious that he knows what he's doing.

JULIA SWEENEY:

I think Lorne is a withholder of praise as a strategy and also because I think he personally feels uncomfortable with it. I remember him stopping me in the hallway and just saying, "I think you're wonderful." It's not like he didn't give me anything. It was more like an aura. It's like in the air. It makes me understand cults. Because you just wanted his approval more, and that was your number one thing. You wanted him to approve of you. And he created an atmosphere that worked with that.

LORNE MICHAELS:

My bet is that Johnny and Ed don't hang together so much now. I could be wrong. I used to say that you get only so many hours that you can be with someone in a lifetime, and you can kind of use it all up in a very intense four or five years or you can spread it over a lifetime. Friendship really needs distance and space. Not that we're overcrowding like rats. But the schedule is built so that after three shows in a row, when people are really getting on each other's nerves, there's a hiatus and you get some distance on it and you appreciate what a good place it is to work.

Early in the nineties, NBC West Coast president Don Ohlmeyer and other executives had begun taking a more aggressive interest in the show, concerned about ratings and giving Michaels lots of unsolicited advice on such matters as who was funny, who wasn't, who should be fired, and suggesting innumerable cosmetic changes. From the beginning, Michaels had resisted NBC's attempts to use the show as a promotional tool— balking, for example, when the network implored him to book Erik Estrada, the star of NBC's CHiPs, *as a host. Ohlmeyer, whom Ebersol had tried to hire to direct* Saturday Night Live *back in the formative days, thought superstars Adam Sandler and Chris Farley were among those who should go. He didn't "get" them and told Michaels they should be fired. NBC brass said the show had grown too costly and accused Michaels, in effect, of coasting. Ohlmeyer even said he thought Michaels spent too much time on the beach at St. Bart's, one of his repertory of longtime haunts, and not enough time streamlining the show. Michaels theorized that one reason for the executives' greater interest in the show was that they felt emboldened by the success they had with* Friends *in prime time; network executives gave themselves credit for putting that ensemble together and then wanted to take a stab at casting* Saturday Night Live *too. An executive with delusions of creativity, like a wounded pig, is a dangerous animal.*

The show suffered a run of bad luck and bad timing. Dana Carvey's departure at the end of the 1992–93 season had been particularly crucial because he took such a large collection of characters and impressions with him; he was a whole stock company himself. Phil Hartman left a year later and gave interviews in which he made nasty cracks about the quality of the show's writing, even though he'd thrived in sketch after sketch. Rather suddenly and concurrently, the press turned hostile, dredging up the old "Saturday Night Dead" slurs to say the show was stale and giving SNL *a relentless trouncing even when the cast was still stellar. Michaels experienced the worst reviews of his career and found some of the attacks distressingly and discouragingly personal. One reviewer wrote that the show had been "a lifeless, humorless corpse for two years, and now it's starting to stink." Others were similarly hostile, if not quite so inelegant: "*Saturday Night Live *is showing its age," "about as amusing as a state funeral," "the show needs a kick in the pants," "Nobody's laughing anymore. You watch it now and sullenly stare at the television."*

In addition to all that, there was dissent from within—crabby campers who joined the cast and almost immediately developed grievances and complaints. If Saturday Night Live *was in yet another transitional phase, these particular growing pains were agonizing, and the more injured the show looked, the more network honchos stepped up their attack, even to the point of leaking to reporters that nothing about* Saturday Night Live *was sacrosanct or untouchable—Lorne Michaels pointedly included. Michaels may have begun to look back fondly even at 1985, the low-rated year he returned as executive producer; it probably looked good compared to 1994, for him the worst year in the show's history.*

For the moment, the fashionable thing was to knock Saturday Night Live. *The sport became so popular that even certain members of the cast joined in.*

LORNE MICHAELS:

Phil Hartman was here eight years. After most shows, he and I would sit together at the party, and there was just a sort of comfort level between the two of us. We obviously loved each other. And when Phil left, the separation was a hard and difficult thing. And then he gave some interview bad-mouthing the next cast, and he didn't like Sandler or whatever, and then he went after me. And I went—Phil? But I think it's how people separate. You suddenly get out of bed and you go, "I didn't like this, I didn't like that." There isn't anyone here who week after week doesn't build their case on how unfairly they've been treated.

I think it's the most natural thing, because they don't have power over their own lives. They submit a piece, and once they've reached some level of fame, the whole world is telling them how good they are. But around here they're dealing with the fact that the writers didn't write anything for them that week, the fact that the writers got up in the morning thinking about themselves and not about them, the fact that the writers sometimes look as if they have more say about things than they do, and the fact that a piece they thought went very well in dress got cut. Just being one of eight or ten or whatever, is really hard after a while. For most of us in the beginning, and I think it's true to this day, their office is nicer than their apartment, and so just about everything in the way they live becomes an improvement once they get here. And then, I think, a lot of people come here and it's their first job, and then within weeks they have an agent, a manager, a publicist, a lawyer, a business manager, and it validates they're actually in show business, because they're talking to people about their career all the time. And after a while, there's not enough money to be made just being here. There's more money to be made by the people who influence them. My job is to hold it together. I hate giving up people, I just do. At the same time, whenever we've gone through big change it's always been kind of intoxicating, and it's kind of what makes the show. If I were still doing the show with the seventies group, I think we'd just all be fried.

AL FRANKEN:

I remember getting a call from someone at the *Philadelphia Inquirer*: "Why doesn't the show take chances?" And I said, "Why don't we take chances? I think we do." And she said, "I'm talking about risky stuff like, you know how *Letterman* does the monkey cam? Now that's risky." And I go, "Okay, that's not 'risky,' it's just a great idea. It's not a *risky* idea. You put a camera on a monkey's head and the monkey runs around the studio. It's great, but you don't know what the word 'risky' means, lady."

JAMES DOWNEY:

I do think the network stepped all over Leno, who they microman-aged to a crazy degree. They basically tried as much as they possibly could to make his show like *Saturday Night Live.* I remember at one point they asked us, "Do you guys have a problem if Phil Hartman is like Jay's sidekick? He can do Clinton or Gorbachev or something." And I remember going, "Actually, yeah, we do. He's in our cast, and if you've seen him three nights or even two nights, it just makes it that much less special."

I remember being mad. I always felt that performers who weren't stand-ups but the type who were very much dependent on writing really should run stuff by us, because they really are representing the show. The only reason Phil could walk on Leno as Bill Clinton without any explanation is that he did Clinton on *Saturday Night Live.* Once you're in that situation, if it's not well written or if it's offensive or stu-pid or otherwise problematic, it hurts us. It's the reason Disney doesn't let people dress up as Mickey Mouse and do car shows and stuff.

I think Lorne did say, "No, you can't do that." Lorne did object to that stuff, but they were very aggressive about it. They sort of looked to the show for ideas, like we were a chop shop or something. Like, "Hey, we saw you do that thing. That's good. Jay could do that." I guess they felt like, "We might need to borrow some things from you guys to really nail down Jay's emerging superiority."

ROBERT WRIGHT:

Quite frankly, the show is always in a period where people are say-ing, "Oh my God, what are we going to do? The cast is not going to be here next year or the year after, what are we going to do?" I've gone through at least three or four of those since I've been here. The worst one was when Don decided he was going to take a big position on the show. I didn't know about it in advance.

What happened is, those nonaggression pacts that Lorne had signed were wearing thin and Don was not willing to be a bystander on *SNL.* Don also didn't travel, so he wouldn't come to New York except under extreme circumstances, and he liked to see his produc-ers in person. He's a very across-the-table kind of guy. And Lorne wasn't out there that much and wasn't interested in having long sessions with Don about details of the show. And I think quite frankly, initially Don was less interested in the talent than he was about the fact that the show wasn't as profitable as he had thought it would be. He thought it could be fixed rather easily, that the show should be and could be a great deal more profitable for NBC. He'd been led to believe that by some of the finance people and some of the other production people on the West Coast. There's always a West Coast–East Coast angle on these sorts of things. He was sending sort of coded messages to Lorne about this, that, and the other thing, and Lorne was doing his own dance around those issues. It was either, "Didn't know that, I'll get on it," or "He's not available, he's gone to Hungary, won't be back for three months." And I think Don just made it a point of writing down every day, "I'm going to catch him on this, we're going to get this done."

WARREN LITTLEFIELD:

We felt that Lorne was isolating himself, and we were looking at a new generation of writer-producer talent that had come up with a show like *Seinfeld*. They hadn't been grown and nurtured in comedy camp. They hadn't worked on *Diff'rent Strokes* and then done *Seinfeld*. These were original voices. We would suggest names and people to Lorne. We didn't know how open he was. Our intent was not to take it away from Lorne. Our intent was to be able to say to Lorne, "Look, they're out there. Their lifelong dream would be to go to New York and work on *SNL*. Maybe you've got to start looking at some of these other kinds of people." Believe me, these were not prime-time situation comedy. They were alternative, unique voices who had put their toe in the water of television and hadn't found out quite what their outlet was.

I think Don was much more focused on, "There's so much wrong." And so those were very, very tough sessions with Lorne. Ultimately what emerged was what we wanted to emerge: Lorne engaged more actively, more time and more energy, a more aggressive pursuit of reinventing the show. I don't think Lorne surrendered control. I think he surrendered to a process that was painful. We were able to keep the show running and the market turned around, and it became a profitable entity again. It became an asset not only creatively but it also became a financial asset as well. Nothing wrong with that.

LORNE MICHAELS:

The network was on a certain level completely justified in saying we're cleaning house, because you couldn't read anywhere anybody saying, "*Saturday Night Live* is doing what it's supposed to be doing," or "These people are funny." We had to let Adam Sandler go with two years on his contract, and Farley with a year. Chris Rock had gone on to *In Living Color*. Spade was allowed to come back in a sort of "David Spade moment" kind of thing. But it was basically, you know, you pull away to turn this all around and just say, "Here we are with a brand-new cast." And Downey couldn't be producer, Downey couldn't be here, and even Herb Sargent was let go. It was just, everybody was let go.

ADAM SANDLER:

The guys at *SNL* protected me a lot. They didn't tell me much. I really didn't even know who Ohlmeyer was. I never met him, I don't think. I just felt if Lorne likes me and if Downey likes me, I'm safe. And then I heard at the end that Lorne was having to fight for me to be on the show. This is what Sandy, my manager, would tell me, that NBC wasn't happy with me. And I'd say, "What's Lorne think?" "Oh, Lorne's happy with you." And I said, "Okay, all right, then we're all set then, right?" And I think at the time Lorne was catching a little bit of flak from them, so he had to listen more than he had in the past.

See, I don't even know if I was fired. I don't know how it was handled. I just remember feeling like, "Did I quit, or did I get fired? I have no idea." But all of a sudden I wasn't on the show anymore. But I was friends with everyone at *Saturday Night Live* still. That's all that counted to me. I never had a tight relationship with NBC. The guys who were important to me were Lorne and Downey and Smigel, of course Herlihy—who is an amazing guy—and a couple of the other writers. It really was creatively the best time of my life. I'm honored to be a member of that bunch of alumni, and I have my best friends from that show. It does feel like we went to war together, even though it was a positive thing. Nobody was scared for their lives, but we stuck it out together, and every Saturday night people were tuning in to laugh, and we wanted to make sure that we got the job done. And we all have a nice bond together.

DON OHLMEYER, *NBC Executive:*

Well, I got into it very straightforward with Lorne. I mean, it's not really my job to talk to Jim Downey. Actually, we would meet twice a year, and like I said, I was very straightforward. I think people pretty much knew where they stood with me in terms of what I felt. I wasn't one of these kind of people that would glad-hand people and then talk behind their backs. I think Jim Downey is maybe as good a political satirist, writer, as there's ever been in television. I think when Jim was the head writer, there were some issues on the show. When you have the talent that was assembled during that period and the shows were as flat as they were, there's some issues somewhere. That was just my perception.

WARREN LITTLEFIELD:

There was one old writer—oh yeah, Jim Downey. Jim's brilliant. He had a wonderful, wonderful career. But Jim, I think some would say, was a little burnt out. He'd done it for a long time. And so finally for Ohlmeyer it became, "You know what? We will not accept anything less than excellence."

JAMES DOWNEY:

I've only met Ohlmeyer three times. He'd been just relentlessly trying to get me fired for like nine months before he ever laid eyes on me. He had this theory that the problem was the show was flat—because we'd come off this gigantic ratings year, '92–'93, which had to do with "Wayne's World." I thought, and most of the writers there thought, the show was clearly in decline. There was like a three-year lag between the ratings we got and the ratings we deserved. We thought it was more '89–'90 that the show was creatively better and that by 1993 we were sort of coasting. We averaged like a 9.5 rating with the "Wayne's World" heat. We haven't seen that in many, many years.

My marriage was falling apart because I was spending way too much time at the show. I remember thinking it's not worth it to do anything embarrassing to keep this job. So I'm not going out of my way to antagonize them, but I'm not going to kiss their ass. Because I could come home and say, "Honey, I was fired." But I could not come home and say, "Honey, I quit. Aren't you proud of me? Now I have to find a new job." So that was the idea.

NORM MACDONALD:

I think Lorne even conceded that changes needed to be made and decided to overhaul. But I think also that nobody liked Jim at the network at that time. He's not a very savvy office politician when it comes to talking to people or anything. He's more like an artist guy who wants to be left alone. He's really into comedy, so he's not that good with the suits.

JAMES DOWNEY:

With the arrival of Ohlmeyer and then NBC doing so well, the basic personality of the network became more aggressive and confident and notey. They were feeling their oats. They used to talk about *Friends* and often contrast *Friends* to *Seinfeld* by saying, "We cast *Friends,*" the implication being that's why the people were more attractive. So they were very confident. It used to be that they would not offer anything except, "My God, you guys are great and we're not here to tell you your job," and then it became, "Just for what it's worth, we loved that, just great," and then it became, "I don't know that this works," and it finally reached a point where it became, "We don't care that it's popular, we don't want you doing this because we don't like it." That's not even a business value. They were so at peace with their own taste and worldview that they were willing to take an economic hit just to have something enacted. That reached its peak I would say in the '94–'95 period.

One of the network's ideas that they were very serious about was, why does it have to be live? And why do you need a guest host, when it's the cast that brings the people back each week? And they bitched about how the live element made it much more expensive and complicated, and how you could go shoot all your *Jeopardy!* sketches in one afternoon.

LORNE MICHAELS:

When it all hit, my son Eddie had just been born and there were some complications. It turned out to be nothing but there was a day and a half or two days of concern. Alice gave birth to him at twelve-thirty, I think, in the afternoon and I still managed to make read-through back at 30 Rock. We had made elaborate preparations in case I couldn't be there—altering the chain of command and all that stuff. But I got back to the office, and it was the week Sarah Jessica Parker hosted, and it was just around the time that we were just being hounded everywhere.

I don't think I'd ever been as scared. You know, I was never scared in the seventies. I think because I was single then, I had already been through rough periods in my life and there was nothing really that was going to scare me—I mean, so what would happen? I would be broke and washed up, and I'd already had that a couple of times.

DON OHLMEYER:

Lorne and I used to have long involved conversations, almost psychoanalytical, about the problems. Sometimes identifying the problems is the most difficult thing. It's very subjective. I would certainly never presume that I know more about doing *Saturday Night Live* than Lorne. I can watch the show and react as a viewer, or I can watch the show and react as somebody who is running the operation and has a vested interest in the success of the show. I can look at the numbers. I can do all these different things. But if you're not there on a day-to-day basis, you don't really know what the problem is.

Lorne knew that there was a problem, but I think he was unsure of exactly what the problem was. Objectively Lorne knew the show could be better. You had to look at what are the strengths and weaknesses of the cast, even though they're very talented. Do we need some fresh blood? Do we need a fresh approach in the writing?

"Ultimatum" is a difficult word. No, I never gave Lorne an ultimatum. But what I basically said to him is, "The show has to get better."

6

Still Crazy After All These Years: 1995–2002

It had been something of a Saturday Night *massacre. Lorne Michaels was forced to fire Adam Sandler and Chris Farley (he was ordered to fire Tim Meadows too, but managed to stay that execution). Veteran Jim Downey was ousted as head writer, Mike Myers had gone to Hollywood to make movies and money.* Saturday Night Live *probably had nowhere to go but up, back up, rebounding as it had done so many times before. It didn't hurt that the likes of Will Ferrell, Cheri Oteri, Darrell Hammond, Chris Kattan, Jimmy Fallon, Ana Gasteyer, Tracy Morgan, Molly Shannon, Horatio Sanz, and Tina Fey were waiting in the wings.*

ALEC BALDWIN, *Host:*

Some of the cast members and writers leave the show and do things that are elevated compared to what they're asked to do on the show, but many of them—this is a terrible thing to say—leave there and become the very thing they made fun of on the show.

One of the oddest elements of the show is that you're standing next to some guy one day doing the show and you think that they're funny, but you turn around and five years later they're getting paid $20 million a movie. There are people I worked with there who I never thought in my wildest dreams that they'd go on to become the apotheosis of movie comedy of their day. So now I'm nice to everybody on the show. No matter who I work with, no matter what a sniveling, drooling wuss they are, I embrace them all like they're my dearest friend and my most respected colleague.

ROBERT WRIGHT, *NBC Chairman and CEO:*

I haven't made that many trips to the seventeenth floor. As a matter of fact, my one official trip to the seventeenth floor—I don't remember the date—was when we had gone through a painful period of recasting, and it was the only time that I was really involved in it. Lorne was really being very good to me. He was humoring me along all the way. He was sending me audition tapes. I was getting really nervous that we were going to do something dumb, that there was so much pressure on Lorne that he would do something that he didn't want to do because he thought the company wanted him to do it.

I was saying to myself, "I've seen this show probably more than anybody at NBC has. I know what's funny on this show and what isn't funny." I really felt that way. So he was sending me tapes that summer, and then when the cast was picked, and I was in complete agreement with the people he'd picked, I marched up to the seventeenth floor, maybe it was just before the season began or just after, and I remember the cast then was Chris Farley, Will Ferrell, Molly Shannon, Chris Kattan just arrived, and Ana and Cheri. I had seen all their tapes, so you kind of feel like you know these people. They didn't know me, but I'd seen their tapes.

So I go up there and I'm very friendly and everything. "Hi, how you doing?" And—oop! They were standing there—Lorne had them all lined up, it was like a wedding, but there were no other people at the wedding except us and Lorne. And they were just like— umphf! "Hi!" "Umphf!" All of a sudden it wasn't cozy at all. And Lorne would say, "No, you can talk! You can talk to him!" And to me, "You can talk to them." So it took a while. We were there about fifteen minutes and I said, "Well, why don't you just tell me how you feel about being on the show?" And Lorne is going, "Tell him what you really think, go ahead, you can say things." I said to Lorne afterward, "I don't think this is really a good idea, Lorne." He said, "I don't know why they did that. They're very comfortable and everything. They're very happy."

LORNE MICHAELS, *Executive Producer:*

I can be pretty savage about people here in terms of what I think their flaws are. I can get abusive. I don't think that what I do between dress and air is terribly nurturing. It's more military, like a drill. My notes tend to be to the point. I think there's a real toughness with people who are funny in the way they've developed their own armor, but some of the people here are made of glass. They can be just very insensitive to other people and at the same time if you pointed out the same thing to them, most of them would be surprised or hurt.

It takes me a long time to understand why I don't like people. I think it's a problem I haven't solved. The idea that people are dumb or not interested always comes as a surprise to me. I always thought I could talk to just about anybody and make myself understood. And when you realize that isn't the case, that either they don't get it or have no interest in it, it takes me a long time to figure that out. Because I go, "Why would you be here? Why would you pick this place to want to work?"

STEVE HIGGINS, *Producer:*

We hear that "it isn't as good as it used to be" thing constantly. I think it probably started on show two in 1975. It's a matter of time before we're going to read "Saturday Night Dead" in the papers again.

A funny thing happened when I got here—Lorne mapped the whole thing out. He told me, "Here's what's going to happen: Ohlmeyer's going to be gone—he's giving us grief now, but he's going to be gone—and somebody else will come in, and by that time the show will be at its height again, but then two years later it'll come down again because the avalanche will start. You'll see 'Saturday Night Dead,' we'll see that for a while, and then it'll be, 'The show is funnier than it's ever been,' and then it'll be, 'The show is worse than it's ever been.'"

And it's worked out exactly like that. And you go, okay, if you're caught up in this historical cycle, you just try to stave off that "the show's not as funny" crap. And the thing is, you wouldn't go to a carpenter's house and go, "Wow, what a crappy job you did on your shelves." Or say to a doctor, "How many patients have you killed?" But people feel free to comment in ways that make you go, "Where do you think you get the nerve?" I think they think they own the show.

You know what? If you like everything in the show, then that's not a good show. If you love every single thing, there's something wrong. It's like pushing the envelope, which is a horrible term, but it's about making that tent big enough so that everybody's included, so that there's something for everybody in the show. You should like *most* of it. But there might be some performance piece that you go, "I just don't get that," and it killed and the audience loves it and you go, "I guess that worked." And that's one thing that Lorne is good at. He'll put enough in that there's always some plus side to it.

JAMES DOWNEY, *Writer:*

Certainly the people at the network did not like the show at all in 1993, 1994, those seasons. When the new group came together in 1995, taking myself out of it, I think that, as much as innocent people were implicitly scapegoated, it was probably necessary that the word be out everywhere that, "No no no, they cleaned house. All the dead-wood's gone. They have a whole new cast. It's all new."

Starting around '95, *Saturday Night Live* became very much a performer's show. There were new innovations limiting what writers could do. Writers had to write one piece for a character and then they could write a premise piece. It was enforcing the idea that "the cast isn't here to bring to life the writers' notions; the writers are there to supply material for the characters that the cast already does." That was a big shift.

That's the biggest way the show has changed: It's come way back to the idea of being a performers' show that features characters. You see the same characters a lot. Writers are the people who never want to repeat stuff. If you're in a writers meeting and your quote-unquote idea for the week is, "I think we can do another Mango," you would be groaned out of the room, whereas performers like repeating stuff and they don't tend to hear, "Why do you guys keep doing Cheerleaders?" When they walk down the street, they get recognized as being on the show, and by and large the people who come up to them don't come up to them to give them shit, they come up to say, "Hey, we love the show."

If someone ran an analysis of the show, I would bet if you take everything in the history of the show that's even been on three times and then from that master list figure out, of the repeat characters, which have racked up the most appearances on the show, I would be willing to bet that of the top ten, seven of them would be from this last period. Things like Mango, Cheerleaders, and so on, whereas in the entire history of the show, there were only four Czech brothers pieces. There were only, I think, seven Conehead sketches. But I promise you there were fifteen Cheerleaders. There had to be. If you said there were eighteen, it wouldn't surprise me.

PAULA PELL, *Writer:*

I got there in '95. That was the year that a huge amount of people didn't come back from the year before, and Lorne kind of cleaned house of everything and started anew. So it was really great because we all came in together. We also didn't have any idea how to do the show. None of us had worked on the show before, and since it's such a different beast than anything else, we all had that attitude that "We're just going to try everything," and it was pretty great. It almost felt like going away to college. Everyone was in all these little dorm rooms. In the hall everyone was getting to know each other. We went out all the time. We were all fairly young. Not many people were married or had kids yet. It was sort of one of those times when everyone was on the same wavelength. Creatively it's hard to come in and figure out what it all is. We were just going forward. We were like, "Screw it," and, "Let's just try." We were all energized, because everyone was thrilled to have this job.

We had one meeting with Lorne where he talked about, "We're going to bring it up again and get it going again." I was aware just as a viewer that they were coming off a bad year. I knew when I first came and met Lorne, before I got hired, he talked about the fact that the show has an arc to it and that it would come back up, a Phoenix rising many times, and this was one of those times we were hoping to bring it back up. It just seemed to have a lot of fatigue and no one was really clicking along together anymore in a creative way. So it seemed like it had a sort of natural death. And his attitude at the time was like, "I've seen it happen before, and I think this is a great new cast and new writers, and I think we can do it again." It was pretty slow at first, and I remember the press at first, there'd be an article that says, "*Saturday*

Night Live is great again," and then the next week it would be, "Oh, I spoke too soon."

Friction between Saturday Night Live *and network executives continued into the second half of the 1990s. Although Jim Downey was held in awe by his peers and Norm Macdonald was Chevy Chase's favorite among all those who succeeded him in the "Update" anchor chair, the team became the target of an essentially one-man crusade. NBC West Coast president Don Ohlmeyer had earlier declared war on Downey as program producer and got him thrown out early in 1995. Downey resurfaced thanks to artful maneuvering by Lorne Michaels, his duties limited mainly to the "Update" segment. That was fine with him but not with Ohlmeyer, who wanted him out of there too. By the 1997–98 season, Ohlmeyer was even more adamant about getting rid of Macdonald—it had turned into a veritable fixation.*

Ironically, Macdonald had originally taken over "Update" with Ohlmeyer's implicit blessing; he'd been adamant at that time that the position not be given to an SNL *veteran who had long wanted it (and was an old pro at ruffling peacock feathers), Al Franken. That had all been private, but now Ohlmeyer's interventions were loud and public. In the entire tumultuous history of the show, it had probably never been the focus of a more explicit conflict between the business and creative sides of the network. Nor had there been a more concentrated assault on the independence and integrity of Lorne Michaels.*

Insiders and outsiders alike, meanwhile, saw it as something other than a coincidence that the Downey-Macdonald "Updates" were mirthfully merciless on the topic of O. J. Simpson, that well-known unconvicted murderer-about-town, who'd hosted the show in its third season and, more significantly, was a longtime golf-playing crony of none other than Don Ohlmeyer.

JAMES DOWNEY:

I don't think anyone needed to tell me particularly—I mean, Lorne had been telling me for two years now—how unhappy Don Ohlmeyer was with me. Ohlmeyer was practically putting out memos saying, "Do not ask or accept advice from this clown." Lorne was probably put in a weird bind when I was doing "Update" with Norm Macdonald, because I know he didn't like that approach to "Update." He thought it was too mean and cold and nasty. So he would have been in a strange position on principle, wanting to fight and run interference for us even though he actually didn't like it that much more than the network did. I think I'm right about this just from knowing him.

NORM MACDONALD, *Cast Member:*

Me and Jim were kind of like alone at *SNL,* you know, especially when the new bunch came in. In many ways they resented Jim, because he was much smarter and funnier than them. And he was like the old crew, you know what I mean? When he went over to "Update," I think they would have been happier to have him gone. After Jim got fired as a producer, I think it shocked the new establishment there that I wanted him to come to do "Update" with me. It was weird for everybody.

Jim liked just doing "Update," because we figured it wasn't that important to the show, you know, and we could just do whatever and they'd leave us alone. I didn't even want to go to dress rehearsal, because I didn't care about the audience reaction at all. It would have been fine with me if we'd never rehearsed it and I could just do the jokes that *I* thought were funny, because I have more faith in me and Jim than I did in any audience. I just like doing jokes I like, and if the audience doesn't like them, then they're wrong, not me.

DON OHLMEYER, *NBC Executive:*

That was part of the problem. Not *part* of the problem; that was the whole problem. I think what you have there, in Norm's statement, is the quintessential issue. When *Saturday Night Live* is really good, they do care what the audience thinks. And when *Saturday Night Live* is not really good, they're kind of doing it for themselves and their pals. That was what I felt was the weakness of "Weekend Update" at that time, which was that they were doing it for themselves. There were a lot of inside references. There were times when you would go an entire "Update" with nothing more than a titter. You can pull out the tapes. I've looked at them—ten times. And looked at them and looked at them and looked at them, because I wanted to make sure I wasn't being an asshole in this.

CHEVY CHASE, *Cast Member:*

Norm said he didn't care if the audience laughed? What's shocking about that? That's sort of the way I felt—that as long as six guys on a couch behind that camera that I was looking into laughed, and I knew those guys, then I was there.

One has to do that, you know, and one has to figure what's going to work and what isn't. Of all the other "Update" guys, the one who was the funniest to me was Norm. Because he just came out and said it. Perhaps that's the writing—Jim Downey and those guys' writing. But it's also Norm's quality of "I don't care." You can take that too far in your life as an entertainer-performer and maybe it would affect—in a negative way—other things that you do. I'm just suggesting that that's a quality that lends itself to being successful, as an "Update" guy and as an actor on *Saturday Night Live,* which is not caring whether people say you're good or not, only that you have your integrity, and that you think it's good.

NORM MACDONALD:

I said "fuck" one time during "Update." Something got caught in my throat and I went, "What the fuck was that?" If I hadn't brought attention to it, I don't think anybody would have even heard it. I pointed it out, because I couldn't believe I said it—although I'm usually shocked that I didn't say it, you know what I mean? It takes a lot of discipline not to say, "fuck." In sketches you've got to say what's on the cards, but in "Update" I would do the joke and then say whatever I wanted afterwards. So when you're just talking like that, you can easily say, "fuck." I like to say it a lot in real life. Anyway, Ohlmeyer said it was cool. He was good about it. He said he knew I didn't do it on purpose. Ohlmeyer should have fired me then, but he was cool.

As for Lorne, he left us alone for the most part. That's what I liked about Lorne. Sometimes he would say, "You don't want to do a joke like that, because you want to avoid a lawsuit," you know? He'd always say, "You don't want to be sued." But he'd let us do the jokes, sometimes even about his friends. He has friends that are super famous and stuff. He was cool about that. I probably wouldn't let people do jokes about friends of mine.

We wanted "Update" to be good, but we didn't think that we had to pander. If the rest of the show was pandering, then we thought we wouldn't have to. So then I started getting the sense that they were unhappy. These people don't come up and talk to you, you just get it third-hand and stuff like that. Ohlmeyer and his crew thought every joke in "Update" should kill, and the audience should be clapping and cheering and stuff. They thought Jay Leno did that every night with his monologues, so why couldn't we do it one night for five minutes, where it would just be wall-to-wall laughter and applause?

My response was, I hate applause. I don't like an audience applauding because to me that's like a cheap kind of high. They kind of control you. They're like, "Yeah, we agree." That's all they're doing, saying they agree with your viewpoint. And while you can applaud voluntarily, you can't laugh voluntarily—you have to laugh involuntarily—so I hate when an audience applauds. I don't want to say things that an audience will agree with, I don't want to say anything that an audience already thinks. And so the thing with "Update" was not to do these same jokes where you said that, you know, Pat Buchanan was a Nazi or some ridiculous thing that wasn't true but that everyone would applaud because they'd already heard it somewhere else. "Update" was never a big pep rally when I was there. It was never a big party. So I think the network started going, "It doesn't seem like as much fun as it should be."

DON OHLMEYER:

What you had then was, you had people tuning out during "Update." And that had never happened before. You never had dropout during "Update."

WARREN LITTLEFIELD, *NBC Executive:*

I think Don wanted to exert control over Lorne in ways that Lorne didn't want to be controlled. It was a battle of wills and egos. I think Norm Macdonald, ultimately, was a symbol. Don just didn't get it. He didn't get Norm Macdonald. Ohlmeyer could be the eight-hundred-

pound gorilla. We said, "You know what? You've got to ask your kid."
We'd sit in a meeting and go, "Don, we disagree. It was funny. It
wasn't a perfect ninety minutes, but it was funny." I don't know;
maybe he was watching it alone at eleven-thirty. It was also before
Don was in rehab.

LORNE MICHAELS:

I remember one night Don and I were having dinner at Morton's
in L.A.—by the bar, where he can smoke—and he would have his
cheeseburger and his glass of milk and his four packs of Marlboros. I
sat there playing with my swordfish thinking, "If he outlives me and it
turns out to be just about gene pool, I'm going to be furious about it."

FRED WOLF, *Writer:*

Ohlmeyer was completely out of line. Norm Macdonald is one of the
funniest guys I ever met, and Jim Downey is the funniest writer I've ever
met. And so if those two guys get together and they put together
"Update," then I have faith that "Update" is a really funny thing coming
from those two guys. I've been on a lot of shows that have been sort of
faltering or whatever. The network decides to step in and alter the original, creative vision and sort of dabble with it—and it's never worked.
I've never seen them improve ratings on any show once they step in.

JAMES DOWNEY:

And the thing that used to drive the network crazy was, why does
he just stare into the camera for a minute after the joke? And we did it
as often as necessary for the audience to get the joke. And there'd
often be a delayed reaction, because some things weren't right there
on the surface.

NORM MACDONALD:

Sometimes I would have to be in something. For a while I had to
do Bob Dole, so I'd fucking have to put on some fucking mask and go
do it, so that would get in the way. All I really cared about was
"Update." But that fucking Bob Dole, man, I wrote a couple of
sketches that I thought were funny for Bob Dole to do, and then all of

a sudden he's the candidate and then I have to appear in people's fucking sketches every week on some lame premise.

One thing I started hearing toward the end was, "You've got to fire Jim." You know, it was almost as if, "You fire Jim and everything will be cool and you can keep going with 'Update.'" I had no interest in anything but "Update."

ANDY BRECKMAN, *Writer:*

I was in the studio the week after O.J. was acquitted and there was this tension in the country because the country was divided and it was this weird sort of thing. It was almost something that was hard to think about, especially in mixed company. You didn't know where people were coming from. And the cold opening that week on *SNL*—you might remember the sketch, I don't know who wrote it and it wasn't even, on paper, that funny of a sketch, and in read-through it didn't kill—but the sketch was this: Tim Meadows as O.J. is back at his old job calling the games at ABC's *Monday Night Football*. And the first joke of the sketch was O.J. on the field doing commentary about a play, and he's doing the thing that Madden does where he writes on the screen and he's joining the marks together—and eventually they spell out "I Did It."

And that was the first joke of the sketch. When he wrote that out, I was in 8H, and the place exploded like—I've never heard a reaction in my life like that, ever. It exploded, but it wasn't just laughter, it was almost a release—like, of course he did it, you know? And thank God somebody said it out loud. And there was applause and laughter. There is no place else that could have done that. Letterman and Leno danced around it, and they were very coy about it, but there was nothing, nothing that came close. And Downey, bless his heart, he was relentless, even after the acquittal, about O.J.

DON OHLMEYER:

My only concern was what I thought was best for the show. I might be wrong or full of shit, but it wasn't like I had some political agenda. The O. J. Simpson thing was over by this time. I put everybody at NBC in a very awkward situation, you know. I was brought up that you don't desert somebody who's been a friend for twenty-seven years because he's at the worst point in his life. My decision to be supportive of O.J. as a person caused a tremendous amount of grief to people at NBC, to my family, to my kids. I did it because I wasn't going to desert somebody who had been my friend for twenty-seven years. But when the whole situation with O.J. started, I called Lorne, I called Jay Leno, and I called Conan. And I said, "Look, this is awkward, but I'm telling you if you in any way lay off this situation out of some concern for what I might think—forget about my feelings, just what I might *think*—you're crazy. You have a job to do. It's the biggest story in the country right now. And you have to deal with it the way you think is best." That was the difficult part of the Norm situation, because it resurrected all the O.J. stuff again. You know, life isn't fair, but that to me was like, what does *this* have to do with *that?*

ROBERT WRIGHT:

Anything about O.J. had an incendiary effect on Don, but Don is a very easy guy to misread. He's so blunt, but you can't necessarily read into the bluntness that he's unfair. I know it sounds contradictory. He can say something that appears to be completely arbitrary, but his actions generally were almost never completely arbitrary.

It would be very easy and consistent to conclude that because Norm said some things about O.J. which were inflammatory to Don that that would be a great reason to get him off the show. But I never found a lot of evidence of that in anything else. He could get very angry about people who were anti-O.J., but doing anything about it from a business standpoint was never part of the agenda. We'll never know the answer to that one. He didn't think Norm was funny. And he probably didn't think the O.J. stuff was. It was like the world against God on O.J. The enemies list was a long list.

WARREN LITTLEFIELD:

Don knew if he ever so much as looked cross-eyed at a television set with anybody from NBC around when Jay was doing an O.J. joke, there would be a problem. Don would stay far away from any comment ever about O.J. He never took it out on Jay, and nobody got more out of O. J. Simpson than Jay Leno did. Don separated himself from saying anything to Jay but, "You're wonderful, you're great."

NORM MACDONALD:

I was in L.A. over Christmas. It was the Christmas that Chris Farley died. I think it was right after Christmas. And they told me that Chris had died and then like three hours later, they told me about "Update," but by that point who cared about "Update"? Because Chris had just died.

Somebody told me Ohlmeyer had said, "I want two things: I want Macdonald fired and I want a 'Best of Chris Farley' ready to go." So then we went to the funeral in Wisconsin. That was really sad. They said, "Ohlmeyer wants you out." I still didn't think it would happen in the middle of the season. And no one would come right out and say it. The first week back from Christmas, no one would come right out and tell me what was going on. Lorne has a hard time telling you bad stuff. I had to do "Update" that Saturday, so I'm like, "Am I doing it or not?" And they're like, "Uh, we don't think you are." So I said, "Somebody's got to tell me I'm fired," but nobody wanted to do it, so they said, "You can phone Ohlmeyer." So I had to phone Ohlmeyer myself. And Ohlmeyer was kind of surprised that I was calling him. He just thought it would be taken care of.

It was kind of weird, you know. I just said, "Well, ha ha ha." He was just kind of good cheer, you know. He said, "Oh, change has got to be made, you understand." And I go, "Well, what's the problem?" And he goes, "It's just not as funny as it should be," and so then I'm like, "You don't think I'm funny?" I said, "People around here are saying it's all you, that they all want me and it's just you that doesn't want me." And then he was kind of surprised. He goes, "Is that what they're saying? They want me to be the bad guy."

DON OHLMEYER:

Lorne's point at the time was, just let it go for the rest of the season and we'll make a change in the summer. And he probably was right. Sometimes I get too wrapped up in something—something that needs to be fixed and it won't be fixed unless we address it. But the Norm thing had been an issue for me for over a year.

*   *   *

The Ohlmeyer era proved to be one of the most difficult periods for Michaels. Everyone knew Ohlmeyer had complaints about the cast, particularly Norm Macdonald and writer Jim Downey. At one point, Michaels, hoping to protect Macdonald and buy time, tried to placate Ohlmeyer with the promise, "If you feel this way at the end of the season, I will make a change."

But as November became December, Ohlmeyer grew increasingly angry and frustrated, calling on Michaels to set up a dinner meeting in Aspen, where both men would be spending the Christmas break.

Then, a week before Christmas, Michaels received word that Chris Farley had died. The funeral would be held in Madison, Wisconsin, Farley's hometown, on the very night Michaels was scheduled to have dinner with Ohlmeyer. Michaels flew to Madison, along with cast member Tim Meadows, attended the funeral, spent time with Farley's family and friends, and flew back to Aspen in time to keep the appointment with Ohlmeyer.

Although Michaels knew the dinner would be difficult, he also thought, perhaps naively, that since he had just buried a young man he truly loved—one whose death had been, unfortunately, drug-related—and had gone through a painful ordeal with Farley's aggrieved family, maybe Ohlmeyer would tread lightly and not be fulminating at full force.

But Ohlmeyer seemed unfazed by the circumstances and in no mood to relent. He looked at Michaels and declared, "Norm's got to go." That's why the firing happened when it did, in the middle of the season. Some believed that if Michaels hadn't been so emotionally drained by Farley's death, he might have been better able to put up a fight and save Macdonald. But it was not to be.

NORM MACDONALD:

I was never bitter. I always understood that Ohlmeyer could fire me, because he was the guy that owned the cameras, so that didn't bother me. Ohlmeyer seemed honest to me about it, you know, straightforward. I was always happy that *SNL* gave me a chance. Other comics, when they were young, wanted to be on Johnny Carson. To me it was like that, you get to be on *Saturday Night Live,* it's a dream come true, and then everything after that is not going to be as good. To me, just getting there was the thing.

WARREN LITTLEFIELD:

Of course myself and others said to Don, "Why are you doing this? What is the agenda? We finish out the year and make the change." I think Don felt he had to send a message, and there are times where Don just felt he had to exert executive power because he could. That public firing was probably the greatest perception ever that it wasn't Lorne's call. That was probably the toughest thing Lorne ever had to endure. Really unfortunate.

NORM MACDONALD:

So then I thought it would be funny to go on *Letterman* and talk about it, because I knew that Letterman had been fired from NBC and stuff like that. I got fired on a Monday, so I called up the people at *Letterman* and said, "Hey, you should have me on, because I got fired. It would be funny if I just said on the show that I got fired, you know?" And so they booked me and I went on. I told Lorne that I'd already been booked on *Letterman* and could I still do it, and maybe I shouldn't do it, and he said, "Go ahead, do it." I didn't tell him that I had done it on purpose.

And I remember Letterman during a break goes, "This is like some Andy Kaufman thing with fake wrestling, right?" And I go, "No, no. It's serious." Like he thought it was just a gag. Then the next day there was like some big reaction at *SNL*. All of a sudden people didn't want me to get fired, because they saw it as some sort of a big network president against the little guy. So then they pretended like they liked me the whole time. Lorne was trying to figure out what to do, because he didn't want it to look like he'd lost control of the show or the network was making decisions for him.

After that, I just tried to get off the show. Ohlmeyer wouldn't let me off; he just wanted me not to do "Update" and do like sketches or whatever. I didn't want to do sketches. So everybody's kind of embarrassed about the whole situation; they just want you gone. But Lorne had always told me, "In the show, you have to have an exit strategy." Which is a way to leave the show in exactly the right way to move on in show business. So I guess after I got fired, my idea was to have an exit strategy—to get out of there without just slinking away after getting fired. And that worked to some extent, in the sense that it gave me a little bit of publicity, which is sort of currency in show business.

TIM HERLIHY, *Writer:*

I'm very good friends with Norm and very good friends with Colin Quinn, so it was tough making that "Update" transition. It was like right around the time Chris Farley died, that first week that we were trying to put together "Weekend Update" with Colin, wondering whether Norm was going to show up or whether it was all going to reverse. We kind of had to plow into it, and put together a whole new set and a whole new everything and try and get Colin ready.

"They're going to fire Norm, they're going to fire Norm"—and, you know, this had been going on for weeks and weeks. And all of a sudden they fired Norm. We just kind of couldn't believe it. There was a real sense of disbelief, and there was a sense that this was just the latest chess move in something that was going to go on for a long, long time.

COLIN QUINN, *Cast Member:*

There was no inkling. Maybe some people knew and we just didn't realize it. But there was no inkling. And I think at that point I was well enough known in the show where I probably would have heard if there was some big rumor flying. I mean, sure, a couple of people knew. But there was no inkling. And Norm had been so good about letting me do pieces on "Update." Not only were me and Norm tight when shooting pool, I lived in the same building as Norm. So it's like, here he is, ten floors below, and I'm hearing this shit.

What happened was, they called me and told me about Norm just because we knew each other. So it's like, "Oh my God!" But here's how I felt: I felt horrible that it wasn't going to be Norm, but—and I even said it to Lorne when I met Lorne after that—if it's not Norm, I'm not going to stand here and say I don't want it. Because I don't want some other guy from outside who I don't think is fucking funny to take the job just because I was being respectful of Norm. And I think Norm felt the same way.

Norm was such an ally of mine, getting all my "Update" features on, that in a way, he had a lot to do with the fact that I would be the guy to take over for him. "Huge whore"—he would say that a lot. And in that Canadian accent of his, it's perfect. Yeah, he's a funny fucking bastard. "Huge whore." You know, if there's one criticism of him, it is that he should have used that on more people.

In retrospect, I could imagine how people would be like, "Quinn's not ready for 'Update.'" But part of being a comedian is the delusion that you should be onstage at all times. Comedians could watch like Robin Williams and Chris Rock go on and the whole audience go crazy, and the whole time I know what they're thinking—even the youngest new guys: "I should come to work this crowd. I'm telling you, I could kill right now." That's how comedians think. I see the young guys looking at me like, "Move over. You had a nice run. Beat it!"

LORNE MICHAELS:

Don's not stupid. Don's not even "evil." But Don is like the greatest high school football coach ever. He'll beat you to within an inch of your life, and he'll force you to do things—but he won't abandon you. I don't think Conan O'Brien would have stayed on the air if not for Don Ohlmeyer.

Colin Quinn's reign as "Update" anchor was relatively short-lived. When the show returned for a new season in the fall of 2000, head writer Tina Fey and cast member Jimmy Fallon took over "Update" and made it a showpiece again. It was no longer a parody of a newscast; now it was just a sexy pair of smart alecks sitting around and making fun of the world. One critic, leveling presumably the ultimate compliment, said that when at their most "ruthless," Fey and Fallon "summon up the finest spirit of Belushi—the anarchic, savage Belushi, the one we all want to remember most fondly in our dreams." Of course, Belushi was never an "Update" anchor, though he did appear occasionally with one of his commentaries, pieces that started out on a calm and reasoned note and rapidly degenerated into hilarious tirades—ending with Belushi twirling himself off his chair and vanishing behind the "Update" desk.

RALPH NADER, *Host:*

In general, on the weekly news "Update" they bat about .275. More than one of four is really good. But there is some redeeming value to it. When the realistic freedom of dialogue and public discourse is restricted in any society, the quality of satire increases. That's why the best satire in the world in the latter half of the twentieth century was in the Soviet Union, like *Krokodil* magazine. Our satire couldn't come close to the satire in the Soviet bloc countries, because it was the only way they could get anything across.

We're moving into that arena now, only it isn't the government that's doing it. It's the censorship of the monetized moguls who run the communications industry and the television-radio industry. I think over time, there've been a lot of stupid and gross things on *Saturday Night Live,* but it does get across some current events with its skits and its "Weekend Update." That is just a reflection of the decay of our culture. When the culture decays and the communications media decay, then something as weak as a .275 hitter on *Saturday Night Live* shines.

TINA FEY, *Cast Member:*

I came here as a writer. I didn't expect to be on-camera, but I had been performing at Second City doing eight shows a week and I was auditioning for other stuff outside as an actor. I never booked commercials and I never got two lines on *Early Edition*—nothing. So I was kind of at a crossroads and thought, "Well, maybe I should just be a writer." I applied for this job as a writer and kind of left it open that if I got the job, that would sort of decide for me what I was going to do for the next stretch of time. After a year or two, I did start to miss performing, so I did a two-woman show with Rachel Dratch in Chicago one summer, and then we did it in New York all of last summer, and also I improvised all the time with the Upright Citizens Brigade down on Twenty-second Street. So we did our show, and I think Lorne came and saw the show last summer. Colin had said he was leaving early in the summer, and then Lorne came and saw the show, and it was Lorne's idea for me and Jimmy to test together to do "Update."

JIMMY FALLON, *Cast Member:*

Originally I didn't even want to do "Update." Honestly, when they asked me if I wanted to do it, I had no idea about the news or anything. I don't read. I read *USA Today;* that's the only thing I read, because it's got colored pictures and stuff. Now I find out the news through setups we do for jokes.

I said "Update" wasn't my bag and didn't want to do it at all. And then Lorne kind of talked me into it. And I said, "The only way I'm going to do it is to do it with two people, because I don't want it to be The Jimmy Fallon Thing." So we look at the auditions—because a lot of the cast auditioned to be "Update" host—and Tina Fey's was awesome. It was great. They were going to hire some other dude, but she was just so cute and so awesome, it was unbelievable. And she had a point of view that I hadn't seen on "Update." So I thought it would be really cool if we both did it, and like immediately Lorne loved it. He knew it right there. He said, yes, definitely: "Tina's going to be the smart, brainy girl, and you're going to be the kind of goofy guy that doesn't do his homework and asks her for answers and stuff." You know, Lorne is brilliant with that stuff. So it was like, "Okay, I like that."

We did a test with just me, Tina, the cameramen, a director, and Lorne. And after one take, he would come out with, "Okay, relax a little bit more." And, "I like Tina on this side and Jim on this side." Lorne said, "What we'll do is, we'll do it until Christmas, because it takes a long time to get into it, and if you hate it or it's not working, we can find something else."

TINA FEY:

All we had from Lorne was that he wanted it to seem that we liked each other, which we do, and that the whole thing was a good time. And underneath that, I know for me, I wanted to make sure I felt that the point of view of the jokes was in keeping with—you know, if I'm reading it—my own point of view of the story. And Lorne said to not worry about it as a parody of the news so much anymore. We use that when it helps us and not worry about it when it doesn't. Because there've been so many parodies and satires of TV newscasts over the years.

Jimmy and I looked at a few tapes when we were preparing our test. We did watch Chevy specifically, because Lorne talked about it. It was an interesting point. He said you have to go out there with a little detachment — "These are the jokes they gave me" — which for me was particularly different, because a lot of times I was writing them. But it is true that to get away with it, you want that sort of playful detachment. Like, we're just out here trying to deal with this. We're not that invested in it.

JIMMY FALLON:

After the first "Update," I was so stressed. When it was over with, I thanked Lorne. I was like, "This is the coolest thing ever." It's such a rush, man. Because I'm wearing a suit, for God's sake. I don't have any suits! I don't! I've got to wear suits now. So I wear suits and talk about the White House and all that stuff. It's cool. Then De Niro came on. It's just fun. It's absolutely fun. I'm peaking soon. It's got to peak, because otherwise I'll go insane, and then where are you?

The way I look at it is, it's mine and Tina's little six-minute thing. It's a theater show. If I want to talk to the audience, I'm going to. One time, the applause sign didn't go on. And it was just dead air. And I was like, "Did they not press the applause button? What's the deal?" Meanwhile, on the cue card it says, "Thank you, everybody." So I am not going to read the card and say, "Thank you, everybody," if no one clapped. Thanks for what? So instead I just said, "Thanks, Tina — and no one else, apparently."

TINA FEY:

We knew that Jimmy was more than charming enough for the two of us. So we'd have that.

ALEC BALDWIN:

I would say the show's less politically wicked than it used to be. Now they make fun of people, but they don't make fun of people and make a political statement at the same time. It doesn't seem that it's as biting satirically as it was before. They should be having a field day with those two huge oil whores that we have in there now, Cheney and Bush. God, you could be just cooking them and eating them every week.

I still think Tina Fey is hysterically funny, though; I think she has the perfect kind of meter and cadence for the news thing. And that's something where you do still have some of the edginess of the show. I used to not even watch the "Weekend Update" segment before, because I thought it was just a lot of tired LaToya Jackson jokes. Now it has some real bite to it, and I think it's because of Tina and Jimmy. They're really funny.

DON OHLMEYER:

"Weekend Update" is what gets you to midnight. You tune in and there'll be a couple of weak sketches, and there might be a sketch that works and then a couple that don't work, and that's the nature of the show. But you grew up knowing that "Weekend Update" was coming. "I'm going to stay tuned until 'Update.'" That's part of the brilliance of Lorne's construction of the show—that you have this thing at midnight that would hold people there for the first half hour even if some of the sketches in the first half hour weren't that strong.

In 1996 and again to an even greater degree in 2000, Saturday Night Live returned to its richest vein of humor, American politics, and in the process the show rejuvenated itself for the umpty-umpth time. The cast was prodigious, the writing team witty and self-confident, the satire biting. Darrell Hammond, one of the most gifted impressionists in the show's mimicry history, mastered Bill Clinton, Jesse Jackson, and the hard-to-impersonate Al Gore (and on nights when announcer Don Pardo was unavailable, Hammond would fill in for him, unbeknownst to viewers, with another spot-on impersonation). Will Ferrell, the cast's most versatile utility player, made his version of George W. Bush easily as iconic as Chevy Chase's Gerald Ford of a quarter-century earlier. Ferrell's impression was accurate, hilarious, and inspired.

The faux Ford and the bogus Bush were blood brothers. Saturday Night Live seemed to have come full circle, back to its roots. Those predicting the show's demise skulked back into the shadows—poised, of course, to return at any given moment. Ratings rose, the show surged again in popularity, and the real Al Gore and his aides studied SNL's

parody of a presidential debate to help understand where Gore had gone
wrong with his own debate performance.

AL GORE, *Host:*

That is true actually. It's not that I set about to use it. It is true though that during the prep for the second debate, somebody brought in the tape—I didn't ask to see it or consciously use it as a tool—but somebody brought it in and said, "You should watch this." And I think it was a way of that person, I can't remember who it was, making a point that the first debate gave grist to the mill for lampooning the sighing and so forth, and that sort of critique that came after the first debate. I think it did have an effect, yes. And I thought it was very funny.

RUDOLPH GIULIANI, *Host:*

Some of my political advisers said it was a bad idea for me to host *Saturday Night Live.* Absolutely. Some of them thought either you could step over the line and do something really offensive to people—it's one thing for comedians to do that, but it's another thing for politicians to do it—or you could really make a fool out of yourself, where you could stand out there for an hour and a half and nobody would laugh at anything.

But of the experiences I had while I was mayor, that was one of the most enjoyable. It was just a great experience. I had been on the show once before that. I had opened the show with Governor Pataki, in which we got into this argument about is it like New York City or New York State? And so I was familiar with the show to that extent. But the idea of doing the whole thing—at first I didn't think I could do it, and Lorne convinced me I could, and I'm glad I did. The response was wonderful. It was absolutely wonderful.

When I hosted, I found that the excitement level of doing live television really adds a tremendous amount to the show. Oh sure, I was nervous. I'd never done that before. I did a lot of public speaking of all different kinds, and I had performed maybe three or four times with the Inner Circle up until then, but I never had to like carry all those different skits. But it was great, great fun.

It was much less difficult than I thought it would be because of Lorne and how professional they all are. They really take you through it and they sort of teach you how to do it. Lorne organizes the show like a lawyer organizes a great trial. He has a whole pattern and format for it. And it turns out that the show was done in the same office building in which I practiced law for four years. So I spent a week preparing it and I felt like I was back preparing for a big trial.

They wanted me to do a whole Mango thing that I thought really was—you know, we didn't want to do that. I thought, "Oh my goodness, that would create quite a stir." Wearing a dress almost accomplished the same thing. Then in the dress-rehearsal version, there were one or two skits that they cut out. They thought other ones were funnier. I remember there was one about the Statue of Liberty, where I played a park ranger giving a description of the Statue of Liberty and like getting out of control, like I was in love with the Statue of Liberty. And there was another one where I did a press conference and there was like a nephew of mine who was jumping all over me. But those were just cut as part of the normal process they go through.

Of the various skits that I did, the one I liked the best was probably the one where I played the taxi driver, and then maybe the one where I played the Italian grandmother was second. In the others I more or less played myself, but in those I got to create a character, and it was just a lot of fun to do that.

Since the night I hosted the show, I've probably dropped by it half a dozen times. Four to six times. I enjoy watching it. I enjoy watching it live as well as watching it on television. I've enjoyed it from the very beginning. I remember Chevy Chase playing President Ford. Now, I worked for President Ford, and loved him, and I still thought the humor was great. It was just great.

DARRELL HAMMOND, *Cast Member:*

The first time I met Lorne I had just had a root canal. I was like dripping, I can remember I felt like blood was going to come pouring out of my mouth. I met him in that studio, no one else in there but a couple of camera people, he shook my hand and asked me to sit down and said to perform. He goes, "You okay?" I said, "Yeah." He goes,

"All right, go ahead, whenever you're ready." That's the first time I met him. I auditioned for him three more times and then I had a long dinner with him after that, and I guess it was shortly after that he hired me.

MARCI KLEIN, *Coproducer:*

Darrell's a huge talent. When his audition tape got put in the machine, I wasn't really paying attention, and all of a sudden he was doing Phil Donahue and I was like, "Holy shit!" I could not believe he sounded so much like the real thing. It almost scared me, because I thought, "He's *too* good."

WILL FERRELL, *Cast Member:*

I was hired for the first nine shows and they were going to pick me up, and that was changed to the next six shows, and after that it was whether you were going to be picked up for the next year. And then after that it was year by year, and so you always feel like you're a little bit on shaky ground. When I got hired, I found an apartment and I was like, "Well, I better take the subway a lot before the first show starts, because once that first show starts I won't be able to take the subway." And I *still* ride the subway, so I don't know.

I think it's different; it's definitely a gradual thing in terms of auditioning and meeting Lorne for the first time. We were seen at the Groundlings, and then there was like the first round of auditions, and then there was a call-back round in which you met with Lorne the day before and then you auditioned again. And then in our case they flew back out and they saw us again at the Groundlings, and it was six weeks before we got hired.

After I made like the first cut, I knew that I was going to have to meet Lorne. I had read somewhere that Adam Sandler did a bit where he humped a chair like a dog when he met Lorne and was signed on the spot. Like, that was it for Adam Sandler. I thought, "When I meet Lorne Michaels, I'm not going to be trite, I'm going to do something funny, I'm going to be really funny."

So my idea was that I filled up a briefcase full of money that I bought at a toy store, and while he was talking to me, I would open the briefcase and start piling fake money on his desk and just say,

"You know what, Lorne, you can talk all you want, but I'm going to walk out of this room, I'm not going to know what happened to this money, you either take it or leave it." That was going to be my big thing—and just walk out.

Well, as soon as I walked in with my briefcase I could tell that the atmosphere was not right for it. Lorne's first thing he said to me was, "Okay, so you're funny, you were funny during the first audition. I hope you're funny tomorrow. Because consistency is what we're looking for." I was just like, oh God. And here's Steve Higgins, who'd been hired the day before, just looking at me. I mean, what comedian walks in with a leather briefcase sitting in their lap? I'm just uncomfortable, knowing I have a briefcase full of fake money. Then it was all superseded by asking me what I was going to plan to audition with the following day.

The second audition was to be like five minutes of what you want to do on the first show. Okay, does that mean stuff that I had done on the first audition that seemed to work, or do you want new stuff? He essentially wanted to see all brand-new stuff, so meanwhile I'm thinking, "Oh my God." So I walked out and they kind of took me through the paces—no, I wouldn't do that, they conveyed to me that they'd seen me do this one thing in the audition and wanted to see if I could cover this other area, and Steve is just looking at me and it's like, "Steve, do you have anything you want to ask Will?" And Steve's like, "Nice briefcase."

So then I walked out, never having opened it, and did the second audition. Then a couple of weeks later Lorne came out to see the Groundlings, and in the following week I had to meet him at the Paramount lot, not knowing that this was "the" meeting. Marci called and said, "Lorne wants to meet with you again, don't worry, it's nothing bad." But I didn't put it together that he was going to be hiring me. I just thought, "Oh, he wants to get to know me."

So here I am at the Paramount lot. I was like, "Damn, I got a second chance, I'm going to bring my briefcase, I'm going to do the money bit here if I'm ever going to do it." And then, "Lorne's ready to see you—oh, you can just set your briefcase down, don't worry about it." We talked for twenty minutes and he told me I was hired. And then I walked out and I just quickly explained to the people outside, "Can you guys just give him some of this fake money? It was this idea I had a long time ago and I never got to do it. That's why I always had this briefcase with me." And then I guess he laughed really hard when he heard the whole thing. I still have the briefcase, yeah.

STEVE HIGGINS:

Around here you brave the storm. That's the only way I can think of it. You just brave it. When it's a sunny day you can frolic on deck, and when it's stormy you cling to the mast. An interesting election year is good for us. This last one with Downey and the cold openings on the debates, that's what really swung everything. People loved the show again. When it's the political stuff, the best is when somebody who's a Democrat goes, "Oh, you really gave it to Bush," and somebody who's a Republican will go, "Oh, you really laid into Gore." That's the reaction we should be getting.

RALPH NADER:

The whole thing in 2000 was bizarre. Here you have this serious presidential campaign, and all of us had to go on these comedy shows like *Saturday Night Live,* because that was the only way we could have more than a sound bite and reach a large audience. This is the land of the free, the home of the brave, 285 million people with endless numbers of channels, and they're all closed off.

JAMES DOWNEY:

Someone did a survey of college students on where they got their political views and information, and television comedy was number one, ahead of newspapers or discussions on campus or even TV news. I don't think it's a crazy thing to say that *SNL* was one of the things that influenced voters in the 2000 election. Certainly after the first debate followed up by the first debate sketch, there was an awful lot of talk. I know that because I was taping the talk-show commentaries. I happened to be watching the Brit Hume show on Fox after the first debate sketch, and something made me think, "Hey, they're going to show a clip from the debate sketch," and that was I think the very first use of it. I kept hearing reports from people that they did it on CNN or there was something on the *Today* show, that sort of thing, and then it became a standard thing that I would keep tabs on. Nowadays they practically have a regular slot. There's a fair-use doctrine or something, they don't have to pay any kind of licensing fee to run a short clip if they're a news program, because they can argue this is a form of news. So, especially on Mondays, they will have a clip of something we did on the show on Saturday.

I thought our first Bush-Gore debate piece was perfectly even-handed. I think maybe some people were used to a more traditional approach where we're only rough on Republicans—at least really rough. The old style of the show was that the way you'd hit Democrats would be to say guys like Carter and Dukakis were just too brainy and intellectual and didn't understand that ordinary people weren't following them, or that they were too detail-oriented and needed to slow down. I guess that's a criticism, but it's nothing like portraying the other side as cretins or criminals.

Over the years I think there have been some heavy-handed elements to the political stuff we've done. I think we've done a lot of good stuff too. To me it's most fun when the tone is silly and there's no anger and our stance is wiseass, uninvolved detachment. I think that works better for everybody. We don't like to think we're getting laughs by just saying, "George W. Bush is an idiot." There has to be more to it than that.

RUDOLPH GIULIANI:

I actually think *Saturday Night Live*'s political humor is among its best. When you think of the imitations of President Ford, plus they had two different great imitations of President Clinton—yeah, I think their political humor has been absolutely terrific. Do I think it has an actual effect on people politically? Gee, I don't know. It doesn't for me because I take it as humor. So when they've made fun of me or made fun of basically my heroes or the Republicans that I like, I know they've made equal fun of Democrats, so it doesn't offend me. I think some people kind of watch it selectively. I don't think it has a big political effect in that sense.

They made equal fun of Gore and Bush, so I think politically it ends up a wash. They never did anything about me that I objected to. They did a great skit of my first inaugural, where my son disrupted the ceremony. I always saw it as humor.

DARRELL HAMMOND:

I got to meet Clinton in the White House, and it was like seeing the largest, strongest, smartest dog in a compound. He was so sure of himself and he so loved being the president, and he seduced everybody in that room. I mean, this guy would walk down the rope line and remember the shit about your sister or your brother that's most crucial to you. That instinct for creating a moment is just gigantic. I've studied Bill Clinton for years, and I haven't once ever caught him posturing or being phony. He just can't. And yet when you see a guy who's that gifted, you think, "Well, he's got to be staging this."

I guess I went about three months before I ever got a handle on him. He was the hardest thing I've ever done, and then my instinct told me: He's doing John Kennedy. He's doing John Kennedy! So I learned Clinton by practicing JFK's inaugural address in a southern accent. At one of those correspondents dinners in Washington, I opened with this joke about Clinton's charisma: "He's the kind of guy that would say to a woman, and get away with it, 'If you would only take your clothes off and let me see you naked, there would be no more white racism, I swear to God.'" And in that split second I looked out the corner of my eye, and it was almost as if I could see that machinery clicking and whirring, and he reached over to the African American woman sitting next to him and gives her a big kiss on the cheek. It was beautiful and the place went nuts and I thought, "How does he do it?" Clinton said something at another correspondents dinner like, "Poor Darrell, what is he going to do when I leave office?"

I spent about twenty minutes alone with Clinton once—him and the shooters; I guess there were a couple of gunmen there from the Secret Service. And man, he was nice as hell to me. Just so complimentary, knew everything I had ever said. He asked me to do him, sure. And I did. One time I did a correspondents dinner where I played his clone. He faked a leg injury and I had to come up and finish the speech, oh yeah, and he was like, "And how would you say this line? How would you say that line?"

With Gore, on the other hand, you could see the puppet and the puppeteer. You know, *The Wizard of Oz*—"Pay no attention to that man behind the curtain"? That was Gore to me. He had no ability to mask what he was feeling or thinking. We could see him trying really hard, and in a way that's kind of endearing.

On *SNL,* we're looking for the jugular. If it comes up on the Republican side, we'll hit it. You can't educate an audience and get them to laugh at the same time; you have to find out what it is that they are feeling at that moment and hit it. They basically should be somewhat in agreement with you in their laughter.

ANDY BRECKMAN:

Lorne defers to Downey to this degree: If Downey says, "I have an idea for a political piece, I don't know what it is, I haven't written it yet, but I will write it," Lorne will block out the six minutes and build the set without having seen or heard the premise. If a Downey sketch is coming in, that's our cold opening, build the set. We'll get the pages maybe the night before, if we're lucky.

DON OHLMEYER:

Downey and Franken are great political satirists. And they always have been. Election years are always very strong years for the show. And they have an ability to get right to the heart of the matter. They don't necessarily stop at the superficial.

I think they've done a fabulous job with—it's a terrible thing to say, but I mean this whole situation with terrorism is such fertile ground for what *SNL* does. It's kind of like playing to their strength. It gives them characters that are in the forefront of the public mind to spoof.

JAMES DOWNEY:

Nowadays, since I came back again after being fired as "Update" guy, I sort of have a mandate to write topical political stuff, although I do other kinds of things too. I'm not always happy—not only with choices made about my own stuff but choices in general. I'd like to see more of the sort of pieces where it's about the premise or the conceit and not about a popular returning character. But at least these days I never have to be in the position of being the guy who's the reason someone else's piece didn't get on, or rewriting someone else, so that's nice. I get to just write.

DARRELL HAMMOND:

I was glad to hear that Ted Koppel likes my impression of him, because I admire him and I don't want him to think I'm a schmuck, you know? I mean some of those guys you just admire. Plus, we didn't really take shots at Koppel. And you can't. How do you take a shot at an esteemed journalist who, by every indication, is a pretty good guy and trying to contribute, you know? You don't take shots at him, what you do is to take him and put him somewhere he would not normally be. In a bathtub, having a bubble bath. You know what I mean.

I actually performed for Koppel at a tribute for him at the Museum of Broadcasting. It's very strange. Because I went there in full Koppel drag. I had the hair and the nose and I had a bit prepared, and they told me that I was to wait until Sam Donaldson got up to give his appreciation of Ted and then I should walk in and interrupt him. And I thought, okay. And so Donaldson is up there, and I walk in and I'm like, "Excuse me?" And when I look into Koppel's eyes, right, I got so scared. And I got so scared I could only say to him, this is what was embarrassing, I could only say it in his voice, I said, "Are you mad at me?" I couldn't help it. And he goes, "No, I'm not mad at you, give me the microphone." And then he takes the mike and he like grabs the wig I'm wearing and he goes, "Roone, you cheap bastard, if you paid me a living wage I could afford a decent rug like this one." And the place went nuts.

The first cast of Saturday Night Live *had lacked one thing that all subsequent groups would enjoy: access to the work of predecessors. When the show was new, it had no models and barely a template. They made it up as they went along, and many improvisations born of desperation became traditions and tenets. Members of succeeding casts were always haunted by the first—its taped work recycled perpetually in reruns—and put to the challenge of trying to equal its impact. In the 1980s, 1990s, and 2000s, the show that had been designed for the TV generation was passed along to the* SNL *generation — talented kids whose earliest memories of watching the show were among their earliest memories of watching, or maybe even doing, anything. Now the* Saturday Night Live *creative team, before the cameras and behind them, included people younger than the show itself, video age babies who'd never known a TV universe without it.*

JIMMY FALLON:

I'm the same age as the show. When I first saw it, I was like seven or eight years old. My parents used to tape it and show me and my sister only the "clean" sketches. The others were too risqué for us, so we couldn't watch the whole thing. They were good censors, because we thought it was a treat just to see anything funny, especially Mr. Bill. I don't know why, but "Wild and Crazy Guys" was our favorite. It was risqué, but we didn't realize as kids what things like birth control devices or tight bulges meant. We were just little kids. We used to perform the sketches at parties, and relatives would be like, "You let your kids say this?" But I had no idea what it meant.

RACHEL DRATCH, *Cast Member:*

I've watched the show since its beginning. I was really young. I'd watch it every Saturday and have friends over and make them stay up to watch the show. It was like a ritual of mine. Gilda Radner was my favorite. Looking back, the thing I loved about her was just — I don't know, you never saw a "woman comedian." There was no separation, no gender thing. Being in Chicago and hearing "women aren't funny" and all that stuff, I liked her the most.

CHERI OTERI, *Cast Member:*

I grew up on the old shows. I remember my mom would let us stay up, because it became such a treat. It was a time when you should have gone to bed but we were up, and I remember to this day my favorites are Bill Murray and Gilda Radner, because I laughed and I related to their characters. I loved their characters. I would recognize when someone else was funny even if they weren't necessarily my type of humor.

When Bill Murray hosted here that time, it was amazing. This writer that I write with, we got into a huge fight. It was a brawl. I mean, screaming and everything. We were screaming so hard at each other. And when you walk out after a fight like that, you're shaking, because you can't believe it got that heated and violent. So I walk out after it's over and there's Bill Murray standing there. He heard the whole thing! And he's like my idol. And this was the first time something like that ever happened. He just looked at me. I felt so ashamed. And the next day I had to sit next to him at rehearsal and I go, "I'm really sorry you had to hear that yesterday." And he said, "Cheri, I felt like I was home."

MOLLY SHANNON, *Cast Member:*

I didn't watch the show as much as other people. I loved Gilda Radner and Bill Murray, but I didn't think about being on *Saturday Night Live* until I was in college. That wasn't always my dream from my whole childhood. It just started in college that I knew I wanted to be on that show.

At NYU, I was a drama major, and I did all of these serious acting classes doing "sense memory," and my God, soooo serious, with all these drama students and *ugh!* And musical thea-tuh. But then we did this revue show, and Adam Sandler was in it, this little comedy sketch show—and it was the best. We made fun of the teachers with little comedy sketches. And I remember it was the most fun. And I thought, "Oh, I like this." We improvised and made stuff up. It felt so free. I loved the improvisation, just using your instincts. And I was like, "Hey, I like this comedy thing." And then I met some guy in L.A. named Rob Muir who I did a show with, who told me, "Comedy is king." And I said, "Is comedy king? Comedy's *king?* Okay." And he said I should think about comedy, and then I really got into it.

The first time I did my Mary Katherine Gallagher character was a long time ago at NYU, in a revue show there. I didn't really base her on anyone. It's just bits and pieces, parts of myself but an exaggerated version of myself, but then there's a lot just made up. I did Mary Katherine Gallagher in that show.

Mary Katherine took a lot of falls. I would bruise myself and cut myself, but I never injured my back or anything. I started to get afraid. At first I didn't think anything of it, it was like punk rock, I actually liked getting bruised. It felt wild and committed and I enjoyed it. But being on TV, so many people would come up to me and go, "Do you get hurt? Do you get hurt? You must get hurt." And after thousands of people asked me, I started to get scared. So then I started to wear padding.

STEVE HIGGINS:

One of the nice things about Tom Davis coming back is that he's such a breath of fresh air. He says, "Oh, you guys are doing a great job." But any of the other writers who leave and come back, it always seems like they're saying, "My high school drama department was better. When I was here it was way better. Now look; they're doing *Ten Little Indians*. Ugh, that's a horrible play." Because most of the people here, this was their first TV job, so they form so many opinions off it, and it's always that high school thing: "My football team was better."

CHRIS KATTAN, *Cast Member:*

When I first saw *SNL* as a kid, I didn't think it was funny. When I first saw the Belushi stuff, I didn't think it was funny. I was watching *Fawlty Towers* and *Monty Python* at that age, and I was hooked on old movies like *Road to Rio* and Abbott and Costello. I was addicted to that stuff. I really got into *Saturday Night Live* when Eddie Murphy came on. He was so relaxed and had so much control and power over the audience and everything that was going on. If there were no laughs he was still so powerful, so relaxed and comfortable. He didn't get nervous, he didn't act like, "Oh my God, this isn't working," and rush through the lines. One time, I don't know what sketch it was, he made some mistake and the audience laughed, and he went, "Shut up!" I was like, "Wow, that was great." It's so great if you can be that relaxed and that confident. Then by the time I got to high school, I wanted to be on *Saturday Night Live*. I didn't know if I was good enough, but I thought, "I actually feel like I might be able to make it on that show, at least I might be able to audition." I just had a gut feeling that I could do it.

Right before I got here, when they had Quentin Tarantino and Tom Arnold as hosts, it wasn't that funny, and I was like, "Oh God, what's happening?" and I was like, "I'm glad I didn't get the show." I actually auditioned with Will and everybody else and I didn't get it, and then months later they asked me to come on out next week all of a sudden. The first couple of years, at least for me, you can't help but take stuff so seriously about getting your sketches in and "is this going to work?" and you stress out so much. I would get so stressed out and so worried about sketches it was just a big waste of energy. But you don't learn that until you kind of let it all go, and then you just relax and you're a better performer.

TRACY MORGAN, *Cast Member:*

I didn't watch the show after Eddie Murphy left. That's how my community is. We stopped watching basically after Eddie left. He was like the blackest thing on TV then. Now everybody has a sitcom. So I don't know if I even want to do prime time after this. But I love doing *Saturday Night Live.* It's late-night. It's live, baby. It's like Jackie Gleason. Once you do this show, you've made TV immortality. I'm going to be on TV the rest of my life. My grandkids will be able to see this. They'll have the marathon on cable on Thanksgiving, the *Saturday Night Live* marathon, and Daddy will be on it.

PAULA PELL:

We have a lot of two-person sketches as opposed to big ensembles of early days. I think it's because of the way we write. We go into little offices with one or two people and someone will have an idea for just one character. I've written some pieces with lots of people in them, but it's hard sometimes if the piece is about a certain character. You have only five minutes to do the sketch and now you have somebody that has to be the center of it. Which is why I think we have a lot of talk shows and a lot of presentational things where it's like, "Hi, I'm My Character."

HORATIO SANZ, *Cast Member:*

I used to watch it when I was eight. In Chicago. My brothers used to watch it. They shared a room and I'd sneak in and watch it with them. I've kind of always in the back of my mind wanted to do it. It had been a dream of mine since I was little. Then in high school you kind of think maybe it's a crazy dream. At one point I toyed with the idea of being in the CIA, but I think you have to join the army first, unless you're really smart. Then my brother started acting in college and I'd go see his plays and it kind of made it more like something I could see. I thought, "Oh, it's more tangible." So I started doing that. I quit college when I started doing improv and I really figured that's what I wanted to do. I was at Columbia College in Chicago. I went to film and television school. And I figure that too is another thing you have to be really good at. If you want to work in the crew, you have to be really good. And I wasn't.

I was in Second City. Everybody would hang out at night, drinking and doing bits. That made it hard to wake up early and make class. Fourteen of us auditioned that year for *SNL*. I've auditioned all my life for things, and even when I've gotten stuff, I didn't really give it my all. Like I auditioned for the Roseanne sketch show and *In Living Color*. And I never really gave it my all. I kind of just fucked around. I guess the reason was I didn't want those other shows, I wanted to wait for this show. I just prepared for this audition really well—more than anything I've ever done. I figured this is my shot and I didn't want it to be like one of those situations where you mess it up and you're like, "Oh well, there will be something else. If I don't get the show at least I can say I did the best I could." They wanted to fly me out the day before; I wanted them to fly me out the week before so I could get acclimated with the city and practice my audition piece. So I went early, put myself in a different hotel, and I just ran my piece, over and over.

I was told by people that I knew on the show, "They don't laugh at auditions. So don't be thrown by it. Keep doing your job." So then when I did hear laughter, that helped me out. I'm thinking, "Oh, this is going better than it normally does." And then I kind of felt really good about the audition. Even if I didn't get the show, I would have felt good about it. And then you go into these meetings, like, "Oh, it's almost done. You have to meet Lorne." So then you're just waiting. And then you meet Lorne and he goes, "You did good. We liked you. I think we'd like to have you on the show." But he doesn't say you're hired. He goes, "Okay, you did good. We're going to bring you out. We're going to bring you out to New York." You kind of want to hear that you're hired. But he doesn't tell you. So I said, "Should I tell my parents I have to move to New York?" And he goes, "Yeah. Tell them you have to move to New York—but don't tell them you'll be on the show." I guess what that means is that having the job somehow doesn't mean you're going to be around in the show.

MOLLY SHANNON:

After NYU drama school, I moved to Los Angeles. I was audition-ing for TV pilots and some commercials and stuff but couldn't really catch a break. There were a lot of young girls my age who were getting pilots, but I wasn't. So I thought, "I'm just going to focus on writing my own show and developing my own characters and improvising." A couple years before I got hired I sent my tape to them, when they hired Ellen Cleghorn, but they didn't respond to my tape, so I just went back and worked on my show and kept writing and developing more characters. This guy Rob Muir and I put together a two-person show called the Rob and Molly Show, and we did that for a couple of years in Los Angeles.

My agent called me and he was like, "Marci Klein is coming to your show—put it together!" I did a show just for her. When I audi-tioned for *Saturday Night Live,* the person who was having the audi-tions for Lorne told me, "Whatever you do, please don't do that Mary Katherine Gallagher character. You'll never get hired. Lorne won't like that, he'll think it's disgusting and dirty." Yeah, she said it was such a disgusting, dirty little character that Lorne wouldn't like it and "whatever you do, don't do that!" For some reason, she just didn't think it was right. I don't want to say her name. But I'll never forget that lady.

TRACY MORGAN:

You know when I first saw Lorne Michaels? I was working at Yan-kee Stadium, before I got into show business. It's where I met my wife fourteen years ago. I used to see Lorne Michaels go in Gate 4 every day. I was selling T-shirts and all that. I was a vendor at Yankee

Stadium. Now look where I'm at. It was so ironic that I met Lorne Michaels like that. And now years later, he's my boss and I'm working on his show. I didn't know him. I was a kid from the ghetto, trying to make a dollar out of fifteen cents.

HORATIO SANZ:

One prevailing frustration is kind of like not knowing where you'll be the same time next year. But I guess a lot of show business is like that. Another reason is sometimes you start thinking you deserve something. You can fall into a situation where you think, "That sucks, I got screwed." But there are so many other factors involved in the show. You have to not get too high with the good and not too low with the bad—to kind of be rational about it. Because whether the host likes something could affect whether it's on the show. Ultimately it's not our show. Lorne's the producer. It's his show. He'll be here for as long as he wants. Some stay longer than others, but it's not our show. It's a shared thing. You have to take those frustrations. Things usually swing around. Like if you have a good week, you'll have a better one next week.

CHRIS KATTAN:

My parents are Zen Buddhists, but that's pretty much the least crazy religion, it's not even a religion really. I had a pretty normal childhood; my parents divorced when I was two and then I lived with my mother and stepfather. My mother left my dad for another man, who was also at the Zen Center thing, but they were friends with people like Leonard Cohen and things like that. We moved to a place called Mount Baldy that was in a mountain, a very secluded area. I lived there from like age four to twelve and I think I went a little crazy up there. I think I really did, because there was nothing to do. I mean, you're in a mountain, and I guess kids should be around other kids. Like at age eight, nine, somewhere around there, they're supposed to be around other kids. And I was not. I mean, except for school. I was a shy kid and I didn't do very many sports and I used to have crushes on somebody every week. I started getting obsessed with other people a little bit—just their personalities. I'd do a lot of observing, but observing while talking with them and stuff like that. I used to get crushes on women like once every three months, a different one. I would never, ever kiss them or anything, because I was not that guy in school, but I would follow them around. That obsession helped me create. It's almost like I started creating for that person—to get in their good graces, in a weird way. I don't know what I'll do when I get married.

CHERI OTERI:

I think some people in the cast have fun crushes on other people, but nothing serious. I guess we're kind of boring—no romances, no drugs. I had an audition once with somebody who used to work here. He's very, very big in the business now. And as soon as I went in for the audition, he went, "Hey, you guys still doing coke over at *SNL*?" Because back when he was here, he was doing it. What *are* we doing, for crying out loud? Oh yeah. Thinking up characters.

TINA FEY:

The seventies and the twenty-first century are just so different. There's no drugs and there's no sex at the show now. I would have been terrified if I was here back in the old days.

MAYA RUDOLPH, *Cast Member:*

We're certainly a much cleaner, healthier generation than past generations. Everybody goes to the gym now—except for me. People are eating right and taking care of themselves and not smoking and not doing drugs. I'm being very general, but it's definitely a reflection of the time and the culture we're living in. To me, it's certainly boring compared to the *Saturday Night Live* of yore. We always make jokes about "I would have died if I'd been here in the seventies. I just wouldn't have made it." And then I also sometimes wish for those days, because I wish I was around when everybody was sleeping with each other. It just sounds like a lot more fun.

CHRIS KATTAN:

When I came here, I heard a lot of Chris Farley stories and stuff like that. And you're like, "Wow, really?" But now there's not too much unhealthiness. Everyone's really healthy. I mean, we all have our neuroses, obviously, or we wouldn't be here, and we wouldn't have characters that are so crazy. That's where our neurosis pops out most likely. I wonder—in the old days, you know, did they perform high? I'm sure I've heard that Belushi was all coked-up when he did this or that—you know, blah, blah, blah. But I just wouldn't be able to function. And I would not want, twenty years from now, to look back and go, "God, I was so coked-up doing Monkey Boy, I forgot what it was like." I'm glad I've done everything sober.

CHERI OTERI:

Believe me, we're not catered to here. You go to L.A., you walk into offices for a meeting or something and they ask, "Would you like a Snapple?" Here we have our refrigerators locked. They lock our refrigerators or they cut back on our beverage consumption. And a lot of us just wait until they have to make popcorn for Lorne and then we all go in like scavengers and eat the popcorn.

KEN AYMONG, *Supervising Producer*:

Actually it was probably me—not some network executive—who gave the order to cut down on the food consumption. There's no question about it: I always look at the financial perspective of the show. I want it to go on forever. I look at the show from a variety of perspectives, and budgetary is certainly one of them. And every so often you sit down and look at it—like, how are you spending your money? It had to do with dinners. Where it became an issue was where I went to the writers and said, "One of the nights has to go away where the entire writing staff is being fed." Or something along those lines. "One of them has to go, and you have to make a choice." And it turned out to be Wednesday. So I'm going to plead guilty to that.

WARREN LITTLEFIELD:

Literally, there was one analysis where somebody said, "You know, villages could survive for quite some time on the weekly food budget for this show." Just insane amounts of stuff. We'd say, "Well, maybe you don't need that after-show party," and they'd go, "We can't do the show if we can't have the party." What everyone goes through that week — I think part of the richness of the experience that everyone feels they are doing something so great, so special, so wonderful, that bonds everybody together, is those after-hour parties.

JIMMY FALLON:

I'm twenty-seven and I look thirty. Because I don't sleep anymore. I feel like I'm getting older fast. That's one thing they don't tell you about the job. You hear stories from other cast members, like, "Hey man, good luck. Hang in there, 'cause this place will kill you. One time I got so angry that I threw a phone out the window." And I'm thinking, I'd have to be mad at the phone company or the phone or something to throw a phone out the window. I'm on the seventeenth floor. Why would I throw anything out the window? I think I'm more humble than that. I'm like, "At least I have a phone!" What made anyone that angry that they got that mad?

ANDY BRECKMAN:

Reruns of the show are syndicated. And what happens is, every time a show is run, you get a little less money. The first time it's rerun, you get I guess close to half your salary — a nice check. And then the second time it's rerun, you get a little less and a little less, and now it's on Comedy Central so often that what me and other writers get is — is just insane. What we get in the mail are piles of checks for seven cents. Just piles of checks. And by the time you write your account number on the back of it and sign each one, your hand hurts. It's an ordeal. And that's what my career at *SNL* is down to now — cramps in the hands and seven-cent checks.

JAMES DOWNEY:

One thing that has definitely changed — and this smells like the network to me — is that in the early years of *Saturday Night Live,* the show would very admirably use its clout when booking music acts. It was like, "We're doing very well, we don't need to book a music act that's going to bring in huge numbers." So we would have some obscure, relatively obscure, or at least interesting choice. Like Sun Ra was on once.

Nowadays the choice of the music seems, to me at least, entirely about getting kids to watch or earning a big rating. I think they've had like the Backstreet Boys on two or three times. And in the old days, that's the kind of thing that would have prompted a full-scale staff revolt. As far as the hosts—I have to admit there have been some in recent years whose names I did not recognize. I just didn't know who they were.

JOHN ZONARS, *Music Coordinator:*

I think the musical philosophy has always been to try to balance established, very famous, and well-known acts like the Rolling Stones with a sort of cutting-edge, not necessarily breaking act, but an act that is sort of avant-garde. The idea of having an avant-garde act is always important I think to Lorne. And essentially no matter who tells you what about the different bookers that were in place and the bookers that are in place now, it's Lorne who books the show.

LORNE MICHAELS:

We're at a place generationally where you can do Britney Spears, where enough people are baby boomers who have kids. And you can put an eighteen-year-old host on, and it will hold the viewers and actually increase the audience.

I would know enough to book Eminem, but I wouldn't presume to pick the song he would sing. Whereas in 1975, I would have been, "What do you mean, you're not doing" this or that song, you know. I think you have to step back and find your role.

ALEC BALDWIN:

I asked Lorne once, "Is there any way the host can very innocently try to influence who the musical guest is?" And Lorne just looked at me very bemused and said, "What did you have in mind?" And I said, "What about someone who's a great singer of standards—how about Rosemary Clooney?" And I thought Lorne was going to swallow his tongue. And then he explained to me the basic rule that governs the musical guest selection: The cost of bringing the musical guest to do the show is often shared by the record company, because it's very expensive to bring them and the crew and all their technical equipment to New York and NBC. And very often it's an artist who is promoting current product, and since it's a promotional tool, the label shares that cost.

JOHN ZONARS:

When we have a musical act perform, the network has evidence that proves that the ratings drop off, and frankly it took me a long time to accept that, because in my world, everyone is worried about the music. We only watched the show when we were kids because we thought the musical act was cool. But the network started telling Lorne that the ratings were dropping off during the musical act and that we should only do one song and that the song should be after "Update." And while they may have a point—I can see how Middle America doesn't care about music, they just want to see the Cheerleaders do their skit—I think it inherently screws up the rhythm of the show.

Considering the gazillions they've earned at the box office—we're talking mythic money—Mike Myers and Eddie Murphy were possibly more revered by the newest breed of Not Ready for Prime Time Players than were Chevy and Gilda and Dan and John. Of course, a good many flop films have been based on SNL skits or have featured former SNL cast members. But the show is obviously still seen as a springboard into Hollywood, and key cast members have no shortage of scripts submitted by eager producers anxious to cash in.

WILL FERRELL:

I think there's a perception that there's like this instantaneous thing that happens, whether it's movie offers or whatever. But it's all very gradual, and even after being on the show for five years you still feel tenuous about your existence. People go, "What a great stepping-stone," but we've all been happy just to have a job. It's like, I mean, initially while you're here, you're just—I mean, there was a part of me that could have quit after the very first time I was on the show. Really. It was like, "Wow, I did it, I was on an episode of *Saturday Night Live,*" and I almost wanted to keep it pristine.

ANDY BRECKMAN:

You can't deny the show is a launching pad unlike any other that I can think of. It's a farm club. It has an amazing batting average. It's like a shot on the old *Tonight Show,* which was so prestigious because it led to so many other things.

MOLLY SHANNON:

Lorne produced *Superstar,* my movie about Mary Katherine Gallagher. Those movies are very cheap to make. They're low-budget, cheap comedies. It maybe cost $14 million and it made $30 million in domestic box office, and then it makes a lot in video, because we have a lot of kids who watch it over and over and over again, and they memorize the lines—little girls and stuff like that. So *Superstar* was a very profitable little venture for Paramount Pictures. One of those low-budget cheapies.

JANEANE GAROFALO, *Cast Member:*

The general attitude over there is that with the Tina Fey regime and the Steve Higgins regime, things started turning around. I think the prevailing attitude had been that women just aren't quite as funny.

MOLLY SHANNON:

First of all, there aren't that many slots for girls. There was me, Ana, and Cheri. So the girls that get there are tough girls, you know. Those are strong women, I would say. We all got along well. I think that either way you just sort of have to take care of yourself. It's not a man-woman thing. They're not going to put something on because it's a girl sketch, they're going to put it on because it's funny. Maybe before that, women had different experiences than I did, but my experience is they're going to put it on if it's funny, not because you're a girl, that's just silly. You're just in competition with yourself.

CHRIS KATTAN:

When I first got on the read-through table, it was very quiet during my sketch, they didn't really laugh at all, and I thought, "God, this is terrible." And then Lorne put the sketch in, it made it in, and it was like the second sketch of the night. So I was really excited and people were just—you know, a featured player has never had their first sketch on in their first week or whatever. So I was very excited that I had.

It was flattering when Lorne said, "You know, you're like the new Mike Myers to me." I was like, "Oh wow." He meant that in a sense of, "You're going to take care of yourself and do your own stuff." And you can see when you watch the old shows that Mike Myers wasn't there throughout other people's sketches. It was more like, here's the Sprockets and here's "Wayne's World" and here's his "Coffee Talk," and that was his stuff. So it's a great way to always be on your toes, and you know, it's good training to only rely on yourself.

DARRELL HAMMOND:

I had no idea that people could be so tired and miserable—because of so much pressure—and yet still be good and still be funny.

JACK HANDEY, *Writer:*

Even today I'll have dreams where it's like late Tuesday night and I don't have an idea for the show. And then Lorne comes into the dream and he's wearing my pants.

DARRELL HAMMOND:

When I came here Lorne told me, "We don't go on the air because the show's ready, we go on because it's eleven-thirty." Here, you're going to be asked to be at your best when you feel your worst. If you're hoarse, have the flu, didn't have time to prepare, didn't sleep well last night, feel depressed—too bad. It's eleven-thirty and it's live, so you've got to change your mental state. Sometimes, by the time you go on, you're so tired you don't even remember why you thought something was ever funny in the first place.

CHERI OTERI:

You get in here and you start doubting yourself. Each week you're auditioning for a show you already got. Each week you're proving yourself. You're starting over week to week. It made me very emotional and unstable. When I did *Just Shoot Me,* Thursday came around and this feeling came over me, this really great peaceful feeling, because I thought, "Oh my God, no matter what, *I'm going to be on the show.* I'm not going to get cut."

Here's the thing I didn't know about *SNL:* I knew that you *could* write, but I didn't know that you pretty much *have to* write if you want to be in the show. There were shows I got cut out of completely! My dad came up from Nashville when we had Garth Brooks, and I was completely cut out of the show.

It was in my third year on the show that I finally stopped being devastated and crying about it. Julia Sweeney said that she had my dressing room, and she told me, "God, how I cried in that room." And it's just the way the show works. But there's no show like it. The good part is that you get to be something different every week. And you get to be seen in front of millions of people. And then I thought, what am I going to do after this? What's going to be as exciting as this? I'll feel good about not having the disappointments, though. I've gotten better at that. Because I was pretty much known as someone who didn't take it very good.

CHRIS KATTAN:

Cheri Oteri and I had one thing in common back when she was on the show: We were really left to write for ourselves. You know, it was pretty much up to us. We could never really assume some writer would take care of us. There are some performers that could assume that. But Cheri and I are more specific, I think. And we had our stock characters, so it was a little difficult for us, and I guess it was a little rough for Cheri. This place can be very unfair, and I think it was a little unfair to her sometimes—like it was up to her every week to come up with something or she's not on the show. Which is a real bummer, and that's happened to me a lot. So I'm like, "Oh God, I guess I've got to come up with a new character for this week," because I am one of the people that can't assume that a writer will take care of me unless that person takes a chance.

TINA FEY:

Certain words chill the audience regardless of context, "rape" being one of them. There's a piece that Adam McKay wrote for Rachel Dratch to do in "Update" that was so funny to all of us, it was about some guys who had written a book about how rape is natural. It was just part of the caveman mentality that lives within all of us and it's part of nature. And Rachel did this "Update" feature as herself talking about how she agreed with the book and how she loved to rape dudes and graphically described these rapes that she had done on men and got into how she was going to rape the two male authors of the book. And Rachel is, you know, pint-sized and adorable—but the audience, even though it was her saying those things, they just could not, did not, go with her on that.

CHERI OTERI:

I talked to Laraine Newman about stress. She talked about how are you going to deal with the pressures because there's so much pressure here. And I was a mess my first three years. I was very emotional. I cried a lot, and it didn't all just have to do with the show. I felt very lonely for some reason. I went to work and then I went home, I went to work and then I went home. Maybe that was my fault, but I don't want to do much outside of work. I don't know why.

I think I don't love New York. I'm from Philadelphia, I'm an East Coast person and I fit in peoplewise here, but I don't know, it's sad here. I feel like I'm always in a building. And I have that bipolar thing too, and I'm claustrophobic, so I always feel like just closed in. You don't see daylight very much, and my office doesn't have a window. You can get an office with a window, but then you have to share with somebody. It was really difficult. It was very, very emotional. But then Laraine gave me good advice. She said, "You know, Cheri, back then therapy wasn't what it is today. Drugs were taken to deal with the pressure, but we were so young. And you didn't think you were abusing it and you didn't think you were taking it for the pressure. You were just partying. But when you party to the point you're emaciated, that's not good." They partied hard back then. And she said, "I can't imagine how you deal with the pressure." And I told her I wasn't dealing with it well for three years. There was no escape, so I was like crying all the time. I would go to bed in disappointment—so much was so very, very emotional. And then I realized it, "I need help with this." And then—I started taking drugs. No, I'm kidding!

*   *   *

In its earliest days, the show's famous "home base" was occupied by a more eclectic array—Raquel Welch, Desi Arnaz, O. J. Simpson, Hugh Hefner, Cicely Tyson, Ralph Nader, Norman Lear, Anthony Perkins, and Miskel Spillman, a little old lady who won an "Anyone Can Host" contest. But still there are surprises—political and sports figures one might not expect take their turn in the show's one-of-a-kind spotlight, or at least make a cameo appearance. Like Robert De Niro popping up to gripe about the way he was impersonated on the show, or Janet Reno busting through a fake wall to make essentially the same complaint.

The best hosts—Steve Martin, Tom Hanks, Christopher Walken, Alec Baldwin, John Goodman—are invited back repeatedly. The worst are, properly enough, dissed and trashed behind their backs once they've gone home.

ELLEN DEGENERES, *Host:*

I can honestly say hosting was probably one of the highlights of my life so far. It was so much fun. I'd never even been to the show, so I didn't even understand the speed of it. When you're watching at home, you don't realize they had to get out of that outfit and into another outfit just during the commercial. So as soon as the camera goes off you're just pulled and people are ripping your clothes off and putting on a different wig and a different outfit. That was another thing to get over too, because I'm the most modest person in the world. So to have people ripping my clothes off and stepping one leg up while someone's putting a wig on and you're half-naked in front of these people—that was a bold move to me.

MARCI KLEIN:

In terms of desirable hosts, we of course always want to get Tom Cruise. I'm always trying for him. Then there are the ones that the writers want, but I don't know how to explain to them that the network might not understand. Like Harvey Keitel, one of my, I thought, really good bookings. But we had to fight for Harvey. To me it's important to have funny shows so that people hear that the shows are funny and then you'll get ratings. It's a longer way to getting a rating, but then there are times where you do a Britney Spears because you know it's going to work. And it gets a big rating and she was really good at it.

I show Lorne the list, but it never gets circulated. No one sees it but him. You know, hopefully, I don't want to spend three weeks on one person. I want to say, "Let's make an offer." Cuba Gooding Jr. is a good example of somebody where I went and I saw *Jerry Maguire* and I came back and I said to Lorne, "I know no one knows who this guy is, but I'm telling you he is going to be a big star from this."

Gary Oldman, who would be my dream host personally, was booked, and on a Thursday night before the Monday that he was supposed to come in, something happened and he had to drop out. I think Tom Hanks came in and really saved us on that one. Gary Sinise was another one. I was so excited. It's always the ones you're like really excited about that drop out. You call in Alec Baldwin, Tom Hanks, John Goodman; John's done it when someone has fallen out. I mean, this is a major thing to ask somebody — "Hey, can you show up in two days?" — when they're not prepared.

No one has ever dropped out during the week of the show, no, because the minute you get here it's too much fun. I mean, honest to God, they are treated so well. When Jackie Chan got here, he said, "I want to get on the plane and go home." And I went, "Ha ha ha." I said, "I promise you on Saturday night at the party, you will be telling me you want to do this again next year." He goes, "Never," but I was right. Some of them freak out when they get here on Monday, but by Saturday they all feel like it's one of the most fun things they've ever done.

You know that nightmare when you didn't study for the exam or you're naked onstage or something? I knew I was really producing the show when I started having dreams about hosts and musical guests not being there. Sometimes I'll be talking to Lorne and I'll go, "How are you not nervous?" I absorb. One host in particular was really nervous. I almost threw up during the monologue because I was so nervous for him.

Gwyneth Paltrow gets more people coming up to her saying, "You were so funny when you hosted *Saturday Night Live*" than there are saying, "You were amazing in *Shakespeare in Love* and congratulations on your Oscar." People recognize when people are good.

GWYNETH PALTROW, *Host:*

For someone like me, who's usually relegated to corsets and British accents, it's really fun to get to do something like hosting. It's great fun for me to play a white girl who wants to talk like a ghetto chick. I never get to do stuff like that otherwise.

The first time I hosted, I felt incredibly nervous—not only about how it would come off but if I would make it through the night, because I adrenalize so much in those situations. When I was walking out to do the monologue, I couldn't feel my hands and feet. But the last time I hosted, I wasn't nervous. I really knew what to expect, and I just felt very free and very lucky to have an opportunity to be ridiculous. I've had experiences where I've been under extreme pressure, an awards show or something like that, but it's very finite. This whole experience lasts for an hour and a half of live television. When you do a play, there's three hundred people sitting there. Not millions.

My mom hosted once in the eighties. She just told me, "It's going to be great," as opposed to kind of chronicling what it was going to be like. She said, "Make sure you do this kind of accent," that type of stuff, and, "Make sure they stretch you as much as possible and do things that you never get to do ordinarily," because this is such a great chance to do that.

In one sketch I played Sharon Stone and got in all kinds of trouble. She was very offended by it. She kind of talked about it a lot in the press and stuff. I think she was very unhappy with it and she felt it was mean-spirited. But then she proceeded to go on TV and stuff and say I was disrespecting all the women that came before me, and stuff like that. She waged a press campaign against me. I look at it like it's a rite of passage to be lampooned on that show. If people are making fun of you on that show, that means you've made it and you're in the cultural lexicon, and it's flattering. I suppose some people are less game for that sort of thing.

ELLEN DEGENERES:

To be honest, there was a time that I was scared of them, because as you know everybody is fodder. They'd made fun of me, especially the whole situation when I met Anne Heche, that whole situation was on a lot. I'm way too sensitive and my feelings got hurt and it was hard. Now I have perspective on it, and they were right to do so, you know?

CAMERON DIAZ, *Host:*

I don't like making fun of other people. I like making fun of myself. I really don't like playing other celebrities and making fun of them. This program is about current events and parodies, which are fun, but I don't want to participate as the person who's doing a parody of a person who's possibly at that moment being humiliated publicly.

GWYNETH PALTROW:

The nicest thing Lorne ever said to me was after the first time I hosted. There was a sketch at the very end of the show where I was supposed to say, "I'm Gwyneth Paltrow and you may know me from *Emma* and all this stuff but what I really like is hardcore porn." And the sketch at dress was like a minute and thirty seconds, and he came up to me and said, "We're unfortunately going to have to cut it out of the live show. I don't want to—I love this thing—but we're going to have to cut it because it's thirty seconds too long. We're over." And I said, "I can do it, I'll shave thirty seconds off." And he was like, "Are you sure?" and I said, "Definitely." And so I did it and I shaved exactly thirty seconds off, and he came up to me after and he said, "No one has ever been able to do that except"—I think it was Bill Murray and someone else—"and no girl, I mean no woman." So I felt very good about myself.

LISA KUDROW, *Host:*

When I hosted, I wasn't really looking at it like, "Wow, I wanted to be part of the cast of this show and I didn't get to do it, and now I'm hosting. Yay for me." It didn't feel like that, because it's too terrifying to host. It's this speeding train, and you feel like there's no choice but to smash into the brick wall.

I didn't feel confident enough to impose my own taste on the sketches. I know some people do, and they are pretty firm with Lorne Michaels and the writers about, "No, this one's no good, I don't want to do that sketch, and you've got to do that sketch." I didn't feel right about that, because I thought, "Lorne Michaels has been doing this for fifteen years and who am I to say that sketch won't work? He thinks it will work." And I deferred a lot.

Thursday or Friday, you're feeling, "No good can come of this! It's not possible this is going to work out." But on Saturday night, when you're behind that door, about to be introduced, you have to gear up, focus, and commit to, "It's going to be just great. It's going to be okay." I'd been told a lot of hosts end up in tears before the show starts. I thought, "Well, at least I'm not crying. It's not *that* bad. So I'm going to be okay."

At Groundlings I had done a lot of live work. It did have that great feeling of you get to own the material when it's live. It's between you and the audience. Unless your mind starts wandering to, "When this is over, then I have to run over there and change into something else." That's when you're in trouble, because you can't then be dealing with the task at hand.

WILL FERRELL:

The worst host was Chevy Chase. He was here the first year that we were here, and then he came back the next year and that was the kicker, the following year. It started right from the Monday pitch; you could just tell something was up. I don't know if he was on something or what, if he took too many back pills that day or something, but he was just kind of going around the room and systematically riffing. First it was on the guys, playfully making fun, until, when he got to one of our female writers, he made some reference like, "Maybe you can give me a hand job later." And I've never seen Lorne more embarrassed and red.

In hindsight, I wish we'd all gotten up and walked out of the room. It was just bad news. I will have to say Chevy's been nothing but nice to me personally, and I think he thinks I'm funny, so I'm cool with him, but yeah, he's been quote-unquote the roughest host. A little snobbish, and he'd yell at someone down the hallway—scream and yell—and you would look at him, and he'd see you were looking at him and he would smile like, "I'm just joking." We'd be like, "No, I don't think you are."

The other kind of classic one—and he wasn't so much abusive, but he was just all over the place—was Tom Arnold. Even Lorne was like, "This will be a bad show, this will be a bad week," and sure enough, it was like, "Oh, this guy is horrible." Once again, though, he wasn't mean. I think you'll find a consensus on the Chevy Chase thing.

ANA GASTEYER, *Cast Member:*

The one miracle is that every host makes it through. I've seen really drunk people make it through, I've seen really stoned people make it through. Everyone makes it through. The system has been around for twenty-seven years now; it's pretty well oiled and sensitive—it just happens.·

Of course, you see a lot of true colors. I mean, even the coolest person in the whole world at some point shits their pants because they're so nervous or so elated that they made it through this terrifying thing and wasn't it fun.

I credit Lorne and Marci and the show for kind of making each host feel likc that was really the most special show, because I've seen people who we've unanimously thought stunk up the barn still really experience elation when it was over and, you know, feel so celebratory and excited by their experience, and it's cute. You see it even in people that are very, very hip and cool.

It's scary. People act like idiots when they're scared. You know, total idiots. Jerry Seinfeld was fearful. Totally fearful. He was very controlling and weird about knowing what sketches had been picked. He was like, "What about this idea?" He made people mad, but then once he knew what sketches had been picked, he was lovely, it was amazing. So everybody has their shtick. Obviously we prefer it when there's somebody like that who brings something to the party—over, you know, somebody who's like, "Well, she's a pretty girl."

CHRIS KATTAN:

There are some weeks where the writers are just kind of unmotivated and it's like, "What are we going to write for this person," you know? She's so generic, she's like this person, or he's like this person, and it's like the same thing again. And then there's the obvious ones, like when Jennifer Lopez was here, it's like, "Oh well, we've got to hit these jokes and these jokes," and then it turns out she doesn't want to make those jokes, so then how can we do it subliminally?

JIMMY FALLON:

It's kind of an amazing thing when you're with a writer. You see the joy in the human face, and not because of what they're writing, or the job of writing it, but the excitement that they're going to unveil a good reference or a good bit, kind of like a mad scientist rubbing his hands together and giggling: "If this monster works, I'm a genius, and if it fails, it's back to the drawing board."

They're excited not about writing it, but about what the audience's reaction will be. It's kind of exciting that way for the writers. Writing itself is tedious. No one ever really enjoys writing until it's done. But you're excited to see people read it, excited to think, "Will they get it? Will they like this line?" It's line by line. It's just cool to watch how insane these guys are.

MOLLY SHANNON:

Kevin Spacey was really great when he came. He was an amazing host. He's just like a machine: "I want to do this, I want to do that." He just creates the whole thing. He just comes in with a plan and he follows it through, and he was like masterful. He was amazing to watch. He just came in and had great ideas and he's funny.

TINA FEY:

Part of the beauty of the show is that at its longest it's only a week; come hell or high water at one A.M. on Sunday, it's done. It's like taking the SATs; they will say, "Put your pencils down," at a certain point. It is best when the host trusts us. It's easiest for us when people come in and trust us. When someone comes in and they're really difficult, it kind of brings us all together against them.

MARCI KLEIN:

The host drives the show much more than people realize. When I first started working here, I was shocked that the host had anything to do with this show. I think people kind of have the image that the host takes a limo in on Saturday after reading their part—they just don't know.

I think the best host that will make a good show is somebody that is confident and trusting enough to let go. When you come here, you need to trust that we're not going to let you go out there and destroy yourself. Lorne and the writers, all of us, really want the hosts to be as good as they can be.

STEVE HIGGINS:

Christopher Walken is always a great show. You can't lose no matter what he does. I love having John Goodman and Alec Baldwin around. Gwyneth Paltrow and Jennifer Aniston were a lot of fun too. We've had some clunker shows, but they all blend together. I think when the hosts come here they're on their best behavior. If they're not, they have everything to lose and nothing to gain.

TINA FEY:

My advice to anyone that hosts: Don't bring your own writers if you want people to love you. That was one thing I thought that Conan O'Brien was very smart about, because he has a staff of writers downstairs but he didn't bring anybody, he came up here and put himself in our hands, which was a good move. Sometimes people with a large entourage can be difficult. It's difficult when a host will have like a publicist in their ear telling them what's funny. That always seems like bad news when you go down to talk to the host in their dressing room and you're talking through a publicist.

Comedy people are hard sometimes, because they have their own kind of comedy that they do and they can be very resistant to what they will and won't do. I think they're usually my least favorite. A host who actually writes on the scripts and hands it back to the writer is usually bad news.

JAMES DOWNEY:

It was ironic when Jerry Seinfeld came, because some of the people he brought used to work here at the show. I can tell you that that approach has a terrible track record. I mean, almost without exception, when they bring writers along their stuff doesn't get on. We will have the read-through without there being any kind of prejudice against them. It's just that often they write stuff that eats it.

HORATIO SANZ:

Tom Green brought in a few of his own writers and was kind of more preoccupied with his image as a guy who doesn't give a fuck. And the show I think suffered.

JON STEWART, *Host*:

It was the first time I'd been asked to host, and I jumped at it immediately. I didn't bring any of my own writers with me; they've got plenty. They're very, very talented people over there who already know their thing, and hopefully I went into it thinking I'd bring a little something to the process and shape it in a way that would give this show a little different flavor than it had the week before. We had a great time doing all that stuff. It's a very collaborative environment. I really had just a mind-blowing good time.

I thought the process that they used to hone material was really smart. The way the show came into focus makes complete sense. It's very linear, it's not arbitrary. There's obviously politics associated with any organization, especially one that's been alive for that long. As the host you obviously are a guest, and it's a different atmosphere. But when you're around some place for a week, you can pick up what's what and who's what and where's what and that kind of shit.

CHERI OTERI:

It makes me feel good when people say, "Yours was my favorite cast." Especially older people who have been around. That just makes me feel good. But I don't feel competitive at all. Why put that pressure on you of what happened before?

RACHEL DRATCH:

Oh my God, I love doing that "Lovers" sketch with Will so much. That comes from when I was in college. There was a professor; my friend had her and kind of got to be friends, and before the break for

Christmas, she asked my friend what she was going to do and she said, "I don't know." And the teacher goes, "Yes — just take it easy — read a book, take a bath, eat a bonbon, spend time with your *luv-uh*." So that became for me and my friend just this big thing we would say all the time, *"luv-uh."* Later Will and I were writing something together and he's like, "What about that 'lover' thing that you said in that other scene?" Those are the funniest things, the things you joke around with friends. So then we developed it. We're like, *eeeuughhh,* you know, when we write it. I laugh so hard, it makes me sick.

The first time at read-through we could not get through it, just like on the show we cannot get through it. I try not to laugh too much, because I don't like it when I'm watching TV and I see someone breaking up all the time; it becomes sort of cheap. But sometimes you just can't help it. I've never been chastised by Lorne for it, but I don't know what happens while he's watching it. Will will just make a face or go like, *"unnhhhh unnhhhhh,"* or something, and it just gets me.

WILL FERRELL:

I'll catch Lorne just like chuckling to himself, something no one ever gets to see, and I don't know if all the times that you don't see him laugh are just part of a façade he has to wear, like being principal or something.

We have these Tuesday night dinners where we will go out with the host. Lorne's a fascinating guy to sit and talk to. The times when Lorne gets frustrated is when — the typical thing of, "What is all the fruit doing in the background there?" Or it will be some suggestion where he's like, "I want you to remove something." Okay, we'll cut that. "No, no, no, but I actually like that." But I thought you said . . . So he can be very vague at times, and the thing you end up losing from a sketch or a piece is a thing. You'll be like, "What did he mean?"

DAN AYKROYD, *Cast Member:*

Some of the greatest moments in a comedian's life are when you are dying. Horatio Sanz and Will Ferrell told me they sometimes watch shows or material they have done on the show that didn't work but that they thought was great, and they sit there and laugh at how dead it is, and at how little the audience is reacting. I remember watching Johnny Carson; Carson was funniest when he was dying.

TINA FEY:

There are a lot of places every week where you're seeking approval. First you want your piece to kill in the read-through. Sometimes your piece kills in the read-through, and even though it doesn't end up in the show, you can still hang your pride on that. Then you want it to work in dress and then you want it to air. If you get some of those things and not all of them, I always figure, well, I got two out of three. At least you can walk with your head held up somewhat. You want the things that you think are genuinely funny first, and then beyond that you start thinking if something has a topicality—that maybe it wasn't in the best shape at the table but it's very topical and we can make it work. And then as the meeting goes on, it comes around to who's not in the show. Who in the cast is not being represented in the show? Well, what do we have for them? Is there anything that worked enough for them at the table that we can make it work better by air?

RICK LUDWIN, *NBC Vice President for Late Night:*

There have been a couple of times where I had to play Judge Wapner in a dispute between broadcast standards and the writers or performers. There was some line in a David Spade "Hollywood Minute," I forget exactly what it was, where broadcast standards said "absolutely unacceptable" and David Spade said, "Well, I'm doing it," and it went back and forth, a ping-pong thing, and finally broadcast standards said, "If you do it, we're going to drop audio." And he said, "Well then, drop audio, but I'm doing it. I'm saying the line." And so he did it. He said the line, and broadcast standards dropped the audio.

Robert Smigel, who pushes the envelope about as far as you can push it on broadcast television, has had a number of dustups. The first time I met Smigel, he and Conan O'Brien were writing partners on *Saturday Night Live*. Conan denies this, but my recollection is they had written the famous penis sketch for Matthew Broderick, with broadcast standards saying, "There's a tonnage issue here. We'll let you say it three times, but we won't let you say it ten times." So there's this odd debate back and forth: "We'll give up this penis but we want to keep that penis."

Another week Smigel did a cartoon about global businesses, GE being one of them, and their connection to Ted Kaczynski, the serial bomber. The notion that global businesses were running the world was basically the theme of the piece. It was a very clever sketch. When I saw it, I immediately passed it on up the line, to whoever was in charge, because I wanted everyone to know what was going on. Standards tentatively okayed it, and we put it on, and it aired once. But then it got pulled from the repeats. And Smigel, I remember, was all upset about it being taken out of the repeats. I said, "Robert, it got on the air. You were not censored. It got on the first time." It got on once—but never again.

ROBERT WRIGHT:

Lorne and I had a couple of issues one time with Smigel on one of his pieces, which I think neither Lorne nor I thought was funny. It was just kind of a GE shot without any point to it. If it had been funnier—there was one done on Jack Welch that was a little funnier that we did run. We didn't stop it. The other one ran, but I think it didn't get repeated. It seemed like it was too pointed without being funny.

ROBERT SMIGEL, *Writer*:

I do raunchy and sometimes nasty stuff, I guess, and I get a lot of attention because Lorne puts my name on the cartoon—but it's embarrassing because there's a million funny people here. I have mixed feelings, because sketch writers in general don't get enough credit. It's a thankless position. You get pretty well paid if you hang out for a while, but there are guys here who are just brilliant that I've worked with and people don't know who they are. One great thing about my cartoons is that people know I wrote them. It's a great thing right there for people to know what you wrote specifically. On this kind of show you're just at the end of a long crawl, and sometimes they don't even have time to run the crawl. I mean, a guy writes one play and everybody knows who he is, even if it's a lousy play, but you can write a hundred great sketches and still be anonymous. I feel lucky to have found a venue that was interesting where I could get this kind of freedom and a little bit of attention.

TOM DAVIS, *Writer:*

Every once in a while, I'll show up and be a guest writer on a show if the coffers are getting low out here. Lorne will let me come back and appear on the show and make some money right away. It's not because they need me or that Lorne particularly was going, "Jeez, I wish Tom Davis would come back to the business." Although the cast and the writers all tell me that they're glad to see me, and I believe them.

Things aren't going well, but I'm a happy guy. I've been separated from my wife for just about three years now. She's still my best friend and I speak to her on a daily basis. My ex-wife is a veterinarian, a really good one. And we have all these animals between us. And they're all getting old now. When she leaves town, I go to her house and all the animals stay there. When I leave town she gets my animals. All my parenting instincts have gone into just a couple of cats and dogs. I think I made the right decision not to have kids. I seem to be a bachelor, 'til the results are in now. I don't mind it. I kind of like living up in the woods, with a couple dogs and cats. And I can go into the city occasionally. That's my life. I live rather modestly, and that's fine with me.

JACK HANDEY:

Lorne has always been very kind about saying there's an open door there, and I think when the show got in trouble with the critics and the ratings about '94, '95, they thought to bring in some of the old guns. And so they brought me in, and I think they brought Robert Smigel back. Lorne and Jim Downey, I think, would encourage me or ask me to come back.

CHRIS KATTAN:

The character of Mango was actually kind of based on an ex-girl-friend. There was a manipulation to her that was incredibly charming. You could nail it like, "Oh, don't you see, you're doing that thing again where it's the whole 'come here, go away' kind of thing, and it's charming and coy and really, really mean." And the joke was that she was a bad dancer but for some ungodly reason, men just fell for her. It's very much like the *Blue Angel* thing too. I don't think I was conscious of it, but it's very *Blue Angel,* you know. I mean, men aren't turning into chickens, but yeah, there is that *Blue Angel* quality. It's really a frightening movie, and in the end the poor guy, I remember him being a chicken.

Monica Lewinsky was going to be revealed as Mango's wife on one show, but Cuba Gooding, who was the host, didn't want to do that. On another show, Mango had a crush on Matt Damon, and then Ben Affleck pretended to be Matt Damon so he could get Mango for himself.

I know some people do think I'm gay. I've had people ask me if I'm bi more than gay. And I'm okay with it, and I like it, because I'm not gay, so actually, for women, it means I'm not threatening. It doesn't bother me too much. I think there's femininity, something feminine, in my characters that's easy for me. The way I move my body and my rhythm—it comes out a little gayish.

JAMES DOWNEY:

There has been a big trend lately where we do an impression of someone and sooner or later you know the real guy is going to do a surprise walk-on and startle the cast. And it's always played as if it's supposed to be threatening: "Oh my God, this is going to be awful, here's the real Alex Trebek, he is going to be bullshit." That kind of makes sense if it's, you know, Mike Tyson, but why is it "dangerous" that the real Tony Danza shows up in our *Who's the Boss?* parody?

At the very least it says that whatever we did, it didn't offend them in any way. I guess it depends on if you really feel strongly that a certain person is so malicious and such a menace that it's important that they really be taken seriously, and here we are with the kid gloves, and the proof that we're not really laying a glove on them is that they'll happily appear on the show.

A thing that actually kind of shocked and stunned me was when Monica Lewinsky was on the show. I guess I can understand the reasons to have her. I don't think she's evil, but it seemed a little trashy. I felt that if you had her, you should at least acknowledge that you were not proud of it.

If I were producing the show, I would have said no to Monica coming on, but I wouldn't say no to Bill Clinton, because he was the president of the United States. But it's something that could never happen. He might agree to do something taped—although if I were him I would like to think that if we called, he would go, "After the shit you assholes have done about me, you have a lot of nerve asking me to do something for you."

I registered my dissent about Monica coming on by writing a couple of sketches, neither of which got on the air. One was about Monica winning "the presidential kneepads," and the history of the kneepads and that kind of thing. I wrote it and called Lorne and said, "Let me try this, it's like painless," because it involved nothing live other than Jimmy Fallon playing Kenny G and Monica Lewinsky standing there and a little bit of voice-over.

Anyway, Monica Lewinsky's publicist read the sketch—I actually watched the guy read it—and after he flipped through it he just went, "Uh-uh. Not interested." And it was like, "Oh, I'm sorry, does she have some long glorious resumé of achievement—or did she blow the president?" There was this attitude like, "Monica Lewinsky does not do kneepad stuff." I thought if I were Monica Lewinsky, I would have a little more sense of humor. I don't remember people forcing her out onstage at gunpoint. It seemed to me she enjoyed the celebrity.

When Gore and Bush did that special, it was different. I don't think by agreeing to appear they were betraying weakness or humiliating themselves or anything, because I think we'd stuck to basically fair commentary on them. I didn't think they'd do it, though, just because I assumed they'd have teams of advisers who would say, "You're nuts to go on a comedy show when you're running for president. It just makes you look altogether too unserious." But I'm glad they did.

Bill Clinton, I think, would be a whole other thing, because a lot of the nature of what we've done about Clinton was about his personal life. And I would like to think that he was really offended by it. Not that the show shouldn't have done it, because he was president and it was all fair game. And I think down the road they will ask him to do something. I would think he wouldn't do it. I'm sure he'll come to a party, though. That's a different thing. Clinton still makes me laugh— though not in a way that I think he would appreciate.

I'm sure there were times especially in the past few years when someone called up and said, "I saw you guys took a shot at me on the show, I'll come on." For the most part, whether they'd put them on is entirely a matter of would it help the show. It can't be a ratings thing in the sense that people heard a rumor that Alex Trebek's going to do a walk-on so everybody tunes in. I guess it's the idea that you have to watch the show every week, because you never know which TV or movie personality is going to show up. I have no way of quantifying it, but I know there's just been an awful lot more in recent years than in the years I was producing.

DARRELL HAMMOND:

You know, sometimes when you get out there you become aware that you'll be funnier if you let the voice slip a little bit and cheat. For instance in *Jeopardy!* when I first did Sean Connery, I had a really accurate Sean Connery. Now what I do is really a bastardization of who he is, because it just seems funnier to me and it's funnier to the writers and it gets more of an audience response. Sometimes they just don't want to see accuracy, they just want it to be funny.

JOHN GOODMAN, *Host:*

I was in town doing a movie—I can't remember if I was hosting the show, I don't think I was—but they needed a Linda Tripp for the cold opening one week. And they called me. Like, I guess there's a resemblance. And then of course I did it a few more times after that.

You know, I always felt a little bad about that. For one thing, after the scandal was over, it was kind of beating a dead horse. I certainly don't like her politics or agree with what she did, but after a while, I felt like I was picking on her.

ALEC BALDWIN:

One time we did an opening with John Goodman, and he blew his lines and he fucked up the biggest joke in our opening and I almost called him an asshole. I think if you watch the tape, I mutter it under my breath. Because he walks away during this Christmas show where he was like the Ghost of Christmas Present, I think I'm literally mumbling the word "asshole" under my breath, because he's bungled the lines and ruined the whole sketch.

The live aspect of the show is to me the most important aspect of the show. It's a challenge. If I was not doing what I'm doing now, I would try to get on the show regularly. It's like getting high, it's like being stoned out of your mind, it's like being shot out of a cannon.

CHRIS PARNELL, *Cast Member:*

I introduced myself to Tom Brokaw in the NBC gym locker room one day. I said, "I'm the guy from *SNL* who does an impression of you." He said, "Oh, right, I've heard of that." We had a pleasant conversation, actually. He told me about the old days of the show, when Belushi and those guys were on and he used to come and watch it with his daughters. And he talked about his daughter having gone to Marci Klein's sweet sixteen birthday party at Studio 54.

He was not naked, no. I think I waited until he was getting into his gym clothes to talk to him. It's a beautiful body, though. Glorious.

Although the Saturday Night Live *casts of the eighties and nineties hardly had the reputation for sybaritic self-indulgence of the original seventies cast, the show's mortality rate continued to be distressingly high. Among the most shocking deaths in the history of the series was that of Phil Hartman, who'd been with the show from the mideighties to the midnineties playing a whole chorus of characters and perfecting particularly deft impressions of Bill Clinton, Ed McMahon, and Frank Sinatra. Hartman was shot to death by his wife, Brynn, who then killed herself.*

Far less unexpected but obviously as tragic was the death of Chris Farley, the tubby and childlike cutup who had tried — too hard and too successfully — to pattern his life and career after John Belushi's. Farley died at the same age, thirty-three, and of essentially the same cause: heedless and delirious excess.

JON LOVITZ, *Cast Member:*

Because Phil could do anything, he had more stuff. He'd be in like eight sketches, you know. He used to go, "God, it's too much," because

I'd have like five sketches, which was great, but he'd be in like eight or ten every week. But he loved doing the show, you know. He did.

The first time Phil was offered the show, he turned it down. And then later on he said yes. I said, "So did you say yes, Phil, because I said you've got to come on and do this?" He said, "Well, no." I said, "Well, why did you say yes?" He said, "Because Joel Silver called me and told me I'd be crazy not to take the job and do it."

I'll say this about missing him: He was my favorite person to work with. He was my older brother. I loved him. I idolized him. I liked him and yet he was like my grandmother—he'd be so excited to see me he just made me feel great about myself. He could do anything. He would just get into something and learn everything about it and go on to the next. The last acting job he had was on a pilot that I did. That was the last job and three weeks later he was killed. It was awful; it was so horrible. In my life there is just a huge gap that will never be filled and part of me just feels lost.

JAN HOOKS, *Cast Member:*

I'll tell you who was really instrumental in getting me through was Mr. Phil Hartman. He was my rock. Luckily, I had a lot of stuff with him. He was just, you know, the Rock of Gibraltar. And we did a *Third Rock* together—less than a month before he died.

TERRY TURNER, *Writer:*

Phil was on the *Third Rock from the Sun* cliffhanger. He played Jan's psychotic boyfriend from Florida. He was on the cliffhanger, and *Third Rock* was coming back the next season. And we were in New York, and we heard that Phil had been shot. We were stunned. I mean, it was one of those things where you think maybe I heard it wrong or maybe when I wake up tomorrow it won't have happened, because he was such a great guy, such a great guy. Everybody liked Phil. Phil was like the centerpoint of the show. He was the thing that held everything together, and he could make the simplest stuff brilliant just by reading it a particular way, by his posture, by his look. We were devastated. I think everybody that knew him was. You couldn't believe that it actually happened.

And it did have an effect I think on everybody, to think, "If that can happen to them, what's to stop it from happening to any of us?" Sitting down to dinner one day, going to a wrap party the next day, and then the next day—you're gone. It was really shocking. Of all the people you would have put into that scenario, the last one you would have picked would have been Phil.

ANDY BRECKMAN:

Just like baseball fans and baseball fanatics put together the best Yankee team ever, so the *Saturday Night Live* dream cast is another game that the writers play—and Phil Hartman makes almost every list.

JAN HOOKS:

My friend Bill Tush at CNN called me. He said, "Jan, there's something coming through on the AP that Phil Hartman committed suicide." And I said, "Oh yeah, right, Bill. Right, yeah. How are you, Bill?" And we chatted and he said, "Wait a minute, wait a minute, there's more information coming through." Then he came back and said, "Jan, it's true. Phil is dead."

I went out and bought chocolate turtle ice cream and, I think, pizza rolls, and just stayed in bed for two days.

MIKE MYERS, *Cast Member:*

I was close to Phil Hartman. We both kind of came from the same place, which is we loved doing characters and came from ensembles. I just worshipped Phil. I looked up to him. I think he's one of the best character-based comedians ever. My office was next to his. I used to just check in with him all the time, just pop into his office and shoot the breeze. He was extremely, extremely supportive and hilarious. He never gave up on a sketch and his work ethic was amazing and I just dug him. I enjoyed everybody, but if you're asking me who was special, I would say Phil Hartman.

I sat beside him at the read-through table. They used to call him "the glue." If he was at a read-through and in a sketch, Phil would be incredibly generous to some rookie writer by selling the hell out of this kid's piece. He would never tank your piece. Afterwards you would just hear "glue, glue, glue" from people around the read-through table. And then someone would always have to tell Phil, "They're not saying 'boo,' they're saying 'glue.' " He just really was a mentor for me.

The day he died was one of the weirdest days of my life. Just complete and utter disbelief, complete and utter despair. I'm sitting here talking about it not believing that we're talking about this. I still can't believe it, I'm still devastated by it. It is a profound sadness that we're sitting here talking about *Saturday Night Live* and the question is about Phil Hartman's death. I can't get over it.

KEVIN NEALON, *Cast Member:*

I was coming back from somewhere, I didn't know if it was a gag or what. I was flying at the Burbank Airport and I was walking from the gate to baggage right through the terminal, and I looked at the TVs over the bar and I saw shots of Phil. I thought, "Oh, he must have a movie coming out."

DAVID SPADE, *Cast Member:*

Toward the end, when Chris was getting too drugged-up and too out of control, it was hard, because I don't drink that much, I drink a little bit. I couldn't keep up with him, and I didn't want to. Plus it was like I used to tell him that he gets a little bit "moody" and "crabby"—which was another way of saying, "tearing the office apart and screaming." It just got to a point where we had different lifestyles. And I was even okay with realizing that he was the funnier one out of the little duo, and that he was being offered more money. Even when we were in movies together, he would be offered three times as much as me. I would just take that as one of the realities of it and not be too offended and say okay. Because *I* would pay him more. He is definitely fun to watch and is definitely a big draw. If I could play off him, and be in the movie with him, that was fine.

We kind of drifted apart toward the end and then started to hang out again, and then talked about what we could do together again, because he said that the only thing people talked about was *Tommy Boy*. And they didn't care about *Beverly Hills Ninja* or whatever else, so he wanted to get back to that. And I said I agreed, that was kind of the consensus at my little camp too.

I was at work when I heard. I fell apart. Mark Gurwitz, my manager, called me on the set during a *Just Shoot Me* rehearsal and said, "I want to tell you because you are going to get hit with all the press in about five minutes." And I walked back onto the set, started to rehearse, and then collapsed and just fell apart, and I had to go into the other room and just cry for twenty minutes straight. I was like hyperventilating, it was too much. It was one of those things that I thought early on, when we were together, that something like that could happen, but he was such a truck that I got to a point when I thought nothing could happen to him. I just couldn't handle what he did, but he was made up differently and he could handle it.

CHRIS ROCK, *Cast Member:*

Farley was crazy, man. He gave me a little part in *Beverly Hills Ninja,* one of the worst movies ever. Nevertheless, it was some money when I needed some money. I think we have the same birthdays too.

Two guys named Chris, hired on the same day, sharing an office, okay. One's a black guy from Bed-Stuy, one's a white guy from Madison, Wisconsin. Now—which one is going to OD? That just goes to show you.

Let's trace back. I remember I was on tour. I saw Chris in Chicago and he was just really fucked up really bad. He just couldn't behave himself. He couldn't put it together for fifteen minutes. He was in my limo and he just couldn't hold it together. And he wanted to show me his apartment, but I couldn't deal with it anymore, so I dropped him off at his place. "Come on, Rock, come on see my place." And we were driving off and I thought that might be the last time I'd see him. And three months later, four months later, I get a message to call Marci. And I called up *SNL* and the switchboard was busy and right then I knew he was dead. And I said, "Ah, fuckin' Chris. The switchboard's never busy. Something must have happened. Ah, shit. Fuck, man. Lost your boy."

ROBERT SMIGEL:

You have arguments and you cry and you have dramatic confrontations where you're begging him to take care of himself and you feel like you're helping. You can do that and feel like you've done something, but the only thing that I had seen that had worked was the actual threat of losing something that was carried out—*Saturday Night Live*. And after that it seemed like people could only make threats, but it was not as easy to cut Chris off from show business. Once you're out in the movie world and you're a movie star, chances are there will always be producers willing to give you work.

BOB ODENKIRK, *Writer:*

Like everybody else, I was worried about Chris the whole time I knew him. I mean, he had terrible drinking problems back at Second City. I think when he got to New York, he got introduced to harder drugs that, of course, made it much, much worse.

There was a *Saturday Night Live* reunion at the Comedy Festival. And we had a "Mr. Show" party, and Chris showed up. He wanted to speak to me, and somebody came to get me, and I went out and Chris was in the alley in a limo with like five asshole party kids from Aspen. They were all smoking pot, and he just looked like—I just knew he wasn't going to make it. He was going to pop. He was bloated and flushed and looked terrible. That was the last time I saw him.

The more interesting thing than seeing him in that state was when I saw him probably a year and a half before that. He was with David Spade at a party in L.A. I'd never seen Chris say no to a drink, but they had a keg at this party and Chris was turning them down. And he seemed incredibly in control—like a different person. He seemed really empowered, whatever he'd been going through, and in control of himself. And I thought that he'd really turned a corner, and that was almost more amazing than seeing him the way he was in Aspen a year later. It was to see him and think, "Wow, there's really hope," you know?

I think his life was pretty chaotic. Between flying around the country and being in these different sorts of spheres of influence—L.A. with his friends, and Chicago with probably a different group of friends, and maybe Madison with his family, and who knows where else when he was on location. I think it's a pretty chaotic lifestyle, and without the structure of *Saturday Night Live* around him, that might have been all Chris needed to get really screwed up.

DAVID SPADE:

On the first day of *Tommy Boy,* he was so nervous he drank twenty-nine cups of cappuccino throughout the day and thought it was a big joke. I thought, I couldn't do that, and if he can do that, and he can drink and he can get up, and he can go out all night and be more chipper in the morning than I am, and I slept fine, then I said, "Okay, we are just built differently." And then when I heard that he had died, I thought, "Yeah, there is some stuff that he can't handle." It goes too far, but when you keep chasing a high like that and you can handle it, then there is no reason not to go to the next level.

TIM HERLIHY:

Chris Farley's death was the most devastating thing that happened while I was there, for sure. Everybody was very emotional and it was very hard that week. That's probably my hardest week. And I feel bad. I think Samuel L. Jackson was the host, and I think everybody was so full of emotion that, you know, we probably could have done a better job.

Chris was such a great weapon in the writers' arsenal. If you were like writing a sketch and you got to page six and nothing was happening, you would just say, okay, "Farley enters." I did that so many times in so many sketches. It was a trick that always worked and never failed, especially in read-through.

NORM MACDONALD:

I never thought Chris would die, because first of all, I don't think anybody will ever die. It just seems like if you're alive you'll stay alive. But also because he was so strong, you know. Like, I would always worry about myself, because I can't drink and I can't smoke and I can't do drugs. I'm always freaked out about like I'm too fragile and I'll die. Spade seems to me like somebody that's very mortal, but Farley was this big, strong guy. It seemed like he could do anything. He was the funniest, that guy. Chris Farley—oh my God.

His comedy was like sophomoric in the best sense of the word. He would just do any crazy thing for a laugh. He'd get naked and act like a little girl. He'd put a pool cue up his ass or something. One time, when I first met him, I was at this retreat right before *Saturday Night Live* started, he just kept breaking me up. You'd laugh and he'd try to do more and more, and then by the end of the night he was like doing his impression of a salad. He'd take all this salad dressing and pour it over his head and then put like tomatoes in his ass and stuff. It was great. He could make anyone laugh—smart or dumb, young or old. If you liked him, if you hated him, it didn't matter.

I did a movie with him; it was like the last movie he ever did. It was the summer of his death, so I saw him then. I worked with him for six weeks. And oh my God, he was big. He had gained a lot of weight. And he was just crazy, reckless, at that point. And when he came back and hosted the show, it was like madness.

ALEC BALDWIN:

I like all of them, but the person I did have a special fondness for was Chris Farley. Even if you were somebody who was on the wagon and didn't drink and didn't take drugs, you wanted to go out and just get completely loaded with Chris. You wanted to go out and be with him and do whatever you had to do and just ingest whatever potion you had to ingest to make you look at life the way Chris did. He was so crazy and free and fun. And he was so childlike in a wonderful way, you thought, "How can I get to where he's at?"

TIM KAZURINSKY, *Cast Member:*

I have a bunch of breakfast buddies in Chicago who were all in Chris Farley's company, and I told the *Trib* I didn't want them writing a thing about how his friends "didn't care." I have breakfast with all the guys in his former company at Second City, and some are AA, and they would not go with him to a place where alcohol was served. They'd say, "Come on over here for breakfast." They would not be a party to his doing drugs, and they did say, "Fuck you, you're killing yourself." Those buddies—one of them was his AA sponsor—they didn't leave him in the lurch. They talked to him all the time, and they just said, "It's your choice. You hang with us, or you die."

When you're getting $6 million a movie, as one of them said, you can buy a lot of new friends overnight. And he did.

AL FRANKEN, *Writer:*

With Belushi we did not know that you died that way. We didn't understand what addiction does and what was going on. With Farley we understood it, he understood it, because he went to rehab about twelve times. He honestly, honestly struggled and tried. He was a wonderful, sweet, loving guy. He was a fan of other people. He loved his family. I don't know what it was. That was really sad.

ROBERT SMIGEL:

After Chris died and I thought about the things that could have been done and talked to people who were close to him, I came to realize that no matter what I felt, no matter how frustrated I was, I hadn't seen a lot of Chris in those last few years. He'd been on the West Coast doing his movies, and every now and then I would hear something or see something and get frustrated and make judgments and confront people—but then I would retreat back into my own problems. So when it came time to talk at Chris's memorial service in New York, there was a part of me that wanted to address my frustration without placing blame on any individuals, because I didn't feel like I was involved enough to make those kind of judgments. So when I spoke, I talked about the disappointment I felt in what had happened, but from my own perspective, and just apologized to Chris personally for whatever I hadn't done. I felt like if anyone heard something in what I said that struck a chord with them, then good, then I could speak for them a little bit too. But at the end of the day, I felt like I could only really speak for my own feelings of letting him down.

Saturday Night Live *had celebrated, in restrained ways, its fifteenth and twentieth anniversaries. There'd been no fifth-anniversary party, of course, because in its fifth year the show had gone all to hell. But it was nothing if not resilient, and that resilience was commemorated in the show's biggest-ever blowout, a three-hour prime-time twenty-fifth-anniversary party on September 26, 1999. Of those still living who'd ever been part of the* SNL *family, Eddie Murphy was probably the only major graduate who stayed away, reputedly out of some ill-defined animosity toward the show that had made him first famous, then rich, then a movie star. Otherwise it was as gala as galas get, with expatriates and former foes burying hatchets to join in the celebration and more than 22 million viewers watching from their homes. Highlights and oddities from a quarter-century of salutary troublemaking passed in review.*

Tom Hanks did the opening monologue, Bill Murray and Paul Shaffer revived Murray's old lounge-singer routine, there were touching tributes to the show's many fallen comrades, and Robert Smigel contributed a cartoon mocking Lorne Michaels, who privately lamented that if he had eliminated Smigel's animated mugging from the show, "Page Six" of the New York Post *would have reported it. Asked about the cartoon later, Smigel insisted it was a labor not of revenge but of admiration, another example of the curious love-hate relationship common to Michaels's professional progeny. America had sometimes hated—well, disliked—*Saturday Night Live *over its fitfully hallowed haul as well, but this was a night to forget all failings, real or imagined—a night to commemorate all the good times and anticipate more to come.*

BILL MURRAY, *Cast Member:*

The old days? I don't really reflect on them. What are the old days—working real hard, sort of that new excitement of having made it, going to the party after the show, and really just sort of competing. It was a competitive time. You threw out there what you had and you saw how it stacked up. Whenever I get together with a few of those guys it sort of comes back.

We spent so much time together so intensely that I guess it's like war buddies or something. You don't have to see them to remember. I don't see the players much at all. I live in the Northeast; most of them live in California. I don't see them very often at all, but when I see them it's great. Like at the twenty-fifth anniversary, we were all there so it was great. Everything they do is fine with me. Anything that happens with them is fine and will always be fine. We just went through too much for me not to wish them well.

You talk about friends for life and stuff, and that's what it is. We'll always be connected; we're sort of working together. I don't know if it's just the reruns, but we're always sort of working together all the time. We sort of went to school together and we're sort of carrying that stuff out into the world. We all have that experience and we're affected by it and we carry it out there. When I see them, I feel like they're doing the same thing I am—they're out there and they have that history and that experience that only the players had, and only they could ever know what it was like. It's sort of a secret in a way. It's like a talisman. It's something we walked away with. We got to walk away not just with the side effect of success, but with the experience. Having the experience was probably the greatest thing.

When I did the twenty-fifth-anniversary show, there was a very warm feeling, a great feeling of like we were all in the same fraternity or sorority, we all like went to the same school somehow, and it was a really small school. I enjoyed people more than I ever did—other guys from other generations and casts and so forth. I felt no feeling like "ugh." Because you always used to feel that this could have been different, or you could have done that a little better or something. But there was none of that feeling at all when we got together again. It was just, "Hey, look at this group." I was able to enjoy everyone so much. I had the best time. It was really delightful.

Tom Davis and I and Paul Shaffer and Marilyn Miller got together to work on something for the show. We went to Paul's apartment and spent like a couple days doing it. Danny came over. It was like a party. Paul opened some really good wine. Somebody rolled a joint. It was hysterical. We just started telling stories—all the time thinking, "We don't want this part of it to end. We don't want this part of it to stop." We were in no rush to write the sketch. I wanted to do a Bruce Springsteen song. I just thought "Badlands" was the right song. And I was arguing with Marilyn. It's great to argue with Marilyn. In the old days, I didn't get Marilyn at first. She used to argue so vociferously, I used to think, "What a bitch this woman is." She's sort of this Jewish princess with a literary bent, and it was always like, "I don't even know how to talk to someone like this." I would just say stuff like, "Marilyn, come on, you're wearing thigh-high boots. How the fuck am I supposed to take you seriously?" That's all I could say to her in my head. I couldn't really argue with her about the point of it, because she didn't get my point of view. She didn't get me at that point. The mistake was always to argue with her about the thing. The right thing to do was always make her laugh. If you could make her laugh, then she could see that you knew what you were talking about, because if you were good enough to make her laugh, you must be funny. And it took me years to figure that out.

So anyway we were arguing about "Badlands." There's some lyric in "Badlands" that's really appropriate for what we did, for what we'd done. It wasn't "Born to Run" and just doing a classic song, which is what we always used to do; "Badlands" was more about what our experience had been. It was really about us. And Paul was like, " 'Badlands'?" And when we started singing the song, his eyes lit up and he got it. He looked at me and he got it. Marilyn was still arguing and Paul said, "It's going to be 'Badlands.' " Paul will listen to everything, he's a fantastic listener, but when he actually speaks, he's speaking because he knows the right answer. So when he got it, it was like, "Great. Now we're there." The writing of it and doing that as a group was really fun. I think we took five or six days to finish it.

Singing the harmony part with Paul to "Badlands" on that show was one of the high points of my entire career. We hit the notes. We pushed the hell out of it. We even put more lyrics in. They wanted to cut lyrics and cut the time and we said, "No, this is what we're going to do," and everybody just got out of the way. And when we did it and we nailed it, I thought, "Bruce Springsteen's got to be liking this."

It was sort of an honor to have the first sketch on that show, I thought. And I thought we just killed. We had a blast. And to really just go out there, cold, and to show them that we still had it, that we can go out there and kill, no warm-up, just walk out there, the show opens up and kills from the first minute—that was great. And then the show just sort of cruised from there on. Everybody was funny, everybody was loose. The show was a success from the first sketch. If the first sketch had died, there would have been tension, there would have been anxiety, people would have pushed a little too hard. God, they did a great show. Everybody did great. Everybody was funny. The party was great; the party went on and on.

TOM HANKS, *Host:*

At the twenty-fifth-reunion show, I remember thinking, "Why did I get saddled with the monologue again? Why am I always the guy with the monologue?" I did the monologue in the fifteenth-anniversary show too, and actually made a joke about it: "I've been elected to come out with what is traditionally the funniest part of the show, the monologue, the host monologue." It's a terrible job. But then again, to go up there and do it on the twenty-fifth-anniversary show, come on, that's a thrill. And an honor.

I think a lot of people who leave go away saying they're never going to come back. They feel just devoured by the experience of doing the show. But as time goes by, I think they realize that, hey, they were part of something that is singular and that there's still nothing else like on TV. I think it's interesting that there have been many, many attempts to try to re-create whatever *Saturday Night Live* does, and they all fail. That's why I found the twenty-fifth-anniversary reunion so emotional, because all these people from different eras who had gone through this quagmire and had been in the trenches and everything, they just forgot about it and were feeling real celebratory. It was a nice evening. Lord knows, it was star-studded as well.

AL FRANKEN:

Saturday Night Live was a very positive experience for all of us. It was like really just a wonderful fucking thing for everybody. There were pressures and there were some people who didn't succeed with the show as much as they would like and may have some feelings about that. But like this last anniversary show was a wonderful experience. Maybe it's just from being older, but everybody sort of didn't care. Like it didn't matter whether you had become a $20 million a movie performer or you were Laraine. Everybody was sort of like, "We did this thing." They might have felt differently ten years ago or something. But it was a great experience. The more people have experience with other things, the more they appreciate what we had.

Of course, I'm sure you've heard some very bitter things too.

ANDY BRECKMAN:

Downey hated the way that Lorne recently had guest stars in as sort of stunts. He'd turn around and there's Joe Pesci or Robert De Niro or Jack Nicholson. Who can we get, who's in town, who can pump this up? My kid brother, David, eleven years younger, he wrote for one year on *Saturday Night Live,* back whenever the Pesci–De Niro thing was, and he was struggling. Because he writes kind of smart, writerly pieces, and they were just looking for stuff to feed characters. He was not getting material on that he could sell at all.

And the first sketch that he officially got on the show survived the cut between dress and air and was slated for the last slot of the show. Lorne had been cutting sketches even during the show, so even being on the final rundown was a little tenuous. But he was officially on and he was thrilled, and it was his first sketch on—and then when Joe Pesci and Robert De Niro, in the middle of that show, made their surprise appearance, the recognition applause in the studio—I didn't have a stopwatch, but it seemed to go on over sixty seconds, it seemed to never end, like a full minute or ninety seconds of recognition applause. And my brother was watching and knew that because of that, his sketch would be bumped. And that just killed him.

MAYA RUDOLPH:

I passed on my first audition because I'd gotten another job offer. But I didn't really want it. This is all I ever really wanted to do. I waited my whole life to be on *Saturday Night Live.* And then when they said come and audition, I'd just been offered a job on a hospital drama called *City of Angels,* a new Steven Bochco series. So I passed on the audition and I was miserable for a month. I was shooting this drama during the week and doing comedy on Sundays. And Steve Higgins came to the theater and he said, "If you don't get picked up for your show, would you be interested in coming back to New York?" And I said, "Yes, please." I never wanted to make that mistake again. So I ended up meeting with Lorne. If interviews are based on how you think you did, I did horribly and should not have gotten the job. I was quite convinced he was not going to give me the job. I didn't feel very secure in the meeting and I was terrified, and I think I ate a piece of popcorn and I was afraid I was going to choke. I just remember being quiet. I'm not a very loud comedian when I'm in one-on-one, and I remember walking back to my hotel thinking, "I will never enter that building again." It was the worst interview of my life. I was an idiot. I was horrible and not convincing.

They brought me in at the end of the twenty-fifth season for the last three shows of that season. I don't think a lot of people had much fair warning that I was coming, as far as what I've been told from the cast. I think I was sort of dropped on them a couple days before I came: "Oh, by the way, this new girl's coming, Maya Rudolph." And I think it definitely made a lot of the women feel, "What does this mean for us? Are we being replaced?" A lot of people were sort of like, "What the hell? We had no idea you were hiring a new cast member at the end of the season."

And I think it made a lot of people feel worried or threatened that things were being shaken up here. That didn't happen—but I was not well received by all.

It was like going to school and everyone already knew where to sit in the cafeteria. There were only three shows left. It was such a hard thing to adapt to, because everyone knew their place and knew what to do and the rhythm of the show and how it works, and I didn't really know anyone here. I was terrified. It was really horrible.

ANA GASTEYER:

I can't speak for other women entirely, but I think that for me the distinct disadvantage of being a woman in any situation—particularly one as competitive as this one—is that I have a really hard time turning off the social-political filter. I don't think that the men in our cast sit around concerning themselves with who likes them and who doesn't as much as I think women do—and as much as I do as a woman. I think that's a feminine quality that I have, that I'm intuitive about interpersonal relationships and I worry about interpersonal relationships and interoffice politics, and I spent a lot of energy concerning myself with that as opposed to like my work getting on the air, and I think that men are just more comfortable with the competition.

I speak to college groups and stuff about being a woman. This era has been clearly less scathed—if that's a word—and if anything, I think we were exalted, for reasons that weren't always clear to me early on, Molly Shannon and Cheri Oteri and I. We got press for it. We got press for being this trifecta of women that turned the show around. I mean, that's what they talked about. I don't think there's such a thing as actual exaltation every day in this place, because there's just too many creative people that need exaltation at any given time. But, you know, we were written up and we were photographed together. That sort of signifies that you've changed a tune, and certainly we heard it anecdotally all the time—that the women are the best thing on the show.

JANEANE GAROFALO:

Life is a boys club. So *SNL* is a reflection of that. But Molly Shannon and Ana Gasteyer and Cheri Oteri and Rachel Dratch and Tina Fey kicked ass. They came in and would not be denied. I'll admit that I was not prepared to deal with the wall of resistance. Molly was. Molly is a much stronger person than me. And she is easily more talented than me.

I'm not being self-deprecating. I think Molly came in and her attitude was right on the money. And it was, "I'll kill you with kindness." But she's fucking very tough. And she is writing and writing and writing and she will not take no for an answer. And she also would not get involved in the bullshit. No gossiping, no nothing. The males were worse gossips than the females. And Molly did not play that game. She didn't get involved with drugs and alcohol. She was there to work.

MAYA RUDOLPH:

I think there's nothing sexier than a funny lady. Funny ladies are pretty damn sexy. There's so much wit and confidence in that, and I love that. I like being a funny lady. I feel I've definitely become more of a woman because of my job—that and turning thirty.

AMY POEHLER, *Cast Member:*

I'm of the school that loves crazy makeup and wigs and teeth. I always want my characters to look uglier than I'm allowed or than I have time for. I think as I've learned through meeting many people that come through here, Vanity is the Death of Comedy. The minute you start feeling you're hot stuff, you're in trouble. I'd much rather have people laugh than go, "Whoo!" I don't want any of that. I think it's pretty hard to be sexy and funny at the same time. Some people can do it, but few can pull it off.

MIKE SHOEMAKER, *Coproducer:*

Lorne always says that producers are supposed to be invisible. So our jobs are really ill defined. To put it simply, Kenny Aymong is studio, Marci Klein is talent, and I kind of cover the connection between the cast and the writers and the producers. But truthfully we overlap, because if there's something that you're good at, you wind up doing it. There's things that Marci does, the way she deals with certain talent, that's genius, but if I were to tell you what it was, it would probably diminish its effectiveness. It's in the way she talks to a host or a cast member. I have to deal with the well-being of a lot of the cast and writers, because they're mine in some ways. When somebody has like a complaint or a problem I'm usually the first stop — for certain people. For other people the first stop is Marci or Steve Higgins. Whenever someone's cut from a sketch, I deliver the bad news. When someone's freaking out, I provide emotional support.

When you're a producer your job is talking to people and getting them to do things you want them to do and yet having them feel that it's their choice and that they're not being forced. The plan of the show is that everyone — cast, writers, performers — they're all doing what they want to do and it's theirs and they own it, and at the same time it's also what we want to do, but we have in some ways to make them feel that it's theirs.

We don't dictate things. The show's like a stampede, and I feel that my job is kind of to keep it going. When someone falls and is about to be trampled, you pick them up and dust them off and kind of send them on their way. You can't really effect change but you can try to avert catastrophes.

JIMMY FALLON:

Mike Shoemaker is a producer, a writer, a therapist. He's the guy people complain to about not being in the show, or "Hey, can you get someone to write something for me?" They'll go to Shoemaker, because they're afraid to embarrass themselves and ask the writers.

When you first get the show, he's the orientation guy. He helps all the new people get acquainted with the place.

Sometimes he forces new writers to sit with a cast member and write something. He does it a lot. That's how I came up with "Jarret's Room," actually, the Internet talk show. I had this idea, he goes, "I'll put you with this new writer, Matt Murray; you sit in the room until you write it." We sat there for four hours and we wrote it.

The show needs Mike. Definitely. I don't know who else I would talk to. He's also a ghost writer, definitely, for "Update." He writes jokes, he punches stuff up. He's been there since Dennis Miller, I think. It's like going to school. His comedy mind is great. I always go to him to bounce stuff off of him. He says, "Oh that's funny" or blah, blah, blah. Saturday mornings, he's always up there with me and Tina writing the jokes, picking what's funny and how to punch it up.

Lorne will come out and say, "You milked it a little bit too long." Like I asked him about the Ian McKellen thing, my reaction after he kissed me. I thought I milked it one beat too long. Lorne goes, "Yes, you did." Ian was more aggressive on the air than at dress, by the way. If you watch it in slow motion, you'll see a little tongue action. He really went for it, man. Anyway, I knew Lorne would tell me the truth, but Shoemaker said, "That was fine. It really worked." He's just always very positive.

All previous mishaps and calamities that had befallen Saturday Night Live *since it was founded were rendered insignificant when, on September 11, 2001, Islamic terrorists flew passenger jets into the twin towers of the World Trade Center—jolting New York, shocking the world. For the producers, writers, and cast of the show, there was a subtext to the tragedy: The twenty-seventh season premiere was eighteen days away. Or was it? Should the fall season be delayed under the circumstances? How much news of the day could decently be satirized by a comedy troupe? Was any attempt to wring laughs out of current events automatically in poor taste?*

On the major decision—whether to air the season premiere in its scheduled time slot—Michaels had to do little deliberation. Mayor Rudolph Giuliani, soon to be named Time *magazine's Man of the Year, asked Michaels to go ahead with the show as a signal that life in New York was going ahead as well. Since first taking office, Giuliani had been a semifrequent visitor to the show, dropping by occasionally during the live telecast as he made his rounds on a Saturday night and having hosted on November 22, 1997. This time, on September 29, he would deliver the first punch line to the first joke to air after the attack.*

First, Michaels's longtime close friend Paul Simon sang his song "The Boxer," a number that Michaels himself requested (though others on the staff found it dubiously appropriate). Onstage, a crowd of New York firemen and policemen listened silently, grim faces panned by the studio cameras. The song over, Michaels stepped up and asked Giuliani if it was all right for Saturday Night Live *to be "funny." Giuliani responded, smiling slightly, "Why start now?" Then, when the laughter subsided, Giuliani exultantly shouted the show's famous opening line.*

Live from New York, New York was alive.

AMY POEHLER:

I was home in the East Village on 9/11. I could see the towers out of my window. All of us who were working on the show at the time called each other to see if everybody was okay, and then after all that died down the next question was, What are we going to do? Do we even have a job? I was thinking they might postpone the show. There was talk about everything coming to a halt. Even thinking about your work, your work in comedy, seemed so kind of frivolous at the time you couldn't even indulge in thinking about it. And then a couple weeks went by and it was like, "Oh yeah, we gotta put on a show." I just remember it being incredibly emotional and Rudy Giuliani being there. It was very tense and very weird.

RUDOLPH GIULIANI:

Lorne asked me if I would appear on the first show they did after September 11. They had visualized what they wanted before they talked to me. In other words, they wanted me and the police commissioner and the fire commissioner, and they wanted a group of firefighters and police officers in order to do something that would honor them. But they also wanted to see if I would appear and in essence make it easier for people to laugh again, basically say to them, "It's okay to laugh."

I don't remember if it was Lorne or Brad Grey who called me and actually wanted to know if I thought it was okay to go ahead with the show, which Letterman had also asked through his producers—whether it was okay to go ahead with that show. Several people had called me to ask me that. I think at *Saturday Night Live,* they were debating whether to do it that week or the next week. And I said not only did I think it was okay to go ahead with the show, I said sooner rather than later. People have to get back into learning how to laugh and cry on the same day, because they're going to be doing it for a long time.

It was a period of time in which I knew I couldn't move people back to normal, but maybe we could at least get them to start doing the things they normally did, to be able to deal with some of the pain they were going through. One of the ways you get through a horrible catastrophic event—like if you lose your mother or your father or a loved one—is you grieve, you mourn, and then you try to get back into your normal way of life. So I pushed them to go ahead with the show.

I thought the show made a tremendous contribution, and I thought the way they handled it—I've seen that tape maybe two or three times since then—was absolutely magnificent. It's hard to watch it and not have a tear in your eye.

I'll tell you what happened the night of the show. I was operating at that point on like two or three hours' sleep per night, and I was going to go home immediately after the opening. I was going to leave after the beginning and not stay for the whole show. And Fire Commissioner Von Essen and I went upstairs to Lorne's office to get our stuff—and we couldn't leave.

And I don't know if that was the funniest *Saturday Night* ever, but to me it was, because it was like I literally hadn't laughed from September 11th up to that point. So it was a little bit like when you go to a restaurant and you're very hungry and the food tastes terrific; you're not sure if the food really is terrific or you're just very hungry.

But we just spent the next hour and a half in Lorne's office just laughing. We couldn't leave. And it was like a release. There were a number of the police officers and firefighters who remained as guests; I could see it was like a release for them too. It was like, "I can laugh now. This is terrific." And I thought they really rose to the occasion. It was a very funny show and a very sensitively done show, because you could easily have made a terrible mistake with a show like that.

WILL FERRELL:
I have a hard time figuring out what the viewpoint of the 9/11 show was. I guess in the final analysis you can't critique it the way you would any other show. Some people said to me, "Great job, it was wonderful," and other people said, "That was lame," because we didn't do really tough sketches. It was a benign show, and maybe that was the best thing to do under the circumstances. The biggest thing I'll take away from it was after the show—talking to firemen and policemen. They just kept thanking us and saying, "Thanks for the break, we really needed it," and we were going, "What?! We should be thanking you." I did get a little bit emotional toward the end, but I still had my hard hat on.

RUDOLPH GIULIANI:
I think they've been unerring in their sensitivity and the way in which they've handled September 11. I was at the show when they did the open with Will Ferrell playing President Bush offering the Bush-Cheney plan for dealing with the suicide bombers, in which they would offer telephone sex as opposed to the seventy-two virgins, and I thought it was hilarious. And I think the night of that show they did the whole thing with Jesse Jackson calling up the Taliban and wanting to go over there and be the one to be called upon to settle it, which was very, very funny.

MARCI KLEIN:
I live downtown near the World Trade Center, and after the tragedy occurred on September 11th, I couldn't get back to my apartment. Like everyone else, I was incredibly upset. I couldn't believe what was happening.

We had been in the midst of planning our first show of the season, which was scheduled to air on September 29th. A couple days after the attack, I told Lorne, "The first show cannot happen. This is not a time to be funny. There is no way we can do a show in two weeks." Lorne told me he thought I was right, but he didn't want to cancel just yet. It was too early. Given that Mayor Giuliani wound up telling us he wanted us to go ahead and do the show, Lorne was right not to have immediately canceled it.

Reese Witherspoon was scheduled to host, and her agent called me and said, "What are you doing, what is going to happen?" I said, "Well, we are going to try and do what we can." Obviously none of us had ever been faced with doing the show under such circumstances, but you can't call it a hardship. We were all lucky enough to be alive and have our families intact. So many people in New York weren't in the same position. I was really proud of the way everyone on the show kept that perspective.

I'll never forget how remarkable Reese wound up being as host. She just did a terrific job and never let the pressure get to her. Reese was a total pro. She showed up with her baby and worked really hard. Everybody was impressed. I will always be grateful for the way she acted. It was such a difficult time for everybody, maybe the most difficult time ever in the history of the show.

But when Mayor Giuliani stood there with the firemen, it was one of the most stirring moments I'd experienced since becoming part of the show. Everyone in the studio audience was just transfixed by it — the Paul Simon song, the firemen and the mayor standing silently and listening. I couldn't help wondering how many of the people watching at home that night had lost someone they loved on September 11, and were perhaps finding some comfort in the way it was done.

Meanwhile, Ben Stiller was supposed to host the following week. Ben was a member of the cast, briefly, back in 1989. We had booked him the previous year because we knew he had a movie coming out in September. He had actually been booked eight months in advance. Now I didn't even know this, but someone in my office had been getting e-mails from Ben Stiller's office in early September with a lot of special requests for him while he was hosting—things like "a groomer," and other stuff. The Friday before Reese hosted, I got a call at 6:30 P.M. from Ben Stiller's publicist. Without the hint of an apology, she just announced that "Ben is dropping out of the show."

Now I will admit that I was still very shaken about September 11, in part because I lived so close to the towers, and I was scared out of my mind, so maybe that helps explain why I just went crazy. I said, "How dare you call and cancel like this? Ben is from New York. He should be fucking showing up with bells on to help the city through this! Haven't you heard what the mayor said?" She started saying he was canceling because of September 11th, and I said, "Wait a second. Reese Witherspoon, who has never done the show, who doesn't even really know if she can handle this—and, unlike Ben, was never even a cast member—is doing the first show. Don't you think Ben ought to maybe rethink it for a second?" And she said to me, "I can't believe you would be so insensitive." I said to her, "Listen, let's just be clear about one thing: The world isn't going to come to an end because Ben Stiller doesn't host *Saturday Night Live*. On the grand scale of things, I just saw three thousand people die out my kitchen window. That's what matters."

I was freaking out. I just said, "Fine. If that's the way he feels, I'm happy to let it go." I think she was surprised. I couldn't believe he would cancel like that. And then I hung up. Someone in my office who had overheard the conversation then said to me, "You don't understand. I think he's dropping out because we were saying no to a lot of stuff that he had wanted while he was hosting." I told her I thought it was more than that: "He's just scared of not being funny."

With that, I call Lorne and tell him what happened. I said, "I disinvited him," and Lorne said, "Fine. We'll get someone else." We were just dumbstruck. Ben never called Lorne, he never called me, he never wrote a letter to the show, nothing. Then, I turn on the fucking TV a couple days later and who do I see but Ben Stiller. He's on *The View,* the *Today* show, he's on every show doing press for his movie. I said to Lorne, "Something's not right here." Turns out they had moved his movie up a week because, they said, the world needed comedy. So what really happened was, Ben's people wanted me to move Ben to the first show and reschedule Reese, you know? I just think it is so wrong what he did.

On the day of the anthrax discovery at 30 Rock, I was at home, and when I called my office after hearing the news, a lot of people there were obviously hysterical. Drew Barrymore was the guest host for that week's show, and she said, "I am going to leave, calm myself down, and go back to my hotel." I completely understood. Then I made sure to tell everyone that if they didn't feel comfortable staying in the building, they should go home. Some people did say, "I am getting out of here, and I will come back when it is fine." It was a very scary situation. Just horrible.

STEVE HIGGINS:

Marci was in control on the anthrax crisis, and so it's one of those things where you go, "Too many cooks spoil the broth. If they need me, they'll call me." I did talk to Drew about it after she talked to the doctor. She was freaked out in the beginning, but then in the end she put on that game face and went ahead with it.

MARCI KLEIN:

I calmed Drew down, but I felt bad for her. Everyone thought she had left town and she didn't. She stayed and she did the show. And this show is really scary to do under the best of circumstances.

ANA GASTEYER:

When I found out I was pregnant, I tried to keep it secret. I was really paranoid. I was a wreck. I just didn't really know how my being pregnant was going to go over. I had a good feeling about it, but I didn't know if they would want me to leave or what. Tom, in wardrobe, I told right away, because he knows my body so well with the weekly fittings—a nightmare, by the way—but I also knew it would be our challenge to keep this kind of under wraps as best we possibly could. Fortunately everyone I work with is such a narcissist, they don't have time to worry about what other people are doing. James, my writer, who I shared an office with, said, "You had gained some weight but you weren't bitching about it, so I kind of knew." You know, it flashed on him: There's an actress in my midst who's not screaming about how fat she is.

When I told Lorne, he didn't seem surprised, but he never really seems surprised about anything. He was fantastic about it, actually. He's a father; he was very supportive. I think he was afraid I was coming in to say I was sick or something had happened. I think he was glad to hear it was good news. He was really cool about making it clear that it wasn't going to impact me in a negative way. Then again, he didn't throw his arms around me, or plant a kiss on me.

My husband and I tried to plan it in such a way that it would work for my career, but you can't really predict conception. It actually happened exactly as I wanted it to. I got pregnant in September, I showed halfway through the season, and I'm due five weeks after the last show of the season. I think Lorne was pleased that my biology had agreed with the format of the show.

In some ways the denial, not telling people, really helped me, because I just had to kind of plow through. I remember when I first started here thinking, "There is no way I'm going to be able to pull an all-nighter." And it's such a routine part of my life now that I think pregnancy fatigue is nothing compared to what we normally go through in a week.

It's worse in the first trimester, and I managed to get through it. I was very careful. I probably had more caffeine than most pregnant women do—not a lot. In a lot of ways it was nice, because it gave me perspective, it gave me like an outside life. This show means so much to people who work here. It's a lifestyle, it's a fraternity, it's a part of everything that you are, so sometimes that's dangerous, because you're in the well and you can't get out of it. It's nice to have something that's also meaningful.

It was really important to me that my work stay consistent. I'm proud that I was able to keep working at the pace that I did. I'm well represented on the show. I have been the entire time I've been here. There are weeks I've been in a shitty mood and say I wish my thing got picked. But I can always figure out the logic; there's always something that makes sense as to why things happen. It's emotional, and I have plenty of moments when I think, "I can't believe my thing got cut," but I just feel that Lorne's predominantly fair with people, and I think he's handled my pregnancy in kind.

The other people in the cast are all completely cute about it. I feel like they're practically going to ask me where babies come from, like, "How's it going to come out?" They're all so young and it's just not really in their sphere. A lot of them touch my belly. I had my dukes up about being written out or not being acknowledged, and I remember being pleasantly surprised that a fair number—especially of the male writers—aren't even really hung up on it. Sometimes I'm pregnant in a sketch, and sometimes I'm not. Sometimes it's just me in a scene, which is really nice, because they can use it as a joke or they don't have to. I made that really clear, because I'm not uptight about it. It's much cuter than I expected.

MAYA RUDOLPH:

My first year here they had a Mother's Day special. I wasn't sure how I was going to deal with it. I have to say being here during that and hearing everybody have fun with their moms and doing funny bits, I was very jealous because my bit was very somber and serious. But in the end I was very happy to share that with my family, not only with my father but with my stepfather too. Because it isn't something you see very often on television. I have a Japanese stepmother and my dad is Jewish and I'm mixed. We are like this motley crew.

Molly Shannon and I both lost our moms when we were really little. You're certainly kind of alone in that when you're growing up, and it's rare to find people, let alone women, who have lost their mothers so young. It's kind of like belonging to a club when you find each other. Molly and I have a similar path that we followed, and it's very interesting to both of us.

I was planning on doing this when I grew up when my mom was still alive, but there's definitely no question that comedy got me through a lot of horrible stuff that I went through as a kid. If my mom didn't have a natural gift to be a singer, I think she would have been a comedian. That's nice to know.

All television shows obviously live or die by ratings. Fortunately for Saturday Night Live, *its ratings built steadily from its first year—already successful—to 1978, a peak year in terms of creativity and Nielsens as well. For that season,* SNL *averaged a 12.6 rating and powerhouse 39 share (a rating is a percentage of all TV homes, and a share is a percentage of TV homes with their sets on at that time). By contrast, for the 2000–01 season, SNL averaged a 5.4 rating and 15 share, but the drop wasn't nearly as dramatic as it sounds, because when the show began it had virtually no competition but old movies on local stations. There weren't hundreds of cable channels; cable was mostly recycled movies, with little original programming.*

Jean Doumanian's experiment in failure, the 1980–81 season, scored the lowest SNL ratings in four years, even though the number of NBC affiliates carrying the show had grown. Dick Ebersol's first year scored a lower average than Doumanian's, but arguably the audience had been chased away and needed to be lured back by positive word-of-mouth. Ebersol kept the audience from slipping away further but did not equal the best ratings of the first five-year period.

Lorne Michaels's return to the show in 1985 didn't electrify the nation either, and the ratings remained virtually the same as in Ebersol's last year. They rose as Michaels reasserted himself and the show regained its status. Throughout the run, of course, the show was treasured by the network for the demographic profile of its viewers—youngish and affluent, the advertisers' favorites—and today networks read demographic tea leaves more religiously than they do the numbers of total viewers and households. Saturday Night Live, *for better or worse, was instrumental in bringing this about.*

Through good times and bad, Saturday Night Live *remained NBC's highest-rated late-night show during the final decade of the twentieth century, generating hundreds of millions in revenues.*

At the start of the new millennium, seasonal averages of a 5.4 rating and 15 share seemed low compared to the 12.6 and 39 of 1978–79, but Saturday Night Live's *ratings were still considered excellent and its demographics exemplary. An attempt by ABC to imitate the show in 1980 with a shrill Los Angeles–based series called* Fridays *lasted only two seasons, but at one point in its first season it briefly outrated Doumanian's version of SNL. Subsequently, SNL handily bumped off such wannabe competitors as a Howard Stern comedy show aired by CBS affiliates, and it easily outpaced MADtv on Fox.*

WARREN LITTLEFIELD:

What's truly amazing is that it's reinvented itself so many, many, many times. And what's equally amazing is that I was a viewer when it first premiered, and I'm a viewer now. I spent a lot of years at NBC—it was part of the crown jewels of the network—but just as a pure come-to-the-set-for-the-joy-of-it experience, I've been there through all those eras. I've been there and watched my children now come there. And there's precious few things in television that have accomplished that.

JAMES DOWNEY:

I think these days Lorne probably takes the network's calls more. I think Lorne's personal tastes are probably much closer to performers than to pure writers. To the extent that the network doesn't agree with the writing staff, Lorne probably agrees on the whole more with the network.

ANDY BRECKMAN:

The problem now is in that room. It's who is or isn't standing up to Lorne, who is maybe taking him on when his instincts are a little low-brow or, you know, too middle-of-the-road, or too safe—who is defending the conceptual writers' pieces in that room. You can almost see by looking at the show what's happening in that room, the room where they do the read-through on Wednesday nights. You can just see it. What's happening, from the little I've seen of the show, is that nobody is defending the smarter pieces, because there always are smarter pieces being written. The read-throughs, by and large, have a great variety. They are, all of them, fifty sketches long. And there's a lot of sketches that are great ideas but could use a little work to make them better, and with a little nurturing over the course of Thursday rewrite could be very strong. But there has to be somebody in the room championing those pieces. And I can just tell, just looking at the show now, that there's nobody standing up to Lorne.

CHRIS PARNELL:

We find out each summer around the first of July if we're coming back or not. So in the summer of 2001, when July first rolled around,

SNL asked the actors waiting for news about their contracts if they could hold out for a couple more weeks because Lorne's mom had passed away, and they asked for time for him to deal with that. And we're all like, okay, fine, whatever. So two weeks go by and then they ask for another extension of another week. Meanwhile, I find out they're auditioning new people for the cast, so I got in touch with the other people who were on the chopping block—Horatio, Maya, and Rachel—and then I heard Maya got brought back and Rachel and Horatio also. And then finally I talked to my manager, and he said, "Lorne's not bringing you back." So it was a pretty big shock. I thought I was doing all right there. I really thought we'd all come back, but it was me that didn't.

I gave up my apartment in New York and moved back to L.A. I kept hearing that I might be coming back, and finally I just told my manager to quit telling me these tales, because he would talk to Lorne and he'd say to me, "Lorne says he might be bringing you back," and I'd get my hopes up and nothing would happen and I'd be disappointed and depressed again. So I said, "Don't tell me anything else unless they want to bring me back for real."

Finally, around the end of February 2002, I was about to test for this pilot and found out that day that *SNL* wanted me to come back for the rest of the season. We were hoping to get a guarantee for the next season too, but we couldn't get that. So I just finally decided that I love the job and I didn't feel ready to go when I was let go. Lorne apologized for putting me through this waiting thing and this sort of limbo situation. He said he wasn't trying to cause me any more pain. The only reference he made was to the budget, that it was a budget issue, and that they'd hired four new cast members. He just blamed it on the budget.

One of the things that made being fired bearable was that there was such a collective outpouring of shock from the writers and other cast members that seemed really sincere. It made me feel like I wasn't just sort of living in some fairyland where I thought everything was okay and it wasn't.

JON STEWART:

As much as I'd like to think I understand television production and understand what it takes to put on a show, I was absolutely knocked out by how they put that show on, just knocked out. The ability of each fiefdom to know their shit, do their shit, and execute at the level they execute was remarkable—really, really impressive to watch. It's unprecedented, it really is.

You don't really think about what effect your presence on the show is going to have. The shit comes all so fast, you don't have time to think about reactions, and if you start thinking about it, about the effect, you're sunk. All you can think about intuitively is, "That looks good, yeah, that's funny, I'll go with that, or that seems a little too didactic." You've got to be into the thing. If you start thinking like, "Maybe that'll get picked up by the wire services," then you're fucked.

MAYA RUDOLPH:

I have a hard time sleeping. I drive myself crazy with worry and I make myself sick with fear from everything in the world. There are certain weeks where I'm frustrated here and certain weeks that I'm mad at myself because I didn't write what I should have written or I've shot myself in the foot. I think if anything, my biggest thing here and my hardest job to get through is just my own personal fear of not being funny and trying to learn how to write. I never really aspired to be a writer, and here I am writing every week on my favorite show in the world. I make myself sick with worry every week about my writing.

But if I start to take any of this stuff personally or worry about how this is working or how much I'm on, I'm going to drive myself nuts. I have to be here far too many years of my life for that. I don't want to be unhappy here.

I'm such a people pleaser that I'm sure I wouldn't let anybody see all the things that are going on in my brain.

I say pretty nasty things in private. I'm a very foul-mouthed young lady. I have a really wonderfully dirty sense of humor. I love really dirty things. You can ask anyone and they'll tell you the same. I get pissed off, but I'm such a Chatty Kathy that everyone ends up hearing about it. I get mad when I'm not in the show or when I fuck up. If I fuck up, I shake and I get embarrassed. For whatever reason, I get nervous here but I don't get that nervous. I get nervous like if my dad's here or if there's a guy I think is cute and is watching the show. I don't get nervous because it's *Saturday Night Live*. I get excited because it's *Saturday Night Live*.

AMY POEHLER:

I'm much too egotistical and insular about my own performance to be able to look at the show as a whole. I've never watched old repeats of *SNL* because I can't bear it. I mean reruns of older seasons of stuff, because if the scene's funny I'm jealous that I didn't think of it. It's too intimidating. I just can't compare myself. I love it so much I can't even watch it.

May 18, 2002, marked the final show of Saturday Night Live's *twenty-seventh season. Winona Ryder was the host, using* SNL *as her "coming out" after being largely reclusive following an arrest for shoplifting. She had been a good soldier throughout the week of rehearsals; she didn't throw any fits, stage any walkouts, or complain about the sketches. If it weren't for some whispers amongst the staff that she had set her sights on Jimmy Fallon, her hosting week would have been almost boring.*

Overshadowing Ryder's appearance was the fact that this was to be the last show for Will Ferrell as a cast member. After seven years, he had decided it was time to move on, despite the fact that Michaels and the rest of the producers and cast wanted him to stay. Much of the show was being designed as a final tribute to Will and his many characters—Alex Trebek, the professor in the "Lovers" sketch, even Neil Diamond.

An hour before dress rehearsal, Neil Diamond called on Michaels's line, and when the assistant said there was a guy on the phone claiming to be Neil Diamond, those sitting around shouted in unison, "Hang up," believing it to be a crank call. Minutes later, when coproducer Marci Klein entered, it turned out she'd been trying to reach him, and it had been the real Neil returning her call. Klein called Diamond back at his hotel and talked him into making an appearance on the show while Will was doing his Diamond parody. To listen to her pitch was to listen to someone who clearly had done this many times before. "It'll be great," she told him. "We'll send a car for you, and you can spend a few minutes with Will figuring out what you want to do." Klein, along with producer Steve Higgins and Michaels, had already decided they didn't want to surprise Ferrell; besides, he already knew that the real Alex Trebek was coming in to help finish out the Jeopardy! sketch. Diamond agreed, and Klein directed her staff to pick him up and gather Will and anyone else involved in the Diamond number at home base at ten-thirty, between dress and air.

With videotaped good-byes from the cast closing out the show, all that remained for the night was the season-ending party, held downstairs at 30 Rock. There was the usual mass gathering of New York chic, and the traditional more private room for Michaels, the cast, writers, and VIP's. Donald Trump stood around and watched, while Yankees pitcher David Wells and his wife hung out with former Yankee ace David Cone. Music blared, many danced, but most of all, people seemed to be taking a deep breath. There would be no pressures Monday to invent material for another host, just the promise of summer. Ana Gasteyer would be having a baby, Jimmy Fallon was running off to do a movie for Woody Allen, Tina Fey was writing a movie for Paramount, and so forth.

WILL FERRELL:

We can't use the word "graduated." I said that to Lorne once and he said, "I hate that word." On my last night, the biggest overriding feeling really was that of it being very surreal. It was emotional at times and then strange in the sense that I had so much to do, and was moving around so much from sketch to sketch that it didn't even really hit me until the very end. And even then I tended to focus on how something played better at dress than it did on air, like I did every week. It got to me more after the show; it was sort of a "retirement party meets a wedding reception." There was a sense of accomplishment but a sense of I was glad it was over. I will miss most the obvious things—the personal relationships and the people. I'll miss most the moments you'll never see: the goofing around during the blocking of sketches on Thursday and Friday. Those were the parts of the week that were the most fun for me. That seventeenth floor has the same feeling of living in a dorm, except that everybody is doing comedy, and I liked that feeling.

What I'll miss the least for sure is the crazy hours, especially

Tuesday night. There really is no reason why we have to come in late on Tuesday and work late and write sketches until seven A.M. It's a remnant of the coke days, I think. It was fun at first in a weird sort of way, but after seven years of doing it, you have to say, "Wait a minute—why do we do it that way?"

On May 21, 2002—a few days after that final show of the season— about 150 members of the Saturday Night Live *family, past and present, gathered in Studio 8H to pay tribute to Audrey Peart Dickman, one of the show's producers from its beginnings in 1975 to 1993, who had died the previous summer. Dickman occupied a special place in the hearts of the show's cast and crew for more than two decades; thus the occasion became a rare moment when the show's past and present met in the show's home studio.*

Chevy Chase chatted amicably with Bill Murray, old animosities gone with the wind, or rather with the passing years. Old-timer Dan Aykroyd joked with new-timers Jimmy Fallon and Tina Fey and Horatio Sanz. Such veteran writers as Rosie Shuster, Marilyn Suzanne Miller, Ann Beatts, Herb Sargent, and Alan Zweibel showed up, like graduates at homecoming.

Lorne welcomed everyone to 8H, made very brief remarks, said he had difficulty speaking about Audrey, and left the stage. Murray, among those memoralizing Dickman, recalled how he used to pick her up in the air and spin her over his head. "She was very light," he said.

Murray said the date marked another milestone, the thirteenth anniversary of Gilda Radner's death. "Audrey's gone, Gilda's gone, Belushi's gone," Murray said, "and there's so many other people that should have gone first. A lot of them are in this room today." Much laughter from the crowd. "Anybody here that wants to admit that they should have died ahead of Audrey?" The question was rhetorical and facetious, but a few people raised their hands.

Michaels stood at the back of the room during the speeches, inescapably and perpetually, if remotely, patriarchal. It is a family, after all—a family of gifted misfits and brilliant oddballs—and it comes together now and then to remember, to celebrate, to mourn—and, no matter how solemn the occasion, to laugh.

ALAN ZWEIBEL, *Writer:*

Emotions are things that I've never really seen Lorne easily verbalize. I was hoping, hoping that there would be something emotional that he would say at Audrey's memorial. Brad Grey, like many others, said it's too bad he has so much trouble emoting. You just assume over the course of years, especially when people have kids, that there's a softening, that there's some sort of emotional acknowledgment, you know. I guess some people it doesn't work with. I can't speak about Lorne authoritatively, I just don't know anymore.

I live in California, so I hadn't seen a lot of those people and combinations of people in many years, and I was affected by it in a very, very profound way. In a wonderful way. I was happy that I had these kinds of feelings. My mind immediately went to, "Jesus, if Lorne dies, are we still going to be able to get together like this? Who's going to throw the party?"

DON OHLMEYER:

I've always admired what Lorne's been able to do for so long. When you think of all the different sketches that have gone into *SNL* since, what, 1975 — when you think of all the things that they've done, there's a lot of chaff among the wheat. But God, the wheat is spectacular.

LORNE MICHAELS:

I tend to think that the most interesting work done each week gets on the air. I think that's what an editor's supposed to do, bring out the best in writers. Do we get the best writers? I think people who want to do this kind of work find us. Now there's *MADtv,* and on cable there's a bunch of these kinds of shows. Conan O'Brien, Leno, do all these sketches. Most of the writers who have been on *The Simpsons* are people who passed through here. *Seinfeld* too.

I've never left here on any Saturday night thinking, "Well, that was a great one." I tend to see only the mistakes. That hasn't changed. Neither has the amount of adrenaline that you produce to get through the show. What has changed is that the hangover of it is generally gone by sometime Sunday, whereas it used to be that a show that didn't work could ruin a whole month. You'd go back and obsess about it. It's like at the beginning you just worry all the time, and when you get older you know when to worry.

Now on the weekend I have kids jumping on me. You can't get out of it with "Daddy worked really, really hard," or "Daddy was up till four-thirty in the morning." The worst thing is when you find that you still have the taste of beer in your mouth and you're getting up and being a dad and it's only been four or five hours since you went to bed.

GWYNETH PALTROW:

Fame is such a weird and distorting thing. I've thought a lot about it, and my theory is that you kind of stop growing at the age you are when you become famous. Because what happens is, people start removing all your obstacles, and if you have no obstacles you don't know who you are. You don't have real perspective on the problems that face you in life, how to surmount them, and what kind of character you have. When you're in the public eye, people project things onto you, and if you take them on yourself, they're very scattering and they can alienate you. Being famous can be very damaging in lots of ways. *Saturday Night Live* is proof of that.

DARRELL HAMMOND:

I try to improve myself every week. It's the only hope I have of making it in show business is to improve. I have to be better than I was. That's the way I look at it, because I'm not a glamour person. If that's what it was all about, then I would just be glamorous. You know, I would love to be a glamour boy, but I'm not.

AMY POEHLER:

We did a show with Queen Latifah as guest host. In one sketch, she and Maya and I were playing this kind of doo-wop group, these sixties girls, and we rehearsed the songs for a couple days beforehand. It was kind of a "Behind the Music" thing. So during the live show, with ten seconds to go before the sketch, we could hear Jena Rositano, the stage manager, talking into her headset saying, "Wait. What? What?? Do you want me to tell them that? Are you kidding me? Are you kidding me?"

MAYA RUDOLPH:

We kept hearing her say into her headset, "Do you want me to tell them that?" Then she said, "Okay." And it was like eight seconds to go, and she looks up and says to us, "You're going to be singing with no music. Five, four, three—" And we had four songs to sing! And you just go, "Ugh." The show goes so smoothly most of the time, we don't realize when it fucks up how bad things can be. We had dance moves and costume changes and songs and harmonies. We had rehearsed it to death and then it just blew up in our faces because there was no music track. That was scary. It was horrible. It was really, really horrible.

AMY POEHLER:

I loved it. We just sang it without the music. And it was one of those things like, "Oh my God, the fuckin' show *is* live. It really is." Of course there's some poor person who screwed up the music who's getting screamed at, but I loved it. I thought it was super exciting. I used to love that about watching the show. I loved being reminded that anything could happen. I loved the screwups. I loved being reminded that it was live.

AL GORE:

The timing of my hosting *Saturday Night Live* was driven mainly by the timing of our book tour, and the timing of my decision to run or not run was driven by the end of the calendar year. And the two just began to converge. It's really interesting the way they fell together, two nights in a row. That was not part of a master plan; it just happened that way. I taped *60 Minutes* on Sunday, just a few hours before it was shown. I didn't make the final decision really until that weekend. What I had intended to do was to wait until the Christmas vacation period, when all of my family was going to be together. And we were going to take a number of days away from everything and everybody, and I was just going to think it through with them and get their feedback. And because of the week of rehearsals, it ended up with the entire family converging in New York that week.

Most of the time when I was not in rehearsals, I was sitting around the suite in the hotel with my family. And the process that I had expected to take place over the Christmas break spontaneously occurred that week because we were all together. I hadn't realized it would happen that way. I knew that once I reached a conclusion one way or the other, I was going to announce it pretty quickly, because I just didn't want to be out there saying disingenuously, "I don't know if I'm going to run," when I really knew that I was or wasn't. So when the family process just emerged, it catalyzed the endgame in my thinking sooner than I expected.

And so midway through that week, I began to lean toward not running. And I tried that idea on for size. And by Saturday I had pretty much decided yeah, I'm not going to do it. But by then the impending performance was a welcome distraction, because you just give yourself over to the vortex of the live performance, and I just put it all on hold until the following day. It actually turned out to be a pretty healthy way to do it, although I wouldn't recommend it to anybody. It just happened.

Absolutely I would have done the sketches I did if I had decided to run for president. I didn't see anything wrong with them. And yes, Tipper and I were really kissing during the opening. Absolutely. I think it was even longer than at the convention.

For me, doing the show was similar to the reason why I love downhill skiing. I am not very good at it, so it takes every ounce of concentration I have in order to avoid killing myself on the way down the mountain, and when I get to the bottom, I feel refreshed because I have not thought about anything other than surviving. And that's pretty much the way that Saturday was.

Oh, it was great fun hosting. I had a blast and so did Tipper. We really enjoyed it a lot. And all of our kids had fun. Our second oldest daughter, Kristin, is a comedy writer working in Hollywood, and she has a number of friends who are on the writing staff at SNL that she knew from the Harvard Lampoon days, so they invited her to come and participate during that week. So we had a little inside track in getting into the minds of what was coming up. That made it even more fun, because we got to hear about a lot of skits that didn't get as far as us.

I had to say no to a few things. If you don't, you're not doing your job as a host. They depend on that. But I didn't say no to very much. I thought they had a tremendous number of good ideas. Now there were some that I thought were funny as hell that I nevertheless wasn't comfortable doing, because I wasn't comfortable saying the words. But I'm sure that's par for the course.

I thought the reaction was really heartening. I still have people come up to me to this day saying, "Hey, really liked you and Tipper on *Saturday Night Live.*" That's just a lot of fun. We had great fun doing it. The show is such a wonderful part of American culture.

JAMES DOWNEY:

If the show were ever canceled, you could never get something like it on again. The idea that the best way to improve it is to cancel it and start over is bullshit. They should definitely keep it on. I don't think a little ratings pressure is the worst thing in the world, but it's probably better not to go crazy over that and give things time. If the show is bad, everyone knows instantly that it's bad. But if it starts to get good again, it seems to take like four years for the word to get around.

I think if Lorne were to step down, the show would very quickly be canceled. I'm absolutely convinced of that—especially at this point. The moment he's replaced, then there's no argument against replacing "that guy." And once that starts to happen, the network will pick that show to pieces. It will get worse and worse and worse, and they will never acknowledge that it was their meddling that made it worse. Besides, I can only imagine the kind of person he'd be replaced with. Believe me, they would not pick some bold young cutting-edge thinker who would startle everyone with his ideas. It would be someone who would make the show much more like the rest of the network.

JEFF ZUCKER, *NBC Universal President and CEO:*

I've been watching the show since I was a little kid. What I remember the most is probably Gilda and Roseanne Roseannadanna.

Having been a producer of the *Today* show for almost ten years, I had a lot of respect for what Lorne does as a producer. And I think the biggest thing an executive can do in those kinds of roles is just support the producers and let their vision speak. There was nothing broken at *Saturday Night Live.* People are fond of saying certain years are better than other years, but at the end of the day, it's all pretty good and pretty special.

I actually think that one of the biggest things I wanted to do when I got my job was address the fact that Lorne and this cast have been totally underutilized by NBC. I can't speak to what happened in relationships before me, but obviously I had a relationship with Lorne from being here in New York, at the *Today* show, and having grown up in New York. I think that that has helped. It's not an accident that we've had a pilot with Lorne each of the last two years, that Tracy Morgan is going to do a show for us, and that we have a development deal with Tina Fey. One of the things that I'm most proud of is that we're tapping into this.

ROBERT WRIGHT:

The show has always been a magnet for criticism, but I would say honestly less so in the last number of years. I don't think it's because the show isn't daring; I think it's because there is so much material on television that offends groups one way or the other that they don't have enough time in a day to write letters to us and the other two hundred shows that they're unhappy about. Today it has to survive not on outrageousness but on extremely good performances and great writing, because in terms of the outrageous aspect—there's just too many places you can go for that.

KEN AYMONG:

I love seeing new people start on this show. A couple years ago I started giving them tickets from their first show that they worked on. I always wish I had had that myself. It's more important, though, for a writer, because that is what this show is; it's a celebration of writing— enhanced by performers, obviously, and the director and Lorne and everybody else who works here. The biggest part of the show to me is the celebration of ideas. That's what I love most about it.

And when you see a new writer start here, they come in with physical comedy in mind—clichés and that sort of thing. But there's inherent talent there. And when I have the opportunity during the course of a season, I say, "I envy you so much. Because from this point on, you're going to look at the world totally different. Now the world gets to service you. All you have to do is see it. And the whole world is going to look different to you now."

I wish I had that gift—to observe. That's the greatest gift I think a writer can have, is to actually observe the human condition, to actually put it down on paper and give an emotion to it.

ROBERT WRIGHT:

I have no idea if the show could survive without Lorne. That's a complete hypothetical. Now *MADtv* has come and stayed and proven that other people can do similar kinds of programming, and Fox has been consistently supportive of that. I just think producing *SNL* is a harder task. You'd have to find people like Lorne to do that. Conan is that kind of a person. I don't know whether Conan wants to be a producer, he wants to be a talent, but he could be a talent, executive producer, or writer. Who's to say? It would be probably fifty-fifty.

LORNE MICHAELS:

I feel old almost every day. I used to remember everything; now I don't. It's also getting harder in the morning to remember my grudges. I have a much harder time holding on to anger other than in the moment. I just lose interest in it. I don't chew over negative things anymore to such a large extent. I'm not great with anger.

There are an enormous number of things that went wrong in my life, a lot of things that were unfair. I'm always going to put a better face on it. That's just the way I was brought up and who I am. People want to believe that I'm someone who at this moment is drinking champagne from a slipper somewhere and on my way into a hot tub with seventy-two virgins or whatever. Fine. I'd much rather my life be perceived as glamorous or stylish than as one of an enormous amount of work that is unceasing. It's a choice: Either you try to make it look easy or you emphasize how hard it is.

My dad never complained—and I admired that.

7

Politica: 2002–2008

CHRISTOPHER WALKEN, *Host:*

I got on a plane shortly after I had hosted and I was sitting next to this woman, and we did the thing that people do on planes, you know—you don't get into each other's space. So we just sat in silence and when the plane was about to land, she looked over at me and said, "It's a great pleasure to meet Colonel Angus." It was funny to have a woman tell me that.

As SNL's twenty-ninth season began on October 4, 2003, the show was still smarting from the departure of the legendary Will Ferrell almost two years earlier. The case could easily be made that Ferrell and Eddie Murphy were the two most important cast members in the show's history. Both were ubiquitous and had the ability to strengthen weak material—to salvage scenes or sketches that would otherwise have died. Other performers had exited in the spring of 2003—among them the ever-physical Chris Kattan and the ever-quirky Tracy Morgan, who'd gotten away with calling Lorne Michaels his "bitch" backstage, an in joke that Michaels found amusing.

Will Forte and Seth Meyers had, meanwhile, proven themselves in the lower ranks and were promoted to full repertory-player status. Luckily, and by now predictably, more reinforcements would find their way to Studio 8H, including the buoyant and versatile Kenan Thompson, who'd costarred as a teenager in two sitcoms on Nickelodeon, the cable channel for kids. Thompson was also subtly symbolic of generational change in the air; he was officially the first SNL *cast member to be younger than the show. Thompson was born in 1978, and the show, of course, began in 1975.*

TRACY MORGAN, *Cast Member:*

It was hard for me to leave, because I had been there for seven years. So you were leaving your friends. It was actually sad. It was bittersweet. That was the end of an era for me. There was no going back. But one door closes, another opens up. I had a TV show in the works, *The Tracy Morgan Show,* which was being produced by NBC, and Lorne was the executive producer. So Lorne knew I was leaving. There was no dramatic thing about telling him. I wasn't shy to talk to him. I'm a man. I'm a grown man.

WILL FORTE, *Cast Member:*

I came in following 2002, right after Will Ferrell had left, so my first show was the first show without him. I feel like at that time, the show was trying to find its new identity. Even though there were still so many wonderful, funny people there, Will was just such a huge part of the show for a long time. So they were trying to figure out what its next phase was going to be.

FRED ARMISEN, *Cast Member:*

I was playing drums in punk bands throughout the '90s and I thought that was where I was going to be headed as far as what I wanted to do. In 1998 I played drums with a band at South by Southwest. I decided I would bring a video camera and interview bands—I don't know why; I just thought it would be a funny thing to do—and do different characters. Previous to that when I was a drummer in a band I found it difficult to get any press or get a lot of attention. So when I did this video where I was interviewing bands, a friend of mine edited it for me and I just sort of distributed it myself. The attention I got from it was very immediate. All of a sudden people wanted to see the tape more than they wanted to come see my band play. So I started showing the video around the country. I traveled to L.A. and San Francisco and little by little all of these certain opportunities unfolded. I got to do some videos for HBO—by HBO I mean HBO Zone; they had another digital channel—and then also there was a music show called *Reverb* so they had me on that. And then I moved to L.A. and just started doing a little bit of stand-up, doing characters. I ended up on Bob Odenkirk's pilot. So all of a sudden I had this tape of me doing characters. My manager at the time sent it to Marci Klein, and then the next thing I knew I was auditioning for *SNL*.

LINDSAY SHOOKUS, *Producer*:

The lore of the audition process has become that Lorne doesn't laugh. Everyone says they are warned in advance that Lorne won't laugh. It's just not true. Lorne will really laugh, and I promise you that Lorne has never hired someone that hasn't made him really laugh. What he won't do is the polite laugh. He won't laugh to make someone feel better when they are bombing. Luckily, there are a couple of us who will.

A few years ago during a camera test in 8H, one of the men auditioning went behind a flat they had set up on the side of the stage, then he stepped out completely naked with his hands between his legs. I think his idea was that he would step out to a roar of laughter and thunderous applause (from all fifteen of us in the room). Instead, the poor naked guy got a whole bunch of silence with a few scattered polite chuckles. He was just standing there, holding his junk, in Studio 8H, in front of Lorne Michaels. You can imagine what an awkward few moments it was when he finished his audition. We're all sitting there, waiting, checking our phones, and watching naked guy collect his props and costumes from all over the stage in silence. Not surprising, but this poor sweet guy was not hired.

FRED ARMISEN:

I prepared so much for my audition that I remember all of it. I went up as Fericito, so then he could introduce all my other characters. I did a self-defense expert, then I did Sam Waterston from *Law & Order,* and then Vin Diesel. And I brought timbales, one of my drums. I really had a lot of stuff. It was an incredible experience. I couldn't believe I was on that stage; I couldn't believe I was doing this. That's how I met Lorne and Tina. For me, it was such a new thing in my life. The whole thing was so surreal and such a dream that I felt very lucky immediately. I didn't feel like, "I hope I get this," I felt like, "Aw, I can't believe I got this far," because it was literally four years out of me having played drums in bands. It really felt like that was the very height of what I can do. It was like, "I can't believe I got to meet Lorne and Tina."

KENAN THOMPSON, *Cast Member:*

I was living in L.A. and I'd flown out to New York to audition for the show. I'd done a couple of auditions, but one was at a comedy club where there was no stage, just a microphone, and kind of angrier people came there. I'd never done stand-up before that point, so that was a little tough for me. Then there was an audition on a stage a couple of days later and that was a little more comfortable. Then a week later they were like, "We want you to audition one more time at the Laugh Factory," *another* comedy club. That was terrifying once again because it was me versus three other stand-up comedians that night, and they, like, tore the roof off the place, 'cause that's what they do. I was very nervous, but the next day I got the call that I was on the show, and I moved from L.A. to New York in two days. My mom was jumping up and down and screaming. I was jumping up and down and screaming—and crying.

FINESSE MITCHELL, *Cast Member:*

They introduced me as a new featured player on "Weekend Update," and I gave a movie report on black people going to see *Crouching Tiger, Hidden Dragon* and finding out they were going to have to read for two and a half hours because the movie had subtitles. It went great. When it was over I walked through the studio high-fiving people like I was Prince after he sang "Purple Rain."

My second host of my first year was Halle Berry, and I was in love with her. All week we had been hitting it off, and we were doing a sketch where I was one of my many characters, doing the ghetto girl Starkeisha, and she was going to be part of that ghetto-girl crew. And when we went to dress rehearsal for the first time to do those characters I was in drag, you know, as a woman, backstage, getting ready to rehearse. I'm standing there in heels, makeup, a wig, and a dress, and

I just saw her look me up and down like, "Oh no, and I liked you, too." It was just this slow-motion look that I saw on her face like, "Oh no, we could've hooked up." And I just looked at her like, "Oh no! Not that look!" And then I thought, "Holy shit. This is it. I just ruined it. I could've been Mr. Berry."

DAN AYKROYD, *Host:*

I had gone back a couple of times to do Bob Dole and was there to do Rush Limbaugh once. Then I came back with [John] Goodman when we were selling *Blues Brothers 2000*. He was host, and I was sort of cohost. But going back to host by myself was totally new. I said to Lorne finally, after years and years and years, "Yes, I will come back and host," and it was fun because I was working with Tom Davis, and I would say we wrote most of that show. We had [Jim] Downey with us, and I was renting—just for the week—an ancient fire hall, a tiny one-carriage fire hall from the 1800s that had been turned into a town house. So we wrote out of there.

I wrote a Fred Garvin piece ["Fred Garvin, Male Prostitute"]. Fred was in an accident but had some parts around that still worked. So I had this elaborate erection machine planned for the side of my leg and was ready to go. We also had written another piece, a Sam Elliott parody—you know how great his voice is—with the premise being that Sam Elliott can sell anything: He can sell you a glass full of metal filings in motor oil and you'll drink it. It was coming down toward that last pocket of the show where there's always kind of interesting, quirky material, and it made for a classic Lorne moment. He came to me and said, "We could do Fred, but we would lose the Sam Elliott piece," and in a minute and a half, Lorne, Tom, and I had to make the decision which piece to do. It was that express decision making that has to be done from time to time, and within twenty seconds the three of us agreed that people had seen the character Fred Garvin, but they had never seen my Sam Elliott impression. So we went for the new.

AL SHARPTON, *Host:*

When I was running for president in 2003, Lorne Michaels called and invited me to host, and it was quite a debate with my campaign staff because people felt that if I did it, it could be risky; we didn't know what was going to happen. And I listened to the debate on both sides and I thought about it and I called Lorne back, and he said, "I cannot guarantee that it won't get risqué, but, you know, we rehearse, so you'll know what's coming." I said, "I'll do it." During rehearsals, he said to me, "Why'd you decide to do it?" I told him, "Because I want the country to know I can laugh at myself." I thought that was important because everybody knew me as a civil rights leader and a guy running for president, and you're always in protest movements angry, and I wanted everyone to understand that I was angry about a cause, I wasn't just a guy that gets up in the morning with a bad attitude.

There were some states that said, "We're not doing it live because he's a candidate," and Jeff Zucker was president of NBC at the time and he said, "To hell with it. We're going with it live anyway." So it became a bigger show because NBC stood up to Iowa and New Hampshire.

LORNE MICHAELS, *Executive Producer:*

I thought he was viable and he behaved great. I think there were maybe six affiliates that dropped out, but it was the right thing to go on with the show.

AL SHARPTON:

Paris Hilton was a late addition, and they told me [that] when they said, "Well, you know, it's going to be hosted by the Reverend Al Sharpton" she said, "Who's Reverend Al Sharpton?" And when they left the dressing room, I looked at my assistant and asked, "Who is Paris Hilton?" because I had no idea who she was. Tracy Morgan had come on in the opening bit saying he looked like me and he was in a tracksuit and with the medallion. In rehearsal, I just said, "I feel good," but on the live show, what no one knew—Tracy, Lorne, anyone—was that I was going to dance. When I said, "I feel good," I did a little bit of footstep, a James Brown dance, so that was my little surprise for Lorne. We got good ratings that night.

LORNE MICHAELS:

Darrell *inhabits* characters. His Bill Clinton *is* Bill Clinton. He had the same power that Dana had with George Bush, which was after a while when you saw George Bush on television, he wasn't enough like George Bush, you know? And in the same way, when you saw Clinton, we could not *not* think of Darrell.

DARRELL HAMMOND, *Cast Member:*

I did W. one time. I remember after dress rehearsal I was hoping it wouldn't make it to air. I didn't like doing it because they were directing me to play it like Will Ferrell had done it, and I didn't want to play it like him. A, it wasn't right to repeat the work that he had created, and B, Will did things differently and he was a friend of mine. He had come up with this creation, and I wanted to come up with my own, but that wasn't going to be available to me and so I moved on. I asked out of it. So I only did him once.

WILL FORTE:

I did not want to do Bush. I was so appreciative of being given the opportunity to be at the show that I would do whatever they would ask. But I'm not an impersonator; that's just not my strong suit. So it was a tricky situation. At that time it was a pretty big cast, too, so I would be doing these George Bush things that I wasn't necessarily comfortable doing and then wouldn't get an opportunity to do the kind of stuff that I wanted to do 'cause they would need to take care of everybody. They would say, "Will's got his Bush thing, so he's taken care of for the show," and then I wouldn't get the more absurd stuff that I really like doing. That all fell by the wayside. It was a tough period.

I think I probably did it for a year, including that fall, when they had all the presidential debate sketches. It was very tough; I was very self-conscious about it, and I didn't particularly feel that I did a very good job. Those presidential election periods and those great debates that I'd seen over the years was a really special thing about the show, but I felt like I was part of the one period that might not have been so great just because I didn't think that I was that good. It's a shame because Seth Meyers did a great John Kerry; he would hold up his end of the deal, but I just didn't give him anything great to play off of.

It was also hard because Will Ferrell was so good at it. I didn't want to see anybody come in and do George Bush after Will Ferrell did it. It was almost like somebody coming in and taking over the role of Church Lady. That's Dana Carvey; nobody else can do Church Lady. And that's kind of what it felt like with George Bush. You can't retire George Bush, because somebody's gotta be him. It was a little bit out of my control. So I apologize to the world for that.

ROBERT SMIGEL, *Writer:*

In the later years on "TV Funhouse" I did more political satire than I generally wanted to, but after Will Ferrell left they did less and less with Bush, and I felt the need to fill that void. Ferrell was incredible and obviously unmatchable, but I had liked Forte's Bush. He had a nice feel for the way Bush would get defensive and kind of whiny, like a little kid. But they weren't using him.

One time I did a particularly dark cartoon called "Torboto," about a robot that tortures people, developed by Dick Cheney to circumvent the Geneva Convention's barring of torture as inhuman. I was worried it was more angry than good, and that night Chappelle was visiting the show. I watched him watching it with his mouth agape. Afterward he looked at me and only said, "You got balls." It confirmed two things for me—that it wasn't that funny, and that *everyone* is afraid of Dick Cheney.

JAMES DOWNEY, *Writer:*

There are ideas that I've had that I thought were funnier than the audience did. I've been doing this so long that I like to try things I've never tried. I like to really see what I can get away with, and sometimes I shock myself. Sometimes it's risky because I'm skating right up to the very edge.

There was one Bush piece I did a couple times in dress that I think died twice and was never on. It was after Abu Ghraib. I knew I was in very dangerous comedy territory, and it was a piece where Bush was trying to justify Abu Ghraib. He was addressing the nation and saying it was an attempt, maybe awkward on our part, to make Iraqis more comfortable with their bodies. There was something about the joy of the nudist lifestyle, and I remember at one point it had a joke like, "Many people have objected to the fact that the detainees were forced to mime sex acts. Now, is it the fact that it was sex acts that you find offensive or is it that it was homosexual sex acts? Think about that, then tell me who's in the wrong here." I thought it was funny. It was a desperate attempt to turn the tables on critics.

One of the problems, I thought, was that it wasn't Will Ferrell doing Bush. We went through so many Bushes, because we had Will, Darrell briefly, Will Forte, and then Jason finally. So this was Will Forte, one of my favorite performers ever, and he did his best, but I think the subject matter was just so disturbing [that] people were like, "No, no, I'm sorry, you're not going to make me laugh about anything that comes within a mile of that." When we did the sketch it was like a death camp in there; the audience was like, "No." There's not laughing, and then there's aggressive silence, where their chins are out and it's like, "I'm so angry you're doing this that I'm going to hold this against the next piece."

ROBERT SMIGEL:

One cartoon I liked, because you didn't see where it was going, was a stop-motion one called "Santa and the States." It was written after Bush beat Kerry on the back of polarizing issues like gay marriage, and the country felt very divided. So Santa is skipping the red states, which, on the map he shows to Rudolph, are labeled DUMB-FUCKISTAN. He makes crude jokes about trailer-park yahoos and this is absolutely killing with the New York studio audience. But then the cartoon starts to turn. You see Santa hanging out with Natalie Merchant and Moby making increasingly smug comments, and finally a blue-state child lectures him on being bigoted for labeling and dismissing red staters as ignorant "for caring about God."

I had supported Kerry but this kind of snobbism had creeped me out, so it felt good to write about it. And yet the next day there were right-wing blogs attacking the cartoon, because it also had a Rush Limbaugh cameo where he becomes the red states' Santa, but it's revealed to be a hallucination—he wakes up over a toilet with OxyContin pills everywhere. So instead of chalking one up for their side, Drudge put the still frame of Rush on the toilet on its front page and labeled the whole thing a disgusting liberal attack. It was kind of funny but mostly sad in the way it reinforced a point of the cartoon: that it's easier and more profitable to keep selling outrage than build any bridges.

Comedy sketches are even more transitory and evanescent than episodes of TV shows: they melt away like snowflakes in the sun. Even so, fans of Saturday Night Live *cherish the memories of enduring sketches from many eras of the show—Richard Pryor and Chevy Chase doing a word-association test, Eddie Murphy playing James Brown in a hot tub, or that whole surreal series of nutty* Jeopardy! *spoofs with Will Ferrell as Alex Trebek and Darrell Hammond as Sean Connery. And a sketch doesn't have to be great to be immortal. One famous (or notorious) example: a "Debbie Downer" sketch from a 2004 show hosted by Lindsay Lohan. This one went viral on the air, in a manner of speaking; Jimmy Fallon was the first to "break," or crack up, and soon everyone at the table— supposedly in a Disney World restaurant—was convulsing in laughter, including Rachel Dratch, who was supposed to maintain a look of sullen anguish as Debbie, a world-class party pooper who likes to dampen everybody's spirits with incongruous references to "deadly terrorist attacks" or "the number one killer of domestic cats." The more they laughed, the more they laughed, until the actors couldn't bear to look at one another for fear of escalating the hysterics.*

LINDSAY LOHAN, *Host:*

I love hosting. It's just a really good energy there, the whole building. It's nice to be around people that are so excited to do what they do and appreciate it and have fun doing it. I will pretty much do anything they ask me to do. It's always fun for me to mock myself and laugh about things that people perceive in the wrong way. It's a great kind of platform to do that.

Sometimes it's hard not to laugh yourself. That's what makes the show so exciting to do. Where else can you do that besides *SNL?*

HORATIO SANZ, *Cast Member:*

Lindsay was so hot at the time. Like, "hot" in both hot physically and hot in her career. She was pretty young, too, and everybody was kinda weird, like the whole building was buzzing with sexuality. She was being set up to be like this super sex-symbol movie star, and that energy kind of came off in the show. It was a very fun, kind of naughty, crazy show. You see these kids, and you're like, "Yeah, there's only so much time these guys have before it all blows up," because they're kind of these little robots being offered up, like with Britney when she was on the show. I mean, she couldn't make a decision without seven of her people chiming in. You feel kind of bad for them, but in a way, sometimes I felt like we were part of the chain that was exploiting them. But the show is what it is. America wants to see those people.

JIMMY FALLON, *Cast Member:*

Rachel had this character who was a bummer person, Debbie Downer. She would just sit around and say things that would bring the room down. We did this sketch where we're at breakfast at Disney World and her line is, "It's official: I can't have children." We all knew that was her line, and we were just waiting for her to say it. And the room was shaking. I'm not kidding, it, like, vibrated, like an earthquake. And we're all looking at her. In my head, I'm like, "Just say your line and fucking get out of the sketch" because Horatio was laughing so hard he was crying.

PAULA PELL, *Writer:*

Rachel had the idea to do that character and so I always wrote the "Debbie Downers" with her. The best scenario ever for people like me who write characters a lot for *SNL* is just to find that character that every person watching has in their life. And it's not very often that you can think of that thing, and when you tap into it, it's pretty amazing.

RACHEL DRATCH, *Cast Member:*

I always loved when things went "wrong" on the show because it reminds you the show really is live. You'd be surprised how many people would ask if the show really is live, so for me that showed the spontaneity, the you-never-know-how-something-will-go quality of the whole thing.

Jimmy and Horatio were laughing really hard at rehearsal and I was thinking, "These guys, they better not mess up my thing with cracking up," even though sometimes it's like we all crack up. But then I don't know what it was—I did the sulk through one of the lines, and I think we were all just giddy from the rehearsal. I can't really explain—it was just a random giggle fit that was completely contagious.

PAULA PELL:

Horatio was wiping tears of laughter out of his eyes with a waffle. It was such an orgasmic experience for a comedy writer. I still hear people referencing it. Even in a drama, it will be like, "Don't be a Debbie Downer about this," and that just cracks us up.

Earlier in the new century there'd been another entry in the annals of unforeseen classics: "More Cowbell," written by Will Ferrell with Donnell Campbell, a playwright friend of his, which proved to be a case study in the genre of ridiculous absurdity. Set in a recording studio, the sketch combined an arcane premise—the 1976 recording of a song by rock group Blue Öyster Cult—with sublime performances and an intentional wardrobe malfunction that revealed Will Ferrell's hairy belly. Fallon, of course, broke, setting off another chain reaction. The sketch became not just iconic but mythic, so that when Ferrell returned to host in 2005, he reprised the character he'd played—Gene Frenkle—this time joining an actual rock group, Queens of the Stone Age, in performance. Naturally, Ferrell had cowbell firmly in hand.

WILL FERRELL, *Host:*

When I went back to host, there was still a fair amount of people that were on the show when I left, so I thought it would probably be fun, but then I realized, "Oh, you kinda can't go home; you can't ever go back home in a way." Even though I was the host, and I knew Horatio Sanz and Amy Poehler and a bunch of people on that cast, all of a sudden— it's not anyone's fault—you're just on the outside. You know everyone has their little bits and inside jokes and you're kind of going, "Oh, what are you guys talking about?" and it used to be, *you* used to be the one who was part of that cast fun. Then the second time I hosted, I knew less people and it actually, in a weird way, was a better show for me. For some reason I was more relaxed. But it is a very strange transition.

JIMMY FALLON:

"Cowbell" was insanity. In dress, it was fine at best, but on-air, everyone upped their game. Will Ferrell wore a shorter shirt so his gut would fly out at the bottom, and Christopher Walken wasn't even talking like a human being. He was yelling, "You gotta have more cowbell" like in a weird cadence. It was one of the funniest things I ever heard. The whole thing was so surreal and dumb. And then Kattan and Will were screwing around, and Kattan pushes Will and somehow knocks his sunglasses off and Will turns his head and looks at me. I saw the eyes of a lunatic. His sweaty stomach was hanging out the bottom of his shirt, his eyes are just staring at me, and that was the moment for my line, and man, oh, man, I just broke. I just couldn't stop.

I was brand-new on the show. I was a stand-up. I didn't know how to play with these people. These guys were professional comedians. They were geniuses. My head hurt me. I had a comedy headache from those guys being too fun.

CHRISTOPHER WALKEN:

A few years after I had done the cowbell sketch, I did a play on Broadway and people brought cowbells to the theater and banged them at the curtain call, and at the stage door, people had special pens and asked me if I would sign their cowbell.

WILL FERRELL:

I went to see him [Walken] in a play a few years ago, and I went backstage after to say hello, and he was talking about the fact that people would bang cowbells at him, and he had a wide smile on his face, and said, "You know, you've ruined my career."

JIMMY FALLON:

I had originally wanted to leave after five years, because Belushi only did five years, and in my head I wanted to be John Belushi. But then I got "Update" and stayed. I never want to stay longer than I have to; as a fan of the show, I like when people leave because that's what makes *Saturday Night Live* work. If you had the same cast that you had from the '70s, this show wouldn't be around. The whole fun of *Saturday Night Live* is people stay and then they leave and then you miss them and then they come back and visit. A part of me hated to leave, but I just had to do it.

TINA FEY, *Cast Member*:

I remember feeling like, "Why are you leaving me? Don't leave me!" Like a spouse.

JIMMY FALLON:

Obviously it was a TV love affair with Tina; I love her so much. She was my partner; she was the best thing that ever happened to my comedy career, to my brain. Doing "Update" with her was my favorite thing in the world. To say good-bye to that was so weirdly sad. I know it's a job, but it's like going to camp and she was my bunkmate. We were really close pals. I talked to her about everything, about all the people I went out with at the time. And I was always asking for her advice. But I knew her career exploded once "Weekend Update" started, so I knew she'd be fine.

LORNE MICHAELS:

You'd have to know Jimmy as well as I do, but I think in Jimmy's head, somehow his reverence for the first five years is such that it's almost codified: you do your five years and then you leave.

JIMMY FALLON:

The first month after I left was just awful. The show came back and I wasn't on? I would watch every show, because I'm a fan, and just be so sad. I started to e-mail Lorne and e-mail Tina—"I don't like this, I don't like that," whatever—just trying to be a part of the show, still, even though I wasn't in the cast. I just loved it so much; I was just happy that there was no dead space, there was no flop in between. Amy and Tina just took it and ran with it, you know, and made it bigger than ever.

LORNE MICHAELS:

I don't know how long Kenan has been here, but no one's going, "God, I wish he'd make room for others." But for Jimmy I think it was a point of integrity rather than self-interest. He didn't think, "You know, Hollywood's calling, I'm going out there." He just thought, "I've done this and I've done it well."

JIMMY FALLON:

I had no plan; I didn't know what to do. You know, you always hope for an Adam Sandler career, or a Mike Myers movie career. And so I said, "I guess I'm going to do movies." Lorne was a bit exasperated, but he said, "Let me know any way I can help." He was just the coolest guy ever. Then he goes, "But also, you know, Conan O'Brien is leaving, and we're going to need a replacement for him. Would you ever want to host a talk show?" I go, "I don't know. I mean, really?" I remember Tina was in the office and Tina goes, "Oh God, stop it. You'd be great! You're Irish, you love to talk to people, and you've got that charm." I just said, "Well, we'll see in five years," because it was some weird deal where Conan signed a thing that said, "You're going to take over *The Tonight Show* in five years." So I had five years to figure my life out knowing that I could have this job.

I tried movies, but they did not work for me. My first big movie was *Taxi* and we got beat out by — what was it, *Alien vs. Predator*? And then I had a move called *Fever Pitch*, with Drew Barrymore, and that got beat out by a movie called *Sahara* with Matthew McConaughey. Those were the ones that felt like the end of my career. But the good thing is I met my wife, Nancy, at *Fever Pitch*.

But Lorne was a man of his word. He called me and said, "Hey, remember I brought up the thing about Conan leaving? Would you want to do this talk show?" I go, "Yeah, but let me ask my wife," so I called Nancy and said, "Lorne is offering me the *Late Night* show." And she goes, "You have to do it. Even if you flop you have to do it because only two other people have done it, Letterman and Conan O'Brien. Just to be on that list, how cool is that?" I go, "All right, I love it, I'm in." And I've got to say, NBC did not want me, they had a list of other people they wanted and told Lorne, "Look, Jimmy Fallon is not hot, he's had two flop movies, you know. We're not into this." And Lorne said, "Well, if you're not into Jimmy then I'm out because I'm bringing him to the party. He's my guest. That's my guy. So if you don't want to do Jimmy, then I don't want to be the producer." It's just pretty cool to tell the story now because the guy believed in me. Why? He didn't have to do that, but I also know I'll never forget it. It was a giant gamble that he didn't have to make. Just so you know, for the rest of my career, I'm going to do everything with Lorne. I owe him so much.

JEFF ZUCKER, *NBC Universal President and CEO:*

The only question we had about Jimmy was whether he was willing to commit and put in the time. Lorne, Jimmy, and I had a dinner together to discuss it, and the rest is history.

LORNE MICHAELS:

After Jimmy left, the way it came down was, Tina and I talked about it, and I said, "I think you should consider Amy because we've never done two women and I think you'd get along great and you will have a different kind of thing." I had spent enough time around the two of them to know that that would be fun. And I think she also wanted to think about doing it herself, and she wanted to know that I had the confidence in her that she could do it by herself. So I said, "If you want to do it by yourself, do it by yourself. I'm good." You know, there was no question that she'd be more than capable of it. I just said, "It's easier with another person, but if you want to do it yourself, do it yourself." And I think she went away for the weekend and on Friday she was doing it herself and by the end of the weekend she called me and said, "I think I'm going to call Amy and do it with her." I think sometimes people have to inhabit and own the decision themselves. Do you know what I mean? Like she definitely could not have been told she had to have Amy. So much of all of this is about confidence and if you don't feel that you have the support then you're going to flop, you know?

TINA FEY:

Well, I remember having the feeling like, "Oh, if I was really a performer at heart, I would be seizing this opportunity to do it alone." And a part of me was like, "I know I'm supposed to want to do it alone." I think we did some screen tests, and I did one alone, and I was thinking, "I don't like it. I feel weird." I don't really work single. It may have been the week of the first show that season and it was this web of crazy late decisions. We kept stalling on it. Lorne was letting me have a say on who I wanted to do it with and whether I wanted to do it alone. And I remember I went down to D.C. on the train to do a now-defunct *LIFE* magazine cover with John McCain—which also ended up being, like, a hilarious weird artifact to have, me and my glasses in a blazer posing with John McCain. It was some kind of "get out the vote" kind of bipartisan, nonpartisan cover. And I remember that it was on the train ride back from D.C. that I realized I didn't want to do it by myself. I called Lorne, I think it was that Monday night, and then I called Amy, saying, "I want you to do this with me." Again, it's all really spousal, it's like a marriage proposal. Like, "I would like you to please be my comedy partner."

AMY POEHLER, *Cast Member:*

The thing about *SNL* is that people leave and everybody says, "How is it going to go on without them?" And then the show goes on and it's such a testament to the structure that Lorne has set up and it's also a testament to the idea that change can be good, and new, fresh, young, interesting people are always around the corner. And when Jimmy left *SNL* I had encouraged Tina to do "Update" by herself because I thought she was so fierce and strong and good at it, and I think that was the discussion for a while. And then there was talk about having Tina have a partner, and that was when in my head I was like, "Oh, I think that partner should be me, and I think that we would be great together." And I remember when we were talking about "Update" Lorne Michaels said to me, "Everything kind of changes once you look into the camera and say your own name." And that was very true, because up until that point, and certainly the many years before on UCB [Upright Citizens Brigade], I was doing a lot of sketches and playing a lot of different people and looking very different all the time. And "Update" was the first time I looked to camera and said my name, and it made a huge difference. Everything kind of changed.

Whenever you're doing comedy the last thing you want to think about is making history. It's a comedy killer, how important what you're doing is. There has to be a certain amount of irreverence in what you're doing. Tina and I were really excited, certainly, to be the first female anchors—and I think we both were glad it was us and not somebody else—but honestly it wasn't something that we really consciously touched upon or talked about, because it was really not as important as just trying to be funny and do a good job. The history part is what people wrote about, and it's nice to have that framing, but like any partnership there has to be that chemistry, and what we were most excited about was the idea of getting to perform together. We knew that we were going to have the chemistry. *SNL* can feel like a very individual and lonely place, so when you get to have a partner, you get to share a similar experience.

We are friends long enough now that she is technically my wife. Though she's yet to agree to take my hand in marriage, I think common law now proves that we are technically comedy wives.

TINA FEY:

You know when a lot of people come to *SNL*, it's their first time on TV, their first time they've been in front of that big an audience. But Amy was fully formed, and we also knew each other. She had plenty of confidence going into it.

AMY POEHLER:

It was very week-to-week. It was kind of like having to find the character of yourself on TV, playing a version of who you were. Tina and I aren't really opposites; people like to think we're like Snow White and Rose Red, but we're actually much more similar than we are different. So we found a rhythm in the way that we did this together. That being said, there was a character of Amy Poehler. You had to discover "what kind of person do I want to be on TV as myself?" and so you would exaggerate certain things. In the beginning there were a lot of writers trying to figure out my voice, and you're just trying to figure out what jokes you can actually deliver. Frankly, it took some time. I don't even want to refer to the first season for me on "Update." It's uncomfortable to me because I feel like my giant eyes are just wider than ever as I try to figure out how to land that plane. It was a new responsibility; it was a steep learning curve and I was very lucky that I was in there with someone like Tina, who had already figured it out and who had become so seasoned so fast.

KEN AYMONG, *Supervising Producer:*

I thought having the two women do "Update" was pretty significant, but more so because they were such strong writers. They had tremendous skills on the writing front, and on the performing side they were really smart and really good on their feet. I've never really bought into the whole gender thing of the show, because throughout the years we've always had great women performers.

TINA FEY:

There have always been women stars on the show, because no matter what's happening in the table-read room, the audience picks who are the stars. Gilda was a star, and in my opinion Jan and Nora and Victoria were stars of that era. But I think we had enough of a shift in the makeup of the writing staff, and we had Beth McCarthy as a female director—we just had more women in that room. And so not for any political reason, but they laughed at things that the women were doing that maybe the men didn't get on the same level. If you were doing your same bit in a room of all white men it's not necessarily going to play the same. I mean, an easy example is—not that these sketches hold up in any way—we used to write, Lori Nasso and I used to write, these parodies of *The View*, and some of the men would say, "What is this, is this a real thing?" And I would go, "Yeah, it's a thing and at least it's a chance for all the women cast to get out." And then it played, and they were like, "Oh, okay." So it wasn't like they were adamantly against it, but if it had only been the guys it wouldn't have played because the real show wasn't on their radar. And so I think by the time, like, Molly and Ana and Cheri did—and again, you know, talk about stars, you cannot say that Cheri Oteri and Molly Shannon were not huge stars at *SNL;* and you had Paula Pell, you had Lori Nasso, you had Cindy Caponera, you had more women in the room — and by the time Maya and Kristen and Amy and Dratch got there they didn't have to do the side work of, like, proving that it made sense for them to be on. They just came in, they killed at the table, they had tremendous confidence, and they got their stuff on.

AMY POEHLER:

It's been, luckily, such a slow and steady climb that it didn't feel like something overnight. So it felt nice. It felt kind of earned. It didn't feel like overnight I became this household name and I hadn't had a body of work behind me. And the person I was doing the work with was someone who, at that point, I had known for almost fifteen years. It wasn't like Tina and I high-fived and then set out every Saturday to change comedy. We just tried to be funny.

BILL HADER, *Cast Member:*

I grew up in Tulsa, Oklahoma, so the idea of being on *Saturday Night Live* was like saying, "I'm going to go colonize Mars." I didn't think it would ever happen.

My audition process was a little crazy. I was performing in a sketch group in a backyard in Van Nuys, and Megan Mullally saw me in that group because her brother-in-law was in the group. So she said, "Hey, you're really funny," and I just said, "Oh, thank you." Then a couple weeks later she called me and said, "I just had dinner with Lorne Michaels and I recommended that he see you for the show because I think you're really funny and they're looking for people like you." The Tina Fey era was winding down and people were starting to leave and they needed new people. I had no management, no agent, no anything. At the time I was working as an assistant editor on *Iron Chef America* and taking classes at Second City in L.A.

When Lorne came to L.A., he came and saw me perform and it went great; it could not have gone any better. He said, "I want to see the show that Megan Mullally saw," and he saw my little sketch group. So our first performance on an actual stage was for Lorne. We had never performed in a theater before. We had just formed. It was really weird. So we did this show, and we killed, it went great and then afterwards Lorne said, "Everyone in the audience were all your friends, weren't they?" And I said, "Yes," and he said, "Okay, I'm going to fly you all out to New York and you're going to do a show where no one knows you." So he flew me out to New York and we did the exact same show and in the front row was Tina Fey and Amy Poehler and Seth Meyers. And it was a writing night, it was a Tuesday night writing night, so they all had this pensive look on their faces like, "We've got to get back and write the show. Why do we have to watch this guy?" And there were a ton of improv students from New York going, "Who the fuck is this guy from L.A.?" And that show went really well. Amy Poehler, I remember specifically, started laughing and it loosened up the whole audience; everyone kind of relaxed. I've always said, "Amy got me the show."

And then nothing happened. But five months later, I got a phone call for an "official audition." I remember going up in the elevator with this guy who had tons of props and I had no props and I was like, "Oh my God, I should have brought props." That was Andy Samberg. That was how I met Andy Samberg. And Andy said he was looking at me going, "Fuck! That guy doesn't need any props!" So we were kind of sizing each other up. I did the audition and then I went back to L.A. A week or two later, I got a manager by this point, and I was with her and she got a phone call and handed me the phone. It was Marci Klein and she goes, "You know you got hired, right?" And I go, "No." And she's like, "Oh. Well, congratulations, you're hired." And I just thought, "Oh wow." And then she goes, "You're going to fly up tomorrow to have this dinner with Lorne. You're flying up with a guy named Andy Samberg, but we don't know if we're going to hire him, so don't tell him anything. Don't tell him you're hired."

So I sat next to Andy on this flight and he's going, "God, I wonder what's going to happen," and it was just crazy awkward and I didn't know what to say. I knew I was hired and was wondering, why would they fly him out and then tell him no, you know? Incidentally, on that plane, in first class, was Judd Apatow and Steve Carell flying to New York to do press for *The 40 Year-Old Virgin,* and the flight got grounded at Dulles airport because of weather and so all the passengers had to hang out. Andy and I were too shy to go over and say hi to Steve Carell and Judd Apatow. We were like, "Wow." We just sat there and stared at them.

One of the most persistent challenges to Saturday Night Live *over the years has been to keep it youthful—to maintain the kind of impudence and unpredictability that made it great in the beginning—and one way to do that was to augment the series with elements that were not "live from New York." Short films were a part of the mix from the beginning, but in the Internet era they assumed new importance on the show. Like the medium of American television itself, they graduated from analog to digital and were substantially transformed.*

The revolution began matter-of-factly, with three junior high school buddies fooling around with newfangled video gear, initially for their own amusement. In time (but not much of it) Digital Shorts made their first appearance on SNL *and became nearly as much of a fixture as "Weekend Update." The guiding stars were cast member and writer Andy Samberg and two exotically named friends, Jorma Taccone and Akiva Schaffer. They had formed a kind of video commune they called the Lonely Island even before they joined* SNL, *then with a go-ahead from Lorne Michaels they began producing weekly pieces.*

They called their videos Digital Shorts because, they would later explain, the production quality was so crappy, so much lower than SNL's *big-time network standard, that they felt they had to distinguish it up front, in the labeling. But Lonely Island proved that filmmaking could now be done—segments conceived, shot, edited, scored, and polished— on the family PC or Mac without looking at all like your uncle Fritz's home movies or even the groin-centric clips that flooded the Internet and the ABC series* America's Funniest Home Videos.

ANDY SAMBERG, *Cast Member:*

I started watching the show when I was eight years old, and I watched, I'd say, every other episode from eight years old until I got hired. When I first started watching, it was people like Dana Carvey and Jon Lovitz and Phil Hartman and then Mike Myers came in and obviously "Wayne's World" was huge for me. And then the next wave that impacted me the most was Sandler, Farley, Spade, and Chris Rock.

LORNE MICHAELS:

I guarantee you that Andy wanted to be Sandler.

AKIVA SCHAFFER, *Writer*:

One of the things that I was interested in very specifically were the short films and music videos that the show had a history of doing every so often—my favorite things like *Men's Synchronized Swimming* or *White Like Me.* I had watched those things over and over again.

ANDY SAMBERG:

Me, Akiva, and Jorma knew each other since junior high school and we linked up after we graduated college in the year 2000 and moved to L.A. and lived together. Akiva and I were both film majors and Jorma was a theater major, and we just started shooting stuff together.

AKIVA SCHAFFER:

Back when we were renting a place on Olympic Boulevard in L.A., I wrote a one-act parody of the Tennessee Williams play *Cat on a Hot Tin Roof* called *Lonely Island,* about how lonely it was on this lonely little island in a sea of traffic—very pseudopoetic and silly. Then when we started making little shorts around the apartment, the opening title would be a shot of it with LONELY ISLAND on the screen. And so by accident that became our name. It's not necessarily a good name; we just got stuck with it.

ANDY SAMBERG:

We thought we were just building stuff on our own, and we had done a few pilots—the Lonely Island did—and all the while I was doing stand-up for I don't know what reason. I always dreamed of being on *SNL* but I didn't think of stand-up as a direct correlation to getting hired there. I even tried, like, a Groundlings audition thing where they place you, but it didn't go well and the style of it didn't feel like it applied to me. It was too much these rules and these games and build characters. I loved *SNL* cast members who had come out of Groundlings but it didn't feel right to me. So we had all this stuff going we were making, but the videos were certainly not why we got hired.

Of the three of us, I was the only one doing stand-up at the time, so they called me first to audition. That went well, which I was shocked by, and because of that somebody said, "So what's the deal with these guys?" And they were like, "They're a group and they work really well together, they have this website with all these videos," and there was material to be looked at if someone cared to look at it. So they brought Jorma and Akiva for an audition and had a writers' meeting with Lorne, and I think all of them went pretty well. They hired me first and then there was a weekend where we had to wait and see if they were going to hire Jorma and Akiva as well, and they— thank goodness—did, as writers.

LORNE MICHAELS:

Jimmy had left the show but was working on the MTV Movie Awards with Mike [Shoemaker] and Steve [Higgins]. Jimmy called me and said, "There's these guys working on the show as writers, and they're the first ones here in the morning and the last ones to leave. I think you should really take a look at them." So all three came in and auditioned and I chose Andy. He was the only one I chose. And Mike, I think with Steve, said, "You know, they make shorts," and I looked at some that they were doing, and they were making a series called *The Boo,* which was a sort of parody of *The O.C.,* and I went, "Okay, bring those two in as writers to work on that."

ANDY SAMBERG:

I think the idea was, "These guys have their own voice, and with Andy as a cast member, we'll have people on the writing staff to help him get that into the show." That is the hardest thing if you become a cast member—translate how you are funny into the show—and I was extraordinarily lucky that they hired those guys, because it's the three of ours' sense of humor that I don't think would have existed if one of us wasn't there.

SETH MEYERS, *Cast Member:*

The three of them were all really talented and they were great people to be around, but their sketches weren't quite working like the stuff they'd done before.

AKIVA SCHAFFER:

We were trying to learn this new skill of writing for *Saturday Night Live,* knowing that what we were really good at was making short films. But we didn't know how to get that onto the show, and we weren't being asked to, either. We knew we had been hired together as a threesome—we're buddies—and our role was to all work on the same team: the team of "getting Andy on the show."

ANDY SAMBERG:

We were still in that place, halfway through our first season, of not knowing if we were making it on the show, to be honest—because you feel things sort of unflow when you first get there, like you have a good table read but the sketch doesn't work well in dress, and it gets cut, or maybe you get something on, but it doesn't go well, or the next week you get shut out. There are so many ways to feel like you are not on solid ground there. We were operating out of fear, not out of confidence.

JORMA TACCONE, *Writer, Director:*

I think we got a little bit frustrated in the way the show works, bringing things to table and not knowing exactly what would work. I think there's a learning curve for everyone who gets to the show. One of the first things we ever wrote for the show was a musical about a boy who's not allowed to wear his shorts at night because his dad's really strict—a musical where Andy's singing and lamenting about why his father is so strict. And then his father, Will Forte, comes in and tells him to stop singing and go to bed, and Andy eventually has a beautiful dream where he floats away on a pair of shorts into the night because all he wants to do is wear his shorts at night. But it did not go over well at the table read at all. It was just such a weird concept. And we started to realize that some of those weirder concepts were things that we just needed to film and present because that was the way to show people that it was potentially good or make sense out of it. Filming it was almost a way to circumvent people not understanding why something was funny. And so one of the first weeks we had off, we went and made a little short called *The Bing Bong Brothers,* which was a takeoff on the Ying Yang Twins' "The Whisper Song," which was this rap song that feels like someone is whispering sexual thoughts into your ear the entire time. And it was just us singing about how we want women to look at us. We borrowed a video camera from Bill Hader's wife, who was working at film school, and shot that really quickly in the West Village and edited it in my apartment, just like on a laptop. Then we were like, "Oh, this is how to get things done, maybe? This is what we've been doing for years; maybe we should try and do it for the show."

COLIN JOST, *Writer:*

They were initially struggling to find their way sketchwise in a live show, and then they went out and shot their first thing, which was *Lettuce,* just a low-budget thing. It wasn't a huge hit but it worked, and it was a new voice.

JORMA TACCONE:

The first time we wrote was teamed up with Will Forte—a conversation between two guys, and while they're having a conversation they start eating heads of lettuce. I wrote a lot of stuff with Will Forte, and stuff with a lot of other people, too. What's so nice about the show is that it does encourage things like that, it does encourage you taking responsibility for your own humor and being able to present it in a way that can be understood by people, why it's funny. I think it is harder for people who go to the show and don't have that luxury of being able to just go off and film it themselves. I think we would have been decent staff writers, but our run at *SNL* would not have been nearly as memorable. We had the distinct advantage of being able to create in that way. And I think there is a lot more opportunity today to do something like that with just you and a camera and a mike and make something funny, which is what you see on YouTube all the time, as opposed to the early Albert Brooks films that needed a 35mm camera and a whole crew and editing for probably a week.

It's so vastly different, the technology nowadays, that you can get something up and have it be late-night quality standards. We edited all those shorts ourselves 'til, like, five, six in the morning. From the moment we stopped shooting them, we were either editing in our offices or on very simple programs on the computer 'til the moment that they aired. That wasn't a possibility even a couple years before we were there, to go and make it all in your office. We would record everyone from Justin Timberlake to Rihanna to Lady Gaga in this shitty little office! It was like inviting someone into your college dorm.

AKIVA SCHAFFER:

When we first decided we were going to make some short films, we specifically didn't want to go pitch and go write it for the table—not to stay under the radar in terms of we didn't want this out, but more to stay under the radar in case we failed. Like, if we made a video for free on our own time and then it comes out badly, there's no embarrassment there. We just can throw it away and no one knows. Whereas if we asked for a big budget and did it in the system and then it turned out stinky, then maybe we'd never get a shot to do it again. We didn't even have to use real edit suites, we just used the computer that we would write on and edit right there. So we'd just turn in the tape because we were afraid to ask permission and have them say no.

So out of fear more than anything else we went and made the very first one, *Lettuce,* for twenty bucks, and then we made *Lazy Sunday* for just the cost of the cab fare.

CHRIS PARNELL, *Cast Member*:

Those guys came to the show with a skill set of how to make these videos already. And they came to me and asked me if I'd go to work on one with them and obviously I said yes. I had no idea it would have the effect it had or the popularity it had.

COLIN JOST:

Lazy Sunday was a huge hit. There hadn't been people doing songs on our show that way probably since Adam Sandler. So it was a combination of a new style, editing it in a funnier and tighter way, and also the music component, which was so strong on its own and was done so well. It was that combination plus Andy being young and having vitality and freshness, and no one had seen him before. It was a great combination. Think about pitching their first couple of digital shorts—pitching Andy and Forte on a stoop, and there's no camera movement and they're talking about a breakup and eating lettuce. No one would be like, "Great! Let's do that!" Or pitching Andy and Chris Parnell rapping about what they do on their Sunday, and you just see some graphic elements on-screen moving around. You'd be like, "All right, but I'd really like to see it first." But they *knew* it was going to be good and they knew they thought it was funny. And that's the biggest thing here: if you feel like something is funny to you, chances are a lot of other people out there will, too.

AKIVA SCHAFFER:

We did *Lazy Sunday* in December of 2005, and by the end of the weekend my brother e-mailed me and told me, "Look at this place where you can watch it online." Because at that point you couldn't watch *SNL* clips online. NBC wasn't putting anything online right after it aired or anything like that. So I was just excited because it was Sunday and I hadn't seen it since we had aired and I was like: "Ooh, I get to watch it again." And that was YouTube.

I have no idea to this day who posted it. And over the next week, as it became kind of a news story, everybody discovered the video and a lot of people discovered YouTube through the video. And then I got so excited: my very first video. I was checking it every day—oh, another ten thousand people saw it, no, a hundred thousand people saw it. By today's standards, if they had five hundred thousand hits it was a huge news story. And it was by far the number one thing on YouTube, but the numbers were not like, obviously, what they are today.

CHRIS PARNELL:

I was home on holiday with my family in Memphis and got a call from Marc Liepis in publicity saying *The New York Times* wanted to do a big interview with me about this "big thing," so that was my first awareness of it. I just feel so lucky to have been a part of that; it was just really cool.

AKIVA SCHAFFER:

My brother noticed a few things on YouTube that he thought could be improved. And he basically did a teeny bit of research and I think the company [YouTube] only really had maybe ten, twelve employees at the time, and he just reached out to them and started talking to them a bunch about it. And in doing so he was looking for a job. And he basically was able to create a job for himself there and started working there from then until well after they sold it to Google. He does not work there anymore.

JORMA TACCONE:

Because *Lazy Sunday* became so popular, I think, we garnered a lot of trust from Lorne and that allowed us to do whatever we wanted to do. And also it wasn't a huge risk because we weren't spending a lot of money making these things. *Lazy Sunday* cost the amount of whatever we spent on videotape and taxi rides to the Upper West Side to go to a theater — cheaper than building sets for a sketch by far. We eventually started getting budgets and shooting things on better cameras and having crew, obviously. In fact, that happened pretty quickly.

ANDY SAMBERG:

All the way up until the year before we got hired, we were still recording *SNL* on VHS tape so we could rewatch sketches we liked. Fred Armisen doing his Native American Comic thing on "Update" — I must have watched that thing, like, thirty times trying to memorize it, it was so great. People always joke to us about how we made YouTube huge, but I think we were more just fortunate in having incredible timing — that we happened to have something people really wanted to watch at the moment computers got fast enough to stream it.

JORMA TACCONE:

So this was the beginning of wanting to see every week how popular something was, because for the first time I think we could quantify the popularity of something we had done in digital hits and downloads.

LORNE MICHAELS:

And then NBC had the classic NBC reaction: sued YouTube. It was suddenly on the front page of the business section, the *Times,* that this start-up called YouTube was being sued by NBC. You know, you would think that somebody would have gone, "Let's just buy this thing or figure it out."

NBC announced at every upfront some new digital strategy, but they didn't have any strategy, obviously, and I wanted SNL.com. I said, "It's idiotic. No kid goes to a corporate site and looks for a show." But they were so fierce about it—"We're building our synergistic NBC.com." And so we weren't allowed to break away. We thought that would have been revolutionary. We would have been Funny or Die or whatever else there was. But they wanted a corporate identity.

SETH MEYERS:

I feel like every so often *SNL* needs a shot of adrenaline to get everybody to pay attention to it again—like those guys and their digital shorts. It just became such a thing that drew people to the show every week. They wanted to see what those guys were going to do. They were as autonomous as anyone has ever been on the show—certainly during the time I was there—in that they would just manage to go off on their own, the three of them, and come up with ideas, week in and week out. They were sort of on a different writing schedule than the rest of the show. As the head writer, I can take no credit for rewriting those spots or giving them suggestions. Every now and then they would shop around ideas, but what those guys pulled off, doing as many of those as they did week in and week out, was unbelievable. The arrival of those guys and the arrival of how people were consuming media on the Web dovetailed together so incredibly well. They were writing sketches every week and we really liked them.

JUSTIN TIMBERLAKE, *Host:*

There was definitely a different energy in their writers' room. It was almost collegiate. The show itself is a bunch of adults who act like children for a living, so obviously they always fit right in. I guess the funniest thing about working with those guys is I feel like most of what we came up with came out of sleep deprivation—when we didn't have time to think about what was PC or not or what would work and what wouldn't. What you have with the Digital Shorts— you have an advantage, which is you have editorial capability. So you can really hit a joke on the nose with the edit.

With *Dick in a Box* we had this loose idea. We're kind of close to the same age so we kind of grew up with that kind of '90s R & B group sound when we were kids, so we had this idea about those groups and how to do a joke about guys who were still stuck in that era. Which wasn't a long era—like half a decade, I think. And so that's the idea we started off on, and then it was kind of like, "How do you get away with them being idiots?" And the best way was for them to be as genuine as possible about the gift they were giving but not totally being at your full wit.

Then the Digital Shorts that came after that were obviously like a spin-off, and then a spin-off of a spin-off. We found that everyone loved those three guys because they were so endearing. So what was so kind of sexist about the lyrics when you looked at the two of them—and this goes back to why you have an advantage with a Digi- tal Short, because you really can, with editorial, you really can hit the joke on the nose with the aesthetic. And I think the fact that we made them look so ridiculous, act so ridiculous, but also so nonintrusive in a way—I think that's what helped it get away with something that seems so misogynistic if it was someone else.

SCARLETT JOHANSSON, *Host:*

I watched the show all the time growing up. We were big *Saturday Night Live* fans in the house, so it was a big family event. We all loved Phil Hartman a lot; we were big Phil Hartman fans. For us it was something that the kids could watch with parents and everybody loved it. That's the great thing about *Saturday Night Live.*

I remember being very happy that there was a rehearsal, because the idea of the show is so abstract you cannot possibly imagine how any of it is going to work, even down to the costume changes. "I have six wig changes in this short period of time and you're going to put fingernails on me and I will have a bald cap and a prosthetic or whatever the hell it calls for?" How it could be possible that you could play a Barbie in one scene and, like, an alien head in another with about a minute and thirty-six seconds in between? It's terrifying. And then of course you have everybody there thinking, "It's old hat," going, "Don't worry, we do this every week. It's going to be fine."

Doing the show is liberating in many ways. I think the thing about *Saturday Night Live,* in order to succeed, is you have to proceed with a kind of reckless abandon, and I think theater has some truth to that, too. I think they probably have more similarities than they do differences. Of course you're there in real time with the audience and I think in both cases the audience wants you to succeed, despite whatever your paranoia might be telling you.

To friends and fans of Julia Louis-Dreyfus, Saturday Night Live *had to be one of the last places they'd expect her to revisit. She'd said being on the show had been anything but a happy experience, particularly in light of the fiercely competitive atmosphere and the drug use she saw. But in 2006, her* Seinfeld *triumph behind her and* SNL *now less cutthroat, Louis-Dreyfus accepted an invitation to return to the show as host. And this time she wasn't bitter.*

Louis-Dreyfus brought backup—her former Seinfeld *castmates Jerry Seinfeld and Jason Alexander—to help with her clever monologue, which ridiculed the so-called* Seinfeld *curse, a lingering myth that held that all four* Seinfeld *stars were doomed to certain failure in anything they attempted after completing the legendary show. The week's guest star was no less than Al Gore, the forty-fifth vice president of the United States, then a busy environmental activist. Gore appeared first in a cold open that envisioned the United States as it might have been under a Gore presidency—which was written by his then-twenty-nine-year-old daughter, former* SNL *staff writer Kristin Gore.*

JULIA LOUIS-DREYFUS, *Host:*

It was like going back in time and fixing things, like if you were a nerd and insecure in high school, then you get to go back and not be the nerd and not be insecure. So from an emotional and psychological point of view, it was pretty remarkable to have that experience. I'm really glad I had it. Because it kind of crystallized a lot of stuff for me. I went back with a lot of experience I didn't have when I was in the cast and I had the added benefit of knowing exactly how the show's done and exactly what I needed to do to protect myself going into the process. And it was great. In addition to that, it was being run by Lorne Michaels and that was a very different creative landscape than it had been when I was a cast member in the '80s. You know, when I hosted in 2006 for the first time, Tina was the head writer, so there was already a very female-friendly culture in place and a plethora of capable, funny, very strong, creative female cast members on the show in addition to writers. Oh, and by the way, it wasn't until, like, halfway through the week that I discovered that I was the first female cast member ever to return as host. Can you imagine that?

I definitely knew that I had to go in with a really strong opener. It's an assload of work to host, at least it was for me, because I didn't want to coast. If you think of the monologue as an SAT exam, that opening is a huge section of your score, and it sets the tone for whether or not you've done a good job. I put a lot of work into it, and I came in with my own material. I wanted to make fun of that whole stupid fucking *Seinfeld* curse shit that was being bandied about and try to poke a hole in it because it was of course absurd.

Even though my time in the beginning there was pretty painful, I'm proud of my association with the show. I feel like I was in the trenches and then to go back was just a kind of personal triumph, a happy one, that's hard to put into words. I think a lot of that is very gender-specific. I think women are better at getting along in a group, frankly. And there are a lot of really funny women in the cast, you know, with Kristen and Maya and Amy and Tina. I'm not suggesting that the men were hostile or aggressive or competitive with one another, but I think there was a culture of friendliness there and I cannot help but think it had sort of an osmosis effect, and I think it came from the ladies. I really do. Because if you think about the material that was popular at the time and successful, you know, characters that came back and stuff, they featured characters that would have a camaraderie between them that was funny, and you can tell it was born out of a friendly environment because the material had a friendliness to it. That's actually when

I met Amy Poehler for the first time and we immediately got along and she's actually become a good friend of mine.

Not every cast member who leaves Saturday Night Live—*and all of them do, eventually—is ushered out with a party and a sketch. Not by a long shot. In fact, most leave quietly when their contracts run out. During the turbulence of the early 1980s, some newly acquired performers were fired before they could appear in a single sketch. At the happy other extreme, Darrell Hammond's talents stayed with the show for fourteen seasons, a record.*

Certainly no one at the show wanted the multitalented Tina Fey to leave; she remains one of the most important writers in SNL *history as well as one of the top "Weekend Update" anchors. It was a huge loss to* SNL *when she departed in 2006. But as the saying goes, It Was Time.*

Two other celebrated women left the show during the same era. Beth McCarthy-Miller was the program's director for eleven years starting in 1995 (succeeding the original, Dave Wilson, who served two terms, 1975–86 and 1989–95) and the first woman to handle that notoriously high-stress job. Rachel Dratch, who left SNL *thinking she was destined for a major role in Fey's* 30 Rock, *got shortchanged by history: the* 30 Rock *gig fell through after the pilot was shot. Dratch was a great TV clown in the tradition of Imogene Coca; her seven years of hilarity on* SNL *comprise an admirable legacy. Among Dratch's best-remembered roles were that of Will Ferrell's spacey New Age "lovah" in a series of uproarious hot-tub sketches and the aforementioned Debbie Downer.*

Horatio Sanz, a versatile and likable SNL *sketch actor, apparently had been at least moderately disgruntled since Adam McKay had left* SNL *as head writer and chafed at being compared to past superstars John Belushi and Chris Farley, mainly because of his portly physique (later trimmed via dieting and exercise). Sanz could do physical comedy handily but clearly preferred material that was more political and cerebral; unfortunately he didn't get a lot of opportunities to do that during his* SNL *tenure.*

Finesse Mitchell, a talented stand-up comic, was a featured player starting in 2003 and became a full cast member in 2005. But the following year he was dropped—the reason given being budget cuts, which can be inflicted on SNL *even if ratings and reviews are good. Mitchell went back to his stand-up career and to roles in sitcoms and comedy movies.*

While Sanz and Dratch were both jettisoned, McCarthy left on her own for perhaps a saner gig, as almost any gig would be. For his part, resident genius Robert Smigel would have one more year before still more budget cuts brought an end to his idiosyncratic tour de force. And Fey? She could have had a lifetime contract if she'd wanted one—but she didn't.

TINA FEY:

My older daughter was born in 2005, and I was in some kind of development deal with NBC. I remember thinking, "Oh, I have to kind of build a bridge to something because you can't stay here forever," as much as anyone would love to stay there forever. And so I thought, "I'm going to try to write this movie *Mean Girls,* I'm going to pitch a sitcom, and I'm going to try to get pregnant and we'll just see what sticks." And all three things overlapped. When my daughter was born in September 2005, I got six weeks off and then I went back a couple shows in, and I remember that season thinking, "Why am I here?" I remember sitting at a table, at the read-through table, listening to someone else's sketch, you know, like the twenty-eighth sketch out of forty, and thinking, "My baby is at home. I gotta get out of here. I can't do this. Why am I here?"

JEFF ZUCKER:

I've been watching the show since I was a little kid. What I remember the most is probably Gilda and Roseanne Roseannadanna.

Having been a producer of the *Today* show for almost ten years, I had a lot of respect for what Lorne does as a producer. And I think the biggest thing an executive can do in those kinds of roles is just support the producers and let their vision speak. There was nothing broken at *Saturday Night Live.* People are fond of saying certain years are better than other years, but at the end of the day, it's all pretty good and pretty special.

I actually think that one of the biggest things I wanted to do when I got my job was address the fact that Lorne and this cast have been totally underutilized by NBC.

Lorne's road to success on NBC, outside of *SNL,* began in the early

2000s. We put *SNL* in prime time with a series of specials and half-hour shows. We also had Lorne do *30 Rock*. He also did *The Tracy Morgan Show* and a few other pilots as well.

LORNE MICHAELS:

Tina was really the first one who went into the television business, so — she did movies, but you know what I mean. So it took how many years for that sensibility to be accessible in prime time or as part of mainstream culture?

RACHEL DRATCH:

I was supposed to go to *30 Rock*, and that — I hate talking about *30 Rock*. It was years ago and that whole thing changed. It was sad. I was kind of on the fence about staying anyway, but I asked, "Can I go back to *SNL*?" And that was the year they were cutting down the cast and, I don't know, budget cuts and blah, blah, blah, so myself, Horatio, and Chris Parnell were all up. I never really know how to spin my exit from *SNL;* the deal was it was a year where they weren't just saying, like, "Yeah, stay for as long as you want." I kind of wish I was able to stick around for a little longer, but back then people left after their seven years, commonly. Now people stay super long.

ROBERT SMIGEL:

Rachel was literally one of my favorite people in the cast. I love people who are natural clowns and just go for it with no hesitation and with abandon. Both Rachel and Horatio made me laugh so hard so many times, and for those guys to be let go, it was impossible for me to feel any anger when financial realities required me to leave. I felt like I dodged a bullet that year by staying one more year.

FINESSE MITCHELL:

When you're a member of the cast, there's a lot of pressure on you outside of *SNL* to bring the funny or bring some sort of change to the show that represents a broader audience of what funny could be. There's a lot of hip and there's a lot of urban and hip-hop out there, and there's so many things that could be funny, but *SNL* doesn't necessarily tap into it because they don't as a whole have that frame of reference. So by the time you're trying to convince them that this is what's really funny and this is what's going on right now, Chappelle would've already done it on *Chappelle's Show*. And then there was the aspect of you may write a joke differently and they just may not get it. Or you may do a reverse joke where sometimes it's kind of obvious that, "Hey, the black guy is butt of the joke, I get it, that's funny," but then sometimes you can write a segment from the black perspective where the white person is the butt of the joke and they don't necessarily get it. Sometimes that was frustrating because you couldn't tell if they didn't want to get it or if they didn't get it.

HORATIO SANZ:

When I first got there, Adam McKay was head writer, and our senses of humor were very similar. He had a way with the show that few people had. I think his intention and our intention was to make *SNL* a little hipper. His shows were really going for something different. There's no one smarter than Adam. He obviously had to go on and start making movies because that's what you do; it just didn't make sense for him to stay any longer. Then when he left I really felt the show was going to a different place. It was almost like the show spit him out. I really didn't like that the show went from strange-funny to being more celebrity-driven—a making fun of celebrities, gossip kind of thing.

I was kind of on autopilot for those last seasons. I was trying to get scenes on, but I wound up in those weird scenes that were on at five to one, at the end of the show. I'd just show up and they'd write funny things for me and I'd kill in these little things, but I didn't necessarily need my own sketch.

FINESSE MITCHELL:

I kind of knew the writing was on the wall for me, that it was my last season; Steve Higgins had told me. He said, "One day, you never know, you might have to come back to host it." So I knew I wasn't coming back. But at that time I was mainly frustrated anyway. I wasn't that happy being there. I wasn't mad or bitter about it, I just wasn't happy. It got to the point where I didn't even remember what made me funny or what my funny was and that's when I thought, "Well, yeah. It's time for a change."

Of course you have those dreams and aspirations going into it if you're the black guy. You're like, "Damn, I'm going to be Eddie Murphy." And when it's not happening and then you're frustrated, it's, "Why am I not Eddie Murphy? I want to be Eddie Murphy by now. It's not happening."

HORATIO SANZ:

I was at home—I think there was an off week—and I started getting calls asking, "Are these rumors true? Are you fired?" I was like, "No. I haven't heard anything about that." And I hadn't! I had actually been in the offices for a few weeks already. After a few calls I called Shoemaker and said, "Is there any truth to this, so I can at least not sound like I'm crazy?" But he said there's no truth to that, as far as he knew. And I believe him. So after that call, when Shoemaker said it wasn't true, I went back and told everyone, "No; there's no truth to this." I said something to the effect of, "It's probably some fucking executive making something up." And I think that that probably pushed things further. I think maybe they were pressuring Lorne, and Lorne was probably still trying to work something out. But at that point, you know, I'd been there eight years so my contract was pretty heavy, you know, because you get more money at that point for every year. I think Lorne discussed, "Maybe we can pay you less or something," but at that point it had been eight years so I felt kind of squirrelly about trying to work there for less money. It felt like a backwards move. I told Lorne if I don't get "Update," this will probably be my last show. And he was like, "No, no, no, I don't want you to quit. And so let's just talk about that later." And so it came as a complete surprise, but also knowing the history of the show and the fact that with my salary they could have hired three new guys, I totally got it. I just wish it would have been a little more forthcoming. It felt a little shitty. I just wish someone could have told me beforehand so I could have left on my own terms. All they had to do was say, "Hey, after this season, we're going to start looking for other people." But being asked to stay and then getting fired? It did sting at first, but I've been cool with it for a while.

CHRIS PARNELL:

After the second stint, after the eighth season, I heard, "Does Chris want to come back for another season?" and I debated it, not because I'd had a bad time, but I just thought, "Maybe this is done." But then I thought, "Look, this is a great job and if they'll have me back for another season, I'll come back." We threw it back in their court, and eventually they came back and said, "No."

When I had been let go the first time, that was the hardest thing I've ever been through. I've been on sitcoms where we did five, eight episodes and get canceled, but nothing ever really compared to that earlier departure in terms of the emotional blow that it was. If, going forward, I never have anything that hits as hard as that, I'll be very lucky. It was a huge letdown and such a major disappointment, and I realized to what extent I'd started defining myself as a cast member of *Saturday Night Live*. It made me start to reevaluate myself and look at myself in a different way.

Between *Lazy Sunday* and "Cowbell," I feel like I was a part of two pretty classic moments on the show. It ushered in a new era, to be sure. When I look back on it, I mostly just feel grateful and thankful to have been a part of the show and for that span of time. Even though getting fired was emotionally hard and a real blow to my confidence and all that, being brought back made me so happy, and I just felt so thankful to be back there and be on the show several more seasons. It was a crazy roller coaster—like somebody said, some high highs and some low lows, and being able to work with the cast members that I did, spanning that original group to who was there when I finished, that was amazing. It all led to some great lasting friendships and certainly for me it not only started my career, it sort of launched me into being able to make a living as an actor, so I have mostly fond memories and just a lot of gratitude to Lorne and everybody there for letting me be a part of it.

I never like to get fired or "let go" from a job, but I was infinitely more okay with it this time.

Even though he had reached the stratosphere of movie stardom, Will Ferrell returned twice in the 2000s to host *SNL*, both times appearing in revivals of his legendary *Jeopardy!* spoof in the straight-man role of emcee Alex Trebek. In this one, from 2009, he jousts with (from left) Kenan Thompson as Bill Cosby, Amy Poehler as Sharon Osbourne, and Darrell Hammond returning to the role of Sean Connery as a mean-spirited prankster. DANA EDELSON/NBCU PHOTO BANK

One of the ancillary honors that go with the presidency is being portrayed in sketches by a cast member of *Saturday Night Live.* The assignment can be less coveted than dreaded, as was the case when Will Forte inherited the role of George W. Bush. DANA EDELSON/NBCU PHOTO BANK

Politicians have been popping up on *Saturday Night Live* since its early days. Still, there had been nothing quite like the hall-of-mirrors encounter in 2008 between Republican vice presidential candidate Sarah Palin (center) and Tina Fey (on monitor), who played Palin on the show. Fey did not want to interact physically with Palin, however, so Lorne Michaels arranged this intermedia moment: the very liberal Baldwin thinks he is standing next to Fey as he complains to Michaels about allowing Palin to appear, unaware that the real Palin is right next to him. DANA EDELSON/NBC

When in doubt, have men dress as women. Beyoncé spoofed her own music video for "Single Ladies" during a November 2008 episode. Masquerading as her backup dancers, and fooling nobody, were (from left) Justin Timberlake, Bobby Moynihan, and Andy Samberg, with Beyoncé herself and episode host Paul Rudd standing by. DANA EDELSON/NBC

MacGruber, one of the maddest *SNL* sketches to emerge from the first decade of the new millennium, had to be pre-taped—partly because each episode ended in an explosion big enough to kill all the characters, although they nonetheless returned in the next chapter. Will Forte (right), who cocreated the spoof with Jorma Taccone, starred as MacGruber with Kristen Wiig (center) as his sidekick. Here, Richard Dean Anderson (left of Wiig), who played MacGyver, makes a guest appearance. DANA EDELSON/NBC

When Betty White hosted the penultimate episode of *SNL'*s 35th season in 2010, she became the oldest person in history to land the gig. Since the episode aired on Mother's Day eve, the show became a celebration of *SNL'*s womanhood, with mom alumni brought back as special guests (from left): Molly Shannon, Amy Poehler, Maya Rudolph, White, Tina Fey, Rachel Dratch, and Ana Gasteyer. DANA EDELSON/NBCU PHOTO BANK

Gathered together for a talk-show sketch on the November 1, 2010, episode, the women of *SNL*, past and present, represent a wide spectrum of comedic talent. From left: Molly Shannon, Maya Rudolph, Tina Fey, Nora Dunn, Andy Cohen (no, not a woman of *SNL*, but the host in the sketch), Ana Gasteyer, Rachel Dratch, Cheri Oteri, and Kristen Wiig. There's not a weak link in the chain. DANA EDELSON/NBC

"You gotta getcher marble columns"—or so it was said, repeatedly, in a commercial spoof that aired in 2006, when Scarlett Johansson had her first shot at hosting *SNL*. Not even the writers and performers know which sketches will catch on with the public, and the silly "Marble Columns"—with Fred Armisen peddling the shabby kitsch—took everyone by surprise. DANA EDELSON/NBCU PHOTO BANK

Many an eccentric-to-insane family has been concocted for *SNL* sketches over the years, but the lip-locking Vogelchecks may outdo all others. Obsessively oral when showing affection, the Vogelchecks eschew mere pecks on cheeks for major mouth-to-mouth osculation, as on this episode from December 2010 with host Paul Rudd (center-left) being warmly greeted by Fred Armisen. DANA EDELSON/NBCU PHOTO BANK

Once the century had turned, *Saturday Night Live* contributed to the Internet revolution by giving virtual free reign to the Lonely Island, an innovative video group formed by performer/writer Andy Samberg and writers/directors Jorma Taccone and Akiva Schaffer. Singer/actor Justin Timberlake appeared in some of the most notorious shorts. From left: Taccone, Schaffer, Lady Gaga, Samberg, and Timberlake. DANA EDELSON/NBC

Kenan Thompson (right) says he'd happily do a "What's Up with That?" sketch every week if they'd let him. No matter how hard this talk show's celebrity guests—like Samuel L. Jackson (to the left of Thompson)—try to contribute to the discussion, Thompson repeatedly breaks into song, and an ensemble of dancers and musicians bursts onto the stage to accompany him. DANA EDELSON/NBCU PHOTO BANK

Although he first appeared in a 2008 sketch, the hilarious character of Manhattan party boy Stefon, created by actor Bill Hader (front-center) and writer John Mulaney, didn't blossom until 2010 when Stefon was moved to "Weekend Update" as a roving night-spot reporter with a crush on anchor Seth Meyers (front-right). DANA EDELSON/NBC

SNL lampooned *The Lawrence Welk Show* three decades after its original network run had ended (in 1971). The sketch always included an appearance by Kristen Wiig (left, of course) as Dooneese, a straggling, oddball singer who had tiny hands and a fascination with Welk's trademark bubbles. Fred Armisen played the bandleader. DANA EDELSON/NBCU PHOTO BANK

Kate McKinnon joined the cast of *Saturday Night Live* in 2012 and, just two years later, won an American Comedy Award as best supporting actress on a TV series. McKinnon's versatility extends to playing male characters when needed—a notable example being her impish impression of teenage heartthrob Justin Bieber. DANA EDELSON/NBCU PHOTO BANK

Seriously funny business: Seth Meyers (right), head writer from 2007 through 2013, huddles with Lorne Michaels backstage during preparations for another week's *Saturday Night Live.* Meyers's reward for a job well done was his own talk show, inheriting *Late Night* from Jimmy Fallon in early 2014 when Fallon moved to *The Tonight Show,* in the process turning Michaels, who produces all the shows, into the new King of Late Night. DANA EDELSON/NBC

FRED ARMISEN:

Tina will always be a personal hero to me. We became very good friends and Tina is everything I want to be. She works so hard and she's so funny. She's not just funny on paper and on-screen, she's a funny person. She's so fast and smart, and the best. She writes sketches like she's making scrambled eggs, like it's nothing. She throws it together and it's just perfect. There's this one that we did called "Frondi" with Ben Affleck where I was this sort of mentally disabled person, and we're on the set of *Gigli* and just wicked quick she just whipped up all the lines and all the structure of it. I will always, always, be in awe of what a hard worker and how fast she is.

TINA FEY:

I would never be where I am today without *SNL*. No way. Nobody would have ever let me be on camera, and then to get a gig like "Weekend Update"—you just can't get any luckier because you are going on TV every week, as yourself, saying, "Hi! This is my name and now I'm telling you jokes." I would probably be teaching improv somewhere or trying to be a playwright in a city that wasn't New York. I don't know where I would be, but no way would I have had the opportunities that I've had since *SNL*.

KEN AYMONG:

The toughest time for me is when a director leaves. You hope you have enough notice so you can get some possible candidates to witness how the show is done because there's no way to describe that without seeing it. There've been just four: Dave Wilson, Paul Miller, Beth, Don. It's amazing.

It's a tough place for a director. I'm the first stage of the interview process for a new director because I need to go over the logistics of how the show is done and what expectations are. And I ask candidates, "Do you think you have a big ego? Can you take input from a lot of people and be expected to follow through on that input?" I'm very frank with them. I tell them, "You have to understand that you're going to be taking instruction from what you consider to be real neophytes in show business. You'll be expected to follow through on the instructions that they give you or the ideas that they have, because that's why we're here." And the last thing I would say to them is, "There is nothing I can do to prepare you for what's going to happen between dress and air. We'll also have situations where we'll have a six-minute sketch and it'll turn into a two-and-a-half-minute sketch and all that beautiful blocking that you did? It's gone. There's going to be a young lady standing behind you who's going to take your script away, and they're going to start changing it like crazy. There's going to be red cross-outs and then there will be a Post-it put on the top of the page, meaning there was a change that happened. I'm not exaggerating: there will be a sea of Post-its."

We have a camera meeting that takes place at a little after eleven o'clock, and the director goes into that meeting. I insist—and Lorne's really great about it—that the lineup meeting that takes place after dress ends by eleven p.m. so that the director has time to turn around his script with all the notes. He'll come downstairs and he'll get his book back. He doesn't know what's in that book yet. All he sees is a sea of Post-its and then he has five anxious cameramen sitting in front of him who want to know what they're doing in that show. At this point we're closing in on eleven fifteen p.m. He has to absorb what's happening on the fly. Post-its all over the floor as he rips them off the page, and there will be another young lady next to him who's taking away stuff that has already been given to him because there's even more changes. And he's relaying these changes that he has to the cameramen, who are wildly confident and comfortable people. They absorb this like there's no tomorrow. Cue cards are a whole separate operation, with each writer expected to be the producer of their own pieces. So each writer is verifying, or should be verifying, that each cue card has everything correct. There are three sets of cue cards, so everything has to match up.

Everything happens in this very short period of time. And that's before we get into the issue of timing, which will be with us all through the show.

SETH MEYERS:

I started on the show as a cast member but I feel like I survived more than anything else by writing. I also was really close friends with the writers. I always thought there was something really exciting about being on the writing staff, and the fact that I wasn't a credited writer was always something that bothered me, especially because I was doing a lot of writing. But then that's true of a lot of cast members on the show. There's nothing you can do about that. When Tina quit, when everyone knew it was Tina's last year, when they asked me if I wanted to be a writing supervisor, I was incredibly flattered, and I felt like it was the first time I would know my role at the show instead of coming in every Monday terrified that this would be the week they "found me out."

AMY POEHLER:

When people leave *SNL* they jump off a train, a moving train, and when you're on the train you just can't believe how the train is going to go on without them, and you hug them and tell them how much you'll miss them, and you wave them good-bye. And then you go back to work. When *you* jump off the train, you stand there and the gravel and dust kicks up in your face and you cough and you watch the train take off and you feel a mixture of, "I can't believe I'm not on the train anymore," and "I'm so excited for where I go next." Some people get off the train and stand at the train station for a really long time, and they don't know where to go next, or they don't have a place to go next, whatever it is, and some people get booted off the train. For some people, the train slows down and they gently step off. When Tina left, I remember a mixture of real sadness that my friend was leaving and real happiness for her because she was going off to do something so great. I've never, ever worried about Tina and what she was going to do next.

SETH MEYERS:

The transition was made easier by the fact that I was stepping in with Amy, who is my closest friend on the show and certainly the person I had worked with the most up to that point. There was as much of a comfort level as you can have stepping into those shoes. I had auditioned for "Update" when Jimmy left, along with Amy and some other people, and that was one of those many times where as much as I would like to have done it I feel the right decision was made, and I thank history for that now. It was nice that I had a chance to audition for it once before the job came up the second time. It started coming into focus on my radar more clearly that I was a lot better at being myself than I was at being other people. A "no-wig" job like that one struck me as a good thing to aim for.

LORNE MICHAELS:

I think Amy believed in Seth and wanted Seth and was very clear about it. I would have been just as happy with Jason. I'm sure we did some tests—we're way too thorough to not have—but in the same way that Tina had to get comfortable with Amy, Amy had to get comfortable with whoever came next. She thought she had a chemistry with Seth, and obviously she did. And they arrived together. Their first show, both of them, was 9/11. So welcome to *Saturday Night Live*. There's cops and Port Authority guys and firemen, and the mayor had been working down at Ground Zero, hadn't been anywhere but Ground Zero, and walked into the studio with a thousand-yard stare. I'm with Paul [Simon], who's doing "The Boxer," and the mayor is there and all the rest, and that's Amy and Seth's debut. I think they bonded really strongly at that. And I think she saw something in Seth, who at that point was a writer and beginning to emerge more and more; she just knew they had something, and she was right. She knew that they could take that to another level that wasn't her-and-Tina.

AMY POEHLER:

Seth is so accomplished that I certainly didn't need to show him any comedy ropes, but it did feel nice to be the senior at the desk, even if it was only a few years, because there's a certain hierarchy, like at any comedy high school. As a freshman you're shown around; in the sophomore year you sort of get the hang of it; junior year you're really cruising; and then senior year you're like, "Oh, *this* is how it's done." Again, I felt that Seth was and is my equal and peer. We started together, so it was nice not to be the one who was starting. I knew we would instantly connect because in many ways I'm the sister he never had, and he's the brother I always wanted. There's such affection, and we share a very similar language, and Seth is so sharp and so incredibly smart. Just as with Tina, I basically felt at times like a car that was riding next to a giant talent truck and was just drafting on their wind.

SETH MEYERS:

I think the only thing you can do as head writer—and by the way, a lot of writers who aren't the head writer do this—is you let it be known to the cast and the other writers that your door is always open and that you're happy to look at their sketch and that you're always happy to make notes on it and suggestions. There's no specific mentoring. Certain people are going to write a certain way, and you try, if you can, to sort of point them sometimes to what the show could use a little bit more of, or how to make their stuff a little bit more show-friendly. At the same time, Lorne doesn't want everybody to become sort of uniform in the way they write, so the trickiest thing as a head writer isn't to try to bring in uniformity but to try to make sure everybody stays unique in the way that they were in their auditions and the way that made Lorne want to have them on board in the first place. Sometimes it's just that if you worked on the show long enough, you can see what a person is good at and help bring what that thing is into the sketch world and make it a little easier.

As head writer, I had to spend much less time on "Update" than on other things. "Update" joke writers worked on it the whole week, and I didn't check in on them until Friday, and then I read through all the jokes to see how good or bad a shape we were in, and then comes a bit more work. Sometimes, obviously, I would write some of the "Update" features and the "test characters," as it were, but I feel like 80 or 85 percent of the work I did on the show was as a *writer*. "Update" was more like the cherry on the cake, my reward. At least that's how I framed it for myself. You work all week trying to make sure everybody else's stuff is as good as it can be, and then you get this incredible piece of real estate where you get to tell jokes for ten minutes.

FRED ARMISEN:

My approach to everything in life is, "Sure, I'll give it a try." I knew they were looking for an Obama, so when Lorne called me into his office and Marci Klein said, "Let Fred do it," and Lorne was like,

"Would you want to try it?" I was just like, "Okay—I'll give it a try." I'm glad he asked. I didn't campaign to do it; it was just an idea that kept growing. They asked me on a Tuesday, and I think I did it that Saturday. I bought Obama's book on iTunes, and I watched videos, and I felt the same kind of surreal feeling as when I did my audition for the show. It was so big that I just thought, "Wow, I can't believe it." The thing that I had on my side is that there were writers there like Jim Downey, so it didn't feel like I had to write anything. I didn't have to be like, "What is Obama saying? What's his thing?" It was all there on the page for me. So I got as much of him down as I could and hoped that over the years I would pick up on more of him.

JAMES DOWNEY:

I would rather have Fred out there doing comedy than just about anybody I can think of, but I'm not sure having him do Obama was a smart casting move. One of the critical things is that Obama has this deep, rich, baritone, while Fred has a voice like mine, more of a tenor. Initially we had a guy who I think does a great Obama; he auditioned for us and he had the same kind of physical presence as Obama— elegant, slender, delicate features. I was really excited because we auditioned him during the strike, before we ever did Obama on the air. He wanted to do the show and we wanted to have him. He had been riding the bench at *MADtv,* where they weren't really using him. But then when they heard we wanted him, they wouldn't let him out of his deal just to keep us from getting him. And then of course we were back on the air and we didn't have any resident person who was really ideal.

FRED ARMISEN:

For some reason, I don't know why—maybe because I don't come from comedy going that far back—I sometimes don't care about things being that accurate or funny. Sometimes I simply think, "Let me just deliver this, and let's see what comes out."

JAMES DOWNEY:

Anybody we picked who was already there was going to have to be playing out of position. It's like asking someone who's five foot seven,

"I'm sorry, but our seven-footer is having back spasms, so you're going to have to cover LeBron tonight. Good luck!" I love Fred, I think he's a genius, and I think he did the very best he could. By the way, he got better and better. In terms of the comedy of it, Fred squeezed every available drop out of that thing. By the fall, it was really about Tina doing Sarah Palin more than it was about presidential candidates.

If I had to describe Obama as a comedy project, I would say, "Degree of difficulty, ten point ten." It's like being a rock climber looking up at a thousand-foot-high face of solid obsidian, polished and oiled. There's not a single thing to grab onto—certainly not a flaw or hook that you can caricature. Gore had these "handles," so did Bush, and Sarah Palin, and even Hillary had them, although Hillary is a much tougher impression. But with Obama it was the phenomenon—less about him and more about the effect he had on other people and the way he changed their behavior. So that's the way I wrote him; he was about what he did to others around him, more about the whole media and political culture. You can imagine the shock, because Hillary had really been the darling of the Democratic Party—certainly establishment Democrats who loved Bill Clinton. She was all of that—*and* she hadn't cheated on anyone. Obama was barely into his second year in the Senate, but he just had it all over Hillary in terms of elegance and style and sophistication and coolness. Plus he had glamour. And he was right about the Iraq War.

The growing library of "Best of" DVDs featuring cast members and hosts from SNL *serves as further evidence of how the show's reach has extended with the help of technology—albeit a fairly simple one in this case. Getting a "Best of" DVD dedicated to your work, with your name and picture plastered on the cover, is more a status symbol than a gold mine for cast members, but ego boosts are obviously much valued in show business, and an eponymous DVD can make a nice reward. In addition, the* SNL *DVD business includes a few boxed sets devoted not to personalities but to entire seasons of the show, including the historic first (1975–76) as well as such specialty items as* SNL *in the '80s, from an NBC clip special; the Digital Shorts; and* The Bad Boys of Saturday

Night Live, *featuring the formidable work of Chris Rock, Chris Farley, Adam Sandler, and others from the 1990s.*

A performer is lucky to get a single DVD devoted to his sketches; one cast member, Will Ferrell, has the honor of being featured on two, released separately. But a "Best of" is definitely a privilege and not a right: Kevin Nealon, for example, though a popular cast member for nine seasons (1986–95), has no "Best of" with his name on it.

DARRELL HAMMOND:

They put out this collection, *The Best of Darrell Hammond.* It really was the *worst* of Darrell Hammond. I should have participated in the compilation of that; it had a lot of my pop flies and ground balls and stuff that shouldn't have been in there. I'm grateful that NBC made sure the DVD never saw the light of day after about a month. I *was* consulted on it, and I suggested three things that did get in: Dan Rather doing a report on anthrax, Tim Russert interviewing John McCain—I was Tim Russert—and one other one. I think it was Sean Connery on *Jeopardy!* and I think it was "I'll take 'The Rapist' for" whatever. In my mind, that got one of the biggest laughs I ever got, but when you watch it, it's not that big of a laugh, so I should have sat in and monitored the whole thing more closely. Someone was making the decisions, and it didn't sell well, and people didn't like it.

ROBERT SMIGEL:

When it was time to make the *Best of Saturday TV Funhouse* DVD, I had the same paranoia that it wasn't enough to sell the product. So for commentary, instead of just droning on with my animators, I brought in people who were the subjects of cartoons—like Bryant Gumbel, James Carville, and Mr. T—to watch them with me. Mr. T went off on all these tangents; he did three minutes on why he has no period after his *T.* So for one of the Mr. T cartoons the commentary is just a nonstop Mr. T ramble, almost entirely unrelated to what you're watching. That's probably my favorite section, although discussing "Ladysmith Black Mambazo in Outer Space" with the actual band was its own sliver of bliss.

At the same time, the online revolution fueling the success of Digital Shorts further shifted the market from DVD to the browser.

JORMA TACCONE:

The first time they showed *Dick in a Box* we were on the studio floor watching and we had this electrifying feeling and we thought, "This is special." We'd thought it was special while we were making it too, and then to feel it had this second life online gave us this other kind of feeling. In a day and a half, *YOLO* got, like, four and a half million hits; it was crazy. It was impossible not to compare yourself to past work. Getting to work with someone as wildly talented as Justin Timberlake, getting to spend maybe four days with him—like any time he wasn't down on the floor rehearsing he'd come up to our shitty little writers' room and work with us on lyrics—*that* was amazing. All of it was amazing.

AKIVA SCHAFFER:

Dick in a Box we thought was pretty inside baseball; we were using songs that people don't necessarily know anymore, from a broad-*SNL*-audience point of view, and the joke was crass and stupid. We were not confident in the least. Timberlake was the only one who was confident. We showed him the script for it, and he read it. We were almost embarrassed to show it to him, but he went, "This is great. We're doing this." I feel like he's the only one who didn't have doubts.

JORMA TACCONE:

It was sort of an order-up kind of thing. Lorne said, "You're making a musical thing with Justin. Just do it." And we were like, "Okay, well, we don't have an idea." And then it was concept Thursday night, start shooting Friday morning, lose Justin for a period of time, end shooting Friday night into Saturday morning, start editing Saturday morning and keep editing 'til the moment that it airs. That became our standard for how we made things. I got so good at knowing how much time we had that if we were done filming something and had fifteen hours until air, I was like, "I can only sleep for half an hour, not forty-five minutes."

COLIN JOST:

One Timberlake sketch that I wrote with Erik Kenward and really loved, but that we never got to do, was Justin playing Michael

McDonald and he opened his own fast-food restaurant and he called it McDonald's. And he was at a piano in his restaurant and he would sing about the deals and also sing about his legal trouble with McDonald's, who were constantly suing him. It was like, "My life is a nightmare / We also have Chicken McNuggets." Timberlake just had the funniest Michael McDonald impression, but we could never figure out how to use it. It's tough to get things into Justin's shows anyway, because he has a bunch of characters that are recurring. Things have to really hit to get in.

JUSTIN TIMBERLAKE:

I think it was the third time I hosted, like right before Mother's Day. We had already done *Dick in a Box,* and so Andy and I knew that we had to do something else, so we came up with the idea for "Mother Lover." Another sketch we had that week was called "Ellis Island," and it was about all of these immigrants coming over and being dropped off on Ellis Island. It was a sketch where I played my great-great-great-great-grandfather and said all of these things about my great-great-great-great-grandson Justin. And at the end of the sketch for "Ellis Island," Andy came on and played Moishe Samberg, who is Andy's great-great-great-great-grandfather, and he prophesied about how Andy, his great-great-grandson, and my great-great-grandson would maybe someday work together, and who knows? They may make something usable. And there were plenty of jokes within that, but the way the show order ran on live television—and I don't even think anyone planned it—this live sketch went into the Digital Short. So you had a sketch where the end of that sketch connects to the next sketch. It was almost like we got like ten minutes of almost linear television. Sketches are so compartmentalized; they're all completely different—and I don't know how many times this had happened on the show or if it ever even happened, but when we ended the "Ellis Island" sketch I walked off, and Lorne was standing there and he grabbed me and said, "Do you realize what just happened?" And I said, "No," and he said, "You just did a sketch to introduce your next sketch within the sketch." He said, "This is one of the most brilliant things to ever happen on the show," and in that moment I realized that no one had really planned it; it was just kind of one of those ser-endipitous moments.

WILL FORTE:

Jorma Taccone was the person with the original idea for *MacGruber*. He kept pitching it to us. John Solomon and I were the other two people involved. We thought it sounded like a pretty dumb idea. We kept saying, "No. Let's do something else."

JORMA TACCONE:

From the moment I pitched *MacGruber* at the show to the moment that the movie was coming out was such an insane experience for me. My original pitch was for the Lance Armstrong show, where I pitched that Lance Armstrong would play MacGyver's stepbrother MacGruber—which makes no sense at all—who defuses bombs by only using pieces of shit and pubic hair, so any time he asks one of his assistants for something he needs, no one wants to touch anything. That was the original pitch. I was terrible at pitching, and it went over really badly. It got huge groans from everyone in the room. But I continued pitching to Forte for about a month that he be MacGruber, and eventually we wrote it—and they are just the best partners in the world to write with, Will and John Solomon. We did all of those together. And so to even get it to be a sketch on the show was shocking, because the pitch went so badly. And the first one we ever did was that initial premise, where he's just this bumbling bomb defuser who is asking for a bunch of dis-gusting items to defuse bombs, and then we quickly realized with Forte that we had this numbskull egotistical *flawed* character that we loved writing for, because anything that you thought of as a problem in someone's life, he had. So he's an alcoholic or a drug addict or he's bad with money or he's a womanizer or he's incredibly vain.

WILL FORTE:

All Jorma would say was, "I have this idea about this character called MacGruber. He's MacGyver's less talented brother." But that was it. You're thinking of sketch ideas, you're not thinking of short film ideas, so I wasn't really into it because it didn't make sense to me as a sketch.

MacGyver had been off for so long, but it wasn't even that. I just wasn't sure. But he was so persistent and kept bringing it up all the time, that kind of to get him to shut up, we all decided, "Well, let's take a crack at it." Jorma is a really funny and smart person, so we thought there was probably something we could find in there. And it's not a crazy idea. But then once we came up with the idea of doing it as a little short and having it in very short, digestible film chunks, we had a lot of fun. Never did we think that it would be anything more than a onetime little short film, so we were pleasantly surprised when people seemed to like the first one. But we didn't think, "Oh, we've *got* to do a second one after this!" After a couple weeks we thought, "Well, let's try a second one." As usual, it was born out of not having any other ideas. A lot of times it's really fun to take a character and explore it on a deeper level. It's one of the most wonderful things about the show, and also one of the tough things.

JORMA TACCONE:

The fact that we not only got it on the show the first time but then got to do another nine sketches of it was amazing. Then Pepsi approached Lorne to do a Super Bowl commercial and he asked us, "Do you want to do this as a Super Bowl commercial?" and we'd already had an idea of doing a sketch where MacGruber sells out. So a Pepsi commercial seemed very much in his wheelhouse. We wanted to do one where he was covered in NASCAR-esque jackets and every kind of Procter & Gamble logo and so it was like, "Yeah, we almost already wrote that." For sixteen hours we shot one with Richard Dean Anderson so he would be in the commercial and then we shot another one with Richard Dean Anderson that was just for the show. We weren't sure that Pepsi would even want this. So we were incredibly lucky at every stage: Just getting on the show was lucky, making ten of them felt lucky, and then getting it through the stage where it aired in the fourth quarter of the Super Bowl—and it was a really close game so that everyone was watching—was great. We were incredibly lucky.

WILL FORTE:

The goal is to be really comfortable onstage and be having fun. You can tell the people who are really having fun, and it took me a while to get rid of the nerves and just really enjoy myself up there. It took, like, five seasons, maybe. I was a real nervous Nellie. It was tricky for a while. And it was also tricky because I came in with Fred Armisen, he was the other new person. Fred was so instantly comfortable—and just *loved* performing. Over the summers he couldn't wait to get back in, whereas I wanted the summers never to end. I was so nervous about going back.

Now, looking back, the experience is something I'll never forget. I still miss it, and I'll always miss it. That's my family. Lorne was so good to me. He's always there for you. It took me a couple of years to realize that. At first I would just get real nervous around him, but he's very open to talking and very friendly, and it really wasn't until toward the end and the *MacGruber* experience, and making the *MacGruber* movie, that I really kinda got to know him. He was so good to us during that period and very supportive and just really stood behind us in a major way and was able to get us into a position to make this movie exactly the way we wanted to do it. I can never thank Lorne enough. I really, really just love the man.

The thirty-third season of Saturday Night Live, *2007–8, set a record that nobody at the show wanted: It was the shortest season ever. The reason was a strike by the members of the Writers Guild of America that shut down production from November 2007 through February 2008. When* SNL *went back into business, momentum was of course lost. The creative team tried to compensate by doing four new consecutive episodes in a row starting February 23, but that just wore everybody out. Runners-up for the dubious distinction of shortest season were the sixth (1980–81) and the thirteenth (1987–88). This one made history in one more way: Because of the dates of the strike, it would be the first season on record not to include a new* SNL *Christmas show. Brian Williams hosted the last show before the strike, on November 5, 2007, with a very special cameo appearance from the man who would be president.*

JAMES DOWNEY:

I wrote a cold open where it was pretty much Hillary congratulating her seven Democratic opponents for the plucky effort and basically making the point: "You keep plugging away and one day you're going to make it. I just know you will." It was sort of condescension mixed with a feeling of entitlement, and she was basically planning the inaugural and talking about the second inaugural. Her counting her chickens was the basic premise. And that was the opening of the first show of that season, and then we only had a couple more—I think it was three more shows and then we had the strike.

BRIAN WILLIAMS, *Host:*

I think I carried the invitation to host around for six months to a year. Lorne extended it to me by telephone; I heard the most imitated voice in the building on the other end of the line: "Mr. Williams, I'd like you to think about hosting our show." And I went into kind of a functioning shock and mostly wanted to talk to my wife and close friends and people I trust and at minimum I walked around mulling for six months. I was obviously concerned and had our research department look up who from my line of work had ever appeared, had ever hosted. I talked to Tom Brokaw about it, I talked to Meredith Brokaw about it, I talked to my wife ad nauseam, I talked to former bosses, some colleagues who I trust. It turned out one of the former journalists from *Nightly News* had appeared but not hosted, and obviously the times have changed. My biggest, deepest, darkest fear was that I was going to flush down the toilet twenty-seven years of hard-earned nonfiction credibility by doing a comedy show. And this story sounds way too convenient to be true but has the added advantage of being true: I was up at a corporate function at 8H, and in the hallway was Chevy Chase. We had crossed paths at a couple of affiliate functions and a couple of upfronts but had never met. Obviously I had spent much of my adult life as a fan, and as a young kid on the Jersey shore I wrote away for tickets and ended up at the show hosted by Broderick Crawford, who I was horrified to see taking oxygen during breaks. I believe it remains on Lorne's list of the top five all-time worst shows.

So I told Chevy my tale of woe and said, "I have a pending invite from Lorne to host the show. What's your opinion, if you don't mind me asking?" And he said, "Well, I'll tell ya, I was a religious Dan Rather viewer for over twenty years, and at the end of Dan's run I was no closer to knowing who he was than at the start. I think you should do it because people will see who you are." And I factored into this decision the fact that I had been going on Jon Stewart's show and back in the day went on Conan's, here in the building, and had been on Dave's show, too. They had been very nice about having me on and it had been an ancillary to my day job. But in the post-9/11 world, where my day job had become so bloody serious, I wanted to be very careful. I had a million warnings to Lorne that I wasn't going to dress in the Oscar Mayer wiener suit and I would have to have right of first refusal over sketches and all of that—but I decided in the end to take the leap. Anytime a dicey role would come up at the table read, they would have a good old time laughing as I struggled with it. And I would say to the group, "This stands a zero chance of ever becoming television, you realize that?" And they would all laugh knowingly. The other thing about my week is, I had to keep working. So I was deprived of the complete *SNL* experience other than the Tuesday all-nighter. I had to keep doing *Nightly News*.

Even that long ago, we still had people who were doggedly covering our business, the television news business, and I was waiting for the column asking, "Which is it? Serious or funny?" But my viewers, God bless them, have always been able to make the delineation. They know that when I say, "Good evening" and I'm surrounded by the backdrop of the *NBC Nightly News* that it's the serious me, and they're smart enough to know that at eleven thirty on a Saturday night, I'm having a little fun. So the cast and I took it one at a time. Seth and I had spent a long night in his office and I sprawled out on his couch and said jokingly, "Do you take dictation?" I was able to do it verbally, and he wrote it down. Obviously this is his line of work and I took all of his advice and he polished it up, but I was still proud to get a writer's credit on that show.

There was a sketch about a sexual predator, and Will Forte wrote it and played the sexual predator. I was actually going to be the straight man and I was fine with it. Lorne cut it for time after dress rehearsal, and it has always bugged me that Jon Hamm played my part several shows later. He owes me. Sketches live forever, man. Even if Lorne kills it, they're going to try to bring it back. It's like an old Coke—still useful years later.

JAMES DOWNEY:

We had a thing where Obama actually appeared on the show, which got a lot of press. I didn't think it was particularly funny, it was just him at a costume party. I didn't write it; I don't want to be too mean about it. I don't know who wrote it. It was more just Obama agreed to do the show so somebody wrote something.

LORNE MICHAELS:

We were contacted by, I think, Howard Wolfson from Hillary's campaign and they wanted to do the first show of the season. Obama was heating up, but they called first, so I said okay. You have to play by those rules. And then, the week of, they bailed. She suddenly had to go do something and I went, "*Really?* You called us and we gave it to you." I think every now and then I get carried away and think we actually do have influence and kind of go, "*What?!*" And then after that we put Obama on—the date when Hillary was supposed to be on. The sense of entitlement which was following her everywhere at that point peaked for me at the bailing—asking for it, being accommodated, and then bailing on it in an election year.

BRIAN WILLIAMS:

If anything, Obama being on the show gave me air cover. I thought, "Well, here's a guy from the nonfiction realm who's going to share this exposure with me." I saw him in the dressing room before the show, but he was in the cold open, before my name was even heard, so his sketch just gave me an extra seven minutes to get nervous.

My chief goal coming out on the stage and down those stairs was A, not to fall, and B, to make eye contact with my wife and two kids. They were up in the guest area; I saw them right away, and that calmed me down.

The digital short was a lot of fun. We shot it all late at night. I ran from the *Nightly News* room to shoot some scenes. We busted into the commissary under the pull-down gate, and we busted into my boss's office. Akiva mostly was the director, but Jorma and Andy, I grew to love all those guys—not knowing Jorma would someday make fictional love with my daughter's fictional character on *Girls*.

HORATIO SANZ:

I don't think the show itself has ever let its freak flag fly in the last twenty years. I think Lorne's very concerned with being neutral so he wants to make fun of everyone. But I think it's hard. He doesn't want the show to be this liberal bash rag. In fact I think he may be a little more conservative than he lets on, and I think he's prideful of the fact that the show doesn't go 100 percent left and bash everything on the right. And you also have Jim Downey, who's basically the Karl Rove of *SNL*. He's always writing the right-wing sketches, and honestly I think a lot of times they're out of tune with the audience. Lorne really loves them and of course Downey's a great writer, brilliant, he's been there forever, but I think Lorne sometimes leans too much on Downey and not enough on guys like Seth. Basically in the last couple of years, it's been Seth going up against Downey to set the show's tone on politics, and I think we could definitely have been harder on the right. They deserved it, and we dropped the ball as far as getting them.

I remember the week that Nancy Pelosi was made speaker; the only thing that we could come up with at the time was, because she was from San Francisco, to make her a dominatrix. I thought that was really, really cheap. And that was just an example of, "Why are we doing this sketch this week when fucking Bush is lying about this, doing this, doing that?" It was pretty frustrating. And it continues to be frustrating. I don't really like watching the political scenes that much anymore, because they're not written in the writers' and actors' tone. They're written like Downey wants to put this message out. And I think that's kind of shitty.

JAMES DOWNEY:

I think my mission is to try to write a funny piece using politics as the subject matter, and so I go with what I think is the most interesting, potentially funny idea that no one else is talking about. What was interesting to me was how things changed. Within a space of about three months, Obama became the trophy wife and Hillary was the wife who put the guy through dental school. Obama came along and Hillary was dumped. There was no pretense about it; the media just abandoned her. It was amazing. It was very unceremonious. It wasn't like I was for Hillary or against Obama. I heard from people who know Obama really well that they knew that the media loved him. They knew that. It's not a politician's job to go, "Look, I don't want to be a rock star. I want to be judged just like any other candidate." Hey, if they're going to be treated like rock stars, that's fine with them.

LORNE MICHAELS:

Smigel had a cartoon that Standards had an issue with that was about racial profiling. Needless to say it was not a subtle and nuanced piece of work. But the laughter was big and it was sort of one way or the other—are you going to play it or not? Standards was saying no and I couldn't quite gauge it because it was playing in front of the audience.

ROBERT SMIGEL:

I had a million notes from Standards over the years, but it wasn't until my last season that the network refused to air a "TV Funhouse." It was a live-action one that was meant to be about racism and profiling, an airline safety video with multilingual narration, and whenever you heard a different language they would cut to people of that nationality. First, typical white Americans, then a Latino family, then a Japanese family, all being instructed about seat belts, overhead compartments, et cetera. Then it cuts to an Arab man and the narrator says, in Arabic, "During the flight, please do not blow up the airplane. The United States is actually a humanitarian nation that is rooted in the concept of freedom," and so on. There were other ethnic groups stereotyped by the narration, but like I said, it was about an ugly subject, profiling, and not racism for racism's sake. When the Standards people freaked, Lorne fought them. He liked it, felt it was "defendable" and could withstand any outrage—remember, this was before hashtags. He ran it at dress and it got laughs—but Standards pushed back hard. They even got someone at NBC human resources to condemn it.

The next week I was there before dress rehearsal and Lorne said, "I have a plan." Obama, in the early stages of his campaign, was doing a cameo in the cold open. Lorne told me he would show my sketch to Obama in his office. "If Obama thinks it's okay, they won't be able to argue it." I just kind of stared blankly and said, "Okay." I mean, I thought it was a brilliant idea, except why would Obama ever give this thing his blessing? What if word got out? "Hey, everybody, that guy over there said it was cool. The one running for president of the country." But I loved Lorne for caring this much and being willing to go that far to get this thing on TV. Anyway, there was nothing else for me to do, so I headed home, and Lorne said to call in an hour.

LORNE MICHAELS:

I showed it to Obama, because if he had any discomfort with it, I didn't want it to appear. We went to one of the back dressing rooms and watched it. He said, "It's funny, but no, I don't think so," and I went, "Okay." So we took it off.

ROBERT SMIGEL:

I called and couldn't reach Lorne, but they did tell me, "It's not in the rundown." And that was it. It felt pretty empty; I'd wasted the show's money on a sketch they couldn't run, and I hadn't even stayed around to see a future president made uncomfortable.

KEN AYMONG:

Strikes are always a killer. I've been through several. We kept everybody on for two or three weeks, hoping it would get resolved, and then it did not, so everybody got laid off. And that particular time, I think they went on strike in November and came back in the end of February, and I remember the network wasn't sure whether we should come back at all, that maybe we should just premiere again the following fall. Lorne fought really hard for us to come back on. It wasn't pleasant.

LORNE MICHAELS:

At best I'm ambivalent about writers' strikes. The one in '89 with Judge Reinhold, we were peaking, and we were going up every week and had a 12 rating or something like that, and then at the end of February we're off the rest of the season. Their first writers' guild strike was 1968 or '69. I'm on *Laugh-In* or *Phyllis Diller,* but we go to the meeting, my partner and I, and the minimum at that point was five hundred dollars a show, and they were fighting for it to be five seventy-five and there were only two people making minimum—me and my partner. And we were going, "We're from Canada. This is an enormous amount of money for us, so don't do it for us," and they said, "No, the labor movement has us…" And so that was my first experience of it.

TINA FEY:

In some ways I feel like *30 Rock* had it worse during the strike because everyone knew that *SNL* was not going to get canceled over it, whereas we could have easily been the victim of "Oh, that show? Just forget it. Never start it back up." So all the writers were feeling a lot of stress around that time. You feel responsibility to the union, and you also feel the pressure of keeping a bunch of people out of work. We marched in the picket lines, but sometimes we would go to the picket line and no one would even see us. There was one down on Wall Street one day and I was like, "This is an exercise in insanity." We were picketing but no one was around. The picket lines in L.A. were comical, everybody ripped and tan and holding a nine-dollar cup of coffee in their hand. It was not a great face of the writers' guild.

LORNE MICHAELS:

You watch people lined up picketing, and they all live west of Doheny, and they're the people who run things.

TINA FEY:

We tried to raise money for people who were out of work and I think Zucker was probably pretty mad about that. I think there was a lot of tension at that time.

ROBERT SMIGEL:

My last cartoon, in February 2008, was *The Obama Files*. It was mostly my wife's idea, actually, about candidate Obama's efforts to distance himself from Jesse Jackson and Al Sharpton without alienating them. It turned out that on the same show, Hillary Clinton made a cameo in the cold open. She was planning to leave right after, but Lorne liked the cartoon, and asked her to hang around for twenty more minutes and watch it. He then introduced me to her and I watched it in her dressing room and it was all fun and exciting. She was laughing a lot at the cartoon. Then about halfway in, I remembered that the ending might not be as much fun. It had Sharpton and Jackson falling through a trapdoor and landing in a "community van" with other political liabilities, including Bill Clinton, who then asks the driver to head for spring break. Relatively tame, but still, it's her husband. Fortunately, Poehler walked in just before then. Hillary still saw it and chuckled politely, but her focus was split and awkwardness was averted. Later I saw Lorne and the first thing out of his mouth was, "I forgot about the Bill part." "Yeah, me too. But she was cool about it." And I assure you, the fact that it was my last cartoon is a total coincidence.

The only thing that was troubling in terms of being let go from the show, which happened in 2008, was having my last season cut in half. That was NBC's move — the execs at the time used the writers' strike to void deals where they could, and they tried to terminate mine in midseason, after the strike ended. Lorne and my agent fought to get me at least one more cartoon, but that was it... a lot of work and salary lost. So yes, it was a little strange for the network to do that to somebody who had been there for so many years. And they were aware I have a boy with autism, and the extra kind of expenses that come with that. Now, the following summer, when "TV Funhouse" was dropped for good, I could understand, because of the budget cuts. I got a personal call from Lorne about it. And Lorne expressed that he'd had to fight to keep the cartoons on the show for the past few years, because they were fairly expensive — if I remember correctly, some were as much as a hundred thousand dollars each. Plus, Digital Shorts came around 2005, I believe, and were phenomenal and probably the most important addition to the show in years.

There was really nothing to feel bad about. I was starting to write movies and making a good living that way. I'd been given an amazing opportunity — making short cartoon sketches was basically something no one else got to do on television. And I got to do it for eleven years. So when it was over, I purposely wouldn't talk about it publicly... I didn't want to cast any negative light on the new season.

Which was hilarious, in retrospect, because that summer Sarah Palin happened and Tina came back and the show had its biggest moment since the '70s.

Saturday Night Live could run on its record when it came to satirizing political figures, including those who held or sought the highest offices in the land. But what was already a stellar tradition would get even more so during the presidential campaign of 2008, when Tina Fey, SNL *writer turned performer, introduced her impression of Republican vice presidential candidate Sarah Palin, governor of Alaska, during a mock debate with Amy Poehler, winningly cast as Hillary Clinton. Before long* SNL *owned the election year.*

Fey would achieve the impressionist's dream: She would become arguably more famous than the person she was impersonating. Although by this point she had retired from the SNL *cast, this gig would prove more than worthy of Fey's time.*

It all started modestly but hilariously back in the early days of SNL, *when Chevy Chase, without makeup or prosthetics and even without mocking any specific gestures or statements, introduced his impression of President Gerald R. Ford in a series of* SNL *debates that boldly brightened an otherwise tepid presidential campaign (asked a question on economics, Chevy, as Ford, protested, "I was told there'd be no math"). Chase's portrait of Ford as a hapless bumbler stuck and haunted the incumbent, who began another tradition when he appeared as himself on* SNL, *despite the pummeling he'd taken, and uttered "Live from New York, it's* Saturday Night," *though he was actually taped from the White House when he said it.*

Presidential politics would, as the saying goes, never be the same.

Chase's Ford, which also broke a long-standing rule against making light of physical threats to a sitting president, began an impressive and often hilarious procession of political impressions that gleefully included Dan Aykroyd's portrayal of Richard M. Nixon dictating his "may-moirs," which began with the book's retail price; Dana Carvey doing the elder George Bush so tellingly that Bush invited Carvey and his wife to a White House sleepover; Phil Hartman and, later, Darrell Hammond as a glib and cocky Bill Clinton (the only president who refused to appear on the show as himself); farceur supreme Will Ferrell as George W. Bush, clueless and half crazy; and Aykroyd again, returning to the show after years away, as Bob Dole, who in a Republican debate kept complaining about his allegedly hardscrabble origins ("Bob Dole didn't have the electric carving knife...").

Even with all that as precedent, Fey took it to a new level, imitating Palin with merciless precision. Her version seemed to eclipse the real thing, emerging as the most reverberant and popular political caricature ever. So it was that at the height of election-year hullabaloo, a British newspaper would acclaim the comedienne, not the politician, as "the most influential woman in America."

TINA FEY:

It was August of 2008, and I was on Fire Island with my husband, Jeff, and it was funny because he had the cover of the *Times* that said "McCain picks running mate," and he said he thought there was a resemblance. I said, "I don't think so. It's just brown hair and glasses." But when we got back to the city, some cousins and old classmates were all saying, "That lady looks like you." At that time, *30 Rock* was not exactly highly rated, and so no one really knew that I wasn't even on *SNL* anymore. In fact, no one remembered that I didn't even really do sketches when I was on. So everyone thought they had the same good idea: that I should play Sarah Palin.

It's funny because I was sort of—arrogantly in my own mind—resisting it, like, "I don't want to play that, and I don't know who's gonna write it, and what if I don't like what they wrote, people are going to think that I wrote it." And at some point I realized that, like, oh, by the way, no one at *SNL* has actually asked me to do this. So I was like, "Oh, right, this is like a little argument that I'm having in my own mind. They haven't asked me to do this, and they don't really need me to do it." Kristen Wiig could certainly have done it with her eyes closed. It wasn't until late that week that Lorne called.

LORNE MICHAELS:

Right after the debate, I'm coming out of my building, the next day, and my doorman, Frank, says, "Mr. Michaels, what a gift! Did you see it last night?" And I go, "Yeah," and he says, "It's Tina Fey!" And I go, "No, Frank, she's not on the show anymore. She's doing her own series." And I'm literally thirty feet away from my apartment and Bobby De Niro's there with his daughter, and he goes, "What a gift." And then I realized this was what everybody was thinking. So I called Tina and said, "I think the audience is demanding that you do it." She said that Saturday was the only day that she could get Oprah Winfrey to appear on *30 Rock*, so she would be filming all day with Oprah. She says, "I can't do it," and I thought, "Kristen can do it," but later that night we talked about it again and Tina said, "Maybe we could rehearse Friday night late? And then I could just come for dress?"

SETH MEYERS:

It was that crazy thing where of course everyone knew we'd do a Sarah Palin sketch and everyone knew Tina would play her. Because of that there was this level of excitement that was both a good and bad thing, because I think we were all fairly terrified that we wouldn't execute on the potential.

Two of the most recognizable women of American politics impersonated by two great women of American comedy—it seemed to be, and was, a formula for surefire success as the thirty-fourth season of Saturday Night Live *got wildly under way on September 13, 2008. Tina Fey, immortally, played Sarah Palin, and Amy Poehler played Hillary Clinton in a sketch most memorable now for the line "I can see Russia from my house," uttered by Fey as Palin but never by Palin herself. (Although Palin said in an interview that parts of Russia could be seen from parts of Alaska, she never said she could see any of it from her house.)*

SETH MEYERS:

The "Russia from the house" line? That was not first draft. I believe I'm going to give credit to Mike Shoemaker for that line. That was the thing about those sketches—you were constantly carrying them around and reading through them for whoever you could get to listen, and people would just constantly pitch jokes.

JAMES DOWNEY:

To be honest with you I didn't even think it was very well written. That's the one that's always played, I think more for politics than for comedy. The first one was the one where it was essentially Hillary going, "I'm smart" and Sarah Palin going, "I'm stupid." I'm smart, I'm stupid, I'm smart, I'm stupid...I thought it was kind of mediocre as a piece of writing, but as performing it was great. The performing is ultimately more important than the writing. It's like good pitching beats good hitting. A performer can lift mediocre material, but even the best-written material, if the performance isn't there, can't make it through that filter.

AMY POEHLER:

You know who I think was most aware of how big that skit was going to be? It was my not-yet-born son, Archibald. Archibald was in my stomach during that sketch doing flips. I think I was probably six to seven months pregnant, playing Hillary at that time, and I remember very specifically the wardrobe department—who, blessedly, kept having to make jackets that fit me in different various sizes during my time there—made a Hillary jacket with a split back because my stomach was so big and I was hiding behind the podium. And when we were doing the sketch, Archie was doing somersaults in my stomach and I was thinking, "Wow, he knows that this is really exciting."

LORNE MICHAELS:

It was at least as powerful as "strategery." You could see perception changing completely. And it's in there—there have been these moments. It's Lovitz as Dukakis going, "I can't believe I'm losing to this guy." Or Chevy as Gerald Ford going, "I was told there would be no math." All of those things that capture something, that perfectly let you know where we are at that moment in our political consciousness. The audience that was suddenly watching Sarah Palin wasn't necessarily the *SNL* audience. Tina crossed over. It made her a huge star.

JOHN McCAIN, *Host:*

Very honestly, the portrayal of her was not fair, but it was certainly well done, and certainly probably the single most watched aspect of the political campaign over any other.

TINA FEY:

When the Internet really thinks they want something, it can easily turn out like, "Well, that wasn't as good as we thought." Having done so much on *SNL*, I was ready to be publicly rejected for it and kind of fine with it. I said, "All right, let's try it. It's probably going to stink." I was surprised that we got away with it.

AMY POEHLER:

Playing Hillary and Sarah Palin was an indication of women taking center stage in politics in a way that I hadn't been able to experience in my time there. I started *SNL* post-9/11; in fact, my first show was two weeks after 9/11 happened, and for the first three or four years of my time there we could barely do anything political. Everyone and everything was so tender, and we had lost Will Ferrell as our Bush. Everything was so bad; the news was so bad. There was a lot of pop-culture stuff, and getting to finally do really deep political parody at the end of my career there felt really satisfying.

Television has been bending, distorting, and misrepresenting reality since it began, long before reality television was a genre, but the mixture of real, surreal, and fake reached a crazy new level when Sarah Palin appeared as herself on Saturday Night Live, *watching and criticizing a sketch in which Tina Fey played her on a previous episode. Coddled gently on camera by producer Lorne Michaels, who was joined by actor Alec Baldwin, Palin didn't actually chat with Fey during the appearance, but the two did walk past each other, and it was Palin who got to shout the show's heraldic signature line, "Live from New York, it's* Saturday Night!*" Later, proving herself a consummate good sport, Palin joined Seth Meyers at the "Update" desk to say she'd decided not to do a planned rap number because "it might just cross the line," but then she joined Meyers gyrating in rap rhythm as Poehler hip-hopped into the song, joined by*

Fred Armisen and Andy Samberg as Eskimos and a guy in a moose costume—altogether a rollicking high point. Thus ended an amazing, mondo-bizarro moment in the history of the show and perhaps in the history of the republic.

LORNE MICHAELS:

I called Alec to come in for it, to be standing with me, because he was the most emblematic liberal at that point. He said he had to introduce a documentary at the Hamptons film festival on that Saturday, so he wouldn't be able to do it. So I said, "Alec, your instincts are always great, but are you telling me you're not going to be here for this thing that the whole world is waiting to see? These two women meeting each other, or at least interacting? You don't want to be here? You'd rather introduce this documentary? Well, you have to do what you have to do. I understand completely. We'll be here."

TINA FEY:

I think I was the one pitching, "Why don't you start her backstage, you know, with Alec, so the crowd won't boo." She had just been booed at a hockey game in Philadelphia, and I thought we had to be cautious. And of course the audience was just happy to see her because she was a star, a media star. Even the New York audience was not feeling their politics at that moment.

LORNE MICHAELS:

Tina was terrified of anything where they would be together looking like an endorsement. When you're standing next to somebody, it's hard, very hard, not to be gracious and not want to see another person in stress, particularly on the show.

Governor Palin got here at four o'clock in the afternoon; she was great. She has wonderful manners—and I honestly don't mean this in a condescending way—but it's that pageant-winner thing. Like, if there were young girls around, she'd spend time, she'd ask questions. It was her daughter's sixteenth birthday. She could not have been more gracious or warmer. She showed up fully dressed, like a candidate would be, and then did everything and didn't question anything.

SARAH PALIN, *Guest:*

I know that they portrayed me as an idiot, and I hated that, and I wanted to come on the show and counter some of that. I love to disarm people. I love to meet them face-to-face, and as a result of being on the show, being able to at least meet, like, Tina Fey's in-laws, whom I adore, that was a valuable connection right there. And to meet Lorne Michaels in person, that was nice. And just all the characters—it was great. But I was certainly aware of how they were portraying me. Unfortunately I have to admit that I was getting used to it. Knowing that that was the reality, you know you make the best of the situation. You either become bitter or you become better, based on the maybe less than ideal circumstances in front of you. *SNL* portrayals of me were less than ideal, but they let me get on there and have some fun and capitalize on what they're doing to me.

KEN AYMONG:

What can I say? The show had been pretty hard on her up to that point, to say the least, but she was amazing. Very easygoing. She didn't hide out, she stayed on the studio floor, and she gladly went along with everything that happened in the show.

SETH MEYERS:

She was incredibly charismatic and game. She couldn't have been friendlier through the whole process, and obviously she would have had every reason to have her guard up. I'm not saying she didn't, but I only had pleasant interactions with her. I felt that the opening sketch, where there were so many moving parts, was the less memorable part of that show, whereas the Amy-Palin rap becomes the part of that show that you always remember. You could just tell in the house; you didn't have to go online to know how that stuff was playing.

The times at *SNL* where I was confident enough that I would just walk out on the floor and watch a piece are few and far between. I pace beneath the bleachers more. But you could just tell it was like "Wayne's World."

PAULA PELL:

That whole time Sarah Palin came to do her little appearance—the actual Sarah Palin—I planned that I was going to come up and talk to her and shake her hand and welcome her and say, "My wife and I are very good people and we live a very socially conscious life and we do a lot for our community, and I just want you to know the face of gay couples and gay people," and I had this whole speech planned. Then I just kind of came up to her in the chaos in the hallway and just nodded and said, "Hi," and walked off. I thought to myself, "I'm such a chickenshit." I was like, "Wow, she's pretty." I just got overwhelmed by the fact that this character who was everywhere on TV was in front of me, and she was real and just ridiculous. So I didn't get my big political moment.

SARAH PALIN:

I'd been a fan and my siblings have been fans of the show since we were quite young. We used to sneak into our TV room so we could watch *SNL*, because our parents thought—or, appropriately, believed—that it was not such a positive thing to be watching. But we snuck into our TV room and we would watch the show. So having an opportunity during the campaign to be on the show was awesome. It was a blast.

SETH MEYERS:

Tina and I, more than anyone else, felt the burden of having to constantly do better with the next one. In the end we probably did six sketches or so in the course of seven or eight weeks. So it was one after the other, and I was just happy in the end that there was never the one that made people go, "Well, that's it; the party's over." And I will say that I wrote the first draft of most of those, but they were always a group effort. Everyone was paying such close attention to that election, including everyone on the writing staff, and everybody had points of view on it. The jokes would always get better as the week went on. People would see Tina and just lose their minds. And then *all* the jokes worked.

SARAH PALIN:

Even today, I'll walk by the TV that's maybe on in our living room and I'll glance up and once in a while I still see that same old Tina Fey, the portrayal of me, and I do a double take. I think, "What am I doing on TV today? Oh! It's Tina Fey." It's weird! What really kills me is that people believe that I said the things that Tina Fey said in her funny comedy sketch. That tells you that yeah, there is that impact on part of the electorate that *SNL* has. Another thing that's significant here is that *SNL* is able to kind of ratchet down what the debate is to a level that is culturally relevant, and that's important and quite significant. So it's important to, again, get on the show, disarm them if you can, and play along with it in order to ultimately get your message out there.

JAMES DOWNEY:

The 2008 election had that really interesting thing going on between Obama and Hillary in the front half, and in the back half you had Tina Fey doing Sarah Palin. I never thought the writing for the Sarah Palin character was particularly great until the last one, the vice presidential debate. But her performance was so incredibly great. It's one of the all-time great political impressions. It's up there to me with Dana Carvey doing Ross Perot and Darrell's Gore. It was just phenomenal. You just got that "Thank you, God" kind of break where you had Sarah Palin and Tina Fey on the planet at the same time. You can't count on getting those kinds of things.

HORATIO SANZ:

I always kind of felt bad when Will Ferrell did his Bush impression, because he was such a good ol' boy that you really didn't think, "Oh, this evil little rich prick whose dad and his friends got him in office." You thought, "Oh, he's just a good old guy I'd like to drink beer with." As funny as Will's impression was, and as funny as that take was, the audience as a whole, the whole country, would probably see that as, "Oh, I like Bush. Because he's Will." You know, if Will hadn't done that impression or at least made him likable, it may have tipped it the other way. I honestly think so. We made up for it. I think Tina's impression basically killed Sarah Palin. I think that helped get rid of Sarah Palin.

SARAH PALIN:

I think *SNL* is egotistical if they believe that it was truly an effect on maybe the public debate about who should lead the country in the next four years. I don't believe that it was that impacting, but certainly it was impacting for a segment of our culture, and I'm a testimony to that because growing up, again with my siblings, we did tune in to *SNL* and we did listen to what it was that they were saying in regards to cultural, or political, or societal jokes—not so much influenced by them, but certainly opening our minds to what it was that *SNL* was trying to portray.

SETH MEYERS:

What made the election campaign for me was the fact that John McCain came on and played himself and Tina played Sarah Palin and they were just standing out there next to each other. It was just as surreal a moment as I can remember on *SNL*. It was great. And I remember between dress and air we added Cindy McCain, who was wonderful as well. It was a really fun night, and when we're talking about a good sport, I think it's hard to find one better than John McCain.

JOHN MCCAIN:

During the campaign itself, I would argue that *Saturday Night Live* has as much impact on younger Americans as any other aspect of a political campaign. A politician, a candidate, cannot control it, but if you don't try, you can be sure that you won't reach them. I certainly had no trepidation about appearing on the show, and despite the failure of the campaign, it was probably the best way I knew to gain communication with the younger voters, who certainly didn't watch the debates and probably didn't come to campaign rallies. Even though they may not pay as much attention as you want, they're pretty well informed as to what's going on politically. Which is why the *Saturday Night Live* skits on politicians are so popular. So it was an incredibly useful way to get in touch with them.

I trust Lorne Michaels and the writers on the show. One of the highlights, frankly, of my political career was when I was able to host

Saturday Night Live, and so when Lorne asked me back, I was really happy to do it. And the skits were good, especially the "McCain-Feingold" skit; people still come up to me and talk about it.

LORNE MICHAELS:

McCain is great with me. He came on that weekend of the election—that Saturday before the Tuesday—and did the thing with Tina, and Cindy came with him. Tina did not want to be in the same shot, but I staged it so that they would just pass each other.

SETH MEYERS:

I can't imagine any outcome where it would have been more tailor-made for comedy than the 2008 election was. From the very beginning, that was the sound of puzzle pieces fitting together, and 2012 I'm very happy with. I feel like we executed it with what we had to deal with, but I don't think any one of us went into it feeling we were going to top 2008.

BRIAN WILLIAMS:

I don't think we can correctly assess, yet, the show's impact on politics or popular culture. The number of times in life people say, "It would make a great sketch on *SNL*" is equaled by the number of times in life people almost knowingly are making judgments on politicians that are based on *SNL* depictions and nothing else. I think it has an immeasurable ability to set the agenda. Now, is it mostly for an audience of the "coastal intelligentsia"? Perhaps, except for the Internet. The Internet has really launched the show in a new way. The Internet has come along like Sweet Pea at the end of a girder and swept up *SNL* into its loving arms.

SARAH PALIN:

If I ran into Tina Fey again today, I would say, "You need to at least pay for my kids' braces or something from all the money that you made off of pretending that you're me! My goodness, you capitalized on that! Can't you contribute a little bit? Jeez!"

AMY POEHLER:

In a very ridiculous way, I was thinking that I had control over when my baby was going to come. I thought, "I'm going to do this last show with Jon Hamm on Saturday, and then I'm going to have the baby on Sunday, and there ya go!" Just five days earlier, I had wrapped the Sarah Palin sketch and still felt like I could finish the show — and then my child Archie had other plans. On Friday night he decided he wanted to start coming and he wanted to get there by Saturday, and so I texted Mike Shoemaker and Seth in the middle of the night and said, "I'm not going to make the show tomorrow." From what I understand, it was really exciting because everyone had these fill-ins for my parts. Elisabeth Moss filled in for herself in a "Mad Men" sketch, and she met Fred Armisen that night, and a year later, on my son's birthday, they were married. That was also the night where Seth had to do "Update" for the first time, and I held my newborn son in my arms as I watched Maya and Kenan sing a song to me and him. Seth tapped on the "Update" desk, which he does now pretty regularly out of a lovely habit, and I felt it was really one of those really incredibly moving moments where all these moments in my life were happening at the same time and I felt my heart crack open.

It was just love with a capital L all over there. Getting it, receiving it, feeling it, seeing this little person, my first son, and seeing the people I loved so much at my job. It felt very real to me and it *is* very real to me. I treasure the love and relationships that I have there and continue to have because of that job.

ABBY ELLIOTT, *Cast Member:*

I sent them a bunch of tapes and then they called me in L.A. to come in and do five minutes onstage. And I really thought it was such a long shot, that there was no way that I could get it, so I wasn't as nervous as I think one would normally be. After the audition I stayed in Connecticut for a couple of days to hang out with my family and we were out to eat, and I got a call saying, "Lorne wants to meet with you on Monday," which usually meant you're being considered for the job. And so I stayed, met with him, and afterward I went off alone and burst into tears in Steve Higgins's office, and he gave me a shot of whiskey. I left for L.A. that night, and when I landed I turned my phone on and I had gotten the job. All my friends knew before I did, and Lorne called my dad and that was really exciting. So I flew back to New York on the red-eye that night and was at the table read the next day.

I came in really young, twenty-one, the youngest female. I was really wide-eyed and didn't have any idea what I was getting into. And that was exciting to me; I wanted to do that. Whatever I was jumping into, it was going to be a shock to my system.

AKIVA SCHAFFER:

With *Jizz in my Pants,* we thought the word *jizz* was filthy, it was really, really dirty, and that there was no way it could ever air. And then Friday night around nine, we were like, "Lorne, we have this video. I have a rough cut here; we can't figure out how to make it clean." Usually Lorne would see our videos for the very first time in dress rehearsal and then if he had a note afterwards he would give it to us and we would do a quick edit between dress and air. In this case we showed it to him on Friday. We knew it was funny, but we couldn't figure out how to make a clean version. And we just wanted to show it to him in case he had ideas or anything and then we were going to work on it through the next week. So he said, "This is for *next week's* show?" And I said, "Here it is," and we played him the dirty version and he said, "I think we could air that." We were shocked; we were very shocked. And then we went all the way up to Jeff Zucker, who happened to be at the show that night. He watched it and said, "Yeah, you can air that—after twelve thirty." So it aired at twelve forty-five, as is. Which shocked me, because I thought *jizz* was a much dirtier word than *dick.*

AMY POEHLER:

Lorne does a very lovely and charming thing, which is he doesn't let you tell him that you're going to leave. He evades it for as long as he can so I don't remember ever really telling him. I think I did in some way, and I think he kept just kind of nodding and being, "Uh-huh. But you'll come back for a few more." And then I remember coming back for a few more.

ROBERT SMIGEL:

That era sort of defied the argument you always hear that "*SNL* needs to have something for everyone…if you don't hate a few sketches, we're not doing our job, et cetera." That cast—especially around my last few years there—had a very consistent sensibility. They worked as a team in a way that I don't really remember ever feeling in any of the eras that I worked there, as great as those other groups were. So many combinations of performers yielded brilliant, weird sketches, like "Potato Chip" with Forte and Sudeikis. Top to bottom, probably the hippest group since the originals—that whole universe that started with Fred and Kristen and Forte and expanded to Samberg and Bill Hader and the rest. And you still had people like Amy and Maya for a hunk of this time. They were great performers and they were all writers…and Seth really let the cast blossom and wrote funny, smart stuff on top of it. I feel like it should be looked at as a golden era, but I don't know if it gets that credit. Maybe it's because of the shadow of Ferrell; they had to follow the greatest cast member ever.

AMY POEHLER:

It feels really good to have people not want you to leave. It's very, very hard to leave, but I felt like it was time to end it. That's when I'd been doing sketch comedy for fifteen years or something and I thought maybe it was time to play one character for a while.

In my fantasy world, Gilda and I would have been best friends. In my fantasy world, Eddie Murphy would've been like, "I don't really think white women are funny, but you're really great." I wish that I had met Phil Hartman. I think about that sometimes. He's someone I would've really liked to have met and worked with, and, sadly, I didn't get that chance. But certainly Gilda. They were such comedy giants for me; I can't really imagine sharing the same air as them. It's interesting: Whenever you parachute into *SNL,* the time that you parachute in, it has to work. I was extremely lucky to come at a time when women were dominating, when my friends were working there, and where I felt like I had some chops having worked at UCB. So I was lucky in the time that I came. I can't imagine what it would be like in a different time, in a *Sliding Doors* universe when I was there at a different time. I don't know how I would've fit in, or if I would've fit in at all, because there's certainly a lot of people that have come through *SNL* who are so supremely talented and didn't quite maybe get to scratch the itch in a way that they did through other jobs. It's really a combination of a lot of things.

ROBERT SMIGEL:

Fred's David Patterson impression actually originated on Night of Too Many Stars, an autism benefit my wife and I do with Jon Stewart for Comedy Central. Lorne actually produced the first one for me at NBC, and *SNL* cast members have always been a huge part of it — Sandler, Ferrell, Tina, Jimmy, Amy, Fred, Maya, and Forte have all done it multiple times. In 2008 Patterson had just taken over as governor after Spitzer's sex scandals and almost immediately confessed — in great detail — to committing adultery. I thought Fred could look just like him, so I asked him to play Patterson for us. We put him at the celebrity phone bank, and while our jokes mostly focused on his eagerness to share TMI, we couldn't resist having him speaking into a stapler instead of a phone. *SNL* took it all way farther with greater success; they made him a complete, very funny regular character. After all the support I'd received from *SNL* it was nice that we could return the favor even a little bit. Much better than a gift bag.

JOHN MULANEY, *Writer*:

One of the strangest things I remember was during my first season, during the fall of 2008. It was a really big time at the show with all the wonderful Sarah Palin stuff. But it was also a nerve-wracking time. I remember the last show at Christmas, Rob Klein and Colin Jost and I wrote an "Update" feature where Fred played Governor David Patterson, the governor of New York. And Fred happened to look identical to David Patterson when he put on a beard. I've never seen someone look more like the person they were impersonating, and we wrote this "Update" feature about New York now that Patterson, who was blind, had taken over from Spitzer.

Fred slid out to the "Update" desk from offstage on a swivel chair but kept sliding, going past Seth. And Lorne, Mike Shoemaker —

everyone—laughed so goddamn hard. It was pretty insane to see Lorne laugh that hard. Colin, Rob, and I were laughing too, but it was amazing to see Lorne like something that much. It was Mike Shoemaker's last show, and we were under the bleachers after Shoemaker ran over and said, "Not a bad way to end this first year. That's pretty cool to see Lorne falling all over himself laughing." And it really was.

Then the next day there were headlines everywhere— "Did *SNL* go too far in Fred playing David Patterson?"—and I had just gotten home for Christmas and I thought, "Oh my God, I'm going to be fired. We're all going to be fired for doing this." I knew enough to know that they thought the piece was really funny and that we had done it with the best intentions. Much to the show's, and Fred's, amazing credit, we kept doing them because Patterson was never the butt of the joke, he was the joke maker. We wrote him like a comedian who burned everyone else, especially New Jersey. Though we didn't want to offend anybody it was kind of interesting to have *The New York Times* saying, "To call this humor sophomoric would be an insult to sophomores," and I was just like, "Oh my God, how *New York Times*-ey." It was a great added, fun element to writing those that we were bothering some people.

One of the most surreal moments was when Governor Patterson came on the show two years later to do a segment with Fred and Seth. The way Governor Patterson and his team would work is that they would record speeches for him so that he could memorize them, and he would listen to the tapes. So they had a blocking rehearsal where he sat at the desk and I'd sit next to him reading the "Update" feature, reading his part and Fred reading his part, so that he would have it on tape. Patterson took home my voice to learn his bit in the "Update" feature. Someone took a photo of me standing next to Patterson, who is laughing, luckily, reading all of these lines that he's going to have to say the next night.

Those Patterson ones—Colin and Rob and I just laughed a lot writing them. It was really fun. Fred was so good at it, and it became just a fully formed character. The added thing of people being pissed off about it, at that age, was kind of exciting.

PAULA PELL:

I've always marveled at the way *SNL* sort of bleeds into everyone's consciousness, and especially living in New York, on Sundays, I would always go to a diner, go eat somewhere, and I would marvel at how many people were talking about *SNL*. And that happens a lot anyway, but during that period of time, there was such constant immersion of connecting *SNL* with just the campaigns. On every news show, they would show a clip. It was just really feeling wonderful and relevant that we were constantly in the forefront of that, and I think that's because Tina and Amy and Seth were writing those debate sketches. The years of *SNL* feeling relevant always kind of come and go, and it's always unique and it's always there in people's consciousness, and people watch it in different eras of their life. But at that moment it felt like *everyone* was watching it. Sarah Palin was just pennies from heaven. An amazing gift to comedy, that woman.

DARRELL HAMMOND:

What was it like after I left? You're talking about living on the moon and then not living on the moon. It's kind of like what astronauts who've walked on the moon talk about when they're playing shuffleboard in Arizona. You were on the moon, but now you don't have those experiences anymore. It's a culture shock.

When I did my last show, it wasn't even acknowledged. Will Ferrell, who was hosting, said something, but it wasn't anything like, "Hey, this is your last show." I mean, he was good when I was there, so it wasn't anything like that. And Will said something again at the "good night." Otherwise people weren't that moved. No one ever really consulted me, partially because I don't know anything about how to put a show like that together.

I wanted to leave after my eleventh year. But there were some people who had advised me very well in my life who kept advising me to stay on, but I knew in my heart of hearts that it wasn't right anymore. By my twelfth year, people didn't even know I was on the show anymore. I knew the scripts were going to stop coming, and they did. I had a giant management agency tell me to stay, I had a thousand people telling me stay, but it wasn't right; it wasn't right.

No one knows how to leave there and no one knows how to get on there. Lorne wanted me to stay, but I felt like I had achieved my dream and that it was time for me to go. It's part of the aesthetic.

I haven't known any place like it. It was just as painful for me to be there when I knew it was wrong.

All of it was frustrating. I never did as well as I wanted to; that's why I never watched reruns, because I thought if I only had one more hour I could have done better.

FINESSE MITCHELL:

I just think I partied too much. I enjoyed New York—I *really* enjoyed New York. I enjoyed being on the show and had I focused more on the show and characters and stuff and really getting better I probably would've been a good five years or six years on the show before I left.

Man, I went out every night. I probably went out every night except Friday night. Yeah, I mean, we got treated great at the clubs, and then there were some hosts that would come in that wanted to go out. So we would take them out on a Thursday night. You know, your Lindsay Lohans, or your Colin Farrells, and then you get that guest that wants to go out. And then Kenan and myself just used to go out so much; we just clubbed, clubbed, and more clubs. And then I had another buddy who was on Broadway and he was from Atlanta. So it was always like three or four of us going out. Staying out until, like, three or four in the morning. Sometimes leaving the house at, like, two in the morning and coming back at, like, you know, four in the morning or five in the morning. But that was the great thing about New York—you could leave so late and they let you right in, and you're drinking for free and meeting people and hanging out. Sometimes we would go clubbing and come back to *SNL* to finish writing on Tuesday night. And in addition to that, *SNL* had some great events that they wanted everybody to go to, so that was kind of special too. You know, go to the Rock and Roll Hall of Fame or Mark Twain Awards at the Kennedy Center. Being a Gemini, you don't like the same things for a long time, but I enjoyed the whole experience.

PAULA PELL:

I had always been just a casual pot smoker. I had never bought pot in New York, and so I bought pot from someone at work. And I had it—like, I'm a super-slow pot smoker, so I'd buy a small amount and have it for, like, weeks and months. And then Shoemaker came into my office one night, and he goes, "I'm going to go see the Kids in the Hall movie. I heard that you're the one who had pot. You're the connection." I said if I'm the connection—the drug connection at *Saturday Night Live* now—then it has fallen. Very far. And it should be ashamed of itself that *I* am the drug connection, because I still have a joint in my jewelry box from, like, 1982. And so it just made me laugh so hard that people were all talking and going, "Yeah, I think Paula smokes pot. Go—I think she has pot." I thought, you know, for a place that, you know, probably had drugs delivered regularly, it just cracked me up how far it had changed.

FRED ARMISEN:

I'm not into drugs; I don't drink. The old casts had their method and I've only heard about it. So all I could do is hear stories and think, "Wow, they made it work." But I wouldn't have been able to do it.

PAULA PELL:

Actors on the show now are just more health-conscious. They'll order from a super-healthy place at work, and you just see people on the show wanting to be healthier in life. The only romances now are just kind of like sweet, open romances that happen when people kind of fell for each other and are going together. There are one or two. But there are very few and very out-in-the-open relationships. None of it is sordid; none of it is outside of marriages. There's just very little scandal there. There's very few Page Six moments with *SNL* anymore. Maybe some of that has trickled down from Lorne, and not that I think he was ever the origin of the debauchery, but, you know, he's raising a family and he's also a health nut. He's certainly healthier than me, and I'm younger than him. I said to Steve Higgins the other day, "You are the age that Lorne was when he hired us," and that really freaked us out. We were like, "Holy shit!" because I thought of him as this elder person when I got hired, and I'm, like, his age now, so...But he's so frickin' healthy, and it just sets the example. I mean, there's some of those dudes who, they stay up all night, you know, and go out and party, and they're young and they can do that and then eat pizza at eight in the morning and they're good with it.

LINDSAY SHOOKUS:

They seem to be a little bit more responsible about going home earlier and making sure they're going to get their beauty sleep. When I started, it felt like it was a little more lively. They would just throw caution to the wind a little bit more, you know? "Well, we'll figure it out." Now it seems a little bit more thought through, and people are much more, like, you know, "Well, I want my trainer appointment in the morning," or they're going to go home so they can look good the next day, which is smart. They're going on-camera. They should look good.

It makes my job easier, so I can't complain too much. It's still a lot of fun, it's just maybe, like, more thought-out fun, where there will be a certain night where people stay for one night as opposed to it all seeming to be one big party. It's like, save it for Saturday, or save it for the writer's party we have one night, you know?

JORMA TACCONE:

We worked all the time. That was my home in an entirely different way. I slept on every couch in the place. The kind of dedication that it takes to make a show like that is the kind of dedication that was there from the moment the show started. People live there; I showered in Lorne's office. I've showered downstairs, probably in the same places that Belushi did all that stuff. I mean, *you live there.* That's your home, and that's the only way to make it happen. My only regret is we never made a documentary about how to make one of those shorts. It's amazing, because that show now looks so seamless. People would often ask us when *SNL* was "filmed." Filmed? It's *live!*

DAN AYKROYD:

It was all-consuming, that's for sure. I think those kids there today suffer from the same thing. They only have one day off: Sunday. But that's got to be one of the greatest jobs in television, working there—for all time. They're very fortunate to be there. I look at Second City as the B.A. program in comedy and improv and writing, and I look at *Saturday Night Live* as the master's program. And then after that point in life, you get your Ph.D. in whatever you go into. So I would say I probably have enough knowledge to teach a graduate-level course in film production now. But definitely *Saturday Night Live* is the master's program.

JOHN MULANEY:

When I first came to the show, I thought, "This thing will be competitive. Some people will be toxic; it'll be very cold." I thought to myself, "This will be a great experience, but this might be really hard, and you could get fired and you'll go back to being a stand-up and it'll be okay." I had to keep telling myself that when I got hired. I started in 2008 and by then Mike Shoemaker and Seth Meyers in particular had created an environment that was so nice. It was a very cool moment in time. The fall of 2008 was amazing for the show, and there was just a great vibe in the air. Everyone wrote together. We had one big rewrite table; all the writers would work with each other; everyone cross-pollinated. It was not a jaded environment; it was really very friendly, very supportive. We were all just together a lot.

COLIN JOST:

We were all fans of the show and knew the lore of the show and so we kind of knew the history of that at the show. We knew that people used to have crazier nights out and do crazier things. I think a bit of it is almost the way people react to their parents, where you learn from that and you're like, "Oh, are these people happy? Are their lives happy? Maybe there's a way for me to deal with it some other way that's not, like, drugs or fighting. Maybe there's a way, maybe in the long run, that's a happier existence, which doesn't make for as good a story but is happier." And I think it's that as much as people being tamer now.

ROBERT SMIGEL:

That era sort of defied that logic that you needed to have the hippest group of people for the show to succeed. The show then not only had the comedy but a consistent level of sophistication I admired. The cast was really working as a team in a way that I don't really remember ever feeling in any of the eras that I worked there. That whole universe that started with Fred and Kristen and Will Forte expanded to Samberg and Bill Hader. They were great performers and they were all writers. I feel like it's looked on as a true golden year. Maybe it's because of the shadow of Ferrell; he's the greatest cast member ever. I remember telling Will that on his last show, and I think it really meant something to him because I had been around for so long.

CHRISTOPHER WALKEN:

A few years ago because of work I literally went around the world. I think I went from New York to Los Angeles, Los Angeles to Australia, then back by way of Singapore. We flew to London, then Paris, then back to New York, and back to Los Angeles. Right around the world. And every hotel that I stayed in, I turn on the TV and there was *SNL*. I'm not sure that people realize the ubiquity of the show. Even in remote places around the world, people watch *SNL*. It's everywhere.

8

One Man's Family: 2008–2014

The election of 2008 and Saturday Night Live *were very good for — and to — each other. When Sarah Palin appeared on the show with pseudo-Sarah, Tina Fey,* SNL *captured its largest audience in fourteen years. The bounty overflowed; even* 30 Rock, *the Fey-Michaels sitcom, saw a big bump in its ratings as Tina-craving viewers followed her to prime time. So it was that a presidential election helped repopularize* Saturday Night Live, *bringing in virgin viewers who'd never watched before as well as returnees who perhaps had strayed for a spell. The obvious question: Could the show hang on to that audience?*

Luckily, SNL's *perpetual search for recurring characters that can pop up several times per season struck gold when Bill Hader, one of the most talented and versatile* SNL *performers of the century so far — and one of the most popular among fellow cast members — introduced Stefon, a sexually adventurous Manhattan party boy. Co-created with writer John Mulaney, Stefon burst forth when he became a special nightlife correspondent for "Weekend Update" with Seth Meyers. Androgynous, jittery, and smoky-voiced, Stefon would describe to Meyers the latest "hottest club in New York" — always some dank cavern populated with oddballs, hipsters, and midgets — and Meyers would plead for more family-friendly haunts. Meyers also chastised Stefon for using the insensitive term* midgets, *and, smitten with Meyers, Stefon finally obliged and changed it: He henceforth would call little people fun-sized, he said. The character caught on quickly, even though Hader violated a cardinal rule of the show by "breaking" — laughing at his own material — at some point in his invariably risible report.*

SETH MEYERS, *Cast Member:*

Bill just showing up was so exciting because we had never quite had someone like him in my time on the show—someone who is both an incredible impressionist and also incredible with characters. And he was doing both. So that was a skill he had that certainly, in that era of the show, he was unparalleled at.

PAUL RUDD, *Host:*

Hader is somebody whose talent is insane. His ear is amazing; it isn't even like he's doing impressions, like Rich Little or somebody. And I've noticed this from just hanging out with the guy. Bill can do anybody. Anybody. He just hears intonations and he can absolutely replicate it. I think of the Alan Alda impression that he did. He'd never done an Alan Alda impression, but that day it was just, "Let's do Alan Alda." And he says, "I'll work on an Alan Alda," and he just did it. He'll home in on something. I know he works on it, but it's an innate ability. He doesn't hang his hat on it either. It's weird; he never even talks about it. All he talks about are books and old movies.

KRISTEN WIIG, *Cast Member:*

What Bill Hader does with his voice is so unique and unbelievable at times, and on top of it he makes the character hilarious. You just find yourself watching him with your mouth open, like, "What the fuck?!"

BILL HADER, *Cast Member:*

John Mulaney and I would write those Stefons. Actually I was more of an editor, and then if something needed a weird voice—I know we did one of Donald Duck having a Vietnam nightmare—those were things that I would come up with: "I can do Donald Duck." Weird sound things were usually me.

JOHN MULANEY, *Writer:*

My initial approach was, "Boy, this is a really weird character and maybe it'll be on about twelve fifty A.M., and that would be a great victory." Bill and I wrote it as a sketch first when Ben Affleck was there, and I remember it was very funny to us; we had a good sense of the character that week that we first wrote it. Stefon and Ben Affleck played brothers who were pitching a movie to a big studio, but they were not on the same page about what the movie was about. So that rhythm of him listing things that it would have was originally in the format of a movie pitch. That sketch aired and did okay; it was like a weirdo thing towards the end of the night, but some people really noticed it. Our friends liked it, and that was really gratifying. The second time we wrote it as a sketch, Stefon was pitching a new restaurant, and his brother that time was Bradley Cooper. A lot of jokes were cool, but it wasn't quite clicking. There were too many people onstage for what was essentially one guy talking. So it wasn't until we put it on "Update" that the added electricity came to it. Then it was either Seth Meyers or Doug Abel who said, "He should describe restaurants, describe clubs," and he quickly became a New York lifestyle consultant.

SETH MEYERS:

I deserve no credit for Stefon other than enjoying setting him up for jokes, but the one thing I will say is, they had originally written it as a sketch, and the one suggestion I had was, every time they would write it as a sketch, any aware host who read the script would see the host had no laughs in the piece—like, it's all Stefon—and if you're a movie star sitting next to Stefon, you probably realize at some point how little people are paying attention to you. So I was the one who suggested—as someone who loves playing a straight man—that "Update" might just be a better home for Stefon, at no point ever expecting it would succeed at the level it did.

BILL HADER:

The first "Update" one we did, we did it at dress, and it went fine. While they were picking sketches for the show, we went over in a corner and there was one line that didn't work—it was a club owner called Amnesia Bernstein, which we thought was funny but got nothing at dress. And then they go, "Meeting!" And I just said, "Oh shit, I gotta go," so I left and told John, "Just put in something." Later, on-air, I got to where it was on the cards, and he had put "club owner Gay Liotta," and that was the first time I saw it—and I started laughing.

And that started this thing where John was like, "Oh, that was fun. I'm going to do this every time now." But these things get highly exaggerated where people say that *every time* I did Stefon there was shit that I didn't know was going to be on the cards; that's not necessarily true.

JOHN MULANEY:

When we did the first one, Bill broke ridiculously. He completely fell apart, which is really funny to me because he felt really bad about breaking on-air. He has a really strong, good work ethic, and he thought each time I would be annoyed at him for breaking—but of course I thought it was awesome. He was trying to keep it together so much that it became fun to put in things purposefully to make him break.

I was also very aware that people can have comedy purity issues with breaking on a live show, but I thought it was so funny and genuine that first time that he laughed, that I just always wanted to keep it funny and genuine by messing with him. I would put in new jokes after dress, and sometimes he would see them right before air; it wasn't like it was the first time he ever saw it on the cue card. I would say, "This is now this, this is now this, this is now that." And then Andy Samberg would stand next to the camera with his arms folded, staring at Bill the whole time, so there was a lot of pressure on trying to make him laugh. It was definitely a group effort.

BILL HADER:

The way I knew that the first one worked was two things: After I finished it, Jim Downey came over to me and went, "That's the funniest thing I've ever seen you do on the show." It was very sweet. And then when I went to the after party, Lorne's assistant was like, "Do you want to go over and sit at Lorne's table?" I remember me and John Mulaney sitting at Lorne's table and him saying that was really great, that was awesome. And then two shows later, I remember John coming up to me on Thursday and saying, "They want another Stefon." And I was like, "Wow! Okay, cool." And when we did that second one it got a giant recognition applause when I rolled out. And I remember seeing Andy Samberg on the other side past the cue cards, standing next to John Mulaney when that was happening, and Andy put his arm around John and hugged him like, "Congratulations, buddy, you got a big hit on the show." It's cool to see that during the sketch, looking out and seeing Andy with John.

JOHN MULANEY:

One time, Spud Webb was mentioned in a club, and all I did was put Spud Webb in again, but just in a different club.

BILL HADER:

Do you know who Spud Webb is? He's this really tiny, tiny basketball player, so I started laughing and then I see Spud Webb is in the second one, which I did not know, so I caught myself, but then Seth went, "Whoa, Spud Webb pulling double duty!" And I was gone. I was completely gone. There was no going back; I was just gone.

JOHN MULANEY:

The biggest one I think ever was when I put in a whole new joke: Stefon asked Seth, "You know Blacula, the black Dracula? Well, this one was the Jewish Dracula." And Seth asked, "What's his name?" And Stefon says, "Sidney Applebaum." I had told him about it right before, and he started really laughing hard, and I said, "Okay don't think about it again. I just told you it's on the cue card." Then on-air you could see his eyes—because it's a longer joke, it's not just a little detail—you could see from his eyes that he was already gone from the beginning of the joke. Then the cue card turned and he sees the whole thing he has to say. That was very satisfying because he broke before he even got to the joke.

BILL HADER:

Another reason I think I broke doing Stefon—without sounding too pretentious—is that the character was very nervous, very tactile, and I would get into this kind of mind-space when I did that character where I was always on the edge. I was just so amped up that one little pinprick and I would start laughing. They gave me this Ed Hardy shirt with these long sleeves so I could kind of hide my face in the sleeves when I broke, and this guy I based it on was a guy who used to serve coffee in Chelsea and was always touching his face—in the way that people on Ecstasy are always touching things—and it just kinda happened where I would cover my face.

Stefon should not be on live television. Where his head's at and his personality are not conducive to delivering the news on live television. He's very nervous.

I went to Lorne at an after party once and I said, "I'm very sorry I keep breaking as Stefon. I'm a little nervous because I've broken every single time I've done it, so now I feel that the audience is waiting for me to break, and I feel a lot of guilt about this." And Lorne said, "Well, if what you're saying isn't funny, then we have a problem. But what you're saying is so outrageous, everyone's laughing. It's when what you're saying isn't funny and you're trying to save the sketch, or you're trying to pull focus away from other performers, or pull focus away from the idea of the sketch and the writing and just trying to pull it all to you, then *that's* when we have a problem." And I said, "Okay." I think Lorne secretly loved it because the audience thought it was great. But I should say for the record, every time I broke, I would get angry with myself. I would laugh up there and then this feeling of guilt would kind of ebb through me of guilt. I'd feel very guilty. So after most Stefons, I'd have my head down and I'd be pissed because I'd laughed.

In my head I was always going, "Don't fuck this up." That became pretty much the prevailing feeling before every single Stefon: "People like this; don't fuck it up." And then it became, "Please, let's not do him as much because we're running out of stuff and I think people are seeing where we're going." It's the same thing that happens with anybody who has a big sketch that the audience really likes. On the Mick Jagger show, I did Stefon, and it was one of the coolest things ever. It got to the point that Seth would start announcing it and all he had to say was, "Well, it's tourist season in New York right now," and everybody would go bonkers. That was a really cool feeling, but then I would get really nervous. Like, "Oh God, there's a lot of expectation on this."

SETH MEYERS:

Another thing—which is more of a credit to Mulaney and Hader than anything else—is Stefon was this great joke-delivery system and he could have come on and been Stefon and it could have worked great without there being this relationship between him and me, but the writers were smart enough to realize that if you have another thing to play on every time he came out, that was another layer to the piece, and it was not just that he went to these nightclubs and there was all this really densely written, detail-oriented writing that I don't think people fully appreciated, but there was this second element that we had this budding relationship.

BILL HADER:

Stefon being "into" Seth was something that just happened naturally. The thing I liked about Stefon was that his being gay was never part of the joke. He was just bad at his job and did a lot of drugs, and you think he might be lying—that these things he talked about might not really be true. And then of course he would be into Seth, and Seth wouldn't like him, so it was just organic that this relationship happened.

The first rule I learned in improv class was that you want to make the other person look good, and that's what Seth did better than anybody. Even when you had kind of a shitty "Update," he would make you look good. It's so easy to play it angry, but he would never get angry. He thought, "I invited these people to 'Weekend Update' for a reason. I want this to work out."

SETH MEYERS:

The approach I had to my era on "Update," which I made early on, which is that a lot of times when people write "Update" features they write the "Update" anchor as frustrated with [the other] character, which makes sense because all the time you're introducing somebody coming out with, like, shopping tips or somebody coming out with how to prepare for a Super Bowl party, and of course they never come out and actually do that; they're immediately off the rails. And someone said to me—a fan basically made the observation—that when I was frustrated with the characters, *they* were also frustrated with the characters. And so I made the decision to be just always delighted with whoever came out on "Weekend Update," Stefon included.

JOHN MULANEY:

I was very surprised to see the number of Stefons we'd done by Bill's last episode. We tried to space them out; we resisted doing them all the time, but by the end we had done a lot. It might've been sixteen or seventeen. Throughout them it seemed kind of natural that Stefon would be attracted to Seth, and then from there, joke by joke, we just started to put together this whole narrative of Stefon trying to steal Seth from his girlfriend—now wife—and it was something that I thought people seemed to like, an added element that was a lot of fun for us. It was very cool to see how bizarrely the whole romance of Seth and Stefon really resonated in the last one that we did.

BILL HADER:

Paul McCartney came up to me and said, "My daughter is a clothing designer." And I was like, "Uh-huh." And he said, "This guy that works with her, he's that way." And he put his hands over his mouth like Stefon, and my wife was behind me and, not quietly, she went, "Oh my God! Paul McCartney is doing your character to you." And I was like, "Thank you, sir. I can die now. Thank you very much. I'm going to go throw up right now." It was crazy having Paul McCartney do your character to you. Robin Williams did the same thing. When he was on the show to do "What's Up with That?" he said, "I love that character that you do." And he started doing it. I was like, "Thank you very much; that's bonkers."

Betty White was actually not the oldest person ever to perform on Saturday Night Live—*jazz great Eubie Blake sang on a 1979 show at the age of ninety-six or ninety-two (depending on whom you ask)—but on May 8, 2010, Betty White, then eighty-eight, became the oldest person ever to host. Her appearance had as much to do with the new as with the old; it came about because of a viewer campaign that began on Facebook at the beginning of the year. Organized loosely as a group called Betty White to*

Host SNL (please?)!, White's Internet "friends" grew into a ground-swell, and she was booked to host the penultimate show of the season. White didn't just stroll lazily through the show either; she was put to work on many sketches, including a new version of "The Delicious Dish," a risqué spoof of an NPR cooking show (earlier versions starred Alec Baldwin) with former cast members Molly Shannon and Ana Gasteyer returning to costar. Lorne Michaels also invited Tina Fey, Amy Poehler, Rachel Dratch, and Maya Rudolph, all mothers, to appear in this, the Mother's Day episode. Ratings went through the Rockefeller Center roof, and the White episode ranked as the biggest event in SNL annals since its election-year triumphs of 2008.

LORNE MICHAELS, *Executive Producer:*

We asked Betty White to host a bunch of times beforehand. I think whenever we'd ask, it just wasn't the right time for her. We were all crazy about her. It worked out great because doing it for the Mother's Day show was a big deal.

BETTY WHITE, *Host:*

I have no idea where the big campaign to get me to host came from. It came out of left field. It seems that somebody put it on — what was it, Tweet? I don't even have a computer, so I don't understand any of that stuff. But they got enough people asking that they invited me to do it. I'd said no about three times over the years. I'm such a California product and the show is so very New York that I thought I'd be like a fish out of water. But they said, "No, we'd really like you to do it," et cetera, and my agent said, "You have to do it," and I said, "No I don't. I don't think so." He said, "Yes you do." Well, I have great faith in my agent, so I said okay. And then I went back to New York and I was panicky. I thought, "What am I doing? Haven't I learned to say no?" I had such qualms.

KEN AYMONG, *Supervising Producer:*

Betty worked just as hard as any other host. She was here late at night doing pre-tapes; she came to every rehearsal. She was amazing.

BETTY WHITE:

I love live television. When I started in the business, for four years I was on five and a half hours a day, six days a week, live—with no script or anything like that. It was just my show, and we had to make it work. So I wasn't afraid of the live aspect of *SNL*. It was fun to get that feeling of immediacy, and I thoroughly enjoyed it.

When I started in television, it was that new thing in the corner of the room where people were actually talking on camera. Comedy shows are altogether different these days. The audience has changed so much. It's a tough audience because they've heard every joke and they've heard every story line and they know where you're going before you even start.

Lorne is a genius. He put things together that made me comfortable on all sides. He's the one who decided to bring the other girls back—not just to support me but because he thought it would be great. So he brought Tina and Amy and all the girls. I was sure happy to be onstage with them.

AMY POEHLER, *Cast Member:*

I was so impressed by her stamina, and she's just *so* sharp. A lot of the ways that the women of *SNL* keep in contact is that we have a text chain where we send pictures of our kids, and it was really cool to have Maya, Tina, Ana, Rachel, Molly, and me and everyone's kids there. It just felt like the circle of life.

MAYA RUDOLPH, *Cast Member:*

When I first started the show they had a Mother's Day special, but that was a rarity; they don't do them every year. Back then I was twenty-seven and had no kids, so it was totally different. One of the things that made our cast able to have this unique experience is that all the women who were there had become mothers. I always think of *SNL* as like being in a comedy war together, like we were all in the same platoon.

LORNE MICHAELS:

Jay-Z coming on and then giving it up for Betty White in that intro before he sang the second song was fabulous.

BETTY WHITE:

I was aware of Jay-Z; it was great to meet him. The whole week was really a delight. I hope it worked. It was such fun to do. We laughed our way through it—all of us. Of course I had to do a lot of eating crow with my agent.

AMY POEHLER:

When I came back to host it was a little strange because your experience there as a cast member is that you're one of many, and then suddenly you're special, and it's kind of hard to buy the idea that you're special enough to be the host. It was strange, but it was also really, really, lovely to be back and not have the same fear of "Am I going to be in anything?" Looking at the show from the point of view of behind that door, and walking out from behind the band, is very strange. The only other time I stood behind the band that way was when we rehearsed musical stuff, but I'd never walked through that door, and that was a big deal for me.

There were these new people when I hosted—it was their first show and I liked watching the experience through their eyes—and I remember how I started doing a thing when I was at *SNL*, which Bill Hader kind of took over and I think Taran does it now, where I would just take the new cast members out to dinner.

VANESSA BAYER, *Cast Member:*

It was so weird meeting cast members and being starstruck by them and then having to act like it was like a normal thing. I remember calling my brother and saying, "Fred e-mailed me"—he e-mailed all the new cast—and Bill took the new cast members out to dinner and they put us in a private room. I had never even been in a private room in a restaurant except for my grandpa's seventy-fifth birthday.

NASIM PEDRAD, *Cast Member:*

I was born in Tehran and came to California when I was about three years old and definitely grew up watching the show as a little kid. *SNL* was my dream job, but I was tucked away in the suburbs and my parents were immigrants and no one knew how to even pronounce my name. I was so removed from the entertainment industry that I'm not sure at a young age I understood it was at all possible. I remember thinking, "It'd be great to be a cast member," but in the same way that it would be great to be an astronaut or Madonna. I had no idea how to get there. I started doing theater in school and eventually majored in theater in college, and I think timing is everything with most things, but especially with *SNL*. I had done a one-woman show called *Me, Myself and Iran* that Tina Fey saw, and she suggested to Lorne that I audition for *SNL*. I also happened to be performing at the Groundlings, so he came out and saw me and after that I got flown out to New York for my first of two auditions. I had definitely heard all of the bad stories about *SNL* but, you know, from another era. I knew Kristen and a couple of other people from the show and they said it had toned down a bit. And I have to say I was still really surprised when I got there as to how kind everybody was to one another.

TARAN KILLAM, *Cast Member:*

My parents watched *SNL*. My first relationship with it was we owned a *Best of Eddie Murphy* VHS that I would watch repeatedly and quote "Buckwheat" and "Learn to Be a Ho" and "Little Richard Simmons" and the tooth fairy sketch. We still have a video of my little brother and I—I think I'm seven or eight, so he's three or four— doing Hans and Franz in our house in Big Bear. And it's an odd thing to be on a show and start to shape the voice of a show that originally shaped who I am, that very much defined for me what I thought was funny and what I thought was cool.

JAY PHAROAH, *Cast Member:*

My comedy came from not having any friends. You know, when you don't have a lot of friends, you talk to yourself and make stuff up and you take this world you've made up and turn it into something that's applicable to comedy. I learned that I could do voices at six and I became one of the funny kids. I made people laugh, and that got me out of a lot of trouble.

I didn't get to do a lot when I was growing up as far as just wilding out, doing what the other neighborhood kids did. I was sheltered. We had a very good base, my mom and dad and I—a kind of Christian base—and that really has helped me. It's kind of like cement, so you don't end up as a crazed celebrity with everybody talking about you on Twitter. That's not gonna happen. But it's a new world to Jay Pharoah. I'm still getting used to it.

BOBBY MOYNIHAN, *Cast Member*:

I spent about six months working on an audition, then I sent in a tape. When I got called to come in and audition, I thought, "There is no way I am going to get it." I auditioned and then the next day they brought me in to talk to Lorne, and I couldn't believe it. I think I waited, like, nine hours on the couch outside his office. It was the LeBron James episode and LeBron James was late, so I had to wait until he had come in and finished everything.

Then I talked to Lorne, and it was like a first date. He just wanted to know everything; he asked me about my family, where I went to school, he asked me if I was a fan of the show. I'm a superfan and so I had a lot to talk about and a lot of questions to ask about the first season and the whole start of it. I remember him saying, "Is there anything in here you like?" And I said, "Oh, I know that's your 'World's Best Boss' mug"—it was from a Steve Carell show, an office sketch—and Lorne goes, "Oh, that mug next to *those Emmys?*" And I was going, "Oh, you set me up for that!"

But he was super nice and wonderful and he said something along the lines—I had a very long beard and very long hair—of, "Why don't you cut your hair and shave your beard and come back?" And I did, but he had left to go to the Emmys, and then they called me back in again and said, "We think we'll start you in January," but it was never definite, and I went, "I think I just got it. I don't know." And then the writers' strike happened, like, the next day, and so for nine months I just sat in my apartment going, "I think I got it, but now it's gone, so I have no idea." I think my hiring was not the first thing on their list, so I just heard nothing for nine months.

Then I heard through the grapevine that the writers' strike was coming to an end and the day it ended I got a call from *SNL* and I was like, "This is it: They're calling to tell me to come to work on Monday," but they were like, "Hey, Maya Rudolph had a baby during the writers' strike so we have to hire a girl," and they hired Casey Wilson and I was just devastated. I thought, "That's it—it didn't happen," and I spent a couple of months in tears and ended up getting a couple of jobs in movies, and then Seth called me out of the blue. I was in Rome, and he said, "We're doing this Web series called *The Line* that Bill Hader and Simon Rich wrote and we'd love for you to play a part in it." And I thought that was my consolation prize, essentially. So I went and did it, and it was my second audition almost, just to see if they could work with me, and after three days they said, "Why don't you come back in and audition for *SNL* again?"

Steve Higgins told me to watch Jimmy Fallon's audition. He said he knew I didn't play guitar and wasn't a big impression guy, but Jimmy did a whole bunch of things. I stayed up three days writing all new stuff. I thought, "I'm going to show them thirty things I could do rather than just three characters and three impressions."

TARAN KILLAM:

The worst news about finding out I was hired on *SNL* was that Will Forte was leaving, because he is truly my favorite cast member of all time. He is just a genius. And we had orbited around each other from the Groundlings theater and so I got to see him at an event after I was hired and he said to me, "It's a marathon, not a sprint," and that was the most valuable piece of advice ever, because you feel you're only as good as your most recent sketch. But it's a show that lives in reflection, and if you can look back on a season and have two pieces that people really talked about, that's a great year. Bill Hader said if you can do two great sketches a season, you do seven seasons, that's fourteen sketches, that's enough for a "Best of" DVD. It's all numbers. We're all part of the matrix. We were writing a sketch this week where they needed a macho guy, and I was the first choice. And Rob Klein said, "Literally, last year you were the sixth choice for the macho guy." It's weird. I came into a show of Jason, Bill, Andy, Fred, Bobby—I was the sixth white guy and now I'm second.

My first season or two there was a *Huffington Post* article that ranked cast members on a weekly basis. They had their own algorithm of screen time—who did what, what is the best sketch—and I was the worst. I was just the worst! It's a dangerous pitfall. With a forty-year history, there's so much to compare yourself to. The shadow grows longer and darker the longer the show goes on. Now we're not just compared to the original '75 cast, we're compared to six generations, versus the people who came before were compared to five. And as the library gets deeper and deeper, a lot of things are similar to stuff that's been done on *SNL*. You also have to get to a place where you just forgive yourself and you say, "Well, my take's going to be different, and I'm going to see it through, and if people laugh, that's the goal."

I'll go home on a break and watch an old episode on TV, and I still cannot believe I'm on *that* show. I still can't believe it's the same show! I came into this thing feeling like, "I don't want to be the one to break it." I still am not at a place where I can go, "Yeah, I'm just like those guys in the old episodes."

Relatively few people who are living or who ever lived have experienced the peculiar and prestigious thrill of looking into an NBC color camera and shouting to several million people at once, "Live from New York, it's Saturday Night*!" Even higher status goes with the honor of hosting the show, a privilege known to a select elite—although lame ringers have slipped through too, later lamented and regretted. Hosting more than once carries with it particular amenities, spoofed in sketches starring celebrities who try to one-up each other with boasts of multiple appearances. That began in 1990, when Steve Martin convened the first gathering of the Five-Timers Club for those who had hosted five times or more.*

As jobs go, it doesn't pay all that well, it requires a full week's unrelenting commitment, and the hours are late and punishing. But hosting Saturday Night Live *is still looked upon as one of the most coveted gigs in television. Hosts are treated well but hardly draped in velvet, although one tradition could be considered a very pleasant perk: Tuesday night dinners given by Lorne Michaels for the host and a smattering of staff from the show at a private room in Lattanzi, a cozy midtown restaurant whose cuisine is classified as Jewish-Italian. It's not a glamorous or trendy place, but it's very comfortable. Invitations to these dinners are much prized.*

BILL HADER:

Lorne would do these host dinners on Tuesday nights. We would write, and then at eight o'clock someone would come to you and say, "Okay, you're going to the host dinner." And then you would go and eat this amazing Italian dinner with Lorne and the host and five or six other cast members, and now you're stuffed on pasta and you're sleepy and yet you have to go back and write more. I never understood why they were on Tuesday nights. I always felt they should be on Monday. Like, after the pitch meeting you could go because everybody just goes home anyways. So why don't we do these on Monday? Ask Lorne and he'll say, "They've always been on Tuesday."

LINDSAY SHOOKUS, *Producer:*

As someone in charge of booking the host, I don't really try to book a host that I think is going to be terrible. It won't do us any favors, you know.

We did once have a host miss a read-through—that's someone not being able to be there to read forty sketches that were supposed to be in their voice. It was Jeff Bridges. He got sick. I remember having to call Lorne and say, "Jeff Bridges cannot come in today." Then we were faced with the idea of picking the twelve sketches of forty that are supposed to really be a showcase of the host—without the host. Obviously we can figure out what's funny, but we don't really know what the host is going to be good at if they're not there. That was a little terrifying.

JUSTIN TIMBERLAKE, *Host:*

I've never had a dress rehearsal go exactly like the show. Most of the people who come to dress are a little closer to the show, more

ONE MAN'S FAMILY: 2008–2014

die-hard fans who want to get to dress rehearsal because they know they get to see sketches that aren't even going to air. The audience for the live show, at least with what I've found, are a slightly more mainstream, slightly more broad group. So there's things you can do in dress rehearsal that are a little more nuanced to the culture of the show, and things you can do in the live show that are more broad. I find that the best rule of thumb is that you have to forget most of what you put together for the week and you just have to play off of the crowd. So if those two hundred people in that audience are responding to what you are doing, I feel then *that* translates to television.

JON HAMM, *Host*:

After the first season that *Mad Men* aired, and Jen and I were in New York at a magazine party or something—I was on the cover of a magazine, which was a very new experience for me as well—and my agent at that time came up to me and said, "You've been asked to host *Saturday Night Live*," and I must have had literally, like, a jaw-dropping thing. Wait—*what?* My agent said, "Yeah, they want you to host," whatever date it was. And Jen and I had literally just booked this trip to Greece and finally I'm done with *Mad Men;* we're finally going on vacation. I'd never been to Greece. The ink wasn't even dry on that thing and they said, "Oh, it's this week," and I said, "I can't do it. I can't: I have this thing." My agent goes, "Okay, all right," and I thought, "Well, that opportunity came and went, but I've got to take care of myself and be a human being." So literally two days later, they asked, "What about this date?" And it's like, "Yes; that I can do." So I remember being amazed and then crestfallen and then equally amazed when it came back to me.

Hosting is an amazing experience. The only thing I can compare it to is the experience of being on a roller coaster, and it's pulling you up the first hill making that clacking sound; that basically is the week. You start hearing this *clack, clack, clack, clack, clack*—you're going up this hill, and you know that the ride's not going to go off the rails, and you also know the ride's going to be over in ninety minutes, but there's this mounting terror that you have to go through this ninety-minute roller-coaster ride. And God bless dress rehearsal, because if it was just one live show it would be a very different experience.

I never had a heart-rate monitor on me but I guarantee you if you had strapped one to my chest at eleven thirty-four all three times that I've hosted, it would be off the charts, and I'm not a guy who gets nervous in that way. But literally, when you're waiting there, you're two inches behind the drum kit, so the drum is, like, touching you in the face because it's a tiny, tiny space—you're literally walking sideways to get onto that set. People think it's a door to a hallway. No. It's a door to a crawl space, basically. And it's you and one of the stage managers. You can't hear anything but the band, and they just shove you out the door, and that's when you crest the hill and you start going on the ride.

SCARLETT JOHANSSON, *Host:*

I feel if you're going to host *Saturday Night Live* as many times as I have, you're fair game at that point to have people make fun of you. Any time I see they're doing some kind of spoof of a scene that I did in a movie, or another actor's playing me, a look-alike or anything, that is an incredibly surreal experience. I saw when Maya did me and I thought she needed more time to fully exploit me the way she could have. I've poked fun at plenty of people when I've hosted—I don't know what would make me, like, less vulnerable to that. I have plenty of opportunities to look like a million bucks. I'd rather look like, I don't know, someone's anus or something, which I know they'll probably turn me into, than look like Marilyn Monroe or whoever. If you're going to do *Saturday Night Live* you want to play the anus, and that's probably the only time you ever want to play the anus. It's not a glamour job.

PAUL RUDD, *Host:*

It's really exciting for me to host the show. I've now hosted it three times and I feel like I have a connection to the show that I never had before I hosted. I live in New York and it's such an important part of the city. I have a very strong affinity for the show. I remember as a kid watching Woody Allen movies made me want to move to New York, made me want to live in New York. There's just something about this city. And there are a few things that I think really encapsulate what New York is, and that we romanticize about it, and so many aspects of *Saturday Night Live* encapsulate that. At the end of the show, when everyone's onstage, as a kid, I would watch that and go, "Oh my God, can you imagine? Now they're going to go to an after party." And then hearing Don Pardo's voice and just even the shots of all the cast members at some different part of the city, whether they're at some sushi restaurant or out on some manhole with steam coming out of it, it was just like, "It's fucking New York, man!" And that music, and then seeing 30 Rock and the marquee. When I'm hosting, I remember pulling up every time and thinking, "Oh my God, there it is." I can't shake it.

SCARLETT JOHANSSON:

My name was once on some little part of a *New Yorker* cover, and I thought, "Oh man, I've really made it. I'm on the cover of the *New Yorker*." And I guess being spoofed on *SNL* is another "I made it" moment.

ROBERT DE NIRO, *Host:*

When I'm doing a movie and it has a particular type of scene, I always imagine it being made fun of on *Saturday Night Live*. I've watched the show ever since it started, and it has always been just a great show.

It's harder to do than some people might think, and there's a little bit of pressure. Some of those skits are funnier than others to me and probably to the audience. But you don't have time to think or worry about this or that, or whether you're good or bad. You just do it and hope for the best.

CAMERON DIAZ, *Host:*

I've never done any theater, so the live part is totally unique for me. But the entire process is completely different. It's obviously something that has been very well cultivated by the powers that be, and by Lorne. You carry a lot of the responsibility as host, but the cast makes you feel like you're capable of doing whatever you need to do, so I always feel like I'm just part of the ensemble. There is pressure, though. You don't want to be the one person who doesn't know how to deliver their lines or the one who screws things up or doesn't understand the pace of things.

CHRIS MARTIN, *Host:*

Gwyneth had done the "Garth and Kat" sketch over the years and I just thought it was fucking incredible, and I love Fred Armisen and Kristen Wiig like everyone else does and I was like, "You know what? I'd really like to do that." So I just asked for their indulgence. And what was it like? It made me realize, "You know what? I'm glad I'm a musician."

For some reason musicians are always drawn to comedians. In fact, I was on a plane with Sacha Baron Cohen, and we were talking about it. He said, "Maybe it's because you spend so much time on tour that you watch all the comedy that's available." A lot of actors want to be musicians, a lot of comedians want to be actors, and I think a lot of musicians secretly think they could be comedians, and sometimes it's good to be reminded, "Stick to your day job."

PAUL RUDD:

I remember one of the things that proved to be tricky the first time I hosted is the whole reading of the cue cards thing, because there's no real lesson in how to do it. It's funny: There are ones that look like, "Oh God, they're totally reading cue cards; they're really bad at it," or they're usually—and I'm guilty of this—actors who like to look at it and then they'll try to look at the actors so that they're not actually looking at the cue cards, but it's the back and forth. When you go back and forth, that makes it look like you're reading cue cards.

It was a strange feeling to do a scene with people and realize they're not even looking at me. We're having a conversation in the scene, and the person is talking to me, but they're just never looking at me. They're only deadlocked right on a cue card so that when the camera cuts to them it looks like they're looking right at me. So those technical things become a little easier after the first time.

JOHN MULANEY:

I introduced Jesse Eisenberg to Mark Zuckerberg. Zuckerberg was on the show, Eisenberg had just played him in *The Social Network,* and they'd never met. Zuckerberg claimed he never saw the movie, and he was going to do an appearance in the monologue. Just by being the writer on the monologue, I'm in charge of it, so I remember getting Jesse—who was hosting—from his dressing room and telling him, "Let's go run it with Mark." I remember bringing Jesse in there with Zuckerberg. Without realizing what I was about to do, I just knocked on the door and said, "Hey, Mark Zuckerberg—Jesse Eisenberg." They're both similar in age, both very nice and polite, maybe on the quiet side. And then I just started laughing so hard, because I couldn't believe that I was the one introducing these two guys. Then Lorne came in and we rehearsed it. There was a lot of money in that room at that moment.

VANESSA BAYER:

One thing you do not think about at all when you're auditioning is that you're going to meet different hosts and musical guests every week. You don't think about the fact that there's going to be some huge celebrity and huge musical group at the show every week and you have to be sort of cool around them. You want them to feel like they're part of the group; you don't want to go, "Oh man, I love you so much." I think I've gotten pretty good at acting cool.

JUSTIN TIMBERLAKE:

Jimmy's the only guy who gets me to break. Actually, I break more than you would think. I broke one time doing one of the Barry Gibb sketches. I broke on the "Family Feud" sketch because Jimmy holds the record for breaking on the show and while the cameras weren't on him when you see me break, it's because I can see in the corner of my eye that he is doubled over, he's laughing so hard, and it just became this thing. For that sketch, it was kind of a serendipitous moment— I'm imitating Jimmy and Jimmy's there laughing and so I guess in a nutshell it explains when Jimmy and I are together on live television— all bets are off. With the Barry Gibb sketches it got to a point where we didn't even rehearse it. We kind of just goofed off in rehearsal because we knew that we were going to kind of go off the cuff with each other. It's one of the few times where Lorne is okay with sort of improvisation within the midst of all these jokes that they've been crafting for a whole week. Because I think that you know with Jimmy and I there's a certain thing to it, especially when it's just Jimmy. I don't think I could take much credit for it, to be honest with you. I mean, there's a certain thing that happens with him where it's almost like the more he breaks the funnier the sketch gets. It's a weird thing.

JIMMY FALLON, *Host:*

Going back to host is a dream come true. It gets even better, if you can believe that. I went back to host and I got the flu. I was so nervous, I think, about hosting, that I got sick. I was just overthinking everything. I asked Tina to come and write something with me and Rachel, and of course she did. It was like, this is where you grew up, so it's like asking your buddies to reunite for a little bit. It meant so much to me as a fan of the show, and I just love that it all came back. We did the Christmas song with Horatio, and it was really kind of a moment. Also we did a great sketch written by Seth Meyers where it was Beethoven and he was introducing his band. It was one of my favorite things that I've ever seen, because Sudeikis, Armisen—we threw in Kattan, Horatio, and everyone scored. We were having a really good time, and I said to myself, "Everyone's in on this: This is a fun night."

That's the best, when you get those vibes, when Studio 8H is rocking so hard that it shakes—the stage actually shakes. The only other time that's happened that way to me was when I did a sketch with Mick Jagger where I was in the mirror looking back at Mick. We wrote that on a Friday night—it was a last-minute sketch—and when we finished it the place was shaking. People were standing up, clapping. I'll never forget that.

HORATIO SANZ, *Cast Member:*

When we went back and did the Christmas thing, they put us all in the same room. So that was very awkward. Tracy had recently written that book where he said something about Kattan being a jerk, or not being nice to people or something—I don't know what it was, but Kattan's father had just died, and the book came out pretty much around the same time. So Kattan came in guns a-blazin', like, "Yeah, Tracy, thanks for saying I'm an asshole in a book, but my dad fucking died." He just kept doing bits about it, but you could tell he was pissed off. Then Tracy came in.

Tracy says a lot of things that I don't think he thinks much about. I don't think he really hated Kattan as much as he was, like, "Those guys were assholes to me, so I'll fuck them up a little bit." Obviously Tracy didn't know about Kattan's dad. Anyway, I guess Shoemaker told them, "Hey, guys, why don't you talk it out if you're going to be in the same room for four days?" And they ironed it out. It had mostly been just bad timing. I think Kattan was not in the best place to get blasted in a book. He ended up doing fine, but it was awkward.

ZOOEY DESCHANEL, *Host:*

I once saw Chris Farley in the gym when I was, like, sixteen. He was at the gym that my parents belonged to, I was on the treadmill, and it was so exciting. He was just walking around the gym, doing bits.

I've been watching *SNL* since I was a kid, when it was on too late for me to stay up, so I would tape it and watch it. I would see the doors that the hosts walked through, and watch them walk down the aisle between the band members. It looks differently when you're back there. It's flat, like a set. It looks like backstage. It's a facade. You're back there, and they have a little monitor, and they say, "Okay, go now." And then you're saying to yourself, "Oh my God, I'm hosting *SNL* right now!"

Between sketches, you get grabbed. It's like when you're in kindergarten and you hold on to the next kid to you. You have to hold on to Donna, the dresser, and she'll lead you through the maze behind the sets, and then you get changed where everybody's changing back there. It's amazing.

ABBY ELLIOTT, *Cast Member:*

You know there's a lot of stuff happening backstage, and people seeing you from the bleachers and you're changing right below them. They have little booths set up behind the stage, sort of underneath the bleachers, so when you're doing these quick wardrobe changes between the scenes, and you're getting your wig taken off or makeup put on and you look up and see people in the bleachers pointing down at you going, "Oh, look!" and you're completely naked. There are definitely places where you can see everything, and you just look up and be, like, "Hi!"

MAYA RUDOLPH:

Going back to host was one of those second-level experiences that make you feel like, "Oh my God, I can't believe this is really happening to me." When you first get hired on the show, you feel that way, like, "My dreams have come true," which is always a strange thing to experience in this day and age, because I feel like no one really expects their dreams to come true anymore. And when you actually have been in that place that long and it becomes your home, and those people become your family, to turn around and host is like a whole other layer of, "Oh my God, I can't believe this is my life."

I think that everybody's experience at *SNL* is different, and the thing that really made coming back so special for me is that the thing I really, really love, the thing I miss the most since I left, was getting to goof around and laugh with my friends. Those particular people make me laugh like nothing else, and the camaraderie and familiarity that you have with each other is so comforting. I had really missed that; it was a homecoming in a lot of ways.

JON HAMM:

It was strange. I just happened to be in town and Lindsay was going to be hosting. I got a call and they asked if I would be interested in doing this thing. It was never a real thing that I was quote unquote "on deck." That was the joke. It was, "Have you got somebody in the wings just in case?" capitalizing on Lindsay Lohan's famous instability, which she was a good sport about. For me it was just another chance to be on the show. Whenever I'm in town they call and say, "Will you do this? We'd love to have you do this—and blah, blah, blah." I say no a lot, too, but I do consider a lot of those people friends and it's nice to be thought of in a positive way. And God, you make so much money doing it—five or six hundred bucks! You can really clean up being a guest star at *SNL*!

LINDSAY LOHAN, *Host:*

It was funny because we actually had another opening. We had a political one where Jon Hamm was going to play Kennedy and we ended up not using that one, but we still wanted Jon to be involved. That's when we just put him in the audience. That was really funny.

MICHAEL SHOEMAKER, *Supervising Producer:*

Lindsay was great. I think you worry about every host until you don't, and there's no way of telling. You can't call a good show on a Wednesday. None of us do. You kind of can't call it until after dress—and even then. Because you never know how air is going to turn out. You never really stop worrying until the after party. Each week you think it's going to go one way, and then a read-through informs you it's going to go in a completely different way, but even with people who are not professionals, if you find a way to make them charming in their unprofessionalism, then you win.

LINDSAY LOHAN:

The last time that I hosted I was really nervous. I hadn't been there in a long time, like four years. I don't know why I was so nervous that time, but I was also going through a transitional phase, just personally, so I didn't feel as comfortable in my own skin.

It was really crazy because the Friday night before, Kristen and a bunch of us had done a pre-tape segment. And we were still in the pre-tape until six A.M. Saturday. Then I had to go to the studio to do photos, so we were up for almost two days straight. When you do pre-tapes, you have to shoot them really early or really late, and we shot this one really late Friday night. It's fun because you're laughing and goofing off the whole time, but it's still grueling. But it's a really good feeling—going there and being around everyone and knowing there is such love there—and that it's completely mutual.

I remember someone in the press said, "She's reading her lines." But *everyone* reads the cards! I actually like to memorize the cards so I don't have to look at them. But I was so nervous in one of the skits, and all the guys kept laughing, and I kept laughing during it.

LINDSAY SHOOKUS:

When Lindsay Lohan first hosted, I was like a kid with her. I've known her for twelve years; the first time she hosted, she was a teenager and I was twenty-two, and I really loved her. She was able to kidsister me each time she came on the show. The last time she hosted, I felt a lot of pressure on my shoulders, and the show's shoulders, to make it a good show.

On a Sunday, the worst thing in the world is if you feel like it wasn't a good show. I really feel like it's on my shoulders to help try and pull out the best version we can for someone, especially if they're not a comedian. With Lindsay, Lorne and myself and the rest of us really wanted to help her put her best foot forward.

BILL HADER:

I really didn't enjoy having Justin Bieber around. I didn't hate the guy, I just wasn't into it. I'm pitching jokes to this kid? I was having a weird week because that was the week I told Lorne that I was leaving the show. I think that whole week was just bad for me. So I partially blamed Justin Bieber for it, I guess. There was one sketch where we all had to dress up as him. I felt like an old man. I'm a father. Why am I dressed up like this guy? What's going on right now? Sometimes you have people who are not your thing and they host the show. But sometimes they surprise me. Someone comes in and you're like, "Ugh—we have this person," and then by the end of the week I'm like, "I love this person!" I have nothing against Taylor Swift, for instance; I just don't listen to her music. And then she came in, and I was thinking, "How wonderful and funny is this girl?! She's so talented." That's how it always is—with the exception of Bieber. He's the only one who lived up to the reputation. I think that's the only time I felt that way in my eight years there.

Without a doubt, when a friend of yours is hosting—for me, someone like Paul Rudd or Seth Rogen or Jonah Hill—odds are you would have a light show. I have no idea why it works out that way. It's so weird. Your friend would be hosting and you'd be really excited, and then you wouldn't be in the show! Or you'd have one good thing in it, and that was it. And you're just going, "How did that happen?" And then along comes someone like Taylor Swift, and that was one of the best episodes I ever had. When she hosted I had a killer episode. And she was a blast.

ROBERT SMIGEL, *Writer:*

Back in 1999, that was the era where you had to try and turn every *SNL* idea into a movie. People had pitched me on *The Ambiguously Gay Duo,* but I didn't go for it—too one-dimensional. Instead, Adam McKay and I wrote an *X-Presidents* movie; I figured the four living ex-presidents were at least *two*-dimensional. That wound up becoming just a graphic novel. Then I had the idea to make Ace and Gary live action, which opened up the characters. Lorne and I talked about using Alec Baldwin, but the rights to the sketch—because it had started on *The Dana Carvey Show*—were very complicated. So it just went away. But five years later, Jim Carrey worked on *Bruce Almighty* with Steve Carell and they got to talking about the idea, and Jim asked if the movie could be developed for him. So Stephen Colbert and I wrote an entire movie script for Jim Carrey and then at the end of the day Jim's advisers decided they didn't want him to wear leotards with a padded ass at this stage in his career, so it disappeared again. Years later Lorne talked to Jon Hamm about the script and he was into it. I was no longer on *SNL* but I suggested we could do a short live Ace and Gary for the show and maybe that could generate some studio interest. Akiva had this great idea that they get zapped into live-action humans, and we got Fallon for Gary, and Colbert and Carell—the cartoon voices—agreed to play the bad guys. I was touched that Carell actually flew in from L.A. just to appear in it as a villain, one that half the audience didn't even realize was Carell, I think, until they saw the credits.

We had a lot of fun shooting, and after that the director, Jason Woliner, and I had to work nonstop at *SNL* for a few days to get the thing done. But then while I still was facing a ton of editing, I got a call to audition for *This Is 40* for Judd, so I snuck out of the edit that day, pretending I was going to be gone for just a half hour, and went to the audition. The truth is, no one would've cared, but I'm a good self-starter when it comes to guilt.

The sketch was presented as a typical "TV Funhouse" and a regular Ace and Gary cartoon, so if I had been watching at home I would have been like, "Oh, this is kind of nice, but really, do we need another one of these?" But within a minute or two it suddenly turned into live action. And it was one of those things that we kept as quiet as we could, so nobody would find out in advance. I just wanted it to be a big surprise on-air.

It was very well received, but obviously it didn't become a movie. It would be pretty expensive for a comedy, in fairness. My agent followed up with the studio and it was, "We want to talk to Robert about a talking-dog movie. There's this thing on the Internet where this dog's mouth is in perfect sync with funny things that a human's saying, and we think that could be a movie, so can we meet about that?" Colbert and I still like the script, though, so someday I'll probably harass Channing Tatum and Taylor Lautner into getting it done.

JAMES DOWNEY, *Writer:*

The biggest risk to doing political comedy is, you always seem to have a choice: Am I going to piss off the audience by trying to get them to laugh when they don't like what I'm saying, or am I going to kiss their ass and get this tremendous wind at my back by sucking up to them and agreeing with them on all the issues and validating their opinions? The second way makes me feel like I cheated. It makes me feel like I won the cross-country race but my mom drove me part of the way. I'm prouder of myself if I go, "Guess what? I know you're probably going to think I'm making a political statement here that you violently disagree with, but I'm going to make you laugh anyway."

I did a piece that got a lot of attention in some circles. Lorne was scared shitless of it and tried to kill it and buried it at the very end of the show. But it was about the Duke lacrosse case and I had Amy doing Nancy Grace. The piece got huge laughs, and I was astonished because it was about rape. One thing audiences know is that there's nothing funny about rape. And the other thing they know is that there's no such thing as a false accusation of rape. That's comedy audience culture, right? It's PC culture. It's the reason why Chris Rock says he cannot get white audiences to laugh about his stuff about "niggers" versus "black people." He goes, "I have a right to say that stuff. But white audiences, I know they like it, but they won't laugh if there's people watching them."

I gotta say I respect more people who head into the teeth of an audience, whether it's going down to the Deep South and making fun of fundamentalist Christianity or going to Manhattan and making fun of PC. I'm sure there are a lot of people in comedy who completely share every fucking detail, jot, and tittle of the Obama administration agenda, and all I can say is: To the extent that you're sincere and that's really the way you feel, then you're a very lucky person because, guess what, you're going to have a very easy career in comedy because audiences will always applaud. They may not laugh but they'll always give you a huge ovation. That's Bill Maher, you know?

LORNE MICHAELS:

In the '70s the thing I dreaded the most was being defined, you know? I wanted to just keep moving forward and to keep changing.

JAMES DOWNEY:

You used to hear all the time, "I'll say this for *Saturday Night Live,* just when you think you know what their take is going to be on something political, they will surprise you and do something different." And that hasn't happened in the last three years of the show. We haven't done anything that anyone would be surprised by. I thought in 2012 we got really repetitive. There were so many Republican debates, and I thought it was a mistake, but the decision was, "If they do a debate, we do a sketch. It's going to be one for one." I thought it ended up being kind of the same thing. There were a lot of Republican gaffes, but we would just sort of dramatize the gaffe as opposed to making a metacomment about it. We were replicating Rick Perry's brain freeze, replicating the booing of the soldier that asked about don't ask, don't tell. Because Jon Stewart is a show that comments on things that happened, it made us feel like, "Stewart made that point." So it felt like we were just sort of echoing what everyone else was doing.

Considering all the dozens of cast members who've left Saturday Night Live *since the first group packed up and followed Lorne Michaels out the door in 1980, it would have been virtually impossible to make a fuss every time somebody split. How did it happen, then, that in May of 2012, cast and crew said elaborate and tearful good-byes to Kristen Wiig in an on-air party disguised as a sketch, with His Lordship Michaels coming out from the wings to dance with Wiig and give her a sweet send-off?*

There were many reasons—at least as many as the number of characters that Wiig had played and helped invent in her seven awe-inspiring seasons on the show. After a period in which SNL *was commended for the number of smart women in key positions both on- and off-camera, such stars as Tina Fey and Amy Poehler had flown the proverbial coop, depleting the female population. To lose Wiig was to lose an entire chorus of recurring characters, a major blow at any time but especially then.*

And that's one of the reasons why she got a party—or, really, an observance, a moment for the show to stop and register an unusually fond farewell. Special guest Jon Hamm, who had earlier appeared in the cold open, also stayed for the good-bye sketch, set at a high school graduation. As the head of the school, host Mick Jagger doled out diplomas to students and told the audience that the one played by Wiig was ready "to become a nun." Then he announced "a song to say good-bye," at which point the band broke into the Rolling Stones' oldie "Ruby Tuesday." Wiig ripped off her black graduation robe and threw it away, and the two of them began to dance.

Before the sketch was over, Wiig danced with everybody—all the men (including Andy Samberg, who literally swept her off her feet and briefly held her in the air) and the remaining women and then, finally, Michaels, who normally dislikes public displays of emotion. But the event met his principal criterion for material on the show: It was funny. Also, it was bittersweet and even poignant.

They were saying good-bye not just to Wiig but also to the characters she and fellow writers had created and perfected—among them Shana, the bosomy office bombshell who made male employees loopy with lust until she went into grotesque, tasteless poses; Mindy, the out-of-it Broadway diva who screwed up all her appearances on a Password-*like game show; Kat, of "Garth and Kat," the chronically unprepared folk duo who tried to fake songs on the spot during "Weekend Update"; the strange woman with the tiny hands who barged into reruns of the Lawrence Welk variety show and plucked at bubbles; and that incorrigibly naughty girl Gilly, who looked upon everyone else in the world as competition for attention and therefore sabotaged them as best she could. Wiig played real people too, all of them with a sardonic edge, whether it was Nancy Pelosi, a tipsy dipso Kathie Lee Gifford, a quirky and baffling Bjork, or Jamie Lee Curtis, who in mock spots for a supposedly healthful yogurt would register its purgative effects right there on-camera.*

Michaels looked genuinely touched as he took his turn dancing with Wiig, then he flashed her a benedictory smile reminiscent of the one that the Scarecrow gave Dorothy before she left Oz for Kansas—a smile that seemed to say, "It's going to be all right."

BILL HADER:

It's a testament to Kristen that she came back after *Bridesmaids* was such a big hit. I'm not going to name names, but some people who were working at the show said, "If that happened to me, I would not come back." She was at the table read, writing sketches, doing everything, and we were like, "You're one of the biggest comedy stars in the world right now and it's so awesome that you're here." That's the funny thing, though, too: The people who came up with Kristen weren't thinking she'd just become a star, because we had already seen what a big star she was. By her first season she would come out on her mark and the audience would just start cheering. I remember I was doing all these impressions and stuff like that and trying so hard to get just one character on the show. And Kristen would so easily get out there and just, boom, boom, boom—like Penelope and this and that. And these things are destroying, they're so good. That was the nice thing about our group. I never felt a sense of jealousy. Everyone was very happy for each other. There was something about her that clicked with the audience. They would get excited. Andy had a very similar thing. It just clicked. After *Lazy Sunday* and those things came out, people would get excited. So we weren't that surprised. It was the newer cast members who were suddenly like, "Holy shit, we're working with this massive star."

KRISTEN WIIG:

Honestly it never crossed my mind to leave the show early. For so many reasons—A, I had a contract for seven years and I wanted to fulfill it. To me it wasn't like, "I'm going to be on this show and then better things are going to come." I wanted to be on the show. It was really hard for me to leave even when I did, and just because *Bridesmaids* made a lot of money didn't affect how I felt being on the show or change my life in that way. I had known pretty much from the beginning that I was going to do seven years and that would be it. Not because I wanted to leave, but seven years is a good chunk of time, and I was excited to try other things and also make way for new people to come in.

I know that Lorne knew I was leaving just from being around the show; we can't really keep any secrets around there. Plus my contract was up and I didn't renegotiate for another year, so he knew. But of course I knew that I still had to sit down with him and talk. I believe we were at dinner and I just said, "Well, are we going to talk about this?" And it was really hard and emotional. The last show of my first season I went up to Lorne and just thanked him; I was just overwhelmed from the year and I got a little choked up, and then when I left, I got *really* choked up. So I started and ended my experience there crying in front of Lorne. It was really, really, really difficult and it's hard for people in the outside world to understand, I think, about leaving that show, because it really is your family. Even the hosts come in and after just spending one week with us it's like we're friends and we know each other and we go through this crazy experience, and that's just one week. So you do that twenty-two times a season for seven years—it becomes your life, and when you leave it's very, very strange.

LORNE MICHAELS:

Colin Jost wrote the Kristen good-bye sketch as a graduation ceremony. At that point, I don't think Andy was 100 percent sure he was
leaving; Jason was agonizing about it. This was the last show of the
season, and Mick was hosting. It was too long at dress, and we just
didn't know whether we'd be doing it—whether there would be time,
especially since it was going to be at the end of the show. And so
because of that I don't think there was a lot of thought given to how
emotional it would be until suddenly there it was and we were doing
it. "Ruby Tuesday" was playing, each cast member danced with her—
it was just a magical thing. People in the audience from the old cast
even came up onstage.

Kristen gave everything to this show her entire time here.

KRISTEN WIIG:

Usually when someone leaves the show, at the table read people
write a good-bye sketch. It gets slipped into the pile so people don't
read it ahead of time, and it's the last sketch of the day, and usually
there are a lot of tears. Colin Jost wrote that sketch and I thought it
was just for the table read, and when it got into the show, I was completely shocked. I was happy because he wrote such a beautiful, sweet,
simple thing and also I knew I wanted to somehow say good-bye but
didn't know how to do it. I didn't know if I should go on "Update"; I
had never been on "Update" as myself, and I didn't want to get up
there and just start bawling my eyes out. We tried thinking of characters leaving, but I couldn't think of anything. It was almost one A.M.
and it was my last show and there wasn't a lot of time left, and there
was an issue of it even making it into the show. So I didn't know if I
was going to be able to say good-bye. I changed clothes quickly, so
that when Mick Jagger's talking I'm putting on my cap and gown and
running out to the stage to sit down. It ended up making the show
and it was just one of the best experiences that I've ever had. I can't
even really put it into words. When Lorne came onstage, that really
got me. I mean, he was there during rehearsal, but it just seemed so
final on-air. He was out there in his suit, and it was just—oh my God,
I could get emotional thinking about it right now.

JON HAMM:

I was incredibly pleased to be asked to be part of that because Kristen is a very good friend of Jen and myself. I love her—she's an insanely talented, lovely human being. It was her last show. She goes, "Will you do something in it?" And I'd never been in the cold open and gotten to say, "Live from New York," but the sketch called for a lot of singing, and I was nervous about that because at that point I had a very injured voice, but for whatever reason adrenaline or something kicked in. Rehearsals were disasters, but I said, "Okay, guys, I promise I'll be able to sing in a normal way." I had taken the red-eye, got there Friday, rehearsed about twice, but I was able to do it, and it was an absolute blast. They had this party for it being the last show of the season; it was insane. And I'm standing there, Jen and I watching, and I said, "How cool is this?" And a guy says, "Yeah, pretty cool, isn't it?" and I turned and it was Mick Jagger!

It was really cool and it was beautiful, in a way that only *SNL* can bring that live experience. It's the last real vestige of *that* that we have.

ERIK KENWARD, *Writer*:

This is not to say anything negative about anyone who came before this, but I would say especially since 2005 or 2006 I have really noticed this feeling of extended family, that people who used to be part of the show now come and go very freely, that people are always available in a way that they weren't my first two or three years at the show. People are not on call, but you always know that if we want them to do something, they will try and make it. For people like Amy Poehler and Seth, certainly, that ideal was very important to them. So I think that started to be more a part of the DNA of the show. Which isn't to say that it wasn't in there before. It just became more pronounced.

We had one of those moments where we were sitting in Lorne's office, it was a Thursday night, and we were talking about what we could possibly do for a cold open. The live *Sound of Music* had just been on that week, and we were talking about when the kids in it made those entrances, they sort of looked like the entrances Kristen's character Denise made in our Lawrence Welk sketches. And then Kristen just happened to come by Lorne's office. She was in the building to do Jimmy's show and stopped by to say hi. We said, "We were just talking about you," and we just started riffing on the idea of this cold open. I remember Lorne said, "Hey, if you guys have something here, just keep talking about it. I'm going to go get a haircut and when I get back we'll make a decision about this." By the time he returned we had the whole thing hammered out. Kristen agreed to do it, and we started calling all of the departments and had the set made. It happened that quickly. This isn't necessarily typical for *SNL* but it's kind of cool when it does happen—when there are lightning-in-a-bottle, let's-put-on-a-show kind of moments. I think that's probably one of the coolest things about *SNL*, when the show is at its best, and the kind of thing that *SNL* can still do that no other show can really do.

It's also a testament to Lorne that he has things organized loosely enough that there is space for things like that to happen. I certainly have worked for people at other jobs or on other gigs, producers who have such a predetermined conception of what a show is going to be that there's no room for new stuff or invention. And putting a piece like that into production on a Friday would be very scary—at the very least, super nerve-wracking—for a lot of people. But for Lorne it's just a matter of course.

DAN AYKROYD, *Host:*

When I went back to do the Justin Timberlake show, it wasn't Lorne that invited me and Steve Martin. It was Justin, because he liked "Wild and Crazy Guys." When he was a kid rehearsing at Disney, he used to watch our reruns, and he always wanted to do that sketch and be one of those characters. So he called Lorne, and Lorne of course wouldn't stand in the way. But the idea of having the old guard back—unless you're talking Kristen Wiig and Will Ferrell and other hot stars of today—it's unlikely that Lorne would call and have me or Chevy back. That's not what the show is now. He's got to develop his new cast. But we're always ready to serve, if it's good and it helps.

The show is about the future; it's about building that legacy in the audience of young people who need this satire, who need to see it.

KRISTEN WIIG:

Being on that show pushes you. The whole week, depending on how you look at it, can be a very stressful week and it can also just be really fun. I think people handle stress differently and I think I just made a decision early on that I wanted to have fun. I know that sounds so simple and stupid, but I just didn't want to leave the show and look back and say, "I wish I would've had more fun." Because when you really think about it, doing *SNL* and working with all of those amazingly funny, cool people is the most "fun" job in the world. Truthfully, sometimes it was really hard. The schedule is difficult. Sometimes you feel like you've done everything you can do and you have no more ideas; sometimes you're so exhausted that you almost fall asleep during rehearsals even if you're standing up. You can never get sick, and you don't see a lot of daylight. Sometimes you work so hard on a sketch and it gets cut and you're gutted. But that being said, it is the best place on earth *because* of how much it challenges you. When you get through it you feel like you've really accomplished something, even if you feel like you had a bad show. And if you did? You have to let it go because the show keeps moving. Show week starts Monday, and you have to show up with new ideas and do it all over again. And you can't wait for it to come.

ANDY SAMBERG, *Cast Member:*

I had told Lorne about my leaving probably the night before. In retrospect, I think maybe I would have been better off making it more clear. It was definitely odd for me, because obviously Kristen got the proper send-off—not only because she announced it but because she was one of the best cast members of all time—and I thought, I kind of did it on my own terms but maybe it would have been nicer and cleaner to have made an actual announcement before the season ended.

There was a big part of me that didn't want to leave. It was the job I'd always wanted. What it came down to is, I just couldn't physically and emotionally do it anymore. Saying good-bye was one of the hardest things I've ever done in my life, because at that point, it's more than just a job, it's family. It's like telling your parents you're moving out, and they're not ready for you to leave. And you're also talking to the guy who gave you the break that changed your life, so you don't want to disappoint him. Lorne said he'd prefer I stayed, but I think he says that to everybody who's going to leave.

Everything I've done in my career, I've always worried about whether Lorne would think it was a good idea; that's always been in the back of my mind. He sticks with you when you leave. I'll never forget how much my life changed because Lorne said, "Yeah, let's give that guy a shot."

FRED ARMISEN, *Cast Member:*

I've known these people for so long and in such close proximity that I felt like, "This is my family," and I know that people say that about casts of TV and movies and other stuff, but ten or eleven years — it's pretty intense. I believe in the way that Lorne picks people for the cast. I really do think there's a DNA for the kind of person that could end up on the show, and I think we all have it in common — just the way we look at things — and I felt close to everyone. It was really great.

ABBY ELLIOTT:

I felt as if that was my family — and then it wasn't. The show is, you know, sliding doors of people. That's sort of how it works, and how it has always worked there, with people coming and going. And it was my time to go.

KATE McKINNON, *Cast Member:*

I was in a holding deal with CBS for pilot season and I had to get out of the deal in order to do the audition for *SNL,* and I was losing half the money from the deal. So it was like a thirty-thousand-dollar audition — which was a lot of money. I was torn if I even wanted to audition because I thought I could have a guarantee of this CBS thing that would let me live for half a year — or I could audition. I'm a very practical person and I thought, "Maybe I shouldn't gamble all this money away." But friends said, "You're insane; you *have* to do it."

I was in Culver City, Los Angeles, when Lorne called. I had been tipped off that I might receive a call but I couldn't imagine that that's what that was. But that's what that was! Lorne said, "I'll cut to the chase: This is your good-news phone call. We would like you to come work for us." I said, "Well, thank you! Really?" I called my manager and my agent because it was really a team effort and I wanted to tell them. We're very close. And *then* I called my mom.

I wasn't that nervous my first night on the show, because I assumed that my sketch would get cut and I wouldn't actually have to do it. I thought, "This is good practice, and I won't have to do it on TV." I was glad when it *didn't* get cut, of course, but I just thought something catastrophic would happen—like my heart would explode and my mother would be watching and have to run to the Long Island Railroad and come and rescue me or something. I wasn't thinking clearly; I was a little overwrought at the time. It was a very stressful week.

FRED ARMISEN:

I was already doing *Portlandia,* and it was already feeling that I should focus more on that. I hinted that maybe I should think about leaving, and then Lorne asked me to stay longer and I thought, "Okay, yes. That feels good," and I knew Bill was staying, so I thought, "Okay, Bill will be there, so we can go through this together." And, "Okay, next year will be my last year." And then when that year came up, I was doing *Portlandia* and having to fly back and forth a lot, and that's when I thought, "This is a lot of flying, and I'm very focused on *Portlandia,* so maybe this is the year to go."

BILL HADER:

After Kristen and Andy left, we were like, "How is this going to work?" That was big. And then John Mulaney left too. That was big. So my last season, Bobby Moynihan just takes it, you know what I mean? He started doing amazing stuff. And working really hard. And Vanessa doing great stuff. Taran. Everyone just raises their game.

VANESSA BAYER:

I wrote Bar Mitzvah Boy with a couple of other people. That was a voice that I had done, a little bar mitzvah boy in my stand-up in

Chicago, and then there was a sketch that was written when I did my first year, and the writers put me in it as the Bar Mitzvah Boy. I don't know why; I guess they knew I was Jewish. So I got to do that voice. And then we were trying to figure out a way to bring it back, and we tried scenes with [me as] Jacob and it didn't exactly work, so we finally figured out to do it on "Update," and then it felt right.

I feel like the character is a version of myself, almost. I went to bar mitzvahs every weekend in the seventh grade. I have a brother who's two years younger and a lot of people who know him think I'm doing an impression of him because of the gestures. You know how little boys are with their hands? How they will wipe their nose or something like that? Their hands are just awkward.

I'm usually really excited just before going on "Update." I always have something in my hand—like ointment—and I always am trying to remember that first line so I can say it without looking at my binder. So a lot of it is me learning that line. Then you can sort of see the audience [from] far stage left so I'm always interested in, like, can they see me or not? And there's a million weird things I can be fixated on, like the chair I sit in has to be the lowest it can be, so I always ask the stage manager if he checked that: "Yeah, I checked it."

BOBBY MOYNIHAN:

When I did Snooki, you could feel the audience go, "We like that you're making fun of her." And I was like, "I'm going to end up being painted orange every week now if this girl keeps on doing stupid things."

NASIM PEDRAD:

Arianna Huffington reached out to me and invited me to the White House Correspondents' Dinner a couple years ago. She was incredibly supportive and seemed to be happy with the impression I was doing of her. It was amazing. I had never really been immersed into the D.C. scene like that. Nobody put me on the spot, but I think that's because Daniel Day-Lewis was at the table next to ours, and he was all anyone could focus on. Including myself.

FRED ARMISEN:

I have never not done Ian Rubbish, ever since I was literally fifteen or sixteen, except for the fact that it's called Ian Rubbish—I've got to give Seth Meyers credit for that. He came up with the concept. He's the one who said, "What if there was a punk who's pro-Thatcher?" because she had just died. That scene of those people from 1977 in London, those are my gods. That was a no-brainer for me.

KENAN THOMPSON, *Cast Member:*

I would do "What's Up with That?" every single show if I could. It's a fun one. I think everybody has fun in it and watching it, so it's like a perfect little storm.

FRED ARMISEN:

"Garth and Kat" was a very simple, very easy thing. Kristen and I used to do it in the hallways on writing night, when I'd see her and we'd just go, "Hey, do you know this song?" And I'd start singing it, and she'd sing along even though it was made up, and we did this so many times that we thought, "We have to do this on 'Update.'" And we just came up with this thing where they thought they were very overly prepared to sing a song, but they were actually very underprepared.

KATE McKINNON:

Bieber wasn't too upset by my impression of him, but he wasn't pleased. I don't think my—I wouldn't want to contribute in any way to a bad situation for him, or make him feel in any way made fun of. I am very, very concerned about making fun of anyone. I don't do anyone that I don't like and I actually really do like him and I want him to know that. That it's coming from a place of admiration and love. Yes, it's a little tricky. But Lorne's style is that nothing can ever be mean, which I completely agree with. And so, you know, we do make fun of people but it's always that we're just, like, taking a kernel of what we find fascinating or entertaining about that person and highlighting it. It's not in the spirit of trying to really cut them down.

BILL HADER:

I had a seven-year contract and extended it when my daughter was born, 'cause I wanted to make a little more money, and then my seventh season, Andy and Kristen left and John Mulaney and Simon Rich left, so all these people that I was used to working with were leaving the show. I was on the fence, and then my eighth season, during the Christmas break, my wife and I decided, "It's time to move to L.A." She's a director and she was getting offers to direct television and we have a family now, we have two kids, so maybe it was time to not do this anymore.

A lot of people wait to tell Lorne at the end of the season, but I was going to be looking for houses in L.A. and I thought it was really disrespectful to do that with him not knowing about it, so I said to him, "Hey, I'm moving to California." People always told me that you cry in those meetings—Kristen said she cried. I think a lot of people cry because it's huge, it's a big, big decision; you're leaving this place where you learned everything. It's leaving home. That was the thing. I thought, "*SNL*'s like college." Dan Aykroyd said it's just a big place where you learn about show business. You learn how to act, write, direct, deal with giant movie stars, deal with failure, deal with giant success, and it just humbles you, and you learn and you grow there and now you're leaving it, into the unknown. And it's not like school, where you graduate; you can stay there as long as you want.

So in the moment where I was telling Lorne, "I'm not graduating, I'm actually leaving my home. You know that's what this is—my family," I thought I was going to pass out. I didn't think I was going to cry, but the room spun. I just thought, "Oh my God, I can't believe I said I'm leaving." And Lorne said, "Well, let's wear this for a while." That was what he said. "Let's see how we feel when May comes around." And I said I was looking at houses and he said okay and that was it. And then I would be on the floor before a cold open and he would walk by and say some little thing like, "You're going to miss this"—you know, very funny and sweet.

FRED ARMISEN:

As the months went, Bill and I just kind of knew. We went through it together and it was really nice when we both were like, "This is our last Christmas show." I talked to Lorne about it, but I think in January or February I made it more clear, and he wanted to keep it more open, which is fair, so it just remained an ongoing discussion until the very last month.

I love *SNL,* I loved it, but I knew it was time to go. It's really strange: When Amy Poehler left, I asked her the same question about knowing when it's time to leave, and she said, "You just know. You know inside. You go, 'I think I'm done.'" And that's exactly what it was like. I thought, "Now I feel like I can go."

BILL HADER:

Lorne doesn't like it when people leave the show, obviously, and I think there's always a part of him that thinks, "You want to leave right now because it's the end of the season and you're tired, but let's see how you're feeling in August, when you haven't been here for a while and it kind of dawns on you that you're not going to have this job, and how much you love the job, and you'll come back."

Lorne doesn't like it when people do big good-byes. For the same reasons he doesn't like send-offs for cast members because he always thinks, "Don't do a big send-off when I can talk you back into staying."

FRED ARMISEN:

I think it was a very clear sort of pass from my Obama to Jay Pharoah's Obama. He did an impression of him that was really good. It was great. It made sense. I'm speaking for Lorne without him actually having said this, but I think maybe he wanted to make sure that Jay was settled into the show before he took on something like that. He just needed a little time there to get himself set. And then Lorne called me about it, and I told him, "I'm a soldier for the show," so whatever he wants me to do, that's what I do. He said that we should talk about changing Obama, as if they were still undecided. I let him know, "Whatever you want—I'll do it, I won't do it, I don't care. I love being on the show. I love doing him, and I'd love to not do him." Jay is so talented. It was also somewhat obvious that I'm not going to be there forever. That was towards the end of my tenure, even though I hadn't announced it. So it made all the sense in the world.

JAY PHAROAH:

I got the call over the summer about doing Obama. Freddie's the best guy in the world, and we talked about it and he was just so supportive, and Lorne was like, "Just work on it and get it ready." And then I was in front of the cameras doing it. Whoo boy, that was scary. My heart was racing. I felt like I almost had a heart attack, there was so much pressure. And I was twenty-four. It's a lot of pressure, especially when it's talked about and in such regard; you don't want to let people down. One thing with Obama's kinda like—he takes a minute...to get...to the point...so I...want two patties...lettuce...two sesame-seed buns...uh...another piece of bread in between.

BILL HADER:

I didn't do any impressions before *SNL*. My manager said, "Part of your audition is going to be impressions," so when we did those shows for Lorne, I was essentially the Italian guy doing impressions, and I had to learn how to do *him*. I think my first one was Al Pacino giving an acceptance speech at the Emmys. I sat in my car and just kept doing it and listening to it. And the trick came where I said, "I shouldn't watch them in movies. I should find interviews or documentary footage." Something felt fresh about that, so you're not just doing their persona from the films, you're doing them more like people.

When I got the show, I didn't really know where I fit in, because I came in with Andy and Kristen and Jason, who were all crazy talents. I felt very lucky, but I said, "Okay, if this is the A-Team, where would I fit into this ensemble?" I thought that I should probably do impressions because that Al Pacino impression went over pretty well. So it was like that. It was never anything that I planned on. It was just, "Oh, that went well, so let's go down that road and that's what this ensemble needs right now. They don't need me doing videos because Andy's doing that. I'd work on characters, but Kristen and Jason are killing it as far as characters are concerned. So let me try to work on some impressions." The political thing came mostly from the writers—Jim Downey, Seth Meyers, people coming to me and saying, "Hey, can you do Tony Blair?" and then you would go and watch Tony Blair before the table reading.

I'd walk in on a Wednesday, which was a table-read day, and I remember Seth Meyers very clearly coming up to me and saying, "Downey just wrote a cold open where you play Eliot Spitzer. Do you have an Eliot Spitzer?" and I said, "Who's Eliot Spitzer?" And Seth is like, "You're an idiot. One, he was our governor." I know nothing. So it was like, "Go watch this tape, watch him give this speech, and figure this out, you dummy." And then I would figure it out and I learned I was a pretty quick study at this stuff. Jim Downey would talk about handles—he taught me about handles. You know, you want to find someone who has a big handle; it's very easy and fun to impersonate them if they have a big handle, something you can grab on to. Obama has no handle, and so Jay did a very good job of finding little things about him. But it's really hard. That's why I think I always liked doing old movie stars, 'cause they have, like, *huge* handles. They're not even real. People now are much more, I don't know—grounded is the most polite way to say it.

James Carville came in when we did those Thursday night specials during the election season. On Thursday morning, Steve Higgins called me and said, "Hey, they're writing a James Carville for you, so go learn James Carville. You're doing it tonight." I found this You-Tube footage of James Carville and started working on it, and then I came in and did it for them in the room and kept working on it more. So when you saw that first one, that was the day of. That would happen to everyone who did impressions.

WILL FERRELL, *Cast Member:*

I think once you've impersonated a president, and then you leave the show, it's like, I get asked in a press junket, "Do you have a good Obama up your sleeve?" and I'm like, "No, I don't at all." A, I'm not an impressionist. Once I left the show, I stopped trying to think of political impressions. But also, Obama is difficult. He's very dry and subtle. And yet you see Jay and the people get it down, and you're like, "Oh, *there's* the impression."

JAY PHAROAH:

I hadn't heard anything from the White House, but then I did an event last year and I heard it from him. It was at Harvey Weinstein's house—very nice; I'd never been there. His house is gorgeous. I thought, "Oh wow, if I can get *this* someday." It was just an opportunity.

I was trying to take my makeup off because I was him *for him* at this event, and he stood right there watching me do it. He was laughing; it was so petrifying. And I heard from his administration that he loves the impression, that he thinks it's great. As long as there's no beef between me and the president, that's good. When that happens, you're Kanye West.

BILL HADER:

Dan Aykroyd pulled me aside after my third episode, and I sat with him and we talked for, like, two hours at the after party. And Dan Aykroyd's like, "Here's what's going to happen: You're going to be really nervous. You're not going to know where you stand. And then the audience is going to understand you, the audience is going to like you, and then you're going to have a couple of seasons where things are going great. And then it's going to turn into you just clocking in. You clock in, you do your stuff, and you clock out, you go home. When you're just clocking in, that's around the time you should go." And that eighth season I kind of felt that. I was like, "Yeah, I come in, I land my stuff, I didn't go to after parties; I had kids." So maybe that subconsciously was there. My third episode he essentially telegraphed my entire career at the show. He was just like, "Here's what's going to happen," and he was 100 percent right. I actually thought about that at my last show. I was like, "Fuck! Dan Aykroyd was right."

As their generation faded from cultural dominance, so baby boomers themselves began departing one by one—not just from the cast but from this mortal coil and vale of tears. As the show celebrated one anniversary after another, the necrology of Saturday Night Live *grew longer and crueler.*

One of the most painful deaths for the show's founders was that of Tom Davis, who had been among the first writers to sign on in 1975. He and fellow comic Al Franken, hired as a team, performed together in addition to writing; their great sketches for others included Dan Aykroyd's uproarious

impersonation of a hemorrhaging Julia Child. Collaborating with Ayk-
royd, Davis memorably created a family of misshapen, beer-swilling outer-
space aliens called the Coneheads; collaborating with Bill Murray, he
created Nick, the lousy lounge singer, who tried imparting lyrics to the
theme from Star Wars, *among other acts of impertinent overreaching.*

Davis and Franken later broke up, Franken said, because of Davis's
troubling problems with addiction. Franken went on to the United States
Senate, of all places, and Davis, who called himself a hippie most of his
life, returned to SNL *for another stint, on his own, from 1986 to 1994.*
His connection to the show lasted beyond that tenure, albeit sporadically
and for financial reasons: As he recalled several years before his death,
"Every once in a while, I'll show up and be a guest writer on a show if
the coffers are getting low out here. Lorne will let me come back and
appear on the show and make some money right away. It's not because
they need me or that Lorne particularly was going, 'Jeez, I wish Tom
Davis would come back to the business.' Although the cast and the writ-
ers all tell me that they're glad to see me, and I believe them." In July of
2012, he died of cancer, his death having no apparent relationship to his
earlier years of drug use. Knowing he was terminal, Davis joked even
about death, referring to it as de-animation and blogging, not long before
the end, "Some of my best friends are dead" and "Fortunately for me, I
have always enjoyed mystery and solitude." Michaels said, "I always
trusted Tom's laugh. I can kinda still hear it."

Charles "Charlie" Rocket could be said to have committed suicide
twice—the first time it was career suicide, when he audibly ad-libbed
the verboten word fuck *during a 1981 sketch spoofing the hit soap* Dallas *and was fired from the show. Rocket, who had been considered a*
bright new hope for the then-struggling program, had anchored "Week-
end Update" for a season and remained an actor after leaving the show.
But tragically, in October of 2005, he walked out into a field near his
Connecticut home and took his life by slitting his throat. Charlie Rocket
was fifty-six; Tom Davis was fifty-nine.

ERIN DOYLE, *Producer:*

When Tom Davis died, we had a memorial at 8H and I was lucky
enough to help Lorne produce it, essentially. We had everyone come

back from those early years. Dan Aykroyd spoke, Bill Murray spoke, Jim Downey spoke, along with a lot of other people. Jane Curtin was there; everyone was there. It kind of made 8H feel like a church. Also, we were able to have the current cast attend, and just watching the old and the new casts mix was really interesting.

Very few people get to choose their families—or have to audition for them. Young people may dream and plan for years about becoming a part of SNL, *but no matter how warmly they are embraced or whether it exceeds their expectations or falls sadly short,* SNL *sends no one away unaffected by the experience.*

JUSTIN TIMBERLAKE:

The last time I hosted Lorne was able to bring in all of the classic, iconic *SNL* giants to be a part of the first sketch. I mean, I grew up watching these people, you know—Martin and Chevy, Tom Hanks, Alec Baldwin, and Candice Bergen. It blew my mind. And that Paul Simon would be part of that moment as well—that blew my mind. I was host and musical guest, and *Three Amigos* was a huge movie in my childhood, so the fact Steve and Martin and Chevy were game to wear the *Three Amigos* costumes to introduce my musical performance is something I will never forget.

CECILY STRONG, *Cast Member:*

I remember when I was about five years old, fighting with every babysitter and telling them my parents let me stay awake late so I could watch the show. That's one of my earliest memories. And then copying every sketch and performing it. My friend Suzanna and I went to this beach lodge in Michigan with my family every vacation, and my parents split up so I got to go with my divorced dad and bring my best friend for a couple of years. I would always direct sketches and make everybody do plays and we would play these two Chicago newspeople, Jim Giovanni and Joe DeMario, and we were just being the superfans, talking about Ditka, and we kept saying, "Cheers to beers," and that kind of thing. We had a VHS of the commercials, I remember, that I watched almost every day; they were my favorites.

It's always been my number one dream. I've always been drawn to the stage and did that all growing up. I got my BFA in theater from CalArts. And now I get to perform live comedy in front of an audience and get to change it every week. It's amazing. I get to dress up, change my hair and makeup. It's Halloween every week.

A month after my first screen test, they told us we were going to be flown out for another one, so I had to come up with a new set of characters and impressions. And every step of the way I was like, "I'm out; I'm done." I kept thinking of all these reasons why they wouldn't choose me, because that's the way my brain works. I even got a weird message from my manager saying, "I just talked to Lindsay and she's saying that casting works in weird ways, and sometimes they don't cast people until midseason." And I thought, "So that all sounds negative. I'm just going to deal with my rejection now." And then, about twenty minutes later, my agent calls and says, "You're being flown out to meet with Lorne." I said, "Is that good?" And he was like, "Well, he's not going to fly you out to tell you that he doesn't like you."

I was hired in this weird limbo of, "We don't know where you'll start; just get out here Monday." I came out prepared to write and was told the Wednesday before the first week that I was going to be on the show. I had to run downstairs to have pictures taken. They didn't have a dress in my size so I was like a stuffed sausage squeezed into a cape dress.

AIDY BRYANT, *Cast Member:*

I think maybe the biggest surprise would be how sort of instantly people respect you in a way that maybe should take you much longer. People immediately, when you have gone through being on *SNL,* even for—I've only been here for two years and yet I feel like people within the industry are, like, really impressed by that and take you seriously much more quickly than if, say, I think if, like, you know, I had just started on a sitcom or something. Just immediately you're like, "Oh, this is the big leagues."

COLIN JOST, *Writer:*

I was a writer, then a writing supervisor—which is just kind of a transitional title—the year before I became head writer, and so I started taking on some of those duties with Seth to start learning that job. It was gradual over the course of three years. There's a lot more anxiety in being head writer. That's the biggest change from writer to head writer. You feel a responsibility for the show. Obviously it's Lorne's show and there's no question about that, but you feel a responsibility. It changes from being a really fun job to being a challenging and stressful job.

What's crazy about the anxiety is that they're your friends, people you hang out with, and before you got that job you were talking to them and saying, "Can you believe this person? That's crazy," and suddenly you have a hand in that and that feels really weird, and you have to start thinking as a producer rather than a writer or cast member. You have to think about what's best for the show and not what's best for your friends. That's at least half the anxiety.

The hardest thing to deal with up front was feeling you should have a strong opinion at every meeting. I'd been in a lot of meetings before, but Lorne was either not asking me what I thought or [not] relying on it. And then suddenly it felt like he was, and that he was giving me leeway to shape the show, which is intimidating.

If certain things don't work, you say, "I should have made that better; I should have seen that it wouldn't work." But there's also a limit to what you can do. You're one in a staff of a lot of people, and a lot can go right or wrong that has nothing to do with you. You're only one small part of it, but you try to do what you can. The beauty of the show is that you start over again the next week, and you don't have many hours to lick your wounds.

BILL HADER:

I never understood the pitch meetings. Wait, I take that back: I *understood* the pitch meetings, I just never *liked* the pitch meetings, because I was never very good at it. A pitch meeting is essentially telling the host, "Here's who you'll be working with this week." And instead of someone shaking their hand and saying "Hi, my name is Bill. I'll be working with you this week," I pitch you an idea. The other reason to do it is if something's happening, if something's in the zeitgeist and it's topical, people can lay claim to it at a pitch meeting. I say that I want to do something about Sarah Palin or whatever, and then they work that out. Or if I say, I have this idea where I play Vincent Price, it's kind of telling the room, "Hey, I'm doing Vincent Price this week, so don't do anything that bumps with it."

TARAN KILLAM:

I think it works differently for different people. For myself, absolutely. You sit down on writing night and it's almost musical—the rhythms, saying something and hearing the rhythm and knowing, "No, that doesn't feel right," because you're also writing for a minimum of four audiences: You're writing for the room on Wednesday, you're writing for Lorne in particular, and then you're writing for the audience that's coming in here—the three hundred tourists, aunts, and uncles that are coming in—and then you're writing for yourself, because you want to be happy with what you do. Bill Hader said it's like this diagram, and you have to find what you think is funny and what the show thinks is funny and the section where they both overlap, and that's the type of material you should be writing for the show.

BILL HADER:

Steve Higgins always talks about Venn diagrams, like, "Here's what you find funny, and here's what the show finds funny," and you have to find that Venn diagram of where both areas overlay. Kristen Wiig, John Mulaney—those are people for whom it's all the same circle. What they naturally like 100 percent works for the show. I felt like I had to find my Venn diagram. It took me four seasons to figure out how to get a thing that I was happy with but that worked for the show. I think for certain people it's just really hard.

FRED ARMISEN:

I think you never know, because even if you and the writers laugh in the office, you still never know. And if everyone laughs at the rehearsal table, you still never know. And even if it goes to dress rehearsal, you're not there. Even if it goes to air and everyone's laughing and it goes great, that second time it doesn't mean that they're gonna be there for you. I actually feel like the only time that I know if something has worked is after it's aired, or even a few months after, to see who's remembered it or who's said something about it on the street. Otherwise you just don't know. It's hard to get a sense of it because it's people talking to you about you, so obviously they're not going to tell you something critical.

AIDY BRYANT:

For my first four or five shows I had almost no lines—maybe one line here, one line the next week. And then all of a sudden I hosted a "presidential debate," and that was, like, a huge switch, and there was a lot on my shoulders for a change. And because it was a town hall debate, it was this really insane cue-card setup where they were shooting over my shoulder, so that meant I could not have any cards in front of me, because they would be in the shot. It was very stressful and very crazy because for a while they were like, "You might have to memorize the whole thing, but we're going to change it," so it was, like, this insane big moment that I could tell was a make or break. Either I could execute it or I couldn't.

Romney and Obama were taking questions from the audience, basically this town hall, and I was Candy Crowley moderating these questions. It was shot in the round, almost, which is really rare for *SNL,* so they had two cue-card guys dressed as extras sitting in the audience with cards at their feet, and any time that they knew that they weren't on-screen, they would stand up and pop up the cards so that I could grab one line and then stick them back down. If you watch that scene, you can see in the background that there are cue-card guys sitting there like extras and then popping up with these cards. It was an insane feeling. And then when it finished, I got to the final thing where I say, "That concludes our debate," and now when I watch it I can fully see in my face I'm like, "Whoo! We made it through!" I'm so overwhelmed and happy. And then I said, "Live from New York," and all of a sudden Tom Hanks was on one side of me and Bill Hader on the other and we ran down this hallway and people had lined the hallway to clap for me, because it was definitely my first big thing on the show.

It was, like, the most special moment of my life, you know?

JAMES DOWNEY:

I used to write this stuff with Al Franken when we started out; I was a standard-issue Harvard graduate commie and Al was, like, a Democratic Party stalwart. He was wherever the party was, and I had contempt for the partisan stuff. And I became more conservative over the years, to the point where I'm now a conservative Democrat, which means in Hollywood terms I'm a McCarthyite, I suppose. But I have to say, and even Franken agrees with me—I've talked to him about this—that the last couple seasons of the show were the only two in the show's history where we were totally like every other comedy show: basically, an arm of the Hollywood Democratic establishment. There was nothing we did politically that in any way set us apart from any other political comedy show. In fact, Stewart was more nuanced. We just stopped doing anything which could even be misinterpreted as a criticism of Obama. We were doing what we had often been unfairly accused of doing, but this time it was true—except our critics just said, "Oh, they've always been that way," and I would go, "No; not so."

It's not a matter of left-right, it's more a matter of "with the pack." We were now with the pack of comedy shows as opposed to being sort of hard to peg, and that had been one of the things I was always proud of about the show.

KATE McKINNON:

Chris Kelly and Sarah Schneider, two brilliant writers, wrote several incarnations of Ann Romney for me to do and then finally landed on that one for "Weekend Update." I had nothing to do with the writing at all, although I had been watching her and although I'm not a Republican, I really liked something about her. There was this quality that was, like, buttoned up, but you could tell that inside, she was a little loose, a little ready to get down. So I really enjoyed her as a character, just playing with that.

PAULA PELL, *Writer*:

A lot of times, people auditioning for *SNL* came from that sea of improvisational comedians—Second City and Groundlings and

UCB—and oftentimes that community of people was not quite as diverse as you would wish. There's plenty of funny gay women and men who do gay content in their comedy, and they are in venues that are within their community, but you really have to try with the Internet and everything to get your stuff out there to where people will see it. Sometimes it was hard because obviously there are far more men than women in a lot of these groups, gay or straight—in the mainstream, at least. And you would sit there and see a whole group of women auditioning and think, "Wow. I know there's gotta be funnier ladies out there. These ladies are funny, but you want those Kristen Wiigs, those brilliant, funny women." You know they exist, but you've got to find them. You've got to get them in there. You've got to audition them.

KATE McKINNON:

I didn't think that anyone was talking about me in the same sense as Kristen Wiig, because that's ludicrous. She's the finest sketch performer that ever lived, and I have not proved myself at all. But I did feel a lot of pressure, personal pressure, because her career at *SNL* was so astounding, and I admired her so much that I held myself to that standard, just internally. And that probably tripped me up a little bit. It drove me a little crazy. I put too much pressure on myself. I eat too much, and I'm a terrible hypochondriac, and I think that I'm going to have an aneurysm or something. I take my pulse a lot.

PAULA PELL:

Kate is of a generation that grew up differently than I did. You know, I'm fifty-one and there was one mainstream movie about two lesbians called *Personal Best* and I had the cassette of it hidden in my drawer. And now when I look at my nieces, who are the same ages as Kate McKinnon, they grew up with MTV and entertainment shows and reality shows, all with tons of gay characters, and episodic shows with tons of gay characters that weren't just about them being gay. They were part of a love triangle; they were part of a medical drama. It's now such a mainstream thing that I don't feel like the pressure was as big on her, but who knows her personal experience with that? I do know that there are lots of young gay girls who love knowing that Kate McKinnon is on there as a cast member, and that they're being represented, because everybody is trying to be represented.

It's also hard to write sketch comedy that spans across all humanity and not have the cast to do those things. As comedy and comedy subjects and pop culture things become more diverse and more interesting, we need the cast to support that, and so I'm really super glad that we're getting a much more diverse cast. It's been a great joy. James Anderson and I, who are best friends and were roommates in college and have worked together at *SNL* for years and years, were about the only gay people on the writing staff for a long time, and that has changed a lot. It's just so wonderful now to know that there's a nice collection of people there that really covers it all.

KATE McKINNON:

I never wanted it to stop me in my life and so far it hasn't — and that's wonderful. I just want to be a regular comedian. That's the banner that I fly. I don't really have much to say about it, I guess. I'm glad I could make a difference and get paid at the same time.

KENAN THOMPSON:

I started watching *SNL* toward the end of the Eddie Murphy years. I was aware of the hot-tub sketch and stuff as a little kid, but it was more what my dad was laughing at. For me it was, like, Sandler and Farley and those guys — Kevin Nealon, Norm, and the others. I had to go backwards to appreciate the earlier things. I wasn't really a fan of Dan Aykroyd and Chevy Chase, 'cause those guys were movie stars. As far as their work on the show, I had to research those years.

LORNE MICHAELS:

Ninety percent of the people working here now weren't alive during the first five years.

KENAN THOMPSON:

It's unbelievably gracious of God to give me this gift. You know what I'm saying? I don't know how else to put it. I can't even watch the show the same way now. It seems like a totally different show now that I'm on it. It's crazy. It's crazy to imagine your picture at some point in that long line of head shots that we have up there on the wall. Eventually you'll get to your picture.

PAUL RUDD:

That show has seen its share of pretty incredible talents, and I always thought Armisen was one of them. There have always been people who have very specific comedic sensibilities that sometimes I thought, "How does it fit in with the show?" When Armisen first joined *SNL,* I wondered. He's so *specifically* funny and so interesting and so left of center. And then he just owned it, and it was so fun to watch his specific kind of thing come through.

FRED ARMISEN:

I'm here with who I love. I'm here with Carrie Brownstein, my soul mate. I'm here with my friends and playing music. I wrote on my guitar strap TYLMIHEARTU—"Thank you, Lorne Michaels, I love you." That's just kind of the way I wanted to do it—I wanted it to be musical. You know that thing in music where it's positive even though it still has little tinges of melancholy to it? I still wanted it to be a sort of happy-sad song.

JAMES DOWNEY:

You get to be a certain age, and it's like I get more and more disconnected from the general thing of the show. First of all, I'm old enough to be their fathers, and then I'm old enough to be their—not grandfathers, I guess, but...I don't know what the future will hold.

SETH MEYERS:

The minute Lorne and I started talking about *Late Night* as a possibility, I made sure I could come back to *SNL* the first half of the season. I was in no way, shape, or form emotionally ready to leave. The timing of it would have meant, I think, that I only had one more show, and I certainly wasn't ready to unpack all my feelings about that in such a short period of time. It's sort of like finding out from your doctor that you have six months to live, and so those last six months are still very vivid and bright—and that's kind of how I felt about *SNL*.

CECILY STRONG:

Every time I have a meeting with Lorne, I assume I'm getting fired. It's like seeing a doctor and you assume they're going to tell you that you have AIDS, even if it's a dentist. So I was really scared and we just chatted for a while and then he said, "I'm going to have you do 'Update.'" I had no idea he was even thinking about it. And then he was like, "Well, I'm going to go; I'm taking someone to dinner." And so then I was just left with Doyle. "What just happened? I'm going to do 'Update'?!" Do I have to change who I am? Does this mean I can't be as outspoken now that I have to represent this brand? Because I've always been "loud-mouthed Chicago kid."

I don't have paparazzi following me; nothing like that is part of my life, but anything I put out there now—I feel so scared about guarding everything. In January, after a show, I was on Twitter and I was getting all these mean ones. Some were really sexist and nasty, and so many were, "Are you pregnant? Are you pregnant?" And I just felt like, "Hey, I have to deal with my body, my own self, my own image issues; why should the public get to weigh in and be bullies about it?" I couldn't decide what to do for months and then I thought, "I'm just going to say one thing, and then after I've said it, I'm only going to address the nicer ones." I think I just said, "No, I'm not pregnant, you bully dickheads" or something along those lines. Then Lorne was on me, for "watch your language" or something. And I said, "Am I allowed to say how I feel? Are we allowed to stick up for ourselves? I'm with you on swear words. My mother would say the same thing, and I trust my mother. Get your point across without swear words. But I want to make sure I have the right to be myself." Figuring all that out has been tough.

CAMERON DIAZ:

They always know who's in town somehow. I'm friends with Adam Levine, so I was planning on coming to the show that week anyway. I was going to go, "Dude, can I get tickets?" but then I got a phone call from Lorne's office and they said we have this sketch we'd like you to be in, and when they said it would be with Adam and with Jerry [Seinfeld] I was like, "Uh, are you kidding me?!" Being sandwiched between Adam and Jerry was a thrill for me. I didn't even care what I had to say.

SETH MEYERS:

What you learn from Lorne and certainly, hopefully, will have learned from me, just as someone who's been there for a long time, is that by design the show has ups and downs, mostly because it's impossible to constantly be rolling out. So you have people who are veterans, people who are new, people who are just coming along, and sometimes that alchemy gets a little off, but if it's such that at any given time you have too many people that are new, that just means that in a year or two, you'll have a great many people who are completely coming into their own.

So it was great to be here this year and for people to watch Kate McKinnon and Vanessa Bayer, who have grown up so much in the last few years, and it's just been a delight to see them do their thing. And to be at the "Update" desk with Cecily is something I'll never forget.

ROB KLEIN, *Writer:*

It's like, oh my God, you lose so many stars of the show or whatever, you know, with Bill, Fred, and Jason, and Andy and Kristen the year before. I mean, obviously that's been the history of the whole show going all the way back and it's always been okay, and the thing that I even remember going back to my first year is, like, Bill Hader was just kind of a guy... and even, like, Bill, Jason, and Fred, when they started, everyone was like, okay, those are just the new guys and they were almost, like, not that distinguishable in some ways. It's like Phil Hartman—he's one of the best people who's ever been on the show. He, the audience, and even the people at the show can't quite see what they're going to become yet. And maybe they don't quite know either, but that's the thing that's made me feel better this year, is remembering back to my first year—even Kristen wasn't necessarily the star of the show. People grow into all of these roles and it happens kind of quickly too.

LINDSAY SHOOKUS:

You can't replace Jason, Fred, and Bill. You can't go out and find the next Bill Hader, just like you can't go out and find the next Will Ferrell. And if you set yourself up for that, you're bound for failure. But if we maybe hire a few extra, maybe we'll find some real gems in there.

BILL HADER:

You have these hosts come in and go, "Hey, I'm on *SNL*, let's party!" And we were like, "Oh, I'm not eating sugar this season." I remember my mother-in-law came in and I won't name the band but friends of the band who played the show said, "Hey, can we, like, hang out in your dressing room and maybe smoke a joint?" and I said, "Yeah, I don't give a shit" — cause I rarely was in my dressing room. And I forgot I told them that and I came after the show with my mother-in-law and there was the band smoking pot and I was like, "Oh, my mother-in-law" and they were like, "Eww" and ran out. And then my father-in-law, who's a judge in Idaho — that was, like, around Christmas — so then we go to Idaho for Christmas and he sits me down and he says, "Your mother-in-law told me about what happened and I just want you to know you've got to watch it with drugs and stuff in your business because I don't want you to get caught with something, and that reflects poorly on you. You've really got to watch it." And I said, "You don't understand: Where I work was founded on pot. If pot didn't exist, there would be no *SNL*. The reason I have this awesome job is that these guys were doing a lot of drugs. So relax; it's all right."

TINA FEY, *Cast Member:*

I think I maybe would have fit in in the Jane Curtin model, which is — I don't think Jane used to, like, do blow with everybody. Jane was, like, already married when she came into the show.

LORNE MICHAELS:

I know how it's written about, and I know what Aykroyd says in interviews about it, because he loves the myth of the old days. After the show, for sure, but during the show, when stuff was getting written? It was just too hard. It was always hard, you know? And I think people loved the idea of that myth, of the '70s myth. Also there was no money for any of it in the first two or three years. That only happened after *Animal House* and that level of success. And it happened mostly with John; Chevy was gone. I wrote with Chevy a lot of times in that first year or year and a half—but he wasn't fucked up.

JAMES ANDERSON, *Writer*:

There are still some people who work there that talk about those days. And I don't know how they ever put on a show. There was some hardcore stuff going on back in the day. And now, you know, the hardcore stuff is, like, tequila shots, basically. That's the hardest thing that's going around. Maybe it's something to do with the era. When it started in the '70s they were more experimental with drugs and stuff. They would get high when they were writing and stuff, back in the day. The high we have is lack of sleep. You're just there until readthrough. So it's coffee, Red Bull, and whatever else.

MAYA RUDOLPH:

Working there is also not just writing sketches and performing them but also checking in with each other and talking to each other about your private life and your family and your, you know, your boyfriend or husband or whatever and your girlfriend or wife. It's knowing that you have to take care of each other, that these are the people that you're with six and a half days out of the week and they see you at your best and your worst and your most tired and eating crap food at four o'clock in the morning and when you're delirious. These are the people that are really taking care of you as well.

LORNE MICHAELS:

When you're the boss, people project onto you. I can generally tell how people got along with their parents or, more specifically, how they got along with their fathers—if they had an adoring one or if they had a contentious one—every time I speak they hear criticism. Gilda Radner called every night to talk about a guy she was breaking up with, and John Belushi would drop by my apartment at three o'clock in the morning to go over things. I remember being in my office somewhere in the end of the first season, and Herb Sargent coming in and saying he had to talk to me. So I said, "What is it?" And he said, "I don't know what to do with my life. What do you think?" He was, like, thirty years older than I was, and I went, "Oh Jesus."

KEN AYMONG:

We now do more prerecorded material than we've ever done before. When we come into a show now, I'll read everything on Wednesday morning before everyone gets here. It's usually about forty scripts, and I would say about ten to twelve of those are prerecorded pieces, whereas years ago, it might be two or three. Over the course of the last five years, with the advent of Digital Shorts, Akiva, Jorma, and Andy and those other guys grew in power, and they were all good. The new writing staff is fairly young, the YouTube generation, and that's the way they're used to seeing things; they think more filmically than we did in the past. We still do the same number of live pieces as well. They're pitted against one another to fight for the airtime.

KATE McKINNON:

I do wonder what it was like not to have the immediate feedback of the Internet the next day. Ultimately I think that all change is bad so, yeah, I think it's more a curse than a blessing, because as I'm rehearsing throughout the week I'm thinking how this is going to live forever—not in some archive but on the Internet and on blogs people are going to write things about. I don't think *SNL* was in the paper every week in 1995. Everyone's a comedian now; everyone's on social media commenting in a joking way, and everything becomes immediate fodder for comedy. Doing sketch comedy has become harder because the pace of it is impossible.

BILL HADER:

I remember Emily Spivey, a writer on the show. I was telling her— oh man, I can't remember the website—so-and-so really didn't like that sketch. Maybe we shouldn't try it again. She was like, "Bill, who the fuck cares? Why are you putting all of your worth into somebody you don't know, you don't know who they are, and they're just spouting shit about you?" And I thought she had a point and I just stopped. It's just like, who the fuck cares? And what I learned later—this is me talking now—was that they would reverse their opinion on things. Someone would love you and say these things, and a year later they hated you. And vice versa. I remember one of the websites hated Herb Welch. They were just like, "Please get rid of this character; it's my least favorite character." And I wasn't reading stuff online, but the people I wrote the sketch with were, and they were like, "Oh yeah, people fucking hate Herb Welch." I did an interview with them for a movie I was in, and they said, "We want to get a comment from you because Herb Welch is in our favorite-sketches-of-the-year thing." And I was like, "Wait—what?" It's this weird yo-yo thing, going up and down and just not knowing. And then it's affecting your work. Then you're sitting in front of your computer going, "Oh, okay, I'm writing this thing that people hate." People don't hate it. It's this one little area. Why would that affect your work? I'd rather have—if a good friend or a colleague or another comedian I respected or someone like that said, "Hey, I like that" or "I'm not really into that" or whatever, then that means something, I guess.

PAULA PELL:

With the Internet, it's just a barrage. Just a barrage of negativity and everyone always says, "Oh, I try not to read that stuff," and it's just bullshit because you know Sunday, they go online and they Google their sketch and they see what people said about it, and that affects them, you know? It affects writers, new writers, and actors.

KATE McKINNON:

I do like to read the Internet. I read every blog every week because I'm just so jazzed that people watch it and I want to know what they liked and what they didn't like, and I've learned to absorb whatever criticism I read, and I really like to see what people have to say about the writing, what they respond to. I feel a little more divorced from it now than I used to be. I would cry initially if I read something negative; I was really out of my mind. Now I take it to heart if I feel it's correct.

CECILY STRONG:

It was almost becoming self-abusive or something, like if I had gotten a lot on that week and other people hadn't. It's like cutting yourself or something to read bad things. You know how it feels. For some reason they like us to be competitive. They like to make it as if it's a competition, and that is the opposite of my happy, healthy place. I like ensembles and supportive environments.

VANESSA BAYER:

I think that no matter what the setup of the cast is, people will always have comments about what it *should* be. People will always have an opinion. When people think about *SNL,* they feel a lot of ownership over it. It's like a sports team; they really have strong opinions about who should be here and what should be on the show and everything, so it is a blessing and a curse. When I was in Facebook, someone would put an article on my page and say, "Oh, they said such a nice thing about you," so I would read it and of course right before that "nice thing" is a dig. So I really try not to look at the Internet anymore. Sometimes my dad will tell me stuff. I think my dad must have figured out how to do a Google alert, 'cause he always knows everything. It was my first season or something and he offhandedly said, "You know, there's a whole page devoted to people who don't like you," and I was like, "Dad, I did *not* know that." I went to Thanksgiving this year and my aunt was like, "Did you know there's a whole thing about your feet online?" There's a thing online where people have a foot thing, people who've been on TV with their feet exposed have a website, but I don't want to promote it in any way. Or maybe I already have!

CECILY STRONG:

I was in Hawaii over the break and I was having just a bad day, just at the pool something happened, I don't even remember what, but I was crying and wearing sunglasses. I cry all the time. And later I see on Twitter somebody wrote, "I'm sitting right beside Cecily at the pool," and I was like, "God, I was crying the whole time." Luckily she can't see, but even in Maui, tucked away, someone sees you.

KENAN THOMPSON:

I used to walk to work a lot, especially when I moved into the city and lived closer to work, and a lot of the FedEx people would shout, "Yeah, what's up, man? Yeah, I seen you on the show! You're funny!" It started with the delivery dudes.

KRISTEN WIIG:

No matter what, a hug from Kenan made everything better.

KENAN THOMPSON:

It's too crazy to focus on that and focus on where you work and focus on who you're coming behind. There's a list of crazy people who have come before. I walk past their pictures in the hall every single day, so it's already in my mind. It'll panic you to death. It really will.

JAY PHAROAH:

You'll have a role here that's not really funny—you're being a team player and everything's about being a team player. In everything. That's how people get to the Super Bowl. I'm sure if Richie Sherman was fighting with the rest of the Seahawks, they wouldn't be anywhere right now. You gotta work together—that's what it's about, man, whatever you get. It's all about whatever you get, being good at it, and having the writers see that and having them see you can do good in those things and then they'll expand your role next time even bigger.

KENAN THOMPSON:

We don't get writers' credits, but everybody writes, you know, for the record. Some actually sit down and write on their own, and some collaborate. I'm more of a collaborator myself. I would say I'm a "super collaborator" 'cause I don't actually type anything. We all write, we all stick to that process. I write every week. That's fine.

KATE McKINNON:

In my mind, this is my last job. I am preparing for that being the reality. Obviously I hope that I have a long career because I would feel bad if I couldn't work. Anything else beyond this would be icing on the cake. I'm putting my money in a tax-free municipal bond fund and just being very practical about savings, so if nothing else happens, then this would be enough. I already got so lucky getting this job. It seems like that would be too much to ask for—to continue to keep doing this—so I'll take it if it comes, but I don't want to hold myself to that standard. That's too much pressure. I've been basically unemployed, or very sporadically employed, for six years before getting this incredible job, and I'm still pretty much "there" in my mind, so this is just a crazy thing that happened.

BOBBY MOYNIHAN:

I'll stay here as long as they'll have me. This was my dream, and I should be thinking more about the future and more about movies, but I'm still worried. When I walk out this door, I want to be able to say to myself, "You did what you wanted to do and be happy with it." Those other jobs are nice and they're not as hectic—nothing is as hectic as this place, and I've been lucky enough to be in a couple of movies—but I love the idea of at two o'clock in the morning someone comes into your office and says something stupid and you go, "That might work," and you write it, and then a year later you've done it five times and you're like, "I can't believe that dumb joke turned into this amazing thing."

When I started, Amy and Darrell were still on the show. It was a completely different place. I feel very lucky that I got to see what I think of as the tail end of "old" *SNL*, the Will Ferrell–Amy Poehler kind of days, and then got to see the meteoric rise of Kristen and Bill and Andy and all those guys, and now I'm getting to see all the new ones. It's crazy. I feel very lucky of my timing on the show. Sometimes I still feel like the new guy, but now that these other new guys are here, I feel like I can give advice and that it's worthy of listening to. I'm in no rush.

MICHAEL SHOEMAKER:

Even if it's a good show, but it was a better dress, people are in a bad mood at the party. That thing that was better before doesn't matter. And yet it still affects them to this day. Like one of Seth's last shows that I went to, and he was like, "Yeah I don't know, it was okay." I was like, "No, this is way better than last week." And he's like, "Yeah but…" And it's just the comparison of dress to air. And they all kind of fall prey to it.

BILL HADER:

I was doing a sketch with Kristen Wiig where I was supposed to throw a milk shake in her face. And I did it perfectly on dress, and then on-air, I threw it and missed her. And it ruined the entire sketch. I totally overshot it, and literally the whole audience gasped. You could just tell it was supposed to be the big blast of the thing. Kristen just kind of froze. Then on the West Coast, they used the one from dress. So the East Coast saw the fuckup, but in the west, and in all the reruns, they played the one from dress. That would happen a lot, where you would do something at dress and be like, "Man, that went great." And then it just wouldn't go as well on-air. If something went good at dress it was jinxed. You're like, "Fuck—it's never going to be that good again." Lorne could tell that I was being very hard on myself. So when that happened with the milk shake, he was like, "Don't worry about it."

ANDY SAMBERG:

One time we did a sketch called "Hamlet Auditions" with Jude Law, 'cause he'd just done *Hamlet* and Bill was doing his great Pacino and he and other people were in a room getting ready to do *Hamlet*, and at one point I come storming in as Nic Cage and I don't think I said two sentences before I do the thing from *Wicker Man* where I'm like, "The beast! The beast!" and run and jump out the window— which is obviously always a fun bit, to go through a window at *SNL*.

And at dress rehearsal I forgot to tuck my head under my arm so I hit the bar, the severed wooden bar, right over my eye and it cut my head open and I just started gushing blood all over the crash mat. And

I had to lie there so I didn't ruin the rest of the sketch as blood poured out of my head. And then finally they broke in, and I popped up and I said to somebody, "Get help! Get a doctor! Get a doctor!" because I was in the next sketch. So Donna, who is in charge of the host's wardrobe and who has been doing it forever and knows every trick in the book, immediately goes, "I got it, I got it," and runs over with some kind of solution or something, holds some stuff up against it and mooshes it down and does some magic thing to my head while my wardrobe guy, Ken, is changing my clothes. So they're still prepping me for the next change, and they got me changed out in time. And I had some weird skin glue stuck to my face for the next sketch and then finally I came out and wiped all the makeup off and got it stapled up.

And then I had to do it again on-air because "Hamlet Auditions" went well. So it was in the live show and I had to go through the window again, knowing I had just busted my head open. But I tucked my head under my arm better this time and I didn't cut myself. The sketch was probably tanking all week and then all of a sudden it went, "Yes, this is the one you have to do!"

NASIM PEDRAD:

You spend all this time working in the hopes that your crazy little idea sees the light of day, and then when it does, it's live television, so things can go wrong, and it's all happening so fast. The instance I'm remembering is the time I had a host accidentally leave our sketch before it was over. The host left early by a minute and a half without even realizing it! Lorne had to rerun an old commercial parody to make up for the lost time. The sketch awkwardly faded to black in the middle of one of our lines, and the whole thing was a mess. But I'd hate to throw the host under the bus, because it kind of wasn't his fault. My favorite part was the host sweetly came up to me during the good-byes and was like, "Hey, we did it." And I did not have the heart to tell him that we certainly did *not*.

KEN AYMONG:

Lorne's terrific when everybody's doing their best and something goes wrong. He can be disappointed, but sometimes he'll just laugh.

It's just one of those things. I remember we had a sketch with Fred Armisen playing a character called Ravish—I actually had it put up online—it was in the ninth act of the show. We did another sketch up at the same location on home base and then we had to do this Ravish talk-show setup during the last break, which was a minute thirty. It was a lot to set in a minute thirty, but between the stagehands and me, we figured we could handle all the pieces. Well, the transition got under way and it was clearly not going to happen. The sketches were in a different order at air than at dress. And there was a three-wall setup on home base, with a chair, a couch, and a table, and a carpet to boot. Carpets are killers up on home base. So when I talk to the stagehands, they're all a very optimistic lot, and they're all, "We can do it." Well, sure enough, the countdown starts and we're not even close. I don't know if it's still up online but I have it on a DVD that I've saved forever, where the stage manager's walking down trying to get some stuff up there and he just goes, "We're screwed." And then the wall wouldn't connect to boot, so we did the whole scene with the wall being held up by three guys. But we made it. It wasn't pretty, but we made it.

ERIN DOYLE:

On Sunday everyone goes away and clears their head, but Lorne comes back on Monday and—even if the show went well and was extremely successful—he still remembers exactly what the problems were on Saturday and will go through the rundown that's on the board in his office on seventeen with us. He sees all the flaws that played. He'll say, "Here's what happened in the cold open; this person missed their cue here"—he can go through the entire show like that. It's kind of a crazy thing, or the way he's built and how he runs this place, but he knows how to break down the show on a very specific level. And then he'll say, "Look, we need to talk to the cast about this, or we need to talk to this department about this." I think every week he's disappointed, but also he can be extremely happy about the show and feel like, "Oh, it went well." The smallest stuff makes him really happy.

KEN AYMONG:

I'm in a weird position because while I've a vested interest that the show be funny, at that point in time for me it's really about the logistics of pulling the show together. On Thursdays I'm still in the early throes of organizing how we're going to do it. I'm in the elemental side of this. Anytime you read a script I'm dealing with what are the seven or eight basic elements of television and every single piece I have to watch out for. Not that I have to create them or anything along those lines, but I have to make sure everybody's on the same path, on the same page. You have the director and the crew, costume design, scenic design, music, graphics, script, and cast—all those elements. And now the show's more complicated than it ever was before. Lorne always turns to me at the end of the thing: "Can you handle this?" I just think about it financially. At that point I'm only thinking about it from a production standpoint. I have a personal criteria in terms of the live show that if we can actually rehearse the live show by Friday at midnight I'm in pretty good shape there. I might have to make concessions on what we'll get to on Saturday but I'll deal with that when we get to it.

JAMES ANDERSON:

When Lorne is laughing, the whole world is laughing. When you're sitting next to Lorne and he's laughing, you're like, "All right, I've done it. I did it."

TARAN KILLAM:

I think at this point people know that as long as Lorne wants to do the show, the show will survive. The interesting aspect is how's it going to transform and who's going to take the reins or step up or what's the new character or piece or segment. What was unique about our generation was that four of us got hired together, and we came into a locked cast. You had Kristen, who I think is one of the greatest performers in the history of the show; you had Andy, who helped change the structure of the show in terms of integrating social media and the Internet; and then Bill, who's just one of the most versatile people of all time, and Jason and Fred. With those people, you don't need anybody else. You really don't. The original cast was seven and adding us four made thirteen. So we were a little superfluous in terms of the necessity of the show.

STEVE HIGGINS, *Supervising Producer:*

This place, you get spoiled when you leave it. You don't deal with people who only care about good; you don't deal [with people] who don't care about how much it costs; you don't deal with people who only care that it's the best possible iteration of that joke or if it's the smartest thing. You deal with people who just want to make money, and you don't know if something's going to make money; you only know if something's good or bad. And that's the thing here: We do pieces on our show that you wouldn't see anywhere else. When you hit it right and you get a great sketch like the Jost one about workers at the Apple factory, you go, "Wow—that's why we're on this earth, that's why we exist in this world, for that kind of thing."

I've worked other places. I've had arguments with people about a two shot and not having a door exposed so if somebody walks in, you're telegraphing the shot or things like that. Here, that's a given— that's already done. You don't have to fight to get your joke in. A twenty-two-year-old writer can come up with some joke that he believes in and can go to Lorne, "I can't change that because it will ruin my piece." This is like the old Hollywood system of stars and writers all under contract, all making movies, except there's a Louis B. Mayer who doesn't want to put his fingers in everything.

If any traces remained of underdog or maverick status for Saturday Night Live, *they were few and fading as 2014 came into view. Considering the crucial cast departures of the previous summer and the continuing controversy over allegedly insufficient ethnic diversity, the* SNL *gang needed a positive boost, and that's just what it got in January at the seventy-first annual Golden Globe Awards, an event that turned into a veritable* SNL *jubilee, with former court jesters now reigning as royalty. The Studio 8H family dominated the telecast even though the show itself didn't win a single major award.*

To establish the SNL *presence right off, alumnae Tina Fey and Amy Poehler returned for their second spin as Globe cohosts; their dual debut in 2013 had managed to put the show on far firmer footing than it had been on in years, back when hosting it was considered a risky gig or a no-win bummer. The two stars brought laughs and class to the production, turning it into an awards show that qualified as actual entertainment.*

As the evening bounced along, Fey and Poehler would see many familiar SNL *personalities march up to accept prizes, including—to his apparent astonishment—Andy Samberg, now named best actor in a comedy or musical for* Brooklyn Nine-Nine, *a comic cop show that also won for best comedy series. As one of its producers, Samberg shared in that prize too. The award was sweeter for Samberg because it was presented by Seth Meyers, who in a matter of weeks would be taking over from Jimmy Fallon as host of NBC's* Late Night, *while Fallon would move from* Late Night *to the holy of holies in this terrain,* The Tonight Show. *Golden Globe history was also made that night, because when Poehler accepted her Golden Globe for starring in the NBC sitcom* Parks and Recreation, *she became the first host of the awards to win one while hosting.*

In occasional reaction shots of the audience, Michaels looked paternal and pleased as his "kids," as well as celebrities whom he considered friends of SNL, *trotted up for their trophies. Michaels's thoughts were probably on the future, not the past; with Fallon's* Tonight Show *and Meyers's* Late Night *coming under his domain, Michaels would soon be the most commanding presence in late-night television—ever—and a dominant oracle in network television generally.*

ANDY SAMBERG:

There is something about being in the *SNL* "stable" that just makes people look at you differently, like being asked to do something like host the *Time* 100 [gala]. A couple of years before, Jimmy had done it, and before that, Seth and Amy had done it. People know you're in New York, they know you're on *SNL,* and so then all of a sudden you're hosting the *Time* 100 and you're making jokes about Sarah Palin and Bill Clinton—about them, and *to* them. *SNL* is the main artery of news and entertainment and everything, and I think that's why it's the best job there is in comedy.

That Golden Globes night was the most surreal and incredible moment. Seth was the groomsman at my wedding; we're very, very good friends. So to have him up there to give me the award made it a hundred times sweeter. We looked at each other like, "What the fuck is happening right now?" That moment of "You're about to be the new host of *Late Night,* and you're handing me a Golden Globe I just won for my new show, and Amy and Tina are hosting and Jimmy is just about to come out and present as the new host of *The Tonight Show,* and Forte is in *Nebraska* and on his way to the stage." The *SNL* connection was pretty incredible.

That Johnny Carson deserved the title King of Late Night was a virtually inarguable position for many years. But in February of 2014, a new consensus would crown a new king: Lorne Michaels not only remained executive producer of SNL *but also became executive producer of* The Tonight Show, *Johnny's old domain—which relocated back to Michaels's beloved New York City after a forty-two-year layover in Los Angeles. Michaels also became executive producer of* Late Night, *hosted by the transplanted Seth Meyers. If the title of king were not enough, Michaels was also hailed as Comedy's Most Important Man . . . Ever by the* Hollywood Reporter.

That importance had grown steadily over the years before exploding in the second decade of the twenty-first century. Michaels's relationship with Conan O'Brien, for instance, dated back to 1988, when he hired O'Brien, an alumnus of The Simpsons *and HBO's* Not Necessarily the News, *as a staff writer on* Saturday Night Live. *Then in 1993, when David Letterman left NBC and his* Late Night *show for CBS and the profitable post-*Tonight *hour threatened to disintegrate, Michaels took a big chance and backed O'Brien to be the new host of a Michaels-produced* Late Night, *standing by him through lacerating early reviews and denunciations from network executives. O'Brien turned the show around, became a hit, and graduated, as his contract stipulated, to* The Tonight Show *upon Jay Leno's departure. Then a tide seemed to turn. Industry insiders and outsiders were surprised that O'Brien did not ask Michaels* *to produce the revamped* Tonight Show, *which promptly imploded, with Leno returning awkwardly and O'Brien, along with executive producer Jeff Ross, exiled to cable.*

JEFF ZUCKER, *Former NBC Universal CEO:*

Unfortunately, Conan and Jeff didn't want Lorne involved with their *Tonight Show*. It's one of the reasons they wanted to do the show in Los Angeles. I'm pretty convinced that if Lorne had been part of the show, none of it would have ended the way it did. Because of my relationship with Lorne, I am sure he would have figured it out and Lorne would have handled it.

STEVE BURKE, *NBC Universal CEO:*

I called Jay and went and saw him on a Sunday afternoon in April 2013. I said to Jay, "I'm not going to *tell* you what we're going to do. You and I are going to *figure out* what we should do. I want to know what you think." I said, "I think we can virtually guarantee you'll be number one if you leave before the Sochi Olympics and you'll guarantee Jimmy a great platform. I think it's actually better for you to leave a little early." And he said, "Okay," just like that. He was a pleasure to work with. Jay said, "Every other time, somebody has come here and told me what to do; they'd already made the decision. You didn't." And I said, "Well, if we tell you to do something, and you don't want to do it, it's not going to work. You have to want to do it." And that made all the difference in the world.

The day after Fallon's *Tonight Show* went on the air, I went down to Lorne's office. I'd only been in his office three or four times and I closed the door and said, "Thank you." He wanted to talk about other stuff, but I said, "No. I'm just here to thank you. I knew you were promoting this—I knew at every dinner you were doing it and I expected it—but it was the right thing and you never pushed me and let me come to it over time."

But not all in Lorne Michaels's kingdom was golden. For Saturday Night Live, *2013 had ended on notes of discord. African American cast members Kenan Thompson and Jay Pharoah were both quoted in the press expressing displeasure at the absence of black women in the show's cast. Thompson, who'd said in an interview that he henceforth refused to dress in drag to make up for the shortage, was assailed from various quarters when he tried to amplify his remarks. One reason that black women were underrepresented on the show over the years, Thompson said, was that "in auditions, they just never find ones that are ready." That prompted a torrent of criticism from those who thought—or claimed— he'd said that there weren't many talented black women in show business. A typically indignant blogger admitted to bashing Thompson not for what he said but for "what he seemed to imply."*

Jay Pharoah made matters worse. "They need to pay attention," he said, publicly scolding SNL producers and talent scouts. Then he recommended a specific black actress, already employed elsewhere, for the cast "because she's black, first of all, and she's really talented." In Pharoah's mind, talent seemed to be coming in second. "She needs to be on SNL," he declared.

One of the show's first responses to the controversy was to satirize it and its own culpability in the minority casting department. Fortuitously enough, Kerry Washington, the black actress who stars on ABC's Scandal, had been booked to host an episode that aired just as the rhetoric escalated. For the cold open, Washington was called upon to play several black women, including First Lady Michelle Obama—dashing on and off the set to change costumes and characters—obviously because there weren't any black women in the cast to play them. SNL got credit for laughing at itself, but some critics took to their keyboards to trounce the show further for an allegedly abysmal record on minority casting.

Audition sessions were convened, the first in SNL history to focus on one particular sex and ethnic group, and as 2014 began, it was grandly announced that Sasheer Zamata, a member of the Upright Citizens Brigade, had been hired. The hubbub subsided, though a few critics still complained about other minorities supposedly underrepresented on the show.

KENAN THOMPSON:

Men in drag has always been a comedy thing. Comedians do it because it's an automatic shock factor, basically. Jerry Lewis and Flip Wilson owned both sides of the spectrum. Everybody's done it, so to me it wasn't that much of a mystery. For me it started doing grandmas. I started doing things so young and it was, "Do a grandma type of a character." And then I got more into current ladies, so it'll be like a Star Jones or a Whoopi Goldberg. I love Whoopi.

JAMES DOWNEY:

I don't think of Kenan having played that many specific black women. Obviously he's done black characters who were women, but I don't remember him ever playing Michelle Obama or anything like that.

LORNE MICHAELS:

I'd personally looked at fifty or sixty [auditions by black women]. But we're always about finding people who are funny. I think when Jay was asked about that, he denied saying it, but it doesn't matter. The point was, we had that many people.

I think what triggered it is that on Tina's show there was that game-show thing. Rob Klein wrote it as this guy's joke with me coming out and, I don't know, I say, "Is it the black one?" and then Kenan says, "I can't believe it. I've been here for, like, nine years, you guys like me..." And he was into a long thing about how he thought he was a son to me. If you look at the script, you'll see that between dress and air, Seth cut it down because he just felt, "Oh, let's just get out on 'Is it the black one?' [It] was a huge laugh at dress." So we didn't get the Kenan reaction, which was the joke for me—you know, even the guy I have known for ten years, I think he's new, and that's how out of touch I am.

KENAN THOMPSON:

It's not good when everybody starts staring at you and like, "What was that?" People take different pieces of a partial quote, basically. If the whole quote was there, it would be much clearer. People can get nasty. It's never my intention to down my own people, that's just crazy, and the way people took it made zero sense as well, but whatever—people make their opinions how they make their opinions. But at the end of the day, Sasheer is here, she's great, Leslie [Jones]'s got a job as a writer, and that's a great day.

JAY PHAROAH:

I learned what happens when you're just not cautious. You have to be cautious, and I've been warned to be *very* cautious. You can't be as relaxed and not on alert for everybody, because there's always stories that people are trying to put out. Things get taken out of context all the time because people that write stories are always looking for what sells.

LORNE MICHAELS:

Literally, Jay didn't know it was a reporter. I thought it was an unfair thing because it wasn't like we didn't have any African Americans auditioning—we had four or five—or that we weren't looking for women. That was my fault. We lost four men, and we had just brought three women in the year before. And we went back and forth and there was one girl we really liked from Chicago. We brought her back thinking that would work. You can tell in the studio. I loved it onstage in Chicago, but unless they're standing on home base and have that other thing, you know—and the worst thing you can do is put someone on who's not ready. The audience makes up their mind quickly; then the writing staff and other people start being favored. You want to be able to protect whoever you bring out.

FINESSE MITCHELL, *Cast Member:*

At first when you get there, you're so excited just to be on the show. Maybe you don't really care that you have to always dress as the woman if we need a black woman—like if we need Oprah you're going to be Gayle [King], or something like that. And you don't necessarily think about it in your first year, and in your second year, you're like, "Man! It's easy to do black women, but it would probably be easier if they just *hired* a black woman." I was very proud of *SNL* for getting somebody this year. It had been a long time, since probably Maya Rudolph. She was mixed, but—you know.

MAYA RUDOLPH:

It didn't have anything to do with me, but I had all kinds of relatives saying, "Your name was in *The New York Times*," and I said, "Really? About what?" I never, never thought of myself on the show as a black female, a black performer, a black cast member, and I don't identify myself that way, so I just did what I normally do, which is watch the whole thing go by and it didn't have anything to do with me. My "black phone" did not ring on the "black desk." Nothing came my way. It didn't have anything to do with me.

LINDSAY SHOOKUS:

I know how things can seem out of context and Jay's still learning and Jay has such a good heart and I adore him. I realize he's still figuring out that, the path of how to talk to people and that not everyone's your friend.

Kenan's a pro and I know at the end of the day he knew exactly what he was trying to say. We're always looking for funny people, and in basic terms, he was like, "It's their jobs, they're going to find somebody, just give them a second." But, you know, it's such a sensitive subject and you have to be very careful.

ERIN DOYLE:

I think everyone felt really bad for Kenan and for Jay. They both love this show and I think most of what they said was misinterpreted in some way. Kenan, especially, felt like what he said was misinterpreted, unfortunately. But, you know, they were fine. This place moves so quickly, sometimes you don't even notice what's happening outside of it.

LORNE MICHAELS:

No one's more loyal to us, and to the show, than Kenan. During the flap about ethnic casting, Kenan was trying to say, "It doesn't work if they're not ready." But you can't use that language anymore. You can't say, "If he's not ready." Believe me, we were protested by Asians, by Latinos, by others. It isn't that you're not doing it, but we are now perceived as a national institution. But we are not taxpayer-funded, you know?

KEN AYMONG:

I just wish it hadn't been *publicly* done. That's all I can really say about it. I just wish it hadn't been that direction. I don't think Lorne really needed a push to do anything. Maybe from a timing standpoint he did; now it certainly does appear that way.

KERRY WASHINGTON, *Host:*

It was so weird because all that stuff about Kenan and what he was saying about the lack of women of color on the show, African American women in particular, came out the week before I was going on. People had this misconception that I was booked because of that controversy, when in fact I had already been booked for a long time! So it was a very strange serendipity that all that unfolded around the same time.

AL SHARPTON, *Host:*

They parodied me during the Obama campaign; they parodied me when I started my TV show. I mean, look: I think that on one level you can get sensitive about how you're being parodied but on another level it's the biggest show of its kind on TV. It makes you relevant, and the assumption is that if they parody you on *SNL* you've made it. I guess the downside is you become the butt of a comedic joke. The upside is that you remain relevant in American pop culture. I've been parodied more than most, but I think of it as a compliment. I just wish Kenan would lose some weight before he does me. I'm not that fat anymore. Kenan needs to take off about fifty pounds to play me.

Lorne called me and said that he wanted me to do a skit around this controversy over not enough black women on *SNL*, and I said, "Fine." We were going to pre-tape it on Friday night; I said that I could do it right after my MSNBC show, so we went up to Lorne's office, taped me coming in and Lorne arguing with Kerry Washington about blacks. She was going on about this "high-powered black leader Sharpton in the audience," and it's like, "Oh wow," 'cause I'm sitting right there in the office. Then at the end of taping, Lorne says, "I wish you could do this live." I was scheduled to preach in Richmond, Virginia, on Sunday morning, and that's why we were pre-taping. And I said, "Well, I don't know," and Kerry said, "You should open the show. You should do the signature line, 'Live from New York, it's *Saturday Night!*'" And I said, "*Now* you're talking." That's when we shifted.

So Lorne had me do the opening thing. I ended up driving eight hours to preach that morning in Virginia, but I know in pop culture what that signature thing means, and so I stayed and did it, got in a car, drove all night to keep my sermon obligation the next morning in Richmond. And I thought it was a powerful punch line, like here she showed the exhaustive thing of trying to play all these black women characters because there were no black women to play them, and I was the one who did the signature part of it by saying, "Yeah, and you won't believe none of this because really, in many ways, the cause is a resigned cause, but live—it's *Saturday Night*." I think the balance of her showing that, and how America sees me as a protest leader at these kinds of things—I thought it was great. Particularly because Lorne had already said that he was going to hire "some black women." I just thought it was good, and I tease Lorne and say, "From '03 to '13—I'm just going to have to wait until '23 for my next appearance."

KERRY WASHINGTON:

The character I play on *Scandal* is this fixer person and I thought, "Oh, this is the ultimate irony"—that I'm being called in to fix this scandal, the *SNL* scandal, even though that wasn't really the case. But I did feel like I wanted to be especially courageous about the work in light of all that. I remember there was back and forth about do we address it or do we not address it, and I was like, "Of course we address it!" We don't *not* address it, we go in and do it, and it took a while to figure out exactly the right way to do it. We had two different cold opens that we worked on, but I love the one we did of me playing all the characters. I was actually with Oprah Winfrey at dinner a few nights later, and we were laughing about it because she texted me right after: "That was awesome!"

There was another pre-taped video piece of Lorne calling me into his office and saying, "We really have enjoyed having you around this week" and basically trying to bamboozle me into signing a seven-year contract with the show—because at that time there were no black women on the show. And I kept saying, "Lorne, I have a job. I have to go back to L.A.," and he said, "Yeah, yeah, I know, it's fine, we'll be totally flexible with you, just sign right here." So it was fun, but it didn't make it into the show. It's better when the cold open is live.

ERIN DOYLE:

It was kind of fun to watch Lorne cut himself from the show.

KERRY WASHINGTON:

Eminem was also really so perfect, because for me there was such fantastic irony of being "the black woman" on the show while there was all this buzz about *not* having a black woman on the show—and then to have this incredible hip-hop icon who is a white man, it's this fantastic juxtaposition. And I am a complete hip-hop child, a product of the hip-hop generation. I grew up in the Bronx in the '80s, and to be able to introduce him and be there while he was performing live, I'll just never forget it. I think he's one of the most talented musicians of our time and a real icon for me, as a member of hip-hop culture. So it was pretty awesome!

PAULA PELL:

I was happy to see the issue being discussed. It was certainly something that I think the show could benefit from, and I'm glad that the discussion happened. I've had experiences even with gay stuff that people got so fired up about. There was a gay sketch that I wrote, or James wrote, back in the day, and they just assumed that there was absolutely no one aware of that at the show, that it's just a bunch of young straight white men. Some people would get so mad. I wrote this sketch for Ellen Page years ago where she was a young girl that came back from a Melissa Etheridge concert, and Andy Samberg was her boyfriend, and it was based on my youth. For a couple of years after my first girlfriend, I was dating guys; I would go to some gay event and come home and was just super-crazy fired up, and I'd be like, "Oh my God, there were just so many women there and they were just so powerful!" I was way too hyped up and excited about where I was at. And so afterwards I had a few people on the Internet bashing it, and some were obviously gay women bashing it in a way that was like, "They need to get a lesbian in *SNL* to write a sketch like that so they can use the right references. Melissa Etheridge is clearly an old, stereotypical lesbian reference." So I wrote the blogger back and said, "I'm the writer and I'm an old dyke, and"—I didn't say "dyke," but I did say, "I'm an old lesbian who still has Melissa Etheridge on cassette in her car, so, you know, sleep well tonight, because your assumption was not correct."

So sometimes I think the show is a good target for people thinking we're completely clueless, and that's just not true. Also, there were many times with auditions, you know, we weren't getting as many diverse people that we needed to, to pick people—you don't want to pick people that aren't funny just because of what community they represent. That is to me in any show—*anything*—tragic, because it is not helping anyone; it's not helping the person that's there, because they're probably not going to be successful, and you know you've got to find them. You've got to find people who are great, and I think because it was an issue that we discussed, we got some really great people to pick from, and picked some really great writers and actors. So it turned out good; it's just always difficult in the middle with all that stuff.

AMY POEHLER:

I will go on record to say that I think Lorne Michaels has done more for women in comedy than anyone I know.

JAMES DOWNEY:

I think that over the long haul, it probably takes care of itself. Kenan has, I would argue, been just a rock for the entire stretch that he's been on the show. This year he has been in my estimation the strongest individual cast member, and sometimes I see him almost single-handedly carry the show. It may be that he's more actually essential to the show this year over some previous years, just because there were other good people too in previous years—I mean, other people about as good as Kenan.

It's not about percentages. They're all individuals. Eddie Murphy dominated the show like probably no other individual ever has; Will Ferrell maybe is a close second. Being a black male doesn't have much to do with that. It's just who he was. I'm sure that he would have been like a superstar in any time that we did the show, but the fact that he was there in a period where he completely dominated wasn't a matter of policy. It was just about his talent and, you know, the environment and so on.

SASHEER ZAMATA, *Cast Member:*

Actually it took me a while even to go back and look up what the interview was. They misconstrued what he was saying. It didn't really matter. I just kind of thank God they said *something,* because that starts this whole search for a black girl. But I didn't really care what they said.

LINDSAY SHOOKUS:

It was stressful just because it was all over the media. It was being covered in a way that I felt like, as it often is, fairly one-sided. I was sensitive because I had to spend three months in the summer traveling all over the country and watching a million DVDs. I had a four-month-old, and I traveled six weeks straight to try and find really funny and talented cast members. You know, the thing that I learned when I first started at *SNL* was "We look for funny." There's always types you might want, but at the end of the day, we hire funny. And so I spent the entire summer looking for funny, and I know what I was looking for. I know I'm just looking for funny people—anyone: women, men, black, white, doesn't matter. And so I really felt that I had unturned a lot of stones, so yeah, I was a little sensitive to the criticism.

I saw Sasheer four years ago at an improv show. She had a three-person improvisation team and I thought immediately she had such a beautiful look and she was really interesting, but she needed a lot of time to grow. I asked her to send me some tape, but she didn't send me a tape that last summer; she decided she wasn't quite ready to send it and so she took her time. So I never really got to see her until I started really searching in the fall. But yeah, Sasheer seemed like a perfect fit once we saw how much she had grown in the last year and a half.

In that time, probably like a three-month period, I'm going to guess, only one agent called me about an African American woman. You know, it was in the papers; everyone was talking about it, it was a huge story for us, and yet no managers or agents were ever calling me saying, "You've got to see my client." It shocked me how much we had to really go out there and search at a different kind of level, because no representation were calling us about any African American women. Even with it being a huge story, like, "Oh, they're going to be looking for somebody."

There's no right thing to say at the end of the day. And all I can say now is I'm really glad that we have Sasheer. Sasheer's a real talent.

SASHEER ZAMATA:

I really tried hard not to look at the Internet. I tried my hardest not to look at articles and stuff like that. All the talk about me possibly being on the show before I auditioned didn't really matter because that's talk that has happened before, and all the blogs talking about a lack of diversity on the show and saying, well, here's a list of funny black women who could be on the show and I was usually on those lists. I would see that because people would post them on Facebook or tag me or e-mail it to me. And I thought, well, it's very nice because if nothing else I'm getting a lot of publicity right now and more traffic to my website, so that's pretty cool. But then it got to the point where they were saying things like, "These are the ladies who are auditioning, and they are going into the studios to audition on Monday," and they had all these details about what was actually happening and that I did not like at all, because I wish I could have just done it inside like everybody else and if I didn't get it, then cool. If that happened, and I didn't get it, then like many comedians I'd go do something else and no one would know. As opposed to everyone knowing that I could have gotten it but then didn't. Or if I got it, then it would be a cool surprise. But everyone knew I had auditioned and was anticipating and waiting to see.

I was in my bed. That's where I was for the previous two weeks. I was in my bed for, like, the whole process. I really didn't want to go out and talk to people. There was a thirty-day period between when I auditioned and when I found out that I was on the show. I didn't want to talk about it, but I guess I saw people at theaters or wherever and it was like, "So do you know anything?" and "What's the process like?"—and I just didn't want to talk to people. So to avoid that, I stayed in bed all the time.

So I was in my bed, my phone was by my side, as it had been for the previous three weeks. And I walked out of my room for two seconds and talked to my roommate and came back and saw a string of calls on my phone. So I called back and it was like, "I'm going to patch you through to Lorne Michaels's office." I was on the bed and had the phone to my ear and they kept me on hold for I don't know how long and I was like, "Why do you still have me waiting? You've already kept me waiting for so long!" And then Lorne got on and he was like, "So this is a happy call," and I was like, "Okay," and I go sinking into the bed. My head was getting more and more buried in the bed the more he spoke, but yes, he was, "We like you, we want you on the show, we think you'll do well." When I hung up, I started screaming. My roommate was there and he could see me and he was like, "Is it good?" I just yelled, "I'm on the show!" And I started jumping up and down.

SETH MEYERS:

I was certainly around when that was going down and it was very exciting. One of the great things about being at *SNL* is being there for someone's first show. Because the show has such great cultural significance, no one gets a job without understanding what it means. To be there for someone's first show is something you'll never forget, and Sasheer's was the last first show I was ever there for, so that has special significance for me.

SASHEER ZAMATA:

I was super excited. I was like, "Let's do it. Let's go ahead and do it." It was a crazy day. I turned my phone off. My mom and her brother are in town: I told them how to get here and be in the audience, but I said, "Now I'm turning my phone off. You can't contact me; I'm not going to turn it on 'til after the show." I knew there was going to be craziness. My phone blew up when there was news I was auditioning. People were texting me and e-mailing me and Tweeting at me. The day I was going into an audition they were like, "Good luck today," and I was like, "Oh, that was so annoying; you shouldn't know this information." And then when I got it—much more: three hundred text messages and a ton of e-mails; it was just too much. So the day of the show I was, "I really don't want to deal with any of this," and I said, "I'm turning off my phone, just shutting it off, and I'm going to focus on what I have to do today."

CECILY STRONG:

You don't win anything in the public. We're going to hire Sasheer and then it's going to be another thing. At the beginning of the year it was: "How will you survive without Jason, Bill, Fred?" And then that's the big controversy all summer: "Is the show dead without Jason, Bill...?" That's the big thing. And then it's the "racist." What's next?

I'm glad to have her. I was so impressed. I was like, "This girl is cool as a cucumber" and just—elegant. Just handling that so well. And it's funny: Nobody noticed the Kerry Washington opening that we did—they had done years ago with Jan Hooks. They did a similar sketch—Jan Hooks kept running out because a new woman was coming in. This was a year where they only had two women, and now the cast, the repertory cast, is 50 percent female for the first time, and it bothered me that why can't we celebrate *that*? We're not even allowed to say that in public because we don't have a woman of the right color. We have two women of color, but they're not the right color. It was an interesting, eye-opening experience just for race in America. Anyways, I thought it was interesting, all the people who were like, "Nasim doesn't count. Biracial doesn't count." It was just interesting to see what counts and what doesn't.

SASHEER ZAMATA:

I think I'm more recognizable than some of the people in the cast because my picture is *everywhere*. I've been stopped almost every day since my first show. I take the subway and I live in Brooklyn and it's changed, but not to the point where I can't go anywhere. Everyone's saying real nice things, but I like my privacy and don't like having attention when I'm not asking for it.

No one expressed more surprise at seeing Seth Meyers on the cover of Time *magazine in January of 2014 than Seth Meyers. The witty and self-effacing SNL head writer, who'd anchored or coanchored "Weekend Update" for seven seasons, Meyers was not named Time's Man of the Year, but the magazine did make him the cover boy when it put out its forecast for the year ahead. The magazine declared Meyers "cerebral and incisive," two sterling qualities that helped him exert a profound influence over the show on the air and behind the scenes.*

SETH MEYERS:

Look, somebody like me doesn't get on the cover of *Time* magazine if it's not a slow news week. Hopefully you can tell by my tone here that I was as surprised as anyone to be on the cover of *Time*. If it had been someone other than me, I would probably be making fun of them. America knows who I am because I was on "Weekend Update." They didn't know who I was when I was just on the show as a cast member. It's the thing Lorne always says about "Update" anchors: You get to tell people your name every week. You do that enough and, certainly in my case, and in Jimmy's case before me, then maybe they'll give you a show with your name on it. Andy, who is as close a friend as I've ever had on the show, was doing some sketch of his that he was going to try to do a second time, and it had not struck me the first time as something that would be recurring, and he mentioned to me, "I was thinking about doing another one of these," and in the way you can be with friends, I went, *"Another one?!"* And he just sort of snapped back: "I don't get ten minutes every week!" I think cast members are still very aware of the advantages that an "Update" anchor has over everyone else.

The whole thing, especially with getting *Late Night* up on its feet, is that I tried so hard to keep the schedule in a way that made the last Saturday feel more like a regular Saturday. There were obviously the added machinations of trying to make sure we figured out how to do the good-bye on "Update," which, with everybody behind us, was sort of easier than I thought it would be.

ANDY SAMBERG:

I love Seth forever, he's the greatest, and one thing I will never forget about Seth is that when I first got hired, he had every reason to ignore me or let me figure it out on my own—you know, a bunch of new people come up every year—but Seth went out of his way to take me under his wing, to help me out, check in on me, and just went totally out of his way to be like an older brother figure and a mentor to me, and I'll never forget that. He didn't have to do it, but he did do it, because he's just a kind, good person.

STEVE BURKE:

I don't see why people were nervous about having Lorne extend his influence. When you have someone like Lorne, and his motivation is good, he makes those around him better every single day. I looked at it and said, "Why not have the Saturday night *fraternity* do as much as they can?" When you watch Jimmy Fallon with Tina Fey and see Amy Poehler on the first Seth Meyers show, why would you not welcome and applaud that?

Part of it is, Lorne comes into their lives at a time that's very special for them. They're young, they've never really had this kind of success, and he's there with them when they go through that. I've never fought in the army, but I would imagine it's the way people feel when they've been on the battlefield together—it's just such a vivid time of their life. So when they are super successful the way Jimmy Fallon is and the way Seth Meyers is, they remember that, and their relationship with Lorne is colored by it.

I think that late night is doing better now on a relative basis as the rest of broadcasting is declining. You get a two and a half demo rating on a Saturday night, you're one of the twenty highest-rated shows on television. But it's not necessarily about every nickel and dime. You look at this big company with twenty-two different businesses—we have a lot of cable channels that make a lot more money than *Saturday Night Live*—but it's right in the core of the DNA of the company, the soul of the company, the heart of the building. When I give somebody a tour of this building, the first place I bring them to is Studio 8H. To me, that's us, that's NBC, that's what we do here.

STEVE HIGGINS:

Chevy left. It's a place designed where people leave. And that's why I believe it's successful too, because each cast and each new staff, it's their show, it's a different show. Lorne's hand isn't so iron-fisted where it's like, "I'm an auteur." It's like, "I'm here to give you an environment where you are free to create things that aren't judged by people who don't do comedy." It's the only show on earth where the writer has a voice, where a writer can go and talk to the cast and the writer is the producer of his piece. Because when Lorne worked on *Laugh-In,* he would see the pieces that he wrote and he'd go, "I didn't do that!" He'd be watching it from a monitor in the writers' building, fifty feet from the stage, and he couldn't go down and talk to anybody, so when he made a show, he wanted to make sure that that was the case. So every new cast brings a new thing. Will's show is different than Sandler's show is different than Andy Samberg's show is different than Seth's—everybody brings their own thing to it and their own personality comes through. And that's why I believe the main reason it's a success—because it's not, "Here's what we do on this show. It's codified. It's all these things" or "This is what makes *Saturday Night Live*—this, this, this, and this." Every year is different. We have lost first Kristen and then Andy and then Bill, Fred, Jason, and Seth and Forte right before that and then Ferrell left—everybody leaves.

But then Kenan and Taran and Bobby, and all the girls, you forget that these girls have only been here two seasons. Everybody stepped up to the plate. Kate, Aidy, Cecily, Vanessa, Nasim, and the rest. All boats rose with the tide. It could have went the other way.

And also, everything takes longer now, that's the thing. TV is so spread out now. It's not like the old days where one appearance on Carson would make your career. Even when I first started, it took people five seasons to really get to know Will Ferrell—and he was in every single sketch. From my memory, it wasn't until he started playing Bush and stuff that people really came to know him. Comedy people loved him instantly, but it's a big country. It takes a long time to get to know anybody. And I think these guys are doing as good as they can.

KENAN THOMPSON:

When you're lucky enough to have a run on *SNL,* you're not really that excited to leave it, but it is one of those inevitable things; you can't stay forever. I've always had my agents and my lawyers and we all sit down and try to go make something happen. But at the end of the day, I've got to go into the room and get the part. The only thing I can do is try to keep my chops up and make sure that they're looking around for different roles and doing their jobs and stuff, and I go to meet the Rob Reiners and the different directors or whatever and try to get that role, basically. That's the ongoing thing as an actor if I want to just be an actor. That also pushes me into wanting to write more for myself and produce things, and that way I don't have to audition all the time. If I can come up with an idea that suits me, and that I can use to convince other people to give me money, and then go do it, that's probably the ultimate, especially for a comedian.

SETH MEYERS:

I think that I've done a really good job of appreciating it while I was there, and I'll sort of always know how special it was to work on that show, and so I was just trying to make the most of the last chance to say good-bye to everybody. You know, probably the easiest thing to mock about the show is those good nights at the end because it seems so strange that people who work together all week would have to hug each other at the end of each show on Saturdays — but there is something very real about needing to have to check in with everybody after everything you've gone through the rest of the week.

BOBBY MOYNIHAN:

I've gotten lucky. Everyone says, like, "*My* 'Update' characters," but it's really me and Seth's characters. We found it together, I feel like. And it's going to be weird doing it with somebody else. One of the great things that will benefit me is I wrote most of the Drunk Uncles and Anthony Crispinos with Colin Jost, who is now going to be the "Update" guy. As a matter of fact, Anthony Crispino is the name of one of his close friends from high school; I met him this summer.

COLIN JOST:

Certain people are easy to write for because they generate funny things themselves and they feel like they're in the range of what your voice is. Cecily and I wrote together a lot. She was someone who I just found really funny and easy to write for. When she did that first one of those, when we wrote that first one, when she performed that on-air, 'cause it must have been one of her first four or five shows ever—she must have had just ice water in her veins, it was just such a happy moment. I remember going to Seth and just being so excited for her, and that's rare. As a writer, all you want is someone who can suck everything out of every joke and get it all out there and know the rhythm of it perfectly enough, and that's a rare thing to have immediately.

DAN AYKROYD:

I can't speak to the present too much. I do think they do a good job on "Update"; they challenge, and they're trying to speak to the power there in some of the things they do, so that's pretty good. We came out of the '60s, and the late '60s into the '70s it was rebel, rebel, rebel. You know, antiestablishment, beware of video commandos. That political sparkle that we had, it might be a little diminished now in terms of the rebel streak, but you look at "Update" and they're pretty bold, might I say.

LENA DUNHAM, *Host:*

I've been an avid watcher. I watch, if not when it's live, then the next day I catch up. And I actually was aware that maybe a *Girls* parody was coming because they had called our location scout about figuring out where some of our spots were. I was filled with excitement, and I actually went over—not to name-drop—to my friend Mindy Kaling's house, who's also great, who's a great comedienne, and we were like, "Oh my God, the *Girls* parody is on," so we turned on *SNL* and it was the first thing after Tina's monologue and we both just started screaming. To be parodied on *SNL*, be it positive or negative, is an honor. It's a cultural institution, one that's been particularly important to me. I didn't grow up in a talk-show-watching house, and I didn't—I was too young to be part of the cult of Letterman. For me, *SNL* was my paradigm of what comedy was supposed to be. I have a collection of Gilda Radner memorabilia. I have a poster of her and a couple of, like, Edie Baskin photographs of Gilda and John Belushi and some little, like, Roseanne Roseannadanna playing cards. Just, like, I love, I'm obsessed with her and obsessed with old-school *SNL* stuff.

Just realizing the full brutality of their schedule and the fact that they managed to do this week in and week out, and make it look easy, was pretty incredible. And also Lorne's level of involvement—I mean, of course you know that he's really a genius, but you think, "Okay, the show's been going on thirty-nine years. At some point Lorne's got to, like, hand this over to a couple of other people. He's got two other shows shooting in the building; he's producing five other shows; he's in a media empire; there's no way he can walk on this floor, making sure everything works." But lo and behold, you know, show night, there he is. And so just that aspect, the intensity and the full engagement, was definitely an incredible thing for me to see. Sketch comedy is broad. But somehow he is able to cut in and just sort of be so incisive about "that moment doesn't feel real" and that's the thing.

It is really amazing how Lorne was able to both express his unique vision and foster the talent, foster the talent of different people. I mean, it's a very impressive thing, and very intoxicating. After I left I couldn't stop thinking about, like, it's a little bit like when you leave summer camp when you're a teenager and all you want to do is talk about your camp friends. My boyfriend was just like, "I love you, I'm so proud of you, you need to stop talking about *SNL*."

TARAN KILLAM:

I think the majority of people who watch the show's sketches now watch them online. I will get compliments from very close friends and family like, "That sketch you did last week was the funniest thing I've ever seen." Well, I'd done it two years ago. There's still the die-hard audience who tune in every Saturday night, but I think the masses at this point are tuning in for segments and are not necessarily watching a full show. The show was built for the Internet before the Internet existed, with these little three-to-five-minute videos and eight to ten of them a week.

"Saturday Night Dead" is a cliché, and "Are they going to survive?" is now less a question of "if" and more a question of "how."

BRIAN WILLIAMS, *Host*:

The thing is, even if you put a blindfold on me, I would know if you sat me in 8H. It has its own smell, a lot of it owing to old paint cans under the rafters. There's no place I would rather be at eleven thirty on a Saturday night, when they set the hands of that clock, and Chris, the stage manager, yells that panicked "Five seconds" to break the tension. Oh my God, there is something absolutely magic. These days I sit in the yellow seats for a couple live shows a year, but mostly I'm home on the couch with my wife and there's never been anything like it. As long as this company is willing to keep going, there are improv troupes doing shows tonight that may not know it yet, but they feature the future stars of *Saturday Night Live*.

Each generation—to borrow a famous quote from another realm of life—each generation gets the *SNL* it deserves.

STEVE BURKE:

Lorne is completely unique. I don't think there's another executive like Lorne. I also think the fact that Lorne has been doing it as long as he has, and loves it as much as he does, gives him the ability to do it better than anybody else could possibly do it. I can't even think of another show that's so identified with a single person. I believe the show itself defies gravity. It breaks so many rules and that's why there's only one. So I think the question of does the show survive after Lorne leaves is real—just obviously not a happy one. But as long as Lorne is vertical, he wants to do the job, and it's a great show, he's going to be doing it.

The great comedian Jack Benny wanted to stay thirty-nine forever—a sentiment unlikely to be shared by those who create and perform Saturday Night Live. *Its thirty-ninth season was by no means one of its most memorable. In fact, it wound up being just what some had predicted for it—a transitional year, driven by a core group of cast members performing material of varying quality that resulted in less-than-auspicious ratings. Nobody wants "transitional year" on their record.*

The season averaged a 4.0 rating, putting it below many previous seasons and way below presidential campaign years, although still making it more popular than many a prime-time show. SNL's ratings have fluctuated for most of the show's roller-coaster history; in the twenty-first century, there has been one new wrinkle: The omnipresent Internet, which has made it possible for millions to see SNL material without ever watching the show. Those added eyes are not counted, at least not yet, by Nielsen.

One truism seems to ring truer than ever: The show is increasingly host and musical-guest dependent. Simply trotting out a hot young actor about to open in a movie doesn't cut it. The larger problem for season thirty-nine was that the repertory company wasn't strong enough, nor the bench deep enough, to draw huge and enthusiastic crowds week in and out.

On a good night, even in a transitional year, the comedy could still click, and a hot cold open would get the show off to an uproarious roar — as on the night that Leonardo DiCaprio surprised host Jonah Hill, joining him to reenact a scene from Titanic mid-monologue. On a bad night, many a viewer had to be scratching their heads and wondering, "What the hell is supposed to be funny about that?"

Fortunately for Saturday Night Live and those who love it, this situation could change tomorrow or the day after that. You just never know. No one does. That's the agony and the ecstasy of the thing.

Even now, Saturday Night Live performers and writers of the future may be limbering up at a junior high school in the Midwest or an inner-city kindergarten or a college humor magazine — watching the show each week, reviewing it with their friends the next morning, irked and lonely on those Saturday nights when there's not a new offering.

And isn't it likely that however often the show is declared to be on the critical list, even those who claim never to watch it anymore would hate like hell to see it go?

America is a country that dotes on itself. It demands perpetual amusement and relishes spoofs of its own passing parade. When Saturday Night Live is at its best, it serves as one big selfie, reflecting an artful vision of who and where we are at the moment. SNL may be the brainchild of one man, but we all seem to have some kind of stake in it, and in its well being.

At a memorial service for the great film critic Pauline Kael, her daughter recalled Kael's unflagging enthusiasm for Saturday Night Live. Kael would invite friends over to watch it, and if they complained about the quality of a particular episode, Kael would say to them dismissively, "Oh well, they're just having a bad night." Everybody has a bad night now and then. It's having had so many good ones that's important — and, after thirty-nine seasons, still astonishing.

9

Lorne

Yes, baskets of popcorn do sit around his office. Yes, he's something of a health nut who takes conscientiously good care of himself. But none of the little details about Lorne Michaels quite compares to one imposing fact: In forty years of live shows, except for a five-year hiatus, he has never missed a single telecast. Whatever was happening in the world at large, or in his own world, Michaels has always been there when Saturday Night Live *went on the air and, ninety minutes later, when it went off. It is indeed a pristine and perfect attendance record, but Michaels doesn't like to talk about it. He thinks it might be "bad juju" — that is, to discuss it would be to tempt fate.*

The show must go on, as the old adage says — but not without Lorne.

ALAN ZWEIBEL, *Writer:*

I remember Gilda used to say that she would search through Lorne's desk hoping that she'd find a note in there that said, "I really like Gilda."

JULIA SWEENEY, *Cast Member:*

I came into the office one day at the end of my first year and said to Christine Zander, "Oh my God, I had a dream about having sex with Lorne last night." And she stopped everything and her body froze and she turned to me, like suddenly it was so like in a cult, and she said, "Julia, we all have those dreams. And I just want you to know it doesn't have anything to do with sex. It has everything to do with power. Maybe that will help you."

STEVE BURKE, *NBC Universal CEO:*

The first time I called Lorne, I said, "Lorne, I'm Steve Burke. You may have read that we just did this deal and I have this list of twenty-five people that I'm calling—Brian Williams, Jeff Zucker, and others—to have breakfast, lunch, or dinner with me sometime in the next month or so to introduce myself, and you're right at the top of my list." There was a long pause and then Lorne said, "Well, breakfast will *never* happen."

ANNE BEATTS, *Writer:*

I've probably had more conversations about Lorne than anybody in my life other than my parents. He was a mentor and a very powerful figure in all of our lives. I do think that he tended to criticize more than to praise, in terms of a management style. But since that also reflected my father, I guess I felt fairly comfortable with that. Maybe he picked people who were dysfunctional in such a way that they did feel comfortable with that.

FRED WOLF, *Writer:*

I had a turbulent family life and my dad wasn't around that much, and I just think Lorne is the greatest. I'd be furious at him and I'd be like really happy sometimes and other times I'd be sullen, but he's just the greatest guy that I've come in contact with, certainly in my career. Some people can get away with everything with him, and some people he just would never give a break to, and you can never really figure out why.

WILL FORTE, *Cast Member:*

At 30 Rock there's the weird elevator system where you have to go down to the sixteenth floor and walk around the corner to take another elevator that will take you down to the bottom floor. We all got into the elevator, and Lorne was walking down the hall toward us. It was a very crowded elevator, and he just said, "It's all right. I'll get the next one." So the elevator doors shut, we go down one floor, the doors open, we walk around to the other elevators, and Lorne is there. It was impossible. It was just like he had a time machine.

And we said, "Lorne! What are you doing there? How did you get here?" And he looked at us and said, "I'm magic."

TINA FEY, *Cast Member:*

He's not terribly effusive. He does not give it out so easily, and that just makes you want to get praise and approval from him more. I think that people who most adamantly deny that they would want that approval are probably the ones who want it the most.

MARILYN SUZANNE MILLER, *Writer:*

I read a thing in the *Times* about Tina Fey and she said something like, "Well, you really want to please Daddy," with regard to Lorne. But Jesus, we thought he was Daddy when I was twenty-five and he was thirty. He was that strict father even when we were kids. You would always look to Lorne for approval. You wanted this father figure to say that was good. But I don't feel by not saying that stuff he was hurting people. He wasn't going, "I'm not speaking to you because your sketch didn't go well." He was that strict father who'd only tell you you did good when you did incredibly good.

I remember once he came up to me and said, "You did good," and that was like him giving me a giant house in the Hamptons and a garage full of cars.

LARAINE NEWMAN, *Cast Member:*

Lorne was so close to our age, and because he was the person he was, he was uncomfortable being "the boss." I don't think he liked the barrier that that put between him and having true friendships with the people he worked with. I think the worst you can say is that he mismanaged or underestimated the impact he had on people who depended on him, and when he couldn't make it good for them, how betrayed they felt. It's tough, but I think that's why a lot of people felt that the rug was pulled out from under them. I did too. I just felt like he was my guardian, you know, he had brought me from Los Angeles to do this show, yet all these people were getting more airtime than I was. I thought, why wasn't he protecting me? Why wasn't he making sure that I had as much time as anybody else? And it's because I was one of many. It's not as if he said to me, "Tough shit," you know, or "That's the way it is," or "Love it or leave it." He really tried to work with me. He really tried.

CHRISTINE ZANDER, *Writer:*

We worked with him before he had children, and I think we were probably all his children before he had children. Lorne somehow manages to be a paternal figure, and I think that's because he enjoys being a father. If he didn't make eye contact with me for a day, I thought, okay, for sure I'm fired. And there would be nothing to support that paranoia.

JANE CURTIN, *Cast Member:*

I think he picked the right profession, because he gets to lord over people who want to kneel at his feet and he doesn't acknowledge them — which makes them work harder.

ANA GASTEYER, *Cast Member:*

I think a lot of us are comfortable with or afflicted by or taken with distant fathers. I'm sure there's a lot of alcoholism in a lot of families connected to the show, that's what I gather. People here are comfortable with chaos. People here are comfortable with distance, with what's not being said, and being able to read what's not being said. So I think that there's a comfort with Lorne's silence for a lot of us.

ADAM SANDLER, *Cast Member:*

Lorne does have a great way of making you feel comfortable. He can also make you feel nervous if he chooses to. But when Lorne would tell a cast member that their skit was funny or you did a good job in a particular bit that you did on the show, it felt great and it really helped your confidence. You felt secure and you felt like, "This guy's seen a lot of different styles of comedy," and he made you feel part of a cool group.

JON LOVITZ, *Cast Member:*

Lorne says I made him like my dad, which I didn't, but he was the boss, you know, and you want to please the boss. But he would say to me, "Come to me with any career problems or any problems you have." I was supposed to do a movie with him and it didn't happen. He blames the studio, and he told a friend of mine that it was my fault, and I got really angry. So then I said stuff about him and it all got back to him, so for four years we really didn't get along. But the last few shows we made up.

I think a lot of us have mixed feelings for Lorne. We're so grateful that he hired us and gave us this opportunity that we'd do anything for him. Then you want his approval. You want approval from your boss and the audience, and he's just not the kind of guy who could do it all the time. I confronted him once, because every Monday he'd be screaming at me. I said, "Lorne, my characters are hit characters, I'm here until seven in the morning, I write three sketches every week." Most of the other people weren't writing for themselves because they didn't know how. I said, "Do you like me? Do you have a problem with me?" Because I was determined not to be afraid of him. And then he goes, "Don't do that, it's too Jewish." I was like, "What? What's too Jewish?" And he says, "Saying you have a problem with me."

PAUL SIMON, *Host:*

That's not true that he was a father figure. No, he wasn't. He was like one of the guys. He wasn't a father figure to me. Not to Michael O'Donoghue. Not to Gilda. But Lorne became the father figure as the cast and writers became younger in comparison to his age. And I think that was one of his big transitional points, when he realized that he wasn't one of their contemporaries; when he wasn't one of the boys and he wasn't looked upon as one of the gang. I think that's when he started to act separate from everybody. He used to wear jeans and a blazer. Then he became a suit-and-tie guy.

CANDICE BERGEN, *Host:*

To me, one of the most—if not the most—interesting aspects is the relationship of Lorne to the cast. And all of the permutations that Lorne, as father figure, or as authority figure, goes through. There's a kind of ambivalence that the cast had for someone who had really found them and put them in this and created their careers. It's just unbelievable the number of talents that have come out of that show. And the resentment of Lorne is consistent with being a father figure and an authority figure—the desperate need for attention and for Lorne's approval. These people went through all of this transference with Lorne as the father figure, with all the attendant complexities of it. The relationship of the cast to Lorne was just very complicated. Even to trying to keep people clean, trying to keep people sober, to keep people straight. I always felt Lorne was never given anywhere near the credit that he deserved for really having such an impact on our culture and on comedy and on television.

DARRELL HAMMOND, *Cast Member:*

He was the boss. He met with me when he needed to meet with me and I think he understood me really well. I didn't know him as well as other people knew him, but I knew him to be a very strong boss. His advice was strong and final.

Anyone can second-guess anyone else, but when we would go out there for the live show, his changes usually worked. He can't always be right, no one can, but he invented this. It's not a sketch show and it's not a comedy show and it's not a variety show or a musical show. It's *Saturday Night Live.* It's his, and he knows how to do it and I don't.

PAULA PELL, *Writer:*

You want to be under those bleachers getting him to laugh so hard that he puts his head down. And now because I have known him for so many years and he's seen me through failures and successes in my professional and personal life, I have a comfort with him now where sometimes if he's giving me shit under the bleachers I'll say, "I can't hear you because the laughter's too loud. When it dies down you can give me that note." And we'll just laugh. I really can give him shit now. Sometimes I'll walk away going, "I can't believe I was just sitting on Lorne's lap and telling him he needs a hug and just squeezing him."

ALAN ZWEIBEL:

Lorne's modus operandi when it came to motivation was, we were a bunch of kids, and if we were denied Daddy's—his—approval, we worked harder and harder to get it. Some thrived on that. Some didn't.

HARRY SHEARER, *Cast Member:*

I found that if you try to approach Lorne on an adult basis, make an appointment, go into his office, wait the requisite two hours, and try to have an adult conversation, you would find a very interesting, polished, smooth discussion that basically led to no results and no change at all. But I found that, as I watched what went on in the show, and sort of heard the stories of the previous years, it became more and more apparent that that was not the way to approach Lorne—that you really had to, if you were a cast member, act out. And if you set fire to wastebaskets, you'd get Lorne's attention much more effectively than if you, you know, scheduled a meeting, waited, and talked like a grown-up with him.

I believed, and I think the evidence pretty much shows, that Lorne's approach to the cast was to try to infantilize them. He wanted them to be like children; he'd be the daddy. That was his preferred way of relating to people. And I didn't particularly want to relate that way.

NORA DUNN, *Cast Member:*

Sometimes I would just get really, really mad and throw a fit to get attention. And then they'd think, "Uh-oh, something has to be done."

You can't help but make this sort of analogy that the show was our mother and Lorne was our father and you wanted to please both of them. You certainly didn't want Lorne to be angry with you. The worst thing you could hear from Lorne was that you had "bad form." He really meant it when he said that, and you really felt badly if you were accused of having "bad form."

RACHEL DRATCH, *Cast Member:*

I wasn't the type to be, like, chatting in his office and going to Yankees games with him, like some people were. A few people who have the same sensibility as him for the whole biz thing get kind of close to him. But I was super shy around him. I would kind of skulk around the hallways, like, "Just happy to be here!"

BILL HADER, *Cast Member:*

The thing I realize about Lorne is that he's a giant fan of show business. He really cares about, and is fascinated by, show business and comedy. When you would just talk to him at an after party, he would loosen up. I had this amazing night where he was with Steve Martin and they were talking to me about comedy albums and then it was like they weren't Lorne Michaels and Steve Martin anymore—these giants in comedy—they were just like me and my friends when we were fifteen and watching *SNL*. They became these two comedy nerds quoting stuff back to each other.

RICHARD DREYFUSS, *Host:*

We certainly were children. Actors can always be children. But Lorne was certainly an adult.

Of course, nobody knew he would do it for thirty years. But he was exactly the same then as he is now. He's got good pace. He's got a great rhythm. He never gets too excited—he never gets too up, he never gets too low. I would personally believe that he's never been to a hockey game in his life.

JOHN GOODMAN, *Host:*

You know, these are sensitive people Lorne has to deal with. A lot of them are people who are going to get hurt, because every once in a while they're going to get their feelings stepped on. That doesn't happen maybe as often as it used to, but it's bound to happen from time to time. And anytime you're dealing with people like that, there's going to be a little hand-holding involved. Obviously Lorne knows this.

DAVID SPADE, *Cast Member:*

When I first read "Hollywood Minute" at read-through, Lorne laughed all the way through it. It was really like having your dad say he liked something, and that was exciting.

JULIA SWEENEY:

I still have approval dreams about Lorne, which is very embarrassing. Like I wake up and I say to myself, "Oh God, how many fucking years does it take before you don't have Lorne showing up in your dreams telling you that you did a good job on something?" I mean, like that's pretty deep into the psyche.

BERNIE BRILLSTEIN, *Manager:*

If I had to make only one deal in my life with the devil or Satan, I'd send Lorne. Because after the conversation was over, they would give him what he wanted. He is the most articulate guy in the world. He doesn't always know if he's right or wrong, but he always makes it sound great.

CHRIS ROCK, *Cast Member:*

How can anyone hate the guy? A lot of people have problems with Lorne. A lot of people I've met from the show come from these great backgrounds, and they're not used to working for people. And you know he hired you to work *for* him, there's no working *with*. You're only working *with* if you count the money at the end of the night. Otherwise you're working *for*. And when you're working for somebody, you're going to have to do shit you don't want to do. And sometimes they're not going to talk to you. And that's what working for people is.

BOB TISCHLER, *Writer:*

I don't have a whole lot of respect for Lorne's opinion. To me, it was better if Bill Murray said he liked a sketch. I just don't think Lorne is creatively terrific. I don't know him that well, but whenever I had a meeting with him, I've walked out of the room going, "I don't even know what the fuck just went on." I don't hold him in the same regard that a lot of people do. I was just never very impressed with him. I thought he spent more time talking about theories of comedy, things that were very nonsubstantive in terms of what we had to do.

BRIAN DOYLE-MURRAY, *Cast Member:*

I was down in Florida working on the movie *Caddyshack* with Harold Ramis and I came back a little late. As soon as I arrived, my brother Bill asked me, "Have you seen Lorne yet?" I said, "No, I haven't seen him." He says, "Don't you realize you're supposed to go kiss the Pope's ring?"

LILY TOMLIN, *Host:*

I don't really want to say a lot about Lorne. I don't think he could accomplish what he has accomplished if he wasn't ambitious. Also he's much more astute politically than someone like me. He would know who to have lunch with. It would never occur to me to have lunch with somebody, or something like that. I've never understood about functioning in the system.

CRAIG KELLEM, *Associate Producer:*

My theory about Lorne is that he is one of these guys whose mother told him every day of his life when he was a kid that he was the most wonderful person in the world and he could do no wrong. Because Lorne just believed in what he was doing, and nobody was going to get in his way. He was determined to get what he wanted, to accomplish what he wanted, and do it the way that he wanted it. If something worried him, he wasn't overt about it. He just figured out what he wanted to do and somehow his willpower outlasted everybody else's resistance.

JANEANE GAROFALO, *Cast Member:*

My secret assumption about Lorne is that he may suffer from such a deep case of self-loathing that if you agree to be on his show and you are nice to him, he cannot respect you. So therefore you are left to wallow in your own despair. He was always very nice to me, but I just presumed that he had to have been aware that the environment was toxic. He had to know that there were so many unhappy people, yet as far as I know, he was never concerned. He rules on the theory of a house divided is a house that's more easily controlled.

ALEC BALDWIN, *Host:*

Lorne is a good friend of mine. I have a lot of respect for him and I admire what he's done and continued to do, and not just because of the longevity. I still think the show from time to time is really funny. Lorne is the glue that holds it together—or doesn't hold it together, as the case may be, because he can be very laissez-faire about how he conducts the whole thing. He lets the whole show kind of sort itself out, the people's wants and desires and egos and everything. Because of my fondness for Lorne and my being around the show so much, I would sometimes look at the people and want to say to them: "There's a very good chance that it's never going to get any better for you than this."

CHRIS ELLIOTT, *Cast Member:*

When people talk about Lorne, "pompous" and "self-centered" usually come up. A lot of people say he enjoys hearing himself talk, and I'm not necessarily saying that in a bad way, because to me that's who he is. It never bugged me. It was always kind of entertaining. I always enjoyed those Monday evening dinners with Lorne and the host. They were always fun. And if you got Lorne and Steve Martin together, the two of them would really go off.

TOM HANKS, *Host:*

I think he's one of the most mesmerizing conversationalists you'll ever meet. He is a fabulous person to sit down and have a dinner conversation with, because it just never stops. Sometimes it's flashy like, "Oh, you know, Mick came over last night, and Mick and I…" You know, "Mick" came by. "I'm going to guess that's Mick Jagger, right?" "Oh, understood." But you know, he's also got kids, he's also got the same vision of the business I think that we all have, that we respond to excellence. You know how a lot of times you'll meet royalty and they're kind of boring? He's not. He's this kind of royalty that ends up being convivial and intelligent and, in some ways, inclusive, even though he has an inclination to tell the same story over and over again if you haven't seen him for a few years. But he's magnificent, well-read, hip company to keep.

BILL MURRAY, *Cast Member:*

I had a different relationship with Lorne than the others, I think. I was adopted. You can love an adopted kid, but there's still something different.

Lorne's social life is different than mine. He travels in a more rarefied circle than mine. He travels the world. He sees it from a different point of view. Part of it's because he's an alien, you know—a Canadian. They have sort of like British echoes that they have to fulfill. They have to go to Wimbledon and they have to do stuff like that that we Americans don't really feel anything about.

When I hosted the show a couple years ago, I remember just turning to Lorne and saying, "God, you really learned how to do this." He was really good at it, much better than I knew or appreciated at the time. I think he's better now than he was in the old days. He used to seem sort of arbitrary sometimes, but he really did learn how to do it. I think given the firepower of that group in the first couple of years, there were a couple people besides him that could have done it.

But he fought the great fights; he really was good at that. He fought the fights against the network. He fought the fights for the best crew. He got the network off our backs, he put us on a different floor, he kept us away from everybody, he gave us the independence that we needed so we didn't feel like we were under a microscope. And it worked. He made great choices. And now just in terms of producing a TV show, he's really good at it.

CANDICE BERGEN:

Well, he's an extraordinarily good friend. He's a wonderful storyteller and he loves to talk. You'd think he wouldn't have time to pay attention to you, but he pays real attention and he's incredibly generous as a friend. And very loyal. He's so smart and perceptive about people; he just gets people so quickly and he's so astute in what he picks up about them. He's amazingly measured and wonderfully witty. I love hearing Lorne's point of view on everything, basically, because I just think what he has to say is so worth hearing. Lorne is only a force for good.

I loved Lorne immediately, as soon as I met him, and he's just one of the people that really matters in my life, and in hundreds of people's lives. When my husband died and there was a tribute for him, without even asking, Lorne had it filmed and had videotapes made. And it was the kind of thing he would do and never even refer to it.

STEVE MARTIN, *Host:*

I think I understand him. I never found him inscrutable. I hear it sometimes said about myself. When you're dealing with all different kinds of people all day, and everyone has a goal toward you, a lot of times you don't fulfill their goal, and then they think, "Oh, uncommunicative," when really it's just that there's no time to fill everyone's goal. Lorne hasn't changed that much. He's Lorne. He's always been a talker, always been kind of wise, always had an overview of how things work.

GWYNETH PALTROW, *Host:*

When I first met him, I was very intimidated by him. I'd never met such a Waspy-seeming Jew in my life. And I was like, where's the "in," you know? I didn't get how to access him at all and I found him very intimidating. And then I sort of feel like I broke through and didn't feel intimidated, and now it's easy to be around him. I am very fond of him. I think he's very smart and a very nice guy, and such a fan of comedy and talent. He's really an amazing person.

The most interesting thing is to kind of be around people like Will Ferrell who talk about Lorne. He carries such weight for all these guys. And they sort of talk about him with love and fear, it's like he stays with them in an extraordinary way. They tell stories of him being very encouraging while also kind of not letting them get a big head about where they are, kind of being discouraging at times in his effort to maintain the hierarchy there. And they're always imitating him, constantly. Everyone imitates Lorne.

NASIM PEDRAD, *Cast Member:*

So much of your time in the beginning is defined by your relationship with Lorne. Lorne's like this father figure meets your boss meets Obi-Wan Kenobi and all you want to do is not disappoint him. In the beginning you don't interact with him constantly, so when you do, stakes are really high. And then if time goes on, you become more comfortable with him and you can start being yourself. Then the next thing you know, you're sitting with him in his office, checking out the fish in his aquarium and telling him about a pair of jeans you really want to buy.

GARRETT MORRIS, *Cast Member:*

There's this commercial with a guy sitting on top of a John Deere machine and the guy says, "How long does a John Deere last?" You know, they're like a Maytag, nobody ever goes to repair these mother-fuckers, right? That commercial has always reminded me of Lorne. Nobody ever had to call the repairman on him.

I was lucky to work for a man like Lorne, who was a great guy and a genius. Two or three times I figured I should've been fired. It wasn't that he was soft, he just dealt with his people a certain way. He knew I was totally dysfunctional. He accepted the responsibility of hiring me, whatever I was. But if you did something wrong he would tell you about it. He would cut me to pieces. It wouldn't take him long to cut you down either—about a minute and a half and I was crawling back to the dressing room. Lorne dug me with all of my flaws, I dig him with all of his. I'm still a Lorne Michaels man.

TOM SCHILLER, *Writer:*

I don't hold anything against Lorne at all. I think he's a shrewd businessman. He realized his dream. He has the power to galvanize people around him who can help him realize his dream, he can make you very excited about the possibilities of exploring your own creativity, and he can get you going. He's good at that.

I was friends with him for a while, but I haven't spoken to him in years. I don't think anyone can get really, totally close to him.

KATE McKINNON, *Cast Member:*

I remember reading that Lorne was a trained concert pianist and loved Rachmaninoff, and I was keeping this bit of information in my back pocket to use in order to bond with him, because I also play the piano and love Rachmaninoff, and I severely wanted him to like me. So I bided my time, and then I found my moment—it was the first time I was going to be saying, "Live from New York, it's *Saturday Night*." I was playing Martha Raddatz in a vice-presidential debate cold open, and he came up to me right before air and said, "Are you all right?" And I said, "Yes," then, timidly, "So I hear you love to play Rachmaninoff." And he said, "No, no. Paul Simon wrote that about me once as a joke." Then he patted me on my back, walked away, and the show started. It's hard to start a conversation with a man who knows and has seen everything.

CARRIE FISHER, *Host:*

Lorne was on my honeymoon, so by all rights I should know Lorne very, very well. He was always like Big Daddy, giving his little comedy treatises and lectures and explaining things to you about comedy. I was really young and I thought I had quite a bit to catch up on. I actually don't know that I did, but that was the feeling I had, because most people were older than I was.

Lorne talks a lot. He's an expert. He liked to warm to his topic. It used to be me and Paul and Lorne and his wife Susan in St. Bart's. He was a little bit dignified, which was funny in combination with Paul's a lot of bit dignified. But they are very close friends. They've been the closest of friends for, my God, thirty years. I liked Lorne because Lorne was much more social than Paul might be. He wanted to stay up and talk, and he was extremely social and he would have people over, and I had grown up that way. It was the way I liked to live. Paul liked to dip into it but also liked to leave and go back and work. He had a more solitary profession.

CONAN O'BRIEN, *Writer:*

Robert Smigel and I were working on this silly pilot for Lorne called "Lookwell," and one night he said, "Let's have dinner and talk it over." So we go to the restaurant and Lorne's there and he's eating a bread stick. And we sit down and he says, "Some friends are going to join us," and I said, "Fine." And we're sitting there for five minutes, and all of a sudden I hear over my shoulder, "What's goin' on?" And I turn around, and it's Paul McCartney and his wife, Linda! And they come over and sit down!

Now if you asked me who I would most want to meet in the world, it's like—well, John Lennon's dead, so I guess Paul McCartney, you know? And now he's sitting right there! So I'm trying to recover while they sit down, and Lorne is gesturing with this bread stick and he goes like, "We've been talking about a TV pilot. Conan, tell them what it's about." And my mind is just frozen. I've just suddenly been handed this ball and I'm completely frozen. Lorne's eating a bread stick and I'm thinking, "Why do I have to talk?"

That was a *huge* night for me. I'm a huge Beatles fan. And I had never met a Beatle. But for Lorne it was just another night, just another dinner.

ELLIOT WALD, *Writer*:

Lorne's had an enormous amount of success and he lives very well. Someone once said if he had his way, the show would be "Live from St. Bart's."

TOM DAVIS, *Writer*:

Lorne a snob? Sure he's a snob. He's a starfucker of the highest order. And all of his close friends know it too. But you just have to get past it. He has a very sweet side. He also, in my opinion, does reward the squeaky wheels—which I sort of resented personally, because I always stuck up for him when he wasn't around. I'm very loyal. Meanwhile, the people who created problems, criticized him in the press, and stuff like that seemed to be rewarded for it, whereas someone like me, who was more protective of him, didn't seem to get the reward. That's the way I interpreted my own personal experience.

I always wanted to be Lorne's friend—in the way that Dan Aykroyd is my pal and Bill Murray is my friend. It just never quite worked out. I think part of it might have been smoking dope in the office. He did then; he doesn't now that he has kids.

I was closest to Lorne in the fourth and fifth year. It was the peak of my influence in the show. And I have great affection for Lorne. I sometimes wish that we were closer. But you know, it's business. He's one of my business associates. And some people become close pals, and with other people it's just a business thing.

ROBIN WILLIAMS, *Host:*

Lorne has that Hotel Algonquin thing going on, filled with all the people he knows and has made and has been around. Kind of like the grand guru of comedy. "Look at what has occurred under my reign"—Emperor Lorne. Careful now—I'll be fucked for life. Be not afraid of him, he knows not where you live now, you're free, boy! He made *Kids in the Hall,* what else can you say? Came from Canada, a frostback, not knowing why, a boy with a vision, a vision in comedy, and then ending up at Brillstein-Grey, and the rest is history.

He likes to schmooze. You come into a meeting with Lorne and he'll tell you how many times he's seen Jack Nicholson that week. It was like, "I was just out with Jack." "Oh, you mean Onassis?" "No! That's Jack-ee, boy."

PENNY MARSHALL, *Guest:*

My mother always said she wanted her ashes spread over Broadway, because she was a tap dancing teacher in the basement of her building in the Bronx. I remember she wanted us to make sure her eyelashes were on. My brother thought there should be a party with tap dancing, which they did do but I didn't go to.

So I was in New York. My mother was donated to science, so you have to understand she just disappeared for a year after she died. They took her. Then all of a sudden her ashes arrived, and so my brother sends me a Ziploc baggie and a candy tin, to New York, part of my mother, because she wanted to be spread over Broadway. So I called Lorne, because he had an office in the Brill Building, and I said, "Lorne, can I use your office? I gotta throw my mother over Broadway." He says, "Excuse me?" So I explained it all to him and he said, "Sure, no problem." Lorne's favorite expression is "No problem."

So I went there with my daughter and a plastic spoon and a Ziploc bag, and we were singing this song from dancing school that my mother ended every show with when she put on shows. And out the window she went. Joe Mantegna, who was in *Glengarry Glen Ross* then, said, "You should have told me, I would have put her onstage. I could have carried her ashes onstage in my pockets." I said, "She wouldn't have liked the play." He said, "It's a Pulitzer Prize play." I said, "She wouldn't have liked it. There was cursing. Lorne's office is fine."

Cut to Paris years later, and my father, who had a stroke in '91, I think, whenever *Awakening* was happening, wouldn't go get therapy or anything. They live for a long time, my family; they don't do well, but they're there. Their hearts won't stop. So I'm in Paris, and my brother called to say my father wasn't looking well. And I asked him, "What should I do? Should I call Lorne?" He calls him Lor-en. "Is Lor-en around? Will Lor-en be in New York?" And ultimately he didn't die that trip, but a couple of years ago I had to call Lorne, because we get cremated in my family. I went to New York with my father in a baggie and I said, "Lorne, I need your office again." He said, "No problem." So I brought my father to the window in a baggie with a spoon, and out the window he went. And I'm trying to brush it off so it doesn't blow back on Lorne's desk, because Lorne never even met my father. And then my grandmother, who was cremated way before, in the seventies, was in a wall that looked like *Hollywood Squares,* out in the Valley, and for some reason my brother recently said, "Why is Nanny there all by herself?" So I don't know if I've got to bring her to New York and call Lorne. I'm not sure yet. But my family goes out Lorne's window.

I love Lorne and I'd do anything for him and at any given time. Not only his talent but his friendship has meant the world to me. Sometimes we're parted for a long time, but you know there's someone there who still understands what you're talking about. Besides, you never know, I may need his window.

ROBERT KLEIN, *Host:*

"Or walk with kings—nor lose the common touch." I know Rudyard Kipling was a racist, but that's still a wonderful poem. Lorne just doesn't have that touch. His arrogance can make me smile. He's just very taken with himself and what he's accomplished. He's certainly done a wonderful job—though I wish he could have done more for Belushi.

BRIAN DOYLE-MURRAY:

Lorne's very hard to get close to. He was kind of isolated, you know. I remember being shocked when we had the Monday night meeting where you meet the host and pitch ideas. That meeting would always start with Lorne being delivered food at his desk, usually sushi. And I always thought that was really weird that he would eat while everyone else was crouching and kneeling before him without any food for themselves. I thought it was a little rude, and I thought it was some kind of a power trip.

GRANT A. TINKER, *Former NBC Chairman:*

I've been in the Grill in Beverly Hills a couple of times, and Lorne will come in, and he will just walk right by me. Which is not the end of my world, but it has always made me wonder, why does he do that?

I have no idea what it comes from. What could it have been? If he says I showed "no interest in *Saturday Night Live*," well, that's true. I mean, not the show as it appeared on television. It was just never appointment viewing for me. And I had no interest in trying to fix a problem that was way down the list of problems that NBC had.

ALBERT BROOKS, *Filmmaker:*

If you interviewed somebody from a movie I made and they said it was the worst set they'd ever worked on, I'd have to take that hit. Here we are thirty years later, and I can remember it all. Lorne was in charge, and he didn't behave very well toward me.

JANEANE GAROFALO:

I waited in his office for hours. And then I decided I would refuse to be embarrassed like that again. You'll wait a lot of hours—that's a power thing. Then, when he realizes you'll do it, he can't respect you. How could he? You've shown him your weakness. You've shown him that you will wait four or five hours and that you'll take it. There's your first mistake.

PAUL SIMON:

For a lot of these people who come out and say nasty things, I think hey, he's not perfect. For the most part, I don't think Lorne ever screwed over anybody. Maybe they didn't like something about Lorne's personality, or maybe they didn't like his judgment or something like that. But he never hurt anybody's career. People from *Saturday Night Live* went on to huge careers, and Lorne didn't have any piece of them. He didn't own them or take them or control them.

He's a decent guy and he's a very powerful guy, and it's unusual to find somebody who's really, really powerful who is that decent. He doesn't push people and throw his weight around. And he never did. He was nasty when he was young, but he mellowed. I think that's why he's a helluva boss to work for, really. You're lucky if Lorne is in your life. For the most part, for most people, their life is improved. I know that's the case with me.

DAMON WAYANS, *Cast Member:*

I have gained an enormous respect for Lorne Michaels and his ability to see beyond his ego. He never said anything but great things about me—even though he fired me. I remember there was a kid on the show who had a drug problem, and Lorne would put him in rehab and take care of him and pay him while he was there and then bring him back to the show. He was like a father to the kid, with the kind of patience that a father would have.

ANDY BRECKMAN, *Writer:*

If there's one thing you can't fault Lorne for, it's the format of the show and how the show comes together, because more than any other show in the history of television, it's withstood the test of time. I mean, that format is fuckin' indestructible, isn't it? If that's all Lorne came up with in his life, I think he'd have earned a place in the television hall of fame.

JON STEWART, *Host:*

Lorne doesn't have much of a track record, so that's why it was really hard to trust him that everything was going to be okay, but I thought, "Well, I'll give this kid a shot and see what he can do for me."

I think the thing that probably strikes me most is, here's a guy who clearly doesn't have to work this hard but still does. And you can only attribute that to either he's insane or he's still excited about the show, he still enjoys it, he still has passion for it, and he still wants it to be good.

LILLY TARTIKOFF:

Lorne *is Saturday Night Live.* I mean, Dick is too. Dick did a fantastic job, and I don't really know how to define who did what—no one's ever going to know, actually. But, you know, there are things that Dick can do. I mean, you would not have Lorne Michaels run NBC Sports. But you would only have Lorne run *Saturday Night Live* and make these movies with those guys. That defines who he is. And that's why he probably has done it for so long, because he probably can't stop.

DANA CARVEY, *Cast Member:*

Lorne had your career and your fate in his hands. He definitely was the centerpiece, because he owned the baseball field. Ultimately, he decided how much you got on-air, how much access you had to your audience. He was like the principal of the school. There was a lot of weighty energy around Lorne. And basically I was just terrified of him the first three or four years—afraid of his power. He could cut you to the quick if he wanted to. He had an acerbic wit. He also could make you feel like a million dollars. He's of the school of very minimal compliment, so that they're weighty when you get them. And they wouldn't be handed out when Church Lady killed, it would be like if I played a cowboy in a scene and I had some funny exit: "I thought your exit as Cowboy Bill was breathtaking." It would be the most obscure detail. And you'd feel like a million dollars.

He's just a great character. There's a great rhythm about him. He's so fun to listen to. He'll go on and on. He'll come up with the weirdest way of looking at things, but we were like his children in a way. He would look down and say, "Kevin's going to do that third-year thing where he asks, 'Who am I in the cast?' Danny went through the same thing. You're going through like that Chevy first-year shall-I-stay? kind of thing." It was great.

BOB ODENKIRK, *Writer:*

Chris Farley came up to me once and he was almost crying. He was in his second month at the show and he said, "I don't get what's going on. Every time I do a bad job, Lorne comes up to me and tells me I just did great, and every time I kill, he comes up to me and says, 'You could work a little harder, you could've done that better.'" Chris's head was spinning.

But if you want to know the greatest thing I ever saw Lorne do, it was the way he wound up treating Chris. I think Lorne was determined not to have what happened to Belushi happen to Chris on his watch. And it seemed to me that Lorne very seriously put it to Chris — every time Chris messed up, he had to go get cleaned up before he could come back on the show. And Lorne seemed to do that even to the detriment of the show, which is to say, he would take Chris off the show even on the Thursday before a show. Lorne really made Chris think about what he was doing, 'cause the most important thing to Chris in the world was performing on that show. That was the goal of his life. And Lorne knew it. And Lorne took it away from him multiple times and forced him to go to rehab. I don't think he ever let Chris slide. And I think that was a great, great thing. An amazing thing, and something I haven't seen anyone else do.

MARCI KLEIN, *Coproducer:*

Sometimes, right before they say "Live," like right before the show starts, when the music is playing, but before the host comes out, I get — it's so pathetic — I start getting misty-eyed and all emotional, because I just can't believe I'm doing this job. I can't believe how much I like this show.

And Lorne gets the same way. That's the moment when I see him get the most excited. I'll look over at him, and his eyes will be popped open, and he'll get on his toes to look out, and he'll be mouthing the intros, and he's just so excited.

MOLLY SHANNON, *Cast Member:*

I did a Mary Katherine Gallagher sketch with Mike Myers and Steven Tyler from Aerosmith, and there was like a brick wall, really balsa wood painted to look like brick, and the stunt people cut the wood so you could break through it fairly easily. But they didn't have enough time to stack the balsa-wood fake bricks and the sketch was starting and I went like, "Oh no, that's the wall I'm supposed to break through, and it's not ready, what am I going to do?" And it was like, "Nine, eight, seven, six...." Oh God, oh shit, the whole sketch — and then Lorne just appeared behind the other side and looked at me like, "Don't let this goof you up. Just do it. Go ahead." And I was just like, "Wow," it helped me a lot that he was there. Stuff like that sort of fuels your performance. And that little private moment between Lorne and me, that's just something that he did do that helped me.

CAROL LEIFER, *Writer:*

I always felt like if Lorne was stony toward you it was pretty impenetrable. I saw him not too long ago and went over to say hello. And it was like the quintessential Lorne moment — "Oh hello, Carol, how are you, what's going on," talking, bullshitting, then a band started playing, with blaring horns. It was real loud music. And Lorne just turned to me and said, "Conversation over." And now that's become a catchphrase among my friends and me — "Conversation over." That's quintessential Lorne.

DICK EBERSOL, *NBC Executive:*

Maybe it's because of his marriage to Alice or having a family, but the Lorne of today has done I think a very, very good job of learning at this stage of his life to delegate. He has, for the first time in the history of the show, the semblance of a real life. And that was never true for Lorne—or me—over the first two decades of the show. I can see it now, though. He doesn't have to live at the show all the time anymore.

AL FRANKEN, *Writer:*

Lorne called the shots. But Lorne is also taking into account a lot of things. He used to try to make sure that everyone was in the show. That was easier to do when the cast was smaller. Sometimes he would put something in just because someone needed something in, psychologically. Sometimes two pieces may bump in a certain kind of way, that other people don't see, the same style of a piece, and they shouldn't run back-to-back. There are just so many factors—you can't get from this set to the other set, there is no configuration in the show where this thing can go in, this sketch can go in but then we have to lose that sketch.

Almost every week, that was the case. Somebody felt bad, and some people take it like, "I am insulted," or "I am just going to take it." Those were people who usually got a lot of stuff, and other people were angry and hurt and depressed, actually. A person could actually get so disheartened and depressed that it affected their ability to create. Certain people actually spiraled out of control or spiraled down to a point where they were having a difficult time emotionally during the year, and it very much hurt their productivity. And it just was a vicious cycle.

GARRY SHANDLING, *Host:*

Lorne's presence was mostly felt on tape day, what I call tape day, which is the day it's done live. On Saturday he would come and he would do the dress rehearsal, the first show in front of an audience, and that's when I went up into his office and just watched him very intuitively reorder the sketches on a big board and cut very intuitively without any doubts. He was really one with that show and the process of selection of what finally aired. He was like a surgeon—very quick, very smart. I certainly don't remember anyone arguing with him.

ANNE BEATTS:

I always felt a little concerned that Lorne never so much as made a pass at me. I thought he was really cute. I remember thinking that he was really cute and interesting.

ROSIE SHUSTER, *Writer:*

The first summer we were separated—I was fourteen, and that was the last separation we had for many, many, many years—he announced that when I came back from Los Angeles he wanted to "pet." So I spent the entire summer straining, pulling, doing my best to grow a set of tits.

ELLEN DEGENERES, *Host:*

To be honest, I thought that Lorne would be a tyrant. He seems to have a reputation of being this really mean kind of scary presence. And he was so nice. Just the reception you get—the first day, when you're brought into his office and he welcomes you and the cast comes in and sits in his office. It's such a warm way to welcome the host and makes you feel good about being there. I don't know what it's like to work with him on a daily basis, but the experience I had with him was great, and he seemed respectful of me. I could feel that he liked me; he made that clear. I really liked him. I really thought I'd be scared of him, and he was so nice and warm. He was great.

And I think he's good-looking. He's a looker. He's a handsome man and he's a good dresser. I like the way he dresses. You know—he's a cutie. I think he knows that. He can't not know that he's cute.

ELLIOTT GOULD, *Host:*

Gilda once said to me at a party after I had hosted, "Look what you've done for Lorne." Perhaps she meant my accomplishments prior to Lorne's success—my coming on the show and working with some degree of consistency on the show and exercising my humility and my sensibility and giving the show everything that I had. Lorne has always been decent to me. And therefore I'm centered with Lorne.

TRACY MORGAN, *Cast Member:*

It's like Luke Skywalker and Obi-Wan Kenobi. Whenever Luke was in trouble, Obi-Wan would come out of nowhere. That's who Lorne Michaels is, he's Obi-Wan. That's what I call him. Everybody has their little nicknames for him. Chris Farley used to call him the Chief. Some people just call him boss. And some people call him Daddy. I call him Obi-Wan.

BOB ODENKIRK:

I mean, the whole thing was weird to me. The whole thing. To me, what was fun about comedy and should have been exciting about *Saturday Night Live* was the whole generational thing, you know, a crazy bunch of people sittin' around making each other laugh with casual chaos and a kind of democracy of chaos. And to go into a place where this one distant and cold guy is in charge and trying to run it the way he ran it decades ago is just weird to me.

WILL FERRELL, *Cast Member:*

Lorne can never tell you that flat-out you're hired, with a hip hip hooray. The way he told me was, "So, we'll bring you out to New York," and I thought, "Oh, another audition." Then he said, "Have you ever lived in New York?" And that's when it hit me: Oh, I got the job. Then I felt self-conscious because I was so relaxed and I wasn't jumping up and down, and so I was like, "Oh, okay." And then I said to Lorne, "Well, I'm going to shake your hand." And he was like, "Do whatever you need to do." And then I walked out.

MARGARET OBERMAN, *Writer:*

I think Lorne Michaels is a very lucky man, that's what I think. He was at the right place at the right time and he recognized some very talented people, and it was the right moment and all those things that maybe come once in a lifetime. I'm not going to say he's not that talented. But he's a producer, and the true talent is what is on the stage.

DANNY DEVITO, *Host:*

What makes Lorne so good as a producer? I think it may be the popcorn. There's a lot of popcorn in his office. He always has big, big bowls of fresh popcorn, and I think that helps. It's really what sets him apart from other producers. And another thing is, he doesn't really care if it drops on the floor. It's like total focus on the board. You could just eat like a slob in that office and he really doesn't give a shit. With him it's really all about the show.

STEVE MARTIN:

He puts people together well. He will suggest something that performers are either too shy or too afraid to suggest. He will encourage partnerships, he'll make the phone call to the person that everybody else'd be afraid to call. And he also has this kind of soft wit and patience. Patience with things and people. He loves the youth that flies around those offices. He gets a lot from it. It keeps him hip, I guess. It keeps him puzzled and it keeps him challenged, because the new thing is sometimes very hard for older people to tolerate and accept, even though we were all once a part of it. He'll let something go that he might not fully understand.

SARAH JESSICA PARKER, *Host:*

Lorne is not necessarily a demonstrative person, but you know you're in good hands. You know it's not a lack of interest on his part; he's overseeing something and doesn't need to be there hands-on all the time. I think he trusts the host that he hires. Look, he's hired you, he must feel fairly confident in your ability to fulfill your obligations, and he feels he doesn't need to baby-sit.

GWYNETH PALTROW:

Lorne can be stingy with praise, but I think you have to be in that environment. They're writing so much each week and the turnover is so fast, you don't want people resting on their laurels and thinking, "Oh, I'm funny, Lorne thinks I'm funny," and then, "Anything I write is funny and good." I think it's very important in terms of keeping the show fresh and edgy and funny and young that nobody relaxes. So I think it's Lorne's job to keep them on their toes.

Some people are able to make it and go on to other things, some people can't, and some people end up killing themselves.

ROBERT SMIGEL, *Writer:*

After my first season I thought I was going to be fired, because Franken said, "Well, I know it's not looking good. I mean, you did great, but it's going to be hard." So I went back to Chicago that summer to work on a stage show. I was really expecting to be fired, and then Lorne brought me in days before the new season and just interviewed me. He asked, "What was your favorite thing you did last season?" It was a very odd kind of short interview. "All right, well, we're just figuring things out." I'd flown from Chicago to talk to him and then all he said was, "I'll let you know." I flew back to Chicago and got another call from him, and he said, "I don't know, you didn't write for the women much." I said, "Well, you know, I just did the best I could, I thought I wrote a lot of good things." "Well, you wrote good showbiz things, but you gave some of the actors a hard time." So he was saying these things and then said, "Okay, get on a plane, come tomorrow." It was so weird.

People get all paranoid about him unless they know him, and as I got to know him over the years, he's a pretty real person and he really is in a very difficult situation. Whether he likes the situation and likes the grief that comes with it, I don't know. It's a very difficult setup here. Everybody's pitted against each other. People have egos and people are insecure and it's a formula for paranoia. When I was producing the Dana Carvey show, I actually got to see some things from the perspective of being in charge, and I called Lorne and said, "I apologize for ever not understanding what your job is."

RACHEL DRATCH:

I never get feedback from Lorne. You always get your notes from some middleman, like, "Lorne wants you to pick up the pace here," or whatever. Sometimes after the show if you did a scene that went really well he'll say something, but he never gets specific like, "Oh my God, when you said that line it cracked me up!" You just have to be able to do without stuff like that.

CHERI OTERI, *Cast Member:*

I don't think you ever really know where you stand with Lorne, and I think that's frustrating, because it's almost like a family, even with its dysfunction, because you want to please him. I always say, "Did Lorne laugh under the bleachers?" I don't have much dialogue with him at all. You live for him to say just once, "Good job." That's the hardest thing, is not having the dialogue that I feel like you should have with your boss.

If you want to see him, he'll see you eventually. But sometimes I think you wish that he would offer things to you. You want a little guidance. But he's not that way. And in a way it's good, because he lets you go and you're very free to do whatever is instinctually there. And the other cool thing is, sometimes they'll say, "He doesn't want you to do that," and I'll go in and I'll say, "I've got to do that, that's important," and he'll say, "Okay." He really trusts our instincts, the performers. I think he's very respectful of what our instincts are.

One time I came back from the summer and he said, "I'd embrace you, but I think I might be coming down with a cold." And I was like, "It's okay, hug me anyway." But I'll go up and I will hug him sometimes and I will kiss him whether he likes it or not, because I feel it. But it's hard when you don't get it back. I understand people who aren't comfortable with stuff like that. They can just give so much. And I guess he's one of those people. He can just give so much, but when you're working for him you really go like, "Anything??? Oh, *nothing,* huh?" Like, "Say 'good show' once. Just say it once." You know? Nothing. And it's like you feel starved sometimes. But then you get used to it, I guess. It's fuckin' crazy, it really is.

CAROL LEIFER:

Lorne and I had such a strange relationship. I don't know what possessed me, but near the end of the season I saw him walking down the hall to go to the elevator, and I hid around the corner, and when he came around the corner I just went, *"Boo!"* And it kind of really startled him. And I remember in the elevator going down going, "I'm sorry if I threw you off with 'boo' there," and he goes, "Whatever." He really wasn't happy that I did it.

CHRISTINE ZANDER:

One week I asked to talk to him after the table read. And I think when you asked to talk to him, I think he was always worried you had a problem and you were going to quit or you were going to confront him. I don't think he really likes confrontation. So after the table read, I went into the office and it was sort of tense, but then I sat down and I just said, "Well, I'm gonna miss next week's table read because I have to have an amniocentesis." And he said, "Oooh, I remember my first amnio," and it was his sister's. But he made it his own. And he was really wonderful about it. We talked for about twenty minutes about how everything would be fine.

It's difficult when you're away from it for a long time to try to remember what made you so crazy or what made you so frustrated, and I think you realize, or at least I did, that a lot of it was in your own head and you can't completely blame him. It's more the combination of people and talent—incredible talent, I think, when I was there, and live television.

ELLIOT WALD:

The only time I met him is when I did a piece on him for the *Chicago Sun-Times* in 1977. He was very charming. I don't really claim to understand Lorne, but if you talk to enough people, you get a sense of Lorne and you realize that in his own way, Lorne was just as hard to work for as Ebersol—and in some ways harder. Lorne is more the smart, neurotic Jewish guy who knows exactly where the buttons on your keyboard are—because he has a similar keyboard himself. Ebersol, on the other hand, is more like a boss. If you cross him, he'll just get mad. Lorne, from all indications, is much more like the diabolical version of yourself. He's manipulative, and he knows exactly how to make people crazy. Someone once called him a psychological terrorist.

CONAN O'BRIEN:

Lorne is very aloof. He's off in his own world. He has a standard joke if you're a rookie writer and he doesn't know you that well. He passed me in the hall once, and he said, "Still with the show?" Then he acted mildly surprised, as if to say, "I thought we got rid of you." And that's his little joke: "Still with the show?"

But I knew I was doing all right, because a few months later—it was late on a Tuesday night—Lorne came into my office. I was sitting at my desk, and he sat on the edge of it and started telling me about this great weekend he had just had in his home on Long Island. "I built a fire and I made some s'mores, and it was really nice, because it was very winterlike." And I was sitting there and thinking, "I can't believe this is happening. Is there someone else in the room? Is there some consequential person in the room? Because I'm certainly not."

ANDY BRECKMAN:

You hear people on the White House staff talking about face time with the president, and that's what goes on here. When Lorne would come into the office and sit for a few minutes, that was almost, you know, a pat on the back, even though there was, literally, *no* pat on the back. Just getting a few minutes of face time with him meant you were of some value to him.

JIMMY FALLON, *Cast Member:*

I talk to Lorne regularly about everything. He's the master. He's been through it all, man. He knows everything. I have to make appointments to see him, because I'll talk to him for an hour if I can. I mean, it's like, "All right, my next issue is this: I'm getting an apartment." And he'll say, "Well, I think you should." Whatever it is, he'll give me advice on it. He's just really great. That's the guy I go to for an answer. He doesn't beat around the bush. He gives you an answer and he takes away all the stress.

JAMES SIGNORELLI, *Director of Commercial Parodies:*

I swear to God—and I've been around this guy for almost thirty years—Lorne has no interest in what you want to talk about. None.

What Lorne thinks is, if you need him to help you solve it, it's not worth solving. And you ultimately are going to solve it yourself, even if he told you a better solution. As Gertrude Stein used to say, "You can't tell nobody what they don't know—not even that they don't know it." And he embodies that. I'll come into his office and say, "Listen, this is what I want to do," and Lorne will say something completely at right angles to it. And I'll go, "Well, I don't think that's really relevant." And he'll just go, "Okay." Meaning—"I'm not listening to what you're saying. This is what I'm saying. And I know that if you do it, you're going to do it, so what are you here for? Let's go do something else. Let's go to dinner."

It's not his job to help me with logistical problems. His job is to look at something and if he thinks it's funny, to laugh with all his heart and soul. When he laughs, America laughs.

CHRIS ELLIOTT:

If you see the movie *Man on the Moon,* you'll see Lorne and Dave Letterman in it, both playing themselves, and it's interesting how they each approached their appearance. Lorne actually tried to make himself look like he looked back when Andy Kaufman was on *Saturday Night Live*—he's barefoot and he's eating with chopsticks in his lounge chair. And then, when they re-created the scene when Andy was with Letterman, Dave has his regular glasses on, which he didn't wear back then. He's wearing his regular suit. He made no attempt whatsoever to act in this movie other than to go through the motions. And in a way it's a lot easier for me to deal with a guy like Dave than it is with Lorne, who's kind of an actor. He's a guy who wants everybody to love him; Dave doesn't give a shit about that. So I seem to be able to read Dave better. The bottom line is, you know, Dave; he's nuts. There's no doubt about it. But he also is what he is. He's never acting, as far as I can tell. He is genuine, and when he's pissed off, he's pissed off, and when he's in a good mood, he's in a good mood. I could never tell any of that with Lorne.

COLIN QUINN, *Cast Member:*

I always thought I could tell how Lorne really felt about things. Even though he doesn't say it most of the time, he does laugh. Like at read-through. He reads all the stage directions, which is a hard thing to do. I've read stage directions before, and it's fuckin' hard. It's a pain in the ass. And he does it every show. You can tell if he likes something or doesn't like it by the way he reads those stage directions. He can be one of the bigger laughers at read-through, but when he doesn't like it, he has no problem just sitting there quietly.

CHEVY CHASE, *Cast Member:*

There's no mystery about who Lorne is to me because we came in on the same level basically. It's just that as time goes on, people become, they're made into a legend by those who are hired and, you know, *Saturday Night Live,* oh, nobody's going to live up to the original cast, nobody can live up to this or that. But there's one thing that stays steady all the way through—Lorne Michaels. Nobody can live up to that, because he put the whole thing together.

He's very nonconfrontational—probably both his strongest and his weakest suit. Lorne is both involved and uninvolved in some ways. His lack of confrontational abilities doesn't serve him well on occasion, because he can't fire anyone. He finds it difficult to fire people. That's a lovely thing too in many ways. But when the chips are down and it comes to artistic integrity versus the network's fear of what a sponsor might or might not say if such and such a sketch is put on, he's there. He'll confront.

Lorne may be frightening to the last five or six casts, to the younger set, as it were. It may be daunting to be around Lorne. I think he may seem intimidating because he seems to know so much. But he's been there all along. He's a real survivor. Anybody who really gets close to him would know that he is a kind and thoughtful guy who doesn't look to hurt others.

ROSIE SHUSTER:

I'm Canadian, and apologies are like mother's milk to us. They just roll off the tongue. "I'm sorry I caught my hand in your car trunk," that kind of thing. I don't think Lorne ever apologized to people for keeping them waiting for a long, long time. Instead, he would drop some names, which was a big soother, and you'd have a tidbit to run back and tell your friends afterwards.

You can't explain Lorne by Canada, that's for sure. There's an adopted British thing happening there. But there are some other elements that got internalized along the way and inside his psyche beside that.

BARBARA GALLAGHER, *NBC Vice President:*

I had one meeting with a unit manager and he made me cry. Lorne found out about it and he was furious. He was very protective. Later on, that guy ends up being indicted in a big unit-manager scandal and sent to prison for embezzling. And Lorne sent me the article with a note that said, "The wheel turns. It turns slowly, but it turns."

ANDY BRECKMAN:

Some executives at Paramount have asked me—because they have that big deal with Lorne where the overhead is quite high—if I know why cast members, once they graduate from *SNL,* don't want to work with Lorne. I'm sure Paramount's idea when they signed Lorne was that he would be able to deliver the Adam Sandlers of the world and be able to feed them that talent, and he hasn't delivered it. I really don't know the answer.

MIKE MYERS, *Cast Member:*

As far as not having Lorne produce the *Austin Powers* films, *Austin Powers* came out of tremendous grief at the loss of my father; it was an homage to my father and all the fun sort of British culture that my father forced all of us, me and my brothers, to watch. I wrote it, I didn't think anybody would make it, I didn't think necessarily it was something Lorne would want to do. There was never a conscious effort not to work with Lorne. I just met different producers out in L.A. because we were living there, and Lorne was in New York. It just happens to be that some people who showed interest in it in its very nascent form are the people I produced it with. It was never a conscious effort to break away from Lorne. I have seen Lorne socially thousands of times. I consider him one of my friends, and certainly one of my teachers. I just met somebody different in L.A. And I actually didn't think necessarily that *Austin* was Lorne's cup of tea.

I am happy to go on record that the character of Dr. Evil in the *Austin Powers* films has really very little to do with Lorne Michaels. It has more to do with a composite of all the bad guys in the James Bond films and the Matt Helm films and *In Like Flint* films. I happen to have a Canadian accent, as does Lorne. It's some vocal quirk which we actually share, being, you know, two guys from Toronto. But for the most part, it really isn't Lorne. It wasn't enough Lorne when I made the first one that I felt it necessary to say anything to him about it in advance. Having said that, Dr. Evil is my favorite character that I've ever done. The only similarity to Lorne is vocally. It's not anything to do with Lorne's character. If anything, he should be honored by it. I would be happy to state very clearly that I do not feel Lorne Michaels is evil. That's a for-the-record type statement.

I have nothing but the utmost respect for Lorne Michaels. He's a Canadian hero to me, to be honest with you. I am in awe of him. I did a project on him in grade eight — or the eighth grade, and I would have said "proe-ject." I was shaking when I met him, and shaking with pride that he's a Canadian. I was never disappointed with how incredibly smart he is. There isn't a day that I don't quote Lorne about some aspect of trying to make sense of show business. It's a situation for which there is no glossary of terms, but Lorne has created a glossary of terms, and I've used it frequently. He's one of the few bosses I've ever worked for who is funnier than I am.

TERRY TURNER, *Writer:*

We didn't have a whole lot of contact with Lorne early on. He would sort of go through the halls on, I guess it was Tuesday night, and wander through and say, "What are you writing, what are you doing?" He was a hard man to reach sometimes. But the signals would be out there. You just had to interpret like he was speaking a foreign language. Later on, Lorne really became a mentor for Bonnie and me. I don't know how it happened or where it began. Then at some point, you know, you're under somebody's wing for so long it never rains on you, but the sun doesn't shine on you either. So you realize that you have to get out from under the wing and do it yourself, see if you can do it.

BERNIE BRILLSTEIN:

No one remembers that Lorne was a great writer, he's a great editor, and his comedy mind is fantastic. But he's two different guys— he's Gatsby and he's Lorne the Canadian. He's two different people. He loves that New York life. In fact, he loves New York more than I do, and I was born there.

DANA CARVEY:

Lorne loves New York because, as he would say, "you've got finance, you've got the theater, and you've got broadcast networks. It's not this sort of one-trick pony."

DAN AYKROYD, *Cast Member:*

I did get mad once and put a hole through a wall in Lorne's office. I punched a hole in it because I was so mad at the way he would give us last-minute changes before air. We would have to run down and give them to the cue card guys, and they would be going crazy and saying, "Are you kidding?! You want us to get *this* on?!" And I just said, at a certain point, we have got to decide what's in and what's out within each sketch—what are the changes and they've got to be done in time, so that you can get them to cards and we aren't standing there with them shuffling cards in front of us on the air. Because everything is read on that show. You can't memorize; it's happening too fast. So I had that one episode when I was mad at him, but I never had any other tense moments with Lorne. And that went away fast.

AL FRANKEN:

After Danny put his fist through the wall, Lorne came in and did his "I'm very disappointed" thing. That's what I remember more than anything else about the incident. Lorne's reaction was of "disappointment"—like a father being disappointed—instead of actual anger. I remember watching that and thinking, "That's a smart way to handle this."

CONAN O'BRIEN:

I remember once he was really mad about a dress that had gone really badly. And we were all packed into that little room afterwards. And he's really pissed. Because this dress didn't go well and a lot of things went wrong. And he's like doing that Lorne thing that he can do sometimes—heavy, heavy sarcasm. Because Lorne will not usually confront you directly. He would just say things like, "Oh, I loved how it had no ending," or "It was brilliant how it just sort of dribbled off." And he's trying to talk about the lousy dress, and I think Bob Odenkirk, who was very junior at that point, whispered to somebody something, and Lorne just went, "Odenkirk, you speak again, I'll break your fucking legs." And it was like the first time I had seen him actually swinging into action and actually beating someone up. It really made me laugh.

KATE JACKSON, *Host:*

I remember when I was hosting, somebody came in and said something to Lorne about John Belushi being in bad shape, and Lorne said, "We're on live at eleven-thirty. He's not allowed to die until after the show."

ANDREW SMITH, *Writer:*

I used to call Lorne every year to see if he had a spot open, until the last time I had a meeting with him. He'd kept me waiting for about an hour and a half or more—a long fuckin' time. And I finally got in there, and then he did his dinner reservations with his assistant during our meeting. Where was dinner going to be, what time was it going to be, that sort of thing. And then that was the end of the meeting. To make matters worse, Lorne still has to be introduced to me every time I meet him. Every time I see him, somebody will have to say, "Lorne, you know Andrew Smith, don't you?" "Oh, yes, yes. Hello." I think he's become a full British subject now in his mind, hasn't he?

BOB TISCHLER:

I have been told so many stories as to who came up with the idea for *Saturday Night Live*. Dick always tried to claim a certain amount of credit, and so does Lorne. I don't know exactly what went on. I can be very critical of the way Lorne works and the way he deals with people and who he is, but the fact remains he is the guy who did put the show together. One of my criticisms is the way he manipulates people, but he did manipulate people to put that show together and to do a good show.

NORMAN LEAR, *Host:*

I have a routine that I've done with my daughter Kate since she was four years old. It's an ancient burlesque kind of sketch. I ask her to help me tell a joke and she tries very hard and messes up and I jump on her for it and she begs for another chance. She messes up in a different way and I jump on her. And it builds and I get angrier and angrier at this child. And it was always terribly funny. I had a wonderful and still have a wonderful relationship with Lorne, and I told him I'd love to do this and he saw it and he said, "Oh God, that's great. We'll do it." But we're now talking the live show. Lorne had somebody making cartoons, I don't remember who it was, and halfway through this live show, I'm about to come out and Lorne says, "I want to run the cartoon" and to cut the sketch with my daughter. So pretty soon I'm out there introducing Boz Scaggs, my music act, and I'm looking at my daughter, who's sitting with her mother and her sister in *such* anticipation. And when it comes time to go to the cartoon, I instead start the thing with Kate, and I bring her up onstage, and we do the routine—which played very well, very well. And Lorne never said a word to me, but I knew he was furious, and he had every right to be. But it was either my daughter or his wrath. And I chose my daughter. In a show business sense, it was not the thing to do. I'm guilty. But Lorne never said anything to me about it. He also never asked me back.

ANNE BEATTS:

I had been out to dinner with my father, and I of course had to go back to work. My father was kind of drunk and against my will insisted on coming back with me to the office. In the hall, he button-holed Lorne and started telling him what he was doing wrong. He was basically telling Lorne how to produce the show. And I was horribly embarrassed and mortified by this. I remember Lorne said to me, "He's not you. Remember, he's not you." I thought that was very kind.

FRED SILVERMAN, *NBC President:*

Lorne and I didn't go out to dinner every night. I think he had a different relationship with Herb Schlosser than he did with me. Maybe he needed more tender loving care at that point in time than I had given him. It's one of those things where you really attack your problem areas. If something is working—like *Saturday Night Live* was—you say, "God bless you," and you just let them alone. I think Lorne mistook that for a lack of love, which really wasn't the case. It wasn't an intentional slight on my part. There were just major fires all over the network. So I think that was part of it. He never felt he had that daily support and tender loving care.

ANDY SAMBERG, *Cast Member:*

He is probably the most iconic off-camera person in the history of comedy, and I don't think that's an exaggeration. On-camera, you have people like Charlie Chaplin—everyone knows him—but in terms of longevity and the quality and the breadth of success, I think Lorne is unmatched. The way he conducts business is very unique because the one thing you can always say about Lorne is he genuinely loves comedy. No matter what complaints people have about him—and I don't really have that many; I've had a good relationship with him pretty much from the beginning—he is in it for the right reason, and that is to make funny quality entertainment. He came up on comedy; he loves it. When somebody is new and funny, he gets really excited. No one is going to ever say that they would compare anyone to Lorne.

STEVE HIGGINS, *Supervising Producer:*

About four years ago, an old cast member came back to host and wanted to redo a sketch they had done at dress that had never made it to air. They loved the piece and said, "I want to do this one thing." So

I mentioned it to Lorne, and he goes, "Yeah, but you know what? There's a weird shot in that piece." I said, "What?" He goes, "There's a weird shot. There's a line that just was off." I go, "Oh, okay. Are you kidding me?" And I walked away and thought, "He's crazy. What is he talking about?" So I went and watched the sketch from dress and there was a weird shot! There it was. It just didn't fit. So four years later, some crappy little sketch that was just at dress is still in his memory bank of things.

When you read about Buster Keaton making movies, you learn he was always left alone. That's what this place is. Lorne keeps everyone away so you don't get noted to death on stuff. So if it's awful, it's our fault. It's funny to me that people go, "He's not there a lot." Well, no—he is. "Oh, but he doesn't come to the tapings." No—he's here every day. "Well, he doesn't blah, blah, blah." No—it's his show, and this is the thing he cares about more than anything else in the world. He loves the other shows, but this is his baby.

BUCK HENRY, *Host:*

I wish he'd make better movies, but then I wish I'd make better movies. So that's no big deal. It wasn't a mistake for him to come back to the show, because it's what he has done the best.

MOLLY SHANNON:

Lorne's a deep thinker. He can analyze anybody. If you want an analysis of somebody, go to him. He's the best. He'll be like, "Well, he's duh duh duh duh duh." He can sum somebody up in like thirty seconds. He's very quick and a very deep thinker and he's very loyal, loyal to a fault. So many of the same people who've worked there for years, these families he's supported, they're still there. The loyalty is phenomenal. He's very loyal. Just rock-solid loyalty like I'd never seen before.

AMY POEHLER, *Cast Member:*

I like to squeeze Lorne a lot and tell him I love him and kiss him and pinch his butt. That's who I am.

MAYA RUDOLPH, *Cast Member:*

I weirdly stopped being nervous around Lorne when I had to go into his office and tell him I was pregnant. But that was my fifth year. Before that, Lorne always made me nervous because I always wanted to be a good girl in front of him and deep down I think I wanted him to think I was great. And I didn't want to piss people off; I was always afraid to speak my mind. But that was also coming from a twenty-seven-year-old with a brand-new job and not knowing where the fuck I was and what the fuck to do and how to do it. I didn't want to get fired. That's what's really going on when you work there. When you look back and you realize, "Oh, he must have thought I was really shy, because I never talked to him and I never really spoke up." I was just a diligent good girl and did my stuff and went home. But once I had to go into his office and tell him I was pregnant—which was, weirdly, a month after Tina had to do the same thing—everything about our relationship changed.

What came first out of that conversation was he was worried because I had done a sketch where I fell through a piano, so he said, "I can't believe I just let you fall through a wire foam piano last week." I hadn't told anybody I was pregnant yet, because I wasn't finished with my first trimester. So he was upset with me that I did that, which was really sweet.

So after I told him I was pregnant, I've always been a lot closer and familial since then. It actually allowed me to speak up and go to his office and start speaking my mind. I just felt really open with him and comfortable with him in a way that I hadn't before. He's probably the most loyal person you will ever know, probably to a fault, because he knows a lot of people, so I don't know how he does that. I love him.

DAVE WILSON, *Director:*

A long time ago, a reporter was interviewing the renowned composer Jerome Kern. The reporter asked Kern what he felt was Irving Berlin's place in American music. Kern answered that Irving Berlin *was* American music. And that's the way I feel about Lorne Michaels. Lorne Michaels *is Saturday Night Live.* He made it a legendary hit. And then he kept reinventing it to reflect that young adult audience's tastes in topical comedy and in popular music.

CHRIS ROCK:

I've never been broke a day since I met Lorne Michaels. When I met Lorne Michaels I lived in a little studio apartment, my family lived in the ghetto for the most part. I met Lorne Michaels, and me and my family have been more than comfortable ever since.

BERNIE BRILLSTEIN:

My dad died in New York and the funeral service was ten-thirty in the morning. The last person I think that's going to be there at ten-thirty in the morning is Lorne. But he was the *first* one. That's Lorne. His depth of feeling, his depth of being hurt, is really tremendous. And so is his depth for enjoyment. He's really the most unique guy I've met with his loyalty. We've been together thirty-some years, and he was romanced by the best of them. But he's never left me.

TIM MEADOWS, *Cast Member:*

I walked around the corner once just as Lorne's children were freeing themselves from their nanny's clutches. I saw him get down on his knees and they ran to him and piled all over him, and I thought, "Man, you've got it goin' on, brother. You got this thing working."

SCARLETT JOHANSSON, *Host:*

It's very rare that you meet people in this industry that have had the experience that Lorne has, that can be charmingly jaded yet still have a curiosity about what's going to work even though you'd think they'd go, "I know what works." He doesn't feel the need to put on that masculine vibrato thing and kind of take control and throw his weight or any of that. He's quietly confident and I think it makes everybody in that working environment feel kind of safe—like they can take a risk and not be shot down.

BILLY CRYSTAL, *Cast Member:*

We had one really nice moment together after all this time at the twenty-fifth-anniversary show, where I came out as Fernando. I had a great four or five minutes, great to be back in the character again, it really was a very strong thing. But Lorne walked me to the mark backstage and met me back there. And he was very warm with me. And that was very nice.

PAUL RUDD, *Host:*

He's one of those guys where it seems like everyone I know who talks about Lorne immediately goes into a "Lorne voice." Nobody can say anything that he said without actually trying to sound like him. He's that iconic, I suppose.

JON HAMM, *Host:*

My favorite thing to do with Lorne—and you get ample opportunity to do this—is listen, because the guy has fifty years or however long he's been in show biz and he has been through every version of every situation that you'll come into, from inspiring you to talking about losing jobs and getting jobs and keeping shows on the network and reinventing shows and just every iteration of every problem you'll ever have. Lorne has been through it all probably seven times. He's a great storyteller and his experience is so wide-ranging that you'd be remiss if you didn't try to take notes.

TOM HANKS:

Lorne invented this thing. It's hard to imagine now the place that Ed Sullivan held in the esteem of the country and the medium of television because he was on every Sunday night. But it was a substantial thing to go on the *Ed Sullivan Show*—just to get the shot in the first place. And then to be called over and shake hands with Ed and maybe even chat with Ed before you went off. When you did Sullivan, it was literally a watermark for anybody's career. And if you did well on Sullivan, it guaranteed you some spot in the firmament. You could say the same thing about the Johnny Carson show. And I think you could say, even though he's not the actual host but he is the godfather of the show, I think you could say the same about Lorne. He is this very particular sort of show business maven that only exists in regularly scheduled television. It doesn't exist in movies. Lorne's produced movies, but other than getting them made, I don't think you could say he's had a resounding influence as a movie producer. But in the medium of TV, where you do a show week after week, Lorne has maintained this level of pacemaking influence that has not altered over the years. *Saturday Night Live* has remained socially relevant literally because of him.

LENA DUNHAM, *Host:*

The energy surrounding Lorne seems to be respect, which is what it's supposed to be because of the fact this is the house that Lorne built. What impressed me so much was his ability to be so decisive. You think to yourself, how are you going to know when something on *SNL* is too broad? Sketch comedy is broad. But somehow he is able to cut in and be incisive about "That moment doesn't feel real" and you look at it and you realize, "Oh, that's why *SNL* works." Because in the midst of the insanity there's these incredibly real, well-observed human moments and Lorne is encouraging those. At the meeting that happens between dress and the show, I can't believe he's saying, "The guest is overlit; that curtain needs to be a shade brighter; you really need to pick up your cue." The fact that he was able to see the big picture and see those little things as well was just crazy. It was someone at the height of their powers, someone who had a complete understanding of a medium that ultimately they had invented. It is really amazing how Lorne was able to both express his unique vision and foster the talents of different people. I mean, it's a very impressive thing—and very intoxicating.

MARILYN SUZANNE MILLER:

I was in Los Angeles writing a novel and found something in my breast the size of a lemon. So I got on a plane an hour later and came back to New York. Within twenty-four hours I knew I had breast cancer. Mine was advanced breast cancer, which is to say I didn't have metastatic breast cancer, but I did have a huge tumor with many nodes, so I had experimental chemo. I told my manager, "I don't want to go back to L.A. I'm too scared." So I was going to stay in New York and have this chemo and radiation. And I was just in shock. At that point I didn't know if I was going to live or die. It was very aggressive cancer.

Lorne had of course been on the phone with me. Everybody from the original show called—the family thing again. Our ties are very emotional. Then one day Lorne called me up. He knew I wanted to be in New York for the treatments and that I had left a job in L.A. And he said, "How'd you like to come back to the show?" And I thought, "Yeah! Love to!" So in the spring I went back. Back home—to *Saturday Night Live*.

CECILY STRONG, *Cast Member:*

Lorne had a meeting with me on my worst day. I looked at him and just started sobbing. On the show right now we're just such a young cast. It's humiliating to admit that anything could get to you. It's humiliating to say, "I've read the bad things that are out there about me." I had talked to my therapist that day and she had asked, "Is there anybody who could give you advice, who knows how to do this, how to navigate this?"

Lorne didn't talk down to me and wasn't upset at me at all. He was very fatherly—he has a really fatherly thing about him. I was crying and I said, "Can I have a hug?"

ALAN ZWEIBEL:

I'd like for God to give me back the time that I invested in trying to figure Lorne out. I would like to have those hours and weeks and months back. I guess it's like someone trying to figure out their parents. There was a real need for validation from him, and now that I've been away from it for so long, when I do see Lorne, there's still that thing where you want him to know that you're doing okay, you want him to be proud. You're like, "Hey, I had a part in this." So there were ill feelings at one time, but they were born out of a different situation.

When most of us got there in '75 and started the show, Lorne's predictions started coming true, and we said, "This guy's a prophet, you know, look at this, everything he's predicting is happening. I'll hitch my wagon to his horse." And then years later, I went to the twenty-fifth-anniversary show. It's funny, because it didn't feel like twenty-five years, but as you looked around and you added up stuff here and there—well, yeah, I guess that does equal twenty-five years.

I was sitting there looking around at the people who were there and coming onstage. I was thinking, look who came through here, look at what it gave birth to, and look at how much money there is in this room right now.

And I thought, "Look what Lorne did. Look at what he's done!"

DAN AYKROYD:

My dad's ninety-five, my mum's ninety-two, and their minds are real sharp. They read the paper every day, they look at television news, and they're right up on everything. It's just the mobility that's the thing, but by the time I'm ninety, there'll be an exoskeleton that I can climb into so I can run down the road and jump up and grab coconuts. That won't be a problem—mobility then—so you can keep the mind straight and the brain straight. With what they're developing now, we'll be hovering everywhere.

Phil Hymes, the lighting director, he's ninety-one this year and he's still there. Don Pardo still does the announce; he's ninety. That studio's had a lot of long careers. Chuck Yeager can go to any jet on the planet now—he's near ninety—get into it, and take off, and he does. So why shouldn't Lorne be there at ninety?!

ANNE BEATTS:

Lorne did have a note from Gilda on his bulletin board that said, "Lorne, I'm happy. Love, Gilda." But enough about Lorne. What about me?

SNL Cast Lists
SEASON BY SEASON

1975–76
Dan Aykroyd
John Belushi
Chevy Chase
Jane Curtin
Garrett Morris
Laraine Newman
Gilda Radner

1976–77
Dan Aykroyd
John Belushi
Chevy Chase
Jane Curtin
Garrett Morris
Bill Murray
Laraine Newman
Gilda Radner

1977–78
Dan Aykroyd
John Belushi
Jane Curtin
Garrett Morris

Bill Murray
Laraine Newman
Gilda Radner

1978–79
Dan Aykroyd
John Belushi
Jane Curtin
Garrett Morris
Bill Murray
Laraine Newman
Gilda Radner

1979–80
Jane Curtin
Garrett Morris
Bill Murray
Laraine Newman
Gilda Radner
Harry Shearer

1980–81
Denny Dillon
Gilbert Gottfried

Gail Matthius
Eddie Murphy
Joe Piscopo
Ann Risley
Charles Rocket

1981–82
Denny Dillon
Brian Doyle-Murray
Robin Duke
Christine Ebersole
Mary Gross
Tim Kazurinsky
Eddie Murphy
Joe Piscopo
Tony Rosato

1982–83
Robin Duke
Mary Gross
Brad Hall
Tim Kazurinsky
Gary Kroeger
Julia Louis-Dreyfus
Eddie Murphy
Joe Piscopo

1983–84
Jim Belushi
Robin Duke
Mary Gross
Brad Hall
Tim Kazurinsky
Gary Kroeger
Julia Louis-Dreyfus
Eddie Murphy
Joe Piscopo

1984–85
Jim Belushi
Billy Crystal
Mary Gross
Christopher Guest
Rich Hall
Gary Kroeger
Julia Louis-Dreyfus
Harry Shearer
Martin Short
Pamela Stephenson

1985–86
Joan Cusack
Robert Downey, Jr.
Nora Dunn
Anthony Michael Hall
Jon Lovitz
Terry Sweeney
Randy Quaid
Danitra Vance

1986–87
Dana Carvey
Nora Dunn
Phil Hartman
Jan Hooks
Victoria Jackson
Jon Lovitz
Dennis Miller
Kevin Nealon

1987–88
Dana Carvey
Nora Dunn
Phil Hartman
Jan Hooks

Victoria Jackson
Jon Lovitz
Dennis Miller
Kevin Nealon

1988–89
Dana Carvey
Nora Dunn
Phil Hartman
Jan Hooks
Victoria Jackson
Jon Lovitz
Dennis Miller
Kevin Nealon
Featuring
A. Whitney Brown
Al Franken
Mike Myers
Ben Stiller

1989–90
Dana Carvey
Nora Dunn
Phil Hartman
Jan Hooks
Victoria Jackson
Jon Lovitz
Dennis Miller
Mike Myers
Kevin Nealon
Featuring
A. Whitney Brown
Al Franken
Adam Sandler
Rob Schneider
David Spade

1990–91
Dana Carvey
Phil Hartman
Jan Hooks
Victoria Jackson
Dennis Miller
Mike Myers
Kevin Nealon
With
Chris Farley
Tim Meadows
Chris Rock
Julia Sweeney
Featuring
A. Whitney Brown
Al Franken
Adam Sandler
Rob Schneider
David Spade

1991–92
Dana Carvey
Chris Farley
Phil Hartman
Victoria Jackson
Mike Myers
Kevin Nealon
Chris Rock
Julia Sweeney
With
Ellen Cleghorne
Siobhan Fallon
Tim Meadows
Adam Sandler
Rob Schneider
David Spade

Featuring
Beth Cahill
Al Franken
Melanie Hutsell
Robert Smigel

1992–93
Dana Carvey
Chris Farley
Phil Hartman
Mike Myers
Kevin Nealon
Chris Rock
Rob Schneider
Julia Sweeney
With
Al Franken
Robert Smigel
Featuring
Ellen Cleghorne
Melanie Hutsell
Tim Meadows
Adam Sandler
David Spade

1993–94
Ellen Cleghorne
Chris Farley
Phil Hartman
Melanie Hutsell
Michael McKean
Tim Meadows
Mike Myers
Kevin Nealon
Adam Sandler
Rob Schneider
David Spade

Julia Sweeney
Featuring
Al Franken
Norm Macdonald
Jay Mohr
Sarah Silverman

1994–95
Morwenna Banks
Ellen Cleghorne
Chris Elliott
Chris Farley
Janeane Garofalo
Norm Macdonald
Michael McKean
Mark McKinney
Tim Meadows
Mike Myers
Kevin Nealon
Adam Sandler
David Spade
Featuring
Al Franken
Laura Kightlinger
Jay Mohr
Molly Shannon

1995–96
Jim Breuer
Will Ferrell
Darrell Hammond
David Koechner
Norm Macdonald
Mark McKinney
Tim Meadows
Cheri Oteri

Molly Shannon
David Spade
Nancy Walls
Featuring
Chris Kattan
Colin Quinn
Fred Wolf

1996–97
Jim Breuer
Will Ferrell
Ana Gasteyer
Darrell Hammond
Chris Kattan
Norm Macdonald
Mark McKinney
Tim Meadows
Tracy Morgan
Cheri Oteri
Molly Shannon
Featuring
Colin Quinn
Fred Wolf

1997–98
Jim Breuer
Will Ferrell
Ana Gasteyer
Darrell Hammond
Chris Kattan
Norm Macdonald
Tim Meadows
Tracy Morgan
Cheri Oteri
Colin Quinn
Molly Shannon

1998–99
Will Ferrell
Ana Gasteyer
Darrell Hammond
Chris Kattan
Tim Meadows
Tracy Morgan
Cheri Oteri
Colin Quinn
Molly Shannon
Featuring
Jimmy Fallon
Chris Parnell
Horatio Sanz

1999–2000
Jimmy Fallon
Will Ferrell
Ana Gasteyer
Darrell Hammond
Chris Kattan
Tim Meadows
Tracy Morgan
Cheri Oteri
Chris Parnell
Colin Quinn
Horatio Sanz
Molly Shannon
Featuring
Rachel Dratch
Maya Rudolph

2000–01
Jimmy Fallon
Will Ferrell
Ana Gasteyer

Darrell Hammond
Chris Kattan
Tracy Morgan
Chris Parnell
Horatio Sanz
Molly Shannon
Featuring
Rachel Dratch
Tina Fey
Jerry Minor
Maya Rudolph

2001–02
Rachel Dratch
Jimmy Fallon
Will Ferrell
Tina Fey
Ana Gasteyer
Darrell Hammond
Chris Kattan
Tracy Morgan
Chris Parnell
Amy Poehler
Maya Rudolph
Horatio Sanz
Featuring
Dean Edwards
Seth Meyers
Jeff Richards

2002–03
Rachel Dratch
Jimmy Fallon
Tina Fey
Darrell Hammond
Chris Kattan

Tracy Morgan
Chris Parnell
Amy Poehler
Maya Rudolph
Horatio Sanz
Featuring
Fred Armisen
Dean Edwards
Will Forte
Seth Meyers
Jeff Richards

2003–04
Rachel Dratch
Jimmy Fallon
Tina Fey
Will Forte
Darrell Hammond
Seth Meyers
Chris Parnell
Amy Poehler
Jeff Richards (Last: #1335)
Maya Rudolph
Horatio Sanz
Featuring
Fred Armisen
Finesse Mitchell
Kenan Thompson

2004–05
Fred Armisen
Rachel Dratch
Tina Fey
Will Forte
Darrell Hammond
Seth Meyers

Chris Parnell
Amy Poehler
Maya Rudolph
Horatio Sanz
Featuring
Finesse Mitchell
Rob Riggle
Kenan Thompson

2005–06
Fred Armisen
Rachel Dratch
Tina Fey
Will Forte
Darrell Hammond
Seth Meyers
Finesse Mitchell
Chris Parnell
Amy Poehler
Maya Rudolph
Horatio Sanz
Kenan Thompson
Featuring
Bill Hader
Andy Samberg
Jason Sudeikis
Kristen Wiig (Start: #1427)

2006–07
Fred Armisen
Will Forte
Bill Hader
Darrell Hammond
Seth Meyers
Amy Poehler
Maya Rudolph

Andy Samberg
Jason Sudeikis
Kenan Thompson
Kristen Wiig

2007–08
Fred Armisen
Will Forte
Bill Hader
Darrell Hammond
Seth Meyers
Amy Poehler
Maya Rudolph (Last: #1522)
Andy Samberg
Jason Sudeikis
Kenan Thompson
Kristen Wiig
Featuring
Casey Wilson (Start: #1524)

2008–09
Fred Armisen
Will Forte
Bill Hader
Darrell Hammond
Seth Meyers
Amy Poehler (Last: #1542)
Andy Samberg
Jason Sudeikis
Kenan Thompson
Kristen Wiig
Featuring
Abby Elliott (Start: #1539)
Bobby Moynihan
Michaela Watkins (Start: #1539)
Casey Wilson

2009–10
Fred Armisen
Will Forte
Bill Hader
Seth Meyers
Andy Samberg
Jason Sudeikis
Kenan Thompson
Kristen Wiig
Featuring
Abby Elliott
Bobby Moynihan
Nasim Pedrad
Jenny Slate

2010–11
Fred Armisen
Abby Elliott
Bill Hader
Seth Meyers
Bobby Moynihan
Andy Samberg
Jason Sudeikis
Kenan Thompson
Kristen Wiig
Featuring
Vanessa Bayer
Paul Brittain
Taran Killam
Nasim Pedrad
Jay Pharoah

2011–12
Fred Armisen
Abby Elliott
Bill Hader

Seth Meyers
Bobby Moynihan
Nasim Pedrad
Andy Samberg
Jason Sudeikis
Kenan Thompson
Kristen Wiig
Featuring
Vanessa Bayer
Paul Brittain (Last: #1610)
Taran Killam
Kate McKinnon (Start: #1616)
Jay Pharoah

2012–13
Fred Armisen
Vanessa Bayer
Bill Hader
Taran Killam
Seth Meyers
Bobby Moynihan
Nasim Pedrad
Jay Pharoah
Jason Sudeikis
Kenan Thompson
Featuring
Aidy Bryant
Kate McKinnon
Tim Robinson
Cecily Strong

2013–14
Vanessa Bayer
Aidy Bryant
Taran Killam
Kate McKinnon

Seth Meyers (Last: #1654)
Bobby Moynihan
Nasim Pedrad
Jay Pharoah
Cecily Strong
Kenan Thompson
Featuring
Beck Bennett

Colin Jost (Start: #1655)
John Milhiser
Kyle Mooney
Mike O'Brien
Noël Wells
Brooks Wheelan
Sasheer Zamata (Start: #1652)

Index

Abba, 68
Abbott and Costello, 456
ABC, 12, 16, 19, 24, 31, 46, 59, 92, 512
Abel, Doug, 610
Ace and Gary, 634
Action Jackson, 322
Affleck, Ben, 483, 565, 609–10
Agnew, Spiro, 162
Albrecht, Chris, 69, 195, 197, 204, 239
Alda, Alan, 609
Alexander, Jason, 557
Ali, Muhammad, 273
Allen, Dayton, 162
Allen, Woody, 41, 184, 185, 198, 322, 517, 625
All in the Family, 66
Ambiguously Gay Duo, The, 634
Ampersand, 392
Anderson, James, 666, 675
Anderson, Richard Dean, 576
Animal House, 95, 121, 177, 242, 244, 380, 666
Aniston, Jennifer, 254, 477
Anthony Crispino character, 695
Antonowsky, Marvin, 19
Apatow, Judd, 546–47, 635
Arledge, Roone, 19, 24, 31, 453
Armisen, Fred: attitude toward show, 662; audition, 527–29; autism benefit, 600; Brownstein and, 662; as cast member, 554, 569–71, 577, 599, 607, 618, 621, 627, 644, 657–58, 662, 676; departure from show, 645, 648–49, 694; on drugs and *SNL,* 604; Fallon and, 629; Fey and, 565; Ian Rubbish character, 647; on Michaels, 649; Moss and, 597; Obama character, 569–71, 649; Palin appearance and, 591; Patterson impression, 600–601
Arnaz, Desi, 93, 214, 470
Arnold, Tom, 457, 475

"Arresting Fat People in Beverly Hills," 18
Arthur, Bea, 112
"Assassination of Buckwheat, The," 234–35
audience: age of, 273, 354, 360, 453–54, 464; black comics and, 382; catch phrases and, 319; Chase and, 122–23; *Dick in a Box* sketch and, 573; Fey as Palin and, 589; as late-night audience, 165; loyalty of, 101, 699; Murphy and, 456; new cast members and, 376; quality of show and, 192; reactions of, 277, 298, 303, 325, 370, 392, 412, 430, 431, 432, 452, 485, 613; sketches and, 126; staff attitudes toward, 159, 346–47, 432, 468; taste of, 266; as television generation, 8, 11, 453–54
Austin Powers, 372, 733
Awakening, 717
Aykroyd, Dan: attitude toward show, 605–6; on John Belushi, 96, 106–7, 108–9, 254; John Belushi and, 35, 77, 98–99, 111, 112, 120, 164, 242, 248, 251, 252; Blues Bar and, 116, 118–19, 189; Blues Brothers and, 120; boys club atmosphere and, 149; as cast member, 33–34, 58, 67, 100, 170, 178; censors and, 143, 145; characters of, 12, 126, 128, 131, 345, 530, 586, 653; Chase and, 80, 94, 125; comedians "dying" during act and, 479–80; as comedy writer, 127, 128, 136, 530, 653; Paula Davis and, 83–84; Tom Davis and, 653, 652–53, 654; Dole and, 344, 530, 587; drug use and, 89, 140, 665–66; Fallon and, 518; Farley and, 355; Fisher and, 127, 164; Hader and, 652; Henry on, 169; hosting and, 642; "Julia Child" sketch and, 126, 133, 652–53; Killer Bees and, 71; Lear on,

112; leaving of, 171, 178; Michaels and, 530; on Michaels, 735, 745; Morris and, 50; movie career of, 177, 530; O'Donoghue and, 96, 127, 128, 163; Radner and, 48, 83, 352; rebellion of, 163; Rock and, 399; Sandler and, 361; screen test and, 46–47; show romances and, 84; Shuster and, 84, 118–19, 120, 131, 141, 167–68; sketches and, 130–31, 134, 135, 140, 143; twenty-fifth-anniversary special and, 496; "Weekend Update" and, 161, 696; on Woodward, 253

Aymong, Ken, 462, 502, 524–25, 544, 592; changes in writers and, 667; diversity issues and, 683–84; episode with Betty White and, 616–17; on live show risks, 673–74; on Michaels, 673–74, 675; on production, 675; writers' strikes and, 583

Baba Wawa sketches, 136
Bacall, Lauren, 106
Bach, Barbara, 277
"Backstage Banter" sketch, 149
Backstreet Boys, 464
Bakker, Jim, 315
Bakker, Tammy Faye, 315
Baldwin, Alec: cast members and, 424; Farley and, 493; Goodman and, 485–86; as host, 340, 389, 405, 470, 471, 477, 616, 654; on Michaels, 710; musical guests and, 464–85; political humor and, 443; Smigel and, 634
Bar Mitzvah Boy, 645–46
Barr, Roseanne, 318, 370
Barrymore, Drew, 509, 540
Basie, Count, 31
Baskin, Edie: on John Belushi, 249; cast photos by, 696–97; drug use and, 89; hosts and, 66; New York pictures of, 49, 60
"Bass-O-Matic" pitchman sketches, 126
Bayer, Vanessa, 618, 628, 645–46, 664, 669, 694
Beatles, 402, 403
Beatts, Anne: John Belushi and, 36, 132, 242; Berle and, 157; Breckman and, 394; on Chase, 98; as comedy writer, 79; departure from show, 188; Dickman and, 518; on Michaels, 173, 701, 724, 737–38, 745; Michaels and, 290–91; Marilyn Suzanne Miller and, 23; on O'Donoghue, 23, 42; pay and, 36; show romances and, 83–84; Shuster on, 42; sketches and, 138, 141, 142; working hours and, 121
Beautiful Phyllis Diller Show, The, 19

"Beauty and the Beast" sketch, 327–28
bee characters. *See* Killer Bees
Beethoven character, 107
Begley, Ed, Jr., 266
Belafonte, Harry, 238
Belushi, Jim: attitude toward show, 228–29; on John Belushi, 245, 251–52; Ebersol and, 222, 226, 273; Kazurinsky and, 249–50; Louis-Dreyfus and, 269; return to show, 258, 260; salaries and, 261; on Woodward, 254
Belushi, John: Aykroyd and, 35, 77, 98–99, 111, 112, 120, 164, 242, 248, 251, 252; Aykroyd on, 96, 106–7, 108–9, 254; Beatts and, 36, 132, 242; Judith Belushi on, 36, 37, 64, 80–81, 106, 108, 243; Berle and, 156–57; *Big Event, The,* 166; Blues Bar and, 117, 118, 189, 252; boys club atmosphere and, 148; Brillstein on, 37, 57, 92, 244–45; as cast member, 37, 38, 100; characters of, 12, 71, 73–74, 107, 128; Chase and, 65, 67, 80, 94, 122–23, 125; Chase on, 34–35, 37, 87; Crystal and, 56; Curtin on, 38, 105, 111, 247; Paula Davis and, 83–84; death of, 242–54, 518; departure from show, 170, 171, 178, 229; drug use and, 87, 88, 105, 106, 108–9, 110–13, 242, 247, 250, 462, 666; Ebersol on, 36–37, 115, 240, 243–44; Elliott and, 386; Farley and, 354, 355, 356, 486; Fey and Fallon compared to, 440; fires and, 37, 115; first show and, 59; Fisher on, 105–6, 127, 247, 250–51; Gould and, 72; Henry on, 169; hosts and, 109–10; impressions and, 106–8; Improv and, 69; Kazurinsky and, 209, 215; Kazurinsky on, 247, 249–50, 251, 253; Killer Bees and, 64, 71; Klein and, 105, 111, 163, 718; Martin on, 105; Michaels and, 111, 666–67, 721, 736; Michaels on, 35–36, 79–80, 98–99, 108, 243, 245, 252–53; military commercials and, 92; Marilyn Suzanne Miller and, 107, 134; Morris and, 129, 249; movie career of, 177; Newman and, 80, 110, 250; Novello and, 338; Pryor and, 71; Radner and, 34, 36, 80; Sandler and, 361; Schiller and, 87, 110; screen test and, 46, 50–51, Shaffer and, 34; Shlien and, 187; Shuster on, 67; sketches and, 132–33; success of, 121, 177, 194, 217, 380; television and, 34–35, 36, 91; women comedy writers and, 80

Belushi, Judith: Aykroyd and, 77; on John
    Belushi, 35, 36, 37, 64, 80–81, 106,
    108, 243; Blues Bar and, 116; drug use
    and, 87; Ebersol and, 214; Kazurinsky
    and, 247
Bennett, Michael, 102
Benny, Jack, 157, 698
Bergen, Candice: as host, 28, 65, 71–72,
    654; on Michaels, 704–5, 711–12;
    Radner and, 81, 83
Berle, Milton, 156–59
Berlin, Irving, 740
Berry, Halle, 529–30
Best of Carson, The, 7
Best of Saturday Night Live, 179, 571–72,
    619, 621
Beverly Hills Cop, 304
Beverly Hills Ninja, 489, 490
Bieber, Justin, 633–34, 647
Big Event, The, 165
"Big Pill" sketch, 330
Bill and Ted, 373
Billy Madison, 378
Bing Bong Brothers, The, 551
Bjork, 637
Blair, Tony, 650
Blake, Eubie, 615
Blake, Robert, 276
Blaustein, Barry: Doumanian era and,
    195–96, 198, 199; Kurtzman and, 218;
    Murphy and, 229, 231, 233, 234, 239;
    Reagan and, 222
Blue Angel, 483
Blue Öyster Cult, 537
Blues Brothers, The, 121, 170, 177, 178, 246,
    372, 380
Blues Brothers band, 110, 118, 120–21
Blues Brothers characters, 35, 107, 120–21
Blues Brothers 2000, 530
Bob Roberts, 367
Bond, Julian, 339
Bowie, David, 118
Brando, Marlon, 51, 166, 253, 405
Breckman, Andy: comedy writers and, 513;
    David and, 265–66, 269; Hartman
    and, 488; hosts and, 281; Lovitz and,
    302; on Michaels, 719–20, 730, 733;
    Michaels and, 291, 452; Marilyn
    Suzanne Miller and, 394; Murphy
    and, 235–36, 237, 238; reruns and,
    463; Saturday Night Live as career
    launching, 466; Simpson and, 434;
    sketches and, 272; walk-ons and, 499
"Breezy Philosopher" sketch, 276
Bridesmaids, 638, 639
Bridges, Jeff, 623
Brillstein, Bernie: on John Belushi, 37, 57,
    92, 244–45; Carvey and, 309; on

Chase, 97; Ebersol and, 244; Garofalo
    and, 390; Grey on, 51; on Michaels,
    17, 24, 25, 33, 39, 44, 292, 708, 735,
    741; Michaels and, 170, 174, 252, 289;
    Michaels on, 17–18, 55; Muppets and,
    76; on Radner, 33; Radner and, 174;
    Saturday Night Live creation and, 22;
    Studio 8H and, 44; Tartikoff and,
    307; Wayans and, 304; Wilson and, 31
Broadcast News, 324
Broderick, Matthew, 480–81
Brokaw, Meredith, 578
Brokaw, Tom, 114, 578
Bromfeld, Valri, 61
Brooklyn Nine-Nine, 677
Brooks, Albert: on Michaels, 718;
    Michaels and, 63–64, 77, 171; Nealon
    and, 314; Saturday Night Live creation
    and, 26–28; Shearer and, 171; short
    films of, 26, 27, 41, 54–55, 59, 63, 65,
    75, 77, 100, 551
Brooks, Garth, 468
Brooks, Jim, 22
Brown, A. Whitney, Lovitz and, 319
Brown, Blair, 243
Brown, James, 535
Brown, Les, 24
Brownstein, Carrie, 662
Bruce Almighty, 634
Bryant, Aidy, 655, 658, 694
Buchanan, Pat, 432
Buckwheat sketches, 223, 233–35
Burke, Steve, 679, 701; on Michaels, 698;
    on Michaels and NBC late night, 693
Burnett, Carol, 43, 73, 130, 131, 174
Burns, Jack, 17
Bush, Barbara, 344
Bush, George H. W., 343, 344–45, 371,
    406, 532, 586
Bush, George W., 443, 444, 449, 450, 451,
    484, 506, 532, 533–34, 571, 581, 587,
    590, 594
Buttafuoco, Joey, 404
Byner, John, 161

Caan, James, 280
Caddyshack, 361, 709
Caesar, Sid, 9, 130, 278–79
Caesar's Hour, 9
Callas, Charlie, 227
Candy, John, 33, 222, 342
Caponera, Cindy, 545
Capote, Truman, 185
Carbon Copy, 279
Carell, Steve, 546–47, 620, 634
Carlin, George: as host, 32, 42, 43, 54, 55,
    58, 60, 62; Michaels and, 25; Saturday
    Night Live creation and, 21

Carney, Art, 13

Carrey, Jim, 254, 294–95, 518, 634

Carson, Johnny: audience of, 21; Aykroyd and, 480; band of, 45–46; Brooks on, 28; and Burbank, 24; Carvey and, 370–71; Chase and, 94; "dying" and, 480; Ebersol on, 29; Hanks and, 301; Jackson and, 311, 312; NBC and, 180; reruns of, 7–8, 9, 19, 20, 29, 188; show as comics' career-launching vehicle, 396, 437, 742

Carter, Jimmy, 345, 450

Carvey, Dana: ad-libbing and, 371; attitude toward show, 399; auditions of, 309, 315–16; George H. W. Bush and, 344–45, 371, 406, 532, 586; characters of, 315–16, 318, 319, 533, 594; comedy writers and, 370–71; departure from show, 407, 416; Downey and, 413; Dunn and, 330; generational split in cast and, 360, 547; Grey and, 309; hosts and, 342, 402; Jackson and, 331; on Michaels, 720–21, 735; Michaels and, 309–10, 317–18, 720–21; movie career of, 372; Murphy and, 232–33; Myers and, 373–74; Rock and, 379, 381; Sandler and, 377, 379; Smigel and, 727; Spade and, 362; Wolf and, 364

Carville, James, 651

Castaneda, Carlos, 90

cast members: airtime of, 9, 75; attendance at events asked of, 603; audience and, 159, 376, 613; auditions, 528–29, 620, 655; band compared to, 45–46; "breaking" and, 479, 608, 610–11, 612–13, 628–29; camera meeting, cue cards, and timing, 566; as celebrities, 105, 362, 520; comedy writers and, 132–33, 148, 294, 318–20, 377–78, 379, 391, 417, 427–28, 454–55, 536, 544, 550, 558, 559, 562, 566–69, 602, 607, 657–58; competition and, 329–30, 360, 396–98, 409, 417, 467–68, 500, 606; consistent sensibility of, 599; deaths of older generation, 652–53; departures of, 193, 302, 539, 542, 545, 557, 559–64, 567, 598, 601, 602–3, 621, 637–45, 648–49, 693–95; director for, 565–66; diversity issues and, 378, 676, 679–91; Doumanian and, 196–97; drug use and, 10, 86, 121, 326, 461, 469, 603–4, 665–66; Ebersol and, 32–33, 36–37, 213, 223, 255, 284; evolution and growth of, 662–64; as extended family, 641–42, 644, 648, 666; Ferrell's importance, 526; first show and, 59, 60–61; Groundlings and, 30, 37, 310, 325, 362–63, 447, 448, 548–49, 619,

621, 659; hosts and, 339–40, 400–401, 558, 618; lesbian/gay members, 659–61 (See also Pell, Paula); Michaels and, 33–39, 52, 79, 288, 308, 360, 400, 426, 514, 598, 703–4, 732–35; Michaels as father figure to, 10, 666–67, 703–4, 713; Michaels and hiring of, 645, 655, 690; military commercials and, 92; Murphy as role model for, 355, 359; Murphy's importance, 526; NBC and, 57, 72, 391, 415, 424, 425, 524; new, welcoming dinner for, 618; as Not Ready for Prime Time Players, 39, 46, 49, 59, 152, 194, 201, 242; opening credits and, 49; premature deaths of, 10, 13, 349, 486; romances of, 10, 83–85, 136–37, 138–39, 168, 271–72, 326, 357, 461, 604; salaries of, 118, 255, 261; *Saturday Night Live* as career launching for, 8, 121, 169, 170, 194, 261, 359, 391, 396, 402, 417, 465–66; *Saturday Night Live* creation and, 25, 26–27, 33–35; schedule of, 213, 603, 605–6; Schlosser and, 169; sketches and, 126–43, 259, 535–37; stars as, 255–67, 286; successes and failures of, 10–11, 424, 498; television and, 159–60; tension between, 331; watching *Saturday Night Live* as children, 454, 619–20, 630, 654–55, 661, 696–97; women stars, 544–45, 637, 659–60, 687 (see also Fey, Tina; Poehler, Amy; *specific women*); younger than the show, 527

Casual Sex?, 329

Catch a Rising Star, 40, 53, 112

Catherine the Great sketch, 109

Catholic League, 339

CBC, 16, 17

CBS, 12, 16, 19, 393, 414, 512

Campbell, Donnell, 537

censors: *Big Event, The,* 166; Blaustein and, 234; Clay and, 332–33; delay and, 43, 71, 332–33; Doumanian and, 198; Ebersol and, 220, 234–35; Franken and, 181; hosts and, 281; Michaels and, 11, 146, 147, 366; Nader and, 441; Novello and, 338; popularity of show and, 100; Pryor and, 71; reactions of, 9; Ron Reagan and, 299; Shuster and, 210–11; sketches and, 142–43, 145, 146, 406; strictness of, 223

Chan, Jackie, 471

Chaplin, Charlie, 738

Chappelle, Dave, 533, 562

Chappelle's Show, 562

Chase, Chevy: *Animal House* and, 95, 666; on John Belushi, 34–35, 37, 87; John

Belushi and, 65–66, 67, 80, 94–95, 122–23, 125; Bergen and, 81; and boys club atmosphere, 148; as cast member, 32–33, 34–35, 67; as comedy writer, 42, 49, 72, 94, 125–26, 273; Paula Davis and, 84; departure from show, 94–97, 100, 124, 126, 693; drug use and, 86–87, 666; on fame, 86; Farley and, 355; first show and, 59, 60; Ford and, 12, 171, 444, 450, 586, 589; Franken and, 162; Hawn and, 95; as host, 122, 122–23, 175, 297, 474; Killer Bees and, 71; Klein and, 26; Macdonald and, 429, 431; Meadows and, 401; on Michaels, 96, 732; Marilyn Suzanne Miller and, 23; movie career, 654; Murray and, 123–25, 518; Murray as replacement for, 101; Nealon and, 325; *New York* magazine cover and, 65; O'Donoghue's wake and, 217; Pryor and, 535; Sandler and, 361; Sargent and, 58; screen test and, 46, 49; show romances and, 84; Shuster on, 66–67; success of, 121, 194, 207; Tomlin and, 93–94; "Weekend Update" and, 9, 49, 64, 67, 74, 122, 123, 145, 410–11, 443; Brian Williams and, 578; Zweibel and, 42, 95

Cheerleader sketches, 428, 465
"cheeseburger cheeseburger," 126, 128–29, 319
Cheney, Dick, 443, 533
Cher, 309
Chico Escuela character, 129
Chippendales sketch, 358
Chris Rock Show, 381
Church Lady sketches, 315–16, 318, 406, 533
City of Angels, 499
Clay, Andrew Dice, 332–37
Cleghorn, Ellen, 459
Clinton, Bill: Carvey and, 407; Downey and, 483–84; Hammond and, 444, 451–52, 532, 586–87; Hartman and, 371, 418, 486, 586–87; lack of appearance on show, 343; *Obama Files* cartoon and, 585; parody debate and, 371–72; Shuster and, 316; *Time* 100 and, 677
Clinton, Hillary, 571, 577–78, 580, 581–82, 584–85, 586, 589, 590
Clooney, Rosemary, 464
Close, Del, 203, 229
Clotworthy, Bill, 142, 210, 234
CNN, 450
Cocker, Joe, 92, 109
Coe, George, 46, 59

"Coffee Talk" sketches, 467
Cohen, Leonard, 460
Cohen, Sacha Baron, 627
Colbert, Stephen, 634, 635
cold open: Carvey as Bush in, 371; as consistent element, 59; Daniels and, 324; DeVito and, 281; Downey political sketches, 449, 452, 577, 651, 714; first, 59; George H. W. Bush doing, 343; Goodman in, 485; Gore in, 557; Hamm in, 637, 641; Hillary in, 584; Kate Jackson and, 152; Lovitz and, 359; Meadows and, 414, 434; Obama in, 580, 582; Sharpton in, 684–85; Washington as multiple black women in, 680, 684–85; Wiig in, 642
Comedy Central, 157, 364, 380, 463, 600
Comedy Store, 309, 338
comedy writers: all-nighters of, 65, 78, 90, 113, 168–69, 177, 192, 268, 271, 285, 319, 384, 388, 394, 518, 671; audience and, 159; Aymong on, 524–25; boys club atmosphere and, 330; careers of, 177, 320–25; cast members and, 132–33, 148, 294, 318–20, 377–78, 379, 391, 417, 427–28, 454–55, 536, 544, 550, 558, 559, 562, 566–69, 602, 607, 657–58; Chase and, 95, 124; competition among, 177, 319, 396–98, 605; departures of, 193; diversity of, 10, 681; Doumanian and, 186, 195–96, 197, 211; drug use and, 10, 113, 240, 606; Ebersol and, 43, 225, 240; experience of, 52, 641–42; Ferrell and, 607; Fey as writer, 558, 559, 565, 567, 602; first show and, 58; food consumption and, 462; gay/lesbian, 659–60; guest writers and, 394; hosts and, 339–40, 470–71, 477–78; Jackson and, 318; Jost as writer, 655–66; Kazurinsky and, 228; Kenward and, 641–42; Meyers as writer, 566–69, 579, 581, 588, 593, 602, 606, 621, 629, 647, 656; Michaels and, 58, 291–92, 347, 394, 428, 513, 519; Morris and, 90; new generation of, 667; pitch meetings and, 656–57; process for, 657–61; quality of, 10; recognition for, 481–82; rewrites and, 347, 394, 413, 606; romances of, 323–24; salaries of, 146–47; *Saturday Night Live* as writer's show, 286; *Saturday Night Live* creation and, 25; Shoemaker and, 503, 606; sketches and, 126–43, 198; stars as cast members and, 261; Tartikoff and, 261; women writers and, 79, 80, 147–50, 335–36, 681; work

comedy writers (*cont.*)
schedule of, 88, 131, 605–6, 643;
writers' strikes and, 211, 214, 279, 577,
578, 583–84, 620
Committee (comedy movement), 39
Cone, David, 517
Coneheads sketches, 12, 126, 128, 140–41,
428, 653
Connery, Sean, 485, 535
Conrad, Robert, 284
Continental Divide, 243
Convy, Bert, 8
Cooley High, 37
Cooper, Bradley, 610
Coppola, Francis Ford, 253
Cosby, Bill, 53
Cosell, Howard, 31, 38, 46, 59, 89, 92
Costas, Bob, 206
Cotton, James, 121
Crawford, Broderick, 155, 578
Credibility Gap, 170
Cronkite, Walter, 47
Cropper, Steve, 121
Crothers, Scatman, 232
Crouching Tiger, Hidden Dragon, 529
Crowley, Jane, 146
Cruise, Tom, 299, 470
Crystal, Billy: Jim Belushi and, 260; as cast
member, 255–56, 260–61; characters
of, 256, 257, 260–61, 263, 264–65,
273; as comedy writer, 273; David
and, 266–67; Downey and, 285; as
host, 255–56, 257; hosts and, 264, 274;
leaving of, 56, 61; on Michaels, 741–
42; movie career of, 256; Murphy and,
380; Palance and, 277; popularity of,
288; as potential cast member, 53–56,
254, 287; schedule and, 263; Shearer
and, 172; Smith and, 281–82; Starr
and, 277–78; Tartikoff and, 257–58,
286–87, 290; Tischler and, 227; Wald
and, 281; Zweibel and, 40–41
Crystal, Janice, 256–57
Culp, Robert, 284
Curtin, Jane: on John Belushi, 38, 105, 111,
247; Blues Bar and, 120; boys club
atmosphere and, 148; as cast member,
38, 93–94, 102–3; Davis memorial and,
654; departure from show, 187; drug use
and, 88, 665; fifth season's last show
and, 185; first show and, 60; on
Michaels, 52, 111, 122, 148, 703; on
Morris, 176; on Newman, 115;
O'Donoghue and, 217; publicity tour
and, 43; on Radner, 140; screen test and,
49; show romances and, 137; Tomlin
and, 93–94; "Weekend Update" and, 74,
103, 111, 122, 123, 145–46, 161, 165

Curtis, Jamie Lee, 637
Cusack, Joan, 288, 300
Czech brothers characters, 126, 134, 135, 428

Dallas, 202, 308
Damon, Matt, 483
Dana Carvey Show, The, 634
Dangerfield, Rodney, 114
Daniels, Greg: as comedy writer, 321–22;
hosts and, 341, 343; Michaels and,
347; Myers and, 346; sketches and,
324; Weathers and, 322
Danza, Tony, 483
David, Larry: Breckman and, 265–66;
Ebersol and, 266, 268, 269; Guest
and, 267; sketches and, 266–67
Davis, Geena, 258
Davis, Paula, 83–84, 163
Davis, Sammy, Jr., 227, 262
Davis, Tom: Aykroyd and, 128, 168, 530,
652–53, 715; on John Belushi, 247;
censors and, 145, 147; as comedy
writer, 297, 65–53; Daniels and, 348;
death of, 652–54; drug use and, 88,
89, 114, 247, 348; famous skits and
characters created by, 652–53; Farley
and, 357; fifth season's last show and,
185; Franken and, 42–43, 348, 652,
653; as guest writer, 482; Higgins
and, 456; Kissinger and, 163; on
Michaels, 715–16; Michaels and, 183,
186, 653; movie career of, 212;
Muppets and, 76; Murray and, 136,
653, 715; Murray-Chase fight and,
125; Novello and, 338; political
humor and, 344; practical jokes and,
90, 150–51; Shuster on, 42; sketches
and, 132, 133, 144–47; Sweeney and,
301; Troggs tape and, 167; twenty-
fifth-anniversary special and, 496;
Wayans and, 303; as writer-producer,
293, 294, 295
Day-Lewis, Daniel, 646
"Death Row Follies," 129
"Debbie Downer" sketches, 535, 536, 559
DeCordova, Fred, 29
"Deep Thoughts," 392
Def Comedy Jam, 381
Degeneres, Ellen, 470, 472–73, 724
"Delicious Dish, The" sketch, 616
Democratic Party, 344
De Niro, Robert, 244, 253, 443, 470, 498,
499, 588, 626
Deschanel, Zooey, 630
DeVito, Danny, 281, 340–41, 726
Diamond, Neil, 516–17
Diaz, Cameron, 473; as host: 626–27,
663–64

Dick in a Box, 556, 573–74

Dickman, Audrey: death of, 518; Doumanian era and, 202; Downey and, 283; sketches and, 143, 144

Digital Shorts, 547–56, 573–74, 585, 667; "Best of" DVDs, 572; Brian Williams and, 580

Diller, Phyllis, 148

Dillon, Denny, 193, 208

Dole, Bob, 344, 433–34, 587

Donahue, Phil, 447

Donaldson, Sam, 453

Don't Look Back in Anger, 110, 242

Douglas, Kirk, 292

Doumanian, Jean: Woody Allen and, 184, 185, 198; Berle and, 158; bias against women and, 192; censors and, 198; comedy writers and, 186, 195–96, 211; Downey and, 296; firing of, 202–3; Gallagher and, 182; Garofalo and, 384; hosts and, 274; Martin and, 134; on Michaels, 92, 186; Michaels and, 183, 184, 186, 192, 289; Murphy and, 193, 201, 229, 230; qualifications of, 192; ratings and, 199, 511–12; title of show and, 92; work ethic of, 199

Downey, James: Armisen and, 570–71; attitude toward show, 523, 662; Aykroyd and, 128, 164–65; boys club atmosphere and, 329; cast members and, 427–28; Clay and, 333; as comedy writer, 297, 533–54, 569–71, 580, 581–82, 662; Daniels and, 322; Tom Davis and, 654; departure from show, 188; diversity issues and, 687–88; Doumanian and, 185; Ebersol and, 223, 285, 296; fifth season's last show and, 185; Franken and, 107–8, 410, 659; Garofalo and, 390, 411; guest writers and, 482; Hader and, 611; Handey and, 347, 392; Hartman and, 326; hosts and, 463–64, 477–78; impressions, advice on doing, 651; Leifer and, 295; Macdonald and, 410, 411–12, 422, 430; Madonna and, 295–96; Michaels and, 183, 186, 413, 421, 424, 429–30, 452, 513, 523; movie career of, 212; Murphy and, 201; Murray and, 283; musical guests and, 463–64; NBC and, 418; Ohlmeyer and, 421, 422, 429, 429, 437, 452; Palance and, 277; political humor and, 344, 345, 392, 412, 421, 449, 450, 452–53, 533–34, 581–82, 594, 635–37, 650; as producer, 295; Rock and, 379; Sandler and, 375, 376, 412, 420; Shearer and, 283; Short and, 272; Simpson and, 434; Spade and, 395;

Wald and, 225; walk-ons and, 483–84, 498; "Weekend Update" and, 429, 430, 431, 434; Wolf and, 412, 433

Downey, Robert, Jr., 288, 292, 297

Doyle, Erin, 653–54, 674, 683, 686

Doyle-Murray, Brian: on John Belushi, 115, 248, 252; Blues Bar and, 117; Ebersol and, 284; fifth season's last show and, 185; on Michaels, 709, 718; Murphy and, 229; Novello and, 338; sketches and, 129; success of show and, 101

Dratch, Rachel: boys club atmosphere and, 501; "Debbie Downer" sketches, 535, 536–37, 559; departure from show, 559, 561; episode with Betty White and, 616, 617; Fallon and, 629; Ferrell and, 479, 559; Fey and, 441, 545, 559; on Michaels, 707, 727–28; watching *Saturday Night Live* as child, 454; "Weekend Update" and, 468–69

"Dr. Death" sketch, 154–55

Dreyfuss, Richard: on John Belushi, 109; John Belushi's impression of, 110; Hammond and, 470; on Michaels, 707; on Radner, 140

Dukakis, Michael, 450, 589

Duke, Robin, 228

Dunham, Corydon, 234–35

Dunham, Lena, 743, 696–97

Dunn, Donald, 121

Dunn, Nora: boys club atmosphere and, 330; as cast member, 288, 544; Clay and, 332, 333–35, 336, 337; departure from show, 407; Jackson and, 331; Lovitz and, 326; on Michaels, 706; Sweeney and, 299

Duvall, Robert, 288

Ebersol, Dick: Abba and, 68; attitude toward show, 220; on John Belushi, 36–37, 115, 240, 243–44; Breckman and, 291; Albert Brooks and, 26, 28; cast members and, 32–33, 36–37, 213, 223, 255–56, 284; on Chase, 32–33, 52, 97; comedy writers and, 43, 225, 240; Crystal and, 256–57, 263, 264, 273; David and, 266, 268, 269; departure from show, 287, 290; Doumanian and, 205; Downey and, 223, 285, 296; on drug use, 87, 88; drug use and, 114; first show and, 60–61 ; Gallagher and, 39, 44; Brad Hall and, 270; hosts and, 274, 277–78, 279, 280–82, 284; Kazurinsky and, 209, 221, 222, 223, 225–26, 240, 284; Louis-Dreyfus and, 272; on Michaels, 722–23; Michaels and, 21, 25, 30, 68, 192, 205, 206, 207,

Ebersol, Dick (*cont.*)
208, 219, 284, 287, 293; Murphy and, 201, 209, 223, 229, 231, 233–34, 235–37, 238, 240, 378; NBC and, 19, 65, 219, 224, 235–36, 284; O'Donoghue and, 207, 215, 216; O'Hara and, 210; Ohlmeyer and, 22, 24, 235; political humor and, 343; ratings and, 511–12; *Saturday Night Live* creation and, 20–22, 23, 24, 29, 205, 737; Schlosser and, 19, 20, 89; sets and, 218; Shearer and, 282–83; Short and, 259; on Shuster, 22; Silverman and, 177, 204, 206, 219–20; sketches and, 218–19, 220, 225; strategy of, 223; Tartikoff and, 204, 205, 206, 219, 238, 255, 256, 274–75, 289, 720; Wald and, 224, 729

Ed Grimley character, 263, 264, 265, 273, 277
Ed Sullivan Show, 16, 18, 40, 742
Eisenberg, Jesse, 628
Eisner, Michael, 408
Ellington, Duke, 31
Elliott, Abby, 597–98, 631, 644
Elliott, Chris: attitude toward show, 385, 386, 390, 404; Garofalo and, 388, 390; hosts and, 404; on Michaels, 710, 731; Travolta and, 401–2
Elliott, Sam, 530
"Ellis Island" sketch, 574
Emily Litella character, 136, 145, 137
Eminem, 464, 686
Entertainment Tonight, 337
Esquire, 26
Estrada, Erik, 415
Etheridge, Melissa, 686–87

Fallon, Jimmy: audition of, 621; autism benefit, 600; Aykroyd and, 518; "breaking" on show, 628; as cast member, 424, 535, 537, 539; comedy writers and, 476; departure from show, 539–41, 542, 567; Dratch and, 536; Ferrell and, 537, 538; Fey and, 539, 540; as host, 629; *Late Night* and, 5, 540–41; Meadows and, 381; Michaels and, 539, 693, 730–31; movie career and, 517, 540; Ryder and, 516; Shoemaker and, 502–3; Smigel and, 634; Timberlake and, 628–29; *The Tonight Show* and, 540, 677, 678, 679; watching *Saturday Night Live* as child, 454; "Weekend Update" and, 440, 442, 443–44, 542; work schedule and, 463
"Family Feud" sketch, 628
"Famous School for Comedians," 27
Farley, Chris: audition of, 360; John Belushi and, 354, 355, 356; "Best of" DVDs and, 572; Carvey and, 407; as

cast member, 548, 630; death of, 436, 437, 439, 486, 489–94; departure from show, 409–10, 420, 424; drug use of, 245, 489, 491, 493, 494; Garofalo and, 389; generational split in cast and, 360; Kattan and, 461–62; Michaels and, 355, 721, 725; movie career of, 490, 493, 494; NBC and, 425; Ohlmeyer and, 415; Rock and, 384; Sandler and, 355, 384; Spade and, 356
"Fast Show, The," 16
Father Sarducci character, 338–39
Fawlty Towers, 456
Fear (rock group), 240
Fellini, Federico, 154, 372
"Fernando's Hideaway" sketches, 264
Ferrell, Will: auditions of, 447–48; autism benefit, 600; "Best of" DVDs and, 572; George W. Bush and, 444, 506, 532, 533, 534, 587, 590, 594; as cast member, 424, 447–48, 526, 599, 607, 671, 694; characters, 537; Chase and, 474; departure from show, 516–17, 526, 527; "dying" during show and, 479–80; Fallon and, 537, 538; as host, 537–38, 602; hot-tub sketches, 559; impressions and, 651; *Jeopardy!* sketches, 535; Kattan and, 457; Meadows and, 381; on Michaels, 725; Michaels and, 479, 712; "More Cowbell" sketch, 537, 538; movie career and, 465; NBC and, 425; September 11 terrorist attacks and, 505; Spade and, 362; Walken and, 538
Fever Pitch, 540
Fey, Tina: Armisen and, 528, 529; autism benefit, 600; Aykroyd and, 518; boys club atmosphere and, 501; as cast member, 424, 441, 696; as comedy writer, 558, 559, 565, 567, 602, 629; departure from show, 559, 560, 567, 637; drug use and, 461, 665; episode with Betty White, 616, 617; Fallon and, 539, 540; Garofalo and, 466; Golden Globe Awards 2014, 676–77, 678; Hader and, 546; hosts and, 476, 477; Michaels and, 541, 587–88, 702; movie career of, 517, 560, 561; Nasim and, 619; NBC and, 524; Palin character, 571, 586–95, 596, 600, 608; Poehler and, 541–43, 545, 568–69; seeking approval and, 480; Shoemaker and, 503; *30 Rock* and, 584, 608; "Weekend Update" and, 440, 441, 442–44, 539, 542–44, 559, 565
First, You Cry, 142
Fisher, Carrie: Aykroyd and, 127, 164; on John Belushi, 105–6, 127, 247,

250–51; as host, 120; on Michaels, 114, 714; on O'Donoghue, 127; Radner and, 139; Simon and, 127, 139, 714
Five-Timers Club, The, 404, 622
Foley, Dave, 345
Ford, Gerald, 12, 80, 81, 171, 343, 444, 450, 586, 589
Ford Fairlane, 336
Forte, Will, 526, 527, 701–2, 678; autism benefit, 600; Bush and, 532–33, 534; as cast member, 550, 576–77, 579, 599, 607; departure from show, 621, 694; Digital Shorts and, 551; MacGruber character and, 575–76, 577; on Michaels, 577
48 Hrs., 236, 238, 380
40 Year Old Virgin, The, 546
Foul Play, 95
Fox (network), 512, 525
Franken, Al: Agnew and, 162; Aykroyd and, 128; on John Belushi, 107–8, 494; Carrey and, 295; cast members and, 359; characters of, 375; Chase and, 126; child of, 150; as comedy writer, 42–43, 297; Daniels and, 347; Tom Davis and, 42–43, 348, 652, 653; departure from show, 410; Downey and, 659; drug use and, 88, 89, 108, 113; Ebersol and, 220; Farley and, 494; first show and, 62; generational split in cast and, 360; Hanks and, 406; hosts and, 342–43, 403; Leifer and, 295; Lovitz and, 319; Mandel and, 364; on Michaels, 723, 735–36; Michaels and, 183, 186, 186; movie career of, 212; Muppets and, 76; Nessen and, 81; Novello and, 338; Ohlmeyer and, 410, 429, 452; political humor and, 344, 345, 659; practical jokes and, 90, 150; Ron Reagan and, 300; on risk, 417; Rock and, 381; Shearer and, 170–71, 173; Silverman and, 179, 180–82, 183; sketches and, 132, 133, 145–46, 147; Smigel and, 727; Sweeney and, 301; Troggs tape and, 167; twenty-fifth-anniversary special and, 498; "Weekend Update" and, 410; as writer-producer, 293, 294
Franken, Franny, 150
"Franken and Davis Show" sketches, 145, 147
Frazier, Walt, 185
Fred Garvin, Male Prostitute sketches, 126, 131, 530
Friday Night Videos, 206
Fridays, 512
Friends, 254, 415, 422

"Frondi," 565
"Frozen Caveman Lawyer" sketch, 327

Gallagher, Barbara: on John Belushi, 242; Albert Brooks and, 64; on Crystal, 54, 56; Doumanian and, 184, 191; on Ebersol, 44; on Michaels, 39–40, 733; Michaels and, 180, 182, 183–84, 733
Gammill, Tom: as comedy writer, 174–75
"Gap Girls" sketches, 403
Garfunkel, Art, 66
Garofalo, Janeane: attitude toward show, 384, 386–87, 389, 390–91; boys club atmosphere and, 501; Downey and, 411; Fey and, 466; on Michaels, 709, 719; Sandler and, 377, 389; Wolf and, 387
Garrison, Jim, 106
"Garth and Kat," 627, 637, 647
Gasteyer, Ana: boys club atmosphere and, 466, 500–501; as cast member, 424, 544, 616; episode with Betty White and, 616, 617; hosts and, 475; on Michaels, 703; NBC and, 425; pregnancy of, 509–11, 517
GE, 367–68, 481
Gibb, Barry, 628–29
Gibson, Mel, 341
Gifford, Kathie Lee, 637
Gilda Live, 170
Girls, 580, 696
Giuliani, Rudolph, 445–46, 450–51, 503–6, 507
Gleason, Jackie, 457
Glengarry Glen Ross, 717
Godspell, 32
Goin' South, 177
Goodbye Girl, The, 110
Gooding, Cuba, Jr., 471, 483
Goodman, John: Aykroyd and, 530; as host, 341, 369, 470, 471, 477; on Michaels, 707; Marilyn Suzanne Miller and, 394; Tripp and, 485
Goodman, Julian, 24
Gore, Al, 444–45, 450, 451, 452, 484, 521–22, 557, 571, 594
Gore, Kristin, 522, 557
Gore, Tipper, 522, 523
Gottfried, Gilbert: attitude toward show, 188, 198; Doumanian era and, 194–95, 197–98, 203; firing of, 204
Gould, Elliot: as host, 72, 147; on Michaels, 724; on Radner, 153, 724
Grade, Lew, 75
Graduate, The, 172
Grant, Cary, 95
Grateful Dead, 174
Great American Dream Machine, 26

Great Gatsby, The, 61
Greek restaurant sketches, 126, 128–29
Green, Tom, 478
Gretzky, Wayne, 402
Grey, Brad: on Brillstein, 51; Carvey and, 309; Garofalo and, 390; Lovitz and, 359; Michaels and, 519; September 11 terrorist attacks and, 505; Wayans and, 304
Gross, Mary: as cast member, 213, 228, 258, 260; Brad Hall and, 220; Louis-Dreyfus and, 270
Groundlings: cast members gleaned from, 30, 37, 310, 325, 362–63, 447, 448, 548–49, 619, 621, 659; Kudrow and, 474
Guest, Christopher: as cast member, 255, 258; characters of, 260; as comedy writer, 273; Crystal and, 273; David and, 267; Downey and, 285; Ebersol and, 257; Kurtzman and, 272; Shearer and, 197, 265; Starr and, 277–78; Tischler and, 256; Wald and, 281
Gulf War, 371
Gurwitz, Mark, 490

Hader, Bill: audition of, 545; Aykroyd's advice to, 652; breaking and, 608, 610–11, 612–13; cast departures and, 645; as cast member, 545–47, 599, 607, 618, 621, 650–51, 658, 664, 675–76; on critics, 667–68; departure from show, 648–49; Digital Shorts and, 551; on drug use and *SNL,* 665; host dinners and, 623; hosts and, 633–64; impressions and, 650–51; live performance versus dress rehearsal mistake, 672; Michaels and, 649, 707; new cast members and, 618, 621; pitch meetings and, 656–57; Stefon character, 608–15; on Venn diagrams, 657; Wiig and, 638–39, 672
Hahn, Jessica, 329
Haley, Bill, 244–45
Half-Hour Comedy Hour, The, 314
Hall, Anthony Michael: attitude toward show, 293; as cast member, 288; Chase and, 298; Ron Reagan and, 298
Hall, Arsenio, 314, 370–71
Hall, Brad: as cast member, 213; as comedy writer, 270; on Ebersol, 218, 220; Louis-Dreyfus and, 271–72; Murphy and, 232; "Weekend Update" and, 284
Hall, Jerry, 347
Hall, Willie, 120
Hallelujah, Baby!, 37
"Hamlet Auditions," 672–73

Hamm, Jon, 742, 579, 624–25, 631–32, 634, 637; cold open and, 637, 641; Wiig and, 641
Hammer, 383
Hammond, Darrell: auditions of, 447; "Best of" DVDs and, 572; as cast member, 424, 559; characters of, 444, 534, 535; Clinton and, 444, 451–52, 532, 586–97; departure from show, 602–3; Dreyfuss and, 470; glamour and, 520; Gore and, 444, 452, 594; Koppel and, 453; on Michaels, 705; work schedule and, 467
Handey, Jack: "Deep Thoughts" and, 392; Farley and, 357; as guest writer, 482; Hartman and, 327; Madonna and, 297; Meadows and, 364; O'Donoghue and, 214, 216–17; rewrites and, 347; Sandler and, 376–77; sketches and, 392; work schedule and, 467
Hangin' with the Homeboys, 360
Hanks, Tom: cast members and, 293–94; Ferrell and, 518; fifteenth-anniversary show and, 497–98; as host, 74–75, 101, 289, 301–2, 340, 342, 402, 404–6, 470, 471, 654, 658; on Michaels, 710–11, 742–43; O'Brien and, 323; Sandler and, 377; sketches and, 301; twenty-fifth-anniversary special and, 495, 497–98
"Hans and Franz" sketch, 318, 319, 325, 619
Hardwick, Cheryl, 214, 328
Harriman, Pamela, 344
Harrison, George, 342–43
Hart and Lorne Hour, The, 17
Hartman, Brynn, 486
Hartman, Phil: Baldwin and, 405; Carvey and, 371, 407; as cast member, 547, 556, 664; Clinton and, 371, 418, 486, 586–87; death of, 486–89; departure from show, 416–17; Franken and, 343; generational split in cast and, 360; Lovitz and, 326; Odenkirk and, 327; Rock and, 381; Sandler and, 379, 416; Sinatra and, 327
Harvard Lampoon, 196, 522
Hawn, Goldie, 95
Hayworth, Rita, 53, 349
HBO: *Not Necessarily the News,* 321, 678; Zone, 528
Heche, Anne, 472
Hee Haw, 17
Hefner, Hugh, 156, 243, 470
Hellzapoppin', 276
Hemion, Dwight, 31
Henry, Buck: *Big Event, The,* 165–66; censors and, 146; characters of, 126,

128, 141, 142; on Chase, 94; Curtin and, 103; fifth season's last show and, 185–86; as host, 72–73, 74, 79, 340; on Michaels, 79, 169, 739; Michaels and, 243; O'Donoghue's wake and, 217; "Weekend Update" and, 165
Henson, Jim, 31, 59, 75
Hepburn, Katharine, 273
Herlihy, Tim: as comedy writer, 395; Farley and, 492; Sandler and, 361–62, 378, 412, 420; "Weekend Update" and, 439
Herman, Nate, 215–16
Herman, Pee-wee, 300
Higgins, Steve: anthrax crisis and, 509; attitude toward show, 676; cast members and, 502, 562, 598, 621, 693–94; Tom Davis and, 456; Ferrell and, 448, 517; Garofalo and, 466; hosts and, 477; Michaels and, 426, 738; political humor and, 449; Rudolph and, 499; Venn diagrams of, 657
Hill, Jonah, 634
Hill, Walter, 236
Hilton, Paris, 531
Hines, Gregory, 286
Hockey Puck Crisis, The, 17
Hogan, Hulk, 264
"Hollywood Minute" sketches, 349, 374, 480, 708
Hollywood Reporter, 678
Hooks, Jan, 544; Bakker and, 315; Clay and, 336; competition and, 329–30, 331; Dunn and, 337; Hartman and, 327–28, 371, 487, 488; hosts and, 341; Jackson and, 314, 316–17; Nealon and, 314; Rock and, 379; Sandler and, 379; stage fright of, 316; women characters and, 691
Houston, Whitney, 383
Howard, Bob, 29
Howdy Doody, 67
Huffington, Arianna, 646
Huffington Post, 621–22
Hughes, John, 293
Hume, Brit, 449
humor, effect of Saturday Night Live on, 8
Hymes, Phil, 745

Ian, Janis, 59
Ian Rubbish character, 647
ICM, 195
"I Married a Monkey" sketch, 225–26
Improv, 40, 69, 310
In Living Color, 303, 378, 381, 382, 395, 412, 419, 458
Iran hostage crisis sketches, 223
It's Pat, 408–9

Jackson, Jesse, 277, 444, 506, 584
Jackson, Kate: on John Belushi, 112; on Michaels, 736; Murray and, 189; on Radner, 152
Jackson, LaToya, 444
Jackson, Michael, 375
Jackson, Reggie, 361
Jackson, Samuel L., 492
Jackson, Victoria: audition of, 310–13, 314; Baldwin and, 405; boys club atmosphere and, 329–30; as cast member, 544; Clay and, 333; comedy writers and, 318–19; departure from show, 406; Dunn and, 331, 338; Hooks and, 317; movie career of, 329; Seagal and, 401; show romances and, 326; Zander and, 328
Jagger, Mick, 25, 30, 253, 347, 402, 613, 629, 637, 640, 641, 710
James, LeBron, 620
"Jarret's Room" sketch, 503
Jay-Z, 617, 618
Jenner, Bruce, 132
Jeopardy! sketches, 485, 517, 535
Jerry Maguire, 471
"Jew, Not a Jew" sketch, 406
Jizz in my Pants, 598
Joel, Billy, 125
Johansson, Scarlett: attitude toward show, 625, 626; growing up with SNL, 556; as host, 556–57, 625; Michaels and, 741
John Belushi Scholarship Fund, 222
Johnson, Lyndon, 149, 223
Jones, Leslie, 681
Joshua Tree Inn, 29, 98
Jost, Colin: attitude toward show, 606; as comedy writer, 573–74, 600, 601, 676, 695–96; on Digital Shorts, 551, 552–53; as head writer, 655–66; Michaels and, 656; Moynihan and, 695; Wiig goodbye sketch, 639
Judy Miller character, 151
"Julia Child" sketch, 126, 133, 652–53
Just Shoot Me, 467, 490

Kaczynski, Ted, 481
Kael, Pauline, 699
Kahling, Mindy, 696
Kahn, Madeline, 72
"Kate and Ali" sketch, 273
Kattan, Chris: auditions of, 456–57; as cast member, 424, 629; characters of, 468, 482–83; childhood of, 460–61; as comedy writer, 468; departure from show, 526; drug use and, 462; Ferrell and, 538; hosts and, 475–76; Morgan and, 629–30; NBC and, 425; sketches

Kattan, Chris (*cont.*)
  and, 466–67; watching *Saturday Night Live* as child, 456
Katzenberg, Jeff, 236, 238
Kaufman, Andy: appearances of, 61, 101; characters of, 54; conceptual art and, 61; Ebersol and, 224; first show and, 59, 61; Letterman and, 438; *Man on the Moon* and, 731; monologues of, 65; Morra and, 55; Nealon and, 314; screen test and, 46, 51
Kazurinsky, Tim: Jim Belushi and, 249–50; on John Belushi, 247, 249–50, 251, 253; John Belushi and, 209, 215; as cast member, 209, 213; comedy writers and, 228; drug use and, 251; Ebersol and, 209, 221, 222, 223, 225–26, 240, 284; Farley and, 493; hosts and, 276; Kurtzman on, 217–18; O'Donoghue and, 210
Keaton, Buster, 739
Keaton, Michael, 281–82
Keitel, Harvey, 470
Kellem, Craig: Belushi and, 57; drug use and, 87; first show and, 58; hosts and, 71; on Michaels, 709; military commercials and, 92; Muppets and, 76; name of show and, 92; NBC and, 44, 60; Pryor and, 70–71; ratings and, 65
Kelly, Chris, 659
Kennedy, Jackie, 82, 185
Kennedy, John F., 234, 451
Kennedy, Mimi, 38
Kenney, Doug: Shaffer and, 34
Kentucky Fried Theater, 21, 22
Kenward, Erik, 573, 641–42; on Michaels, 642
Kern, Jerome, 740
Kerry, John, 533, 534
Kids in the Hall, 345
Kids in the Hall, 604, 716
Killam, Taran, 618, 619, 621, 657, 676, 694, 697
Killer Bees, 59, 62, 64, 71, 72, 75, 194, 361
Kimble, Billy, 364
Kinison, Sam, 281, 309, 333, 352
Kipling, Rudyard, 718
Kissinger, Henry, 163
Klein, Marci, 362–63, 387; anthrax crisis and, 509; Armisen and, 528; Brokaw and, 486; Diamond and, 516; Farley and, 490; Ferrell and, 448; Hader and, 546; Hammond and, 447; hosts and, 470–71, 475, 476–77; on Michaels, 721–22; September 11 terrorist attacks and, 506–9; Shannon and, 459; talent and, 502
Klein, Rob (writer), 600, 601, 621, 664

Klein, Robert (host); John Belushi and, 105, 111, 163, 718; as host, 68, 105; live television and, 67; on Michaels, 18, 718; on Radner, 152; *Saturday Night Live* creation and, 26
Knights of Columbus meeting sketches, 129
Koch, Ed, 227
Koppel, Ted, 453
Kristofferson, Kris, 155
Kroeger, Gary, 260, 272, 276–77
Kudrow, Lisa, 254, 362–63, 473–74
Kuhn, Bowie, 62
Kurtzman, Andrew: Caesar and, 278–79; David and, 269; Doumanian era and, 193; Ebersol and, 223, 224; Guest and, 272; hosts and, 278–79; Kazurinsky and, 217–18; stars as cast members and, 260

"Ladysmith Black Mambazo in Outer Space," 572
Lamb Chop, 76
Landis, John: *Animal House* and, 95, 121; on Michaels, 39; Murphy and, 236; Murray-Chase fight and, 125; O'Donoghue and, 106; Shuster and, 120; *Three Amigos* and, 290
"Land Shark" sketch, 81, 82
Lane, Nathan, 232
Larry Sanders, 385
Lasser, Louise, 155–56
Late Night, 5, 540–41, 662, 677, 678, 692; Michaels as producer, 677, 678
Later, 206
Late Show with David Letterman, 365, 678
Lattanzi restaurant, 622–23
Laugh Factory, 529
Lautner, Taylor, 635
Laverne and Shirley, 63, 152, 166
Law, Jude, 672
Lawrence, Martin, 381
Lazy Sunday, 552–54, 564, 638
Lear, Norman, 112, 470, 737
Lee, Christopher, 154–55
Lee, Eugene: on Michaels, 40; office location and, 88–89; on Wilson, 45
Lee, Frannie, 165
Leifer, Carol: boys club atmosphere and, 329; as comedy writer, 295, 300; on Michaels, 722, 728–29; Michaels and, 305
Lemmings, 26
Lennon, John, 74, 106, 242
Leno, Jay, 20, 418, 432, 434, 435–36, 519, 678, 679
Letterman, Dave: Carson and, 20; CBS and, 678; Downey and, 212; Elliott

and, 404, 731; fans of, 696; Gammill
    and, 175; Giuliani and, 505;
    Macdonald and, 438; O'Brien and,
    321, 393; Simpson and, 434; Stringer
    ·and, 414
Lettuce, 551, 552
Levy, Eugene, 32, 281
Levy, Neil: on Aykroyd, 164; on John
    Belushi, 112–13, 243; Doumanian era
    and, 200–201, 202; drug use and, 89;
    on Ebersol, 207–8; first show and, 58;
    Lennon and McCartney and, 74;
    Murphy and, 229–30, 231; on NBC,
    68; O'Hara and, 210; on Radner, 139;
    Reiner and, 63; salaries and, 146–47;
    Saturday Night Live creation and, 25;
    stars and, 155–56
Lewinsky, Monica, 483–84
Lewis, Jerry, 276, 680
Lewis, Shari, 76
Liepis, Marc, 553
LIFE magazine, 542
Limbaugh, Rush, 530, 534–35
"Limo for a Lame-O," 179, 180–82
Lindsay, John, 185
Lisa Loopner character, 12, 136, 137, 138.
    See also Nerds sketches
Little, Rich, 8, 22, 162, 370, 609
"Little Chocolate Doughnuts" sketch, 132
Littlefield, Warren: Downey and, 421;
    food consumption and, 462–63;
    Michaels and, 419, 432–33; O'Connor
    and, 368; Ohlmeyer and, 435–36, 438;
    success of show and, 513; Tartikoff
    and, 181, 307–8
Lohan, Lindsay, 535–36, 631, 632–33
Lonely Island, 547, 548
Lopez, Jennifer, 475–76
Lornettes, 311, 323
Lou Goldman character, 267
Louis-Dreyfus, Julia: attitude toward
    show, 270–71, 557; as cast member,
    213, 228, 258, 260; David and, 269–
    70, 271; drug use and, 271; Ebersol
    and, 272; Hall and, 271–72; return to
    SNL, 557–59
"Lovers" sketch, 478–79, 516, 559
Lovitz, Jon: Breckman and, 302; Carvey
    and, 374; as cast member, 288, 547;
    characters of, 288, 292, 300; Chase
    and, 297; competition and, 319–21;
    departure from show, 407; DeVito and,
    340–41; Dukakis character, 589; Dunn
    and, 330; Franken and, 294; Hartman
    and, 326, 486–87; Jackson and, 318; on
    Michaels, 703–4; Michaels and, 359;
    movie career of, 292, 320; sketches
    and, 327; Smigel and, 308

Ludwin, Rick, 156–57, 332–33, 348–49,
    368, 480–81

McCain, Cindy, 595, 596
McCain, John, 542, 572, 589, 595–96
McCarthy-Miller, Beth, 544, 559, 560, 565
McCartney, Linda, 309–10, 715
McCartney, Paul, 74, 92, 309–10, 402, 403,
    615, 715
McConaughey, Matthew, 540
Macdonald, Norm: Breckman and, 394;
    Downey and, 410, 411–12, 422, 430;
    Farley and, 492–93; firing of, 436, 437,
    439; Michaels and, 437; Ohlmeyer
    and, 429, 430, 431, 432–33, 435, 436,
    437; Rock and, 382; "Weekend
    Update" and, 410–12, 429–34, 436,
    438, 439; Wolf and, 364
MacGruber, 575–76
MacGyver, 576
McKay, Adam, 468, 559, 562, 634
McKean, Michael, 258
McKellen, Ian, 503
McKinnon, Kate: as cast member, 644–45,
    647, 660–61, 664, 671, 694;
    impersonation of Ann Romney, 659;
    on Internet feedback, 668–69; on
    Michaels, 647; on pace of sketch
    comedy, 667
McMahon, Ed, 486
Madden, John, 280–81, 434
Mad magazine, 96
Mad Men, 624
"Mad Men" sketch, 597
Madonna, 295–97, 375
MADtv, 512, 519, 525, 570
Maher, Bill, 636
Mailer, Norman, 102, 241
Malkovich, John, 413
Malone, Tom, 120
Mandel, David: attitude toward show, 397,
    398–99; departure from show, 409;
    Downey and, 412–13; Franken and,
    364; Rock and, 383
Mango sketches, 427, 428, 446, 482–83
Man on the Moon, 731
Manson, Charles, 172
Mantegna, Joe, 717
Marini, Lou, 121
Marley, Bob, 366
Marshall, Garry, 22
Marshall, Penny: on John Belushi, 115,
    250; *Big Event, The,* 165–66; Blues
    Bar and, 119; on Fisher, 164; on
    Michaels, 63, 716–17; on Radner, 152;
    show romances and, 136–37
Marshall, Peter, 48
Martin, Andrea, 32, 255, 258

Martin, Billy, 308

Martin, Chris, 627

Martin, Steve: on Aykroyd, 164; on John Belushi, 105; Blues Bar and, 119–20; Farley and, 357; first show and, 61; as host, 340, 354–55, 470, 622, 642; on Michaels, 712, 726; Michaels and, 133–34, 290, 707, 710; Nealon and, 314; O'Brien and, 322; Pross and, 174; Radner and, 151, 350; *Saturday Night Live* creation and, 21; sketches and, 134, 135, 654; taboo topics and, 126–27

Marx, Harpo, 242

Mary Katherine Gallagher character, 455–56, 459, 466, 722

Mary Tyler Moore Show, The, 22, 35

*M*A*S*H,* 72

Mason, James, 50

Master Thespian character, 288, 292

Matthau, Walter, 133

Matthius, Gail, 193

Mature, Victor, 53

Mazursky, Paul, 154

Me, Myself and Iran, 619

Meadows, Tim: Chase and, 401; Farley and, 409–10; Handey and, 364; on Michaels, 741; Michaels and, 414, 424, 437; Rock and, 380–81, 382; Sandler and, 409–10; Seagal and, 400–401; Simpson and, 434; Spade and, 409–10; worst year on *SNL,* 409–10

Mean Girls, 560

Meatballs, 177

Menendez brothers sketch, 413

Merchant, Natalie, 534

Meyer, George, 296, 297

Meyers, Seth, 526, 532, 546, 555, 596, 693, 694; attitude toward show, 641, 662–63, 672, 695; as comedy writer, 566–69, 579, 581, 588, 593, 602, 606, 621, 629, 647, 656; departure from show, 692, 694, 695; diversity issues and, 690; on evolution of cast, 664; Fey and, 588; Golden Globe Awards 2014, 677, 678; Hader and, 609, 610, 613–14, 651; *Late Night* and, 5, 677, 678, 692; Moynihan and, 695; Palin and, 590, 592; Poehler and, 567–69, 597; political humor and, 650, 651; Samberg and, 678, 692–93; *Time* magazine cover, 691–92; "Weekend Update" and, 567–68, 569, 590, 597, 608, 610, 613, 614–15

MGM, 13

Miami Vice, 303

Michaels, Alice, 423, 722

Michaels, Eddie, 423

Michaels, Lorne: ad-libbing and, 160, 371; all-nighters and, 78; on Arnaz, 93; auditions and, 528, 545–45, 597, 620, 681; Aykroyd-Shuster relationship and, 168; Beatts on, 173, 701, 724, 737–38, 745; on John Belushi, 35–36, 79–80, 98–99, 108, 243, 245, 252–52, 253; John Belushi and, 111, 666–67, 721, 736; on Berle, 158–59; *Big Event, The,* 166; boys club atmosphere and, 148, 149–50, 329; breaking on camera and, 479, 613; on Brillstein, 17–18; on Albert Brooks, 27, 63–64; Albert Brooks and, 64, 77, 171; Carson and, 9; Carvey and, 309–10, 317–18, 407; cast departures and, 637–40, 643, 644, 648–49, 693–94; cast members and, 33–39, 52, 79, 288, 308, 360, 400, 426, 514, 542, 545–46, 645, 650, 693, 704–6, 732–35; censors and, 11, 146, 147, 366, 582, 598; Chase and, 96, 97, 121; Chase on, 96, 732; Clay and, 332–34, 336–37; as comedy writer, 414, 735; comedy writers and, 58, 291–92, 347, 394, 428, 513, 519, 569, 653; conceptual art and, 61; Crystal and, 54–56; Curtin on, 52, 111, 122, 148, 703; departure from show, 182–83, 190, 191, 193; Dickman and, 518; Digital Shorts and, 547, 548, 549; diversity issues and, 681–91; Doumanian and, 183, 184, 186, 192, 289; Downey and, 635–36; dress of, 165; on drug use, 87; drug use and, 18–19, 87, 111, 114, 604; Dunn and, 330, 333–34; Ebersol and, 21, 25, 30, 68, 192, 205, 206, 207, 208, 218, 284, 287, 293; Emmys, 620; episode with Betty White and, 616, 617; Fallon and, 442, 503, 539, 540–41; Farley and, 355, 437; as father figure, 10, 666–67, 701, 702, 703–9, 713, 714, 719, 721, 735; Ferrell and, 516, 517; Fey and, 561, 587–88, 589; fifth season's last show and, 186; first show and, 60; Ford and, 81; Forte on, 701–2; Franken and, 162, 410; Garofalo and, 387, 388, 391; Gasteyer and, 510; *Gilda Live* and, 170, 179; growing-up years, 16–17; Hammond and, 532; Hartman and, 416–17; on Henry, 73, 78; Henry on, 79, 169, 739; Higgins and, 426–27; hosts and, 155–56, 161–62, 277, 333–34, 342, 445–46, 470–71, 475, 530, 578–79, 596, 622–23, 642, 664, 724; Kattan and, 466–67; Kaufman and, 61; Lennon and McCartney and, 74; lifestyle of, 700; Lovitz and, 320–21,

359; Macdonald and, 431, 436; McCain and, 595–96; marriage to Shuster, 18, 22, 120, 167–68; Martin and, 133–34, 707; maturity of, 604–5; Meyers and, 568; military commercials and, 92; mistakes or screw-ups, show reviews, and, 673–74; Morris and, 176; movie career of, 183, 212, 289, 372–73, 466, 634; Muppets and, 76; Murphy and, 380; Murray and, 104, 104–5; Murray-Chase fight and, 125; musical guests and, 68, 69, 464; Myers and, 345–46, 372–73; on myth of the old days, 665–66; name of show and, 92; NBC and, 39, 44–45, 60, 62, 68, 71, 174, 320, 369, 376, 414, 415, 416, 418–23, 429, 513, 555, 560–61, 711, 732; Obama and, 580; O'Brien and, 322, 393, 678–79; O'Connor and, 366, 367, 368; O'Donoghue's wake and, 217; Ohlmeyer and, 320, 410, 415, 418–23, 423, 426, 433, 435, 436, 437, 438, 440, 519; pace of show and, 65; Palin and, 590–91; Poehler and, 542, 568, 598; political humor and, 343–44, 345–46, 581, 587–88, 589; Pryor and, 70–71; Radner and, 48, 666, 700, 704, 745; ratings and, 512; reaction to show, 479; redefining comedy and, 75; reruns and, 98, 287; return to show, 10, 287, 288–91; reviews and, 66; Rock and, 360–61; salary of, 92; Samberg and, 548, 549; Sandler and, 376, 420; Sanz and, 563; *Saturday Night Live* as hit show, 64–65, 99, 698; *Saturday Night Live* creation and, 8, 21, 22, 23–30, 205, 737; *Saturday Night Live* criticism and, 354–55; Schiller and, 407; screen tests and, 46–47; September 11 terrorist attacks and, 505, 507, 508, 568; Shaffer and, 167; Sharpton and, 531, 684–85; Shearer and, 170, 171, 172, 173, 197; Shore on, 16–17; Shuster on, 15, 18, 149–50, 724, 732–33; Silverman and, 174, 179–81; sketches and, 140; Spade and, 374; staff's reflections on, 700–745; star on Hollywood Walk of Fame, 94; Sweeney and, 408, 414–15; Tartikoff and, 180, 183, 289, 290, 295, 307; on television, 35–36; Timberlake and, 574; *Tonight Show, Late Night,* and producing, 5, 677, 678–79, 693, 697; twenty-fifth-anniversary special and, 495; vision of, 636, 642, 647, 694, 697; walk-ons and, 498; Wayans and, 303–5, 306, 307; Wiig departure and, 637–

40; Wolf and, 396; work ethic of, 78; work schedule and, 131, 525; writers' strikes and, 583–84; Zweibel and, 40–42; Zweibel on, 519, 700, 706, 744

Mike Douglas Show, The, 195

Miller, Dennis: Clay and, 337; departure from show, 325, 407; Rock and, 381; Sandler and, 379; "Weekend Update" and, 288, 294, 411; Wolf and, 364

Miller, Glenn, 31

Miller, Henry, 154

Miller, Marilyn Suzanne: John Belushi and, 107, 135; boys club atmosphere and, 149; Breckman and, 394; as comedy writer, 22–23, 79; Dickman and, 518; drug use and, 88; Franken and, 416; on Michaels, 702, 743–44; Murphy and, 230; Myers and, 394; practical jokes and, 90; Radner and, 140, 152–53, 351; Sandler and, 377; *Saturday Night Live* creation and, 23; Shaffer and, 131; show romances and, 85; Shuster on, 42; sketches and, 134–35, 136; twenty-fifth-anniversary special and, 496–97

Miller, Paul, 565

Minkman character, 260

Minnelli, Liza, 269

Minow, Newton, 91

Mr. Bill, 101, 454

"Mr. Monopoly" sketch, 302–3, 304

"Mister Robinson's Neighborhood" sketches, 223

Mr. T, 264, 572

Mitchell, Finesse, 529–30, 559–60, 561–63, 603; on black women absent from cast, 682

Mitchell, Joni, 189

Mitchum, Robert, 342

Moby, 534

Mohr, Jay, 410

Mom and Dad Save the World, 321

Montana, Joe, 402

Monty Python, 38, 39, 41, 352, 456

Moore, Demi, 327

Moore, Dudley, 238, 307

Moore, Mary Tyler, 35

"More Cowbell" sketch, 537, 538, 564

Morgan, Tracy: book by, 629–30; as cast member, 424, 531; departure from show, 526, 527; Kattan and, 629–30; on Michaels, 725; Michaels and, 459–60, 526; Murphy and, 457; NBC and, 524; Rock and, 381

Morra, Buddy, 53, 256, 290

Morris, Garrett: John Belushi and, 129, 249; *Big Event, The,* 165–66; as cast member, 37, 38–39, 90–91, 100, 148;

Morris, Garrett (*cont.*)
  characters of, 12, 129; as comedy
    writer, 38–39, 50; drug use and, 175–
    76, 137; fifth season's last show and,
    185; on Michaels, 713; screen test and,
    46, 50; Shearer and, 172–73
Moss, Elisabeth, 597
"Mother Lover" sketch, 574
Mount, Thom, 95
Moynihan, Bobby, 620–21, 645, 646, 671,
  694, 695
Muir, Rob, 455, 459
Mulaney, John: attitude toward show, 606;
  as comedy writer, 628, 657; departure
  from show, 645; Hader and, 611, 614;
  on Michaels, 600–601; Stefon
  character and, 608, 609–10, 611–12,
  614, 615; on "Weekend Update" and
  Patterson impersonation, 600–601;
  Zuckerberg and, 628
Mullally, Megan, 545
Muppets, 59, 75–76, 100
Muppet Show, The, 75
Murphy, Eddie: "Best of" DVD, 619; cabs
  and, 236; characters of, 223, 232–36,
  535; as cast member, 526, 687;
  departure from show, 261; Doumanian
  and, 193, 201, 229, 230; Doumanian era
  and, 200–201, 202, 203, 254; Ebersol
  and, 201, 209, 223, 229, 231, 233–34,
  235–37, 238, 240, 378; fifteenth-
  anniversary special and, 348–49, 380; as
  host, 239; hosts and, 274; Kattan and,
  456; Morgan and, 457; movie career of,
  236–37, 238, 255, 465; Piscopo and, 229,
  234, 239; reruns of shows and, 287;
  Rock and, 378, 380; as role model, 355,
  359, 563; success of, 236, 238, 239, 378,
  380; twenty-fifth-anniversary special
  and, 494; Wayans and, 306
Murphy, Matt, 121
Murray, Bill: ad-libbing and, 160; on John
  Belushi, 109–10, 246, 248; Blues Bar
  and, 117; as cast member, 103–5;
  characters of, 12, 48, 128, 495, 653; on
  Chase, 124–25; Chase and, 123–25,
  518; as Chase's replacement, 101;
  Curtin and, 49, 103, 123; Tom Davis
  and, 653, 654; departure from show,
  188–89; Dickman and, 518–19;
  Doumanian era and, 193–94; fame
  and, 178; fifth season's last show and,
  185; first show of, 103–4; as host, 219,
  711; on Michaels, 711; movie career
  of, 177; Murphy compared to, 230;
  old days and, 495–97; Oteri and, 454–
  55; Prime Time Players and, 59; Pross
  and, 174; Radner and, 136–37, 151–52,

351–52; Sandler and, 361; Schlosser
  and, 169; screen test and, 46, 48;
  Shannon and, 455; Shearer and, 171–
  72; sketches and, 130, 135–39, 144;
  Tischler and, 708; twenty-fifth-
  anniversary special and, 495, 496–97
Murray, Matt, 503
Myers, Mike: Carvey and, 373–74; as cast
  member, 345–46, 547; departure from
  show, 424; Franken and, 375;
  Hartman and, 488–89; Kattan and,
  466–67; on Michaels, 733–34;
  Marilyn Suzanne Miller and, 394;
  movie career of, 360, 372, 424, 465,
  540; Nealon and, 320; O'Brien and,
  346; Radner and, 350; Rock and, 379,
  381; Shannon and, 722; Spade and,
  362; Tartikoff and, 372–73
Myers, Peter, 350

Nader, Ralph, 339, 405, 441, 449, 470
Nasso, Lori, 544, 545
Nat X sketch, 378
National Lampoon, 23, 42, 96, 364, 392
National Lampoon Radio Hour: John
  Belushi and, 34, 67, 80, 82, 246; Judith
  Belushi and, 214; comedy writers and,
  52; Goodman and, 341; Radner and,
  82; Shaffer and, 34; Tomlin and, 69
National Lampoon Show, 39, 46
National Lampoon's Vacation, 298
Native American Comic, 554
NBC: *Big Event, The,* 165; cast members
  and, 57, 72, 391, 415, 424, 425, 524;
  Chase and, 97; comedy writers and,
  36; conservatism of, 222; criticism of,
  355; Doumanian and, 191–92, 205;
  Downey and, 418, 422; Ebersol and,
  19, 65, 219, 224, 235–36, 284; Fallon
  and, 541; Fey and, 560; GE as owner
  of, 367; Brad Hall and, 270; hosts and,
  470, 531; Michaels and, 39, 44–45, 60,
  62, 68, 71, 174, 191, 320, 369, 376, 414,
  415, 416, 418–23, 429, 513, 560–61,
  693, 711, 732; mistakes of, 65; Morgan
  and, 527; Murphy and, 202; musical
  guests and, 464–65; music library of,
  70; publicity tour and, 43; RCA as
  owners of, 19; Robbins and, 367;
  Saturday Night Live creation and, 7–8,
  21–22, 24, 27, 28–29, 31; stations
  carrying show and, 58; Studio 8H
  and, 21, 44, 528, 629, 653–54, 693,
  698; success of show and, 91;
  Tartikoff and, 275–76; writers' strike
  and, 585; YouTube and online
  viewing, 553, 555; Zucker and,
  560–61

NBC Nightly News, 578, 579, 580
NBC's Saturday Night, 8
Nealon, Kevin: as cast member, 314, 572; characters of, 318–19; Daniels and, 322; Farley and, 358–59; generational split in cast and, 360; Hartman and, 489; Hooks and, 314–15; hosts and, 402; Sandler and, 379; Sweeney and, 369; "Weekend Update" and, 325, 328, 410; Wolf and, 364
Nebraska, 678
Neighbors, 253
Nelson, Willie, 120
Nerds sketches, 90, 101, 103, 126, 128, 136, 137–39, 142, 167
Nessen, Ron, 57, 81, 339
New Jack City, 379
Newman, Laraine: Aykroyd and, 38, 84, 128; John Belushi and, 80, 110, 250; Blues Bar and, 118; boys club atmosphere and, 148–49; as cast member, 37–38, 100; characters of, 12, 128; departure from show, 186–87; drug use and, 114, 153; fifth season's last show and, 185; Gould and, 72; Improv and, 69; Kudrow and, 362; on Michaels, 702–3; Murray and, 351; Murray-Chase fight and, 125; Oteri and, 469; on Radner, 153, 154–55; screen test and, 46, 47; show romances and, 137, 168; sketches and, 141–42, 143; success and, 101; Tomlin and, 93; Troggs tape and, 167
Newman, Paul, 185
Newman, Randy, 290
New Orleans, 165
"News for the hard of hearing" sketches, 170
New Show, The, 289, 290
Newsweek, 75, 177
New York City, as site for *Saturday Night Live,* 21, 24, 40, 69, 77, 103, 625–26
New York magazine, 65
New Yorker magazine, 626
New York Post, 241, 335, 495
New York Times, 66, 553, 601, 682
Nichols, Mike, 102
Nicholson, Jack, 498, 716
Nickelodeon, 526
Nick the Lounge Singer sketches, 48, 135–36, 495, 653
Nightline, 334, 337
Night of Too Many Stars, 600
Night Shift, 281
1941, 244
Nixon, Richard, 19, 162, 586
Noble Rot, 243
Nolte, Nick, 239

Norris, Pam: Doumanian era and, 191, 196, 198, 199, 204; Doumanian on, 196; Ebersol and, 221; Murphy and, 231–32, 237; O'Donoghue and, 209
Not Necessarily the News, 321, 678
Not Ready for Prime Time Players: cast members as, 39, 46, 49, 59, 152, 194, 201, 242
Novello, Don: advertising and, 161; John Belushi and, 243; characters of, 338–39; Ebersol and, 219; sketches and, 128–29, 338–39; on Zappa, 156

Obama, Barack, 569–71, 577, 580, 581–83, 649, 652, 659; impressions of, difficulty with, 651
Obama, Michelle, 680
Obama Files, The, 584–85
Oberman, Margaret: boys club atmosphere, 271; Ebersol and, 284, 285–86; hosts and, 276, 281–82, 284; Louis-Dreyfus and, 271–72; on Michaels, 725; Murphy and, 230, 236, 238
O'Brien, Conan: attitude toward show, 324–25; censors and, 480–81; as comedy writer, 321–22; as host, 477; hosts and, 323; Kudrow and, 363; on Michaels, 714–15, 730, 736; Michaels and, 322, 393, 540, 678–79; Myers and, 346; Ohlmeyer and, 435; Smigel and, 364–65; television show of, 519, 579; Wright and, 525
O'Connor, Cardinal, 339
O'Connor, Carroll, 112
O'Connor, John J., 66
O'Connor, Sinead, 365–67
Odd Couple, The, 22, 63
Odenkirk, Bob: Armisen and, 528; Clay and, 333; Farley and, 354, 491; Hartman and, 327; hosts and, 342; on Michaels, 721, 725; Myers and, 346; O'Brien and, 736; Sandler and, 376; Smigel and, 313, 364–65; Steinbrenner and, 323
O'Donnell, Rosie, 309
O'Donoghue, Michael: Abba and, 68; attitude toward show and, 209–11; Aykroyd and, 96, 127, 128, 163; band and, 70; Beatts on, 23, 42; John Belushi and, 36; *Big Event, The,* 165–66; Blues Bar and, 116–17; as comedy writer, 72; Paula Davis and, 83–84, 163; death of, 216–17; drug use and, 89; Ebersol and, 207–8, 215, 216; Elvis's death and, 106; firing of, 216; first show and, 59; Franken and, 163; Goodman and, 341; Handey on, 214;

O'Donoghue, Michael (*cont.*)
  Michaels and, 206–7, 704; Marilyn
  Suzanne Miller and, 23; Muppets
  and, 75–76; Murray-Chase fight and,
  125; Shuster on, 42; Tomlin and, 127;
  Zweibel and, 75–76
O'Hara, Catherine, 210
Ohlmeyer, Don: Downey and, 420, 421, 422,
  429, 437, 452; Ebersol and, 22, 24, 235;
  Franken and, 410, 429, 452; Letterman
  and, 393; Macdonald and, 429, 430, 431,
  432–33, 435, 436, 437; Michaels and,
  320, 410, 415, 418–21, 423, 426, 433, 435,
  436, 437, 438, 440, 519; role in show,
  415, 418–23, 426, 565; Simpson and,
  429, 435; "Weekend Update" and, 444
Oldman, Gary, 471
Oteri, Cheri: boys club atmosphere and,
  466, 500, 501; as cast member, 424,
  544, 545; characters of, 468; as
  comedy writer, 467–68; competition
  and, 467–68, 478; drug use and, 461;
  on Michaels, 728; NBC and, 425;
  Newman and, 469; watching *Saturday
  Night Live* as child, 454–55
Outer Limits, The, 35

Pacino, Al, 650
Page, Ellen, 686
Palance, Jack, 277
Palin, Michael, 281–82
Palin, Sarah, 571, 586–95, 596, 600, 602,
  608, 677; appearance on *SNL,* 590–93
Paltrow, Gwyneth, 471, 520; as host, 471,
  472, 473, 477, 627, 712, 726–27
Paper Chase, The, 292
Paramount, 183, 212, 236, 289, 372, 466, 733
Pardo, Don: as announcer, 59, 380, 625,
  745; Crystal and, 53; Hammond
  and, 444
Parker, Sarah Jessica, 423, 726
Parks and Recreation, 677
Parnell, Chris, 486, 513–14; Digital Shorts
  and, 552, 553; departure from show,
  561, 564
Parton, Dolly, 341
Pataki, Governor, 445
Pathological Liar character, 288, 292, 300,
  319–20
"Pat Stevens Show" sketch, 326
Patterson, David, 600–601
PBS, 26
Pedrad, Nasim, 618–19, 646, 673, 694, 713
Pell, Paula, 428–29, 457, 536, 537, 545, 592,
  705; drug use of, 604; on gay writers
  and performers, 659–61, 686–87; on
  Internet criticism, 668; on Michaels,
  604–5

Pelosi, Nancy, 581, 637
Penn and Teller, 61
People magazine, 249, 328, 374
Pepsi, 576
"Perfume for One-Night Stands"
  commercial parody, 154
Perkins, Anthony, 470
Perot, H. Ross, 371–72, 594
Perry, Rick, 637
Pesci, Joe, 498, 499
Pharoah, Jay, 619–20; diversity issues and,
  679–80, 682, 683; Obama character,
  649, 650, 651–52; on teamwork, 670
Phyllis Diller, 583
Pickett, Lenny, 369
Pick-Up Artist, 310
Piscopo, Joe: on John Belushi, 247;
  Doumanian era and, 193, 197, 200;
  Ebersol and, 209, 235, 240; firing of,
  255, 261; Murphy and, 229, 234, 239;
  Sinatra and, 226–27, 262, 327; Wald
  and, 230
Pleasence, Donald, 280
Poehler, Amy; attitude toward the show,
  516, 543, 641; autism benefit, 600; cast
  departures and, 542–43, 540; as cast
  member, 545, 558, 585, 599–600, 618,
  636, 671; on comedy, 501–2; comedy
  writing and, 602; departure from
  show, 567, 598, 599–600, 637, 649;
  episode with Betty White and, 616,
  617, 618; Ferrell and, 537; Fey and,
  541–44, 545, 569; Golden Globe
  Awards 2014, 676–77, 678; Hader and,
  546; as host, 618; impression of
  Hillary Clinton, 586, 588, 589, 590;
  Louis-Dreyfus and, 559; Meyers and,
  567–69; Michaels and, 598, 687, 739;
  9/11 terrorist attacks and, 504; Palin
  appearance and, 590–91; pregnancy
  of, 589, 597; Rudolph and live show
  glitch, 520–21; "Weekend Update"
  and, 541, 542–43, 544
Pomerantz, Hart, 17
Portlandia, 645
"Potato Chip" sketch, 599
Presley, Elvis, 106, 229, 244
Preston, Billy, 59
Price, Jeff, 218
Prime Time Players, 46, 59
Professor Backwards character, 9
"Prom Night" sketch, 139
Pross, Max, 174, 175
Pryor, Richard, 21, 25, 70–71, 73, 98, 134,
  236, 535

Quaid, Randy, 288, 303, 305, 347, 399
Queen Latifah, 520

Queens of the Stone Age, 537
Quinn, Colin: Macdonald and, 439–40; on
    Michaels, 732; "Weekend Update"
    and, 439–40

Radner, Gilda: all-nighters and, 169;
    Aykroyd and, 48, 83, 352; John
    Belushi and, 34, 36, 80; Bergen and,
    81; Berle and, 157, 158; boys club
    atmosphere and, 149; as cast member,
    33, 38, 100, 544; characters of, 12,
    136, 137, 138, 145, 151, 523, 560;
    comedy writers and, 177; Crystal and,
    55–56; Curtin and, 103, 111, 140;
    death of, 349–53, 518; departure
    from show, 192; Dratch and, 454;
    eating problems of, 152–54; fifth
    season's last show and, 185; *Gilda
    Live* and, 170, 177, 179; Gould and,
    72, 724; Improv and, 69; influence of,
    696–97; Michaels and, 48, 48, 700,
    704, 745; Marilyn Suzanne Miller
    and, 140, 152–53, 351; Morris and,
    129; Murray and, 136–39, 151–52,
    351–52; Oteri and, 454; screen test
    and, 46, 48; Shaffer and, 32; Shannon
    and, 455; Shearer and, 176; Simon
    and, 136, 139; sketches and, 136–39,
    141–42, 144; Smith and, 324; success
    and, 101, 102, 194; Tomlin and, 93;
    variety hour for, 173–74, 179; Zucker
    and, 523; Zweibel on, 82–83, 85, 91,
    192, 700
Ramis, Harold, 709
Raphael, Mickey, 120
Rather, Dan, 572, 578
RCA: criticism of *Saturday Night Live* and,
    20; as NBC owners, 19; *Saturday
    Night Live* as cocoon and, 188
Reagan, Nancy, 299–300, 331
Reagan, Ron, 298–300
Reagan, Ronald, 171, 225, 234, 260, 270,
    344
Redgrave, Lynn, 276
refrigerator repairman sketches, 145
Reiner, Rob, 63, 65, 286
Reinhold, Judge, 343, 583
Reitman, Ivan, 95
"Relatives of the Rich and Famous"
    sketch, 260
Reno, Janet, 343, 470
Revenge of the Nerds movies, 138
Reverb, 528
Reynolds, Burt, 19
Rhoda, 22–23
Rice, Donna, 329
Rich, Simon, 621
Richards, Keith, 118, 402

Right Stuff, The, 149
Rink, The, 270
Riperton, Minnie, 82
Risky Business, 299
Risley, Ann, 193
Road to Rio, 456
Robbins, Jerome, 102
Robbins, Tim, 367–68
Robertson, Pat, 344
Robillard, Duke, 120
Rock, Chris: attitude toward show, 379,
    381, 383, 383–84, 399, 414; "Best of"
    DVDs and, 572; as cast member, 378,
    380–81, 382, 395, 548, 636; departure
    from show, 395, 412, 420; Farley and,
    357, 490; as featured player, 378; hosts
    and, 382; on Michaels, 708, 741;
    movie career of, 379, 382; Sandler
    and, 360–61, 378, 379, 384; Spade
    and, 356
Rocket, Charles, 193, 202, 205; death of,
    653
Rocky, 278
Rogen, Seth, 634
Rolling Stones, 464
Rollins, Jack, 18, 26, 55
Romney, Ann, 659
Ronstadt, Linda, 8, 21
Roomful of Blues, 120
Rooney, Mickey, 232
Roseanne Roseannadanna character, 82,
    136, 523, 560, 696
Rositano, Jena, 520
Ross, Diana, 331
Ross, Jeff, 679
Rowan and Martin's Laugh-In, 8, 17, 21, 69,
    583, 694
Rubin, Alan, 121
Rudd, Paul, 625–26, 627, 634; on Armisen,
    662
Rudin, Bill, 29
Rudolph, Maya: attitude toward show,
    515–16, 617, 631; auditions and, 499;
    autism benefit, 600; boys club
    atmosphere and, 501; as cast member,
    545, 558, 599, 666; diversity issues
    and, 682–83; drug use and, 461;
    episode with Betty White and, 616,
    617; hiring of, 500; as host, 631;
    Johansson and, 625; live show glitch,
    520–21; on Michaels, 740; Mother's
    Day special and, 511; Poehler and,
    597; pregnancy of, 621; Radner and,
    81–82
Running Scared, 286
Russert, Tim, 572
Ryan, Meg, 232
Ryder, Winona, 516

Sadat, Anwar, 172
Sahara, 540
Salute to Sir Lew Grade, A, 30–31
Samberg, Andy, 546–47, 599, 607, 621, 686, 694, 738; attitude toward show, 547–48; audience and, 638; departure from show, 640, 643–44, 645; Digital Shorts, Internet, and, 547–56, 580, 650, 667, 675; Golden Globe Awards 2014, 677, 678; Hader and, 611–12, 650; "Hamlet Auditions" and, 672–73; Meyers and, 677, 678, 692–93; Michaels and, 548, 549; Palin appearance and, 591; Timberlake and, 574–75; *Time* 100 hosting, 677–78; Wiig farewell and, 637
Samurai character, 12, 71, 73–74, 107
"Samurai Deli" sketch, 73
"Samurai Hotel" sketch, 71, 73
"Samurai Stockbroker" sketch, 73–74
Sandler, Adam: audition of, 360; autism benefit, 600; "Best of" DVDs and, 572; boys club atmosphere and, 329; Carvey and, 407; as cast member, 548; as comedy writer, 363, 375–76; departure from show, 409–10, 420, 424; Downey and, 375, 376, 412; dress rehearsal versus live, 377; Farley and, 355, 384; Ferrell and, 447; Garofalo and, 377, 389; generational split in cast and, 360; Hartman and, 416; hosts and, 361; Macdonald and, 410; on Michaels, 703; movie career of, 378, 540; Ohlmeyer and, 415, 420; Rock and, 360–61, 378, 379; Shannon and, 455; Spade and, 356, 384; success of, 376; Wolf and, 364
"Santa and the States" sketch, 534
Sanz, Horatio: auditions of, 458; Aykroyd and, 518; as cast member, 424, 536, 537, 559, 562; Christmas song and, 629–30; departure from show, 559, 561, 563–64; "dying" during show and, 479–80; Ferrell and, 538; hosts and, 460, 478; McKay and, 562; Michaels and, 458–59, 581; political humor and, 581; watching *Saturday Night Live* as child, 457
Sargent, Herb: on John Belushi, 106; Chase and, 58; Dickman and, 518; Elliott and, 385; firing of, 420; Louis-Dreyfus and, 271; Michaels and, 289, 667; Marilyn Suzanne Miller and, 22; Murphy and, 238; Not Ready for Prime Time Players and, 59; practical jokes and, 90; Pryor and, 70–71; "Weekend Update" and, 411
Saturday Night, 31, 58

"Saturday Night Dead," 293, 294, 416, 426, 697
"Saturday Night Lifeless," 387
Saturday Night Live: after-show party, 116–17, 462–63, 605, 611, 613, 652, 672; anthrax scare and, 10, 509; "Best of" DVDs, 179, 571–72, 619, 621; as boys club, 79, 147–50, 192, 271, 329, 387, 388, 389, 466, 500–501, 558; cancellation of, 11, 274, 308; Christmas show, 577; cold open and, 59, 152, 281, 324, 343, 359, 371, 414, 434, 449, 452, 485, 557, 580, 582, 584, 637, 641, 642, 648, 651, 674, 680, 684–85, 714; comedy sketches, 535; competition of, 12; creation of, 7–8, 15, 19–30, 205, 737; Digital Shorts, 547–56; Doumanian era and, 191–205; dress rehearsal versus live, 377, 520–21, 623–24, 632, 641, 672–73; Ebersol era and, 204–29; elections and, 344, 449–52, 595–95, 602, 608, 636–37, 651, 658; Emmys won by, 72, 99, 134, 620; established comedy stars as cast members and, 255; fifteenth-anniversary special, 46, 348–49, 380, 494; first show, 54–63; generational change on, 661, 671, 675–76, 698; as global, 607, 699; golden age of, 100–101, 121, 160, 188; Golden Globe Awards 2014, 676–77; hosting of, 622–35, 699; Internet and, 596, 615–16, 621, 667–70, 675, 699; as live show, 43, 67, 210, 225, 237, 285, 306, 332–33, 365, 366, 379, 422, 445, 467, 472, 486, 520–21, 531, 536–37, 605, 611, 617, 626, 641, 673–74; musical guests and, 9, 68, 69, 214, 240, 258, 280, 463–64, 699; oldest host, 615–18; opening credits and, 49, 59, 60; pitch meetings, 656–57; popularity of, 12, 100, 165, 192, 444, 602, 697; prestige of, 11, 606, 626, 655, 696; in prime time, specials, 560–61; ratings of, 65, 173, 199, 261, 296, 297, 332, 334, 337, 416, 421, 433, 444, 463–64, 465, 470–71, 511–13, 523, 608, 699; recurring characters, importance of, 608; reruns of, 98, 453, 463, 495, 516; return of iconic stars of, 654; reviews of, 65–66, 75, 77, 416, 601; satirizing political figures and, 586–96, 600–601; September 11 terrorist attacks and, 503–9, 568, 590; shortest seasons of, 577; and Studio 8H, 21, 44–45, 52, 578, 677, 693; success of, 101–4, 176–77, 191, 525; theme music and, 45; thirty-ninth season, 698–99; as

trendsetter, 7, 15, 61–62, 66, 69, 75,
159, 192; twenty-fifth-anniversary
special, 46, 348, 494–95, 744; writers'
strikes and, 577, 578, 583–84, 620;
youthfulness of, 547, 555–56
Saturday Night Live with Howard Cosell,
59, 89, 92
Scaggs, Boz, 737
Scandal, 680, 685
Schaffer, Akiva, 547, 548, 549, 550, 552,
553, 554, 573, 580, 598, 667
Schiller, Bob, 19
Schiller, Tom: John Belushi and, 87, 110; as
comedy writer, 291; departure from
show, 407; on Michaels, 18–19, 29–30,
713; movie career of, 212; on Radner,
154; "Samurai Hotel" and, 73; short
films of, 100, 110, 242; spirituality of,
57; success of show and, 102
Schlosser, Herbert: cast members and,
169; Ebersol and, 19, 20, 21, 88; first
show and, 62; Michaels and, 738;
Saturday Night Live creation and, 8,
19, 20–21, 24, 28, 30; Studio 8H and,
45; success of show and, 91
Schneider, Rob, 364, 379, 413
Schneider, Sarah, 659
Schneider, Suzy, 329
Schreiber, Avery, 17
Scott, Lynn, 118
Scott, Tom, 118
Scott, Willard, 393
SCTV, 228, 255, 258–59, 262–63, 264, 285
Seagal, Steven, 336, 400–401
Second City: Aykroyd and, 33–34, 35, 83,
120, 606; Jim Belushi and, 222, 251;
John Belushi and, 35, 247; cast
members gleaned from, 30, 213, 545,
659; as comedy movement, 39; Farley
and, 491; Fey and, 441; Kazurinsky
and, 228, 240, 247, 249; Michaels's
contacts with, 23; Murray and, 188;
Myers and, 345; Sanz and, 458
second cop sketches, 104, 135
Secunda, Barry, 206
Segelstein, Irwin, 203
Seinfeld, 266, 267, 269, 271, 398, 409, 410,
419, 422, 519, 557, 558
Seinfeld, Jerry, 475, 477, 557
Sellers, Peter, 322
September 11 terrorist attacks, 503–9, 568
Sgt. Bilko, 399
Shaffer, Paul: audience and, 162; band
and, 32; as comedy writer, 78, 131;
hosts and, 156; on Michaels, 32;
Michaels and, 121; Murray and, 495;
performing opportunities and, 167;
Radner and, 34; Shearer and, 172;

Short and, 258; show romances and,
84; sketches and, 136; twenty-fifth-
anniversary special and, 496, 497
Shandling, Garry, 76, 723
Shannon, Molly: auditions of, 459; boys
club atmosphere and, 466, 500, 501;
as cast member, 424, 544, 545, 616;
characters of, 455–56, 459; episode
with Betty White and, 616, 617; Farley
and, 358; hosts and, 476; on Michaels,
722, 739; movie career of, 466; NBC
and, 425; Rudolph and, 511; watching
Saturday Night Live as child, 455
Sharpton, Al, 530–31, 584, 585, 684–85
Shearer, Harry: as cast member, 169–70,
171–72, 176, 255, 258; characters of,
260, 265; on Chase, 175; as comedy
writer, 273; Crystal and, 264; David
and, 266; departure from show, 282;
Doumanian era and, 197; Ebersol
and, 257; on Michaels, 706; Michaels
and, 170, 171, 172, 173, 197
Sheffield, David: on Belushi, 252;
Doumanian era and, 195, 196–97;
Ebersol era and, 220, 223; hosts and,
276, 280; Murphy and, 229, 231, 234
Shlien, Robin: censors and, 143; departure
from show, 187; Doumanian and,
184–85; drug use and, 113–14, 141;
Ebersol and, 279–80; Murphy and,
233; O'Donoghue and, 216; sketches
and, 141; success of show and, 102
Shoemaker, Mike, 413, 502–3, 563, 588,
597, 600–601, 606, 630; Lohan
and, 632
Shookus, Lindsay: diversity issues and,
683, 688–89; Lohan as host and, 633;
as producer, 528, 605, 623, 665
Shore, Howard: band and, 31, 70, 120; on
John Belushi, 120; on Hefner, 156;
hosts and, 70; on Michaels, 15–16;
musical guests and, 68; pay of, 77–78;
screen test and, 46, 51; Studio 8H
and, 44; theme music and, 45
Short, Martin: as cast member, 255, 258–
59; characters of, 264, 265; as comedy
writer, 272–73, 273; departure from
show, 407; Downey and, 285; Ebersol
and, 257; hosts and, 274, 277; Myers
and, 345; popularity of, 288; salary
and, 261; schedule and, 262–63;
Shaffer and, 32; Shearer and, 265,
283; Starr and, 278; Wald and, 281
Shrek, 176
Shuster, Frank, 16, 19
Shuster, Rosie: all-nighters and, 168–69;
Aykroyd and, 84, 118–19, 120, 131,
141, 168; Berle and, 157; Blues Bar

Shuster, Rosie (*cont.*)
  and, 118–19; boys club atmosphere
  and, 79, 149–50; Carvey and, 315–16;
  censors and, 210–11; on Chase, 66–67;
  as comedy writer, 79; comedy writers
  and, 42; Paula Davis and, 84; departure
  from show, 188; Dickman and, 518; on
  Ebersol, 22; Ebersol on, 22; first show
  and, 61; marriage to Michaels, 18, 22,
  120, 167–68; on Michaels, 15, 18,
  149–50, 724, 732–33; on Radner, 154;
  show romances and, 85; sketches and,
  136–39, 141–43; Southern and, 210–11;
  working hours and, 103
Signorelli, James: advertising and, 161;
  audience and, 165; on John Belushi,
  132–33; on Michaels, 131, 730–31; on
  Radner, 102; sketches and, 129
Silver, Joel, 487
Silverman, Fred: attitude toward show,
  177, 178–79; John Belushi's
  impression of, 107–9; Doumanian
  and, 184, 202; Ebersol and, 177, 204,
  206, 219–20; Franken and, 179, 180,
  181–82, 183, 186; on Michaels, 738;
  O'Donoghue and, 216; Radner and,
  173–74, 179; ratings and, 173; on
  Schlosser, 20; Tartikoff and, 274
"Silverman in the Bunker" sketch, 216
Simon, Paul: Fisher and, 127, 139, 714;
  Garofalo and, 388; Hanks and, 405;
  as host, 62–63, 66; Levy and, 25; on
  Michaels, 719; Michaels and, 95, 568,
  704, 714; Nealon and, 402; Radner
  and, 136, 139; September 11 terrorist
  attacks and, 504, 507; success of show
  and, 103
Simon, Sam, 394
Simpson, O. J., 429, 434, 470
Simpsons, The, 13, 410, 519, 678
Sinatra, Frank, 226–27, 262, 327, 486
Sinatra, Tina, 327
Sinise, Gary, 471
60 Minutes, 38, 260, 521
Smigel, Robert: Armisen as Patterson and,
  600; attitude toward show, 606–7;
  autism benefit, 600; "Best of" DVDs
  and, 572; Carvey and, 370; on cast
  members, 599; censors and, 480–81,
  582–83; departure from show, 560,
  561, 585–86; Dratch and, 561; Farley
  and, 490–91, 494; Jackson and, 318;
  Madonna and, 296; Meadows and,
  364; on Michaels, 727; Michaels and,
  308, 495, 714–15; movie career, 634–
  35; Myers and, 346; O'Brien and, 393;
  Odenkirk and, 313, 364–65; political
  humor and, 533, 534–35, 584–85, 600;

Sandler and, 375, 376, 420; Sanz and,
  561; "TV Funhouse" sketch with
  Fallon, Colbert, and Carell, 634–35
Smith, Andrew: Doumanian era and, 194;
  Ebersol era and, 219, 221–22; on
  Michaels, 736; Michaels and, 287;
  Piscopo and, 228; Puerto Rican maid
  and, 137; sketches and, 259; stars as
  cast members and, 259, 281–82
Smith, Gary, 31
Smith, G. E., 150, 324
Smits, Jimmy, 363
Smothers Brothers, 414
Smothers Brothers Show, 338
Snyder, Tom, 162, 180
Soap, 255, 256, 257
Social Network, The, 628
Solomon, Will and John, 575
Sonny and Cher, 43
Southern, Terry, 210–11
Spacek, Sissy, 134
Spacey, Kevin, 476
Spade, David: attitude toward show, 399,
  404; Carvey and, 371–72, 407; as cast
  member, 548; censors and, 480;
  characters of, 374–75; departure from
  show, 395–96, 409–10, 420; Farley
  and, 356, 358, 489–90, 492; on
  Michaels, 708; movie career of, 396;
  Murphy and, 349; Myers and, 362;
  Rock and, 384; Sandler and, 356, 384;
  Seagal and, 400–401; Wolf and, 364
Spears, Britney, 464, 471, 536
Special Bulletin, 235
Spielberg, Steven, 194
Spillman, Miskel, 470
Spinal Tap, 258
"Spit-Take Talk Show" sketch, 270
Spitzer, Eliot, 600, 651
Spivey, Emily, 667–68
Springsteen, Bruce, 496–97
Starkeisha character, 529
Starr, Kenneth, 316
Starr, Ringo, 277–78
Star Wars, 127
Stefon character, 608–15
Steiger, Rod, 51
Stein, Gertrude, 731
Steinberg, David, 33
Steinbrenner, George, 323
Stephenson, Pamela, 255, 258
Stern, Howard, 512
Stevens, Connie, 24
Stewart, Jon, 478, 515, 579, 600, 637, 659,
  720
Stewart, Patrick, 408
Stewart, Rod, 280
Stiller, Ben, 385, 507–8

Sting, 328
St. James, Susan, 279
Stone, Sharon, 472
Stringer, Howard, 414
Strong, Cecily, 654–55, 663, 669, 691, 694, 695–96
Stuart Smalley character, 375
Studio One, 9
"Stunt Baby" sketches, 126, 142
Sudeikis, Jason, 534, 599, 621, 629, 650, 676; departure from show, 640, 694
Sullivan, Ed, 13, 28, 742
Sumo wrestlers sketches, 144, 145
Sun Ra, 463
Superstar, 466
Swayze, Patrick, 358
Sweeney, Julia: as cast member, 362; characters of, 369–70; departure from show, 408; on Michaels, 700, 708; Michaels and, 408, 414–15; Oteri and, 468; Seagal and, 401; Smits and, 363
Sweeney, Terry: attitude toward show, 306; as cast member, 288, 295; Chase and, 297; Dunn and, 330; Franken and, 301; as gay, 305; Ron Reagan and, 299–300
Swift, Taylor, 633, 634

"Taboosters, The" sketch, 210–11
Taccone, Jorma, 547, 548, 549, 550, 551–52, 554, 573, 667; attitude toward show, 605; MacGruber character and, 575–76; Pepsi commercial, 576; Brian Williams and, 580
Tanen, Ned, 95
Tarantino, Quentin, 457
Tartikoff, Brandon: attitude toward show, 204–5, 274; Jim Belushi and, 222; cancellation of show and, 11, 274, 290, 295, 307; cancer of, 274–75; Carvey and, 309; comedy writers and, 261; Crystal and, 258; Doumanian and, 183, 184, 186, 204; Ebersol and, 204, 205–6, 219, 238, 255, 256, 274–75, 289; Franken and, 181; as host, 275–76; Michaels and, 180, 183, 289, 290, 295; Myers and, 372–73; Silverman and, 181
Tartikoff, Calla, 274
Tartikoff, Lilly, 257–58, 274, 275–76, 720
"Tarzan, Tonto, and Frankenstein" sketch, 326
Tatum, Channing, 635
Taxi, 281, 340, 540
Taylor, James, 118, 167, 248, 402
Tebet, Dave, 29, 60
television: John Belushi's attitude toward, 34, 35, 36, 91; comedy sketches and,
535; effect of *Saturday Night Live* on, 8, 9, 51, 69, 75, 85–86, 100, 101, 159–60, 212; Michaels on, 35–36; reality distortion and, 590; Zweibel on, 91
television generation, 8, 11, 453–54
Temple, Shirley, 131
terrorism, 10, 452, 503–9
Third Rock from the Sun, 487
30 Rock (30 Rockefeller Plaza), 24, 36, 103, 122, 205, 233, 358, 385, 403, 423, 509, 517, 626, 701
30 Rock (TV series), 559, 561, 584, 587, 588, 608
This Is 40, 635
Thomas, Danny, 157, 368
Thomas, Dave, 32, 345
Thomas, Pam, 345
Thompson, Kenan: audition, 529; as cast member, 526–27, 540, 597, 603, 647, 661–62, 694; on celebrity, 670; comedy writing and, 670; departure from show, 694–95; diversity issues and, 679–81, 683; generational differences on *SNL* and, 661; impression of Al Sharpton, 684; on performing in drag, 680–81; Wiig and, 670
Three Amigos, 289–90, 654
Thurm, Nathan, 260
Timberlake, Justin, 555–56, 573–75, 623–24, 628–29, 642, 654
Time magazine, 691–92
Tinker, Grant A.: attitude toward show, 214, 221; censors and, 234, 235; on Michaels, 718; on Schlosser, 20–21; Tartikoff and, 274
Tischler, Bob: on John Belushi, 246; as comedy writer, 211; Crystal and, 263–64; Ebersol and, 224; Guest and, 256; on Michaels, 708–9, 737; O'Donoghue and, 209, 211–12, 215, 216; Piscopo and, 227; Second City and, 213; Shearer and, 282; stars as cast members and, 267
Titters (Beatts), 23
Today show, 450, 523, 524, 560
Todd DiLaMuca character, 128, 138–39. *See also* Nerds sketches
To Kill a Mockingbird, 288
Tomlin, Lily: John Belushi and, 69; and boys club atmosphere, 148; as host, 66, 70, 127; on Michaels, 18, 709; Michaels and, 25, 148–49, 414; Marilyn Suzanne Miller and, 42, 142; Newman and, 37–38, 93; *Saturday Night Live* creation and, 21; *Saturday Night Live* originality and, 69; specials of, 8, 18, 37–38, 69, 148–49

Tommy Boy, 356, 489, 492
Tomorrow, 24
Tonight Show: as career launching for comics, 396, 466, 742; Chase and, 94; Fallon and, 5, 540, 677, 678, 679; Franken and, 42–43; Jackson and, 312; Leno and, 678, 679; as live-on-tape, 365; Martin and, 134; Michaels and, 162, 677, 678–79; music of, 31; O'Brien and, 678–79; as profitable, 173; reruns of, 7–8, 9, 19, 20, 29, 38, 188; *Saturday Night Live* hosts and, 29
Tootsie, 278
"Torboto" (cartoon), 533
Toscanini, Arturo, 12
Townsend, Robert, 200–201, 306
Tracy Morgan Show, 527, 561
Trading Places, 236–37, 380
Trainspotting, 118
Traviesas, Herminio, 145
Travis, Randy, 342
Travolta, John, 317–18, 401–2
Trebeck, Alex, 483, 485, 516, 517
Trinity Square Repertory Company, 40
Tripp, Linda, 485
Troggs tape, 167
Trump, Donald, 517
Turner, Bonnie: attitude toward show, 391–92; boys club atmosphere and, 329; Church Lady sketches and, 315; Clay and, 335; as comedy writer, 313; departure from show, 407; Hooks and, 371; Michaels and, 734
Turner, Terry: attitude toward show, 310, 313, 391–92; Carvey and, 315; Clay and, 335; departure from show, 407; elevators and, 347; Hartman and, 487–88; Jackson and, 332; on Michaels, 734–35; Myers and, 373
Turner, Tina, 280
Tush, Bill, 488
"TV Funhouse," 533, 582, 585; "Best of" DVD, 572; Ace and Gary cartoon/live sketch, 634–35
Twilight Zone, The (film), 236
Twilight Zone, The (television show), 35
Tyler, Steven, 722
Tyson, Cicely, 470
Tyson, Mike, 483

Uncle Roy sketches, 126, 141–42
Upright Citizens Brigade (UCB), 441, 542, 599, 659, 680
Urban Cowboy, 183

Vance, Danitra: as cast member, 288, 294
Variety, 24

Vedder, Eddie, 402
View, The, 544
Village Voice, 23, 36
Vinton, Bobby, 48

Wagner, Jane, 18, 69
Wald, Elliot: attitude toward show, 232; David and, 267–68; Downey and, 225; Ebersol and, 224, 729; Louis-Dreyfus and, 271; on Michaels, 715, 729; Murphy and, 230, 239; O'Donoghue and, 215–16; schedule and, 285; Shearer and, 260; stars as cast members and, 261–62
Walken, Christopher, 470, 477, 526, 538, 607
Wall Street Journal, 329
Warner Brothers, 183, 289
Washington, Kerry, 680, 684, 685, 686, 691
Wayans, Damon: Breckman and, 302–3; departure from show, 302, 303, 304–5, 306; Madonna and, 296; on Michaels, 719; Michaels and, 303, 304–5, 306, 307; Rock and, 378
Wayne's World, 372, 373
"Wayne's World" sketches, 346–47, 373, 381, 402, 406, 421, 467, 547, 592
Webb, Spud, 612
"Weekend Update": Armisen and, 554, 647; Aykroyd and, 161; Bayer and, 646; Chase and, 9, 49, 64, 67, 74, 122, 123, 145, 411, 443; Curtin and, 74, 103, 111, 122, 123, 145–46, 161, 165; David and, 268; Downey and, 429–30, 431, 434; Dratch and, 468–69; Fallon and, 440, 442–44, 539, 567, 692; Fey and, 440, 441, 442–44, 539, 542–44, 559, 565; Hader as Stefon, 608–15; Jost and, 695–96; Kazurinsky and, 284; Macdonald and, 410–12, 429–34, 436, 438, 439; Meyers and, 567–68, 569, 590, 597, 608, 610, 613–15, 692; Dennis Miller and, 288, 294, 411; Mitchell and, 529; Murray and, 160; Nader and, 441; Nealon and, 325, 328, 410; Odenkirk and, 313; Patterson and, 600–601; Poehler and, 541, 542–43, 544; popularity of, 12; Quinn and, 439–40; Shoemaker and, 503; special interest groups and, 11; as star maker, 692; Strong and, 663, 664; Wiig and, 647; Zweibel and, 67, 143–46
Weis, Gary, 100
Welch, Jack, 481
Welch, Raquel, 470
Welcome Back, Kotter, 401
Wells, David, 517
Wernick, Sandy, 17, 21
West, Johnny, 336

"What's Up with That?," 647
"Whiners, The," 223
White, Betty, 615–18
White, Larry, 22
Widettes, 103
Wiig, Kristen: attitude toward show, 643; as cast member, 558, 587, 588, 599, 607, 619, 627, 632, 642, 647, 657, 660, 664, 671, 675; characters of, 638, 641–42, 650; departure from show, 637–41, 643, 645, 648, 664, 694; Hader and, 609, 638, 650, 672; impersonations by, 638; movie career, 638, 639; Thompson and, 670
"Wild and Crazy Guys" sketches, 454
Wilder, Gene, 351
"Wild Thing," 167
"William Holden Drinking Helmet, The" sketch, 276
William Morris, 97, 310
Williams, Brian, 577, 578–79, 580, 596, 697–98
Williams, Cindy, 152, 165, 166
Williams, Robin: on Belushi, 244; Blues Bar and, 116, 252; as host, 237; on Michaels, 716; on Stefon, 615
Wilson, Casey, 621
Wilson, Dave: ad-libbing and, 160; comedy writers and, 52; as director, 45, 559, 565; Doumanian era and, 202; Ebersol and, 221, 241; Mandel and, 398; on Michaels, 32, 740; musical guests and, 68–69, 368; *Saturday Night Live* creation and, 31; screen tests and, 47, 52
Wilson, Flip, 92, 680
Winfrey, Oprah, 300, 588, 685
Wired (Woodward), 112, 253
Witherspoon, Reese, 507–8
Wiz, The, 176
Wolf, Fred: attitude toward show, 399–400; cast members and, 364; competition and, 396–21; Farley and, 356, 357, 358; Garofalo and, 387, 388–89; on Michaels, 701; Ohlmeyer and, 433; Rock and, 378–79, 382–83, 412; Spade and, 374–75
Wolfson, Howard, 580
"Womb, The" sketch, 270
Wonder, Stevie, 227, 280
Woodward, Bob, 112, 254
Wright, Robert: attitude toward show, 524; censors and, 481; Father Sarducci and, 339; Michaels and, 425, 524; O'Brien and, 393; Ohlmeyer and, 393, 418–19; Simpson and, 435

X-Presidents, 634

Yeager, Chuck, 745
YouTube, 551, 553, 554, 555
Your Hit Parade, 43
Your Show of Shows, 9, 66, 130, 278

Zamata, Sasheer, 680, 681, 688–91
Zander, Christine: Dunn and, 330; Hartman and, 409; Jackson and, 328; on Michaels, 703, 729; Sweeney and, 363, 370, 700
Zappa, Frank, 156
Zonars, John, 365–67, 464, 465
Zucker, Jeff, 523, 531, 541, 560–61, 583, 598; *Tonight Show* and, 679
Zuckerberg, Mark, 628
Zweibel, Alan: on John Belushi, 177; on Berle, 157–58; *Big Event, The,* 165–66; burnout and, 174; cast members and, 79; on Chase, 95, 125–26; as comedy writer, 40–42; departure from show, 187, 192; Dickman and, 518; on Michaels, 519, 700, 706, 744–45; Muppets and, 75–76; practical jokes and, 90; on Radner, 82–83, 85, 91, 192, 700; Radner and, 155, 192; Samurai sketches and, 73; success of show and, 102; "Weekend Update" and, 67, 143–46; work ethic and, 98

About the Authors

James Andrew Miller is an award-winning journalist who has served as senior executive producer in the news business, and has also worked on the entertainment side of television production and development. He received his B.A. from Occidental College, his M.Litt. from Oxford University, and his M.B.A. from Harvard University, all with honors. Along with Tom Shales, he is the author of the #1 bestseller *Those Guys Have All the Fun: Inside the World of ESPN.*

Tom Shales is America's foremost television critic, having won the Pulitzer Prize for Criticism in 1988. For twenty-five years, he was film critic for National Public Radio.